Microsoft® Office 2008 for Mac
Step by Step

Joan Preppernau

PUBLISHED BY
Microsoft Press
A Division of Microsoft Corporation
One Microsoft Way
Redmond, Washington 98052-6399

Library of Congress Control Number: 2008929791

Printed and bound in the United States of America.

1 2 3 4 5 6 7 8 9   QWT   3 2 1 0 9 8

Distributed in Canada by H.B. Fenn and Company Ltd.

A CIP catalogue record for this book is available from the British Library.

Microsoft Press books are available through booksellers and distributors worldwide. For further information about international editions, contact your local Microsoft Corporation office or contact Microsoft Press International directly at fax (425) 936-7329. Visit our Web site at www.microsoft.com/mspress/. Send comments to mspinput@microsoft.com.

Microsoft, Microsoft Press, Access, Encarta, Entourage, Excel, Expression, Fluent, Hotmail, MS, MS-DOS, MSN, OneNote, Outlook, PivotTable, PowerPoint, SharePoint, SmartArt, Visual Basic, Windows, Windows Live, and Windows Vista are either registered trademarks or trademarks of the Microsoft group of companies. Other product and company names mentioned herein may be the trademarks of their respective owners.

The example companies, organizations, products, domain names, e-mail addresses, logos, people, places, and events depicted herein are fictitious. No association with any real company, organization, product, domain name, e-mail address, logo, person, place, or event is intended or should be inferred.

This book expresses the author's views and opinions. The information contained in this book is provided without any express, statutory, or implied warranties. Neither the authors, Microsoft Corporation, nor its resellers or distributors will be held liable for any damages caused or alleged to be caused either directly or indirectly by this book.

Acquisitions Editor: Juliana Aldous Atkinson
Developmental Editor: Sandra Haynes
Project Editor: Rosemary Caperton
Editorial Production: Online Training Solutions, Inc.
Technical Reviewer: Charles Preppernau

Body Part No. X15-04041

Contents

Introducing Microsoft Office 2008 for Mac..................................... xiii

   Program Overview xiii

   New Features xiv

      New in Office 2008 xiv

      New in Word 2008 xiv

      New in Excel 2008 xv

      New in PowerPoint 2008 xv

      New in Entourage 2008 xv

   Let's Get Started! xvi

Features and Conventions of This Book xvii

Using the Companion Content xxi

   Practice Files.. xxi

      Using the Practice Files.................................... xxi

      Removing the Practice Files................................ xxi

      Practice File List xxii

   Bonus Web Content xxiii

   Minimum System Requirements................................. xxiv

Getting Help xxv

   Getting Help with This Book and Its Companion Content............... xxv

   Getting Help with an Office 2008 Program xxvi

About the Author.. xxvii

Quick Reference

   Microsoft Office 2008 for Mac Q-3

   Microsoft Word 2008 for Mac................................. Q-21

   Microsoft Excel 2008 for Mac Q-39

   Microsoft PowerPoint 2008 for Mac Q-55

   Microsoft Entourage 2008 for Mac Q-69

What do you think of this book? We want to hear from you!

Microsoft is interested in hearing your feedback so we can continually improve our books and learning resources for you. To participate in a brief online survey, please visit:

www.microsoft.com/learning/booksurvey/

Part I   **Office Basics**

1   Explore and Manage the Office Interface   3

Start an Office Program 4
    Sidebar: Mouse Manners 5
Find Your Way Around File Windows. 6
Give Instructions in an Office Program 8
    Menus and the Menu Bar. 9
    Toolbars. 11
    The Elements Gallery. 14
    The Toolbox 16
Use and Configure Program-Specific Features and Functions. 19
    Word Tools and Preferences 19
    Sidebar: Update and Enhance Office Programs .22
    Excel Tools and Preferences. 24
    PowerPoint Tools and Preferences 26
Personalize Program Functionality. 27
    Store Your Information for Reuse 29
    Change the Gallery Color Scheme 31
Practice Working with Windows and Commands 32
Key Points 41

2   Practice Basic Office File Skills   43

Open, Save, and Close Office Files 44
    Sidebar: Choose the Right File Format. 46
Practice Opening, Saving, and Closing Office Files 47
View Office Files. 56
    Change the View 56
    Change the Magnification 57
    Split and Arrange Document and Workbook Windows 58
Find and Replace Content and Formatting. 60
    Word Search Options 60
    Excel Search Options. 64
    PowerPoint Search Options 65
Practice Replacing Content and Formatting. 66
Print Office Files. 69
Key Points 73

3   Work in Office Programs   75

View and Move Around in Word Documents. 76
Move Around in Document Content 77
Practice Viewing and Moving Around in Documents. 80
Sidebar: Change the Units of Measurement 86
Practice Moving Around in Document Content. 90
Sidebar: Word File Formats 92
View and Move Around in Excel Workbooks 92
Sidebar: Maximize Screen Real Estate 96
Practice Viewing and Moving Around in Workbooks. 98
Sidebar: Display Formulas in a Worksheet. 100
Sidebar: Excel File Formats. 104
View and Move Around in PowerPoint Presentations. .106
Practice Viewing and Moving Around in Presentations 108
Sidebar: PowerPoint File Formats 114
Key Points 117

Part II   Create Basic Office Files

4   Create Word Documents   121

Create a Basic Document 122
Create a Document 122
Enter Text 124
Sidebar: Insert or Link To External Content. 125
Practice Creating and Populating Documents 126
Create a Document from a Project Template. 132
The Project Gallery 132
Project Templates 135
Work with Word Publications 136
Work with Word Notebooks 138
Practice Creating Documents from Project Templates .142
Create a Personalized Project Template. 147
Practice Creating Custom Templates 148
Key Points 152
Sidebar: Bonus Web Content. 153

5   Create Excel Workbooks   **155**

Create a Basic Workbook. 156

    Sidebar: How Much Data Can I Store in a Workbook? 157

Enter Data on a Sheet. 158

Resize Columns and Rows 160

    Sidebar: Hide Columns and Rows. 161

Fill Cells with a Series of Data 161

Practice Creating and Populating Workbooks 163

Create a Workbook or Sheet from a Project Template. 170

Practice Creating Workbooks and Sheets from Templates 175

Key Points. 179

6   Create PowerPoint Presentations   **181**

Create a Basic Presentation 182

Add Slides to a Presentation 183

    Add Blank Slides. 183

    Insert Slides from Other Presentations 184

    Sidebar: Remove Slides from a Presentation. 184

Practice Inserting Slides from Other Presentations 185

Add Content to Slides. 188

    Sidebar: About Slide Masters. 188

    Work with Layout Placeholders. 188

    Insert Content in a Placeholder. 189

    Modify Text. 191

Create a Presentation from the Project Gallery 192

    Create a Presentation Based on an Office Theme Template 193

    Create a Presentation Based on a Project Template .193

    Sidebar: Special Presentation Themes 195

Practice Creating Presentations 196

Create a Presentation from a Word Document 203

Practice Exporting and Importing Presentation Outlines. 205

Key Points 208

    Sidebar: Bonus Web Content. 209

Part III   **Work with Office File Content**

7   Work with Word Document Content   213

Edit Document Text. 214

Insert and Delete Text. 214

Select Text. 214

Copy and Move Text. 216

Undo Changes 219

Practice Manipulating Text 220

Sidebar: Let Word Take Care of the Details. 221

Automatically Display Current Information in a Document. 225

Work with Office Themes. 228

Practice Applying Themes and Color Schemes 231

Work with Styles 236

Manage Document Templates 239

Practice Applying and Modifying Styles and Document Templates. 241

Check Spelling and Grammar 253

Key Points 256

Sidebar: Bonus Web Content. 257

8   Work with Excel Sheet Content   259

Edit Worksheet Data. 260

Change Cell Content. 260

Change Worksheet Structure. 260

Restrict the Content Allowed in a Cell 262

Automatically Format Cells Based on Content. 264

Create Charts in Workbooks 265

Choose a Chart Type. 265

Modify a Chart. 266

Practice Creating Charts from Worksheet Data 267

Create Charts in Documents and Presentations. 277

Insert or Link to an Existing Chart. 277

Create a Chart on a Page or Slide. 279

Manage Sheets. 281
    Add and Remove Sheets. 282
    Sidebar: Hide Sheets 284
    Copy or Move Sheets 285
    Organize Sheets. 285
    Assign Sheet Names 286
Practice Working with Sheets and Data. 286
Key Points 293

9   Create Excel Formulas   295
Understand Functions. 296
    Numeric Functions. 297
    Text Functions 299
    Generic Functions 299
Create Simple Formulas 300
Reference Worksheets and Workbooks. 304
Use Absolute and Relative References. 305
Reference Named Cells and Ranges. 306
Practice Creating Formulas 308
Key Points 315

10   Work with PowerPoint Slide Content   317
Format Slide Text. 318
Customize a Slide Background 320
Add a Watermark to a Slide. 321
    Sidebar: Work with Presentation Color Schemes 324
Practice Formatting Slide Backgrounds. 326
    Sidebar: Move Slides in a Presentation 337
Change the Layout of a Slide. 337
    Sidebar: Work with Slide Masters 339
Change Standard Slide Settings 339
Run a Slide Show 340
Key Points 343
    Sidebar: Bonus Web Content. 343

Part IV   **Enhance Office File Content**

11   Format Office File Content   347

Control Page Setup 348

Set the Page Size 348

Set the Page Orientation 349

Set the Document Margins 350

Insert Page and Section Breaks 351

Format Paragraphs 353

Indent Paragraphs 353

Align Text Horizontally 354

Align Text Vertically 355

Add Borders and Shading 356

Practice Changing the Size and Appearance of Paragraphs 358

Format Characters 363

Sidebar: Case and Character Formatting 366

Sidebar: Apply Existing Formatting to Other Content 367

Practice Formatting Characters 368

Format Worksheet Cells and Cell Contents 375

Format Numeric Data 375

Merge Cells 375

Draw Borders by Hand 376

Set Up a Sheet for Printing 377

Key Points 379

12   Create and Insert Graphics   381

Insert and Modify Shapes 382

Insert Commercial Clip Art 386

Sidebar: Add Images to the Clip Gallery 388

Insert Symbols as Text or Graphics 390

Insert Your Own Photos 391

Practice Inserting and Modifying Images 393

Sidebar: Check Whether Graphic Effects Are
Compatible with Earlier Program Versions 400

Create Professional Diagrams 401
   Create a Diagram from Scratch 402
   Modify a Diagram 403
Practice Creating and Modifying Diagrams 404
Key Points 411

13   **Review Word Documents**   **413**

Revise a Document 414
Give Feedback on Document Content. 416
Practice Reviewing Documents. 417
Key Points 427

14   **Add Finishing Document Elements**   **429**

Add Professional Cover Pages. 430
Practice Adding Cover Pages. 431
Add Headers and Footers 434
   Sidebar: Insert and Format Page Numbers. 436
Practice Adding Headers and Footers 436
   Sidebar: Add a Watermark to a Document. 440
Create a Table of Contents. 442
Practice Creating Tables of Contents 445
Create an Index 450
Practice Creating Indexes. 454
Create a Bibliography 462
Key Points 465

Part V   **Stay In Touch and On Time**

15   **Communicate Online**   **469**

Work in Entourage 470
Personalize Entourage 474
Connect to Your E-Mail Account. 475
   Sidebar: Work with Exchange Accounts. 476
Create and Send E-Mail Messages 484
   Address Messages 484
   Attach Files 485
   Save Message Drafts. 486
   Send Messages. 486

Practice Creating and Sending E-Mail Messages 487
Enhance Message Content. 492
  Format Message Text 492
  Research Words and Phrases. 493
  Create E-Mail Signatures 496
Reply To and Forward Messages. 499
Practice Responding to Messages 500
Delete Messages 503
  Sidebar: Schedule Actions to Occur Automatically 504
Practice Deleting Messages. 505
Key Points 509

16   Manage Contacts and Schedules   511

Work in the Address Book. 512
  View, Sort, and Filter Records in the Address Book. 512
Work with Contact Records. 513
  Work in the Contact Window 514
  Create a Contact Record. 515
  Sidebar: Linking Entourage Items. 517
Work with Contact Groups 518
Flag Items for Follow Up 519
Assign Categories to Items 521
Work in the Calendar 523
  Display Different Views of a Calendar 524
  Display Your To Do List. 525
Schedule a Calendar Event. 526
Practice Working with Your Calendar 528
Search for Information 531
Key Points 532

Glossary G-533
Index. I-539

What do you think of this book? We want to hear from you!

Microsoft is interested in hearing your feedback so we can continually improve our books and learning resources for you. To participate in a brief online survey, please visit:

www.microsoft.com/learning/booksurvey/

Introducing
Microsoft Office 2008 for Mac

Microsoft Office 2008 for Mac is a collection of programs, tools, and utilities you can use to manage and present information of all sorts. To meet the varying needs of individuals and organizations, there are three editions of Office 2008. This book is based on the Home and Student Edition, which includes Microsoft Word 2008 for Mac, Microsoft Excel 2008 for Mac, Microsoft PowerPoint 2008 for Mac, Microsoft Entourage 2008 for Mac, and Microsoft Messenger for Mac. The standard edition of Office 2008 also includes Microsoft Exchange Server Support and Automator Actions for Workflows. The Special Media Edition includes all of the above, plus Microsoft Expression Media.

Microsoft Office 2008 for Mac Step by Step includes in-depth coverage of Word, Excel, PowerPoint, and Entourage, which are the core programs of all three editions.

From time to time, Microsoft releases service packs containing updates to the programs in your installation of Office. This book was written against Office 2008 Service Pack 1 (SP1), which fixed several problems with the original release of Office 2008 and provided additional functionality for the core programs. By the time you read this, additional service packs might be available.

Program Overview

Each of the programs discussed in this book has a particular purpose, as follows:

- **Word.** A sophisticated word-processing program with which you can quickly and efficiently author and format documents.
- **Excel.** A powerful spreadsheet program with which you can perform calculations on and analyze data.
- **PowerPoint.** A full-featured program with which you can develop and present dynamic, professional-looking presentations.
- **Entourage.** An information-management program that handles your e-mail messages, schedule, tasks, and contacts.
- **Messenger.** A dynamic program that allows you to easily communicate with your co-workers regardless of their location or time zone.

Because Office 2008 has been designed as an integrated suite, many of the tasks you perform in each of the component programs are carried out in the same way, using the same kinds of tools and techniques. Rather than repeat the instruction for each program, we identify the common techniques for tasks such as formatting and working with graphics, and then show you what is different for each program.

New Features

Those of you who are upgrading from Office 2004 have a treat in store! Office 2008 is more powerful than its predecessor, as well as easier and more intuitive to use. Here are lists of the new features of Office 2008 that you will learn about in *Microsoft Office 2008 for Mac Step by Step* or its accompanying Web articles.

New in Office 2008

- **Office Toolbox.** Common to Word, Excel, and PowerPoint, the Toolbox contains most of the tools you will use for tasks such as formatting and inserting graphics.
- **Elements Gallery.** Another common feature, you use this gallery to perform many tasks in all three programs.
- **Themes.** These enable you to create documents, worksheets, and presentations with a common look.
- **SmartArt graphics.** With the new SmartArt feature, you can create professional-looking diagrams of processes and relationships in any document, worksheet, or presentation.
- **New file formats (Office Open XML Formats).** These file formats make it easy to share files with Windows-based computers, as well as reduce file sizes and improve data recovery.

New in Word 2008

- **Publishing Layout view.** In this new environment for desktop publishing, you can use professionally designed templates and powerful layout tools to create sophisticated Word publications.
- **Notebook Layout view.** This view has been enhanced so that you can personalize your Word notebooks.
- **Document elements.** You can quickly add preformatted elements, such as cover pages, headers and footers, and tables of contents to your documents.
- **Mail merge.** An improved and streamlined Mail Merge Manager now makes it easy to quickly merge documents and data to produce customized mass mailings.

New in Excel 2008

- **Bigger sheets.** You have more than 1 million rows and more than 16 thousand columns to play with!

- **New charting features.** Now you can use advanced formatting options to create precisely the effect you want.

- **Formula Builder.** This powerful tool helps you create formulas without stressing about function names and syntax.

- **Formula AutoComplete.** You type the beginning of a formula and then choose from valid options. It's that simple!

New in PowerPoint 2008

- **New themes, layouts, and Quick Styles.** With these professionally designed formatting options, you can quickly produce visually exciting slides that will catch your audience's attention.

- **Special effects.** When you need to add even more pizzazz, you can add effects such as 3-D, bevels, gradients, reflections, shadows, and glows.

- **Table styles.** You can use dynamic, built-in table styles to instantly format table headings, columns, and rows so that the information displayed in the table is easier to read and interpret.

- **Custom slide layouts.** If none of the existing slide layouts precisely fits your needs, you can easily create your own and specify the content placeholders, background, color scheme, and graphics you want.

New in Entourage 2008

- **Information management.** Spotlight search, categories, and the Favorites Bar are among the many features you can use to find, organize, and filter Entourage items.

- **Meeting management.** Setting up and updating meetings, accepting or declining meeting invitations, and communicating with participants is now easier with the new Calendar interface.

- **Out of Office messages.** You can schedule internal and external messages to occur automatically without having to specifically turn them on and off. (Available only for Exchange accounts.)

- **Junk and phishing message protection.** New detection capabilities and protection levels help you make your e-mail more secure than in earlier Entourage versions.

Let's Get Started!

The programs in Office 2008 are fun to use, and after you become familiar with basic tools and techniques for working in Office programs, there is practically no limit to the types of files you can create. This book gives you straightforward instructions for using Word, Excel, PowerPoint, and Entourage. It takes you from knowing little (or nothing) about any of the programs to a level of expertise that will enable you to create attractive, professional-looking documents, worksheets, and presentations that you can be proud to distribute to friends and family or colleagues and teachers. It also shows you how to use Entourage to stay in touch with the important people in your life and to keep track of your time and your tasks. We look forward to showing you around Microsoft Office 2008 for Mac.

Features and Conventions of This Book

The practice exercises in this book have been designed to lead you step by step through some of the tasks you are most likely to want to perform in the following programs, which are available in any edition of Microsoft Office 2008 for Mac: Microsoft Word 2008 for Mac, Microsoft Excel 2008 for Mac, Microsoft PowerPoint 2008 for Mac, and Microsoft Entourage 2008 for Mac.

This book is divided into five parts, each covering a related set of tasks or features. This makes it easier to identify skills and methods you can use in more than one Office 2008 program.

If, after reading the book and completing the practice exercises in each chapter, you later need help remembering how to perform a procedure, the following features of this book will help you locate specific information:

- **Detailed table of contents.** Scan this listing of the topics and sidebars within each chapter to quickly find the information you want.
- **Quick Reference.** Find simple instructions for performing tasks and procedures covered in detail elsewhere in the book. In addition to the generic instructions, the Quick Reference includes tables of keyboard shortcuts that you can use to perform many common tasks.
- **Chapter thumb tabs.** Easily locate the beginning of the chapter you want.
- **Topic-specific running heads.** Within a chapter, quickly locate the topic you want by looking at the running heads of odd-numbered pages.
- **Glossary.** Look up the meaning of a word or the definition of a concept.
- **Detailed index.** Look up specific tasks and features, and general concepts, in the index, which has been carefully crafted with the reader in mind.

You can save time when reading this book and working through the practice exercises by understanding how special instructions, keys to press, buttons to click, and other conventions are indicated in this book.

Convention	Meaning
	This icon at the end of a chapter introduction indicates information about the practice files you will use when working through the exercises in the chapter.
SET UP	This paragraph preceding a step-by-step exercise indicates the practice files or programs that you will use when working through the exercise, and any requirements you should attend to before beginning the exercise.
CLEAN UP	This paragraph following a step-by-step exercise indicates actions you should take to restore your system after completing the exercise, and provides instructions for closing open files or programs before moving on to another topic.
1 2	Blue numbered steps guide you through hands-on exercises in each topic.
1 2	Black numbered steps guide you through procedures in sidebars and in expository text.
→	An arrow indicates a procedure that has only one step. Multiple arrows indicate multiple one-step options for achieving the desired results.
Practice Makes Perfect!	This paragraph at the beginning of each chapter indicates the location of the practice files that you will use in the chapter's step-by-step exercises.
Note	These paragraphs provide information pertinent to the preceding step or paragraph.
Troubleshooting	These paragraphs warn you of potential missteps that might prevent you from continuing with the exercise.

Convention	Meaning
Tip	These paragraphs provide a helpful hint or shortcut that makes working through a task easier, or information about other available options.
See Also	These paragraphs direct you to more information about a given topic elsewhere in this book.
Resources	These paragraphs direct you to learning resources external to the book.
Bonus Web Content	These paragraphs direct you to articles and exercises that are available from the book's companion Web site, located at *www.microsoft.com/mspress/companion/9780735626171*.
Interface elements	In steps, the names of keyboard keys and program elements, such as buttons, commands, and dialog boxes, are shown in black bold characters.
	The first time in an exercise that you are told to click a button, or when the insertion point changes to an alternative shape, a picture of the button or insertion point appears in the left margin.
Control+Tab	A plus sign (+) between two key names means that you must hold down the first key while you press the second key. For example, "Press **Control+Tab**" means "Hold down the **Control** key while you press the **Tab** key."
User input	Text that you are supposed to type is shown in blue bold characters.
Glossary terms	Terms explained in the glossary are shown in blue italic type.
Item and screen element names	A variety of item and screen element names, such as file, folder and sheet tab names, placholder text, and emphasized words, are shown in italic characters.

Using the Companion Content

The companion content for this book includes practice files you can use as you work through the book's exercises. By using practice files, you won't have to spend time creating sample files that contain all the elements necessary to experiment with the features and skills we're discussing. Instead, you can jump right in and concentrate on learning how to use the programs.

In addition to the practice files, the companion content includes fully searchable electronic versions of this book and of the fifth edition of the award-winning *Microsoft Computer Dictionary*—the ultimate reference for the home or office with definitions and explanations of more than 10,000 technical terms!

Practice Files

Before you can use the practice files, you must install them on your computer. When properly installed, the files are stored on your hard-disk in chapter-specific subfolders of the *~/Documents/Microsoft Press/2008OfficeMacSBS/* folder. If you install the practice files to a location other than the default, you will need to substitute that path within the exercises.

Using the Practice Files

Each exercise is preceded by a SET UP paragraph listing the files needed for that exercise and explaining any preparations you should make before you start, and followed by a CLEAN UP paragraph explaining anything you need to do to restore your system before you continue.

Removing the Practice Files

You can free up hard disk space by removing the practice files. To do so, navigate in the Finder to the *~/Documents/Microsoft Press/* folder. To delete all the book's practice files, right-click the *2008OfficeMacSBS* folder, and then click Move To Trash.

> **Note** The companion content for this book does not contain the Microsoft Office 2008 for Mac software. You should purchase and install that program before using this book.

Practice File List

Chapter	Folder	File
Chapter 1: Explore and Manage the Office Interface	None	None
Chapter 2: Practice Basic Office File Skills	*OfficeSkills*	*BookSeries.docx* *ColorDesign.pptx* *CompanyMeeting.pptx* *Loan.xlsx*
Chapter 3: Work in Office Programs	*OfficePrograms*	*BookSeries.docx* *Introducing.pptx* *InvestmentCalculator.xlsx* *Loan.xlsx* *OfficeProcedures.docx*
Chapter 4: Create Word Documents	*CreateDocuments*	*AnnouncePlanner.docx*
Chapter 5: Create Excel Workbooks	*CreateWorkbooks*	*EmptyFolder.txt*
Chapter 6: Create PowerPoint Presentations	*CreatePresentations*	*Introducing.pptx* *SalesMeeting.pptx* *SalesPlanning.pptx*
Chapter 7: Work with Word Document Content	*WorkDocuments*	*FallNewsletter.docx* *SBSTemplate.dotx* *SeriesDescription.docx* *Unstyled.docx*
Chapter 8: Work with Excel Sheet Content	*WorkSheets*	*AirQuality.xlsx* *CookieSalesByTroop.xlsx*
Chapter 9: Create Excel Formulas	*CreateFormulas*	*AnnualSales.xlsx*
Chapter 10: Work with PowerPoint Slide Content	*WorkSlides*	*MyVacation.pptx*
Chapter 11: Format Office File Content	*FormatContent*	*Bamboo.docx* *OfficeDocs.docx*
Chapter 12: Create and Insert Graphics	*CreateGraphics*	*Kids1.jpg* *Panda1.jpg* *SummerActivities.pptx*
Chapter 13: Review Word Documents	*ReviewDocuments*	*Fairytale.docx*
Chapter 14: Add Finishing Document Elements	*FinishDocuments*	*Contents.docx* *FrostKing1.docx* *FrostKing2.docx* *Index.docx*
Chapter 15: Communicate Online	*Communicate*	*Fairytale.docx* *Smiley.png*
Chapter 16: Manage Contacts and Schedules	None	None

Bonus Web Content

While researching and developing content about Microsoft Office 2008 for Mac, we ended up with far more information than would fit into the printed book. The additional content is available, as articles and exercises, from the book's companion Web site, which is located at:

www.microsoft.com/mspress/companion/9780735626171

Bonus content available from the companion Web site includes articles such as these, and others that may be posted from time to time:

- "Add Timings to Slides in PowerPoint 2008 for Mac"
- "Animate Slide Content in PowerPoint 2008 for Mac"
- "Animate Slide Transitions in PowerPoint 2008 for Mac"
- "Create a Self-Running Presentation in PowerPoint 2008 for Mac"
- "Organize Text in Columns in Word 2008 for Mac"
- "Organize Text in Lists in Word 2008 for Mac"
- "Perform Calculations in a Table in Word 2008 for Mac"
- "Practice Working with Slide Masters in PowerPoint 2008 for Mac"
- "Prepare Speaker Notes and Handouts for Presentations in PowerPoint 2008 for Mac"
- "Present Text in a Tabular List in Word 2008 for Mac"
- "Restructuring Content in Outline View in Word 2008 for Mac"
- "Work with Publication Elements in Word 2008 for Mac"
- "Work with Tables in PowerPoint 2008 for Mac"
- "Work with Tables in Word 2008 for Mac"

Digital Content for Digital Book Readers: If you bought a digital-only edition of this book, you can access the print edition's companion content online.

Visit *www.microsoft.com/mspress/companion/9780735626171* to get your downloadable content. This content is always up-to-date and available to all readers.

Minimum System Requirements

This book includes discussions of the following programs in the Home & Student Edition of Office 2008 for Mac:

- Microsoft Office Word 2008 for Mac
- Microsoft Office Excel 2008 for Mac
- Microsoft Office PowerPoint 2008 for Mac
- Microsoft Office Entourage 2008 for Mac

To install and run these programs, your computer needs to meet the following minimum requirements:

- Processor: Intel, PowerPC G5, or PowerPC G4 (500 MHz or faster) processor
- Operating System: Mac OS X version 10.4.9 or later
- Memory: 512 megabytes (MB) of RAM
- Hard Disk: 1.5 gigabytes (GB) of available disk space

> **Tip** Hard disk requirements will vary depending on configuration; custom installation choices might require more or less hard disk space.

- Display: 1024 x 768 or higher resolution monitor
- Drive: DVD-ROM
- Peripherals: Keyboard and mouse or compatible pointing device
- Miscellaneous: HFS+ hard disk format file format (also known as Mac OS Extended or HFS Plus); Microsoft Entourage and certain features require Internet access

In addition to the hardware, software, and connections required to run Office 2008, you will need the following to successfully complete the exercises in this book:

- Word 2008, Excel 2008, PowerPoint 2008, and Entourage 2008
- 25 MB of available hard disk space for the practice files

Getting Help

Every effort has been made to ensure the accuracy of this book and its companion content. If you run into problems, please contact the appropriate source, listed in the following sections, for help and assistance.

Getting Help with This Book and Its Companion Content

If your question or issue concerns the content of this book or its companion content, please first consult the Microsoft Press Book and CD Support page, located at:

www.microsoft.com/learning/support/books/

From this page, you can access information about replacement books and CDs, and locate the errata page, which contains corrections for known content issues. You can also report content issues if you find an error in the book that doesn't yet appear on the book's errata page.

To locate the errata page for a specific book, enter the book's ISBN (located in the white box in the lower-left corner of the back cover), including hyphens, into the search box on the Microsoft Help and Support site, which is located at:

support.microsoft.com

Another place to look for helpful information is on this book's companion Web site, where we'll be posting additional articles and exercises that didn't fit into the printed book, and practice files necessary for the exercises. You can find the companion Web site at:

www.microsoft.com/mspress/companion/9780735626171

If you don't find the help you're looking for from any of these resources, you can send comments or questions to Microsoft Learning Technical Support at:

mspinput@microsoft.com

Or you can contact me (the author) through my blog, which is located at:

joanpreppernau.spaces.live.com

Constructive feedback, error reports, and questions that help to shape future versions of this and other books are always welcome.

Getting Help with an Office 2008 Program

If your question is about a specific Office 2008 program, and not about the content of this book, your first recourse is the program's Help system. This system is a combination of information that was stored on your computer when you installed Office 2008 for Mac (Offline Help) and, if your computer is connected to the Internet, the most up-to-date information available online from Microsoft (Online Help). You can find general or specific Help information in several ways:

- You can display a ScreenTip containing a description of a toolbar button, or of a button, command, setting, or action in the Toolbox, by pointing to the item.
- You can display the program's Help system by using any of these methods:
  - → In Word, Excel, or PowerPoint, click the purple **Help** button at the right end of the Standard toolbar.
  - → On the **Help** menu of any program, click the Help item specific to that program (for example, Excel Help).
  - → In any program, press **Command+?** (Command+Question Mark).
- In an operating system-related dialog box (for example, the **Print** dialog box), you can display Mac Help system information specific to that dialog box by clicking the **Help** button located in its lower-left corner.

If you don't find the information you need in the program's Help system, consult the Office 2008 for Mac Solution Center, which is part of the Microsoft Help and Support site located at:

support.microsoft.com

From the home page of the site, point to Self Support Options (in the Support Options list in the left pane) and click Product Solution Centers. In the Office Products section of the Select A Product Solution Center page, click Office 2008 For Mac (or, if it's not listed, start entering the product name in the Quick Product Finder box at the top of the page and then, in the list that appears, click the product you're looking for help with).

Additional information is available from the Help and How-To section of the Mactopia site, which is located at:

www.microsoft.com/mac/

About the Author

Joan Preppernau has worked in the training and certification industry for 12 years. As President of Online Training Solutions, Inc. (OTSI), Joan is responsible for guiding the translation of technical information and requirements into useful, relevant, and measurable training, learning, and certification deliverables. Joan is a Microsoft Certified Technology Specialist, a Microsoft Certified Application Specialist Instructor, and the author or coauthor of more than two dozen books about Windows and Office (for Windows and for Mac).

Joan enjoys a blissful life in America's Finest City—San Diego, California—with her husband, Barry, and their young daughter, Trinity, who has appropriated one of Mommy's laptops so she can write her own book about computers—and will undoubtedly create a bestseller as soon as she masters basic reading and writing skills.

Online Training Solutions, Inc. (OTSI)

OTSI specializes in the design, creation, and production of Office and Windows training products for information workers and home computer users. For more information about OTSI, visit:

www.otsi.com

America's Finest Publishing Team

To borrow a phrase, it takes a village to write a book. This book would really and truly not exist without the support of these creative, intelligent, encouraging, and witty members of the OTSI publishing team:

- Charles Preppernau, who reviewed all the exercises to locate errors, omissions, and necessary clarifications, so that you (hopefully) won't find any.
- Debbie Berman, who patiently processed—and reprocessed—the hundreds of graphics that provide important visual references and reinforcement.
- Jaime Odell, who did a superb job copyediting the text and catching the many errors resulting from my fingers functioning separately from my brain.
- Jan Bednarczuk, who was willing to step in whenever required.
- Jean Trenary, who managed the production processes, provided constant support, encouragement, and sanity checks, and laid out the book so beautifully.
- Jeanne Craver, who provided graphic processing support.
- Joyce Cox, who helped to start me on this path 25 years ago, and has been an incredible mentor and partner for the past 10 years, provided invaluable input throughout the process and created the amazing Quick Reference section. Many of the practice files and file concepts are Joyce's work.
- Kathy Krause, who provided superb developmental input and managed the content creation processes with dedication, perseverance, and a great attitude.
- Lisa Van Every, who provided production support when InDesign got cranky.
- Marlene Lambert, who provided support for the always-cranky indexing tools.
- Rob Carr, who helped to organize the companion content.
- Susie Bayers, who gathered information and tracked book elements along the way.

We're especially thankful to the support staff at home who make it possible for our team members to devote so much of their time and attention to these projects.

Thanks also to Seth Maislin and the Potomac Indexing team for the detailed index, and to the many people at Microsoft Press and Microsoft Learning who supported this book through its inception, creation, and release, including Juliana Aldous, Rosemary Caperton, Elizabeth Hansford, Sandra Haynes, Bill Teel, Charlotte Twiss, and Michael Zuberbier.

Quick Reference

Microsoft Office 2008 for Mac Q-3

Microsoft Word 2008 for Mac. Q-21

Microsoft Excel 2008 for Mac Q-39

Microsoft PowerPoint 2008 for Mac Q-55

Microsoft Entourage 2008 for Mac Q-69

Microsoft Office 2008 for Mac

Office 2008 Keyboard Shortcuts... Q-4
Basic Office 2008 Skills Q-6
    Closing files and programs Q-6
    Dialog boxes Q-6
    Document windows Q-6
    Elements Gallery Q-6
    Opening files Q-7
    Preferences dialog box...Q-7
    Saving files Q-7
    Selecting text... Q-8
    Starting and activating programs Q-8
    Toolbars and the toolbar area Q-9
    Toolbox Q-9
Simple Instructions for Doing Things in Office 2008 ....Q-10
    AutoCorrect Q-10
    Clip art Q-10
    Compatibility reports..Q-10
    Diagrams Q-11
    Editing content Q-11
    Finding and replacing text and formatting Q-12
    Font Book..Q-13
    Format Painter..Q-13
    Formatting graphics...Q-13
    Formatting Palette Q-14
    Formatting text manually Q-14
    Page setup Q-14
    Photos and pictures Q-14
    Printing files..Q-15
    Program preferences Q-15
    Project Gallery..Q-16
    Reference tools Q-16
    Saving files Q-16
    Shapes...Q-17
    SmartArt diagrams Q-17
    Software Update..Q-18
    Status bar Q-18
    Symbols..Q-18
    System control..Q-18
    Themes Q-18
    User information..Q-19
    Viewing files..Q-19

Office 2008 Keyboard Shortcuts

You can quickly perform tasks by using keyboard shortcuts—one or more keys that you press on the keyboard to complete a task. For example, pressing Command+P opens the Print dialog box.

> **Note** Keyboard shortcut descriptions refer to the U.S. keyboard layout. Keys on other keyboard layouts might not correspond to the keys on a U.S. keyboard. Keyboard shortcuts for laptop computers might also differ.

Working with files, programs, and tools

To	Press
Create a new file or item	Command+N
Save	Command+S
Print	Command+P
Open a file	Command+O
Close a file	Command+W
Quit the current program	Command+Q
Hide the current program	Command+H
Switch to the next program	Command+Tab
Switch to the previous program	Shift+Command+Tab
Hide other programs	Command+Option+H
Minimize the window	Command+M
View Reference Tools (Entourage)	Shift+Command+Option+R
View Reference Tools (Excel, PowerPoint, Word)	Command+Option+R
Open the Project Gallery	Shift+Command+P
Open the Preferences dialog box	Command+Comma

Dialog boxes

To	Press
Move to the next box, option, control, or command	Tab
Move to the previous box, option, control, or command	Shift+Tab
Exit a dialog box or cancel an action	Escape
Perform the action assigned to a default button	Return

Editing

To	Press
Undo the last change	Command+Z
Redo or repeat the last action	Command+Y
Cut the selection to the Clipboard	Command+X
Copy the selection to the Clipboard	Command+C
Copy the selection to the Scrapbook	Shift+Command+C
Paste from the Clipboard	Command+V
Paste from the Scrapbook	Shift+Command+V
Select All	Command+A
Display the Find dialog box	Command+F
Delete one character to the left	Delete
Delete one character to the right	Del or Clear

Formatting

To	Press
Apply or remove bold formatting	Command+B
Apply or remove an underline	Command+U
Apply or remove italic formatting	Command+I
Insert hyperlink	Command+K

Moving around in text

To	Press
One character to the left	Left Arrow
One character to the right	Right Arrow
One line up	Up Arrow
One line down	Down Arrow
To the beginning of a word or one word to the left	Option+Left Arrow
One word to the right	Option+Right Arrow
To the end of a line	Command+Right Arrow or End
To the beginning of a line	Command+Left Arrow or Home
To the beginning of a paragraph or up one paragraph	Option+Up Arrow
Down one paragraph	Option+Down Arrow
Display the Find dialog box	Command+F

Basic Office 2008 Skills

These basic skills are either unrelated to a specific program feature, or necessary to know in order to complete other sets of instructions.

Closing files and programs

To close an Office file

→ Click **Close** on the **File** menu.

→ Click the **Close** button in the upper-left corner of the window.

To close an Office file and quit the program

→ Click **Quit** on the **File** menu.

To quit a program

→ Click **Quit <Program>** on the **<Program>** menu.

To force an unresponsive program to quit

1. Click **Force Quit** on the **Apple** menu.
2. In the **Force Quit Applications** dialog box, click the program, and click **Force Quit**.
3. In the confirmation message box, click **Force Quit** again.

Dialog boxes

To move a dialog box

→ Drag its title bar.

Document windows

See Also "Viewing files" later in this Quick Reference section

To close a document window

→ Click the red **Close** button at the left end of the window's title bar.

To temporarily hide a document window

→ Click the yellow **Minimize** button at the left end of the title bar.

To change the size of the document window

→ Drag the resize handle.

To restore the default document window size

→ Click the green **Restore** button at the left end of the title bar.

Elements Gallery

To display or hide a gallery

→ Click the tab of the gallery you want to display.

→ Click the active tab to hide a gallery.

→ Double-click any inactive tab to hide a gallery.

To open or close the Elements Gallery

→ Click the **Gallery** button on the Standard toolbar.

→ Click **Elements Gallery** on the **View** menu.

→ Click the active Elements Gallery tab.

→ Double-click an inactive Elements Gallery tab,.

To manage the behavior and appearance of the Elements Gallery

→ On the **Gallery** page of the **Preferences** dialog box, select the **General** and **Appearance** options you want.

Opening files

To start an Office 2008 program and open a document

→ Double-click the Office file in the Finder.

→ Right-click the document and click **Open**.

To open an existing Office file

→ Open a document you have worked with recently by pointing to **Open Recent** on the **File** menu and then clicking the file you want.

Or

1. Click **Open** on the **File** menu, or click the **Open** button on the Standard toolbar.

2. In the **Open** dialog box, navigate to the file you want to open, and then do one of the following:

   ● Open the original file for editing by double-clicking the file.

   ● Open the file for viewing only by clicking **Read-Only** in the **Open** list and then clicking **Open**.

   ● Open a copy of the file by clicking **Copy** in the **Open** list and then clicking **Open**.

Preferences dialog box

To display the Preferences dialog box for the active program

→ Click **Preferences** on the **<Program>** menu.

To display a specific page of preferences

→ In the **Preferences** dialog box, click the icon for that page.

→ In the **Search** box in the upper-right corner of the **Preferences** dialog box, enter a search term related to the desired setting to spotlight the appropriate page.

To return to the list of preferences

→ At the top of the active page, click the **Show All** button.

Saving files

To save a file for the first time

1. Click **Save** on the **File** menu, or click the **Save** button on the Standard toolbar.

2. In the **Save As** pane, navigate to the folder where you want to save the file, assign a name to the file, and then click **Save**.

To save changes to an existing file

→ Click the **Save** button on the Standard toolbar.

To save a copy with a different name or in a different location

1. Click **Save As** on the **File** menu.
2. In the **Save As** pane, navigate to the folder where you want to save the copy of the file, or assign a different name to the file, and then click **Save**.

To create a new folder while saving a file

1. Display the navigation area of the **Save As** pane, and click **New Folder**.
2. In the **New Folder** dialog box, replace *untitled folder* with the name you want, and click **Create**.

Selecting text

See Also "Office 2008 Keyboard Shortcuts" earlier in this Quick Reference section

To select text

→ Select an individual word by double-clicking it.

→ Select adjacent words, lines, or paragraphs by dragging through them.

→ Select adjacent words, lines, or paragraphs by positioning the insertion point at the beginning of the text, holding down the **Shift** key, and either pressing an arrow key or clicking at the end of the text you want to select.

→ Select a sentence by clicking anywhere in the sentence while holding down the **Command** key.

→ Select a line by clicking the selection area to the left of the line.

→ Select a paragraph by triple-clicking it, or by double-clicking the selection area to the left of the paragraph.

→ Select an entire document by triple-clicking anywhere in the selection area.

To select noncontiguous blocks of text

→ Select the first block of text, and then hold down the **Command** key while selecting additional blocks.

To release selected text

→ Click in the document window anywhere other than in the selected text or selection area.

Starting and activating programs

To start or switch to an Office 2008 program

→ Click the program icon in the Dock.

To start an Office 2008 program and open a document

→ Double-click an Office file in the Finder.

→ Right-click the document in the Finder and click **Open**.

To start an Office 2008 program from the Finder

→ In the Finder, open the *Applications* folder and then the *Microsoft Office 2008* folder. Then do one of the following:
- Double-click the program you want to run.
- Right-click the program and click **Open**.

To open the Project Gallery

→ Click the **Project Gallery** icon in the Dock.

→ Click **Project Gallery** on the **File** menu.

Toolbars and the toolbar area

To display or hide a toolbar

→ Point to **Toolbars** on the **View** menu, and then click the name of the toolbar you want to display or hide.

→ Right-click anywhere in the toolbar area (not on the title bar), point to **Toolbars** on the shortcut menu that appears, and then click the name of the toolbar you want to display or hide.

To move a floating toolbar

→ Drag its title bar.

To manage the appearance and content of the toolbar area

→ Display or hide the toolbar area by clicking the **Hide Toolbars** button in the upper-right corner of the document window.

→ Display or hide icon labels in the toolbar area by right-clicking in the toolbar area and then clicking **Icon Only**.

Toolbox

To manage the appearance and content of the Toolbox

→ Display or hide the Toolbox by clicking the **Toolbox** button on the Standard toolbar.

→ Switch palettes by clicking the palette buttons at the top of the Toolbox, or by choosing the palette you want from the **View** menu.

→ Minimize the Toolbox by double-clicking its title bar. Double-click again to restore the Toolbox.

→ When the Toolbox is minimized, display a palette by clicking its button.

→ Move the Toolbox on the screen by dragging it by its title bar.

→ Dock the Toolbox by dragging it close to the left or right edge of the screen.

→ Swivel the Toolbox to display the Toolbox Settings pane by clicking the Settings button.

→ Control how and when the Toolbox closes by using the commands at the top of the Toolbox Settings pane.

→ Control what appears on each Toolbox palette by using the commands at the bottom of the Toolbox Settings pane.

→ Change the color scheme of the Toolbox from the **Gallery** page of the **Preferences** dialog box.

Simple Instructions for Doing Things in Office 2008

The generic instructions in this topic apply to the core Office 2008 programs: Microsoft Word 2008 for Mac, Microsoft Excel 2008 for Mac, and Microsoft PowerPoint 2008 for Mac.

AutoCorrect

To add a misspelled word to the AutoCorrect list

→ On the **AutoCorrect** page of the **Preferences** dialog box, enter the misspelled word in the **Replace** box and the correct spelling in the **With** box.

To cancel an AutoCorrect replacement

→ Click the **Undo** button on the Standard toolbar before you type anything else.

→ Click the **AutoCorrect Options** button, and then click **Undo**, **Change back to**, or **Stop Automatically Correcting**.

To manage AutoCorrect

→ On the **AutoCorrect** page of the **Preferences** dialog box, select or configure options for automatically correcting text and formatting as you type.

Clip art

To view the available clip art

→ Display the **Clip Art** page of the **Object Palette**.

→ Change the size of the images in the preview window by moving the slider at the bottom of the palette.

To insert a clip

→ On the **Clip Art** page of the **Object Palette**, click **Clip Art** in the category list, click the clip you want, and then drag it to the document, worksheet, or slide.

To add an image to the Clip Gallery

1. Open the **Clip Gallery** by clicking **Clip Art** on the **Insert** menu.
2. Click **Online** to display the Microsoft Office Online Web site, and search for the image you want.
3. Select the **Add to selection basket** check box adjacent to the image.
4. Use the links in the **Selection Basket** pane on the left side of the screen to preview the selected clip and download it.
5. After the clip is downloaded, navigate to the **Downloads** window or to the *Downloads* folder in your user profile, right-click the file, and click **Open**.

Compatibility reports

To check the compatibility of a document with other versions

→ In the Toolbox, click the **Compatibility Report** button.

→ On the **View** menu, under **Toolbox**, click **Compatibility Report**.

To identify the cause of a compatibility issue

→ In the **Compatibility Report** palette, click an item in the **Results** list to activate the specific document element that generated the warning.

To remove a warning from the Results list

→ Click the warning and then, in the **Ignore** list, click **Ignore Once** to remove the currently selected warning, **Ignore All** to remove all current instances of the warning, or **Don't Show Again** to stop generating the warning.

To manage the Compatibility Report feature

→ On the **Compatibility** page of the **Preferences** dialog box, select or configure options that control the behavior of the **Compatibility Report** palette and file settings that affect compatibility with previous program versions.

Diagrams

See "SmartArt diagrams" later in this Quick Reference section

Editing content

See Also "Office 2008 Keyboard Shortcuts" earlier in this Quick Reference section

To start a new paragraph or a new line at the insertion point

→ Start a new paragraph by pressing **Return**.

→ Start a new line within the same paragraph by pressing **Shift+Return**.

To insert text

→ Click to position the insertion point, and begin typing.

To delete content

→ Click to position the insertion point, and then press the **Delete** key to delete the character to the left or press the **Del** key to delete the character to the right.

To copy selected content to the Clipboard

→ Click **Copy** on the **Edit** menu.

To paste content from the Clipboard

→ Position the insertion point where you want to insert the clipping, and then click **Paste** on the **Edit** menu.

To change the default pasting operation

→ After pasting, click the **Paste Options** button and click the option you want.

To combine two paragraphs

→ Delete the paragraph mark at the end of the first paragraph.

To move selected content by dragging

→ Point to the selection, press and hold the mouse button, drag the selection to its new location, and release the mouse button.

To move selected text via the Clipboard

1. Click **Cut** on the **Edit** menu.
2. Position the insertion point in the location in which you want to insert the clipping, and then click **Paste** on the **Edit** menu.

To undo or redo a change

→ Undo the last action by clicking the **Undo** button on the Standard toolbar.
→ Undo multiple actions by clicking the earliest action you want to undo in the **Undo** list.
→ Redo the last action by clicking the **Redo** button on the Standard toolbar.
→ Redo multiple actions by clicking the earliest action you want to redo in the **Redo** list.

To control how the program behaves when you are editing an Office file

→ On the **Edit** page of the **Preferences** dialog box, select or configure options that control how the program behaves while you are editing a document.

Finding and replacing text and formatting

To find a search term

1. Click **Find** on the **Edit** menu.
2. On the **Find** page of the **Find and Replace** dialog box, type the term you want to locate in the **Find what** box, and then click **Find Next**.

To refine a search

1. Display the **Find** page of the **Find and Replace** dialog box, and enter the search term.
2. If necessary, click the **Expand** button. On the expanded **Find** page, select options to more specifically define the search.

To find a special character

1. Display the expanded **Find** page of the **Find and Replace** dialog box.
2. In the **Special** list, click the character you want to search for, and then either click **Find Next** or select the **Highlight all items found in** check box and click **Find All**.
3. Click **Close**.

To replace a search term

1. Click **Replace** on the **Edit** menu, or if the **Find** page of the **Find and Replace** dialog box is already displayed, click the **Replace** button.
2. On the **Replace** page, type the term you want to locate in the **Find what** box and the replacement term in the **Replace with** box, and then do one of the following:
   - Locate and select the next occurrence of the search term by clicking **Find Next**. When you find an occurrence you want to replace, click **Replace**.
   - Replace all occurrences in the document by clicking **Replace All**.
3. Click **Close**.

To replace formatting (Word and Excel)

See Also "To replace a font throughout a presentation" in the "PowerPoint 2008 for Mac" Quick Reference section

1. Display the expanded **Replace** page of the **Find and Replace** dialog box, and enter the **Find what** and **Replace with** terms, if any.
2. Select the type of formatting you want to search for in the **Format** list, and the type you want to replace it with.
3. Either click **Find Next** and **Replace**, or click **Replace All**.
4. Click **Close**.

Font Book

To open the Font Book

→ Click **Font Book** in the */Applications/* folder.

Format Painter

To copy formatting from a selection and apply it to only one other location

→ Click the **Format Painter** button on the Standard toolbar, and then either click a single content item or drag across multiple contiguous items to apply the formatting.

To copy formatting from a selection and apply it to multiple locations

1. On the Standard toolbar, double-click the **Format Painter** button.
2. Click or drag across each item you want to apply formatting to.
3. Press the **Escape** key to release the Format Painter.

Formatting graphics

To change the size of a graphic

→ Drag a corner handle to resize a shape while maintaining its aspect ratio.
→ Drag the top or bottom handle to change the height of the shape.
→ Drag a side handle to change the width of the shape.
→ Precisely resize the graphic by right-clicking it, clicking **Format Shape**, and then setting the height, width, or scale on the **Size** page of the **Format Object** dialog box.

To rotate a graphic

→ Drag a green rotation handle to rotate the shape in a clockwise or counterclockwise direction.
→ If necessary, display a green rotation handle by opening the **Size, Rotation, and Ordering** panel of the **Formatting Palette**, clicking the **Rotate** button, and then clicking **Free Rotate**.
→ Rotate precisely by right-clicking the shape, clicking **Format Shape**, and then on the **Size** page of the **Format Shape** dialog box, setting an exact degree of rotation.

To change the stacking order, distribution, or alignment

→ Right-click the shape whose stacking order you want to change, point to **Arrange**, and then click one of the options.

Formatting Palette

To display the Formatting Palette

→ In the Toolbox, click the **Formatting Palette** button.

→ On the **View** menu, under **Toolbox**, click **Formatting Palette**.

Formatting text manually

See Also "Formatting text manually" in the "Word 2008 for Mac" Quick Reference section

To change the font of selected text

→ In the **Font** panel of the **Formatting Palette**, in the **Font Name** list, click the font you want.

To vary the look of text without changing the font

→ Change the font size by clicking the size you want in the **Size** list in the **Font** panel.

→ Increase or decrease the font size in set increments by sliding the **Size** control in the **Font** panel.

→ Change the font style by clicking a style button on the Formatting toolbar or by clicking the style in the **Font** panel.

→ Change the font color to a different theme or standard color by clicking the color you want in the **Font Color** list in the **Font** panel.

Page setup

To control the size and orientation of printed files

→ Set the page size by changing the **Paper Size** setting in the **Page Setup** dialog box.

→ Orient content vertically or horizontally on the page by clicking the corresponding button in the **Page Setup** panel of the **Formatting Palette**, or in the **Page Setup** dialog box.

→ Define the printable area of the page by setting the left, right, top, and bottom margins in the **Document Margins** panel of the **Formatting Palette**.

Photos and pictures

To insert an image from a file

→ Point to **Picture** on the **Insert** menu, and then click **From File**.

→ On the **Photos** page of the **Object Palette**, double-click the image or drag it to the page.

To add a folder or library to the Photos page

1. In the category list at the top of the **Photos** page, click **Other Library Or Folder**.

2. In the lower-left corner of the **Open Library Or Folder** dialog box, click **Show iPhoto Libraries** or **Show Image Folders** to indicate the type of folder you want to add.

3. Select the image folder or iPhoto library you want to add to the **Object Palette**, and then click **Choose**.

To format a selected picture

→ Apply a preset Quick Style, shadow, glow, reflection, or three-dimensional effect from the corresponding tab in the **Quick Styles and Effects** panel of the **Formatting Palette**.

→ Apply a custom shadow effect from the **Shadow** panel of the **Formatting Palette**.

→ Apply a custom reflection effect from the **Reflection** panel of the **Formatting Palette**.

→ Apply a monotone color wash by clicking the **Recolor** button in the **Picture** panel of the **Formatting Palette** and then in the picture, clicking an area of the color you want to set as transparent.

→ Crop the picture by clicking the **Crop** button in the **Picture** panel and then dragging the corner and side handles that appear.

→ Cut the picture into a shape by clicking the **Change Shape** button in the **Picture** panel, pointing to the shape group, and then clicking the shape you want.

→ Make one color in the picture transparent (so that you can see through the picture to its background) by clicking the **Set Transparent Color** button in the **Picture** panel and then, in the picture, clicking the color you want to make transparent.

→ Apply a specialized image effect (Distortion, Stylize, Color Adjustment, Color Effect, Blur, Sharpen, or Halftone Effect) by clicking **Effects** in the **Picture** panel and then, in the **Image Effects** dialog box, clicking the effect you want and, if necessary, adjusting the default effect settings.

→ Replace the current picture with another while retaining the shape and effects, by clicking the **Replace** button in the **Picture** panel and then, in the **Choose a Picture** window, double-clicking the replacement picture.

Printing files

To print the contents of a file by using the default settings

→ Click the **Print** button on the Standard toolbar.

To print part of a file or to print by using non-default settings

→ Click **Print** on the **File** menu, choose the settings you want in the **Print** dialog box, and then click **Print**.

To preview a file before printing

→ In the **Print** dialog box, select the **Show Quick Preview** check box and view each page in turn in the **Quick Preview** pane by clicking the **Next** and **Previous** buttons below the pane.

Program preferences

To control basic settings specific to a program

→ On the **General** page of the **Preferences** dialog box, select and configure options that control general settings, such as menu, sound, and appearance options.

To control the display of content and program elements (such as scroll bars)

→ On the **View** page of the **Preferences** dialog box, select and configure options that control how a program displays a file and which types of objects appear on screen.

To control the information saved with an Office file and the save frequency of AutoRecover versions

→ On the **Save** page of the **Preferences** dialog box, select or configure options for how the program saves files.

Project Gallery

To display the Project Gallery

→ Click **Project Gallery** on the **File** menu.

→ Click the **Microsoft Project Gallery** icon in the Dock.

→ Double-click **Microsoft Project Gallery** in the */Applications/Microsoft Office 2008/Office/* folder.

To manage the behavior and appearance of the Project Gallery

→ On the **Settings** page of the **Project Gallery**, select the **General**, **Documents and Wizards**, and **File Locations** options you want.

Reference tools

To display reference information for a word or phrase

→ Type the word or phrase in the **Search** box at the top of the **Reference Tools** palette and then press **Return**.

To research alternatives for a word by using the thesaurus

1. In the **Reference Tools** palette of the Toolbox, expand the **Thesaurus** panel.
2. In the **Search** box at the top of the palette, enter the word or phrase you want to look up and then press **Return**.
3. In the **Meanings** list, click the meaning that is most representative of the meaning you want to convey.
4. Research a suggested synonym further by clicking it and then clicking the **Look Up** button.
5. Insert a synonym from the list by clicking it and then clicking the **Insert** button.

To translate a word or phrase into another language

→ Right-click the word, or select and right-click the phrase, and then click **Translate**.
   Or
1. In the **Reference Tools** palette of the Toolbox, expand the **Translation** panel.
2. In the **Translation** panel, choose the original language in the **From** list, and the language you want to translate to in the **To** list.
3. Enter the word or phrase you want to translate In the **Search** box at the top of the palette and then press **Return**.

Saving files

To set the default locations in which Word looks for and saves files

→ On the **File Locations** page of the **Preferences** dialog box, click **Documents**, **Clipart pictures**, **User templates**, **Workgroup templates**, **User options**, **AutoRecover files**, **Tools**, or **Startup**, and then click **Modify**. In the **Choose a Folder** dialog box, select the folder and then click **Choose**.

Shapes

To insert a shape

→ Insert a shape at its default size by clicking it on the **Shapes** page of the **Office Palette** and then clicking the document, worksheet, or slide.

→ Insert a custom-sized shape by clicking it on the **Shapes** page and then dragging across the document, worksheet, or slide.

→ Insert a shape with equal horizontal and vertical dimensions by holding down the **Shift** key while you drag.

To format a shape

→ Make any of the following modifications from the **Formatting Palette** (in Word, Excel, and PowerPoint), from the **Format AutoShape** dialog box (in Word), or from the **Format Shape** dialog box (in PowerPoint):

  - Change the dimensions and angle of rotation.
  - Change the fill color and outline color.
  - Add shadows, glows, reflections, and three-dimensional effects.

To display the Format AutoShape or Format Shape dialog box

→ Right-click the shape and then click **Format AutoShape** or **Format Shape**.

To add text to a selected shape

→ Click in the text area of the shape to activate the insertion point, or right-click the shape and click **Add Text**. Then type the text that you want the shape to display.

→ Format the text by right-clicking the shape, clicking **Format Text**, and then in the **Format Text** dialog box, choosing the options you want.

SmartArt diagrams

To insert a diagram

1. Display the **SmartArt Graphics** tab of the Elements Gallery, click the button for the type of diagram you want, and then click the diagram thumbnail.

2. In the **Text** pane, click a placeholder and type the text you want to appear in the corresponding shape.

3. To promote, demote, add, and remove shapes, click the buttons on the **Text Pane** window toolbar.

To modify a diagram

→ Add and remove shapes, and edit the text that appears in the shapes, by making changes in the **Text** pane.

→ Move a shape within a diagram by dragging it.

→ Remove a shape from a diagram by selecting it and then pressing the **Del** key.

→ Use the options in the panels of the **Formatting Palette** of the Toolbox to make changes such as the following:

  - Switch to a different layout of the same type or of a different type.
  - Add shading and three-dimensional effects to all the shapes in a diagram.
  - Change the color scheme.

- Change an individual shape—for example, you can change a square into a star to make it stand out.
- Apply a built-in shape style.
- Change the color, outline, or effect of a shape.

Software Update

To configure the Software Update feature to automatically check for and download updates

1. In the Dock, click the **System Preferences** icon.
2. In the **System Preferences** window, under **System, click Software Update**.
3. In the **Software Update** window, select the **Check for updates** check box and the **Download important updates automatically** check box.
4. In the **Check for updates** list, choose the update frequency (**Daily**, **Weekly**, or **Monthly**).

To manually check for updates

→ Click the **Check Now** button on the **Software Update** page of the **System Preferences** dialog box.

Status bar

To turn the display of information on the status bar off and on

→ Right-click the status bar and click the item you want to turn on or off.

Symbols

To insert a symbol

→ On the **Symbol** page of the **Object Palette**, click the category you want in the category list, click the symbol you want, and then drag it to the document, worksheet, or slide.

→ To insert the symbol as a text character rather than a movable, resizable image, click an insertion point before dragging the symbol.

System control

To access commands for controlling your Mac

→ Click the **Apple** icon at the left end of any menu bar and then click the command you want.

Themes

To apply a different theme

→ Click the thumbnail of the theme you want in the **Document Theme** gallery of the **Formatting Palette**.

To change the color scheme

→ In the **Document Theme** gallery, click the color scheme you want in the **Colors** list.

To change the font scheme

→ In the **Document Theme** gallery, click the font scheme you want in the **Fonts** list.

User information

To edit user information in Word, PowerPoint, and Excel

→ On the page of the **Preferences** dialog box listed for each program, enter the information you want to appear in all programs:

- Word: The **User Information** page
- PowerPoint: The **Advanced** page
- Excel: The **General** page

To edit user information in Entourage

→ In the Address Book, create a contact record containing your information. Then on the **Contact** menu, click **This Contact Is Me**.

Viewing files

To change the view

→ Click commands on the **View** menu.

→ Click buttons on the **View** toolbar in the lower-left corner of the window.

See Also the additional techniques in the "Viewing" topics in the "Word 2008 for Mac," "Excel 2008 for Mac," and "PowerPoint 2008 for Mac" Quick Reference sections

To change the magnification

→ Choose a specific magnification level or way of fitting the content in the window from the **Zoom** list on the Standard toolbar

→ Click **Zoom** on the **View** menu, select the magnification you want in the **Zoom** dialog box, and click **OK**.

To scroll parts of a file into view

→ Move up or down by clicking the scroll arrows at either end of the vertical scroll bar. Move left or right by clicking the scroll arrows at either end of the horizontal scroll bar.

→ Move in bigger increments by clicking the scroll bar on either side of the scroll box.

→ Drag the scroll box on the scroll bar until the part of the document you want to view is visible.

To open a second window for the same file

→ Click **New Window** on the **Window** menu.

To view two or more files of the same type at the same time

→ In Excel, click **Arrange** on the **Window** menu, select the arrangement you want in the **Arrange Windows** dialog box, and click **OK**.

→ In PowerPoint and Word, click **Arrange All** on the **Window** menu to automatically arrange the open windows of that program.

To bring all documents from the same program to the front of a stack

→ Click **Bring To Front** on the **Window** menu.

Microsoft Word 2008 for Mac

Word 2008 Keyboard Shortcuts Q-22
Simple Instructions for Doing Things in Word 2008 . . . . .Q-26
    Bibliography. Q-26
    Borders and shading Q-26
    Charts Q-26
    Comments Q-27
    Copying and pasting content Q-28
    Cover pages Q-28
    Document formatting Q-28
    Document properties. Q-28
    Document templates Q-29
    Finding text Q-29
    Formatting text by using styles Q-29
    Formatting text manually Q-30
    Formatting paragraphs Q-31
    Headers and footers. Q-31
    Hiding text Q-32
    Index Q-32
    Inserting and linking to files Q-33
    Inserting information fields. Q-33
    New documents Q-33
    Page breaks Q-34
    Page numbers Q-34
    Ruler Q-34
    Section breaks. Q-35
    Spelling and Grammar. Q-35
    Tables of contents (TOCs) Q-35
    Tracking changes. Q-36
    Viewing documents Q-37
    Watermarks Q-38

Word 2008 Keyboard Shortcuts

Moving the cursor

To move	Press
One paragraph up	Command+Up Arrow
One paragraph down	Command+Down Arrow
Up one screen (scrolling)	Page Up
Down one screen (scrolling)	Page Down
To the top of the next page	Command+Page Down
To the top of the previous page	Command+Page Up
To the end of a document	Command+End
To the beginning of a document	Command+Home
To a previous edit, or the location of the most recent edit since the document was last saved	Shift+F5

Selecting text and graphics

To extend a selection	Press
Select multiple items that are not next to each other	Select the first item that you want, hold down Command, and then select any additional items
One character to the right	Shift+Right Arrow
One character to the left	Shift+Left Arrow
One word to the right	Shift+Option+Right Arrow
One word to the left	Shift+Option+Left Arrow
To the end of a line	Shift+Command+Right Arrow or Shift+End
To the beginning of a line	Shift+Command+Left Arrow or Shift+Home
One line down	Shift+Down Arrow
One line up	Shift+Up Arrow
To the end of a paragraph	Shift+Command+Down Arrow
To the beginning of a paragraph	Shift+Command+Up Arrow
One screen down	Shift+Page Down
One screen up	Shift+Page Up
To the beginning of a document	Shift+Command+Home
To the end of a document	Shift+Command+End
To the end of a window	Option+Shift+Command+Page Down

Editing text and graphics

To	Press
Create AutoText	Option+F3
Paste the Spike contents	Shift+Command+F3
Delete one word to the left	Command+Delete
Delete one word to the right	Command+Del
Cut to the Spike	Command+F3

Aligning and formatting paragraphs

To	Press
Center a paragraph	Command+E
Justify a paragraph	Command+J
Left align a paragraph	Command+L
Right align a paragraph	Command+R
Indent a paragraph from the left	Control+Shift+M
Remove a paragraph indent from the left	Shift+Command+M
Create a hanging indent	Command+T
Remove a hanging indent	Shift+Command+T
Apply a style	Shift+Command+S
Start AutoFormat	Command+Option+K
Apply the Normal style	Shift+Command+N
Apply the Heading 1 style	Command+Option+1
Apply the Heading 2 style	Command+Option+2
Apply the Heading 3 style	Command+Option+3
Apply the List style	Shift+Command+L

Inserting paragraphs and tab characters in a table

To insert	Press
New paragraphs in a cell	Return
Tab characters in a cell	Option+Tab

Formatting characters

To	Press
Change the font	Shift+Command+F
Increase the font size	Shift+Command+>
Decrease the font size	Shift+Command+<
Increase the font size by 1 point	Command+]
Decrease the font size by 1 point	Command+[
Display the Font dialog box	Command+D
Change the case of letters	Shift+F3
Format in all capital letters	Shift+Command+A
Underline words but not spaces	Shift+Command+W
Double-underline text	Shift+Command+D
Format in all small capital letters	Shift+Command+K
Apply subscript formatting (automatic spacing)	Command+Equal Sign
Apply superscript formatting (automatic spacing)	Shift+Command+Plus Sign
Remove manual character formatting	Control+Spacebar

Selecting text and graphics in a table

To	Press
Select the next cell's contents	Tab
Select the preceding cell's contents	Shift+Tab
Extend a selection to adjacent cells	Hold down Shift and press an arrow key repeatedly
Select a column	Click in the column's top or bottom cell, hold down Shift and press Up Arrow or Down Arrow repeatedly
Extend a selection (or block)	Shift+Command+F8, and then use the arrow keys; press Command+Period to cancel selection mode
Reduce the selection size	Shift+F8
Select multiple cells, columns, or rows that are not next to each other	Select the first item you want, hold down Command, and then select any additional items

Moving around in a table

To	Press
Move to the next cell	Tab (If the cursor is in the last cell of a table, pressing Tab adds a new row)
Move to the preceding cell	Shift+Tab
Move to the preceding or next row	Up Arrow or Down Arrow
Move to the first cell in the row	Control+Home
Move to the last cell in the row	Control+End
Move to the first cell in the column	Control+Page Up
Move to the last cell in the column	Control+Page Down
Start a new paragraph	Return
Add a new row at the bottom of the table	Tab at the end of the last row
Add text before a table at the beginning of a document	Return at the beginning of the first cell

Reviewing documents

To	Press
Insert a comment	Command+Option+A
Turn track changes on or off	Shift+Command+E
Go to the end of a comment	End
Go to the beginning of the list of comments	Command+Home
Go to the end of the list of comments	Command+End

Printing and previewing documents

To	Press
Switch in or out of Print Preview	Command+Option+I

Simple Instructions for Doing Things in Word 2008

Bibliography

To record source information

1. In the Toolbox, display the **Citations** palette, and choose a citation style from the **Citation Style** list.
2. Click the **Create New Source** button and supply the source information.
3. Click **OK** to display the citation in the **Citations Manager**.

To insert citations

1. Position the insertion point in the citation location—usually immediately following the citation or in a footnote.
2. In the **Citations Manager**, select the citation style you want, and then double-click the source you want to cite.

To compile a bibliography

1. Position the insertion point at the end of the document or on the page where you want the bibliography to appear.
2. Display the **Bibliography** group on the **Document Elements** tab of the Elements Gallery and select from the list the citation style you want to use.
3. In the gallery, click either the **Bibliography** thumbnail or the **Works Cited** thumbnail.

Borders and shading

To put a border around the active paragraph

→ In the **Borders and Shading** panel of the **Formatting Palette**, click the **Type** button in the **Borders** area, and then in the **Border Type** gallery, click the border you want.

→ Click **Borders and Shading** on the **Format** menu. On the **Borders** page of the **Borders and Shading** dialog box, click the setting, style, color, and width of the border you want, and then set and clear individual borders by clicking the **Preview** diagram.

To shade the background of a paragraph

→ Display the **Borders and Shading** panel of the **Formatting Palette**, click the **Fill color** button in the **Shading** area, and then in the **Fill Color** gallery, click the color you want.

To remove formatting from a paragraph

→ Click the **Clear Formatting** on the **Edit** menu.

Charts

To insert or link to an Excel chart

1. Ensure that the chart is saved on its own chart sheet.
2. Click the **Object** on the **Insert** menu.
3. In the **Object** dialog box, click **Microsoft Excel Chart**, and then in the lower-left corner, click **From File**.
4. In the **Insert as Object** dialog box, navigate to and click the workbook containing the chart you want to insert.

5. If you want to maintain a link from the inserted chart to the source workbook, select the **Link to File** check box.

6. If you want to insert an icon linking to the source workbook, rather than inserting the chart itself, select the **Display as Icon** check box.

7. In the **Insert as Object** dialog box, click **Insert**.

To create a chart directly in a document

1. Position the insertion point where you want the chart to appear, and then either click **Chart** on the **Insert** menu or display the **Charts** tab of the Elements Gallery.

2. Display the chart gallery you want, and then click the chart type.

3. Enter the data you want to plot in the Excel worksheet that appears, and then close the workbook window.

To make changes to an embedded chart

→ Right-click the chart and click **Edit Data** to open the workbook containing the chart data.

→ Right-click any chart element (such as legend, axis, or gridlines) to display formatting options for that element.

→ Double-click a data series to display the **Format** dialog box for the data series, in which you can format the fill, line, shadow, scale, plot direction, data labels, or other settings appropriate to the chart type.

→ On the **Charts** tab of the Elements Gallery, click a different chart type to change the chart without affecting the data.

Comments

To insert a comment

1. Select the text to which the comment refers and click the **New Comment** button on the Reviewing toolbar or **Comment** on the **Insert** menu.

2. Type the comment in the balloon that appears (in Print Layout view) or in the Reviewing pane (in Normal view).

To manage comments

→ Display the reviewer's name and the date and time the comment was inserted by pointing to either the commented text or the balloon.

→ Jump from balloon to balloon by clicking the **Next** or **Previous** button on the Reviewing toolbar.

→ Edit a comment by clicking its balloon and using normal editing techniques.

→ Delete a comment by clicking the **X** button in the balloon or by clicking the **Reject Change/ Delete Comment** button on the Reviewing toolbar.

→ Respond to a comment by adding text to an existing balloon.

→ Attach a new balloon to the same text by clicking the balloon and then clicking the **New Comment** button on the Reviewing toolbar.

→ Turn off the display of comment balloons by clicking **Comments** in the **Show** list on the Reviewing toolbar.

→ Display only the comments of a specific person by clicking the **Show** button, pointing to **Reviewers**, and then clicking the names of the reviewers whose comments you don't want to see.

To display the Reviewing pane

→ Click the **Reviewing Pane** button on the Reviewing toolbar. Click the button again to hide the pane.

→ Change the size of the Reviewing pane by dragging its upper border by the **Resize** handle.

Copying and pasting content

See Also "Word 2008 Keyboard Shortcuts" earlier in this Quick Reference section

To display the Scrapbook

→ Open the Toolbox and then, if the **Scrapbook** is not already displayed, click the **Scrapbook** button on the Toolbox menu bar.

To copy selected content to the Scrapbook

→ Display the Scrapbook, and then click **Copy to Scrapbook** on the **Edit** menu.

To paste a selected scrap from the Scrapbook

→ In the **Scrapbook**, click the **Paste** button.

→ Click **Paste from Scrapbook** on the **Edit** menu.

To move noncontiguous content from multiple locations via the Spike

1. Cut selected content to the Spike by pressing **Command+F3**.
2. Position the insertion point where you want to insert the content collection, and then paste the Spike contents by pressing **Command+Shift+F3**.

Cover pages

To insert a cover page

→ In the Elements Gallery, click the cover page design you want in the **Cover Pages** group on the **Document Elements** tab. Then customize the cover page with your own information.

To delete a cover page

→ Point to any part of the page, click the button that appears near the upper-left corner of the page, and then click **Remove Cover Page**.

Document formatting

To change the margins or header and footer location of a document

→ Click **Document** on the **Format** menu, make the necessary changes in the **Document** dialog box, and click **OK**.

Document properties

To view the properties attached to a document

→ Click **Properties** on the **File** menu.

To enter additional properties

→ Enter the information on the **Summary** or **Custom** page of the **Properties** dialog box.

Document templates

To start a new document based on a template

1. Open the **Project Gallery**, and display the **New** page.
2. In the **Show** list, click **Word Documents**, and then in the **Category** list, click the type of template you want.
3. In the **Template** list, click the template. Then click **Open**.

To display the master page of a template

→ Click the **Master Pages** tab in the lower-right corner of the document window.

To save a document as a template

1. Click **Save As** on the **File** menu, and in the **Save As** dialog box, assign the template a name.
2. In the **Format** list, click **Word template (.dotx)**. Then click **Save**.

To start a new document based on a template you have saved

→ In the **Project Gallery**, click **My Templates** in the **Category** list, and then double-click the template you want in the **Template** list.

To attach a different template to a document

1. Click **Templates and Add-Ins** on the **Tools** menu.
2. In the **Templates and Add-Ins** dialog box, click **Attach**.
3. In the **Choose a File** dialog box, locate and click the template you want to attach and then click **Open**.
4. In the **Templates and Add-ins** dialog box, select the **Automatically update document styles** check box. Then click **OK**.

Finding text

To find text with specific formatting

1. Display the expanded **Find** page of the **Find and Replace** dialog box, and enter the search term, if any.
2. In the **Format** list, click the type of formatting you want to search for, and then either click **Find Next** or select the **Highlight all items found in** check box and click **Find All**.
3. Click **Close**.

Formatting text by using styles

To apply a character style

1. Select the text, and display the **Styles** panel of the **Formatting Palette** or the **Style** list on the Formatting toolbar.
2. Click the character style you want.

To apply a paragraph style, list style, or table style

1. Click anywhere in the paragraph, list, or table, and display the **Styles** panel of the **Formatting Palette** or the **Style** list on the Formatting toolbar.
2. Click the paragraph style, list style, or table style you want.

To display all the available styles

→ At the bottom of the **Styles** panel, click the **List** arrow, and then click **All styles**.

To create a new style

1. Click the **New Style** button in the **Styles** panel.
2. In the **New Style** dialog box, specify the following:
   - The name of the new style
   - The type of style you want to create
3. Do one of the following:
   - If you are creating a paragraph style, specify its base style (if any), and the style for the paragraphs that follow it, and its formatting.
   - If you are creating a character, list, or table style, supply the information specific to that style type.
   - If you want to save the style with the current template, select the **Add to template** check box.
4. Click **OK** to close the **New Style** dialog box.

To modify an existing style

1. In the **Styles** panel, point to the style you want to modify, click the arrow that appears, and then, in the list, click **Modify Style**.
2. In the **Modify Style** dialog box, make simple changes to the formatting of the selected style. Or select the aspect you want to change from the **Format** list, make your selections, and click **OK**.
3. Click **OK** to close the **Modify Style** dialog box.

Formatting text manually

See Also "Formatting text manually" in the "Office 2008 for Mac" Quick Reference section

To vary the look of text without changing the font

→ Change the font color to a nonstandard color by clicking **More Colors** in the **Font Color** list, in the **Font** panel of the **Formatting Palette**. In the **Colors** dialog box, click the color you want on one of the tabs of the dialog box. Then click **OK**.

→ Change the font effect by displaying the **Font** dialog box, making changes in the **Effects** area, and clicking **OK**.

To make multiple formatting changes in one place

→ Click **Font** on the **Format** menu, and change options in the **Font** dialog box.

To change the spacing between characters

1. Display the **Font** dialog box, and click the **Character Spacing** button.
2. In the **Spacing** list, click the option you want. Then in the **By** box, increase or decrease the setting.
3. Click **OK**.

To highlight selected text

→ In the **Font** panel of the **Formatting Palette**, click the **Highlight** arrow, and then click the color you want.

To highlight multiple blocks of text

→ In the **Font** panel of the **Formatting Palette**, click the **Highlight** arrow, click the color you want, and then drag the highlighter tool across the text you want to highlight.

→ Click the **Highlight** button or press **Escape** to turn off the highlighter.

To change the case of selected text

→ Hold down the **Shift** key and press the **F3** key until the text is formatted with the case you want.

To repeat a formatting command

→ Click **Repeat <formatting>** on the **Edit** menu.

> **See Also** "Format Painter" in the "Office 2008 for Mac" Quick Reference section

To return a paragraph to its default formatting

→ Click the **Clear Formatting** on the **Edit** menu.

Formatting paragraphs

See Also "Borders and shading" earlier in this Quick Reference section

To indent a paragraph

→ In the **Alignment and Spacing** panel of the **Formatting Palette**, enter or select the indentation (in inches) in the **Left**, **Right**, and **First** boxes.

→ Drag the indent markers on the horizontal ruler.

To change the horizontal alignment of a paragraph

→ In the **Alignment and Spacing** panel of the **Formatting Palette**, click the **Align Text Left**, **Align Center**, **Align Text Right**, or **Justify** button next to **Horizontal**.

To start a new centered or right-aligned paragraph

→ Point to the center or right side of a blank area of the page, and when the pointer's shape changes to an I-beam with appropriately aligned text attached, double-click to create a pre-aligned paragraph.

To change the line spacing of a paragraph

→ In the **Alignment and Spacing** panel of the **Formatting Palette**, click the **Single Space**, **1.5 Space**, or **Double Space** button next to **Line Spacing**.

To add space before or after paragraphs

→ In the **Alignment and Spacing** panel of the **Formatting Palette**, enter or select the space (in points) in the **Before** and **After** boxes.

Headers and footers

See Also "Page numbers" later in this Quick Reference section

To insert a themed header or footer

1. Display the **Document Elements** tab of the Elements Gallery.
2. In the **Header** group or the **Footer** group, select from the **Insert as** list the pages you want the header or footer to appear on—**Even Pages**, **Odd Pages**, or **All Pages**.
3. In the **Header** gallery or **Footer** gallery, click the element you want to insert.
4. Scroll to a page displaying the header or footer, and replace any placeholders with the appropriate content.

To hide the document text while working with a header or footer

→ Select the **Hide Body Text** check box in the **Header And Footer** panel of the **Formatting Palette**.

Hiding text

To hide a selection

→ Click **Font** on the **Format** menu, select the **Hidden** check box in the **Font** dialog box, and then click **OK**.

To display text that is formatted as hidden

→ Click the **Show** button on the Standard toolbar.

To print text that is formatted as hidden

→ On the **Print** page of the **Preferences** dialog box, select the **Hidden Text** check box.

Index

To display the Mark Index Entry dialog box

→ Click **Index and Tables** on the **Insert** menu. Then on the **Index** page of the **Index and Tables** dialog box, click **Mark Entry**.

To mark index entries

1. With the **Mark Index Entry** dialog box displayed, select the word or phrase you want to index, and then click anywhere in the **Mark Index Entry** dialog box to activate it.
2. If necessary, adjust the entry to specify the following:
   - Whether the entry is a main index entry or a subentry
   - Whether the entry is a cross-reference, a single-page entry, or a page-range entry
   - The formatting of the page number associated with the entry
3. Click **Mark** to insert the index entry adjacent to the selection, or click **Mark All** to insert the entry adjacent to all occurrences of the selection.
4. When you finish marking entries, close the **Mark Index Entry** dialog box.

To display index entries in a document

→ Click the **Show** button on the Standard toolbar.

To delete an index entry

→ Select the entire hidden field and press the **Delete** key.

To create an index based on the index entries marked in a document

1. Position the insertion point where you want the index to appear, and ensure that index entries are hidden.
2. Click **Index and Tables** on the **Insert** menu, and on the **Index** page of the **Index and Tables** dialog box, specify the following:
   - Whether the index formatting should use styles from the current template or be based on a predefined format
   - The number of columns
   - The page number alignment and the type of tab leaders
   - Whether subentries should be indented on separate lines below the main entries or appear on the same line as the main entries
   - Whether words beginning with accented letters should appear in their own sections or be alphabetized as if they had no accents

3. Click the **Modify** button, specify paragraph and character styling for each level of index entry in the **Style** dialog box, and click **OK**.
4. Click **OK** to close the **Index and Tables** dialog box.

To update an index
→ Right-click the index and click **Update Field**.

Inserting and linking to files

To insert an entire file
1. Click **File** on the **Insert** menu.
2. In the **Insert File** dialog box, navigate to the folder where the file is stored, click the file, and then click **Insert**.

To link to a file
1. Click **File** on the **Insert** menu.
2. In the **Insert File** dialog box, navigate to the folder where the file is stored, and click the file.
3. Select the **Link to file** check box, and then click **Insert**.

Inserting information fields

To insert the current date or time
1. Click **Date and Time** on the **Insert** menu.
2. In the **Date and Time** dialog box, click the date and/or time format you want.
3. To insert the date or time as a field rather than as static text, select the **Update automatically** check box.
4. Click **OK**.

To insert other information fields
1. Click **Field** on the **Insert** menu.
2. In the **Field** dialog box, click the category of information and then the field you want.
3. To change the default options for the field, click **Options**, and in the **Field Options** dialog box, choose the settings you want and then click **OK**.
4. Click **OK**.

To display the codes that control the information displayed in a field
→ Right-click the field and click **Toggle Field Codes**.

To manually update information in a field
→ Right-click the field and click **Update Field**.

New documents

To start a new document
- Start a new document of the same type as the one you were last working in, click the **New** button on the Standard toolbar.
- Start a blank document of a specific type by choosing the type you want from the **New** list on the Standard toolbar.

Page breaks

To insert a manual page break

→ Point to **Break** on the **Insert** menu, and then click **Page Break**.

→ Press **Shift+Enter** (using the **Enter** key on the numeric keypad).

To control how Word breaks pages

→ Display the **Paragraph** dialog box by clicking **Paragraph** on the **Format** menu. Change any of the following options on the **Line and Page Breaks** page of the dialog box, and click **OK**:

- Select the **Widow/Orphan Control** check box to avoid breaking a page with the last line of a paragraph by itself at the top of a page or the first line of a paragraph by itself at the bottom of a page.
- Select the **Keep With Next** check box to avoid breaking a page between the selected paragraph and the following paragraph.
- Select the **Keep Lines Together** check box to avoid breaking a page within a paragraph.
- Select the **Page Break Before** check box to avoid breaking a page before the selected paragraph.

To remove a page break

→ Click to the left of the break and then press the **Del** key.

→ Click at the beginning of the content immediately following the break and then press the **Delete** key.

Page numbers

See Also "Headers and footers" earlier in this Quick Reference section

To insert only page numbers in a header or footer

1. Click **Page Numbers** on the **Insert** menu.
2. In the **Page Numbers** dialog box, specify the position (**Top** or **Bottom**) and alignment (**Left**, **Center**, **Right**, **Inside**, or **Outside**) of the page numbers.
3. Click **OK**.

To change the numbering scheme

1. In the **Page Numbers** dialog box, click **Format**.
2. If you want to precede page numbers with chapter numbers, select the **Include chapter number** check box and set the style and separator.
3. If you want to start at a page number other than 1, click **Start at** and enter the starting page number. Then click **OK**.

Ruler

To display or hide the ruler

→ Click **Ruler** on the **View** menu.

To temporarily display a hidden ruler

→ Point to the top of the document window to display the horizontal ruler or the left side of the document window to display the vertical ruler.

To change the unit of measure

→ On the **General** page of the **Preferences** dialog box, in the **Measurement Units** list, click **Centimeters**, **Inches**, **Millimeters**, **Picas**, or **Points**.

Section breaks

To insert a section break

→ Point to **Break** on the **Insert** menu, click one of the following, and then click **OK**:
- Click **Next Page** to start the following section on the next page.
- Click **Continuous** to start a new section without affecting page breaks.
- Click **Odd Page** to start the following section on the next odd-numbered page.
- Click **Even Page** to start the following section on the next even-numbered page.

To remove a section break

→ Click to the left of the break and then press the **Del** key.
→ Click at the beginning of the content immediately following the break and then press the **Delete** key.

Spelling and Grammar

See Also "AutoCorrect" in the "Office 2008 for Mac" Quick Reference section

To correct the spelling or grammar of an underlined word or phrase

→ Right-click the underlined word or phrase to display suggested corrections, and then click the suggested spelling you want or, if none of the suggestions is correct, manually enter the correct spelling.

To check the spelling and grammar of an entire document

1. With the insertion point at the top of the document, click **Spelling And Grammar** on the **Tools** menu.
2. If Word displays the **Spelling and Grammar** dialog box, do one of the following:
- Click the correct spelling in the **Suggestions** box, and then click **Change** to change this instance of the misspelling or **Change All** to change all instances in the document.
- Click **Ignore** to leave the selected word as-is.
- Click **Ignore All** to skip all instances of the selected word or grammatical issue.
- Click   to add the selected word to the default dictionary.

To change the Spelling And Grammar feature settings

→ On the **Spelling and Grammar** page of the **Preferences** dialog box, select or configure options related to checking for, showing or hiding, ignoring, and correcting spelling and grammar errors.

Tables of contents (TOCs)

To insert a standard TOC

1. Click to position the insertion point where you want to insert the TOC, and then display the **Document Elements** tab of the Elements Gallery.
2. Display the **Tables of Contents** gallery, and do one of the following:
- With **Heading Styles** selected in the left pane, click the style of TOC you want.
- With **Manual Formatting** selected in the left pane, click the style of TOC you want to insert formatted placeholders for.

To insert a custom table of contents

1. Click **Index and Tables** on the **Insert** menu.
2. In the **Formats** pane of the **Index and Tables** dialog box, click the style variation you want. Then in the **Show levels** list, click the number of levels, and in the **Tab leader** list, click the style of leaders.
3. Click the **Options** button, and in the **Table of Contents Options** dialog box, place a number from 1 through 9 in the **TOC Level** box for any style you want to include in the TOC. Then click **OK**.
4. On the **Table of Contents** page of the **Index and Tables** dialog box, click **Modify**. Then in the **Style** dialog box, modify the font, paragraph, tabs, border, and other formatting of these styles as necessary, and click **OK** in each of the open dialog boxes.

To update a table of contents

→ Right-click the TOC and click **Update Field**. In the **Update Table of Contents** dialog box, click **Update page numbers only** or **Update entire table**. Then click **OK**.

To move a table of contents

→ Drag the TOC frame's move handle (the three dots in the upper-left corner).

To delete a table of contents

→ Click the arrow at the right end of the **Table of Contents** tab and then click **Remove Table of Contents**.

Tracking changes

To turn on the Track Changes feature

→ On the status bar, click the **TRK** button.

Or

1. Point to **Track Changes** on the **Tools** menu, and then click **Highlight Changes**.
2. In the **Highlight Changes** dialog box, select the **Track changes while editing** check box, and then click **OK**.

To specify how you want Word to indicate changes

→ On the **Track Changes** page of the **Preferences** dialog box, select or configure options for inserted and deleted text, changed formatting and lines, comments, and balloons.

To manage the display of tracked changes

→ Track changes without showing them on the screen by clicking **Final** in the **Display for Review** list on the Reviewing toolbar.
→ Redisplay the revisions by clicking **Final Showing Markup** in the **Display for Review** list.
→ Display the original version, with or without revisions, by clicking **Original** or **Original Showing Markup** in the **Display for Review** list.
→ Select the types of revisions that you want to display—for example, only comments or only insertions and deletions—from the **Show** list on the Reviewing toolbar.
→ Display or hide the revisions of specific reviewers from the **Show** list.

To accept or reject a tracked change from its balloon

→ Click check mark button or the **X** button.

To accept or reject tracked changes from the Reviewing toolbar

→ Move forward or backward from one tracked change to another by clicking the **Next** or **Previous** button.

→ Incorporate a selected change into the document by clicking the **Accept Change** button.

→ Undo the selected change or restore the original text by clicking the **Reject Change** button.

→ Accept or reject multiple changes by selecting a block of text containing changes you want to process and then clicking the **Accept Change** or **Reject Change** button.

→ Accept all the changes at once by clicking the **Accept** arrow and then clicking **Accept All Changes in Document**.

→ Reject all the changes at once by clicking the **Reject** arrow and then clicking **Reject All Changes in Document**.

→ Accept or reject only certain types of changes or changes from specific reviewers by displaying only the changes you want to accept or reject, clicking the **Accept** or **Reject** arrow, and then clicking **All Changes Shown** in the list.

To handle tracked changes from the Accept Or Reject Changes dialog box

1. Point to **Track Changes** on the **Tools** menu, and then click **Accept or Reject Changes**.

2. In the **Accept or Reject Changes** dialog box, move from change to change, accepting or rejecting as appropriate.

3. When you have resolved all the tracked changes, click **OK** to acknowledge the message box, and click **Close** to close the **Accept or Reject Changes** dialog box.

Viewing documents

See Also "Word 2008 Keyboard Shortcuts" earlier in this Quick Reference section

To move to the next or previous page

→ At the bottom of the vertical scroll bar, click the **Next Page** button or **Previous Page** button.

To move to the next object of a specific type

→ At the bottom of the vertical scroll bar, click the **Select Browse Object** button, and then click the icon for the type of object you want to move to.

→ Display the **Go To** page of the **Find and Replace** dialog box, click the type of object in the **Go to what** list, click the specific object in the **Enter** list, and then click **Next**.

To jump to a specific page

→ Click the **Navigation** button on the Standard toolbar, and then in the Navigation pane, click the thumbnail of the page you want.

To jump to a specific heading

→ In a document with heading styles applied, display the Navigation pane, click **Document Map**, and then click the heading you want.

To change the Document Map view

→ With the Document Map displayed, right-click the Navigation pane, and then click the option you want.

To view more than one page at a time

→ Click the **Zoom** arrow on the Standard toolbar, and then click **Two Pages**.
   Or
1. In the **Zoom** list, click **Many Pages**, and then click the page picker.
2. Drag the pointer down and to the right to expand the page picker so that it displays the number of pages you want.
3. Click the icon representing the configuration you want, and then click **OK**.

To display or hide non-printing characters

→ Click the **Show** button on the Standard toolbar.

Watermarks

To create a graphic watermark in a document

1. Click **Watermark** on the **Insert** menu.
2. In the **Insert Watermark** dialog box, click **Picture**, and then click the **Select Picture** button.
3. In the **Choose a Picture** dialog box, navigate to and double-click the image file you want.
4. If necessary, change the percentage in the **Scale** box. Then click **OK**.

To create a text watermark in a document

1. Click **Watermark** on the **Insert** menu.
2. In the **Insert Watermark** dialog box, click **Text**.
3. In the **Text** box, type the characters you want to display behind the document text.
4. Choose the font and font size. Apply bold and/or italic formatting if you want. Set the font color and then the transparency. Finally, choose horizontal or diagonal orientation.
5. Click **OK**.

Microsoft Excel 2008 for Mac

Excel 2008 Keyboard Shortcuts Q-40
Simple Instructions for Doing Things in Excel 2008 . . . . Q-46
    Charts Q-46
    Columns, rows, and cells Q-46
    Conditional formatting Q-47
    Editing cell data Q-47
    Errors Q-48
    Filling cells Q-48
    Formatting cells and cell contents Q-48
    Formulas Q-49
    Headers and footers Q-49
    Importing data Q-49
    New workbooks Q-50
    Number formatting Q-50
    Page breaks Q-50
    Page setup Q-50
    Print area Q-50
    Protection Q-50
    Range names Q-51
    References Q-51
    Restricting content Q-51
    Saving files Q-52
    Selecting cells and data Q-52
    Sheets Q-52
    Viewing worksheets Q-53
    Workbook templates Q-54

Excel 2008 Keyboard Shortcuts

Moving and scrolling in a sheet or workbook

To	Press
Move one cell up, down, left, or right	An arrow key
Move to the edge of the current data region	Control+arrow key
Move to the beginning of the sheet	Control+Home
Move to the last cell in use on the sheet, which is the cell at the intersection of the rightmost column and the bottom row (in the lower-right corner); or the cell opposite the home cell, which is typically A1	Control+End
Move up one screen	Page Up
Move down one screen	Page Down
Move one screen to the left	Option+Page Up
Move one screen to the right	Option+Page Down
Move to the next sheet in the workbook	Control+Page Down
Move to the previous sheet in the workbook	Control+Page Up
Move to the next workbook or window	Control+Tab
Move to the previous workbook or window	Control+Shift+Tab
Move to the next pane in a workbook that has been split	F6
Move to the previous pane in a workbook that has been split	Shift+F6
Scroll to display the active cell	Control+Delete
Display the Go To dialog box	Control+G
Repeat the last Find action (Find Next)	Command+G
Move between unlocked cells on a protected sheet	Tab

Entering data on a sheet

To	Press
Complete a cell entry and move down in the selection	Return
Start a new line in the same cell	Control+Option+Return
Fill the selected cell range with the text that you type	Control+Return
Complete a cell entry and move up in the selection	Shift+Return
Complete a cell entry and move to the right in the selection	Tab
Complete a cell entry and move to the left in the selection	Shift+Tab
Cancel a cell entry	Escape
Delete the character to the left of the insertion point, or delete the selection	Delete
Delete the character to the right of the insertion point, or delete the selection	Del
Delete text to the end of the line	Control+Del
Move one character up, down, left, or right	An arrow key
Repeat the last action	Command+Y
Edit a cell comment	Shift+F2
Fill down	Control+D
Fill to the right	Control+R
Define a name	Control+L

Working with a selection

To	Press
Clear the contents of the selection	Delete
Delete the selection	Control+Hyphen
Turn on Show Formulas view	Control+Shift+Plus Sign
Move from top to bottom within the selection	Return
Move from bottom to top within the selection	Shift+Return
Move from left to right within the selection, or move down one cell if only one column is selected	Tab
Move from right to left within the selection, or move up one cell if only one column is selected	Shift+Tab
Move clockwise to the next corner of the selection	Control+Period
Move to the right between nonadjacent selections	Control+Option+Right Arrow
Move to the left between nonadjacent selections	Control+Option+Left Arrow

Formatting and editing data

To	Press
Display the Style dialog box	Shift+Command+L
Display the Format Cells dialog box	Command+1
Apply the general number format	Control+Shift+~
Apply the currency format with two decimal places (negative numbers appear in red with parentheses)	Control+Shift+$
Apply the percentage format with no decimal places	Control+Shift+%
Apply the exponential number format with two decimal places	Control+Shift+^
Apply the date format with the day, month, and year	Control+Shift+#
Apply the time format with the hour and minute, and indicate A.M. or P.M.	Control+Shift+@
Apply the number format with two decimal places, thousands separator, and minus sign (-) for negative values	Control+Shift+!
Apply the outline border around the selected cells	Command+Option+Zero
Add an outline border to the right of the selection	Command+Option+Right Arrow
Add an outline border to the left of the selection	Command+Option+Left Arrow
Add an outline border to the top of the selection	Command+Option+Up Arrow
Add an outline border to the bottom of the selection	Command+Option+Down Arrow
Remove outline borders	Command+Option+Hyphen
Apply or remove strikethrough formatting	Shift+Command+Underline
Hide rows	Control+9
Unhide rows	Control+Shift+(
Hide columns	Control+Zero
Unhide columns	Control+Shift+)
Add or remove the shadow font style	Shift+Command+W
Add or remove the outline font style	Shift+Command+D
Edit the active cell	Control+U
Cancel an entry in the cell or the formula bar	Escape
Edit the active cell and then clear it, or delete the preceding character in the active cell as you edit the cell contents	Delete
Paste text into the active cell	Command+V
Complete a cell entry	Return
Enter a formula as an array formula	Control+Shift+Return
Display the Formula Builder after you type a valid function name in a formula	Control+A

Working in cells or the Formula bar

To	Press
Edit the active cell and then clear it, or delete the preceding character in the active cell as you edit the cell contents	Delete
Complete a cell entry	Return
Enter a formula as an array formula	Control+Shift+Return
Cancel an entry in the cell or formula bar	Escape
Display the Formula Builder after you type a valid function name in a formula	Control+A
Insert a hyperlink	Command+K
Activate a hyperlink	Return (in a cell with a hyperlink)
Edit the active cell and position the insertion point at the end of the line	Control+U
Open the Formula Builder	Shift+F3
Calculate all sheets in all open workbooks	Command+=
Calculate the active sheet	Shift+Command+=
Start a formula	=
Alternate the formula reference style among absolute, relative, and mixed	Command+T
Insert the AutoSum formula	Shift+Command+T
Enter the date	Control+Semicolon (;)
Enter the time	Command+Semicolon (;)
Copy the value from the cell above the active cell into the cell or the formula bar	Control+Shift+Inch Mark (")
Alternate between displaying cell values and displaying cell formulas	Control+Grave Accent (`)
Copy a formula from the cell above the active cell into the cell or the formula bar	Control+Apostrophe (')
Display the AutoComplete list	Option+Down Arrow
Define a name	Control+L

Selecting cells, columns, or rows

To	Press
Select the current region around the active cell (the current region is an area enclosed by blank rows and blank columns)	Control+Shift+Asterisk
Extend the selection by one cell	Shift+arrow key
Extend the selection to the last nonblank cell in the same column or row as the active cell	Control+Shift+arrow key
Extend the selection to the beginning of the row	Shift+Home
Extend the selection to the beginning of the sheet	Control+Shift+Home
Extend the selection to the last cell used on the sheet (lower-right corner)	Control+Shift+End
Select the entire column	Control+Spacebar
Select the entire row	Shift+Spacebar
Select only the active cell when multiple cells are selected	Shift+Delete
Extend the selection down one screen	Shift+Page Down
Extend the selection up one screen	Shift+Page Up
With an object selected, select all objects on a sheet	Control+Shift+Spacebar
Alternate among hiding objects, displaying objects, and displaying placeholders for objects	Control+6
Show or hide the Standard toolbar	Control+7
Turn on the capability to extend a selection by using the arrow keys	F8
Add another range of cells to the selection; or use the arrow keys to move to the start of the range you want to add, and then press F8 and the arrow keys to select the next range	Shift+F8
Select all cells with comments	Shift+Command+O
Select cells in a row that don't match the value in the active cell in that row	Control+\
Select only cells that are directly referred to by formulas in the selection	Control+Shift+|
Select cells in a column that don't match the value in the active cell in that column	Control+[
Select all cells that are directly or indirectly referred to by formulas in the selection	Control+Shift+{
Select only cells with formulas that refer directly to the active cell	Control+]
Select all cells with formulas that refer directly or indirectly to the active cell	Control+Shift+}
Select only visible cells in the current selection	Shift+Command+Z

Charts

To	Press
Cycle through chart object selection	An arrow key
Alternate among hiding chart objects, displaying chart objects, and displaying placeholders for chart objects	Control+6

Toolbars

To	Press
Make the first button on a floating toolbar active	Option+F10
Select the next button or menu on the active toolbar	Tab
Select the previous button or menu on the active toolbar	Shift+Tab
When a toolbar is active, select the next toolbar	Control+Tab
When a toolbar is active, select the previous toolbar	Control+Shift+Tab
Perform the action assigned to the selected button	Return

Windows

To	Press
Move to the next pane in a workbook that has been split	F6
Move to the previous pane in a workbook that has been split	Shift+F6
Switch to the next workbook window	Command+F6
Switch to the previous workbook window	Shift+Command+F6
Maximize or restore the workbook window	Control+F10

Simple Instructions for Doing Things in Excel 2008

Charts

To plot the data in selected cells as a chart

→ Click the chart category on the **Charts** tab of the Elements Gallery, and then click the specific chart type.

To change the chart type

→ Activate the chart and click a different chart type on the **Charts** tab of the Elements Gallery.

To format a chart

→ Select the part of the chart you want to format, and then choose formatting options such as the following:

- Add data labels by right-clicking the chart and clicking **Add Data Labels**.
- Add a title by displaying the **Chart Options** panel of the **Formatting Palette**, clicking the title placeholder, and then typing the title.
- Display axes by displaying the **Chart Options** panel of the **Formatting Palette** and clicking the **Show** option you want.
- Display gridlines by displaying the **Chart Options** panel of the **Formatting Palette** and clicking the **Major** and **Minor** options you want.
- Modify the position of the legend by displaying the **Chart Options** panel of the **Formatting Palette** and clicking the option you want in the **Legend** list.
- Double-click a data series to display its **Format** dialog box, in which you can format the fill, line, shadow, scale, plot direction, data labels, or other settings appropriate to the chart type.

To add data to an existing chart

1. Right-click the chart and click **Select Data**.
2. In the **Select Data Source** dialog box, change the data range in the **Chart data range** dialog box. Then click **OK**.

To move a chart to its own sheet

1. Right-click the chart (not a chart element) and click **Move Chart**.
2. In the **Move Chart** dialog box, click **New sheet**. In the New sheet box, enter a name for the chart sheet. Then click **OK**.

Columns, rows, and cells

To resize a column or row

→ Drag the separator that is to the right of the column heading to the left or right.

→ Drag the separator that is below the row heading up or down.

→ Precisely fit a column to its contents by double-clicking the separator to the right of the column. Or point to **Columns** on the **Format** menu, and click **AutoFit Selection**.

→ Precisely fit the height of a row to its contents by double-clicking the separator below the row. Or point to **Rows** on the **Format** menu, and click **AutoFit Selection**.

→ Right-click a column heading or a selection of several column headings, click **Column Width**, specify the exact width in the **Column Width** dialog box, and click **OK**.

→ Right-click a row heading or a selection of several row headings, click **Row Height**, specify the exact height in the **Row Height** dialog box, and click **OK**.

To hide a column or row

→ Right-click a column heading or row heading or a selection of several headings, and click **Hide**.

→ Unhide the column or row by selecting the flanking headings, right-clicking the selection, and clicking **Unhide**.

To insert columns, rows, or cells

→ Insert a new column by selecting the column that will appear to the right of the new column and then clicking **Columns** on the **Insert** menu.

→ Insert multiple new columns by selecting that number of columns to the right of where you want the new columns to appear and then clicking **Columns** on the **Insert** menu.

→ Insert a new row by selecting the row that will appear below the new row and then clicking **Rows** on the **Insert** menu.

→ Insert multiple new rows by selecting that number of rows below where you want the new rows to appear and then clicking **Rows** on the **Insert** menu.

→ Insert cell(s) by selecting the cell(s) that will appear to the right or below the new cell(s) and then clicking **Cells** on the **Insert** menu. Then in the **Insert** dialog box, specify the direction you want to shift the selection to make room for the new cell(s).

To delete selected columns, rows, or cells

→ Delete selected columns or rows by clicking **Delete** on the **Edit** menu.

→ Delete selected cells by clicking **Delete** on the **Edit** menu and then in the **Delete** dialog box, specifying the direction you want the remaining content to move to fill the gap left by the deleted cells.

Conditional formatting

To automatically format cells that meet certain criteria

1. Select the cells, and click **Conditional Formatting** on the **Format** menu.

2. In the **Conditional Formatting** dialog box, specify the first condition for the formatting, and then click the **Format** button.

3. In the **Format Cells** dialog box, specify the font, border, and/or pattern formats for cells meeting the condition. Then click **OK**.

4. To set additional conditions for the selected cell range, click **Add** and then repeat steps 2 and 3.

Editing cell data

To cut, copy, or delete selected text

→ Use the standard menu commands, keys, and keyboard shortcuts.

To delete all the text in a cell

→ Activate the cell by clicking it once, and then press **Delete**.

Errors

To control how Excel checks for errors in workbooks

→ On the **Error Checking** page of the **Preferences** dialog box, select or configure options for background error checking, ignored errors, error-indicator colors, and error-checking rules.

Filling cells

To fill a series of cells with a series of data

→ Enter the first series element into the cell you want the series to start in, and then drag the cell's fill handle down or to the right to increase the series, or up or to the left to decrease the series.

To fill a series backward

→ Enter the first two series items in the first two cells, select the two cells, and then drag the fill handle of the selection.

To adjust the content or formatting of a filled series

→ After releasing the fill handle, click the **Auto Fill Options** button that appears, and choose the option you want.

To copy the contents of a cell into a series of cells

1. Select the cell, and drag the cell's fill handle across the series of cells.
2. After releasing the fill handle, click the **Auto Fill Options** button that appears, and click **Copy Cells**.

To create a custom list

→ On the **Custom Lists** page of the **Preferences** dialog box, with **NEW LIST** selected in the **Custom lists** box, enter the list items in the **List entries** box. Then click **Add**.

Formatting cells and cell contents

See Also "Borders and shading," "Formatting text manually," "Formatting text by using styles," and "Formatting paragraphs" in the "Word 2008 for Mac" Quick Reference section

To change the default font

→ On the **General** page of the **Preferences** dialog box, choose the font you want from the **Standard font** list.

To format numerical data

→ Choose the format you want from the **Number** panel of the **Formatting Palette**.

To merge selected cells

→ Select two or more cells you want to merge. Click the **Merge and Center** button on the Formatting toolbar, or select the **Merge cells** check box in the **Alignment and Spacing** panel of the **Formatting Palette**.

To draw borders manually

1. Display the Border Drawing toolbar by clicking the **Draw Border** button in the **Borders and Shading** panel of the **Formatting Palette**.
2. Select the line style and weight from the **Border Style** list, and the line color from the **Border Color** gallery.
3. Do one of the following:
   - Draw a single line by dragging along the cell separator.
   - Create a set of lines by dragging diagonally across the range of cells.

Formulas

To display the Formula Bar

→ Click **Formula Bar** on the **View** menu.
→ Resize the **Formula Bar** by dragging its lower-right corner.

To create a formula

→ Type the formula directly into the worksheet cell in which you want the results to appear, following the prompts as necessary.
→ Display the **Formula Bar**, and type the formula into the box, following the prompts as necessary.
→ Display the **Formula Builder** in the Toolbox, double-click the function you want to use, and enter the required information in the set of cells at the bottom of the **Formula Builder**.

To display formulas instead of their results

→ On the **View** page of the **Preferences** dialog box, select the **Show formulas** check box in the **Window options** area.

Headers and footers

To add headers and footers to a worksheet or list sheet

→ In Page Layout view, double-click in the header or footer area. Add the content you want, and then double-click the sheet to close the header or footer.

To display the date or time in the active header or footer

→ On the floating **Header & Footer** toolbar, click the **Insert Date** or **Insert Time** button.

Importing data

To insert an entire file

1. Click the **Import** button on the Standard toolbar.
2. In the **Import** dialog box, click the type of data you want to import, and then click **Import**.
3. In the **Choose A File** dialog box, locate the data file you want to import and then click **Get Data**.
4. Follow the Text Import Wizard instructions to select and map the data you want to import to fields in a new list sheet. Then click **Finish** at the end of the process.

New workbooks

To start a new workbook

→ Click the **New** button on the Standard toolbar.

Number formatting

To specify the number of decimal places used in a selected cell range

→ Click **Cells** on the **Format** menu. On the **Number** page of the **Format Cells** dialog box, click the number format you want and then, in the **Decimal Places** list, select or enter a number from **0** through **30**.

Page breaks

To insert a manual page break

→ Select a cell in the row below the intended page break, and then click **Page Break** on the **Insert** menu.

Page setup

See Also "Page setup" in the "Office 2008 for Mac" Quick Reference section

To control the appearance of a worksheet when printed

→ Scale content to a specific percentage of the actual size by entering or selecting the percentage in the **Adjust to** box in the **Page Setup** panel of the **Formatting Palette**.

→ Fit content onto a specific number of pages by selecting the **Fit to** check box in the **Page Setup** panel of the **Formatting Palette** and then entering or selecting the number of pages in the **Page(s) wide** and **Page(s) tall** boxes.

→ Display or hide gridlines and column/row headings by selecting or clearing the corresponding **View** check boxes in the **Page Setup** panel of the **Formatting Palette**.

→ Print row and column titles by clicking the **Print Titles** button in the **Page Setup** panel of the **Formatting Palette**.

Print area

To specify the area of a worksheet to be printed

→ Designate selected cells as the print area by pointing to **Print Area** on the **File** menu and then clicking **Set Print Area**.

→ Add selected cells to an existing print area by pointing to **Print Area** on the **File** menu and clicking **Add to Print Area**.

→ Clear the print area by pointing to **Print Area** on the **File** menu and clicking **Clear Print Area**.

Protection

To protect a worksheet or workbook from changes by unauthorized people

→ In the **Save As** dialog box, click **Options**. Then in the **Save Options** dialog box, enter a password in the **Password to modify** dialog box.

→ Point to **Protection** on the **Tools** menu, and then click **Protect Sheet**. In the **Protect Sheet** dialog box, select the **Contents**, **Objects**, and/or **Scenarios** check boxes. If you want to allow changes by authorized people, enter a password in the **Password** box and distribute the password to authorized people.

→ Point to **Protection** on the **Tools** menu, and then click **Protect Workbook**. In the **Protect Workbook** dialog box, select the **Structure** and/or **Windows** check boxes. If you want to allow changes by authorized people, enter a password in the **Password** box and distribute the password to authorized people.

Range names

To name a selected range of cells

→ In the **Name** box at the left end of the **Formula Bar**, type the range name, and then press **Return**.

Or

1. Point to **Name** on the **Insert** menu, and then click **Define**.
2. In the **Define Name** dialog box, verify or change the range name and cell range, and then click **Add**.

References

To reference a range

→ Enter a relative reference by typing the first and last cells in the range, separated by a colon:

A1:B5

→ Enter an absolute reference by typing dollar signs ($) to the left of any part of the reference you want to be absolute:

$A1:$B5

A$1: B$5

$A$1:$B$5

To reference a named range

→ Use the range name in place of the cell range. No special punctuation is necessary.

To reference a cell or cell range on another sheet

→ Type the sheet name followed by an exclamation mark (!).

Sheet2!A1:B5

To reference a cell or cell range in another workbook

→ Type the workbook name and extension enclosed in square brackets, followed by the sheet you want within that workbook. Enclose the entire reference in single quotation marks, and follow the close quotation mark with an exclamation mark (!).

'[Workbook2.xlsx]Sheet2'!A1:B5

Restricting content

To control the content entered in a list column

→ Double-click the column heading, and in the **Column Settings** dialog box, specify the following:

- Formatting appropriate to the type of data you expect the column to contain
- The value to appear by default in all the cells in the column
- Whether duplicate values are allowed
- Data validation criteria and messages to guide data entry

Saving files

To set the default location in which Excel looks for and saves files

→ On the **General** page of the **Preferences** dialog box, click the **Select** button to the right of **Preferred file location**. In the **Choose a Folder** dialog box, select the folder and then click **Choose**.

Selecting cells and data

To select a single cell, column, or row

→ Click the cell, column heading, or row heading.

To select contiguous cells, columns, or rows

→ Point to the first cell, column heading, or row heading, and drag through to the last one.

To select noncontiguous cells, columns, or rows

1. Select the first cell, column heading, or row heading.
2. Hold down the **Command** key, and click the other cells, columns, or rows you want to include in the selection.

To select a cell for editing

→ Double-click the cell to activate the insertion point, and then click or use the keyboard navigation keys to position the insertion point where you want it.

To select cell data

→ Drag across the data, or hold down the **Shift** key and press the navigation keys.

Sheets

To insert a new sheet

→ Insert a new worksheet by clicking the **Insert Sheet** button at the right end of the sheet tabs.
→ Insert a new chart sheet or list sheet by pointing to the **Sheet** button on the **Insert** menu and then clicking **Chart Sheet** or **List Sheet**.
→ Insert a specialized sheet from the Project Gallery or the Elements Gallery.

To hide the active sheet

→ Point to **Sheet** on the **Format** menu and click **Hide**.

To display a hidden sheet

→ Point to **Sheet** on the **Format** menu, click **Unhide**, click the sheet you want, and click **OK**.

To move or copy a sheet

→ Move a sheet within a workbook by dragging its sheet tab.
→ Move the sheet to a different workbook by dragging it from one workbook window to the other.
→ Copy the sheet to a different workbook by dragging it while holding down the secondary mouse button.
  Or

1. Right-click the sheet and click **Move or Copy**.
2. In the **Move or Copy** dialog box, specify the target location of the sheet in the **To book** list.
3. If you want to create a copy of the sheet at the selected location, select the **Create a copy** check box. Then click **OK**.

To rename a sheet

→ Double-click the sheet tab, type the name, and press **Return**.

→ Right-click the sheet tab, click **Rename**, type the name, and press **Return**.

Viewing worksheets

See Also "Excel 2008 Keyboard Shortcuts" earlier in this Quick Reference section

To change the default view of new sheets

→ On the **View** page of the **Preferences** dialog box, in the **Settings** area, choose the view you want from the **Preferred view for new sheets** list.

To hide window elements to view more of a worksheet

→ Hide row and column headings by clearing the **View** check box to the right of **Headings** in the **Page Setup** panel of the **Formatting Palette**, or by clearing the **Show row and column Headings** check box on the **View** page of the **Preferences** dialog box.

→ Hide sheet tabs by clearing the **Show sheet tabs** check box on the **View** page of the **Preferences** dialog box.

→ Hide scroll bars by clearing the **Show vertical scroll bar** or **Show horizontal scroll bar** check box on the **View** page of the **Preferences** dialog box.

→ Hide the formula bar by clicking its **Close** button, by clicking **Formula Bar** on the **View** menu, or by clearing the **Show formula bar** check box on the **View** page of the **Preferences** dialog box.

→ Hide the status bar by clicking **Status Bar** on the **View** menu, or by clearing the **Show status bar** check box on the **View** page of the **Preferences** dialog box.

To view more than one part of a workbook at the same time

→ Drag the **Split** bar located at the top of the vertical scrollbar downward, and then, in each pane, display the parts of the workbook you want to view.

To arrange only the windows for the active workbook

1. Click **Arrange** on the **Window** menu, and select the arrangement you want in the **Arrange Windows** dialog box.
2. Select the **Windows of active workbook** check box, and then click **OK**.

To move to a specific cell, named range, or worksheet element

→ Display the **Go To** dialog box by clicking **Go To** on the **Edit** menu. Click a named location, enter a cell reference in the **Reference** box, or click **Special** and, in the **Go To Special** dialog box, click the type of element you want to go to. Then click **OK** in the open dialog box(es).

Workbook templates

To start a new workbook based on a template

1. Open the Project Gallery, and display the **New** page.
2. In the **Show** list, click **Excel Workbooks**, and then in the **Category** list, click either **Home Essentials** or **Ledger Sheets**.
3. In the **Template** list, click the template you want. Then click **Open**.

To add a standard ledger sheet to the active workbook

1. At the top of the workbook window, click the **Sheets** button.
2. On the **Sheets** tab of the Elements Gallery, click the button for the category of ledger sheets you want.
3. Click the template you want.

To save a workbook as a template

1. Click **Save As** on the **File** menu, and in the **Save As** dialog box, assign the template a name
2. In the **Format** list, click **Excel Template (.xltx)**. Then click **Save**.

To start a new workbook based on a template you have saved in the default location

→ In the Project Gallery, click **My Templates** in the **Category** list, and then double-click the template you want in the **Template** list.

Microsoft PowerPoint 2008 for Mac

PowerPoint 2008 Keyboard Shortcuts Q-56
Simple Instructions for Doing Things in PowerPoint 2008 . . . . Q-60
    Adding content Q-60
    Adding slides Q-60
    AutoFitting Q-60
    Backgrounds Q-61
    Bulleted and numbered lists Q-62
    Charts Q-62
    Deleting slides Q-62
    Color schemes Q-62
    Delivering a slide show Q-63
    Ending a slide show Q-64
    Formatting text Q-64
    Headers and footers Q-64
    Inserting slides Q-64
    New presentations Q-64
    Moving and sizing content placeholders Q-65
    Moving slides Q-65
    Outlines Q-65
    Photos and pictures Q-65
    Presentation templates Q-65
    Saving files Q-66
    Selecting slides and text Q-66
    Slide layouts Q-67
    Themes Q-67
    Viewing slides Q-67
    Watermarks Q-68

PowerPoint 2008 Keyboard Shortcuts

Moving around in text

To move	Press
To the beginning of a word or one word to the left	Option+Left Arrow
One word to the right	Option+Right Arrow
To the beginning of a paragraph or up one paragraph	Option+Up Arrow
Down one paragraph	Option+Down Arrow
To the end of a text box	Option+End
To the beginning of a text box	Option+Home

Editing text and objects

To	Press
Duplicate the selected object	Command+D
Increase the font size	Shift+Command+>
Decrease the font size	Shift+Command+<
Change the case of letters	Shift+F3
Apply subscript formatting	Command+Equal Sign
Apply superscript formatting	Command+Plus Sign on the numeric keypad
Center a paragraph	Command+E
Justify a paragraph	Command+J
Left align a paragraph	Command+L
Right align a paragraph	Command+R
Open the Format Text dialog box	Command+T

Working in presentations

To	Press
Insert a new slide	Control+M or Shift+Command+N
Zoom in	Shift+Command+Plus Sign
Zoom out	Shift+Command+Minus Sign
Make a copy of the selected slide in outline view, Slide Sorter view, or in the outline pane in Normal view	Command+D
Make a copy of the selected slide in notes page view, or in the slides pane or notes pane in Normal view	Shift+Command+D
Open a presentation	Command+O
Save a presentation with a different name, location, or file format	Shift+Command+S
Find text, formatting, and special items	Command+F
Find and replace text, specific formatting, and special items	Control+H
Check spelling	Command+Option+L or F7
Insert a hyperlink	Command+K
Cancel a command, such as Save As	Escape
Duplicate the selected slide	Shift+Command+D

Changing views

To	Press
Show or hide guides	Command+G
Switch to Handout Master view	Shift+click Slide Sorter View
Switch to Slide Master view	Shift+click Normal View
Activate the presenter tools	Shift+click Slide Show
Switch to Normal view	Control+Shift+Z
Switch to Slide Sorter view	Control+Shift+V
Switch to Notes view	Control+Shift+T
Expand the outline pane in Normal view	Control+Shift+X
Switch to Slide view	Control+Shift+C

Selecting text

To select	Press
One character to the right	Shift+Right Arrow
One character to the left	Shift+Left Arrow
From the insertion point to the same point one line up	Shift+Up Arrow
From the insertion point to the same point one line down	Shift+Down Arrow
All text to the start of the line	Shift+Home
All text to the end of the line	Shift+End
From the insertion point to the end of the paragraph	Shift+Option+Down Arrow
From the insertion point to the beginning of the paragraph	Shift+Option+Up Arrow
From the insertion point to the beginning of the text box	Shift+Option+Home
From the insertion point to the end of the text box	Shift+Option+End

Working in a table

To	Press
Move to the next cell	Tab
Move to the preceding cell	Shift+Tab
Move to the next line or row	Down Arrow
Move to the preceding line or row	Up Arrow
Start a new paragraph in a cell	Return
Add a new row at the bottom of the table	Tab at the end of the last row

Presenting a slide show

To	Press
Perform the next animation or advance to the next slide	N, Return, Page Down, Right Arrow, Down Arrow, Enter, or the Spacebar (or click the mouse button)
Return to the previous animation or return to the previous slide	P, Page Up, Left Arrow, Up Arrow, or Delete
Go to slide number	The number of the slide that you want to view, and then press Return
Display a black screen, or return to the slide show from a black screen	B or Period
Display a white screen, or return to the slide show from a white screen	W or Comma
Stop or restart an automatic slide show	S or Plus Sign
Start a slide show from the first slide	Control+Shift+S or Command+Return
Start a slide show from the current slide	Control+Shift+B
End a slide show	Escape, Command+Period, or Hyphen
Erase on-screen annotations	E
Go to next hidden slide if the next slide is hidden	H
Redisplay hidden pointer and/or change the pointer to a pen	Command+P
Redisplay hidden pointer and/or change the pointer to an arrow	Command+A
Hide the pointer and button immediately	Control+H
Hide the pointer and button in 10 seconds	Command+U
Show or hide the arrow pointer	A or Equal Sign
Display the contextual menu	Hold down Control and click the mouse button

Simple Instructions for Doing Things in PowerPoint 2008

Adding content

To add text to a slide

→ On the slide, click the appropriate placeholder and type the text.

→ On the **Outline** page of the Navigation pane, click in the outline where you want to add content, and type the text.

See Also "PowerPoint 2008 Keyboard Shortcuts" earlier in this Quick Reference section

To create a text box

→ Click the Text Box button on the Standard toolbar, or click **Text Box** on the **Insert** menu, and then drag on the slide to define the text box area.

To add other content to a slide

→ Insert a table, chart, SmartArt graphic, image file, clip art image, or movie clip by clicking the corresponding control and then following the instructions that appear.

Adding slides

To add a new slide with the default layout after the current slide

→ Click **New Slide** on the **Insert** menu.

To add a new slide with the layout you select

→ In the Elements Gallery, click the layout you want on the **Slide Layouts** tab.

To insert a slide from an existing presentation after the current slide

1. Point to **Slides From** on the **Insert** menu, and then click **Other Presentation**.
2. In the **Choose A File** dialog box, navigate to the folder where the existing presentation is located, and click the presentation.
3. With the **Select slides to insert** option selected, click **Insert**.
4. In the Slide Finder, click the thumbnail for the slide you want and click **Insert**. Then click **Close**.

AutoFitting

To prevent the auto fitting of text to its placeholder

→ When PowerPoint changes the font size to fit the text into the box, click the **AutoFit Options** button that appears, and then click **Stop Fitting Text to This Placeholder**.

Backgrounds

See Also "Watermarks" later in this Quick Reference section

To apply a solid color to a slide background

→ In the **Slide Background** panel of the **Formatting Palette**, click the background color and, optionally, the style you want.

Or

1. Click **Slide Background** on the **Format** menu.
2. On the **Solid** page of the **Format Background** dialog box, expand the **Color** gallery and click the color you want.
3. Click **Apply** to apply the background to only the current slide, or **Apply to All** to apply the background to all slides in the presentation.

To apply a gradient to a slide background

1. On the **Gradient** page of the **Format Background** dialog box, select **Linear**, **Radial**, **Rectangular**, **Path**, or **From Title** in the **Style** box.
2. For each gradient slider, click the slider, choose the color from the **Color** list, and choose the transparency from the **Transparency** slider.
3. To add a color halfway between the current slider and the next stopping point to its right, click **Add Color**.
4. Click **Apply** to apply the background to only the current slide, or **Apply to All** to apply the background to all slides in the presentation.

To add a texture to the slide background

1. On the **Texture** page of the **Format Background** dialog box, click the texture you want and then, using the **Transparency** slider, set its transparency.
2. Click **Apply** to apply the background to only the current slide, or **Apply to All** to apply the background to all slides in the presentation.

To add a picture to the slide background

1. On the **Picture** page of the **Format Background** dialog box, click the **Choose a Picture** button.
2. In the **Choose a Picture** window, navigate to and click the picture you want, and then click **Insert**.
3. On the **Picture** page of the **Format Background** dialog box, set the **Transparency**, and if you want, select the **Tile** check box.
4. Click **Apply** to apply the background to only the current slide, or **Apply to All** to apply the background to all slides in the presentation.

To hide the background graphics of a slide

→ With the slide displayed, select the **Hide Background Graphics** check box in the **Slide Background** panel of the **Formatting Palette**.

Bulleted and numbered lists

To change the level of an item

→ On the **Outline** page of the Navigation pane, click the item whose level you want to change. Then do one of the following:

- Demote the item by clicking the **Increase Indent** button on the Formatting toolbar or by clicking the **Increase List Level** button in the **Bullets and Numbering** panel of the **Formatting Palette**.
- Promote the item by clicking the **Decrease Indent** button on the Formatting toolbar or by clicking the **Decrease List Level** button in the **Bullets and Numbering** panel.

See Also "PowerPoint 2008 Keyboard Shortcuts" earlier in this Quick Reference section

To convert a bulleted (unordered) list to a numbered (ordered) list

→ Select the list items you want to change, and then click the **Numbering** button on the Formatting toolbar or in the **Bullets and Numbering** panel.

To change the style, color, or size of the numbers or letters or to specify a starting number or letter

→ Make a selection in the **Style** list in the **Bullets and Numbering** panel.

→ Display the **Format Text** dialog box by clicking **Bullets and Numbering** on the **Format** menu, or by right-clicking the list and then clicking **Bullets and Numbering**. Then make a selection on the **Numbering** page.

To convert a bulleted list to normal text

1. Click the active **Bullets** button in the **Bullets and Numbering** panel or on the Formatting toolbar to remove the bullet character or number.
2. Display the **Paragraph** page of the **Format Text** dialog box in one of these ways:
   - Click **Paragraph** on the **Format** menu.
   - Right-click the selected text and then click **Paragraph**.
3. On the **Paragraph** page of the **Format Text** dialog box, under **Indentation**, click **(None)** in the **Special** list, and change the **Before Text** measurement to **0"**.

Charts

See "Charts" in the "Word 2008 for Mac" Quick Reference section

Deleting slides

To remove one slide

→ Delete the current slide by clicking **Delete Slide** on the **Edit** menu.

→ Right-click any slide in the Navigation pane and click **Delete Slide**.

To remove multiple slides

→ Select the slides in the Navigation pane or in Slide Sorter view. Then right-click the selection and click **Delete Slide**.

Color schemes

To display a presentation's color scheme

→ Click **Theme Colors** on the **Format** menu.

To change a theme element to another color

1. In the **Create Theme Colors** dialog box, click the colored icon to the left of the theme element name, and then click the **Change Color** button.
2. In the **Colors** dialog box, select the color you want to use for the specified theme element from the **Color Wheel**, **Color Sliders**, **Color Palettes**, **Image Palettes**, or **Crayons** page, and then click **OK**.
3. If you want to save the customized color scheme for reuse, enter a name for the color scheme in the **Name** box.
4. Click the **Apply to All** button to apply your changes to the active presentation.

Delivering a slide show

See Also "PowerPoint 2008 Keyboard Shortcuts" earlier in this Quick Reference section

To start a slide show from within PowerPoint

→ Click **View Slide Show** on the **Slide Show** menu.
→ Click the **Slide Show** button on the Standard toolbar.
→ Click the **Slide Show** button on the **View** menu (in the lower-left corner of the window).

To move in sequence through the slides in a show

→ Without moving the mouse, click the primary button.
→ Press the **N**, **Return**, **Page Down**, **Right Arrow**, or **Down Arrow** key.
→ Press the **Spacebar**.

To move nonlinearly

→ Move to the previous slide by pressing the **P**, **Page Up**, **Left Arrow**, **Up Arrow**, or **Delete** key.
→ Move to the first slide by pressing the **Home** key.
→ Move to a specific slide by typing the slide number and pressing **Return**.
→ Move to the last slide in a presentation by pressing the **End** key.

To use the commands on the Slide Show menu

→ Display the menu by clicking the button that appears in the lower-left corner of the slide when you move the mouse.
→ Move between slides by clicking **Next**, **Previous**, or **Last Viewed**, or by clicking **Go To Slide** and then clicking the specific slide you want to display.
→ Hide the slide show without closing it by clicking **Black Screen**. Redisplay the slide show by clicking the screen. Redisplay the slide show and move to another slide by pressing the key corresponding to the movement.
→ Display the slides in a custom slide show by clicking **Custom Show** and then clicking the show you want.
→ Display a list of keyboard shortcuts for carrying out slide show tasks by clicking **Help**.
→ Hide the pointer or change its form by pointing to **Pointer Options** and then doing one of the following
  - Click the pointer format you want.
  - Point to **Pen Color**, click the color you want, and then make annotations on the slide.
→ Change an on-screen event by pointing to **Screen** and then doing one of the following:
  - Click **Pause** to pause a self-running presentation.
  - Click **Erase Pen** to remove annotations from the slide.

To stop a slide show before the end

→ Press the **Escape** key.

→ Click **End Show** on the **Slide Show** menu.

Ending slide show

To add a black slide to the end of a slide show

→ On the **View** page of the **Preferences** dialog box, select the **End with black slide** check box in the **Slide Show** area.

Formatting text

See Also "Borders and shading," "Formatting text manually," "Formatting text by using styles," and "Formatting paragraphs" in the "Word 2008 for Mac" Quick Reference section

To replace a font throughout a presentation

1. Click **Replace Fonts** on the **Format** menu.
2. In the **Replace Font** dialog box, click the font you want to change in the **Replace** list, and click the new font in the **With** list.
3. Click **Replace**, and then click **Close**.

To increase or decrease the font size

→ Increase the size by clicking the **Grow Font** button in the **Font** panel of the **Formatting Palette**.

→ Decrease the size by clicking the **Shrink Font** button in the same pane.

Headers and footers

To set up standard slide footer content

1. In the **Page Setup** dialog box, click **Header/Footer**.
2. On the **Slide** page of the **Header and Footer** dialog box, select the **Date and time**, **Slide number**, and/or **Footer** check boxes, and provide the information associated with your selections.
3. Click **Apply** to apply the footer to the current slide or click **Apply All** to apply it to all slides in the presentation.

To set up standard header and footer content for notes and handouts

1. In the **Page Setup** dialog box, click **Header/Footer**.
2. On the **Notes and Handouts** page of the **Header and Footer** dialog box, select the **Date and time**, **Header**, **Page number**, and/or **Footer** check boxes, and provide the information associated with your selections. Then click **Apply to All**.

Inserting slides

See Also "Adding slides" earlier in this Quick Reference section

New presentations

To start a new presentation

→ Click the **New** button on the Standard toolbar.

Moving and sizing content placeholders

To move a layout placeholder

→ Point to the placeholder, and when the pointer changes to a four-headed arrow, drag the placeholder to its new location.

To resize a layout placeholder

→ Click its border to activate the resize and rotate handles, and then drag the resize handles.

To restore a layout placeholder to its original position and size

→ Reapply the original slide layout.

Moving slides

To rearrange a presentation

→ On the **Slides** tab of the Navigation pane, drag slides up and down to change their order.

→ In Slide Sorter view, drag slide thumbnails into the order you want.

Outlines

To import a Word outline as a presentation

1. Click the **Open** button on the Standard toolbar.
2. In the **Open** dialog box, navigate to the folder where the outline file is located, and click the file. Then click **Open**.

To export an outline from Word as a presentation

1. In the Word document, apply heading styles to the outline elements you want to use in the presentation. Use the Heading 1 style for slide titles, Heading 2 for first-level bulleted list items, and Heading 3 for second-level list items.
2. Point to **Send To** on the **File** menu, and then click **PowerPoint**.

To export a presentation as a Word outline

1. Display the **Save As** dialog box, navigate to the folder where you want to store the outline, and assign a name in the **Save As** box.
2. Click **Outline / Rich Text Format (.rtf)** in the **Format** list. Then click **Save**.

Photos and pictures

See Also "Photos and pictures" in the "Office 2008 for Mac" Quick Reference section

To insert a photo or picture

1. In the content placeholder, click the **Add Picture** icon.
2. In the **Choose a Picture** dialog box, navigate to the folder where the picture file is stored, click the file, and then click **Insert**.

Presentation templates

To start a new presentation based on a template

1. Open the **Project Gallery**, and display the **New** page.
2. In the **Show** list, click **PowerPoint Documents**, and then in the **Category** list, click either **Presentations** or **Office Themes**.
3. In the **Template** list, click the template you want. Then click **Open**.

To save a presentation as a template

1. Click **Save As** on the **File** menu, and in the **Save As** dialog box, assign the template a name.
2. In the **Format** list, click **PowerPoint Template (.potx)**. Then click **Save**.

To start a new presentation based on a template you have saved

→   In the Project Gallery, click **My Templates** in the **Category** list, and then double-click the template you want in the **Template** list.

To save the theme from a template for use in other presentations

1. Create a presentation from the template. Then on the **File** menu, click **Save As**.
2. In the **Save As** dialog box, click **Office Theme (.thmx)** in the **Format** list.
3. In the **Save As** box, enter an appropriate name for the theme, and click **Save**.

To apply a saved theme to the open presentation

1. Point to **Theme** on the **Format** menu, and then click **From File**.
2. In the **Choose Themed Document or Slide Template** dialog box, ensure that the *My Themes* folder is displayed, click the theme you saved, and then click **Apply**.

Saving files

To set the default location in which PowerPoint saves files

→   On the **Advanced** page of the **Preferences** dialog box, click the **Select** button to the right of **Default file location**. In the **Choose a Folder** dialog box, select the folder and then click **Choose**.

Selecting slides and text

See Also "PowerPoint 2008 Keyboard Shortcuts" earlier in this Quick Reference section

To select contiguous slides

→   Select the first slide on the **Slides** page or the **Outline** page of the Navigation pane, press and hold the **Shift** key, and click the last slide in the set.

To select noncontiguous slides

→   Select the first slide on the **Slides** page of the Navigation pane, press and hold the **Command** key, and click the each additional slide in the set.
→   Select the first slide on the **Outline** page of the Navigation pane, press and hold the **Control** key, and click the each additional slide in the set.

To select text on a slide

→   Select an individual word by double-clicking it.
→   Select adjacent words, lines, or paragraphs by dragging through them.
→   Select adjacent words, lines, or paragraphs by positioning the insertion point at the beginning of the text, holding down the **Shift** key, and either pressing an arrow key or clicking at the end of the text you want to select.
→   Select the title and all the text on a slide by clicking its slide icon on the **Outline** page of the Navigation pane.
→   Select an entire list item by clicking its bullet or number on either the **Outline** page or the slide.
→   Select all the text in a placeholder by clicking inside the placeholder and then clicking **Select All** on the **Edit** menu.

Slide layouts

To create a slide based on a slide layout

→ On the **Slide Layouts** tab of the Elements Gallery, click **Insert new slide** in the left pane. Then click the thumbnail of the slide layout you want to apply.

To format existing slides with a different slide layout

1. Display one slide in Normal view, or select one or more slides in Slide Sorter view.
2. On the **Slide Layouts** tab of the Elements Gallery, click **Apply to slide** in the left pane.
3. Click the thumbnail of the slide layout you want to apply.

To make changes to a slide layout

See "Slide masters" later in this Quick Reference section

Slide masters

To display the slide masters of the current presentation

→ Point to **Master** on the **View** menu, and then click **Slide Master**.

To change the layout of all slides based on the same slide layout

1. Display the slide masters. In the Navigation pane, click the slide layout you want to change.
2. Make the changes you want to the text boxes, fonts, graphics, and other elements of the slide layout. Then, on the Master toolbar, click **Close Master**.

Themes

See "Themes" in the "Office 2008 for Mac" Quick Reference section

Viewing slides

See Also "PowerPoint 2008 Keyboard Shortcuts" earlier in this Quick Reference section

To hide window elements to view more of a slide

→ Change the size of the panes in Normal view by dragging the splitter bar between the Navigation pane and the Slide pane left or right, or between the Slide pane and the Notes pane up or down.

→ Hide the Navigation pane by clicking the **Close** button in its upper-right corner.

To display a slide at the maximum size supported by the presentation window

→ Press **Control+Shift+C**.

To move between slides

→ On the **Slides** page of the Navigation pane, click the slide you want to display.

→ On the **Outline** page of the Navigation pane, click the number, icon, title or text of the slide you want to display.

→ On the **Outline** page of the Navigation pane, press the **Right Arrow** key to move from slide to slide.

→ Use the vertical scroll bar on the right side of the Slide pane.

→ Click the **Previous Slide** or **Next Slide** button at the bottom of the Slide pane scroll bar.

To display only slide titles in the Outline page

→ Right-click the Navigation pane, point to **Collapse**, and then click **Collapse All**.

Watermarks

To insert a WordArt watermark

1. Display the slide in Normal view, and select a style from the **WordArt** tab of the Elements Gallery.
2. Replace the *Your Text Here* placeholder with your watermark text, and then select the text.
3. In the **Colors, Weights, and Fills** panel of the **Formatting Palette**, set the **Fill Transparency** to a number between 65% and 90%.
4. If the WordArt design includes an outline, set the **Line Transparency** to a number between 65% and 100%.
5. Size and position the WordArt where you want it to appear on the slide.

To insert a watermark with text in a shape

1. Display the slide in Normal view, and display the **Object Palette** in the Toolbox.
2. Insert the shape, and then size and position it where you want it to appear on the slide.
3. Add text to the shape by typing it directly, by double-clicking in the center of the shape, or by right-clicking the shape and then clicking **Add Text**.
4. Select the shape, and in the **Colors, Weights, and Fills** panel of the **Formatting Palette**, choose **No Fill** in the **Fill Color** list, and choose **No Line** in the **Line Color** list. Then set the **Fill Transparency** of the shape to **100%**.
5. Select the text, and in the **Colors, Weights, and Fills** panel, choose the color you want the text to be. Then set the **Fill Transparency** of the text to a number between 65% and 90%.

To create a picture watermark

1. From the **Object Palette**, insert an image or photo.
2. Size and position the picture where you want it to appear on the slide.
3. With the picture selected, set the **Transparency** in the **Picture** panel of the **Formatting Palette** to a number between 65% and 90%.

Microsoft Entourage 2008 for Mac

Entourage 2008 Keyboard Shortcuts Q-70

Simple Instructions for Doing Things in Entourage 2008. . . . . .Q-74

    Address Book. Q-74

    Calendar Q-74

    Categories Q-75

    Contact groups Q-76

    Contact records. Q-76

    Displaying modules Q-76

    E-mail accounts. Q-76

    E-mail messages Q-77

    E-mail signatures. Q-79

    Favorites Bar. Q-79

    Flagging for follow up Q-80

    Folder list Q-80

    Mini Calendar Q-80

    Preview pane Q-80

    Scheduling Entourage events Q-80

    Searching items. Q-81

    To Do list. Q-81

    Toolbar Q-81

Entourage 2008 Keyboard Shortcuts

Windows and dialog boxes

To	Press
Show or hide the folder list	Command+B
Create a new item of the default module type	Command+N
Open a new Entourage window	Shift+Command+Option+N
Go to the Mail view	Command+1
Open the Message list in a new window	Command+Option+1
Go to the Address Book view	Command+2
Open the Address Book in a new window	Command+Option+2
Go to Calendar view	Command+3
Open the Calendar in a new window	Command+Option+3
Go to Notes view	Command+4
Open the Notes list in a new window	Command+Option+4
Go to Tasks view	Command+5
Open the Tasks list in a new window	Command+Option+5
Go to Project Center view	Command+6
Open the Project Center in a new window	Command+Option+6
Open the Progress window or make it the active window	Command+7
Open the error log or make it the active window	Command+8
Cycle forward through open windows	Command+Tilde (~)
Cycle back through open windows	Shift+Command+Tilde (~)
Open the selected item	Command+O
Move forward through boxes in a dialog box	Tab
Move back through boxes in a dialog box	Shift+Tab
Move forward through tabs in a dialog box	Control+Tab
Move back through tabs in a dialog box	Shift+Control+Tab

Modules and lists

To	Press
Duplicate the selected item	Command+D
Delete the selected item	Command+Delete
Show or hide the Preview pane	Command+\
Cancel the selection of all items	Shift+Command+A
Close the current open item and open the previous item in the list	Command+[
Close the current open item and open the next item in the list	Command+]

Message list

To	Press
Open the Message list in a new window	Shift+Command+Option+N
Create a new folder	Shift+Command+N

Calendar

To	Press
Switch the view to include today	Command+T
Open the Go To Date dialog box	Shift+Command+T
Move to the previous calendar period (day, week, work week, or month) corresponding to the view	Command+[
Move to the next calendar period	Command+]

Messages

To	Press
Send the open message	Command+Return
Send and receive all messages	Command+K
Save the open message and store it in the Drafts folder	Command+S
Add an attachment to the open message	Command+E
Check spelling in the open message	Command+Option+L
Check recipient names in the open messages	Command+Option+C
Reply to the sender of the message	Command+R
Reply to all	Shift+Command+R
Reply only to the sender of a mailing list message	Command+Option+R
Forward the message	Command+J
Mark the selected message as junk mail	Shift+Command+J
Mark the selected message as not junk mail	Shift+Command+Option+J
Add the sender of the selected message to the Address Book	Command+Option+C
Move the selected message to a folder	Shift+Command+Option+M
Decrease the display size of text in an open message or in the Preview pane	Command+Hyphen (-)
Increase the display size of text in an open message or in the Preview pane	Command+=
Display the previous unread message	Control+[
Display the next unread message	Control+]
Scroll down to the next screen of text or, if you are at the end of a message, display the next unread message	Spacebar
Scroll up to the previous screen of text	Shift+Spacebar
Scroll down to the next screen of text	Option+Spacebar
Scroll down through a message slowly and continuously	Hold down Spacebar
Delete the active message and display the previous message	Command+Option+[
Delete the active message and display the next message	Command+Option+]
Delete the active message and display the previous unread message	Control+Option+[
Delete the active message and display the next unread message	Control+Option+]
Delete the active message and, if the message window is open, close it	Command+Option+Delete

Flagging items

To	Press
Flag the selected item with a due date of Today	Control+1
Flag the selected item with a due date of Tomorrow	Control+2
Flag the selected item with a due date of This Week	Control+3
Flag the selected item with a due date of Next Week	Control+4
Flag the selected item with a due date of No Due Date	Control+5
Mark the selected item as Complete	Control+0
Clear the selected item's flag	Command+Option+ Apostrophe (')

Printing

To	Press
Print one copy of an item with the default settings	Command+Option+P

Search

To	Press
Find text in items	Command+F
Find the next instance of the text you searched for in an item	Command+G
Find the next instance of the selected text	Shift+Command+G
Cancel a search in progress	Command+Period (.)
Perform an Advanced Search	Command+Option+F

Simple Instructions for Doing Things in Entourage 2008

Address Book

To change the displayed fields

→ Point to **Columns** on the **View** menu or right-click any column heading, and then click field names on the list that appears.

To change the display order of contact records

→ Click the heading of the column you want to sort by.

→ Change the order of the sort column (high/low or low/high) by clicking the heading a second time.

To send an e-mail message or instant message to a contact

→ In the Address Book, click the contact record. Then on the toolbar, click **E-mail** or **Chat**.

To invite a contact to a meeting

→ In the Address Book, click the contact record. Then on the toolbar, click **Invite**.

To display, open, and create contact record links

→ In the contact record, click the **Links** button. In the **Links To** window, click **To New** or **To Existing** and then, in the list, click the type of item you want to link to. In the dialog box that opens, create or locate the item.

→ In the Address Book, click in the **Links** column and then click **Link To Existing Link** or **To New**. In the list, click the type of item you want to link to. Then in the dialog box that opens, create or locate the item.

Calendar

To create a calendar event

1. Click the **New** button on the Calendar window toolbar.

2. In the **New Event** window, enter the name of the event in the **Subject** box and its location in the **Location** box.

3. In the **Start** box, select the date of the event or, if it's a multi-day event, the first day.

4. If the event is not tied to a specific time span, select the **All-day event** check box. If it starts and finishes at specific times, enter that information in the **Start** and **End** boxes.

5. If the event will recur on a regular schedule, click the **Occurs** list and then click the frequency of recurrence.

6. If you want to change the reminder time, select the units and number of units in the lists to the right of the **Reminder** check box, or clear the check box.

7. If you want to block out time for travel, select the **Travel time** check box and, in the lists, select the amount of travel time and the relationship to the event.

8. Click the **Status** button and, in the list, click **Busy**, **Free**, **Tentative**, or **Out Of Office**.

9. Add any notes or other information, close the event window, and then click **Save** in the message box.

To change the calendar display

→ Move to the current day by clicking the **Today** button on the toolbar.

→ Move to the previous or next time period by clicking the left or right arrows to the left of the time period.

→ Display a specific date or range of dates by clicking or dragging to select them in the Mini Calendar.

→ Change the view by clicking the toolbar buttons or by clicking the view you want on the **Calendar** menu.

→ Change the time period displayed in the large calendar by doing the following:

● Display the month that appears in the Mini Calendar by clicking the month name in the Mini Calendar.

● Display a week that appears in the Mini Calendar by clicking the margin to the left of that week in the Mini Calendar.

● Display a specific day by clicking that day in the Mini Calendar.

Categories

To assign one category to an item

→ Right-click the item, point to **Categories**, and then click the category.

→ Select the item in the module window, click the **Categories** arrow on the program window toolbar, and then click the category you want to assign.

→ Open the item in its item window, click the **Categories** arrow on the item window toolbar, and then click the category you want to assign.

To assign multiple categories to an open or selected item

1. Click the **Categories** button on the program window or item window toolbar.

2. In the **Assign Categories** dialog box, select the check boxes of the categories you want to assign. (Assign a category and select its color by clicking the category name and clicking the **Set Primary** button before selecting its check box.)

3. Click **OK**.

To display only items with a specific category assigned to them

→ Click the category name in the **Views** section of the Folder list.

To manage categories

→ Display the Categories window by clicking **Edit Categories** in any of the **Categories** lists.

→ Create a new category by clicking the **New** button.

→ Change the name of a category by double-clicking the name, editing it, and pressing **Return**.

→ Change the color associated with a category by clicking its color box and then clicking the color you want.

→ Delete a category and remove any assignments of that category by clicking the category name, clicking the **Delete** button, and clicking **Delete** in the message box.

Contact groups

To create a contact group

1. On the Address Book toolbar, click the **New** arrow and then, in the list, click **Group**.

2. In the **Group** window, enter the group name and click the **Add** button.

3. In the text box, enter the name (if you have a contact record for the person) or e-mail address of each group member. Press **Tab** after each entry to start a new line, or **Return** to finish.

4. If you want the e-mail messages you send to this group to display only the group name and not the addresses of the group members, select the **Don't show addresses when sending to group** check box.

5. Close the group window and click **Save** in the message box.

Contact records

See Also "Address Book" earlier in Quick Reference section

To create a contact record

1. On the Address Book toolbar, click the **New** button. Or from any module, click the **New** arrow and then, in the list, click **Contact**.

2. In the **Create Contact** window, enter a basic name and other information you want to record. (Display additional fields by clicking the **More** button in the lower-right corner of the window.)

3. Close the contact window and click **Save** in the message box.

To make changes to a contact record

1. In the Address Book, double-click the contact record you want to edit, and in the contact record window, make any changes, additions, or deletions.

2. Close the contact window and click **Save** in the message box.

To link a contact record

1. Open the contact record window, click the **Links** button on the toolbar, and then click **Open Links**.

2. In the **Links To** window, click the **To New** button or the **To Existing** button and then, in the list, click the type of item you want to link to.

3. Select or create the item, and then close the open windows.

Displaying modules

To switch between modules

→ Click the module buttons that appear at the left end of the toolbar in every module.

E-mail accounts

To automatically configure an account

1. Click **Accounts** on the **Tools** menu.

2. In the **Accounts** dialog box, click the **New** button, and then click **Mail** (or, to connect to an Exchange account, click **Exchange**).

3. On the **Set Up a Mail Account** page of the **Account Setup Assistant**, enter the e-mail account you want to connect to in the **E-mail address** box.

4. Click the **Next** button to submit the account for automatic configuration.

5. If the automatic configuration was successful, click the **Next** button to display the **Verify and Complete Settings** page. Verify your name and e-mail address, and enter the password required to access the account.

6. If the automatic configuration was *not* successful, click the **Next** button to display a more complete version of the **Verify and Complete Settings** page. Enter the information required to access the account.

7. Click the **Next** button to display the **Optional: Verify Settings** page, and then click the **Verify My Settings** button.

8. If the verification fails, click the **Back** button to return to the **Verify and Complete Settings** page. The settings that failed verification are now indicated in red. Correct the information in these fields, and then click the **Next** button to return to the **Optional: Verify Settings** page.

9. After the verification succeeds, click the **Next** button to display the **Setup Complete** page. Enter the name by which you want to identify the account. If you want the account to appear in your Entourage contact record, and to be updated at regular intervals with other accounts, leave the check boxes selected; otherwise, clear the ones you don't want to apply. Then click **Finish**.

To manually configure an account

1. Click **Accounts** on the **Tools** menu and then click the **New** button (not its arrow).

2. In the **Account Type** list, click the type of account you want to connect to (**POP, IMAP, Exchange**, or **Windows Live Hotmail**). Then click **OK**.

3. Enter the requested information in the **Edit Account** dialog box.

4. If your incoming server requires special information, click the **Click here for advanced receiving options** button in the **Receiving mail** section to display a box of options specific to the incoming server. Select the check boxes that are pertinent to your account, and then close the box.

5. If your outgoing server requires special information, click the **Click here for advanced sending options** button in the **Sending mail** section to display a box of options specific to the outgoing server. Select the check boxes that are pertinent to your account, and then close the box.

6. In the **Edit Account** dialog box, click **OK**.

E-mail messages

To start a new message

→ In the Mail module, click the **New Mail Message** button on the toolbar.

→ In any other module, click **Message** in the **New** list on the toolbar.

To address a message

→ Type the intended recipient's e-mail address into the **To**, **Cc**, or **Bcc** box, separating multiple addresses by using commas or by pressing **Return**.

→ If Entourage displays a list of matching names or addresses, click the correct one, and then press **Tab** or **Return** to insert the entire name or address in the box.

To format a message

→ Format the text by clicking buttons on the message header toolbar.

→ Format the background with a color by clicking the **Background** arrow on the message header toolbar and then clicking the color you want.

→ Format the background with a picture by clicking the **Insert** button on the message window toolbar and then clicking **Background Picture**. In the **Choose a File** dialog box, select the picture you want and then click **Choose**.

→ Remove a background picture by clicking **Remove Background Picture** on the **Message** menu.

→ Insert clip art images, symbols, pictures, and other graphics from the **Object Palette** of the Toolbox.

To send a message

→ Click the **Send** button on the toolbar.

To attach files

→ Click the **Attach** button on the toolbar, select the file you want to attach in the **Choose Attachment** dialog box, and then click **Open**.

→ Change the attachment settings by clicking the right-pointing triangle to the left of the **Attachments** label, clicking the box below the **Attachments** list, and then clicking the options you want.

To save message drafts

→ Close the message without sending it, and then click **Save as Draft** in the warning message that appears.

→ Resume work on a draft message by clicking the **Drafts** folder in the Folder list, double-clicking the message, and composing and sending the message as usual.

To specify the account from which to send a message

→ Click the account in the **From** list at the top of the message header.

To reply to or forward a message

→ Click the **Reply**, **Reply To All**, or **Forward** button in the message window or on the Standard toolbar. Then adjust or enter the recipients' addresses, type your message, and send as usual.

To display the actions you have taken with a message

→ If you've taken only one action, it is documented at the top of the yellow bar in the message header, in the message window or Preview pane.

→ If you've taken multiple actions, click the **History** link at the right end of the yellow bar in the message header, in the message window or Preview pane.

To delete a message

→ Move a message to the Deleted Items folder by clicking the message header in the Mail pane and then clicking the **Delete** button on the toolbar or pressing the **Delete** key.

→ Move a message to the Deleted Items folder by right-clicking the message header in the Mail pane and clicking **Delete Message**.

→ Permanently delete a message by displaying the contents of the **Deleted Items** folder, clicking the message header or selecting multiple messages in the Mail pane, clicking the **Delete** button on the toolbar or pressing the **Delete** key, and then clicking **Delete** in the message box.

→ Manually empty the **Deleted Items** folder by right-clicking the folder in the Folder list, and then clicking **Empty Deleted Items**.

→ Have Entourage automatically empty the **Deleted Items** folder by setting up a schedule for this task.

See Also "Scheduling Entourage events" later in this Quick Reference section

E-mail signatures

To create an e-mail signature

1. Click **Signatures** on the **Tools** menu. Then in the **Signatures** dialog box, click the **New** button.
2. In the **Name** box, enter a name by which you will identify this signature and then press the **Tab** key.
3. In the content box, enter the text of your e-mail signature. Apply formatting by using the commands available on the toolbar above the content box.
4. Insert a picture, background picture, sound, or movie by pointing to **Insert** on the **Message** menu, and then clicking the type of item. In the **Choose a File** dialog box that opens, select the specific item, and then click **Choose**.
5. Close the signature window. If Entourage displays a dialog box prompting you to save the signature, click **Save**.

To specify a signature to be inserted in all new messages

1. Open the **Edit Account** dialog box by using one of these methods:
   - In the Folder list, right-click the account header, and then click **Edit Account**.
   - Click **Accounts** on the **Tools** menu. Then in the **Accounts** dialog box, double-click the account name.
2. In the **Edit Account** dialog box, display the **Options** page.
3. In the **Default signature** list, click the signature you want to appear at the bottom of each message sent from this account.
4. Click **OK**.

To remove an automatically inserted signature

→ Select and delete the signature as you would any other text.

To manually insert a signature

→ Point to **Signature** on the **Message** menu, and then click the signature you want to insert.

Favorites Bar

To add a folder or view

→ Right-click the folder or view in the Folder list, and then click **Add To Favorites Bar**.

To remove a folder or view

→ Right-click the target folder or view in the Folder list, and then click **Remove From Favorites Bar**.

Flagging for follow up

To remind yourself of a task, appointment, or flagged item

→ Right-click an item, point to **To Do**, and click the due date you want.

→ Right-click an item, point to **To Do**, and click **Add Reminder** to open the **Dates and Reminder** dialog box, in which you can set start and due dates and specify when the reminder should appear.

To mark a flagged item as complete

→ Click its flag icon.

→ Right-click it, point to **To Do**, and click **Mark As Complete**.

Folder list

To customize the Folder list pane

→ Hide or show the pane by clicking **Hide Folder List** or **Show Folder List** on the **View** menu.

→ Change the width of the pane by dragging the vertical frame divider separating it from the content pane to its right.

→ Change the height of the pane by dragging the horizontal frame divider separating it from the Mini Calendar below.

Mini Calendar

To open or close the Mini Calendar

→ Click the **Expand/Collapse** button at the left end of the status bar.

To move to a different month

→ Click the arrows on the left and right sides of the pane header.

→ Return to the current month by clicking the dot in the center of the header.

To change the number of months displayed

→ Drag the horizontal divider at the top of the pane or the vertical divider on the right side of the pane.

Preview pane

To open, close, or move the pane

→ Point to **Preview Pane** on the **View** menu and then click **On Right**, **Below List**, or **None**.

Scheduling Entourage events

To set up a scheduled event

1. Click **Schedules** on the **Tools** menu.

2. In the **Schedules** window, click the **New** button.

3. In the **Edit Schedule** dialog box, specify one or more occurrences, and one or more actions. Then click **OK**.

4. Close the **Schedules** dialog box.

Searching items

To locate any Entourage item containing a specific search term

→ Enter the search term in the **Search** box in the upper-right corner of the Entourage program window. Then in the **Quick Filter**, click a button to set the scope.

To sort the search results

→ Click the heading of the column you want to sort by.

To Do list

To display the To Do list in the Calendar window

→ Click the **To Do List** button on the toolbar.

To add a task to the To Do list (and simultaneously to the Tasks list)

→ Type the task description in the **Create a task** box at the bottom of the **To Do List** pane.

→ Assign a due date to the task as you create it by clicking the **Options** button, and then clicking the due date you want to assign.

To open a To Do list item in a window

→ Double-click it in the To Do list.

Toolbar

To hide or show the toolbar

→ Click the **Hide Toolbar Area** button.

→ Click **Hide Toolbar** or **Show Toolbar** on the **View** menu.

To customize the toolbar

→ Add buttons to the toolbar by clicking **Customize Toolbar** on the **View** menu (or in the Calendar module, on the **Calendar** menu) and then dragging commands to the toolbar from the dialog box that appears.

→ Specify whether icons and/or text should appear on toolbar buttons by choosing **Icon & Text**, **Icon Only**, or **Text Only** in the **Show** list. To display small icons, choose **Icon & Text** or **Icons Only**, and then select the **Use Small Size** check box.

Part I
Office Basics

1 Explore and Manage the Office Interface 3

2 Practice Basic Office File Skills. 43

3 Work in Office Programs 75

Chapter at a Glance

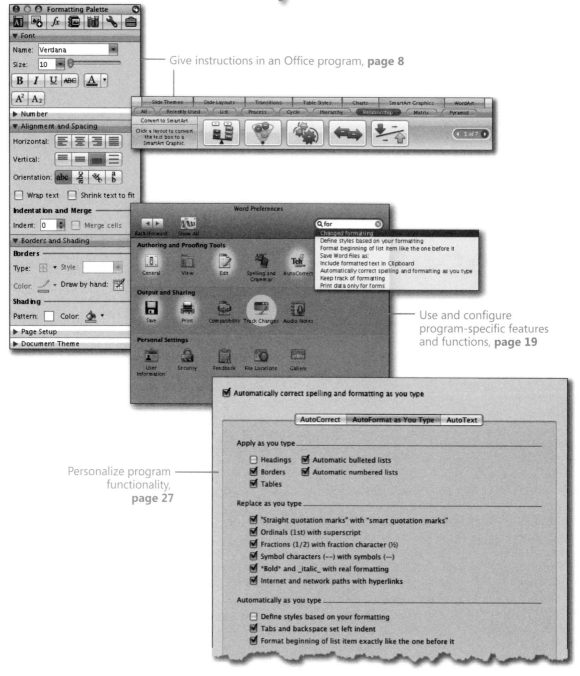

Give instructions in an Office program, **page 8**

Use and configure program-specific features and functions, **page 19**

Personalize program functionality, **page 27**

1 Explore and Manage the Office Interface

In this chapter, you will learn how to

✔ Start an Office program.

✔ Find your way around file windows.

✔ Give instructions in an Office program.

✔ Use and configure program-specific features and functions.

✔ Personalize program functionality.

The 2008 release of Microsoft Office for Mac is one of the most sophisticated business productivity programs available today. With Office, it's easier than ever to efficiently create a wide range of business and personal documents, from a simple letter to a complex worksheet to a professional-looking presentation. The Office programs have been designed to make powerful features more accessible, and as a result, even novice users will be able to work productively with Office after only a brief introduction.

Programs in the Office 2008 for Mac Home & Student Edition—particularly Microsoft Word 2008 for Mac, Microsoft Excel 2008 for Mac, and Microsoft PowerPoint 2008 for Mac—share many common *interface* elements. After you become familiar with and comfortable using one program, it will be comparatively simple to apply your experience to another.

Each of the programs that are part of Office 2008 for Mac provides several methods of giving commands when working with the program, with a file, or in a file. Three of the programs—Word, Excel, and PowerPoint—have very similar sets of tools. (In this book we'll refer to these three programs collectively as *the primary Office programs*.) Microsoft Entourage 2008 for Mac shares some of the same tools, as does, to a lesser extent, Microsoft Messenger for Mac.

In this chapter, you'll learn about tools that are common to the primary Office programs and tools that are specific to Word, to Excel, and to PowerPoint. Then you'll learn about ways in which you can personalize the appearance and behavior of a program to best suit your needs and working style.

See Also You can find handy keyboard shortcuts, simple instructions for performing common tasks, and other useful information in the Quick Reference section at the beginning of this book.

> **Practice Makes Perfect!** You won't need any practice files to complete the exercises in this chapter. See "Using the Companion Content" at the beginning of this book for information about practice files.

Start an Office Program

You can start an Office 2008 program in several ways:

- Click the program icon in the Dock. If the program isn't yet running, clicking the icon makes it bounce, indicating that the program is starting. If the program is already running, clicking the icon switches to that program.

- In the *Finder*, open the *Applications* folder and then the *Microsoft Office 2008* folder. (The Office programs and their supporting utilities are installed in this folder.) In the folder, double-click the program you want to run, or right-click it and then click **Open**.

- Double-click an Office file in the Finder, or right-click it and then click **Open**, to start the relevant program and open the file at the same time.

See Also You'll walk through the process of starting a program in "Practice Working with Windows and Commands" later in this chapter. You can see images of the Dock and the Finder procedures in that topic.

> **Note** The terms *application* and *program* refer to the same thing. In this book we consistently use the term *program*, to simplify things. You might see the term *application* used in the Mac or Office interface. When referring to labeled interface elements, we'll use the term that appears in the interface. We also use the term *Office file* to refer collectively to Word documents, Excel workbooks, and PowerPoint presentations. We'll talk more about this in Chapter 2, "Practice Basic Office File Skills."

Mouse Manners

Computer mice come in all shapes, sizes, and colors. These days, most have a significant amount of functionality built in, but the basics remain the same. Here's a quick rundown of mouse actions and the way we refer to them in this book:

- **Point.** Move the mouse so that the on-screen mouse pointer rests over the specified object.
- **Click.** Point to the specified on-screen element (usually a button, link, or command), and then press and release the *primary mouse button* once.
- **Right-click.** Point to the specified on-screen element, and then press and release the *secondary mouse button* once.
- **Drag.** Point to the specified on-screen element, press and hold down the primary mouse button, move the pointer (usually to select content or move something), and then release the button.
- **Right-click and drag.** Point to the specified on-screen element, press and hold down the secondary mouse button, move the pointer, and then release the button.

The left mouse button is traditionally the primary mouse button, and clicking instructions are given that way in this book and in other computer documentation. If you're left-handed or just want to change things up, you can switch the primary and secondary buttons, so that clicking the right mouse button carries out click operations, and clicking the left mouse button carries out right-click operations. (If you do that, you'll just need to do the opposite of whatever the instructions say.)

To change the way the Mac operating system interprets mouse clicks:

1. Click the **System Preferences** icon in the Dock to open the **System Preferences** window.

2. In the **Hardware** section, click **Keyboard & Mouse**.

   From the Keyboard & Mouse page that opens, you can change the tracking, scrolling, and double-clicking speeds, set the primary mouse button, and specify whether and how you want to use a keyboard/mouse combination to zoom in on window content.

   Any changes you make on the Keyboard & Mouse page take effect immediately.

Find Your Way Around File Windows

Each Office file opens in its own window, with its own set of docked toolbars and Elements Gallery. Every file window includes a specific set of elements, including the following:

- **Title bar.** The title bar displays the name of the active document. At the left end of the title bar are the three familiar buttons that have the same function in all programs. You can close the window by clicking the red Close button, temporarily hide the window by clicking the yellow Minimize button, and return the window to its default size by clicking the green Restore button.

The Hide Toolbars button, which we'll discuss in "Toolbars" later in this chapter, is at the right end of the title bar.

- **Scroll bars.** You click on either side of the scroll box or drag the scroll box to move the document, but not the insertion point, in that direction. The horizontal scroll bar is visible only when the document content exceeds the width of the window; the vertical scroll bar is visible only when the document content exceeds the height of the window.

    You can change the effects of clicking in the scroll bar from the Appearance page of the System Preferences window. (This feature is controlled by the operating system rather than the program.)

- **Scroll arrows.** You click an arrow to move the document (but not the insertion point) one line up or down, or a short way left or right; or click and hold a scroll arrow to continuously scroll the document.

    You can change the location of the scroll arrows from the Appearances page of the System Preferences window. (This feature is also controlled by the operating system.)

- **Status bar.** Across the bottom of the program window, the status bar displays information about the current document. You can turn off the display of an item by right-clicking the status bar and then clicking that item.

- **View toolbar.** Located at the left end of the status bar, the View toolbar displays buttons for the common document views. Other views might be available from the Views menu.

  See Also For information about adjusting the view of an Office file, see "Change the View" in Chapter 2, "Practice Basic Office File Skills."

- **Resize handle.** You drag this handle to change the size of the window.

While working through the exercises in this book, you'll have the opportunity to use all these window elements.

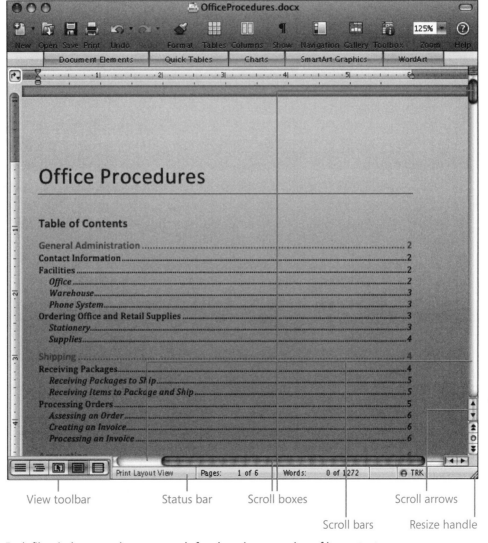

Each file window contains many tools for changing your view of its content.

Give Instructions in an Office Program

When Word, Excel, or PowerPoint first starts, a *splash screen* appears, identifying the program and providing distraction while program resources load in the background. Then the program menu bar appears at the top of the screen, followed by a document window. Depending on the state of the program when it was last closed, the Toolbox might also open. Your screen will look something like this:

A typical window configuration. You can control the active document from the menu bar or Toolbox, and access Office programs from the Dock.

> **Note** What you see on your screen might not match the graphics in this book exactly. The screens in this book were captured on a monitor set to a resolution of 1024 × 768 pixels with the Dock open at the bottom of the desktop.

You can give instructions in an Office 2008 program in many ways. You can choose *commands* from a menu, click buttons on a toolbar or in a toolbox, choose features from a gallery of options, or use keyboard shortcuts. In this section, we'll examine menus, toolbars, and toolboxes in the primary Office programs. Later in this chapter, we'll discuss *interface elements* that are specific to each program.

> **Tip** Many Office for Mac keyboard shortcuts use the Command key in conjunction with another key. On a modern Macintosh keyboard, the Command key might be labeled with the word *Command* or with the infinite loop symbol, which looks like this: ⌘. (On older Mac keyboards the Command key was labeled with an apple. For that reason, many long-time Mac users refer to this key as the "open apple" key.) On a Windows keyboard, the Command key is labeled with the Windows logo (a waving flag), and is commonly referred to as *the Windows key* or *the Windows Logo key*. On a Macintosh running Mac OS X, both of these keys perform the same function, so if you connect a Windows keyboard to your Mac, you can use the same keyboard shortcuts as you would on a Mac keyboard.

Resources Throughout this book we include information about keyboard shortcuts you can use to give commands without using the mouse. You can access a full list of keyboard shortcuts for Office and for the individual programs by searching for "keyboard shortcuts" in the program's Help file.

Menus and the Menu Bar

Each Office program, when active, displays a full-width menu bar across the top of the screen. The menu bar includes a program menu with links to program information, preferences, and commands; eight common menus; and from one to four menus that are specific to the current program.

The Excel menu bar

> **Note** Word, Excel, and PowerPoint don't have integrated program windows displaying one set of program controls and multiple files. Instead, each program has the independent menu bar and file-specific windows.

The menus common to Word, Excel, PowerPoint, and Entourage are:

- **The program menu.** You manage the program, rather than files or content, by using commands on this menu.

- **File.** You manage files by using commands on this menu. You can open, save, close, and create files; preview and print documents; or send document content to other people or programs. You can also view and manage file properties.

- **Edit.** You manage content by using commands on this menu. You can select, copy, cut, and paste text and graphics; find and replace specific text or formatting; and move around in the document.

- **View.** You control the display of the document and of various program tools by using commands on this menu.

- **Insert.** You insert or link to document parts, specialized content, visual elements, multimedia elements, and other elements by using commands on this menu.

- **Format.** You apply character and paragraph formatting to selected content, and set up layout options, by using commands on this menu.

- **Tools.** This menu provides access to very useful research tools, including a thesaurus and dictionary, tools for managing documents, wizards to assist you with creating documents, and other goodies.

- **Window.** You manage the display of file windows by using the commands on this menu.

- **Help.** You access the computer Help system and the Office program Help system from this menu, as well as online resources for program information and updates.

> **Tip** You can go directly to a program's Help file by clicking the Help button on the Standard toolbar in the program instead of going through the Help menu on the program's menu bar.

See Also For information about menus specific to Word, Excel, and PowerPoint, see the program-specific topics in "Use and Configure Program-Specific Features and Functions" later in this chapter.

> **Tip** Clicking the Apple icon at the left end of any menu bar displays a menu of commands for controlling your Mac. You can access software updates and software compatible with your Mac operating system, set system preferences and control the appearance of the Dock, and open applications, documents, and servers you have recently accessed. You also have options for shutting down applications and for shutting down or logging off from your Mac.

The menus are followed by a series of icons linking to features specific to your computer. These might include things like AppleScripts and Automator workflows, Time Machine, Bluetooth, AirPort, and SuperDrive. At the right end of the menu bar are the volume control, date and time, and the *Spotlight* search control.

> **Note** Automator is a Mac program that helps you automate tasks that you perform frequently. Office 2008 for Mac (the full version, not the Home & Student Edition) and Office 2008 for Mac Special Media Edition come with sample Automator workflows, and you can create your own.

The menu bar is a separate entity from the file window. The menu bar remains open as long as the program is running; even if you don't have a document open.

Toolbars

Each of the primary Office programs includes certain general-use toolbars that, when open, appear in the toolbar area at the top of the file window, and might also include context-specific floating toolbars. A toolbar is a container for buttons that you click to perform a task and lists from which you select options.

Word, Excel, and PowerPoint all include the Standard toolbar and the Formatting toolbar.

The Standard toolbar in each program includes basic commands such as New, Open, Save, Print, Undo, and Redo; buttons to toggle the display of the Elements Gallery and the Toolbox; the Zoom commands; and a link to the Help file. In addition, the Standard toolbar in each program includes a few program-specific commands.

See Also For information about the toolbars in the Word, Excel, and PowerPoint file windows, see the program-specific "Tools and Preferences" sections later in this chapter.

The Formatting toolbar is also available in each of the primary Office programs. As the name implies, this toolbar hosts commands you use to format text and paragraphs. (Formatting commands specific to tables, charts, graphics, and other visual elements appear on specialized toolbars, in the Elements Gallery, or in item-specific dialog boxes.)

By default, the Standard toolbar appears at the top of each Word, Excel, or PowerPoint file window. Other toolbars are hidden until you choose to display them or they are necessary to the task you're performing at the time.

You can display and hide toolbars in these ways:

→ On the **View** menu, point to **Toolbars**, and then click the name of the toolbar you want to display.

→ Right-click anywhere in the toolbar area (not on the title bar), point to **Toolbars** on the shortcut menu that appears, and then click the name of the toolbar you want to display.

On both Toolbars submenus, a check mark in front of a toolbar name indicates that the toolbar is open. If you have other file windows (for the same program) open when you change the toolbar configuration, the additional toolbars appear in each window the next time you activate the window.

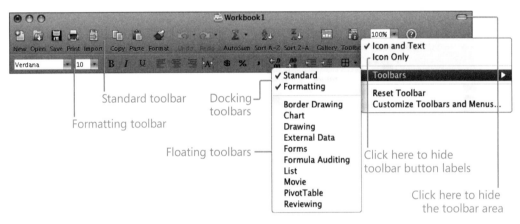

Common commands for working with content are available from the Standard and Formatting toolbars.

> **Tip** If you find the toolbar area is taking up too much space in the window, you can make it smaller by displaying only the icons (and not the labels), or you can hide it altogether by clicking the Hide Toolbars button located in the upper-right corner of the window. (This doesn't affect other open file windows for the same program.)

On the Toolbars submenus (available from the View menu or from the toolbar area shortcut menu) the toolbars listed above the horizontal line are those that will appear in the toolbar area at the top of the file window; we refer to these as docking toolbars. The toolbars listed below the line are floating toolbars. Floating toolbars can be horizontal or vertical, or they might present a gallery of choices in a rectangle.

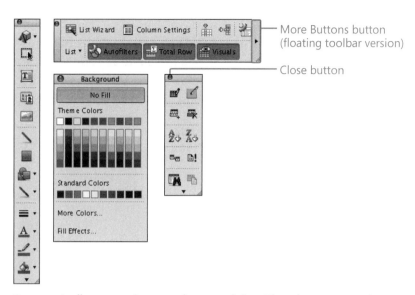

More Buttons button
(floating toolbar version)

Close button

Program toolbars come in many shapes and sizes. They show commands in different ways, including as buttons, as text, or in a gallery.

You can open a floating toolbar at any time by pointing to Toolbars on the View menu and then clicking the toolbar you want, or by right-clicking the toolbar area, pointing to Toolbars, and then clicking the toolbar you want. You can close a floating toolbar by clicking its Close button or by clicking its name (to remove the preceding check mark) on the View menu or the Toolbar menu.

You can't remove a docking toolbar from the toolbar area, but you can move a floating toolbar anywhere on the screen (including outside of the file window) by dragging its *title bar*.

Commands on toolbars are represented as buttons or, less frequently, as lists or *galleries*. By default, the button name appears below each button icon, and pointing to a button displays a ScreenTip that describes what the button does.

Point to any toolbar button to display a description of its function.

Tip When more toolbar content is available than can be shown on a docked toolbar, the More Buttons button appears at the right end of the toolbar. Click this button to display a list of additional buttons and commands.

Some buttons have arrows, but not all arrows are alike. If you point to a button and both the button icon and the arrow are in the same box, clicking the button displays options for refining the action of the button. If you point to a button and the arrow is in its own box separate from the button icon, clicking the button carries out that action with the button's current settings. If you want to change those settings, you need to click the arrow to see the available options.

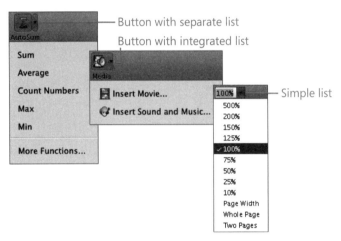

Many commands and options are available from lists.

> **Tip** To select an item from a list, click the arrow shown to the right of the button or list box to expand the list, and then click the item you want.

The Elements Gallery

The Elements Gallery is a new feature in Office 2008; available only in the primary Office programs—Word, Excel, and PowerPoint. (Entourage and MSN Messenger do not have Elements Galleries.) A similar feature, the Microsoft Office Fluent user interface Ribbon, was introduced in Office 2007 for Windows. The Elements Gallery and Ribbon represent a radical change in the way commands are made available within the program. A significant difference between the Elements Gallery and the Ribbon is that in the primary Office 2007 for Windows programs, the Ribbon has entirely replaced *all* menus and toolbars. (Microsoft implemented this concept in a pre-release version of Office 2008 for Mac, and it wasn't well received.) Office 2008 still includes the traditional menus and toolbars, as well as an improved Toolbox and the new Elements Gallery.

The Elements Gallery is located at the top of the content pane, below the toolbar area. By default, only the gallery tabs are visible. You can display the gallery by clicking any tab, and hide it by clicking the active tab or double-clicking any inactive tab.

See Also You can change the program settings so that the Elements Gallery opens automatically when you start a program. For information about changing Elements Gallery settings, including the color and transparency of the Elements Gallery, see "Personalize Program Functionality" later in this chapter.

From the Elements Gallery, you can insert a variety of document elements into an *Office file*:

- In Word, you can insert cover pages, headers, and footers into a document and tables of contents, bibliographies, Quick Tables, charts, SmartArt graphics, and WordArt from the Elements Gallery onto a page.

- In Excel, you can insert worksheets into a workbook, and charts, SmartArt graphics, and WordArt from the Elements Gallery into a worksheet.

- In PowerPoint, you can apply themes to a presentation, apply layouts and transitions to slides, and insert professional-looking tables, charts, SmartArt graphics, and WordArt from the Elements Gallery onto slides.

The Elements Gallery is divided into sections, called *tabs*. One type of document element is available from each tab. For example:

- From the Excel Elements Gallery, you can insert Sheets, Charts, SmartArt Graphics, and WordArt.

- From the PowerPoint Elements Gallery, you can insert Slide Themes, Slide Layouts, Transitions, Table Styles, Charts, SmartArt Graphics, and WordArt.

The elements on each tab are organized into *groups*, usually related to the style of the element represented on the tab. Each group contains *thumbnails* representing the document element you can insert or apply by clicking the icon.

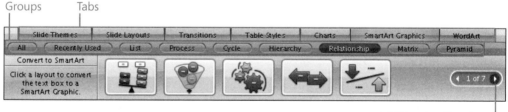

From the PowerPoint Elements Gallery, you can insert a wide variety of slide elements.

See Also To learn about creating really cool graphics like the ones shown here, see "Create Professional Diagrams" in Chapter 12, "Create and Insert Graphics."

Depending on your screen resolution, the size of the program window, and the number of thumbnails in a group, all the thumbnails in a group might not fit in the Elements Gallery at one time. When that happens, navigation buttons at the right end of the gallery indicate the number of additional gallery pages.

When you point to thumbnails in the Elements Gallery, the active thumbnail gets bigger than the others. If you don't like this effect, you can turn it off by following the instructions in "Change the Gallery Color Scheme" later in this chapter. As you point to each thumbnail, its name appears in the upper-left corner of the gallery page.

The Toolbox

The Toolbox displays the commands and settings you are likely to need when working with an Office file. The first time you start Word, Excel, or PowerPoint, the program's Toolbox opens, to the right of the file window, displaying the Formatting Palette.

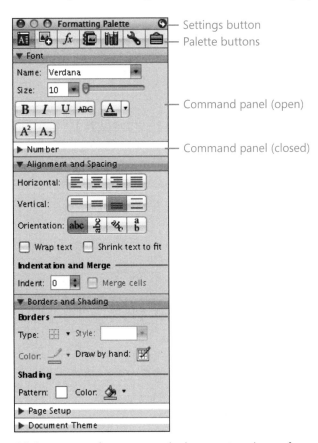

All the common font, paragraph, document, and page formatting options are available from the Formatting Palette.

Each program's Toolbox includes multiple *palettes*, and each palette can include multiple *panels* of commands. The result is that you can perform nearly any function within an Office file by using the commands available from the Toolbox. The Toolboxes for all three programs include these common palettes (the icon representing each palette is shown to the left of its description):

- **Formatting Palette.** This palette is a convenient central location for the tools you use to format text, paragraphs, tables, charts, pictures, and other document elements.

- **Object Palette.** From this palette, which is new in Office 2008, you can insert shapes, symbols, clip art, or pictures into an Office file.

- **Scrapbook palette.** This is a convenient central storage location for content snippets and files that you want to reuse elsewhere. The Scrapbook is shared by Word, Excel, and PowerPoint, so you can retrieve stored content from a program other than the one you saved it in.

  You can organize content in the Scrapbook palette by assigning keywords to a clipping or file (let's call these scraps, collectively) and by assigning scraps to categories or to projects that you're tracking in the Project Center (a feature of Entourage).

- **Reference Tools palette.** Tools on this palette give you direct access to a thesaurus, the Encarta encyclopedia, single-language dictionaries that provide definitions of English, French, German, Japanese, and Spanish words; a bilingual dictionary that provides definitions and translations of simplified or traditional Chinese, English, French, German, Italian, Japanese, Korean, and Spanish words; and a cool translation tool that you can use to translate phrases in simplified or traditional Chinese, Dutch, English, French, German, Greek, Italian, Japanese, Korean, Portuguese (Brazilian), Russian, and Spanish.

- **Compatibility Report palette.** From this palette, you can check the compatibility of your Office file with other versions of Office, for Mac or for Windows.

- **Project Palette.** From this palette, you have access to all the information about projects that you're tracking in the Project Center, and a link to the Project Center.

  See Also For information about tracking Office files, time, people, and information about a project in the Project Center, see Chapter 16, "Store and Retrieve Information."

Each program includes one additional palette:

- The Word Toolbox includes the Citations palette. From this palette, you can insert appropriately formatted bibliographic citations into a document.

  See Also For information about using the Citations palette, see the sidebar "Create a Bibliography" in Chapter 14, "Add Finishing Document Elements."

- The Excel Toolbox includes the Formula Builder palette. From this palette, you can locate mathematical functions that are appropriate to the operation you want to perform. You can then fill in the information required by the function, and the Formula Builder inserts the complete formula into your worksheet.

  See Also For information about using the Formula Builder palette, see "Create Simple Formulas" in Chapter 9, "Create Excel Formulas."

- The PowerPoint Toolbox includes the Custom Animation palette. From this palette, you can add entrance, emphasis, and exit animation effects, or multimedia actions, to selected slides. You can preview and modify the effects directly in the Custom Animation palette.

  Bonus Web Content For information about using the Custom Animation palette, see "Animate Slide Content in PowerPoint 2008 for Mac" on the book's companion Web site at *www.microsoft.com/mspress/companion/9780735626171.*

You can manage the appearance and content of the Toolbox in several ways:

- You can display and hide the Toolbox by clicking the **Toolbox** button on the Standard toolbar.

- You can switch palettes by clicking the palette buttons at the top of the Toolbox, or by choosing the palette you want from the **View** menu.

- You can minimize the Toolbox by double-clicking its title bar. The minimized toolbox displays only the title bar and the palette buttons. You can display a palette by clicking its button, or redisplay the Toolbox in its previous state by double-clicking its title bar.

- You can move the Toolbox around on the screen. It is designed to dock tidily at the right or left side of the file window, but it can also float. When you drop the Toolbox very close to the left or right edge of the screen, it docks itself.

Clicking the Settings button swivels the Toolbox to display the Toolbox Settings pane. Using the commands at the top of the pane, you can control how and when the Toolbox closes. Using the commands at the bottom of the pane, you can control what appears on each palette.

You can choose which panels appear on each Toolbox palette.

Use and Configure Program-Specific Features and Functions

In this topic, we'll discuss menus, toolbars, tools, and settings that are specific to Word, to Excel, and to PowerPoint.

Word Tools and Preferences

Word 2008 for Mac provides a specific set of tools designed to simplify the process of creating excellent documents. You can organize information on the page by using tables, tabs, and columns, and add a variety of professional formatting and visual content. On-screen rulers help you lay out information precisely and consistently. To enhance the review and collaboration processes, you can track changes made to a document, insert comments, and compare and merge two documents. You can also use the handy wizards that guide you through the process of creating form letters, envelopes, labels, and letters.

The Word menu bar includes the common menus discussed in "Menus and the Menu Bar" earlier in this chapter, each of which hosts commands tailored for document creation and management. In addition, you can access specialized tools and commands from these three menus:

- **Font.** You can ensure that your document visually supports your intended message by formatting text with any of the more than 100 fonts in this list. Each font name on the menu is shown in that font face (although you can turn this off and view them all as plain text if you prefer). If you know the general characteristics you want in a font, you can quickly find one that represents those characteristics by browsing preselected font collections.

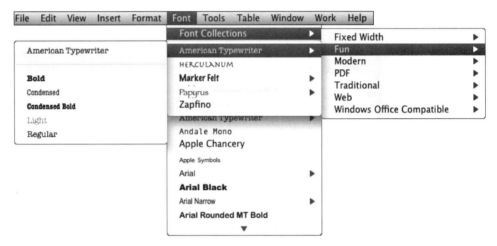

- **Table.** You can organize information (or an entire page) in a clean, structured format by presenting it in a *table*. You can create a table from scratch or convert existing text to a tabular format, and then manage the appearance of the table content, by using the commands on this menu. Word unfortunately does not support the latest breed of table formats that is available in PowerPoint 2008 for Mac and throughout the 2007 Office system for Windows. It does still support the table formats of previous versions of Word, including simple, classic, colorful, contemporary, and other table formats.

- **Work.** You can add current documents in progress or files you frequently access to the Work menu so that you have immediate access to all of them from one location. If you store documents in different folders on your computer, the Work menu provides a convenient central directory, and you don't have to navigate through the file storage structure (or even remember where you've stored a file) to open the document you want. That being said, it's very difficult to remove a document from the Work menu when you no longer want to have it there. Dozens of blog posts and articles exist that give instructions for programmatically invoking the removal of items from the Work menu, but you might not want to get caught up in such a complex process.

The Word document–specific commands and tools are also available from an extensive collection of toolbars. This program has 10 specialized toolbars in addition to the Standard and Formatting toolbars discussed in "Toolbars" earlier in this chapter:

- Three docking toolbars (Contact, Reviewing, and Tables And Borders) display commands and tools that you might want to access frequently.

- Seven floating toolbars (AutoText, Background, Database, Drawing, Forms, Movie, and Speech) display commands that you will need only when working with those program functions.

In addition to the standard Preferences pages described in "Personalize Program Functionality" later in this chapter, the Word Preferences dialog box includes these seven pages on which you can tweak settings specific to Word:

- Spelling And Grammar
- Print
- Track Changes
- Audio Notes
- User Information
- Security
- File Locations

Update and Enhance Office Programs

From time to time, Microsoft makes changes to the Office 2008 for Mac software. These changes might include new features, improved functionality, or revisions to guard against newly discovered security threats. These updates are available to you through the Software Update feature of your Mac, which you can configure from the System Preferences dialog box.

If you have configured Software Update to automatically check for and download updates, the Software Update icon will bounce around in the Dock when an update is available to install. You can manually check for updates by clicking the Check Now button on the Software Update page of the System Preferences dialog box.

You can also locate updates to the Office 2008 for Mac software, as well as other, related programs and tools, on the Mactopia Downloads page at

www.microsoft.com/mac/downloads/

In Word and PowerPoint, the AutoCorrect group on the Preferences page also provides access to the AutoFormat As You Type settings. This feature controls the automatic application of certain types of text and paragraph formatting.

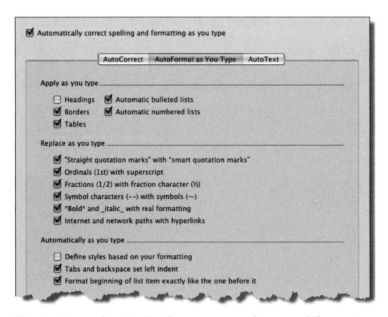

The AutoFormat function handles some types of paragraph formatting, so you don't have to.

In Word only, the AutoCorrect group provides access to the AutoText settings. With this feature, you can enter a word or phrase without typing the entire entry. You store the text you want to enter as AutoText, and select the Show AutoComplete Tip check box.

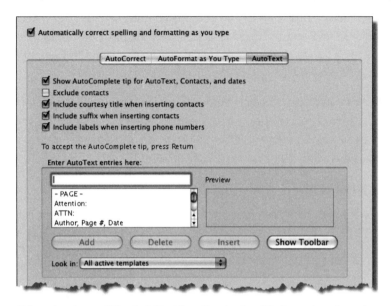

Take advantage of the AutoText function to simplify the entry of words and phrases you frequently employ.

When you type the beginning of the stored text in a document, the suggested completion appears in a ScreenTip above the insertion point. To enter the stored text, simply press the Return key.

Excel Tools and Preferences

Excel 2008 for Mac incorporates a specific set of tools you can use to track, calculate, and present data. Most of the workbook- and worksheet-specific commands in Excel fit neatly into the structure provided by the common menus discussed in "Menus and the Menu Bar" earlier in this chapter. Excel incorporates only one additional menu, the Data menu, which hosts commands and tools specific to working with numeric data and text stored in an Excel workbook or in an external data source.

Excel-specific commands are grouped on nine floating toolbars (Border Drawing, Chart, External Data, Forms, Formula Auditing, List, Movie, PivotTable, and Reviewing) that appear automatically when relevant information is selected; for example, the PivotTable toolbar appears when you click a cell in a PivotTable.

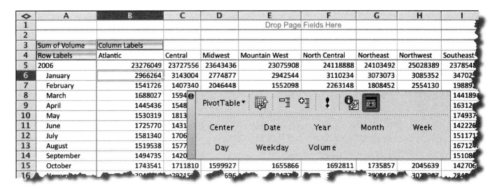

The PivotTable floating toolbar opens when you click any part of a PivotTable.

In addition to the standard Preferences pages described in "Personalize Program Functionality" later in this chapter, the Excel Preferences dialog box includes these seven pages on which you can adjust settings specific to Excel:

- **Chart.** For the chart, you can specify how Excel plots empty and hidden cells. For charts in general, you can choose whether ScreenTips appear when you point to chart names and data markers.
- **Color.** You can modify the set of colors (40 in all) available in the program.

● **Calculation.** You can specify whether calculated fields update automatically as source data changes, and specify the maximum iterations used for goal seeking and for resolving circular references. For the active workbook only, you can choose to have Excel format all values with a specific number of decimal places, the system starting date from which Excel calculates values (the Macintosh and Windows systems vary in this respect), and whether Excel saves values of linked data sources with the worksheet.

● **Error Checking.** You can specify the types of errors Excel flags for review. To avoid irritating false errors, adjust the Error Checking preferences to match the way you work.

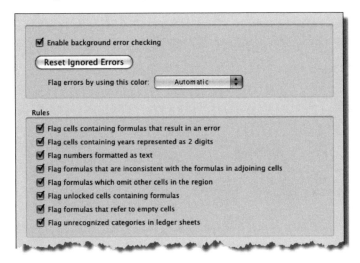

● **Custom Lists.** You can create custom data sets for use when filling cells and sorting data.

● **AutoComplete.** You can choose when and for what types of data the AutoComplete list appears, and how it functions.

● **Security.** You can protect a worksheet or workbook from changes by unauthorized people, automatically remove personal information from the file when you save it, and display a warning when opening a file that contains macros.

PowerPoint Tools and Preferences

PowerPoint 2008 for Mac provides a specific set of tools that control the creation of professional presentations from beginning to end and cover a variety of delivery methods, including live presentation, Web presentation, electronic transmission, and print. PowerPoint presentations are intended to deliver information in a more visual than text-based fashion, so this program includes tools centered around creating snazzy graphics, incorporating interactive content, animating slide content, and transitioning effectively between slides—in other words, features that help to attract and keep a viewer's attention.

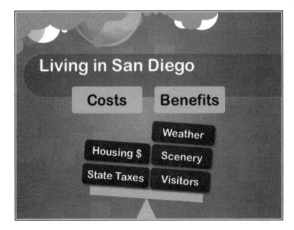

PowerPoint 2008 provides many tools for creating a visually appealing presentation.

PowerPoint incorporates only one menu other than the standard menus described in "Menus and the Menu Bar" earlier in this chapter. The Slide Show menu hosts commands and tools specific to the process of preparing a presentation to be shown as a slide show. Three specialized docking toolbars (Outlining, Reviewing, and Tables And Borders) display commands and tools that you might want to access frequently.

In addition to the standard Preferences pages described in the next topic, "Personalize Program Functionality," the PowerPoint Preferences dialog box includes these two pages on which you can control settings specific to PowerPoint:

- **Spelling.** Although not as extensive as the Spelling And Grammar utility in Word, PowerPoint does offer a basic spell-checking utility.

- **Advanced.** On the Advanced page, you can set the default location in which PowerPoint looks for files, and you can update the limited user information required by PowerPoint.

Personalize Program Functionality

You can change the appearance and behavior of an Office program in many ways. You can manage the program options in Word, Excel, PowerPoint, or Entourage by clicking Preferences on the program menu (for example, the Word menu) that is on the menu bar to the right of the Apple menu.

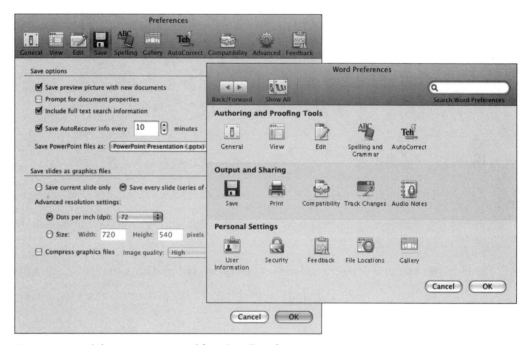

You can control the appearance and functionality of a program from the Preferences dialog box.

> **Tip** To quickly display the Preferences dialog box for the active program, press Command+Comma.

Each Preferences dialog box displays buttons representing groups of program settings. Clicking a button displays the program settings specific to that group. In Word and Excel, you can enter terms related to the program settings that you want to change into the Search box located in the upper-right corner of the Preferences dialog box. A list of topics containing the search term appears instantly, and as you continue to type, Spotlight filters the list and spotlights the icons representing the dialog boxes from which you can set the options shown in the list.

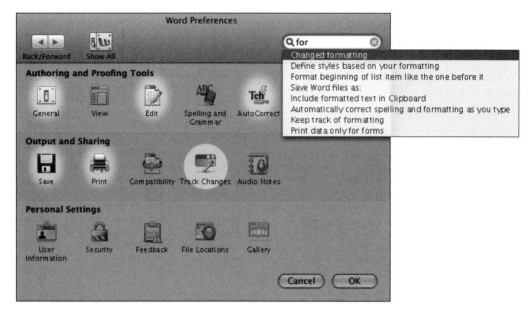

Groups containing relevant information are spotlighted as you enter text into the Search box.

The Preferences dialog boxes for Word, Excel, and PowerPoint all include these eight setting groups:

- **General.** The commands on this page control basic settings specific to the program.

- **View.** These commands control the display of content and program elements (such as scroll bars).

- **Edit.** These commands control the way the program behaves when you're typing, pasting, or moving content within an Office file.

- **Save.** These commands control the information saved with each Office file and the frequency with which the program saves temporary AutoRecover versions of your documents. If the program crashes and you haven't recently saved open Office files, AutoRecover is your very good friend!

- **Gallery.** With these commands, you can customize the appearance and activity of the Elements Gallery.

- **AutoCorrect.** These commands let you control the AutoCorrect feature that corrects common misspellings and typing errors, applies basic capitalization rules, and changes certain character combinations to symbols. (For example, AutoCorrect will change (c) to ©, a copyright symbol.)

  See Also For information about other features accessed through the AutoCorrect group, see "Word Tools and Preferences" earlier in this chapter.

- **Compatibility.** These commands control settings related to the Compatibility Report feature.
- **Feedback.** With these commands, you can opt into or out of the Microsoft Customer Experience Improvement Program. If you do participate, a background utility collects anonymous data about your computer and your usage of Microsoft software and services, and transmits that data, from time to time, to Microsoft. This doesn't affect the speed of your computer.

In this topic, we discuss some of the ways you can personalize Office that are common to all the programs.

Store Your Information for Reuse

During the installation process, the Office 2008 programs import the user information you provided during the computer setup process. This might include your name, initials, company, address, telephone number, and e-mail address. Office programs display and use this information. For example, your user name appears on the program splash screens, in comments you insert into Office files, when setting up an e-mail account, and in the properties saved with files you create.

If the current user information isn't yours, contains an error, or just doesn't say what you want it to, you can easily change it. Changes you make to your user information from Word, Excel, PowerPoint, or Entourage are immediately reflected in the other programs. All the Office programs have access to the user information you supply in any one program. The programs will automatically refer to the up-to-date information when you create documents.

Each of the Office programs stores only the information that will be used in that program:

- PowerPoint stores only your name and initials. You can edit these by clicking the Advanced button in the PowerPoint Preferences dialog box.
- Excel stores only your name. You can edit this by clicking the General button in the Excel Preferences dialog box.
- Word stores quite a bit of information, if you provide it. You can use the stored information in your documents; for example, in letters and on envelopes. Documents you create from the Project Gallery might include pertinent information from your user profile. For example, a fax cover page created from the Project Gallery automatically displays your company name.
- Entourage creates a *contact record* in the Address Book by using the available personal information.

To change your Office user information or save more information as part of your personal contact record, from Word, follow these steps:

1. In the **Word Preferences** dialog box, under **Personal Settings**, click the **User Information** button.

2. In the **User Information** dialog box, change any of the basic data shown; or click **More** to open a multipage dialog box in which you can record and manage your home, work, and personal information.

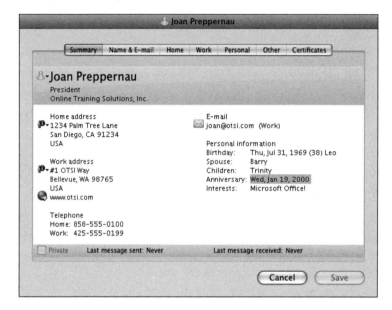

The content in this dialog box is the same as that shown in your Entourage contact record.

Change the Gallery Color Scheme

Each of the Office programs has an associated color—blue for Word, green for Excel, orange for PowerPoint, and purple for Entourage. These colors are visible on the program icons in the Dock, on the file icons in the Finder, on the program splash screens, and in the Elements Gallery and Toolbox in Word, Excel, and PowerPoint.

You can change the color scheme of the Elements Gallery and Toolbox, or customize the appearance and performance of the Elements Gallery, from the Gallery page of the Preferences dialog box.

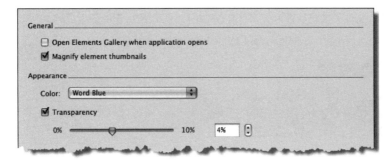

You can change the color and transparency of the Elements Gallery.

In the General area, you can control whether the Elements Gallery opens automatically when you start a program, and whether the element thumbnails increase in size when you point to them in the Elements Gallery.

In the Appearance area, you can change the color displayed in the Elements Gallery and Toolbox from the program-specific color to graphite, and control the transparency (on a scale from 0 to 10 percent) of the Elements Gallery.

Practice Working with Windows and Commands

In this exercise, you'll practice the skills we've discussed in this chapter while investigating the ways of giving instructions in Word 2008. First, you'll practice some basic window-management skills. Then you'll explore the Word menus, toolbars, Toolbox, and Elements Gallery. Finally, you'll look at the many aspects of Word you can control from the Word Preferences dialog box.

 SET UP You won't need any practice files to complete this exercise; just follow along with the steps.

1. In the Dock, click the **Microsoft Word** program icon.

Or

Open the Finder. In the Navigation pane, under **PLACES**, click **Applications**. Open the *Microsoft Office 2008* folder, and then double-click **Microsoft Word**.

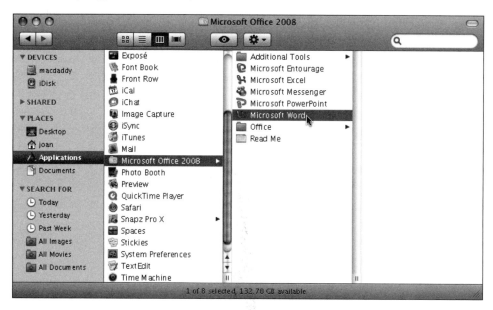

If the Word program icon is visible in the Dock, it bounces to indicate that the program is starting. The Word splash screen appears, followed by a blank document.

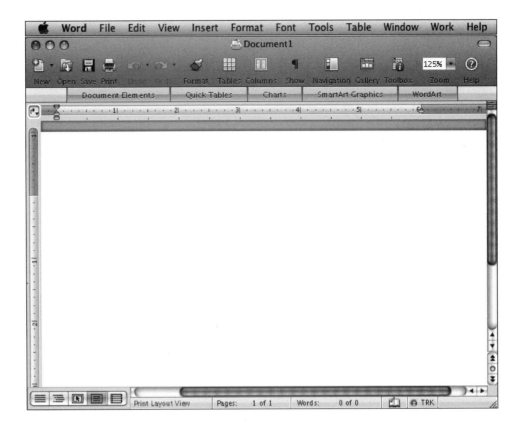

> **Note** We're not showing you the non-program related controls at the right end of the menu bar, but there will most likely be some there. The horizontal and vertical *rulers* shown here might not be visible, depending on your previous use of the Office programs. If the *Toolbox* opens, ignore it for now—we'll talk about it later in this exercise.

The name *Document1* is shown in the title bar. Word gives a sequential name to each of the temporary documents you open during a program session. (Quitting the program resets the temporary file-naming scheme.) At this point, the document is only temporary; it hasn't been saved anywhere on your computer.

2. Point to the red, yellow, and green window controls in the upper-left corner of the window.

Symbols appear in the colored dots to indicate the purpose of each button.

3. Click the green **Restore** button.

   The window resizes slightly to fill the available space between the menu bar and the Dock (or the bottom of the screen, if you're not displaying the Dock). This is the default Word document window size and location.

4. Point to the **resize handle** in the lower-right corner of the document window. The shape of the mouse pointer does not change to indicate that the handle is active.

5. Drag up and to the left until the window is about half its previous size.

   See Also For information about dragging, see the sidebar "Mouse Manners" earlier in this chapter.

6. Point to the title bar at the top of the document window. Then drag the window to the center of your screen.

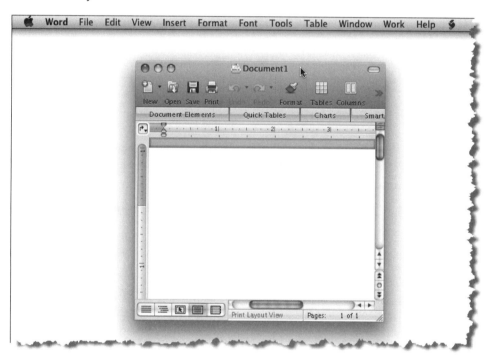

7. Click the **Restore** button, look at the results of this action, and then click it again.

   The window switches between its default size and location and the size and location you chose.

8. At the left end of the title bar, click the yellow **Minimize** button.

The window disappears. It has been minimized to the Dock. A thumbnail of the document appears in the Files area at the right end of the Dock. The thumbnail is identified as a Word document by the Word icon (the blue *W*) in its lower-right corner.

9. Point to the document thumbnail.

   A ScreenTip appears, displaying the name of the document.

10. In the Dock, click the **Document1** thumbnail.

    Or

    In the Dock, click the **Microsoft Word** icon.

    The document window returns to its previous size and location.

11. If the Standard toolbar is not open beneath the title bar, point to **Toolbars** on the **View** menu, and then click **Standard**. If any other toolbars are open (as indicated by a check mark on the **Toolbars** submenu, use the same method to close them.

> **Note** In this book, when the Standard toolbar is the only active toolbar, we refer to it in exercises simply as "the toolbar." For example, an exercise might instruct you to click the Save button on the toolbar, rather than specifying the Standard toolbar. When multiple toolbars are active, we refer to each by name to avoid confusion.

12. Restore the document window to its default size and location. Then point to each button on the toolbar to display its active outline and ScreenTip.

    The outlines indicate which buttons have separate or integrated lists, and each ScreenTip provides an explanation of the button's purpose.

13. On the Word menu bar, click **View**. Then on the **View** menu, point to **Toolbars**.

The Toolbars submenu appears, displaying a list of the toolbars available in Word 2008. The check mark to the left of *Standard* indicates that the Standard toolbar is open.

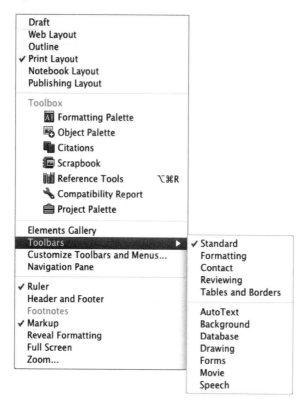

14. On the **Toolbars** submenu, click **Formatting**.

The Formatting toolbar opens below the Standard toolbar. These two toolbars contain commands you will frequently use when working in a Word document. The chevron at the right end of the Formatting toolbar indicates that the toolbars contain more buttons than can be shown.

> **Troubleshooting** If your screen settings aren't the same as ours, all the buttons might be shown on the Formatting toolbar. If the More Buttons button isn't at the right end of the Formatting toolbar, skip to step 16.

15. At the right end of the Formatting toolbar, click the **More Buttons** button to display the additional buttons.

16. If the Toolbox isn't already open, click the **Toolbox** button on the Standard toolbar. Or, if the **Formatting Palette** is not active in the open Toolbox, click **Formatting Palette** in the **Toolbox** section of the **View** menu.

The Toolbox opens, displaying the Formatting Palette.

17. In the **Formatting Palette**, click panel titles to open or close panels so that only the **Font** panel, the **Alignment and Spacing** panel, and the **Bullets and Numbering** panel are open.

18. Compare the buttons available on the Formatting toolbar to the buttons in the three open panels of the **Formatting Palette**. Then click the **Format** menu and compare the commands available from that menu to the commands on the toolbar and in the Toolbox.

Bonus Web Content For information about bulleted and numbered lists, see "Organize Text in Lists in Word 2008 for Mac" on the book's companion Web site, at *www.microsoft.com/mspress/companion/9780735626171*.

The three command structures provide very similar sets of commands. When working in the primary Office programs, you can use the command structure that you're most comfortable with.

See Also In this exercise we're only looking at the commands, not using them. For information about font and paragraph formatting commands, see Chapter 11, "Format Office File Content."

 19. On the Standard toolbar, click the **Gallery** button.

The Elements Gallery expands to display the Document Elements tab, which is divided into five groups. The first page of the Cover Pages group is visible. The navigation controls at the right end of the group indicate that additional Cover Page designs are available.

Navigation controls

20. On the **Document Elements** tab, in the **Cover Pages** group, click the arrow to display the next page of thumbnails. Repeat this until you've viewed all the thumbnails.

Word 2008 provides 17 cover page choices, each with a distinctive graphic design.

See Also For information about creating cover pages, see "Add Professional Cover Pages" in Chapter 14, "Add Finishing Document Elements."

21. On the **Document Elements** tab, click **Table of Contents**. In the **Table of Contents** group, point to the first thumbnail.

The thumbnail magnifies to indicate that it is active, and the name of the selected design (*Classic*) replaces the words *Insert a Table of Contents* at the left end of the gallery.

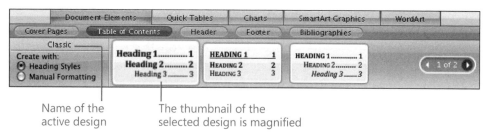

Name of the active design

The thumbnail of the selected design is magnified

22. At the left end of the gallery, click **Manual Formatting**.

The thumbnails change to reflect the selection.

23. View the rest of the groups on the Document Elements tab—**Header**, **Footer**, and **Bibliographies**. Then view the **Quick Tables**, **Charts**, **SmartArt Graphics**, and **WordArt** tabs.

We'll work with each of these tabs in later chapters.

24. When you finish investigating the Elements Gallery, click the active tab once.

The Elements Gallery closes so that only the tabs are visible.

25. Right-click in the toolbar area (to the right of the **Help** button, for example), point to toolbars, and then click **Formatting**.

The Formatting toolbar closes.

26. Right-click again in the toolbar area, and then click **Icon Only**.

The button labels disappear from the Standard toolbar and the buttons reposition themselves. Without the labels, the toolbar buttons take up significantly less space and present a much tidier appearance.

27. On the toolbar, click the **Toolbox** button. Then in the upper-right corner of the document window, click the **Hide Toolbars** button.

The document window is now very tidy, with fewer things to distract you from the document content (if there was any).

28. On the **Word** menu, click **Preferences**.

The Word Preferences dialog box opens.

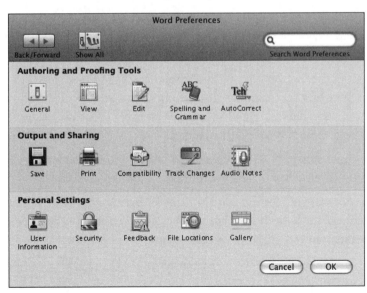

29. Under **Authoring and Proofing Tools**, click **Edit**.

The Edit page of the Preferences dialog box opens.

30. Point to **Drag-and-drop text editing**.

A description of the feature appears in the Description Of Preference box at the bottom of the page.

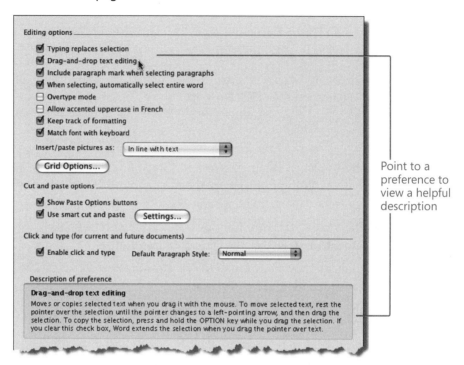

Point to a preference to view a helpful description

31. Point to any other options that interest you, and then at the top of the page, click the **Show All** button to return to the preference group listing.

32. Investigate other options in the **Preferences** dialog box, and try out the Spotlight search feature by typing a feature name in the **Search** box to locate the preference group(s) containing related settings. When you finish, click **Cancel** to close the dialog box without making any changes.

33. Use the techniques you've learned to redisplay the toolbar area and the toolbar button labels. Then on the **Word** menu, click **Quit Word**.

34. On your own, repeat the concepts of this exercise in Excel and PowerPoint to familiarize yourself with the available commands for personalizing the programs. We'll investigate these programs in later chapters.

CLEAN UP When you finish experimenting, close any open Office documents and quit the Office programs.

Key Points

- You can give instructions in an Office program in many ways, such as choosing a command on a menu, clicking a button on a toolbar or in the Toolbox, and using keyboard shortcuts. You can choose the method you're most comfortable with.

- The primary Office programs share many of the same menus and toolbars.

- You can hide or display toolbars, the Elements Gallery, and the Toolbox to declutter your working environment.

- The Elements Gallery contains preformatted document parts that you can insert into an Office file.

- You can personalize your Office installation by providing information about yourself, such as your name, address, telephone number, and the name of the company you work for.

- You can change the way program features work from the Preferences dialog box of each specific program.

Chapter at a Glance

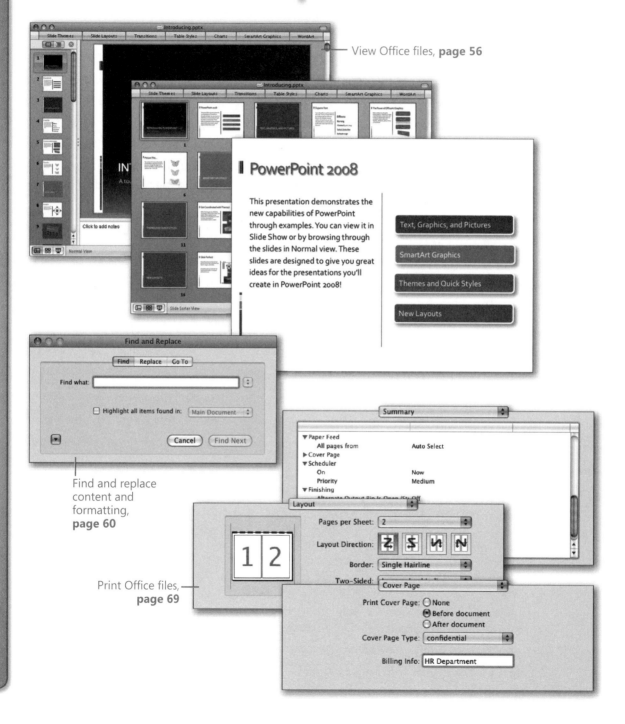

View Office files, **page 56**

Find and replace content and formatting, **page 60**

Print Office files, **page 69**

2 Practice Basic Office File Skills

In this chapter, you will learn how to

- ✔ Open, save, and close Office files.
- ✔ View Office files.
- ✔ Find and replace content and formatting.
- ✔ Print Office files.

Files created in each program in the Microsoft Office system are identified by different names: Microsoft Word files are *documents*, Microsoft Excel files are *workbooks*, and Microsoft PowerPoint files are *presentations*. In this book, we refer collectively to all three of these file types as *Office files*.

Although Word, Excel, and PowerPoint are different programs with very different purposes, many of the ways in which you interact with the programs and the Office files you create are similar, if not identical. Microsoft has designed the programs with as many common elements as possible so that you don't need to spend as much time learning basic program skills. Instead, you can apply the tools and techniques you learn when using one program to other programs within Office 2008.

In this chapter, you'll learn common skills you can use to open, save, close, and view Office files in Microsoft Word 2008 for Mac, Microsoft Excel 2008 for Mac, and Microsoft PowerPoint 2008 for Mac. Then you'll learn about finding and replacing information in an Office file. Finally, you'll learn about printing Office files.

See Also You can find handy keyboard shortcuts, simple instructions for performing common tasks, and other useful information in the Quick Reference section at the beginning of this book.

Practice Makes Perfect! The practice files you will use to complete the exercises in this chapter are in the *OfficeSkills* practice file folder. See "Using the Companion Content" at the beginning of this book for information about installing and locating the practice files.

Open, Save, and Close Office Files

You open an existing document, workbook, or presentation from within the appropriate program by clicking the Open button on the toolbar, by clicking Open on the File menu, or by pressing Command+O. Any of these commands displays the Open dialog box.

The first time you display the Open dialog box, it opens to your *Documents* folder. If you display the dialog box again in the same program session, it displays the contents of whatever folder you last used. You move between folders by using standard browsing techniques.

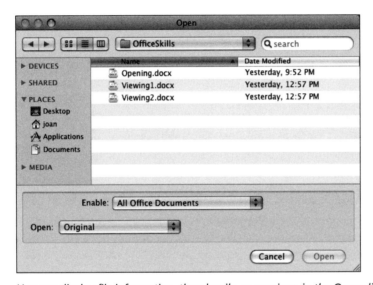

You can display file information, thumbnails, or previews in the Open dialog box.

> **Tip** From the Open list in the lower-left corner of the Open dialog box, you can choose the way you want to open the selected file. The default option is Original, which opens the file and allows edits (provided the file is not designated as *read-only*). Your other options are Read-Only, which opens the file but doesn't allow changes, and Copy, which creates and opens a copy of the file.

Each file you create is temporary until you save it as a file with a unique name or storage location. To save a file for the first time, you click the Save button on the toolbar, click Save on the File menu, or press Command+S. Each action displays the Save As dialog box, in which you can assign a file name and select a location.

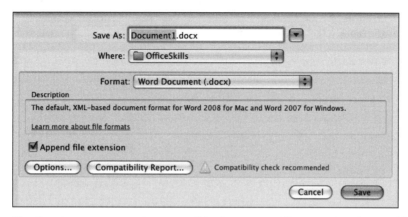

The first time you save a document, Word suggests a file name, location, and format.

If you want to save the file in a folder other than the one shown in the Where box, you can choose a standard location from the Where list or click the Expand button to the right of the Save As box to display a navigation area in which you can choose the folder you want. If you want to create a new folder in which to store the file, you can click the New Folder button that appears in the lower-left corner of the Save As dialog box when the navigation area is open.

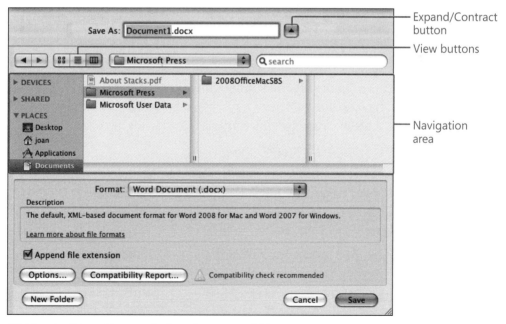

Clicking the Expand button displays the storage folder structure.

Choose the Right File Format

With the new Office Open XML Formats, you can use a lot of great program features and save the same amount of content in a much smaller file than the formats used by earlier versions of Office. Other programs can easily access and use content in these formats, which can be very useful in certain situations. If you create files that will be opened only in Office 2008 for Mac or the 2007 Office system for Windows, these file formats are the right choice for you.

If you'll be sharing files with people who are running earlier versions of the Office programs, they can access those files by installing a free file converter that will allow them to open files saved in the following file formats:

- Word Document (.docx)
- Word Macro-Enabled Document (.docm)
- PowerPoint Presentation (.pptx)
- PowerPoint Show (.ppsx)
- PowerPoint Template (.potx)

See Also For information about the file formats available in Office 2008, see the sidebars "Word File Formats," "Excel File Formats," and "PowerPoint File Formats" in Chapter 3, "Work in Office Programs."

Two file converters are available:

- **Office Open XML File Format Converter for Mac.** This converter supports Office 2004 and Office v. X running on Mac OS X 10.4.8 (Tiger) and later and is available from the Office for Mac Downloads page at

  www.microsoft.com/mac/downloads/

- **Microsoft Office Compatibility Pack for Word, Excel, and PowerPoint 2007 File Formats.** This converter supports Office 2000, Office XP, and Office 2003 running on Windows 2000 or later and is available from the Microsoft Download Center at

  www.microsoft.com/downloads/

> **Note** Before installing either the File Format Converter or the Compatibility Pack, the people with whom you want to share files should install any available service packs or high-priority updates for their operating system or their version of Office.

> **Tip** You can change the way files are displayed in the navigation area of the Save As dialog box independently of the way they're displayed in the Finder. Click the View buttons located near the top of the Save As dialog box to switch among icon view, list view, and column view.

After you save a file the first time, you can save changes simply by clicking the Save button on the toolbar. The new version of the file then overwrites the previous version. If you want to keep both the new version and the previous version, click Save As on the File menu, and then save the new version with a different name or in a different location. (You cannot store two files with the same name and file format in the same folder.)

Each Office file opens in its own window. You can close an individual file by clicking the Close button (the red dot) in the upper-left corner of its window, clicking Close on the File menu, or pressing Command+W. After you close all the open files, the program continues to run. You can close all open files and quit the program by clicking Quit on the File menu or pressing Command+Q.

Practice Opening, Saving, and Closing Office Files

In this exercise, you'll practice opening, saving, and closing Office files by using a variety of methods. You'll open an existing Word document and save it with a new name; open a copy of an existing Excel workbook and save the copy in the same folder; and then open an existing PowerPoint presentation in read-only mode and save an editable version in a different folder. Finally, you'll close the files and quit the programs.

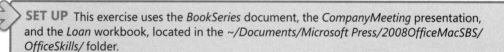

SET UP This exercise uses the *BookSeries* document, the *CompanyMeeting* presentation, and the *Loan* workbook, located in the *~/Documents/Microsoft Press/2008OfficeMacSBS/ OfficeSkills/* folder.

1. Start Word.

    The Word menu bar appears at the top of the screen, and a temporary document opens.

2. On the **File** menu, click **Open**.

    > **Note** If the toolbar area is hidden, click the Hide Toolbars button in the upper-right corner of the document window. If no toolbars are open, right-click an empty place in the toolbar area, and then point to Toolbars. On the submenu, toolbars preceded by check marks are open. To make your window look like ours, open the Standard toolbar and close all other toolbars.

See Also For more information about the Standard toolbar, see "Toolbars" in Chapter 1, "Explore and Manage the Office Interface."

The Open dialog box opens, showing the contents of the *Documents* folder or the folder you used for your last open or save action in this session.

> **Tip** If a dialog box is hiding the text you want to work with, you can move the dialog box on the screen by dragging its title bar.

3. If the dialog box does not display the contents of your *Documents* folder, click **Documents** in the sidebar of the navigation area.

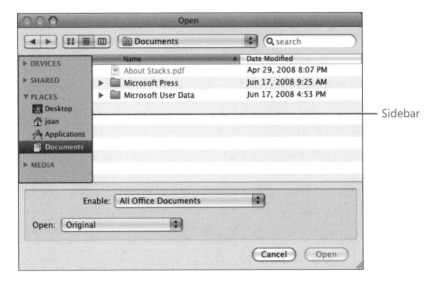

Sidebar

> **Note** If the contents of your Open navigation area aren't arranged as shown here, click the List View button on the toolbar.

4. Double-click the *Microsoft Press* folder, double-click the *2008OfficeMacSBS* folder, and then double-click the *OfficeSkills* folder.

5. Click the *BookSeries* document and then, with **Original** selected in the **Open** list, click the **Open** button.

The temporary document closes, and the *BookSeries* document opens.

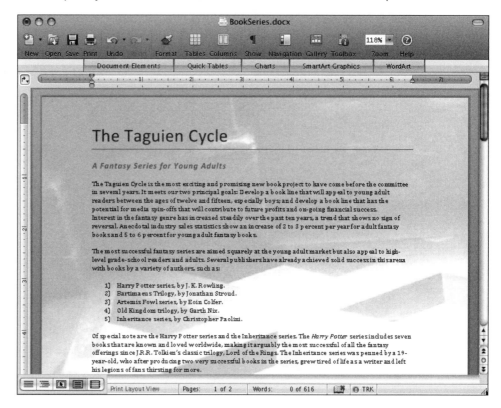

> **Note** If the Standard toolbar is not open, display it now.

6. On the Word menu bar, on the **File** menu, click **Save As**.

The Save As dialog box opens, displaying the contents of the *OfficeSkills* folder. The current document title appears in the Save As box, selected for editing.

Expand/Contract button

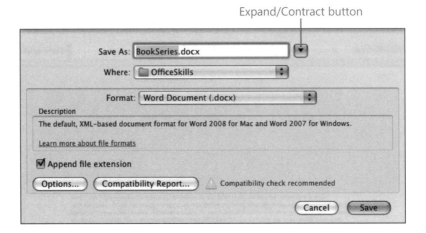

Note If your Save As dialog box is expanded to display the navigation area, click the Contract button to the right of the Save As box.

7. In the **Save As** box, replace *BookSeries* with PressRelease. Then click **Save**.

   Word saves a second version of the file, with the new name, in the *OfficeSkills* folder.

8. On the toolbar, click the **Open** button. In the **Open** dialog box displaying the contents of the *OfficeSkills* folder, ensure that **All Office Documents** appears in the **Enable** box.

   Tip You can filter the files displayed in the navigation area by choosing the file type you want to see from the Enable list.

9. Click the *Loan* workbook. In the **Open** list, click **Copy**. Then click **Open**.

A message box appears, notifying you that the *Loan* workbook was created in Excel.

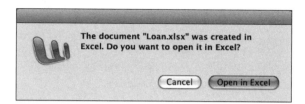

10. Click **Open in Excel**.

Excel starts, and a copy of the *Loan* workbook, named *Loan1*, opens. The copy is only a temporary file until you save it.

11. On the toolbar, click the **Save** button.

The Save As dialog box opens, prompting you to save the workbook as *Loan1* in your *Documents* folder.

12. Click the **Expand** button to the right of the **Save As** box.

The Save As dialog box expands to display a navigation area consisting of the sidebar and the contents of your *Documents* folder.

Note If the contents of your navigation area aren't arranged as shown here, click the Column View button on the toolbar.

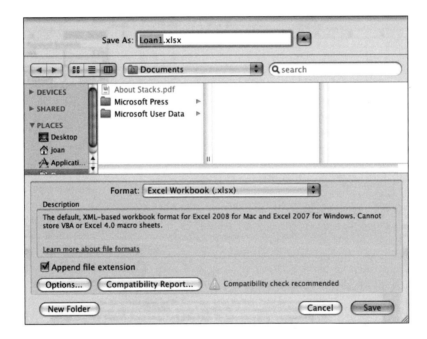

Tip The file formats available in the Format list in the Save As dialog box vary depending on whether a ledger sheet, chart sheet, or other type of sheet is active.

13. Click *Microsoft Press* in the first column, click *2008OfficeMacSBS* in the second column, and click *OfficeSkills* in the third column. Then click **Save**.

14. On the toolbar, click the **Open** button. In the **Open** dialog box displaying the contents of the *OfficeSkills* folder, click the *CompanyMeeting* presentation.

15. In the **Open** list, click **Read-Only**. Then click **Open**, and in the message box that appears, click **Open in PowerPoint**.

The *CompanyMeeting* presentation opens. A notation on the title bar indicates that the file is read-only.

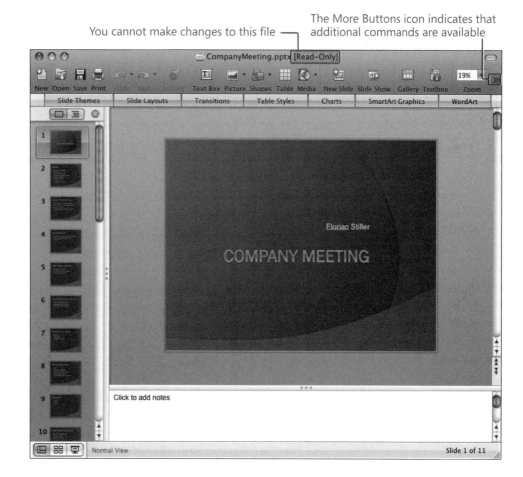

You cannot make changes to this file ⎯

The More Buttons icon indicates that additional commands are available

16. Click the **Save** button.

A message box appears, giving you the option of saving changes under a different file name.

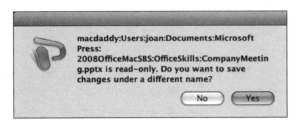

17. In the message box, click **Yes**.

The Save As dialog box opens.

18. Click the **Expand** button.

The Save As dialog box expands to display the sidebar and the contents of the *OfficeSkills* folder.

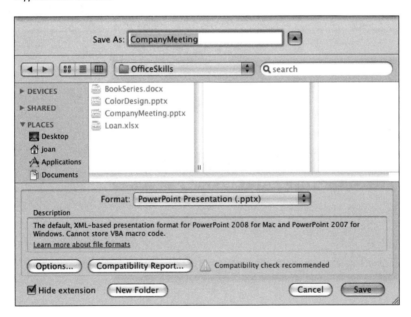

19. At the bottom of the **Save As** dialog box, click **New Folder**.

The New Folder dialog box opens.

20. Replace *untitled folder* with Final, and then click **Create**.

The *Final* folder appears in the file list and is selected.

21. Click **Save**.

PowerPoint saves the *CompanyMeeting* presentation in the *Final* folder. [Read-Only] disappears from the title bar to indicate that you are now working in the new version and can make changes to the file.

22. On the **PowerPoint** menu, click **Quit PowerPoint**.

The open presentation and the PowerPoint menu bar close, and the *Loan1* workbook becomes active.

23. On the Excel menu bar, on the **File** menu, click **Close**.

The open workbook closes, but the Excel menu bar remains visible.

24. With the Excel menu bar active, press **Command+Q** to quit Excel.

The Excel menu bar disappears and the *PressRelease* document becomes active.

 25. Click the **Close** button at the left end of the document window title bar to close the *PressRelease* document.

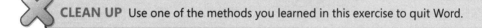 **CLEAN UP** Use one of the methods you learned in this exercise to quit Word.

View Office Files

Depending on the way you're working in a file, you may find it more effective to work in a view other than the default, to change the magnification so that you can see more or less detail, or to view multiple parts of a file or multiple files at one time.

Change the View

You switch among views of an Office file by using commands on the View menu or by clicking the buttons on the View toolbar in the lower-left corner of the window. Each program offers its own set of views that are appropriate to its content. For example, you can display a PowerPoint presentation in Normal view, Slide Sorter view, and Slide Show view. We discuss the views available in each program in Chapter 3, "Work in Office Programs."

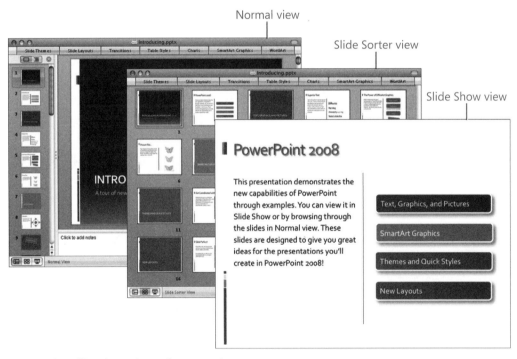

PowerPoint offers three views of presentation content.

Change the Magnification

You can change the magnification of any Office file by choosing a magnification level from the Zoom list on the Standard toolbar, by entering a magnification level in the Zoom box, or by clicking Zoom on the View menu and selecting the magnification you want in the Zoom dialog box. You can select a specific magnification level or fit the content to the window.

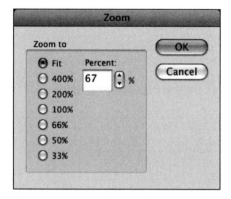

Change the magnification level of a file to show more or less detail.

The options in the Zoom dialog box vary depending on the type of Office file you're viewing. The range of magnification varies by program, as follows:

Program	Magnification range
Excel	10 percent to 400 percent
PowerPoint	10 percent to 400 percent
Word	10 percent to 500 percent

See Also In addition to changing the view of the file content, you can display and hide the toolbar area, the Elements Gallery, the Toolbox, and program-specific tools. For information, see Chapter 1, "Explore and Manage the Office Interface."

Split and Arrange Document and Workbook Windows

Office files often contain multiple units of content that you will want to view and manipulate—a presentation is made up of multiple slides, a workbook of multiple worksheets, and a document of multiple pages.

In Excel and Word, you can split the window into separate panes. Each pane has its own set of scroll bars, so you can view two areas of a worksheet or document at the same time. To split a window, drag the Split bar (at the top of the vertical scrollbar) down.

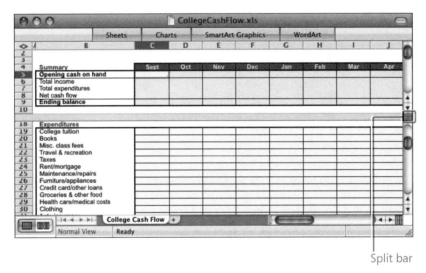

Split bar

Display two views of one workbook or document by splitting the window.

> **Tip** Excel 2008 supports up to four panes in each window.

If you want to display more than one file on the screen, you can arrange and work with the separate windows. When you're working with several open Office files of the same type (documents, workbooks, or presentations), you can automatically arrange all the open files by clicking Arrange or Arrange All on the Window menu. Clicking Arrange opens the Arrange dialog box, in which you can choose a Tiled, Horizontal, Vertical, or Cascade window arrangement.

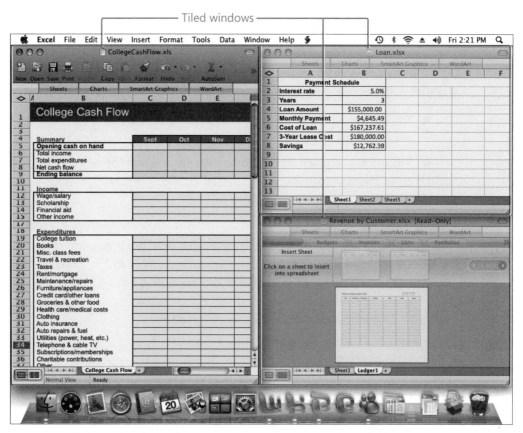

Arrange multiple workbooks on the screen by using the commands available on the Window menu.

Each window retains its own set of scroll bars, but the scroll bars of only the active window are visible.

If you're working with several Office files of different types, you can bring all the files of one type to the front of the stack by clicking Bring All To Front on the Window menu of the relevant program.

Find and Replace Content and Formatting

You can use the Find and Replace features to locate or change information in any Office file. With minor variations, the Find and Replace features work the same in all of the Office 2008 for Mac programs:

- You use the Find feature to search for information, such as a character, word, phrase, format, or style.

- You use the Replace feature to replace instances of the search term or format with other terms or formats.

Word Search Options

Word 2008 for Mac provides significantly more search options and replace options than other Office 2008 programs. Clicking Find on the Edit menu, or pressing Command+F, displays the Find page of the Find And Replace dialog box.

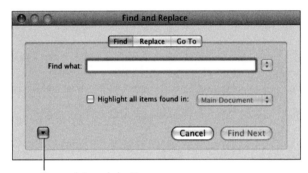

Expand Search button

You can move between instances of specified text in a document,
or highlight all instances in the document.

After you enter the search term you want to locate in the Find What box, you can click Find Next to locate and select the next occurrence of that text, or select the Highlight All Items Found In check box and then click Find All to highlight all occurrences of the search term in the document.

> **Tip** If you find an error in a document while conducting a search, you can edit the document content without closing the Find And Replace dialog box. Simply click the document, make the change, and then click the Find And Replace dialog box to reactivate it.

You can specify additional search options by clicking the Expand Search button.

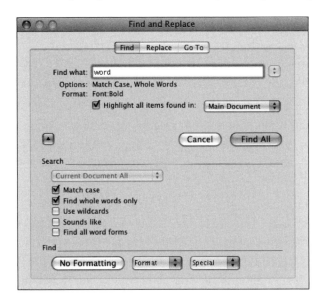

In Word, you can search for content that meets very specific criteria.

In the expanded Find And Replace dialog box, you can select any or all of the check boxes:

● Select the Match Case check box to match the capitalization of the search term as you have entered it in the Find What box.

● Select the Find Whole Words Only check box to find only whole-word occurrences of the Find What text.

● If you want to check that your usage of two similar words, such as *effect* and *affect*, is correct, select the Use Wildcards check box and then enter a wildcard character in the Find What box to locate variable information. The two most common wild-card characters are:

　○ The ? (question mark), which stands for *any single character in this location.*

　○ The * (asterisk), which stands for *any number of characters in this location.*

Resources For a full list of wildcard characters and guidelines for using them, see the topic "Wildcard characters you can use when searching" in the Word Help system.

● Select the Sounds Like check box to find occurrences of the search term that sound the same but are spelled differently, such as *there* and *their.*

● Select the Find All Word Forms check box to find multiple forms of the search term, such as *plan*, *planned*, and *planning.*

By using the lists in the Search and Find areas, you can:

- Guide the scope and direction of the search.

- Include special characters such as paragraph marks, tab characters, or graphics in the search term, by selecting the character from the Special list. Doing so inserts a special code identifying the character (such as ^p for paragraph mark) in the Find What box.

- Specify the format of the search term, or indicate that you want to search for *any* text formatted with a specific character format, paragraph format, or style, by displaying the Format list and then clicking the type of formatting you want to search for. Options include Font, Paragraph, Tabs, Language, Frame, Style, and Highlight.

If you know that you want to substitute one word or phrase for another, you can use the Replace feature to find each occurrence of the text you want to change and replace it with different text. Clicking the Replace button at the top of the Find And Replace dialog box, or clicking Replace on the Edit menu, displays the Replace page of the Find And Replace dialog box, which is the same as the Find page with an additional Replace With text box.

On the Replace page, you can do the following:

- Click Find Next to locate and select the next occurrence of the search term.

- Click Replace to replace the selected occurrence of the search term with the replacement specified in the Replace With box and move to the next occurrence.

- Click Replace All to replace all occurrences with the specified replacement.

In addition to searching for words and phrases, in Word 2008, you can search for a specific type of character, paragraph, tab, language, frame, or style formatting, or search for highlighting, and replace the specified formatting with different formatting.

To replace a format with a different format:

1. On the **Edit** menu, click **Replace** (or press **Shift+Command+H**).

    The Find And Replace dialog box opens, displaying the Replace page.

2. Click to position the insertion point in the **Find what** box, and then click the **Expand** button to display additional search options. In the **Find** area, in the **Format** list, click the type of formatting you want to search for.

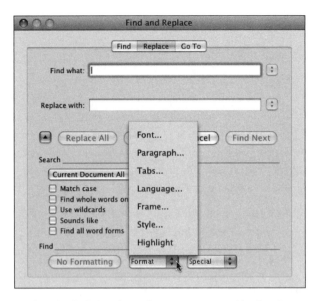

3. In the **Find** dialog box that opens, specify the formatting you want to find.

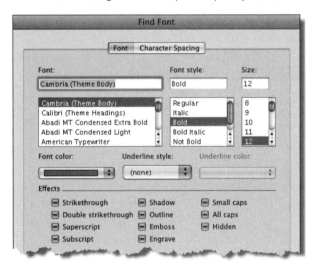

4. Click **OK** in the **Find** dialog box. Move the insertion point to the **Replace with** text box and repeat step 2, specifying the formatting you want to substitute for the Find What formatting. Then click **OK** in the **Replace** dialog box.

The Find And Replace dialog box reflects your choices.

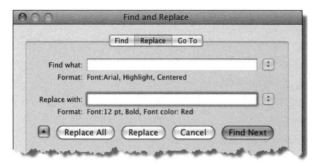

5. Click **Replace All** to replace every instance of the Find What formatting with the Replace With formatting, or click **Find Next** to search for the first occurrence of the format, and then click **Replace** to replace that one instance and move to the next.

Excel Search Options

The Find and Replace functions in Excel 2008 for Mac are designed to locate information in worksheet cells. Clicking Find on the Edit menu or pressing Command+F displays the Find dialog box.

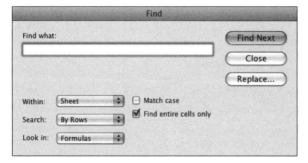

In Excel, you can locate specific text in formulas, values, and comments.

You can restrict the search operation to the current worksheet or search the entire workbook, specify the direction of the search (by rows or by columns), and specify what aspect of each cell will be evaluated (formulas, values, or comments). You have the options of matching the case of the search term as you enter it in the Find What box, and of specifying whether to find all cells containing the search term or only those cells that contain nothing but the search term.

Clicking Replace in the Find dialog box or on the Edit menu displays the Replace dialog box, in which you can specify a replacement term.

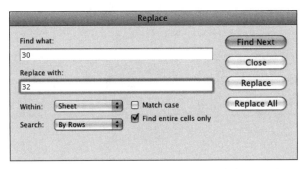

You can find and replace content on a worksheet or throughout an entire workbook.

PowerPoint Search Options

PowerPoint 2008 for Mac provides the following search and replace options:

● You can locate specific text within a presentation from the Find dialog box, which you open by clicking Find on the Edit menu or pressing Command+F. You can specify whether PowerPoint should locate matches with the exact capitalization or case—that is, if you specify *person*, PowerPoint will not locate *Person*—and whether it should locate matches for the entire text—that is, if you specify *person*, PowerPoint will not locate *personal*.

● You can replace specific text with other text from the Replace dialog box, which you open by clicking Replace in the Find dialog box or by clicking Replace on the Edit menu. You can approve the replacement of each instance of the search term, or replace all instances of the search term in the presentation in one operation. You have the options of matching the case of the search term and of excluding variations on the search term.

● You can change all instances of a font within a presentation to another font. You can specify only the font name, not the size, weight, or any other attribute.

Practice Replacing Content and Formatting

In this exercise, you'll replace text and formatting in a PowerPoint presentation. You can use many of the techniques you'll practice in this exercise in other Office 2008 programs.

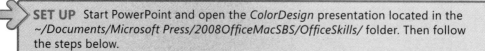

SET UP   Start PowerPoint and open the *ColorDesign* presentation located in the *~/Documents/Microsoft Press/2008OfficeMacSBS/OfficeSkills/* folder. Then follow the steps below.

1. On the **Edit** menu, click **Replace** (or press **Control+H**).

   The Replace dialog box opens.

2. In the **Find what** box, type verdigris, and then press **Tab**.

3. In the **Replace with** box, type Verdigris.

4. Select the **Match case** check box to locate text that exactly matches the capitalization you specified and replace it with the capitalization you specified.

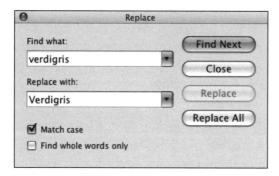

5. In the **Replace** dialog box, click **Find Next**.

   PowerPoint finds and selects the word *verdigris* on Slide 3.

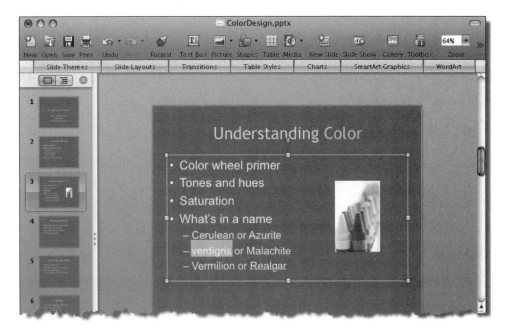

6. In the **Replace** dialog box, click **Replace**.

PowerPoint replaces *verdigris* with *Verdigris*, and then locates the next match, on Slide 5.

7. In the **Replace** dialog box, click **Replace All**.

A message box notifies you that PowerPoint has finished searching the presentation and that the Replace All operation changed two additional occurrences of the search term.

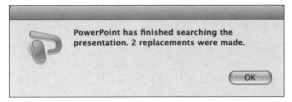

8. In the message box, click **OK**, and then in the **Replace** dialog box, click **Close**.

9. On the **Format** menu, click **Replace Fonts**.

The Replace Font dialog box opens.

10. With *Arial* selected in the **Replace** list, click **American Typewriter** in the **With** list.

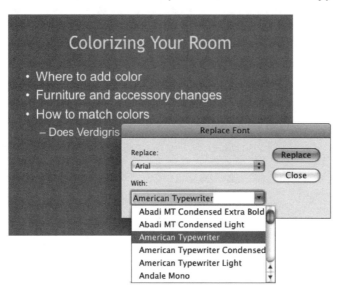

11. In the **Replace Font** dialog box, click **Replace**.

The slide text changes to the American Typewriter font.

12. In the **Replace** list, click **Trebuchet MS**. Scroll the **With** list, and click **Cooper Black**. Then click **Replace**.

The slide title text changes. Your slides now have an entirely different look!

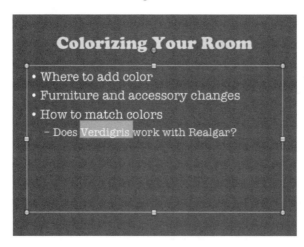

13. In the **Replace Font** dialog box, click **Close**.

 CLEAN UP Close the *ColorDesign* presentation without saving your changes, and quit PowerPoint.

Print Office Files

Although the concept of a "paperless office" is wonderful, possible, and certainly a goal that we are actively working toward at our company, it is still very necessary to print the documents, worksheets, and—perhaps to a lesser degree—slides you create in the Office programs.

 You can quickly print one copy of an entire Office file on the default printer, with the default print settings, by clicking the Print button on the Standard toolbar.

If you want to print only part of the file or multiple copies, print non-standard file elements such as notes or comments, or change any other print setting, open the Print dialog box by clicking Print on the File menu or by pressing Command+P.

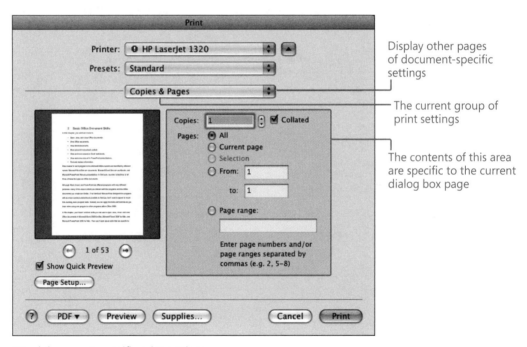

Word document–specific print settings

From the Print dialog box, you still have the option of printing the file with the default print settings—simply click Print and you're done. Or you can change any of a multitude of settings—some which aren't obvious because they're located on different pages of the dialog box. From the list immediately above the settings area, you can access any of the following groups of settings:

- Copies & Pages
- Layout
- Color Matching
- Paper Handling
- Paper Feed

- Cover Page
- Scheduler
- Finishing
- Image Quality

From the same list, you can also display a non-editable Summary page listing all the current print settings.

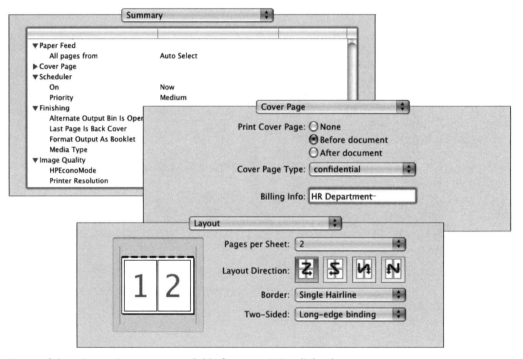

Some of the print setting groups available from any Print dialog box

The settings available from the Copies & Pages page of the Print dialog box vary between programs, but the other pages are the same in all programs.

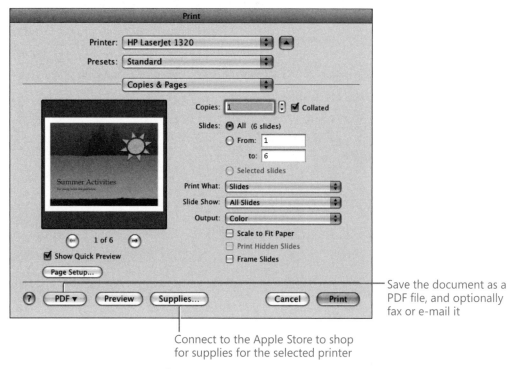

Connect to the Apple Store to shop for supplies for the selected printer

Save the document as a PDF file, and optionally fax or e-mail it

PowerPoint presentation–specific print settings

Before you print a file, it's usually a good idea to check how it will look on paper by previewing it. Previewing is essential for multipage files but is helpful even for one-page files. In the Print dialog box, the Quick Preview pane displays a small version of one page at a time; you can move forward and backward by clicking the Next and Previous buttons below the pane.

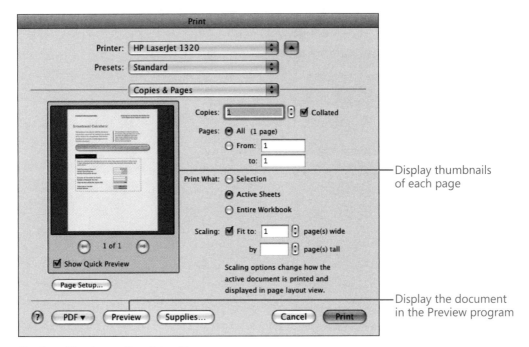

Excel workbook–specific print settings

To display a full-size, non-editable version of the file as it will be printed, click the Preview button to open the file in the Preview program (installed with the Mac OS).

Key Points

- Word, Excel, and PowerPoint share many of the same features and commands, so you don't need to have a whole new set of skills for each program.

- You can save Office files in the new Office XML File Formats, as well as other formats that are compatible with older program versions. Files saved in the Office XML File Formats can be opened in Office 2008 programs on a Macintosh computer or in Office 2007 programs on a Windows computer.

- To simplify the process of working with a lot of content or with several Office files, you can display and arrange multiple windows on the computer screen.

- The Find and Replace features make it simple to quickly locate or change text or formatting in a document, workbook, or presentation.

- You can quickly print any Office file with the default print settings by clicking the Print button on the Standard toolbar. You also have the option of specifying which pages to print and how many copies, as well as selecting settings related to page layout, color matching, paper handling, paper feed, cover pages, scheduled printing, finishing, and image quality.

Chapter at a Glance

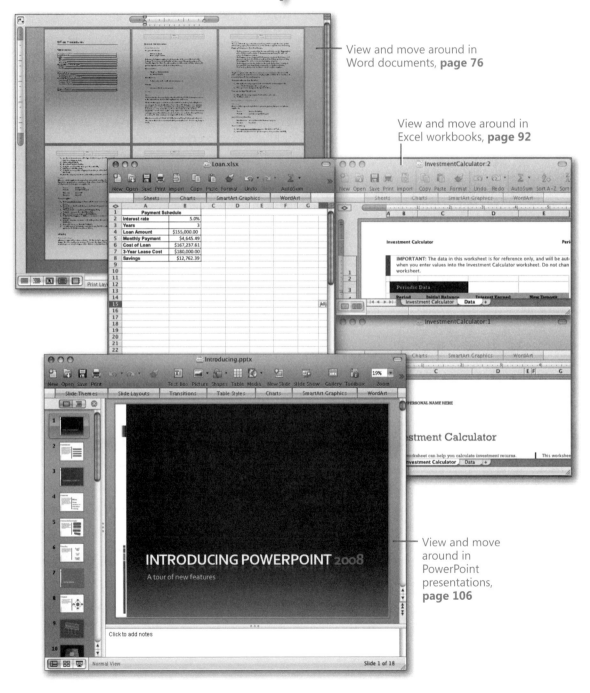

View and move around in Word documents, **page 76**

View and move around in Excel workbooks, **page 92**

View and move around in PowerPoint presentations, **page 106**

3 Work in Office Programs

In this chapter, you will learn how to

- ✔ View and move around in Word documents.
- ✔ Move around in document content.
- ✔ View and move around in Excel workbooks.
- ✔ View and move around in PowerPoint presentations.

Before we get started with the process of creating Microsoft Word documents, Microsoft Excel workbooks, and Microsoft PowerPoint presentations, we'll spend a bit of time practicing the ways that you view and move around in each of these core Office programs. Then in later chapters, we won't need to give specific instructions for changing views, moving to different pages or slides, and so on.

Word, Excel, and PowerPoint each offer multiple views of files. Some views depict a file exactly as it will appear in print; others display more information on the screen. You can easily switch between views, and choose the best view for your needs at a specific time.

Word, Excel, and PowerPoint also offer multiple ways of moving around in file content. You can use menu commands, on-screen navigation tools, and keyboard shortcuts to move a variety of directions and distances.

In this chapter, you'll learn about skills that are specific to viewing and moving around in Word documents, Excel worksheets and workbooks, and PowerPoint slides and presentations.

See Also You can find handy keyboard shortcuts, simple instructions for performing common tasks, and other useful information in the Quick Reference section at the beginning of this book.

Practice Makes Perfect! The practice files you will use to complete the exercises in this chapter are in the *OfficePrograms* practice file folder. See "Using the Companion Content" at the beginning of this book for information about installing and locating the practice files.

View and Move Around in Word Documents

You can look at the content of a document in any of the following views:

- **Print Layout view.** This is the default view for working in a Word document. This view displays a document on the screen the way it will look when printed. You can see elements such as margins, page breaks, headers and footers, and *watermarks*.

- **Draft view.** This view displays the text of a document with a simplified layout so that you can type and edit quickly. Paragraph and font formatting and styles are visible, but images, text box content, headers and footers, and other graphic elements are not visible.

- **Outline view.** This view displays the structure of a document as nested levels of headings and body text, and provides tools for viewing and changing its hierarchy.

- **Web Layout view.** This view displays a document on the screen the way it will look when viewed in a Web browser. You can see backgrounds, AutoShapes, and other effects. You can also see how text wraps to fit the window and how graphics are positioned.

In addition to these four views, Word 2008 provides two working environments in which you can create and manage specialized content. You can create original content in these views or import other content into them:

- **Notebook Layout view.** This environment turns your document into an electronic notebook in which you can create and organize handwritten and electronic information, including audio clips.

- **Publishing Layout view.** This environment, which is new in Office 2008, provides desktop publishing tools and designer templates that are not available in other views, so you can easily create a newsletter or other professional-looking publication.

See Also For information about creating documents in Notebook Layout view and Publishing Layout view, see "Work with Word Notebooks" and "Work with Word Publications" in Chapter 4, "Create Word Documents."

You can switch between views of a document by using the following methods:

→ On the **View** menu, click the name of the view you want.

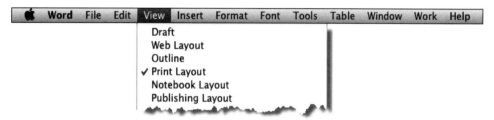

→ On the View toolbar in the lower-left corner of the window, click the button for the view you want.

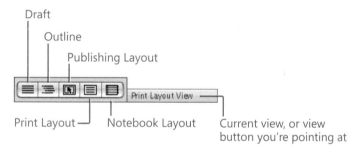

Move Around in Document Content

You can move around in an open document in several ways. To move around in a document without changing the location of the insertion point, you can use the vertical and horizontal scroll bars as follows:

● Click the scroll arrows to move the document window up or down by a line, or left or right by a few characters.

● Click above or below the vertical scroll box to move up or down one screen, or click to the left or right of the horizontal scroll box to move left or right one screen.

● Drag the scroll box on the scroll bar to display the part of the document corresponding to the location of the scroll box. For example, dragging the scroll box to the middle of the scroll bar displays the middle of the document.

You can also move around in a document in ways that do move the insertion point. To place the insertion point at a particular location, you simply click there. To move the insertion point back or forward a page, you can click the Previous Page and Next Page buttons below the vertical scroll bar.

You can also press a key or a *key combination* on the keyboard to move the insertion point. For example, you can press the Home key to move the insertion point to the left end of a line or press Command+Home to move it to the beginning of the document.

> **Tip** The location of the insertion point is displayed on the status bar. By default, the status bar tells you which page the insertion point is on. The Live Word Count feature tells you which word out of all the words in the document it is in. To turn Live Word Count on or off, display the Word Preferences dialog box, click View, and then in the Window area, select or clear the Live Word Count check box.

You can use the keyboard shortcuts listed in the following table to move the insertion point around in a document.

To move...	Press...
To the left one character	Left Arrow
To the right one character	Right Arrow
To the left one word	Option+Left Arrow
Right one word	Option+Right Arrow
To the beginning of the current line	Home or Command+Left Arrow
To the end of the current line	End or Command+Right Arrow
Up one line	Up Arrow
Down one line	Down Arrow
Up one screen	Page Up
Down one screen	Page Down
To the beginning of the current or previous paragraph	Command+Up Arrow or Option+Up Arrow
To the beginning of the next paragraph	Command+Down Arrow or Option+Down Arrow
To the beginning of the previous page	Command+Page Up
To the beginning of the next page	Command+Page Down
To the beginning of the document	Command+Home
To the end of the document	Command+End

In a long document, you might want to move quickly among elements of a certain type; for example, from graphic to graphic. You can click the Select Browse Object button at the bottom of the vertical scroll bar and then make a choice in the palette of browsing options that appears, such as Browse By Page or Browse By Graphic.

To move to a specific page, section, line, bookmark, comment, footnote, endnote, field, table, graphic, equation, object, or heading:

1. Press **F5** to display the **Go To** page of the **Find and Replace** dialog box.

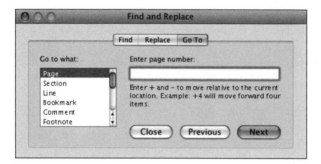

2. In the **Go to what** list, click the type of element you want to jump to.

   The Enter box changes to reflect the selected element.

3. In the **Enter** box, type the name or number of the specific element you want to move to, or type <User Input>+ or <User Input>- followed by the number of items you want to move forward or backward.

   Or

   In the **Enter** list, click the specific element you want to move to.

4. Click **Next**.

Practice Viewing and Moving Around in Documents

In this exercise, you'll look at a formatted Word document in the two views you're most likely to use while working with documents: Print Layout view and Draft view, and then in a view you'll use less often: Web Layout view. First you'll explore the many ways you can view and move around in a document in Print Layout view, and then you'll look at the same document in Draft view and Web Layout view.

 SET UP This exercise uses the *OfficeProcedures* document located in the *~/Documents/ Microsoft Press/2008OfficeMacSBS/OfficePrograms/* folder. Start Word, and then follow the steps below.

1. Open the *OfficeProcedures* document.

   The document opens in Print Layout view.

2. Scroll through the document, noting the features that are visible.

   The document consists of six pages. Each page has a gradient color background. On all pages but the first, a header appears at the top of the page and the page number appears in the lower-right corner. The document headings are formatted by using styles.

   See Also For information about styles, see "Work with Styles" in Chapter 7, "Work with Word Document Content." For information about headers and footers, see "Add Headers and Footers" in Chapter 14, "Add Finishing Document Elements."

 3. Press **Command+Home** to move to the top of the document. On the toolbar, click the **Zoom** arrow, and then in the list, click **Page Width**.

   The magnification level changes to display the depiction of the printed page within the width of the document window. The Zoom setting changes to reflect the new magnification level.

Current magnification

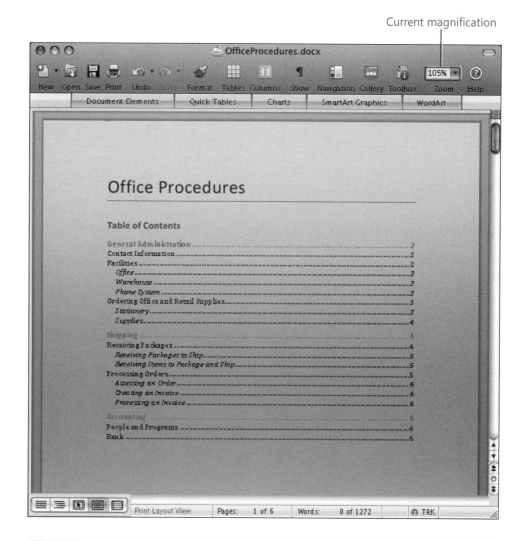

Note Depending on the size of your screen, the size of the document window, and the screen resolution, the magnification levels shown in your Zoom box might not match those shown here. That's okay! You can still complete the exercise as written.

4. In the **Zoom** list, click **Whole Page**.

The entire first page appears in the document window. Note that the insertion point is still active at the beginning of the document. You can insert, edit, select, and format content at any magnification level.

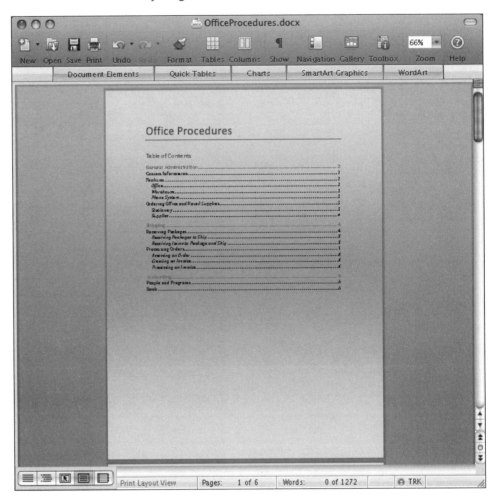

5. In the **Zoom** list, click **Two Pages**.

The magnification changes so that you can see the document in sets of two pages side by side.

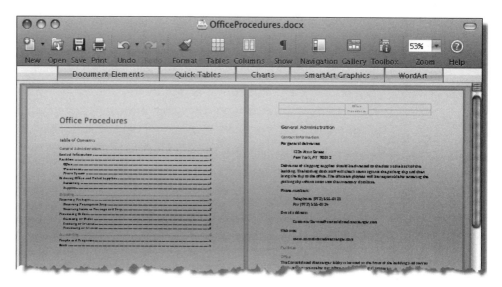

 6. Below the vertical scroll bar, click the **Next Page** button (you might need to click it twice) to display the third and fourth pages of the document.

7. On the **View** menu, click **Zoom**. In the **Zoom** dialog box, with **Many Pages** selected, click the page picker.

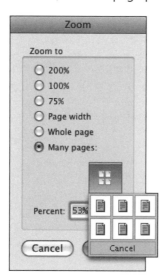

8. In the expanded page picker, point to (but don't click) the page icon in the second column of the second row.

    2 x 2 Pages appears at the bottom of the page picker.

9. Move or drag the pointer down and to the right to further expand the page picker. See how far you can go! Then click the icon representing the **2 x 3 Pages** configuration.

    The magnification level in the Percent box changes to reflect your choice, but the page display doesn't yet change.

10. In the **Zoom** dialog box, click **OK**.

    The six pages of the document now appear in the document window. Even at this magnification, you can see details such as font colors, underlining, headers and footers, and headings.

11. On the **View** menu, click **Ruler**.

    Horizontal and vertical rulers appear above and to the left of the active page. On the rulers, the active area of the page is white and the margins are blue.

12. Press **Command+Page Down**.

    The insertion point moves to the top of the text on the second page. Indicators on the status bar show that the insertion point is now on page 4 of 6 and in word 589 of 1272.

    When the insertion point moved to the second page, the horizontal ruler also moved. At this magnification, the measurements untis on the ruler aren't legible.

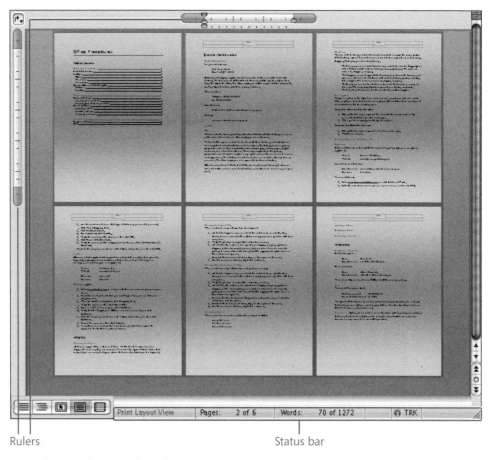

Rulers   Status bar

13. In the **Zoom** list, click **Page Width**.

The markings on the ruler are clearly visible at this magnification level. The blue areas at the left and right ends of the horizontal ruler and the top and bottom ends of the vertical ruler indicate the page margins. The indent markers denote the left and right indents of the active paragraph.

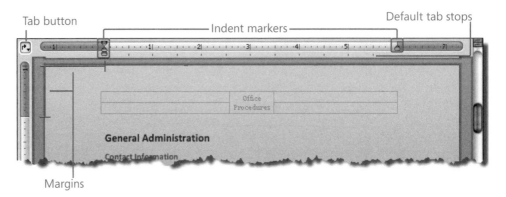

On the horizontal ruler, gray lines below the units of measurement indicate the positions of the default tab stops. You can set custom tab stops by using the Tab button at the intersection of the horizontal and vertical rulers.

See Also For information about indents, see "Indent Paragraphs" in Chapter 11, "Format Office File Content."

Bonus Web Content For information about tab stops, see "Present Text in a Tabular List in Word 2008 for Mac" on the book's companion Web site at *www.microsoft.com/ mspress/companion/9780735626171.*

Change the Units of Measurement

Measurements on the ruler reflect the units of measurement associated with *your* installation of Office 2008 for Mac. In this book, we show inches, but your computer might show metric units. You can change the units of measurement displayed on the ruler and in dialog boxes to inches, centimeters, millimeters, points, or picas, depending on your needs.

To change the units of measurement:

1. Click **Preferences** on the **Word** menu (or press **Command+Comma**).

2. In the **Word Preferences** dialog box, under **Authoring and Proofing Tools**, click **General**.

3. In the **General** dialog box, in the **Measurement Units** list, click the type of units you want. Then click **OK**.

Changing the units of measurement in one Office 2008 program does not affect the units displayed by other Office programs or by your operating system.

---

14. In the **Zoom** list, click **150%**.

   The document text is clearly visible at this magnification.

15. On the toolbar, click the **Navigation** button.

The Navigation pane opens on the left side of the document window, displaying thumbnails of the document pages.

Navigation pane

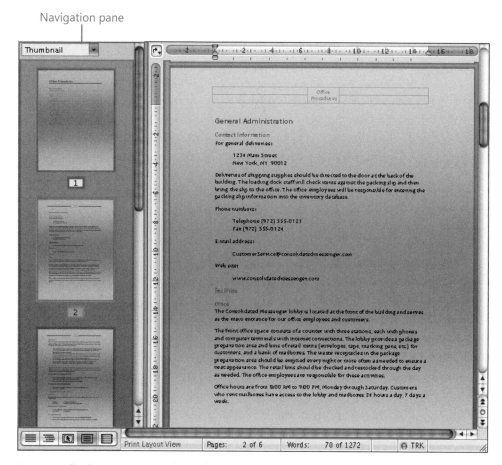

You can display any page of the document by clicking its thumbnail in the Navigation pane. You can resize the thumbnails and change the number displayed by dragging the right border of the Navigation pane to the left or right.

16. In the list at the top of the Navigation pane, click **Document Map**.

The Navigation pane changes to display the Document Map—a hierarchical view of the headings in the document. In the Document Map, the first heading on the active page is selected.

17. In the **Document Map**, click the **Shipping** heading.

Word displays the page containing the selected heading.

18. Right-click anywhere in the Navigation pane.

A menu of Document Map options appears.

Arrows pointing down indicate that subheadings are displayed

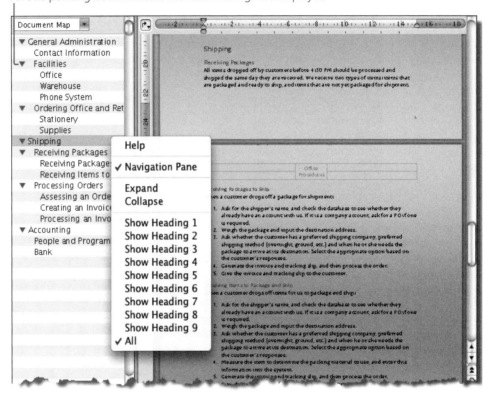

19. On the shortcut menu, click **Show Heading 2**.

The Document Map contracts to display only first- and second-level headings.

20. In the **Document Map**, click **Receiving Packages**.

The selected heading moves to the top of the document window.

21. To the left of **Receiving Packages**, click the right-pointing arrow.

The Document Map displays the previously hidden subheadings.

22. On the toolbar, click the **Navigation** button.

The Document Map closes.

23. On the toolbar, click the **Show** button.

Non-printing characters such as spaces, tabs, paragraph marks, and table delimiters become visible.

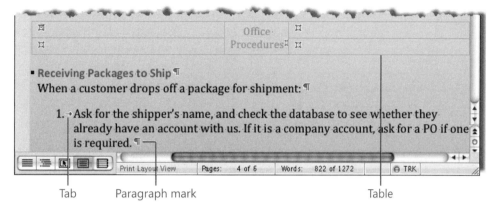

Tab   Paragraph mark   Table

 24. Click the **Show** button again to hide the non-printing characters. Then on the View toolbar, click the **Draft View** button.

The page background, headers, and footers disappear, and a simpler view of the document content is displayed, at 100 percent magnification.

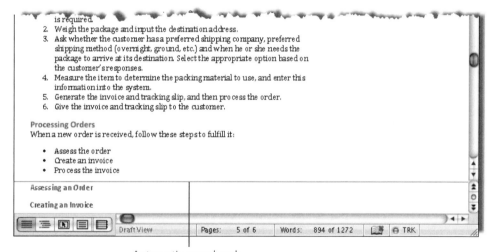

Automatic page break

Blue horizontal lines indicate automatic page breaks. A partial horizontal line and the words *Page Break* indicate a manual page break. You can see an example of this following the table of contents.

See Also For information about inserting discretionary page breaks, see "Insert Page and Section Breaks" in Chapter 11, "Format Office File Content."

25. Scroll through the document. Note the characteristics of Draft view and consider situations in which you will find it useful to work in this view.

26. On the **View** menu, click **Web Layout**. Scroll through this view of the document, which shows how it will appear in a Web browser if you save it as a Web page. When you finish, click **Print Layout** on the View menu to return to the original view.

 CLEAN UP Hide the ruler, and then close the *OfficeProcedures* document without saving your changes.

Practice Moving Around in Document Content

In this exercise, you'll practice ways of moving around in a Word document.

 SET UP Open the *BookSeries* document located in the *~/Documents/Microsoft Press/2008OfficeMacSBS/OfficePrograms/* folder.

1. In the document subtitle, click once at the end of the paragraph to position the insertion point.

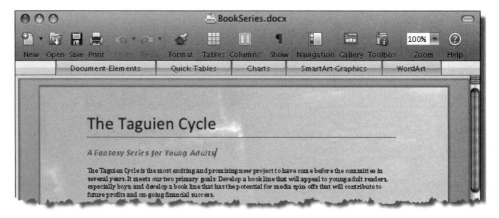

2. Press the **Home** key to move the insertion point to the beginning of the line.

3. Press the **Right Arrow** key two times to move the insertion point to the beginning of the word *Fantasy*.

4. Press **Option+Right Arrow** once to move to the beginning of the word *Series*.

5. Press the **End** key to move the insertion point to the end of the line.

6. Press **Command+End** to move the insertion point to the end of the document.

7. Press **Command+Home** to move the insertion point to the beginning of the document.

8. At the bottom of the vertical scroll bar, click the **Next Page** button to move to the top of the second page.

9. Click once in the vertical scroll bar above the scroll box to move the document up one screen.

   Note that the location of the insertion point does not change—only your view of the document changes.

10. Drag the vertical scroll box to the top of the vertical scroll bar.

    The beginning of the document comes into view.

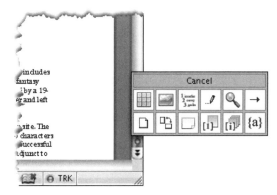

11. Click to the left of the title to place the insertion point at the beginning of the document, and then at the bottom of the vertical scroll bar, click the **Select Browse Object** button.

    A gallery of browsing choices opens. You can move to the next instance of an object by clicking the button that represents that object type.

12. Point to each button in the gallery.

    As you point to each button, the type of object it represents appears at the top of the gallery.

13. Click the **Browse by Page** button.

    The insertion point moves from the beginning of page 1 to the beginning of page 2.

CLEAN UP Close the *BookSeries* document and quit Word.

Word File Formats

When saving files in Word 2008, you can choose from several file formats. For most purposes, the Word Document (.docx) format will be appropriate; this is the Office Open XML Format compatible with Word 2008 for Mac and Word 2007 for Windows.

> **Tip** Microsoft Visual Basic for Applications (VBA) macros don't run in Word 2008, and the Word Document (.docx) file format doesn't save macro code. If your document includes VBA macro code that you want to preserve, save your file in the Word Macro-Enabled Document (.docm) or Word Macro-Enabled Template (.dotm) file format.

Other common file formats include:

- **Word 97–2004 Document (.doc).** The default document format for previous versions of Word (Word 98–Word 2004 for Mac and Word 97–Word 2003 for Windows).

- **Word Template (.dotx).** A format for XML-based templates containing document content and settings such as styles, page layout, AutoText entries, custom keyboard shortcut assignments, and menus.

- **Word 97–2004 Template (.dot).** The document template format for previous versions of Word (Word 98–Word 2004 for Mac and Word 97–Word 2003 for Windows).

View and Move Around in Excel Workbooks

Excel provides two views of worksheet content:

- **Normal view.** This view displays the content in each worksheet as one large cell grid. The ruler is not available in Normal view.

- **Page Layout view.** This is the default view for a new workbook. This view displays worksheet pages as they will appear when printed. Headers and footers are visible. Pages that do not contain content appear gray.

> **Tip** To change the default view, display the Excel Preferences dialog box and then, under Authoring, click View. On the View page, in the Settings area, choose the view you want from the Preferred View For New Sheets list. Then click OK.

- **Rich Text Format (.rtf).** A formatted document format that other applications, including compatible Microsoft programs, can read and interpret.

- **Plain Text (.txt).** An unformatted text file format that uses the Mac Extended ASCII character set. Select this format only if the destination program cannot read any of the other available file formats.

- **Web Page (.htm).** A format for HTML documents for display in a Web browser on a Macintosh or Windows computer.

- **Portable Document Format (PDF).** A file format that exactly preserves document content and formatting for display on any Mac or Windows computer.

Word 2008 also supports several specialty document formats:

- You can save a document in these formats: Word Macro-Enabled Document (.docm), Word Macro-Enabled Template (.dotm), Word XML Document (.xml), Word 2003 XML Document (.xml), Single File Web Page (.mht), Word Document Stationery (.doc), and Word 4.0–6.0/95 Compatible (.rtf).

- You can save files containing dictionary words and terms in the Speller Custom Dictionary (.dic) format or the Speller Exclude Dictionary (.dic) format.

- You can save the font, color scheme, and background of the document as an Office Theme (.thmx) that you can apply to another Office 2008 file.

Resources For more information about Word file formats, see the topic "File formats for saving documents" in the Word Help system.

You can switch between views of a worksheet by using the following methods:

→ On the **View** menu, click the name of the view you want.

→ On the View toolbar, click the button for the view you want.

 — Page Layout

Normal

Tip The View toolbar is located on the status bar. In Excel, you can hide the status bar—for example, to save screen real estate or simplify the window—by clicking Status Bar on the View menu. A check mark indicates when the status bar is active.

The following table lists several ways of using keyboard keys to move around in a worksheet. In addition to these methods, you can move between cells by pressing the Tab and Return keys. You can move one cell to the right by pressing the Tab key, or one cell to the left by pressing Shift+Tab. The Return key moves you to different locations depending on your recent activity, as follows:

- If you've been entering data vertically—for example, supplying information in one column of a worksheet—pressing the Return key moves down one cell.

- If you've been entering data horizontally—for example, creating a table of data or entering data in a table from left to right—pressing Return moves to the farthest left cell of the next row of the data entry range.

In addition to the Tab, Shift+Tab, and Return keyboard shortcuts, you can use the keyboard shortcuts described in the following table to move around in a worksheet or workbook, or between workbooks.

To move...	Press...
Up, down, left, or right one cell	Up Arrow, Down Arrow, Left Arrow, or Right Arrow
To an edge of the current data region	Control+Arrow key
To the beginning of the row	Home
To the beginning of the sheet	Control+Home
To the last populated cell (the intersection of the rightmost column of data and the bottom row of data)	Control+End
Up or down one screen	Page Up or Page Down
To the left one screen	Option+Page Up
To the right one screen	Option+Page Down
To the next worksheet	Control+Page Down
To the previous worksheet	Control+Page Up
To the next pane in a split worksheet	F6
To the previous pane	Shift+F6
To the next workbook or window	Control+Tab
To the previous workbook or window	Control+Shift+Tab

To move to a specific cell, named range, or worksheet element:

1. Press **Control+G** to open the **Go To** dialog box.

2. Click the location you want to jump to, or enter a cell reference in the **Reference** box.

   Or

   Click the **Special** button to display the **Go To Special** dialog box. Then select the type of element you want to locate.

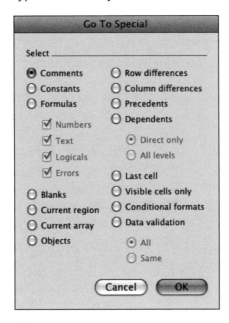

3. Click **OK**.

Maximize Screen Real Estate

When working with a large amount of data, with multiple workbooks, or on a small screen, the amount of available desktop working space—the screen real estate—becomes quite valuable. You can increase the available horizontal and vertical space in an Excel workbook window in several ways. The following table lists ways of increasing screen real estate.

Space savings	Action	Method
Horizontal and vertical	Display the window at a large size	Click Full Screen on the View menu. Or Click the Maximize button at the left end of the title bar.
Horizontal and vertical	Decrease the magnification level	Click 75%, 50%, or smaller in the Zoom list.
Horizontal and vertical	Work in Normal view	Click the Normal View button on the View toolbar.
Horizontal and vertical	Hide the row and column headings	In the Page Setup panel of the Formatting Palette, clear the View check box to the right of Headings. Or On the View page of the Excel Preferences dialog box, in the Window Options area, clear the Show Row And Column Headings check box, and then click OK.
Vertical	Hide the Formula Bar	On the View page of the Excel Preferences dialog box, in the Settings area, clear the Show Formula Bar check box, and then click OK.

Space savings	Action	Method
Vertical	Close the Elements Gallery	Click the Gallery button on the toolbar. Or Click Elements Gallery on the View menu.
Vertical	Hide the toolbar area	Click Full Screen on the View menu. Or Deselect all the toolbars on the Toolbars submenu of the View menu or on the toolbar area context menu.
Vertical	Hide the status bar	On the View page of the Excel Preferences dialog box, in the Settings area, clear the Show Status Bar check box, and then click OK.
Vertical	Hide the sheet tabs	On the View page of the Excel Preferences dialog box, in the Window Options area, clear the Show Sheet Tabs check box, and then click OK.
Vertical	Hide the horizontal scroll bar	On the View page of the Excel Preferences dialog box, in the Window Options area, clear the Show Horizontal Scroll Bar check box, and then click OK.
Horizontal	Hide the vertical scroll bar	On the View page of the Excel Preferences dialog box, in the Window Options area, clear the Show Vertical Scroll Bar check box, and then click OK.

The net effect of making all of the above changes is a workbook window displaying only the title bar, the Elements Gallery tabs, and the worksheet content.

Practice Viewing and Moving Around in Workbooks

In this exercise, you'll look at different views of an Excel workbook and experiment with ways you can move around in workbooks and worksheets. You'll create a second instance of a workbook and open another workbook; then you'll have Excel arrange the open windows in various ways. You can use many of the techniques you'll practice in this exercise in other Office 2008 programs.

> **SET UP** This exercise uses the *InvestmentCalculator* and *Loan* workbooks located in the *~/Documents/Microsoft Press/2008OfficeMacSBS/OfficePrograms/* folder. Start Excel, and then follow the steps below.

1. Open the *InvestmentCalculator* workbook.

    The workbook opens in Page Layout view.

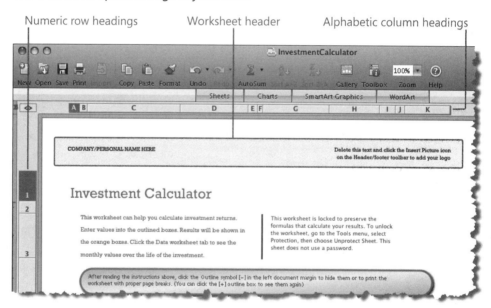

2. If the entire page width isn't visible as shown in the preceding graphic, click the green **Restore** button on the left end of the window header and then, in the **Zoom** list, click **100%**.

    This workbook includes two worksheets: *Investment Calculator* and *Data*. The worksheet header information is visible at the top of the worksheet, above Row 1.

3. Click the **Data** worksheet tab.

The information on this worksheet occupies a total of 16 pages: 2 pages across and 8 pages down.

4. On the **View** menu, click **Formula Bar**.

The Formula Bar opens below the Excel menu bar. Notice that the Formula Bar, unlike most toolbars, is not integrated into the workbook window. It remains visible when Excel is active, regardless of whether a workbook is open.

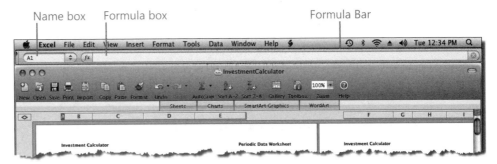

5. Press **Command+End** to move to the last occupied cell on the worksheet.

> **Tip** By pressing Command+End, you can locate content that's outside of your intended worksheet layout.

The cell reference (F364) appears in the Name box on the Formula Bar, and the formula calculating the cell value ($325,235.79) appears in the formula box.

6. Drag the vertical scroll box to the bottom of the scroll bar.

The worksheet content in the window moves so that only the last row is visible.

7. Click the **Scroll Up** button on the vertical scroll bar three times.

Rows 361 through 364 (displaying periods 357 through 361) are visible.

8. Click one time at the end of the content in the formula box.

The formula appears in cell F364 in place of its results. Cell references in the formula, and the corresponding cells in the worksheet, are identified by color.

9. Click anywhere in the formula.

A ScreenTip displays the correct formula syntax.

References to cells in other
worksheets don't change color

Formula syntax

Color coding maps cell
references to worksheet cells

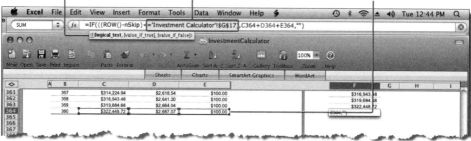

See Also   For information about Excel formulas, see Chapter 9, "Create Excel Formulas."

 10. Press the **Escape** key to deactivate the Formula Bar without making changes. Then click the red **Close** button at the left end of the Formula Bar to close it.

Display Formulas in a Worksheet

You can turn on a feature that enables the display of formulas directly in worksheet cells rather than only in the Formula Bar.

To turn on the formula display feature:

1. Click **Preferences** on the **Excel** menu (or press **Command+Comma**).

2. In the **Excel Preferences** dialog box, under **Authoring**, click **View**.

3. In the **View** dialog box, in the **Window options** area, select the **Show formulas** check box. Then click **OK**.

After you turn on the feature, you can toggle the display of formulas by pressing Control+` (the grave accent character found under the tilde, to the left of the number 1 key, on most keyboards).

> **Tip**   If the status bar that contains the View toolbar is hidden, click Status Bar on the View menu to display it.

---

 11. On the View toolbar in the lower-left corner of the workbook window, click the **Normal View** button.

The page layout representations, such as the headers and page margins, disappear.

12. Press the **Home** key to move to cell A364, at the beginning of the active row.

13. Press the **Page Up** key twice to move up two screens.

14. Press **Control+Page Up** to move to the *Investment Calculator* worksheet.

15. On the **Window** menu, click **New Window**.

Excel opens a second instance of the *InvestmentCalculator* workbook and appends numbers to the workbook names in the window title bars.

16. Drag the *InvestmentCalculator:2* window down, by its title bar, so both windows are visible.

17. In the *InvestmentCalculator:2* window, click the **Data** worksheet tab.

18. On the **File** menu, point to **Open Recent**, and then in the list, click *Loan.xlsx*.

> **Troubleshooting** If the Loan workbook doesn't appear in the Open Recent list, open it from the *~/Documents/Microsoft Press/2008OfficeMacSBS/OfficePrograms/* folder.

You now have three open Excel workbook windows, containing different content, arranged in layers.

19. On the **Window** menu, click **Arrange**.

The Arrange Windows dialog box opens, depicting the most recent arrangement selection. If you haven't previously arranged windows, the Tiled arrangement is selected.

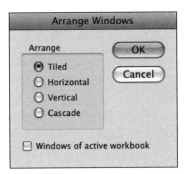

20. In the **Arrange** area, click **Tiled**. Then click **OK**.

Excel arranges the workbook windows so that all three are visible. In a tiled layout with an odd number of windows, the workbook that is active at the time of the arrangement (in this case, the Loan workbook) occupies the largest window.

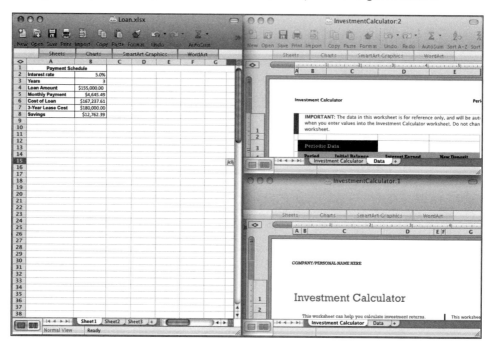

21. Open the **Arrange** dialog box, click **Cascade**, and then click **OK**.

Excel stacks the three windows in neat layers, with the title bar of each window visible.

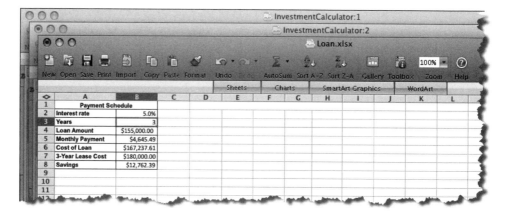

22. Press **Control+Tab** to cycle through the open windows. End with the *InvestmentCalculator:2* window active.

23. Open the **Arrange** dialog box, click **Vertical,** and select the **Windows of active workbook** check box. Then click **OK.**

Excel arranges only the two *InvestmentCalculator* windows in vertical columns.

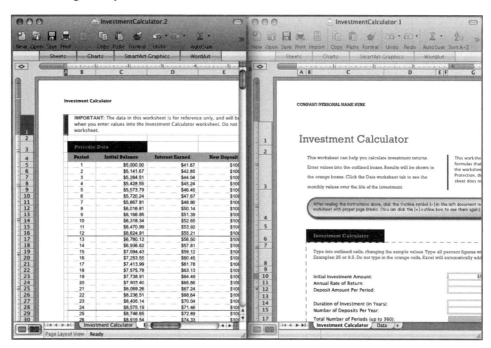

24. Close either of the *InvestmentCalculator* windows.

The window number disappears from the end of the workbook name in the title bar of the remaining window.

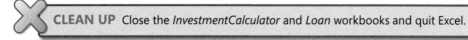

CLEAN UP Close the *InvestmentCalculator* and *Loan* workbooks and quit Excel.

Excel File Formats

When saving files in Excel 2008, you can choose from many file formats. For a standard workbook, the new Office Open XML Format common to Excel 2008 for Mac and Excel 2007 for Windows, Excel Workbook (.xlsx), provides the most functionality and is the best choice, provided you don't need to share the file with people using an earlier version of Excel.

> **Tip** VBA macros don't run in Excel 2008, and the Excel Workbook (.xlsx) file format doesn't save macro code or Excel 4.0 macro sheets. If your workbook includes VBA macro code that you want to preserve, save your file in the Excel 97–2004 Workbook (.xls), Excel 97–2004 Template (.xlt), Excel Macro-Enabled Workbook (.xlsm), Excel Macro-Enabled Template (.xltm), Excel 5.0/95 Workbook (.xls), or Excel 97–2004 & 5.0/95 Workbook (.xls) file format. When saving a worksheet containing macro code that you want to preserve, use the Excel Add-In (.xlam) or Excel 97–2004 Add-In (.xla) file format.

Other common file formats include:

- **Excel 97–2004 Workbook (.xls).** The default workbook format for previous versions of Excel (Excel 98–Excel 2004 for Mac and Excel 97–Excel 2003 for Windows).

- **Excel Template (.xltx).** A format for XML-based templates containing workbook settings such as formatting, headings, formulas, and custom toolbars.

- **Excel 97–2004 Template (.xlt).** The workbook template format for previous versions of Excel (Excel 98–Excel 2004 for Mac and Excel 97–Excel 2003 for Windows).

- **Comma Separated Values (.csv).** An unformatted file format containing the data from the active worksheet, with cell values separated by commas.

- **Web Page (.htm).** A formatted HTML document format for display in a Web browser on a Macintosh or Windows computer.

- **Portable Document Format (PDF).** A file format that exactly preserves document content and formatting for display on any Mac or Windows computer.

Excel 2008 also supports several specialty workbook and worksheet formats:

- You can save a workbook in the following formats: Excel Binary Workbook (.xlsb), Excel Macro-Enabled Workbook (.xlsm), Excel Macro-Enabled Template (.xltm), Excel 2004 XML Spreadsheet (.xml), Single File Web Page (.mht), Excel 5.0/95 Workbook (.xls), and Excel 97–2004 & 5.0/95 Workbook (.xls).

- You can save or export the data on the active worksheet in the following formats: Excel Add-In (.xlam), Excel 97–2004 Add-In (.xla), UTF-16 Unicode Text (.txt), Tab Delimited Text (.txt), Windows Formatted Text (.txt), MS-DOS Formatted Text (.txt), Windows Comma Separated (.csv), MS-DOS Comma Separated (.csv), Space Delimited Text (.prn), Data Interchange Format (.dif), and Symbolic Link (.slk).

Resources For more information about Excel file formats, see the topic "File formats for saving workbooks" in the Excel Help system.

View and Move Around in PowerPoint Presentations

PowerPoint provides four views of presentation content. You can edit slide content in these two views:

- **Normal view.** This is the default view. This view displays three panes:
  - ○ The Navigation pane, which displays either the Slides page showing thumbnails of the slides in the active presentation or the Outline page showing an outline view of the text in the presentation.
  - ○ The Slide pane, which shows the currently selected slide as it will appear in the presentation.
  - ○ The Notes pane, which provides a place for entering notes about the current slide. These notes might be related to the development of the slide or they might be speaker notes that you will refer to when delivering the presentation.

  You can change the size of the panes in Normal view by dragging the splitter bars between the Navigation pane and the Slide pane left or right, and by dragging the splitter bar between the Slide pane and the Notes pane up or down. You can close the Navigation pane by clicking the Close button in its upper-right corner, and restore it by clicking the Normal view button on the View toolbar.

- **Slide view.** This view displays the current slide at the maximum size supported by the open presentation window.

> **Tip** Slide view is not available from the View menu or from the View toolbar. You can access it only by using the keyboard shortcut Control+Shift+C.

You can't edit slide content in the following two views:

- **Slide Sorter view.** This view displays thumbnails of every slide in the presentation. You can insert and delete slides; rearrange slides by dragging, copying, cutting, and pasting; and select multiple slides to set a common property, such as a transition or a theme.

- **Slide Show view.** This view displays the full-screen slide show of your presentation.

See Also For information about entering text on PowerPoint slides, see "Add Content to Slides" in Chapter 6, "Create PowerPoint Presentations."

You can switch between views of a presentation by using the following methods:

→ On the **View** menu, click the name of the view you want.

→ On the View toolbar, click the button for the view you want.

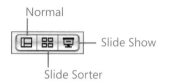

To move between slides, do any of the following:

● On the **Slides** page of the Navigation pane, use the vertical scroll bar on the right side of the Navigation pane to access all the slides. Click the slide you want to display.

● Use the vertical scroll bar on the right side of the Slide pane.

● Click the **Previous Slide** or **Next Slide** button at the bottom of the Slide pane scroll bar.

● Press the **Up Arrow**, **Left Arrow**, or **Page Up** key to move to the previous slide, and the **Down Arrow**, **Right Arrow**, or **Page Down** key to move to the next slide.

When a text box is active, you can use the keyboard shortcuts described in the following table to move around in slide text.

To move...	Press...
To the left one charactert	Left Arrow
To the right one character	Right Arrow
To the beginning of the current word, or to the left one word	Option+Left Arrow
To the right one word	Option+Right Arrow
To the beginning of a line	Home
To the end of a line	End
Up one line	Up Arrow
Down one line	Down Arrow
To the beginning of a paragraph, or up one paragraph	Option+Up Arrow
Down one paragraph	Option+Down Arrow
To the beginning of a text box	Option+Home
To the end of a text box	Option+End

Practice Viewing and Moving Around in Presentations

In this exercise, you'll look at different views of a PowerPoint presentation and experiment with ways you can move around in presentations and on slides.

> **SET UP** This exercise uses the *Introducing* presentation located in the *~/Documents/ Microsoft Press/2008OfficeMacSBS/OfficePrograms/* folder. Start PowerPoint, and then follow the steps below.

1. Open the *Introducing* presentation.

   The presentation opens in Normal view. In the lower-right corner of the presentation window, PowerPoint displays the total number of slides and the position of the current slide. The current slide is indicated in the Navigation pane by a blue selection box.

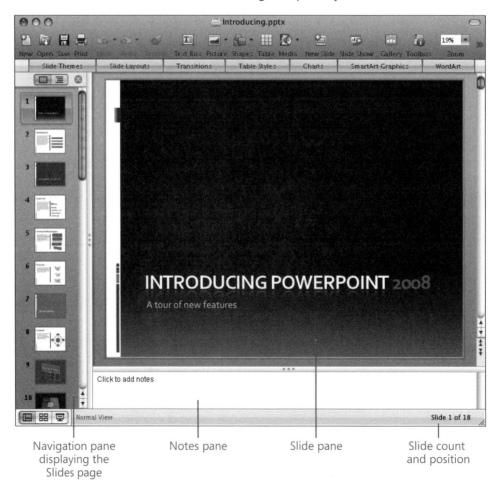

Navigation pane displaying the Slides page

Notes pane

Slide pane

Slide count and position

2. In the Navigation pane, on the Slides page, click **Slide 8**.

> **Tip** You can scroll the Navigation pane to bring more thumbnails into view.

 3. At the bottom of the scroll bar on the right side of the Slide pane, click the **Next Slide** button to move to **Slide 9**.

 4. Click the **Previous Slide** button to move back to **Slide 8**.

5. Drag the Slide pane scroll box slowly down to the bottom of the scroll bar, releasing the mouse button when the **Slide 18** ScreenTip appears.

As you move down the scroll bar, a ScreenTip tells you the number and title (if there is one) of the slide that will be displayed if you release the mouse button at that point.

6. Press the **Page Up** key until **Slide 14** appears.

7. Click and hold at the top end of the Slide pane scroll bar.

PowerPoint moves through all the slides in the presentation and ends with Slide 1.

 8. In the Navigation pane, click the **Outline** button.

The Navigation pane changes to display the Outline page. The current slide is indicated in the Navigation pane by a gray selection box.

9. Press the **Right Arrow** key to move to **Slide 2**. Compare the content in the Navigation pane with the content shown on the slide.

The Outline page displays the slide title and the text contained in the text box.

10. In the Navigation pane, click the number, icon, title, or text for **Slide 4**.

Slide 4 appears in the Slide pane. Clicking any part of the slide representation on the Outline page displays the slide.

11. Press **Control+Shift+X**.

The Navigation pane expands to fill about 75 percent of the presentation window. This view is useful when you want to view or edit the text of several slides at one time.

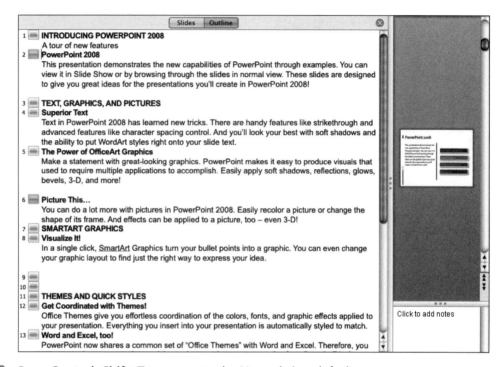

12. Press **Control+Shift+Z** to return to the Normal view defaults.

13. Right-click an empty area of the Navigation pane, point to **Collapse**, and then click **Collapse All**.

The Outline page of the Navigation pane now displays only the slide titles. Slides containing only graphics don't have a title, only a slide number and icon.

The current slide is indicated in the Navigation pane by a light blue selection box.

Selection box

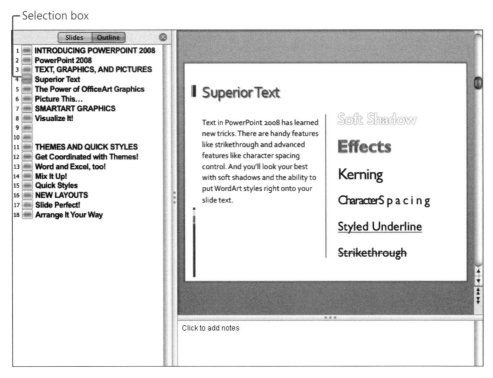

 14. On the View toolbar in the lower-left corner of the presentation window, click the **Slide Sorter View** button (or press **Control+Shift+V**).

The Navigation pane and Notes pane close. All the slides now appear as thumbnails in one large pane. The current slide is indicated in the Slides pane by a light blue selection box.

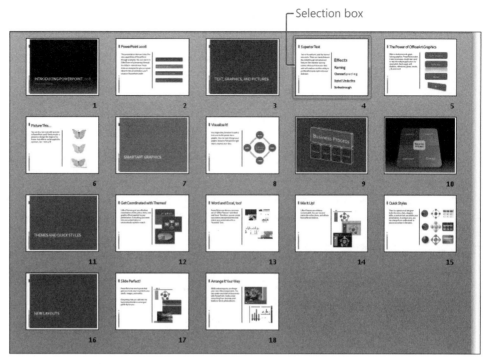

Selection box

15. Double-click **Slide 15**.

PowerPoint displays the presentation in Normal view, with Slide 15 active.

16. Press **Control+Shift+C** to switch to Slide view.

The Navigation pane and Notes pane close. PowerPoint displays the current slide at the maximum size supported by the presentation window.

17. On the View toolbar, click the **Slide Show** button (or press **Control+Shift+S**).

PowerPoint displays a full-screen view of the first slide in the presentation.

PowerPoint File Formats

From PowerPoint 2008, you can save a presentation in many different formats. PowerPoint Presentation (.pptx) is the new Office XML File Format for PowerPoint 2008 for Mac and PowerPoint 2007 for Windows. This default format provides the most functionality.

> **Tip** VBA macros don't run in PowerPoint 2008, and the PowerPoint Presentation (.pptx) file format doesn't save macro code. If your presentation includes VBA macro code that you want to preserve, save your file in the PowerPoint Macro-Enabled Presentation (.pptm), PowerPoint Macro-Enabled Template (.potm), or PowerPoint Macro-Enabled Show (.ppsm) file format.

Other common file formats include:

- **PowerPoint 97–2004 Presentation (.ppt).** The default presentation format for previous versions of PowerPoint (PowerPoint 98–PowerPoint 2004 for Mac and PowerPoint 97–PowerPoint 2003 for Windows).

- **PowerPoint Template (.potx).** A format for XML-based templates containing presentation settings such as fonts, color schemes, slide layouts, and graphics.

- **PowerPoint 97–2004 Template (.pot).** The presentation template format for previous versions of PowerPoint (PowerPoint 98–PowerPoint 2004 for Mac and PowerPoint 97–PowerPoint 2003 for Windows).

- **PowerPoint Package.** A format for a portable package of all the files required by your presentation, including images, sound, and movies.

- **Movie (.mov).** An animated video format that you can play in the QuickTime Player.

- **Web Page (.htm).** A formatted HTML document format for display in a Web browser on a Macintosh or Windows computer.

- **Portable Document Format (PDF).** A file format that exactly preserves document content and formatting for display on any Macintosh or Windows computer.

PowerPoint 2008 also supports several specialty presentation formats:

- You can save a presentation in any of the following formats: PowerPoint Show (.ppsx), PowerPoint 97–2004 Show (.pps), PowerPoint Macro-Enabled Presentation (.pptm), PowerPoint Macro-Enabled Template (.potm), PowerPoint Macro-Enabled Show (.ppsm), and Outline/Rich Text Format (.rtf).

- You can save or export the slides of a presentation as individual files in any of the following formats: JPEG Image (.jpg), Portable Network Graphics (.png), Graphics Interchange Format (.gif), Bitmap (.bmp), and Tagged Image File (.tif).

- You can save the font, color scheme, and background of the presentation as an Office Theme (.thmx) that you can apply to another Office 2008 file.

Resources For more information about PowerPoint file formats, see the topic "File formats for saving presentations" in the PowerPoint Help system.

18. Move the mouse.

The pointer becomes visible, and the Slide Show Options button appears in the lower-left corner of the screen. Clicking this button displays a list of slide show options.

See Also For information about presenting a slide show, see "Run a Slide Show" in Chapter 10, "Work with PowerPoint Slide Content."

19. Click anywhere on the slide (not on the Slide Show Options button).

The slide show advances to the next slide.

20. Press the **Right Arrow** key.

The slide show advances to the next slide.

21. Continue through the presentation, using any of the following methods:

- To advance to the next slide, press **N**, **Return**, **Page Down**, **Right Arrow**, **Down Arrow**, or the **Spacebar**, or click the mouse.

- To return to the previous slide, press **P**, **Page Up**, **Left Arrow**, **Up Arrow**, or **Delete**.

As you move through the presentation, read the information on the slides to gain a better overview of PowerPoint 2008 and the variety of features we'll discuss later in this book.

> **Tip** To stop a slide show before you reach the end, press the Escape key.

After the last slide, the slide show closes and you return to Slide view.

> **Tip** If you prefer, you can have PowerPoint end all slide shows with a black slide so that you have time to wrap up before closing the presentation. To turn on this function, display the PowerPoint Preferences dialog box, click the View button, and in the Slide Show area, select the End With Black Slide check box. Then click OK.

 CLEAN UP Switch to Normal view and display the Slides page in the Navigation pane. Then close the *Introducing* presentation without saving your changes, and quit PowerPoint.

Key Points

- Each Office program offers a variety of ways to view and move around through the Office files you are working with. You can move around by using the mouse or convenient keyboard shortcuts.

- Word, Excel, and PowerPoint each offer multiple views of files. You can easily switch between views by clicking the buttons on the View toolbar at the left end of the status bar.

- In Word, the default view is Print Layout view. In this view a document appears on your screen exactly as it will appear on the printed page. You can also work with documents in Draft, Outline, and Web Layout views.

- Print Layout view is also the default view of Excel workbooks. In Print Layout view, you can display horizontal and vertical rulers that indicate the boundaries of the printed page and other information. Another option is to view a worksheet in Normal view, which displays one large cell grid.

- The default view of a PowerPoint presentation is Normal view. In Normal view, you have access to a list of slides or an outline of the presentation in the Navigation pane, an editable version of the active slide, and an area in which you can enter speaker notes associated with the slide. You can also display slides at full window size in Slide view, display thumbnails of the entire presentation in Slide Sorter view, or display a slide show of the presentation in Slide Show view.

Part II
Create Basic Office Files

4 Create Word Documents 121

5 Create Excel Workbooks. 155

6 Create PowerPoint Presentations 181

Chapter at a Glance

Create a basic document, **page 122**

Work with Word publications, **page 136**

Create a document from a project template, **page 132**

4 Create Word Documents

In this chapter, you will learn how to

- ✔ Create a basic document.
- ✔ Create a document from a project template.
- ✔ Work with Word publications.
- ✔ Work with Word notebooks.
- ✔ Create a personalized project template.

Microsoft Word is the most popular word-processing program in use today. In the beginning, Word provided a welcome improvement on the traditional typewriter, allowing changes and corrections within a document, without the use of correction fluid. As we continue moving toward the concept of a "paperless" society, Word has grown into a rich, fully featured program that makes it easy to create attractive, well-organized documents that are ideal for a variety of distribution methods.

In this chapter, we'll explore the various documents you can create in Microsoft Word 2008 for Mac. We'll start from scratch with a blank document and investigate the *properties* that are already assigned to the document when you create it. Then we'll explore ways of entering text—from scratch, from the document properties, and from another file or program. We'll investigate the variety of complex and useful documents available as templates from the Microsoft Project Gallery, and wrap up the chapter by creating templates of your own.

See Also You can find handy keyboard shortcuts, simple instructions for performing common tasks, and other useful information in the Quick Reference section at the beginning of this book.

Practice Makes Perfect! The practice file you will use to complete the exercises in this chapter is in the *CreateDocuments* practice file folder. See "Using the Companion Content" at the beginning of this book for information about installing and locating the practice files.

Create a Basic Document

Although Microsoft Word 2008 for Mac is the simplest program to use in the Home & Student Edition of Microsoft Office 2008 for Mac, its capabilities are vast. In its most basic format, a Word document might be nothing more than a page of text, much like you would create on a typewriter (for those of us who remember that far back). You can modify simple text by adding character formatting, such as colored fonts and bold or italic effects, and paragraph formatting, such as alignment and spacing.

The basic Word document supports content such as formatted text and graphics, lists and tables, page formatting, electronic bookmarks and hyperlinks that are available when viewing the file electronically (for example, on a computer, through a Web browser, or through a mobile application), fields displaying dynamic content, functions, and formulas. Word offers a variety of file storage and delivery options. You can save a document in a simpler format, such as a text file; in a secure format, such as a PDF file; or in a more complex format, such as a Web page.

Create a Document

When Word starts, a new temporary document opens: either a blank document, a blank Notebook Layout document, or a blank Publishing Layout document, depending on which you were last working in. You can create a new document of one of these types by selecting the document type from the New list on the toolbar.

A new blank document created in Word 2008 looks like nothing more than a blank page, but in reality it already contains a variety of information, such as styles, margins, and properties. Some of this information is pulled from your user information, and some is stored as part of the *document template* on which the blank document is based.

> **Note** The default document template is *Normal.dotm*. In the file extension, *dot* stands for *document template*, and the *m* indicates that it's a *macro-enabled* template.

You can see the information associated with a document in various places, including the Properties dialog box, the Page Setup dialog box, and the Style dialog box.

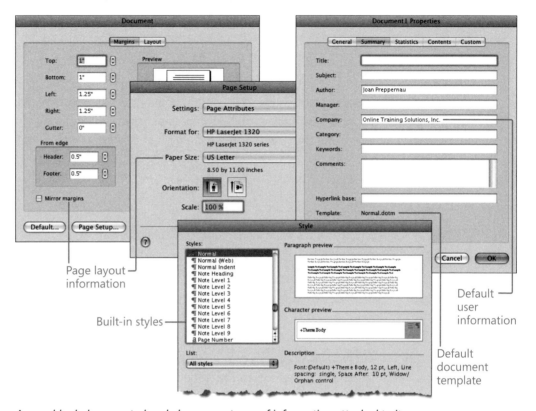

Page layout information

Built-in styles

Default user information

Default document template

A new, blank document already has many types of information attached to it.

See Also For information about document templates, see "Manage Document Templates" in Chapter 7, "Work with Word Document Content."

Enter Text

The blinking insertion point in the document window indicates the location where the next *character* (or image, table, or other document element) you enter will appear. When the insertion point reaches the right margin, the word you are typing moves to the next line. To start a new *paragraph*, you press the Return key. To start a new line but not a new paragraph, you can insert a manual line break by pressing Shift+Return.

When you are viewing hidden characters in a document, a paragraph mark indicates the end of each paragraph containing text, an image, or other content, and a bent arrow indicates a manual line break within a paragraph. These characters are visible when hidden text is shown.

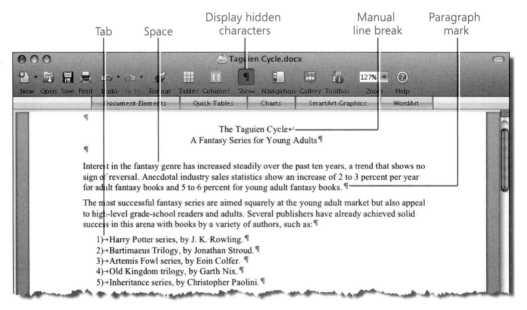

A paragraph mark indicates the end of a paragraph. A bent arrow indicates a manual line break.

The paragraph mark carries with it the formatting assigned to that paragraph. In the days before the *Format Painter*, a simple way of transferring multiple paragraph format settings to another paragraph was to copy the paragraph mark at the end of the source paragraph and paste it at the end of the target paragraph.

See Also For information about paragraph formatting, see "Format Paragraphs" in Chapter 11, "Format Office File Content." For information about the Format Painter, see the sidebar "Apply Existing Formatting to Other Content," also in Chapter 11.

The basic method of entering text into a document is by typing. You can also insert text that you cut, copy, or *import* from another file, text that has been saved as *AutoText*, or the document properties and other information saved with the document.

See Also For information about saving text as AutoText, see "Word Tools and Preferences" in Chapter 1, "Explore and Manage the Office Interface." For information about inserting images, see Chapter 12, "Create and Insert Graphics."

Insert or Link To External Content

You can easily incorporate the text of one document into another, without opening the source document, by inserting or linking to the source file:

- Inserting a file inserts the entire contents of the source file into your document at the insertion point, retaining the paragraph and character formatting of the source file.

- Linking to a file inserts a field displaying the contents of the linked file, with character and paragraph formatting intact. Content and formatting changes made to the linked file are reflected in your document when you update the field. You can edit the linked content in your document, but any changes you make will be overwritten when you update the field.

You can insert or link to content created in other programs, such as Microsoft Excel. Word converts the contents of the source file to text before inserting the content or the link to the content.

Practice Creating and Populating Documents

In this exercise, you'll create a new document, look at the information already contained in the document, and then add content to it by typing and by inserting the contents of an external file.

> **SET UP** You'll create your own practice file in this exercise, and also use the *AnnouncePlanner* document located in the *~/Documents/Microsoft Press/2008OfficeMacSBS/CreateDocuments/* folder. Quit Word if it's running, so we can start from scratch.

1. Start Word.

   When Word starts, a temporary document named *Document1* opens in the default Print Layout view. Blank documents created during each program session are numbered consecutively, regardless of the document type.

   See Also For information about different ways of viewing a Word document, see "Change the View" in Chapter 2, "Practice Basic Office File Skills."

2. On the toolbar, click the **New** arrow.

   The New list expands to display the types of blank documents you can create.

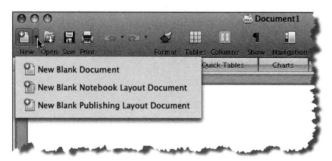

> **Tip** Each document type is represented in the New list by a *slightly* different icon: the New Blank Document icon is a blank page, the New Blank Notebook Layout Document icon is a lined page, and the New Blank Publishing Layout Document icon is a page with the print area outlined. On the toolbar, the New button displays the icon of the most recently created document type. You can create a new document of that type by clicking the button instead of the arrow.

3. In the **New** list, click **New Blank Document**.

   A second temporary document, *Document2*, opens. Both of the open documents exist only in the computer's temporary memory until you save and name them.

4. On the Word menu bar, on the **File** menu, click **Properties**.

   The Document2 Properties dialog box opens, displaying the Summary page.

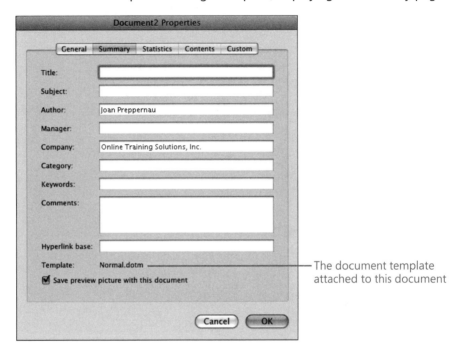

The document template attached to this document

5. Look at the **General**, **Summary**, **Statistics**, **Contents**, and **Custom** pages of the dialog box to see the information that is already stored with the blank document.

   You can change the current properties, or enter additional information that you want to save with the document, on the Summary page and on the Custom page.

6. In the **Document2 Properties** dialog box, click **Cancel**.

7. On the **Format** menu, click **Document**.

The Document dialog box opens.

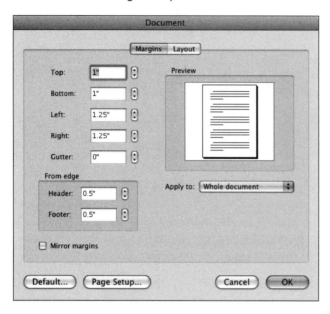

The page margins and header and footer location have been set by the currently attached document template, *Normal.dotm*.

8. In the **Document** dialog box, click **Cancel**.

9. On the **View** menu, point to **Toolbars**, and then click **Formatting**.

The Formatting toolbar opens at the top of the document window, below the Standard toolbar.

10. With the insertion point blinking at the beginning of the new document, type Decorators, Get Ready for a Change!

The text appears in the new document. On the Formatting toolbar, you can see the style and alignment of the current paragraph and the font, font size, and font formatting of the text, all of which have been set by the *Normal* document template.

Paragraph style   Font name, size, and formatting   Paragraph alignment

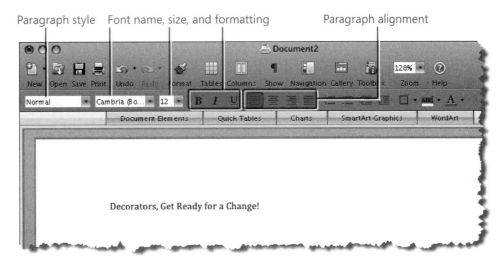

Decorators, Get Ready for a Change!

11. Press the **Return** key to begin a new paragraph. Then type With spring just around the corner, let's start making those home decor changes you've been thinking about all winter.

When you press the Spacebar after typing the letters d-e-c-o-r, Word changes the word from *decor* (with a plain "e") to *décor* (with an accented "é"). This occurred because the word pairing *decor/décor* is in the standard *AutoCorrect* word list.

See Also For information about the AutoCorrect, AutoFormat, and AutoText functions, see "Word Tools and Preferences" and "Personalize Program Functionality" in Chapter 1, "Explore and Manage the Office Interface."

12. Press the **Spacebar**, and then type Let's introduce fresh new color. Let's add some accessories. Let's come up with a great plan for a room to love.

Notice that you did not need to press Return when the insertion point reached the right margin, because the text wrapped to the next line.

> **Note** If a red wavy line appears under a word or phrase, Word is flagging a possible error. For now, ignore any errors.

13. Press **Return** to begin a new paragraph. Then on the **Insert** menu, click **File**.

> **Note** The ellipsis (...) following the File command indicates that clicking the command opens a dialog box and requires further action on your part.

The Insert File dialog box opens, displaying its most recent configuration and file storage location.

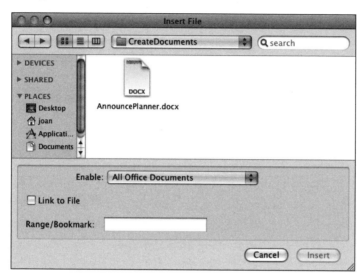

14. If the dialog box doesn't already display the contents of the *~/Documents/ Microsoft Press/2008OfficeMacSBS/CreateDocuments/* folder, navigate to that folder. Then click (don't double-click) the *AnnouncePlanner* document.

See Also For information about dialog box views and navigation, see "Open, Save, and Close Office Files" in Chapter 2, "Practice Basic Office File Skills."

At the bottom of the dialog box, notice the options to link to the file and to insert or link to a specific range of content in the file.

15. In the **Insert File** dialog box, click **Insert**.

Word inserts the contents of the selected document. The inserted text retains the font formatting of the original document.

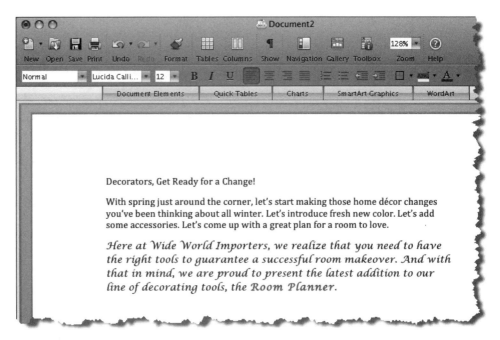

16. On the Standard toolbar, click the **Save** button.

The Save As dialog box descends, displaying the contents of the *CreateDocuments* folder. In the Save As box, Word suggests *Decorators*, the first word in the document, as a possible name for this file.

17. With *Decorators* selected in the **Save As** box, type Planner Announcement.

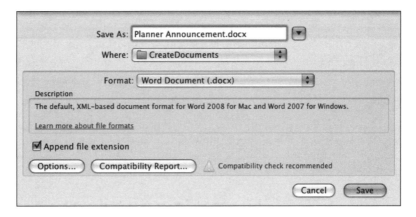

See Also Your Save As dialog box might look different from the one shown here. For information about expanding and working in the Save As dialog box, see "Open, Save, and Close Office Files" in Chapter 2, "Practice Basic Office File Skills."

18. In the **Save As** dialog box, click **Save**.

The Save As dialog box closes, Word saves the file in the *CreateDocuments* folder, and the name of the document, *Planner Announcement*, appears on the title bar of the document window.

 CLEAN UP Hide the Formatting toolbar. Then close the *Planner Announcement* file and the *Document1* file.

Create a Document from a Project Template

When you want to quickly create an effective, visually attractive document, one of the most efficient methods is to leverage design work already done for you by other people. (Although this might be considered plagiarism in another context, Microsoft is quite willing to let you take credit for all the hard work when you produce a document using their designs.)

The Project Gallery

The Project Gallery, installed with Microsoft Office 2008 for Mac, gives you access to approximately 160 ready-made, professionally designed project templates, as well as Office files that you've recently accessed. (Not all the templates are for Word projects—some are for Microsoft Excel 2008, Microsoft PowerPoint 2008, and Microsoft Entourage 2008.) Some of these projects can be used as is; others are designed as *templates* to which you must add your own information. You can personalize any aspect of any project by changing the text, formatting, size, shape, and other design elements.

See Also This topic discusses the pre-populated project templates available from the Project Gallery. We'll specifically discuss document templates—the base files that define styles within a document—in "Manage Document Templates" in Chapter 7, "Work with Word Document Content."

To open the Project Gallery, click the Microsoft Project Gallery icon in the Dock, or open it from the */Applications/Microsoft Office 2008/Office/* folder.

Project Gallery pages   Search for a specific template

Category list   Template list   Filter by file type

The New page of the Project Gallery in Thumbnails view. You can change the display of project templates in the Template list by clicking the View buttons located above the Category list.

The Project Gallery includes four pages:

- The New page displays project templates for creating new Office documents.

- The Recent page displays a list of Office files you have worked with in the past two months. You can filter the list by day or week.

- From the Project Center page, you can open Office files that are part of a project you have set up in the Project Center.

- From the Settings page, you can refine the default Project Gallery settings and specify the types of templates and wizards you want to have available.

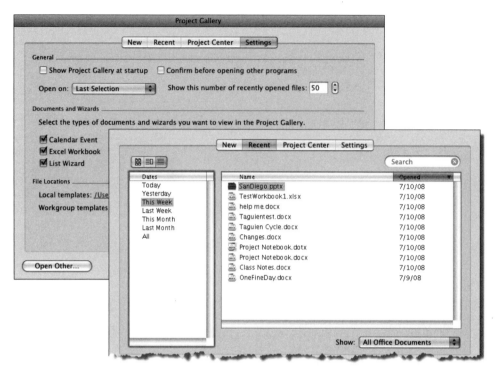

From the Project Gallery, you can create new documents or locate and open recent documents.

Three views of the Project Gallery are available:

- **Thumbnails view** displays (you guessed it) thumbnail views and names of the project templates that fit the current filter or search criteria. In this view, a maximum of six thumbnails are visible in the Template list at a time. This is the default view.

- **Details view** displays the names and file types of the category's project templates, and the thumbnail, name, file type, file size, and creation/modification dates of the selected template. In this view, up to 14 templates are visible in the Template list at a time.

- **List view** displays only the names and file types of the category's project templates. Up to 14 templates are visible in the Template list.

The Category list is displayed on the left side of the Project Gallery in all three views.

Project Templates

Clicking a category or subcategory in the Category list displays project templates of that type in the Template list. By default, project templates of all types are visible. You can filter the Template list to display templates for only a certain program by selecting that program from the Show list. If no templates of the selected category and file type are available, the Template list displays a generic graphic in Thumbnails view or a blank list in Details view or List view.

In Thumbnails view, this screen indicates that no project templates are available in the selected category or subcategory. This screen also appears—somewhat misleadingly—when you select a category that has subcategories.

Choosing a project template from the Project Gallery creates a temporary Office file based on the selected template, and opens that file in the appropriate program and view. Depending on the project template you select, the file content might be basically final other than changes you want to make, or it might contain *placeholders* or *greeked text* for you to replace with your own information. You replace these with your own text by clicking either type of placeholder and then typing the replacement. If you aren't going to use a placeholder, you simply delete it. After you make the changes you want, you name the file and save it to your *Documents* folder or other storage location, or save it as a custom template.

> **Note** The changes you make in a file created from a project template affect only that file, not the template it is based on.

See Also For information about saving changed documents as templates, see "Create a Personalized Project Template" later in this chapter.

Work with Word Publications

Many of the project templates available from the Project Gallery are for creating publishing projects that support the tools provided in Publishing Layout view. You can create these same publications from the Publication Templates tab of the Elements Gallery in a Word document window.

Word publications, which are new in Word 2008 for Mac, are professionally designed publishing projects of diverse types, appropriate for both business and personal use. Publication categories include:

- Awards
- Brochures
- Business cards
- Catalogs
- CD labels
- Flyers
- Invitations

- Menus
- Newsletters
- Postcards
- Posters
- Programs
- Signs

In contrast to a standard Word document in which content is laid out continuously in paragraphs, the individual pages of a Word publication are each laid out separately, with text in text boxes, and graphics. Typical content might include graphic objects (such as pictures, OfficeArt shapes, SmartArt graphics, tables, or charts) placed directly on the page and sections of text inserted in text boxes that set the text apart from the main document content. Longer sections of text might run between two or more linked text boxes. You can link a text box to another on the same page or anywhere else within the publication; Word manages the flow of the text between the text boxes in the order you specify.

See Also For more information about working with graphic objects, including shapes, Clip Art, and pictures, see Chapter 12, "Create and Insert Graphics."

> **Tip** Many of the shapes available from the Objects Gallery of the Toolbox have integrated text boxes. You can insert text into a shape text base, and link the shape text boxes in the same way you do freestanding text boxes.

Each publication consists of one or more master pages upon which content is built. Each master page defines common elements—page background, borders, images or image *drop zones*, page numbers, text, and other elements—that appear on all publication pages based on that master page.

Workspace   Publishing Layout tools   Traditional placeholders

In this simple Word publication, the formatted placeholder text is the only element that is not part of the master page.

You work with Word publications in Publishing Layout view. Special features of this view include the *workspace*; tools for managing pages and master pages, shapes and lines, and text boxes; and a variety of guides to help you precisely position content on pages.

> **Note** You can display a publication and edit its content in a view other than Publishing Layout view, but you won't have all the great Publishing Layout tools at your fingertips. You can display and work with a regular Word document in Publishing Layout view.

Work with Word Notebooks

Word notebooks are specialized documents in which you can record and organize various types of information, including typed and handwritten notes, drawings, images, and audio clips. Word notebooks are a simplified version of the notebooks you can create by using Microsoft Office OneNote for Windows.

Each Word notebook is divided into *sections*. The default notebook template creates three sections; you can add or remove sections to suit your needs. In Notebook Layout view, each section appears to contain only one page that supports scads of content, but in fact the content you insert is divided by Word onto separate pages in accordance with the document page setup. These pages are visible when you switch to a view such as Page Layout view, or when you preview the document before printing it.

By default, notebooks open in Notebook Layout view. The notebook appears to be just that—a ring-bound notebook—sitting on a colored background. The default visual representation is called Simple Contemporary. Other display options are Lucent Glass, Bright Academic, Snow Gloss, and Beige Plastique—each varies only slightly, such as in color scheme, tab shape and size, and minor design features. You can display the notebook in any of these designs, each with or without the notebook rings on the left side. (When you choose to display the notebook without the rings, the corresponding holes still appear on the pages.) To change the visual representation of the notebook, click the Appearance button on the toolbar and then click the representation you want.

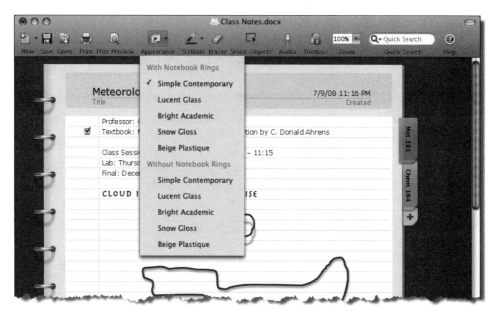

You can choose from five notebook representations, each with or without notebook rings.

In Notebook Layout view, the notebook appears on a colored background called the workspace. (In some other programs, this is referred to as a pasteboard.) The Word notebook workspace doesn't provide functionality as it does in OneNote, but you can change its color and texture from the default Graphite to any of 13 other background options, including 6 different wood tones with realistic grain representations. To change the workspace background, click Customize Workspace on the status bar and then click the background you want.

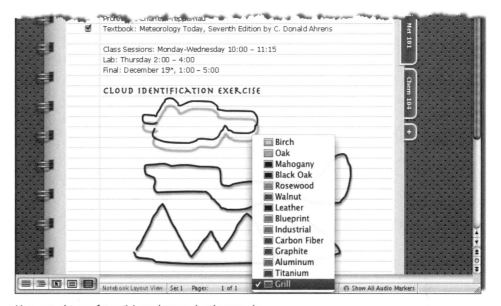

You can choose from 14 workspace backgrounds.

Note You can display a notebook and edit its content in a view other than Notebook Layout view, although the fancy notebook functionality won't be available. In other views, each section starts a new page. You can't display a regular Word document in Notebook Layout view; you must first reformat it. When you switch to Notebook Layout view from a regular document, Word gives you the option of reformatting the document for use in Notebook Layout view.

You can insert text, graphics, handwritten notes, and audio notes into a notebook. If appropriate, you can organize the collection of notes in a multilevel outline.

By using the commands available from the Formatting Palette, you can format and organize content in each section.

In Notebook Layout view, the Formatting Palette displays additional panels of commands specific to organizing notebooks.

 Handwritten notes are called *Scribbles*. To scribble in your notebook, click the Scribble arrow on the toolbar and then, from the list, select the pen you want to use. You can choose from Medium Point, Fine Point, and Very Fine Point, and specify any color (by using the standard color grid or choosing a color from the Color Wheel, Color Sliders, Color Palettes, Image Palettes, or Crayons). In Scribble mode, the mouse pointer looks like a pen. After you choose the width and color of the pen, hold the pen over the page, press and hold the primary mouse button, and scribble as you please.

When you release the pen, Word converts the Scribble to a graphic, complete with handles for moving and resizing it. Additional scribbling with the same pen can be incorporated into the same graphic. You can group and arrange Scribbles, control the way text on the page wraps around a Scribble, fill areas of a Scribble with color, and change the color, weight, style, and endpoints of the original lines. You can also control the existence and appearance of shadows cast by the Scribble. The only thing that remains static is the shape or pattern you originally scribbled.

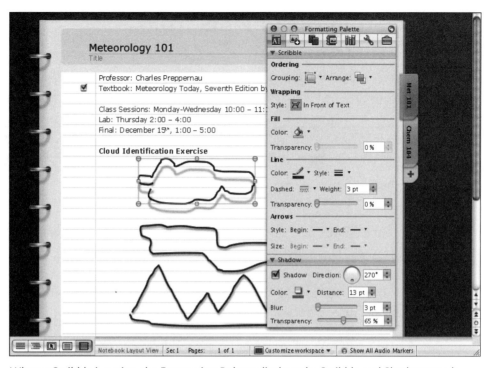

When a Scribble is active, the Formatting Palette displays the Scribble and Shadow panels.

If your computer system includes a microphone (built-in or otherwise) you can record audio notes to go along with other notebook content. Each notebook supports one audio recording. The audio notes you record are synchronized with your actions on the notebook page. As you play back an audio note, the audio icon appears in the left margin of the page and follows the movement of the insertion point on the page and between sections during the recording. To create an audio note, click the Audio button on the toolbar and then use the commands on the Audio toolbar to start, pause, stop, or play back the recording.

Clicking the Audio button displays the Audio Notes toolbar with standard audio recording controls.

Practice Creating Documents from Project Templates

In this exercise, you'll explore the Project Gallery and the Word publication templates available therein. Then you'll create a brochure based on one of the project templates.

SET UP Everything you need for this exercise is provided by Microsoft Word.

1. In the Dock, click the **Microsoft Project Gallery** icon.

   Or

   With the Word, Excel, PowerPoint, or Entourage menu bar active, click **Project Gallery** on the **File** menu (or press **Shift+Command+P**).

   The Project Gallery opens, displaying the New page in Thumbnails view. Blank Documents is selected in the Category list, and the available templates for creating blank documents appear in the Template list.

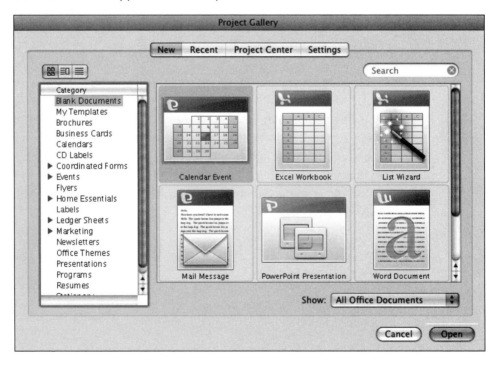

> **Tip** By default, the Project Gallery displays the page—New, Recent, Project Center, or Settings—that was active when it was most recently closed. If you would prefer that the Project Gallery open to a specific page each time, display the Settings page and then, in the Open On list, click the default starting page you want.

2. Scroll the **Template** list to view the eight available blank file templates.

> **Note** Templates that you create will appear in the My Templates category.

The color of the thumbnail header and the stylized program initial (matching the program icons in the Dock) indicate the program in which each project template opens its resulting document.

3. In the **Show** list, click **Word Documents**.

The Template list now displays only three blank document templates: Word Document, Word Notebook Layout, and Word Publishing Layout. These are the same three templates available from the New list on the Standard toolbar in the Word window, which we looked at earlier in this chapter.

4. In the **Category** list, click the arrow to the left of **Events**.

The Template list does not change, but the Events category expands to reveal four subcategories: Awards, Invitations, Postcards, and Posters.

> **Tip** Clicking a top-level category name (instead of its arrow) displays the generic Project Gallery page. Templates are available only from the subcategories.

5. Click the **Posters** subcategory.

The Template list displays thumbnails of four poster templates.

6. Above the **Category** list, click the **Details View** button.

The Template list changes to a list (with the first template already selected), and the Details pane appears, displaying additional information about the selected template.

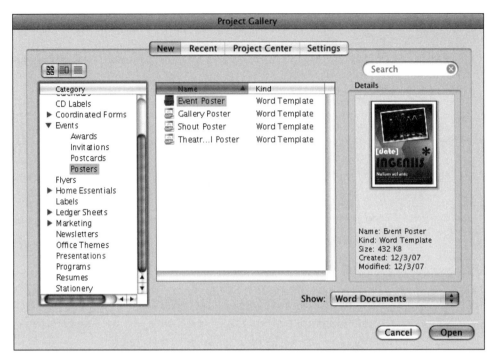

7. At the top of the **Template** list, click the **Name** header.

   The sort order of the templates changes. You can sort the list by either the name or the kind of template by clicking the corresponding header, and reverse the sort order by clicking the header again.

8. Click the **Thumbnails View** button to return to the default view.

   Notice that the sort order you selected in Details view is not active in Thumbnails view. You can't change the sort order of the thumbnails from alphabetical.

9. Scroll the **Category** list to see the available project templates, and end by clicking **Brochures**. In the **Template** list, click **Float Trifold Brochure**. Then click **Open**.

   A full-color brochure opens on the default Publishing Layout view workspace, which resembles an oak desktop. The toolbar displays the specialized Publishing Layout tools.

   The Pages section of the status bar indicates that the brochure is a two-page document.

   > **Tip** To move to a specific page of a document, click Pages on the status bar (or press Command+G) to display the Go To page of the Find And Replace dialog box. Enter the number of the page you want to move to, and then click Go To or press Return.

10. Click below the scroll box on the vertical scroll bar to display the second page of the brochure.

The brochure includes graphics, greeked text, and—if you supplied them as part of your user information—your default address and Web page. The two pages represent the outside and inside of a tri-fold brochure, which you can create by printing this publication double-sided.

> **Tip** The publication settings do not automatically turn on the Two-Sided printing option. If your printer is capable of double-sided printing, you will need to turn on that option (on the Layout page of the Print dialog box) before printing the brochure. If you plan to print a lot of copies of the brochure, you can supply the publication file to a commercial printing company and they will handle the printing niceties.

Address and Web page
from your user profile   Greeked text

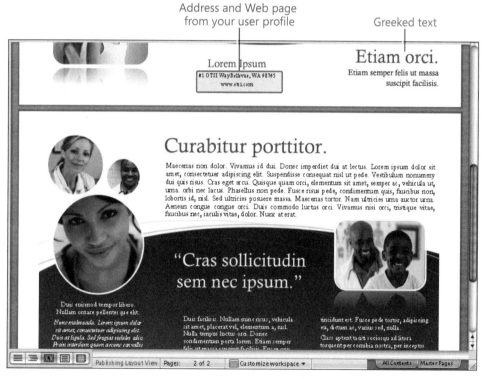

See Also You can provide standard information for use in documents such as this by populating the User Information window or the pages of your personal address card. You access these resources from the Word Preferences dialog box. For more information, see "Personalize Program Functionality" in Chapter 1, "Explore and Manage the Office Interface."

11. In the lower-right corner of the document window, click the **Master Pages** tab.

12. If necessary, click the **More Buttons** button at the right end of the toolbar to display the **Zoom** list. In the **Zoom** list, click **Whole Page**. Then scroll the window to view each of the two master pages.

Each master page defines a different page background.

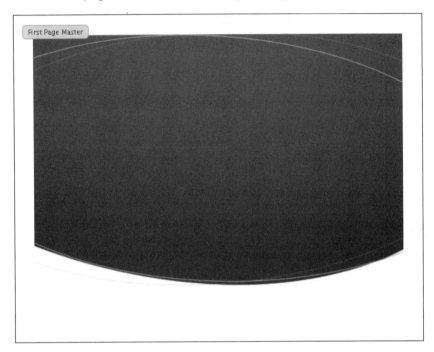

13. In the lower-right corner of the document window, click the **All Contents** tab to return to the populated publication.

You can work more with the text and graphics in this Word publication and with the special tools available in Publishing Layout view. In this exercise, though, we're concentrating on the simple process of creating a document from a project template, so we'll wrap things up.

14. On the toolbar, click the **Save** button. In the **Save As** dialog box, name the publication Doctor Brochure and save it, with the other practice files from this chapter, in the *~/Documents/Microsoft Press/2008OfficeMacSBS/CreateDocuments/* folder.

 CLEAN UP Close the *Doctor Brochure* publication.

Create a Personalized Project Template

In addition to using the Project Gallery templates, you can create your own. If you routinely create the same type of document, such as a monthly financial report, you can create and format the document once and then save it as a template on which to base future versions of that type of document. You can save your new template with text in it, which is handy if you create many documents with only slight variations. Or you can delete the text so that a document based on it will open as a new, blank document with the styles already defined and ready to apply to whatever content you enter.

To save even more time, you can create a document based on one of the project templates, modify it—for example, by adding your own name and address—and then save the modified project template with a different name. The next time you need to create this type of document, you can use your personalized version rather than the standard project template. You can save the content and formatting of any document as a custom project template that you can use to create other, similar documents. Project templates you create and save in the Project Gallery are available from the My Templates category.

In this topic, we discuss creating a custom project template by using a Word notebook as an example, but you can follow the same steps with any type of Office file.

To save the active document as a project template:

1. On the **File** menu, click **Save As**.

2. In the **Save As** dialog box, enter a generic name for the template in the **Save As** box. Then in the **Format** list, click **Word template (.dotx)**.

> **Note** If you want people who are running older versions of Word to be able to use the template, click Word 97–2004 Template instead.

   The folder in the Where box changes to *My Templates*.

3. In the **Save As** dialog box, click **Save**.

> **Tip** If you and other members of your organization frequently create standard documents such as newsletters, you can establish and maintain consistency across the organization by developing and distributing custom project templates. Templates that you save in the Word Template format can be opened in Word 2008 for Mac and Word 2007 for Windows.

Custom templates saved in your *My Templates* folder are available to you from the My Templates list in the Project Gallery. By default, your *My Templates* folder is located in this folder:

~/Library/Application Support/Microsoft/Office/User Templates/

The *My Publication Templates* and *My Themes* folders are also at this location. This is obviously not an easy path to follow, but you probably won't have a reason to. However, if someone else sends you a custom template, save it to this folder so you can access it from the Project Gallery.

Practice Creating Custom Templates

In this exercise, you'll personalize a standard Word notebook and then save it as a project template.

 SET UP You don't need any practice files for this exercise. Open the Project Gallery and display the Blank Documents category.

1. In the **Template** list, click **Word Notebook Layout**. Then click **Open**.

   A blank Word notebook opens in Notebook Layout view.

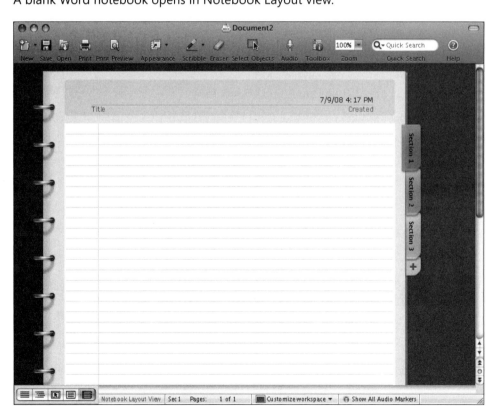

The notebook includes three sections identified by section tabs of different colors. The header area at the top of the page is the same color as the tab of the section the page falls in.

> **Note** When you print a notebook, each section starts on a separate page. You can print an entire notebook or only the active section. Section names (on the section tab), background colors, and rule lines don't print.

2. With **Section 1** active, click at the left end of the **Title** line, type Status at a Glance, and then press the **Tab** key.

The insertion point moves to the first line of the notebook page, and a round dot appears in the left margin. The round dot, which we'll call the *paragraph selector*, indicates the first line of the current paragraph. You can select a paragraph (for example, to format or move it) by clicking the paragraph selector.

3. Type the following text, and then press the **Return** key:

Provide a brief synopsis of the project status.

The insertion point and paragraph selector move to the next line.

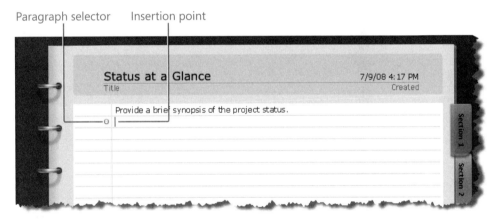

4. Right-click the **Section 1** tab, and then click **Rename Tab**. With the tab name active, type Status.

5. Repeat step 4 first to rename the **Section 2** tab as Schedule, and then to rename the **Section 3** tab as Team.

6. Display the **Schedule** section, and enter Project Schedule on the **Title** line.

7. Display the **Team** section. Enter Project Team on the **Title** line, press **Return** to create a second line, and then type Roles and Responsibilities.

8. Click the **Add Section** button below the **Team** tab.

   A new section, Section 4, appears and is active. The new section tab is gray, as is the tab above it.

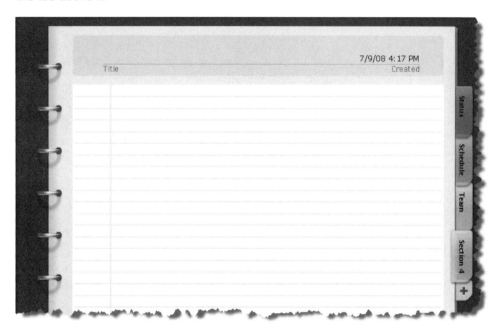

9. Change the name of **Section 4** to Tools, and the section title to Programs and Utilities. Then right-click the section tab, point to **Section Color**, and click **Orange**.

   You have created a generic project management notebook.

10. On the **File** menu, click **Save As**.

    The Save As dialog box slides out from the toolbar.

11. In the **Save As** box, type Project Notebook. Then in the **Format** list, click **Word Template (.dotx)**.

    The folder shown in the Where box changes to *My Templates*.

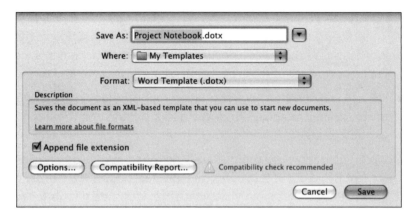

12. In the **Save As** dialog box, click **Save**.

The status bar displays the progress as Word saves the document. When it is finished, the template name appears in the title bar.

13. Close the *Project Notebook* template, and then open the Project Gallery.

14. In the **Category** list, click **My Templates**.

Your personalized template appears in the Template list.

Your custom project template!

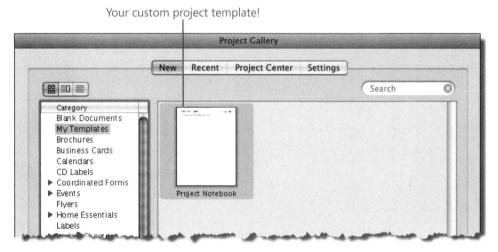

15. In the **Template** list, double-click **Project Notebook**.

Word opens a new, untitled document based on the selected template.

CLEAN UP Close the new document and then quit Word.

Key Points

- Word includes three basic document types: blank documents, notebooks, and publications. Each of these has a special purpose, view, and toolset.

- You can take the effort out of creating sophisticated documents by using one of the predefined templates from Word as a starting point. You can also create your own templates.

- Word publications are professionally designed publishing projects for which text content is laid out in text boxes on individual pages. You work with Word publications in Publishing Layout view, which provides special tools for working with the page layout. You can open a publication in another view, and you can open standard documents in Publishing Layout view.

- Word notebooks are specialized documents in which you can record and organize various types of information, including typed and handwritten notes, drawings, images, and audio clips. You work with Word notebooks in Notebook Layout view. You can't open a non-notebook document in Notebook Layout view. You can convert a regular document to a notebook, but some formatting might be lost.

Bonus Web Content

You can find the following articles about additional Word 2008 features on the book's companion Web site, at *www.microsoft.com/mspress/companion/9780735626171*:

- "Organize Text in Columns in Word 2008 for Mac"
- "Organize Text in Lists in Word 2008 for Mac"
- "Perform Calculations in a Table in Word 2008 for Mac"
- "Present Text in a Tabular List in Word 2008 for Mac"
- "Restructuring Content in Outline View in Word 2008 for Mac"
- "Work with Publication Elements in Word 2008 for Mac"
- "Work with Tables in Word 2008 for Mac"

Chapter at a Glance

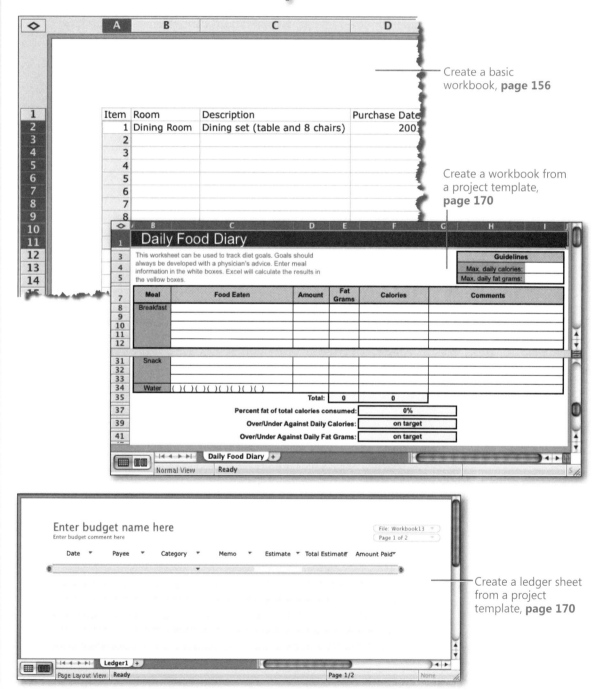

Create a basic workbook, **page 156**

Create a workbook from a project template, **page 170**

Create a ledger sheet from a project template, **page 170**

5 Create Excel Workbooks

In this chapter, you will learn how to

- ✔ Create a basic workbook.
- ✔ Enter data on a sheet.
- ✔ Resize columns and rows.
- ✔ Fill cells with a series of data.
- ✔ Create a workbook or sheet from a project template.

You might hear it said that Microsoft Excel is the most popular database program in the world, because people tend to store a lot of data in Excel workbooks. However, that's not actually its intended purpose. In fact, Excel is a powerful tool for tracking, charting, analyzing, and sharing information so that you can make informed business decisions.

The basic Excel file is a *workbook*. The structure of an Excel workbook is more complex than that of a Microsoft Word document, because a workbook can contain more than one sheet of independent or linked information. Thankfully, in the 2008 version of Excel, Microsoft saw fit to include only one sheet in a standard blank workbook. One sheet is usually all you need. Older versions of Excel created three sheets in each workbook, so you had to delete the two you didn't use. But of course, most people didn't bother to delete them, so there are probably billions of unused sheets now taking up hard disk space.

In this chapter, you'll learn about workbooks, sheets, and data. You'll create workbooks and worksheets to store information, and you'll practice various methods of entering information into worksheets.

See Also You can find handy keyboard shortcuts, simple instructions for performing common tasks, and other useful information in the Quick Reference section at the beginning of this book.

> **Practice Makes Perfect!** You won't need any practice files to complete the exercises in this chapter, but you'll save the files you create in the *CreateWorkbooks* practice file folder. See "Using the Companion Content" at the beginning of this book for information about practice files.

Create a Basic Workbook

The basic file you create in Excel 2008 for Mac is a workbook, saved in the Excel Workbook (.xlsx) file format. If your workbook content warrants it, you can save a workbook in a binary file format (to aid compatibility with previous versions) or macro-enabled file format (to enable macros within the workbook). These files are also referred to as workbooks. In this chapter, we examine simple workbooks in which you store, manage, calculate, and present simple data. (Don't worry—we're saving the hard bits for later chapters.)

One thing that is simpler in Excel than in Word is that you can create only one type of workbook by clicking the New button—a blank workbook. You don't need to choose a specific type of workbook or worry about which type of workbook will be created.

Regardless of the type of workbook you end up with, every workbook starts out in the simple Workbook format. When you save the workbook, you can choose a different format. (If your workbook contains programmatic content, Excel might automatically select a binary or macro-enabled format in the Save As dialog box.)

If the file format you choose doesn't support a type of content contained in the workbook, Excel warns you. For example, if you use fancy formatting in your workbook and try to save it in the Excel 97–2004 Workbook (.xls) format, Excel displays a cautionary message that the content might not be available in the new format.

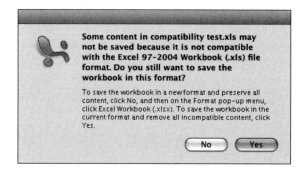

Excel warns you if the file you're saving contains elements that aren't compatible with the selected file type.

> **Note** Content in a workbook is stored on *sheets*. In addition to the basic blank sheet (which we refer to as a *worksheet* to differentiate it from the others), you can create *chart sheets* and *list sheets*. Each has a different appearance and purpose. For more information about the different sheet types, see "Manage Sheets" in Chapter 8, "Work with Excel Sheet Content."

How Much Data Can I Store in a Workbook?

If you plan to manage large data sets in Excel, you'll be happy to know that you can store a lot of information in an Excel workbook. Excel 2008 supports the storage of significantly more data than earlier versions of Excel. You can now store *more than 1 million rows of data* in one worksheet. Specific limits include those listed in these tables.

Workbook or sheet specification	Maximum
Worksheet size	1,048,576 rows by 16,384 columns
Column width	255 characters
Visible characters in a cell	1024
Total characters in a cell, visible in the formula bar	32,767
Characters in a header or footer	255
Sheets in a workbook	Depends on available memory
Colors in a workbook	56
Conditional formats	3
Panes in a window	4
Undo levels	16
Entries in a filter list	10,000 (255 characters maximum)

Calculation specification	Maximum
Number precision	15 digits
Largest positive number	9.99999999999999E+307
Largest negative number	−9.99999999999999E+307
Length of formula	8,192 characters
Arguments in a function	255
Nested functions	64

Charting specification	Maximum
Charts in a workbook	255
Data series in a chart	255
Data points in a chart	256,000
Data points in a data series (2-D charts)	32,000
Data points in a data series (3-D charts)	4,000

Resources **For more information on this interesting subject, see the topic "Specifications and limits for Excel 2008" in the Excel Help system.**

Enter Data on a Sheet

After you create a workbook, you enter data into it—specifically, you enter the data into a worksheet contained within the workbook.

What exactly is this data we're referring to? When you think of "data," you might envision the opening screen from the movie *The Matrix*, with millions of little green characters you're supposed to be able to read even though they're streaming down the screen backward or in Kanji (a writing system for the Japanese language that uses pictorial characters).

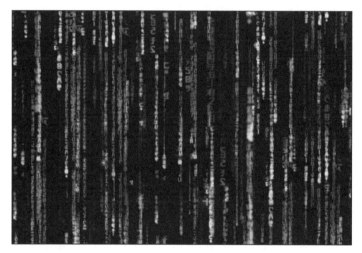

Digital rain, from the movie The Matrix, *as a representation of data.*

> **Totally Random Thought**   After the release of the first *Matrix* movie, a lot of people installed screensavers depicting the *Matrix* code—you can find a lot of versions on the Web, some three-dimensional. The official *Matrix* site at *whatisthematrix.warnerbros.com* offers a Mac version. If you're a *Matrix* fan, take a look at the "About the Author" section of this book and see if you notice anything interesting.

You probably have your own concept of data. To avoid confusion, we should define the term, because we use it a lot in this book. *Data* is the plural of *datum*, which is a piece of information, a point of reference, or a given fact.

> **Note**   The singular form *datum* is rarely used. In this book, we use *data* to refer to both singular and plural instances.

The Microsoft Encarta Dictionary offers two definitions of data:

1. *factual information*

   Information, often in the form of facts or figures obtained from experiments or surveys, used as a basis for making calculations or drawing conclusions.

2. *information for computer processing*

   Information, e.g. numbers, text, images, and sounds, in a form that is suitable for storage in or processing by a computer.

In this book, we'll use the word *data* to refer to any type of information you store and manage in your Excel workbook.

You can use Excel to track simple data, such as a packing list for frequent travelers, or complex data, such as an analysis of annual sales. If you need to work with a large quantity of data, you're in luck—you can store up to 1000 pages of data in a worksheet.

An Excel worksheet is composed of rows and columns of *cells* that contain values, or *data points*, that make up a *data series*. To enter data in an individual cell—the intersection of a row and column—you click the cell to select it, and start typing.

You can select an entire column by clicking the *column heading*—the box containing a letter at the top of each column—and an entire row by clicking the *row heading*—the box containing a number to the left of each row. You can select the entire worksheet by clicking the Select All button—the box at the junction of the column headings and row headings.

You can enter data into a worksheet or list sheet by typing, copying or *filling* data that already exists in the sheet, pasting data that you've copied from another source (such as a Word document, a Web page, or a sheet from another workbook), or importing data from another file.

> **Tip** You can import data into Excel 2008 from a text file containing values separated by commas, tabs, or spaces; from a local HTML file; or from a FileMaker Pro database. To import data from one of these sources, click the Import button on the Standard toolbar. In the Import dialog box that opens, click the data type you want to import, and then click Import. In the Choose A File dialog box, locate the data file you want to import, and then click Get Data. The Text Import Wizard guides you through the process of selecting and mapping the data you want to import to fields in a new list sheet.

See Also For information about ensuring that cell content meets specific requirements, see "Restrict the Content Allowed in a Cell" in Chapter 8, "Work with Excel Sheet Content."

Resize Columns and Rows

A worksheet is divided into alphabetically named columns (A, B, C, and so on) and numerically named rows (1, 2, 3, and so on). The column letters and row numbers are indicated by the column headings and row headings that appear by default above and to the left of the worksheet. The columns of each new worksheet are of equal width, and the rows are of equal height.

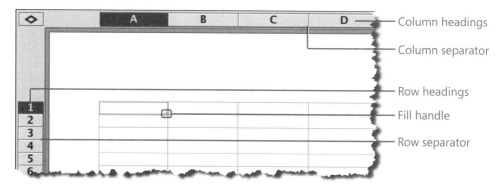

A new worksheet is neatly divided into columns and rows.

A cell is named with the column letter and the row number of the column and row that intersect at that point (for example, A1). If you enter more data into a cell than it can display, some of the data will not be visible, except when the cell is active. You can increase the size of a cell by increasing the width of its column or the height of its row. Of course, this affects the width and height of all the cells in the column or row—you can't change the size of an individual cell.

You can resize columns and rows in several ways:

- You can drag the separator that is to the right of the column heading to the left or right.

- You can drag the separator that is below the row heading up or down.

- You can resize a column to precisely fit the width of its contents by double-clicking the separator to the right of the column.

- You can resize a row to precisely fit the height of its contents by double-clicking the separator below the row.

- You can specify the exact width of one or more selected columns in the Column Width dialog box, and the exact height of one or more selected rows in the Row Height dialog box.

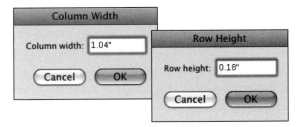

You display these dialog boxes by right-clicking the column or row heading, or right-clicking anywhere in a selection of column or row headings, and then clicking Column Width or Row Height. Changes you make in the dialog box affect the selected columns or rows.

Hide Columns and Rows

You can easily hide a row or column of a worksheet—for example, so that it doesn't take up space on the screen or appear in a printed report. To hide one row or column, right-click the row heading or column heading, and then click Hide. To hide multiple rows or columns, select the rows or columns you want to hide (you can't select both rows and columns at the same time), right-click anywhere in the selection, and then click Hide.

A hidden row or column retains its row number or column letter. When a row or column is hidden, the headings on either side change to blue, and the column selector between the flanking headings is twice as wide as usual.

To unhide a hidden row or column, drag across the flanking headings, right-click the selection, and then click Unhide.

Fill Cells with a Series of Data

You can very quickly enter a logical data series (such as 1, 2, 3 or Monday, Tuesday, Wednesday) in contiguous cells by using the Auto Fill feature. By default, Excel recognizes the days of the week, the months of the year, and any numeric series, including dates and times. You can easily create a custom fill series by adding the series to the Custom Lists page of the Excel Preferences dialog box.

To fill a series of cells with a series of data, you start by entering the first series element into the cell you want the series to start in. (The first element doesn't have to be the first entry in a list; Excel will start the series with any entry, and repeat the series to fill the number of destination cells you select.) Then drag the cell's fill handle down or to the right to increase the series, or up or to the left to decrease the series. If you want the series to fill backward (Friday, Thursday, Wednesday, and so on) enter the first two series items in the first two cells, select the two cells, and then drag the fill handle of the selection.

When you release the fill handle, the Auto Fill Options button appears. This is a *smart button*. Clicking the button displays a menu of options tailored specifically for the type of data series you're filling.

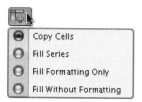

The Auto Fill Options menu adapts to reflect the logical data series.

These basic fill options always appear on the Auto Fill Options menu:

- **Copy Cells.** By selecting this option, you can copy the content of the source cell into the selected destination cells.

- **Fill Formatting Only.** By selecting this option, you can copy the font and cell formatting of the source cell into the destination cells.

- **Fill Without Formatting.** By selecting this option, you can copy the content of a single source cell or fill a series based on multiple source cells, while maintaining the original formatting of the destination cells.

If Excel recognizes the source cell or cells as belonging to any known series, the Auto Fill Options menu includes the Fill Series option. By selecting this option, you can fill the destination cells with a logical series based on the source cell or cells.

If the source cell content is a day of the week, the Auto Fill Options menu includes the Fill Days and Fill Weekdays options. If the source cell content is a date, the menu includes those two options as well as the Fill Months and Fill Years options.

Practice Creating and Populating Workbooks

In this exercise, you'll first create a blank workbook. You'll enter information into a worksheet and resize columns so that you can see the information. Then you'll create additional data by copying and filling data series.

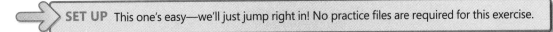

SET UP This one's easy—we'll just jump right in! No practice files are required for this exercise.

1. Start Excel. (If Excel is already started, you're a step ahead of the game.)

   As with Word, starting the program (without opening a specific workbook) creates a blank temporary file—in Excel, this is a workbook named *Workbook1*.

2. On the toolbar, click the **New** button.

   A blank workbook opens in Page Layout view, which is the default view for new workbooks. The upper-left cell, cell A1, is active. This is indicated by the blue outline of cell A1 and the shading of the column A heading and the row 1 heading.

   > **Note** In Page Layout view, pages that don't contain content are shaded. This makes it easy to determine whether any cells on a page contain content.

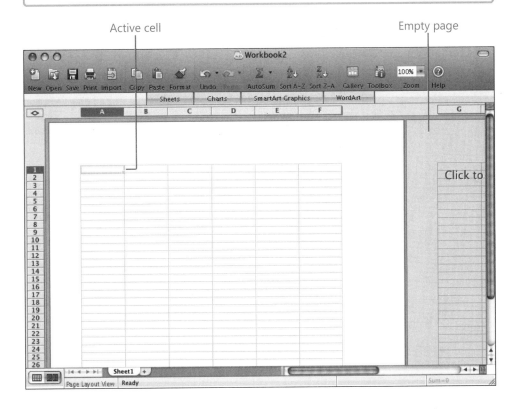

> **Note** The horizontal and vertical rulers might appear at the top and on the left side of the worksheet, outside of the column and row headings. Because they're not necessary for this exercise, you can hide the rulers by clicking Ruler on the View menu.

3. With cell **A1** active, type Item.

As you type, the text entry box for the cell you're typing in pops up from the surrounding worksheet. This nifty little feature, which you won't find in Excel 2007 for Windows, makes it much easier to distinguish the content of the active cell from that of the surrounding cells. Most conveniently, though, the pop-up displays all the text in the cell, so if there is more text than can be displayed in the cell, you can see it all while you're editing it.

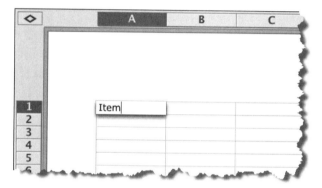

While you're entering text, a blinking insertion point appears in the cell.

> **Note** You can increase the Zoom level, as we've done here, to make it easier to see the worksheet content.

4. Press the **Tab** key.

Cell B1 becomes active. Notice that now there is no visible insertion point in the active cell.

5. In cell **B1**, type Room. Press **Tab** to move to cell **C1**, and type Description. Press **Tab** to move to cell **D1**, and type Purchase Date.

As you type the final letter of the word *Date*, the text exceeds the width of the cell, and the text entry box expands to two columns wide.

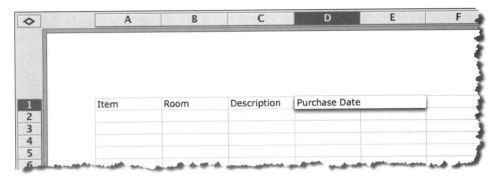

6. Press **Tab** to move to cell **E1**, and type Purchase Price. Then press **Return**.

   Pressing Return indicates to Excel that you've reached the end of the information you're entering in this row. The cell selector moves to the cell that Excel perceives as the first in the series of data you're entering. In this case, that should be cell A2. If you stopped to experiment with anything between steps 4 and 6, it might be cell B2 or C2.

7. Type the following data into cells **A2** through **E2**:

In cell...	Type...
A2	1
B2	Dining Room
C2	Dining set (table and 8 chairs)
D2	2007
E2	2600

   When you finish, press **Return**.

   Some of the data isn't visible because it's larger than the cell it's in, so let's adjust the column width.

   > **Note** The default worksheet font is 10-point Verdana. You can change the default font from the General page of the Excel Preferences dialog box. For example, you might want to use a larger font that is easier to see, use a smaller font to fit more on a page, or consistently use a font that is part of your corporate branding scheme.

8. Point to the column **C** heading. When the pointer changes to a downward-pointing arrow, drag to the right through column **E**.

9. Hold down the **Command** key, and then click the column **A** heading.

Columns A, C, D, and E are now selected.

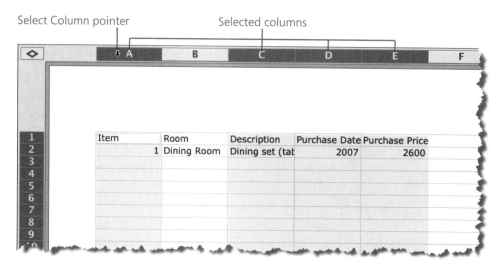

> **Note** When you select one or more cells, the corresponding column and row headings appear shaded.

10. Point to the column separator to the right of column **A**. When the pointer changes to a double-headed horizontal arrow, double-click.

The width of each of the four selected columns changes to precisely fit its widest content.

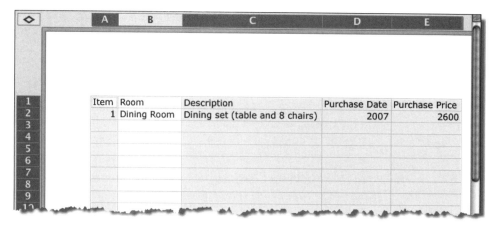

> **Tip** If you have difficulty resizing the selected columns by double-clicking the column separator, you can instead point to Columns on the Format menu, and then click AutoFit Selection.

Later in this book we'll apply character and paragraph formatting to the actual cell content.

11. Click cell **A2**, which contains the number *1*.

 12. Point to the fill handle in the lower-right corner of the active cell. When the pointer changes to a black plus sign, drag down through cell **A11**.

As you drag, the pointer changes to a diamond, with small arrows in the upper-left and lower-right corners, and a small box displays the value that will be entered in the cell.

When you release the mouse button, the number *1* appears in cells A2 through A11. The Auto Fill Options button appears outside the lower-right corner of the filled selection. If you don't click this button, it will disappear on its own shortly.

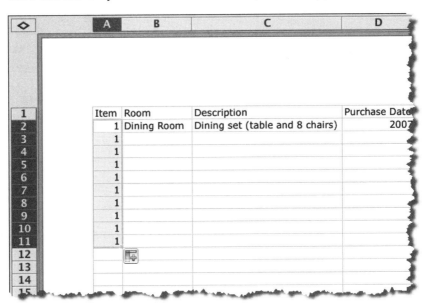

13. Click the **Auto Fill Options** button to display a menu of options for filling the selected cells.

The Copy Cells option is currently selected. As a result, all the cells are filled with a replica of the initially selected cell.

14. On the **Auto Fill Options** menu, click **Fill Series**.

The contents of cells A2 through A11 change from a series of 1s to the numbers 1 through 10. The Auto Fill Options button remains available in case you want to choose a different option.

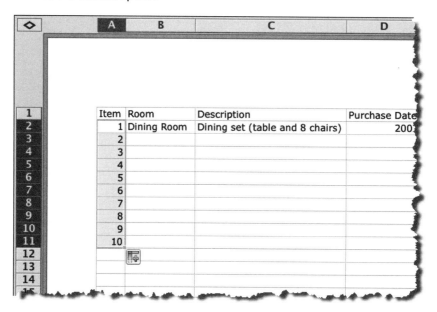

> **Tip** Auto Fill is one of the few actions that you can't undo. If you Auto Fill a selection and don't like the results, delete the filled data (but not the original base data) and start again.

We'll do more with this worksheet later.

 15. On the toolbar, click **Save** (or press **Command+S**).

The Save As dialog box opens. Notice that Excel suggests *Workbook2* as the file name, rather than suggesting the first word in the file, as Word does.

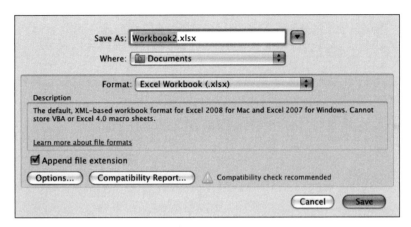

16. In the **Save As** box, replace the suggested file name with My Inventory.

 17. If the *navigation area* isn't already visible in the **Save As** dialog box, click the **Expand** button to display it. Navigate to the *~/Documents/Microsoft Press/ 2008OfficeMacSBS/CreateWorkbooks/* folder.

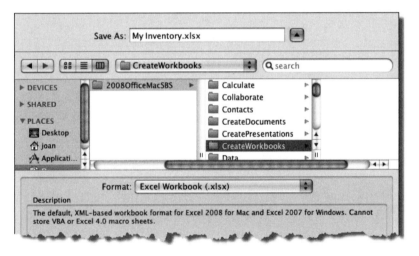

18. In the **Save As** dialog box, click **Save**.

Excel saves the workbook, and the new file name appears on its title bar.

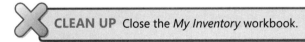

CLEAN UP Close the *My Inventory* workbook.

Create a Workbook or Sheet from a Project Template

In Chapter 4, "Create Word Documents," we discussed the Microsoft Project Gallery, from which you can create a variety of blank or purpose-specific Office documents from templates. Several Excel workbook templates are available in the Project Gallery, mostly centering around the collection and management of financial data, with a few random list-keeping solutions thrown in. Each project template creates a workbook containing a single-sheet solution.

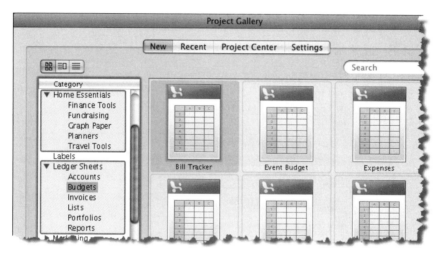

Only the Home Essentials and Ledger Sheets categories include Excel project templates.

Other than the blank sheet templates, all the Excel templates in the Project Gallery are in the Home Essentials and Ledger Sheets categories. (And in the same vein, all the project templates in those categories are Excel templates.)

Here's a misleading feature of the Project Gallery to watch out for: The Category list *always* displays *all* the category names, regardless of what filter is applied. There is no visible indicator of whether a category includes one or more project templates matching the filter you choose in the Show list. The only way to determine whether a category includes a specific type of template is to click the category or subcategory name. If the category doesn't include templates of the selected type—for example, if you select Excel Documents in the Show list and then click anything other than a subcategory of the Home Essentials or Ledger Sheets category—the Template list displays only the Project Gallery splash screen.

Document type filter

You must click a category in the list to find out whether it includes templates matching the selected document type.

The Home Essentials category includes 23 templates. The templates in this category create colorful worksheets containing basic built-in calculation functions. You work in these sheets in Normal view.

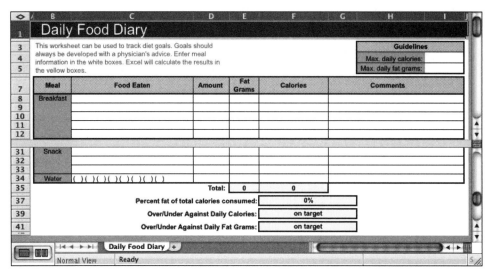

A typical Home Essentials project

The Home Essentials category includes templates to create the following worksheets:

- **Finance Tools.** You can use these 9 templates to create worksheets to plan and analyze budgets, cash flow, leases, loans, and investments:

    - Home Budget
    - College Cash Flow
    - Investment Calculator
    - Investment Projections
    - Loan and Credit Planner
    - Standard Loan
    - Car Loan Comparison
    - Car Loan Worksheet
    - Car Lease vs Purchase

- **Fundraising.** You can use these 3 templates to create worksheets to plan a fundraising event and track the results:

    - Event Budget Worksheet
    - Donations Log
    - Pledge Log

- **Graph Paper.** You can use these 6 templates to create worksheets that depict graph paper of different grid configurations:

    - Plain Grid
    - Plain Small Grid
    - Plain Large Grid
    - 5x5 Grid
    - 5x5 Small Grid
    - 10x10 Grid

You can enter data into the graph paper on your computer or print it out and take it with you. The graph paper worksheets don't include any built-in calculations.

- **Planners.** You can use these 3 templates to create worksheets to schedule important maintenance tasks for your tummy and your car:

  ○ Daily Food Planner   ○ Vehicle Repair Log

  ○ Meal Planner

- **Travel Tools.** Planning a road trip? You can plan and track your trip by creating worksheets from these 2 templates:

  ○ Itinerary   ○ Vehicle Road Trip Log

The Ledger Sheets category includes 30 templates that create professional-looking ledger pages with the built-in functionality of list pages. You work in these sheets in Page Layout view.

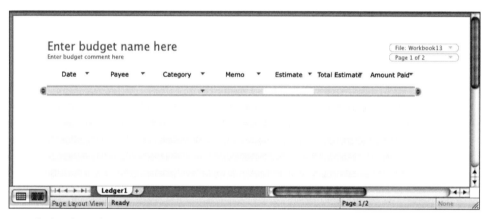

A typical Ledger Sheets project

The Ledger Sheets category includes templates to create the following list sheets:

- **Accounts.** You can track information about bank and credit card accounts by creating worksheets from these 6 templates:

  ○ Business Checkbook   ○ Savings Passbook

  ○ Personal Checkbook   ○ Account Balance

  ○ Checking Ledger   ○ Credit Card Statement

- **Budgets.** You can forecast and track income and expenses by creating worksheets from these 6 templates:

  ○ Home Budget   ○ Bill Tracker

  ○ Travel Budget   ○ Expenses

  ○ Event Budget   ○ Income

- **Invoices.** If you have a small business but don't use an accounting program that generates invoices, you can issue invoices by creating worksheets from these 3 templates:

  - Service Invoice
  - Retail Invoice
  - Wholesale Invoice

  You can use the invoices created from the templates as is or personalize them with your company information.

- **Lists.** You can keep track of a variety of information by creating worksheets from these 10 templates:

  - Address List
  - E-mail List
  - Shopping List
  - Guest List
  - Gift List
  - Thank You List
  - Phone List
  - Phone Call Log
  - Inventory
  - Vehicle Maintenance

- **Portfolios.** You can track your investments by creating worksheets from these 2 templates:

  - Stocks
  - Funds

- **Reports.** You can report financial invoice and expense information by creating worksheets from these 3 templates:

  - Customer Statement
  - Outstanding Invoices
  - Expense Report

You'll notice in the lists above that there are some purposes for which multiple templates exist. Select the template that most closely addresses your information management needs, and then modify it to make it your own. In addition to the project templates, you can create a standard blank workbook or create a list by using a wizard. These options are available from the Blank Documents category.

All of the Ledger Sheets project templates that are available from the Project Gallery are also available from the Sheets tab of the Elements Gallery. Creating a sheet from the Elements Gallery inserts it into the existing workbook.

See Also For information about the Elements Gallery, see "The Elements Gallery" in Chapter 1, "Explore and Manage the Office Interface."

Practice Creating Workbooks and Sheets from Templates

In this exercise, you'll create a workbook from the Project Gallery and a ledger sheet from the Elements Gallery.

SET UP Start Excel, if it isn't already open. No practice files are required for this exercise.

1. On the **File** menu, click **Project Gallery** (or press **Shift+Command+P**).

   The Project Gallery opens, displaying the Blank Documents category.

2. In the **Category** list, expand the **Home Essentials** category, and then click **Finance Tools**.

   The project template thumbnails give you an idea of what each worksheet will look like.

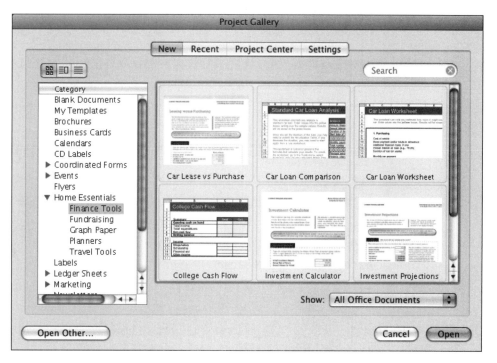

3. Scroll to the end of the **Template** list, and click the **Monthly Home Budget** thumbnail. Then in the **Project Gallery**, click **Open**.

Excel opens a temporary, untitled workbook in Normal view, containing one worksheet named *Monthly Home Budget*.

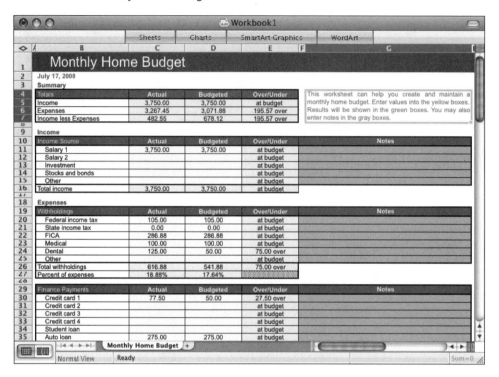

> **Note** No toolbars are necessary in this exercise, so we've hidden the toolbar area to save screen real estate.

You can use the Monthly Home Budget worksheet to track your planned and actual monthly income and expenses. Instructions in cell G4 provide information about how to use the worksheet.

4. On the **File** menu, click **Save As**.

The Save As dialog box opens. Excel suggests a file name. Notice that the suggested file format is *Excel 97–2004 Workbook (.xls)*, rather than the default Excel 2008 file format, *Excel Workbook (.xlsx)*. This is a good indicator that the original template was created in an earlier version of Excel.

The suggested file format reflects
the format of the original template

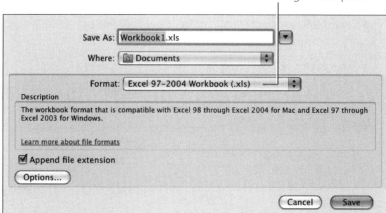

5. In the **Save As** box, replace the suggested file name with My Budget.

6. If the folder structure isn't already visible in the **Save As** dialog box, click the **Expand** button to display it.

7. Navigate to the *~/Documents/Microsoft Press/2008OfficeMacSBS/ CreateWorkbooks/* folder. In the **Format** list, click **Excel Workbook (.xlsx)**.

You can save a file created from an
older template in the new file format

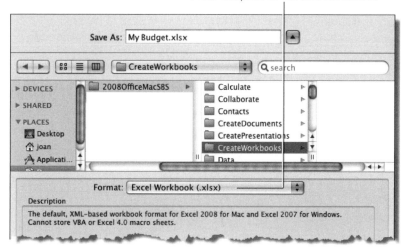

8. In the **Save As** dialog box, click **Save**.

Excel saves the workbook in the new file format. Other than the name on the title bar, no change is apparent, but you now have access to all of the Excel 2008 for Mac functionality.

9. At the top of the workbook window, click the **Sheets** button.

The Sheets tab of the Elements Gallery expands. Each subcategory of the Ledger Sheets Project Gallery category has a corresponding group button at the top of the tab.

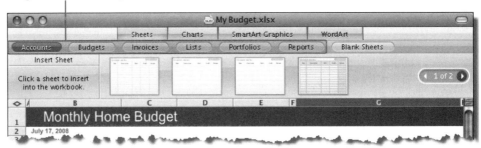

Groups corresponding to the Ledger Sheets subcategories

> **Note**   You can display more sheet thumbnails at one time by widening the workbook window. We're sticking with the smaller window so that all the graphics in this exercise look similar.

10. Click the **Budgets** button to display that group of ledger sheets.

11. Point to each of the ledger sheets to display its name in the style name area at the left end of the gallery. When you come to the *Home Budget* sheet, click it.

Excel inserts a sheet named *Ledger1* in the *My Budget* workbook, to the right of the *Monthly Home Budget* sheet. The ledger sheet is sized so that the entire sheet is visible in the window.

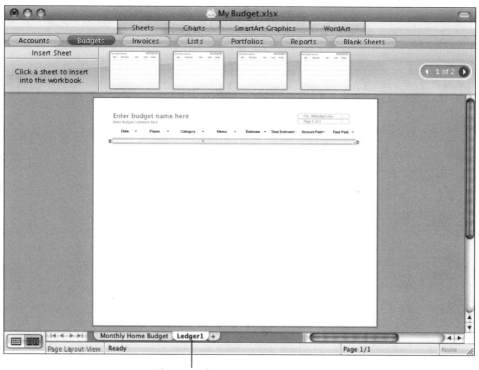

The new sheet

 CLEAN UP Close the *My Budget* workbook without saving your changes.

Key Points

- You can create workbooks, worksheets, chart sheets, and list sheets from scratch or from templates.

- You can populate worksheets by typing, pasting, or importing data.

- If a cell contains more data than can be displayed in the existing space, you can resize the cell by dragging or double-clicking the column selector or row selector, or by specifying the size in the Column Width or Row Height dialog box.

- You can fill adjacent cells with a series of data based on at least one entry. If none of the standard alphanumeric series fits your needs, you can easily create a custom fill series.

Chapter at a Glance

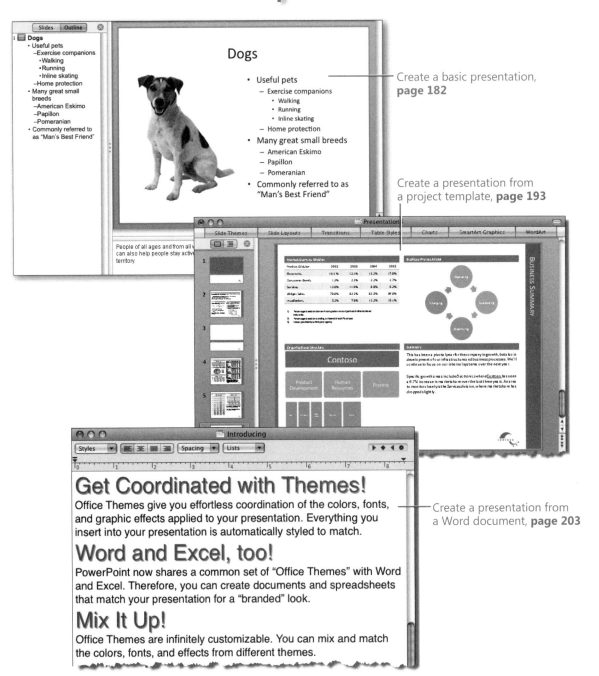

Create a basic presentation, **page 182**

Create a presentation from a project template, **page 193**

Create a presentation from a Word document, **page 203**

6 Create PowerPoint Presentations

In this chapter, you will learn how to

✔ Create a basic presentation.

✔ Add slides to a presentation.

✔ Add content to slides.

✔ Create a presentation from the Project Gallery.

✔ Create a presentation from a Word document.

You can create a Microsoft PowerPoint presentation in several ways. For example, you can add slides and slide content to a blank presentation, create a presentation based on a template from the Microsoft Project Gallery, create a populated presentation by importing an outline document into PowerPoint, or modify an existing presentation.

In this chapter, you'll create presentations from scratch, from a template, and by importing an outline. You'll add slides to a presentation, both from the Elements Gallery and by importing them from another presentation. Then you'll populate the slides with text.

See Also You can find handy keyboard shortcuts, simple instructions for performing common tasks, and other useful information in the Quick Reference section at the beginning of this book.

Practice Makes Perfect! The practice files you will use to complete the exercises in this chapter are in the *CreatePresentations* practice file folder. See "Using the Companion Content" at the beginning of this book for information about installing and locating the practice files.

Create a Basic Presentation

Each time you start PowerPoint, it displays a temporary presentation, just as Microsoft Word displays a blank document and Microsoft Excel a blank workbook. You can create a plain, blank presentation from within PowerPoint by clicking New Presentation on the File menu (or pressing Command+N).

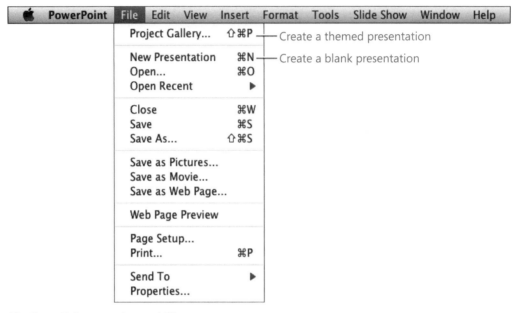

The PowerPoint menu bar and File menu

Alternatively, you can create a presentation that already has an Office theme applied, or a pre-populated presentation, by clicking Project Gallery on the File menu.

The new presentation, whether blank, themed, or pre-populated, is a temporary file until you save it. If you close the file without saving it, the file and its contents will be entirely removed from the computer.

See Also For information about creating presentations that are already formatted with a graphic theme, see "Create a Presentation Based on an Office Theme Template" later in this chapter.

Add Slides to a Presentation

When you create a new presentation that isn't based on a project template, PowerPoint supplies only a title slide and leaves it to you to add the other slides you want.

Add Blank Slides

You can add a slide with the default layout, immediately after the current slide, by clicking New Slide on the Insert menu. You can add a slide with a different layout by selecting the layout you want from the Slide Layouts tab of the Elements Gallery.

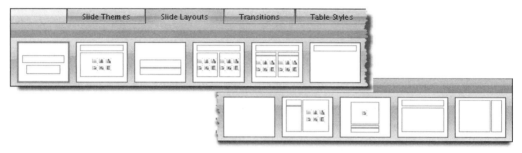

Many standard slide layouts are available from the Slide Layouts tab of the Elements Gallery.

The basic slide layouts that are available in any new presentation include the following:

- Presentation and section openers:
  - Title Slide
  - Section Header
- Content:
  - Title Only
  - Title and Content
  - Title and Vertical Text
  - Vertical Title and Text
  - Content with Caption
  - Picture with Caption
  - Two Content
  - Comparison

In addition to these, a blank slide layout on which you can insert whatever content holders you want is available. Presentations created from the Project Gallery can also include purpose-specific slide layouts.

Bonus Web Content For information about custom slide layouts, see "Practice Working with Slide Masters in PowerPoint 2008 for Mac" on the book's companion Web site at *www.microsoft.com/mspress/companion/9780735626171.*

Insert Slides from Other Presentations

If your presentations often include one or more slides that provide the same information, you don't have to recreate the slides for each presentation. For example, if you create a slide that shows your company's product development cycle for a new product presentation, you might want to use variations of that same slide in a new product presentations. You can easily insert a slide from one presentation in a specific location into a different presentation. The slide will assume the formatting of its new presentation.

To insert a slide from another presentation into the current presentation:

1. Point to **Slides From** on the **Insert** menu, and then click **Other Presentations**.

2. In the **Choose a File** dialog box that opens, select the presentation containing the slide(s) you want to insert.

3. To insert the entire presentation, click **Insert all slides**, and then click **Insert**.

4. To insert only specific slides, click **Select slides to insert**, and then click **Insert**. In the **Slide Finder** that opens, select the slide(s) you want to insert, click **Insert**, and then click **Close**.

Remove Slides from a Presentation

When you're working in Normal view, an easy way to remove a slide from a presentation is to right-click the slide in the Navigation pane, and then click Delete Slide. Using this method, you can delete any slide regardless of which slide is currently displayed.

To delete multiple slides at one time, select those slides in the Navigation pane or in Slide Sorter view, right-click any selected slide, and then click Delete Slide.

> **Tip** To select contiguous slides on the Slides or Outline page of the Navigation pane, click the first slide, press and hold the Shift key, and click the second slide. To select noncontiguous slides on the Slides page, click a slide, press and hold the Command key, and then click each additional slide. To select noncontiguous slides on the Outline page, click a slide, press and hold the Control key, and then click each additional slide.

You can delete the currently displayed slide by clicking Delete Slide on the Edit menu.

Practice Inserting Slides from Other Presentations

In this exercise, you'll insert slides from one presentation into another.

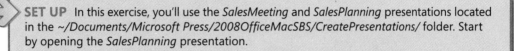

1. On the **Slides** page of the Navigation pane, click **Slide 3**.

   Note that all the slides in this presentation have white backgrounds.

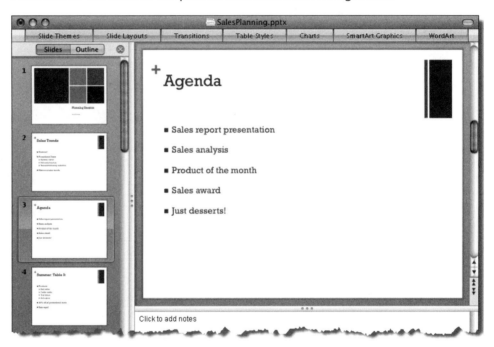

2. On the **Insert** menu, point to **Slides From**, and then click **Other Presentation**.

   The Choose A File dialog box opens.

3. If the dialog box doesn't already display the contents of the *CreatePresentations* folder, navigate to that folder. Then click the *SalesMeeting* presentation.

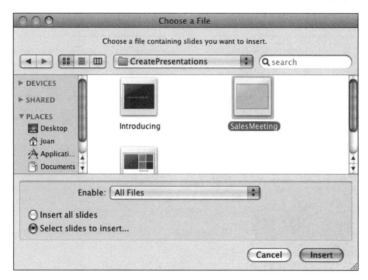

4. With the **Select slides to insert** option selected, click **Insert**.

The Slide Finder opens, displaying thumbnails and titles of all the slides in the *SalesMeeting* presentation. Note that all the slides in this presentation have patterned blue backgrounds.

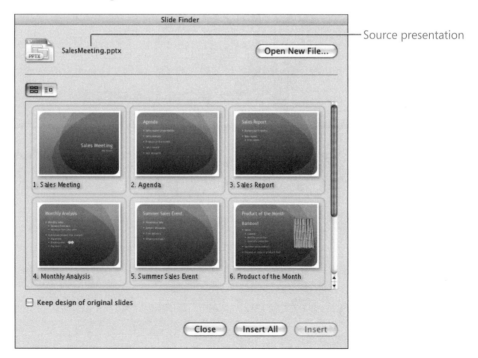

Source presentation

5. In the **Slide Finder**, scroll the pane, and click the thumbnail for **Slide 7**, titled *Bamboo Product Line*.

The thumbnail depicts a slide with a blue patterned background, a white title, and a table. The table has a blue header row and, if you look closely, blue cell outlines.

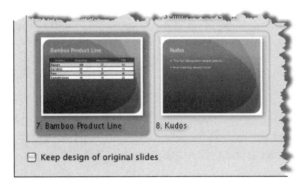

> **Tip** If you want the slide to retain its original formatting, select the Keep Design Of Original Slides check box in the Slide Finder before inserting the slide.

6. In the **Slide Finder**, click **Insert**.

PowerPoint inserts the selected slide from the *SalesMeeting* presentation as Slide 4 in the *SalesPlanning* presentation. The new slide has the white background of the other slides in the destination presentation, and the table has a purple header and outlines. It's not obvious from what we could previously see, but the font has also changed to that of the *SalesPlanning* presentation.

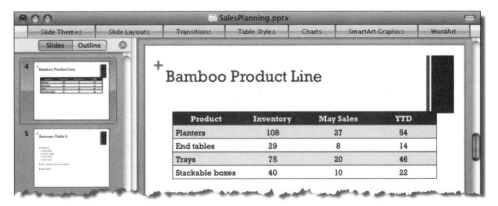

 CLEAN UP Close the *SalesPlanning* presentation without saving your changes.

Add Content to Slides

In Normal view, *layout placeholders* indicate where you can insert different types of slide content. For example, a Title And Content slide has placeholders for a title and for a bulleted list or a graphic element such as a table, chart, picture, or movie clip.

You can enter content on a slide either into the layout placeholders that are already in place or directly onto the slide.

About Slide Masters

The base content of a slide—the default position of layout placeholders, the default fonts and colors of text within text placeholders, and any background graphics that appear on all pages of a certain type—are stored with the *slide masters*. Certain slide master elements aren't editable on the slide; you can change them only from the slide master.

Using slide masters, you can efficiently apply structure, formatting, and standard base content (such as textual or graphic elements) to a slide or group of slides. Each of the slide layouts available from the Elements Gallery corresponds to a slide master. You can change the structure, formatting, or base content of all the slides that have a specific layout by editing the slide master.

Bonus Web Content   For more information about slide masters, see "Practice Working with Slide Masters in PowerPoint 2008 for Mac" on the book's companion Web site at *www.microsoft.com/mspress/companion/9780735626171*.

Work with Layout Placeholders

In Normal view, layout placeholders look like boxes. When you are viewing a slide in Slide Sorter view or in a slide show, the placeholders aren't visible. Any content you enter into a placeholder is visible in all three views.

Tip   If you don't enter content into a placeholder, that area will simply appear to be empty—so you don't need to delete unused placeholders before you deliver a presentation.

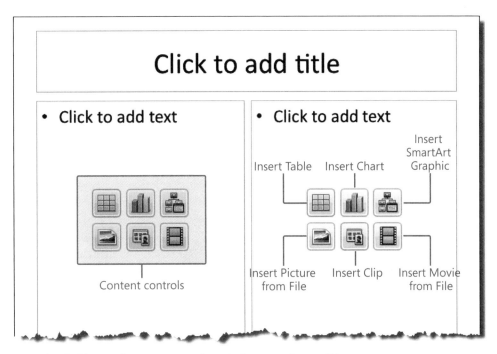

Text placeholders and content controls make it easy to insert slide content.

Insert Content in a Placeholder

When you point to a placeholder on a slide, or to text on the Outline page of the Navigation pane, the pointer changes to an I-beam. When you click the placeholder or text, a blinking insertion point appears where you clicked, to indicate where characters will appear when you type. As you type, the text appears both on the slide and in the outline.

You can add text and graphic elements to a slide by following these guides in the layout placeholders:

● To enter a slide title, click the words *Click to add title*, type the slide title, and then press **Return**.

● To enter bulleted text, click the words *Click to add text* in the content holder, type the text of the first bulleted list item, and then press **Return** to create another list item.

See Also For information about formatting lists and paragraphs, see "Format Slide Text" in Chapter 10, "Work with PowerPoint Slide Content."

● To insert a table, chart, SmartArt graphic, image file, clip art image, or movie clip, click the corresponding control, and then follow the instructions that appear.

Alternatively, you can enter text on the Outline page of the Navigation pane, where the text of the presentation is displayed in outline form.

Clip art from the Microsoft Clip Gallery   Slide title   Multilevel list

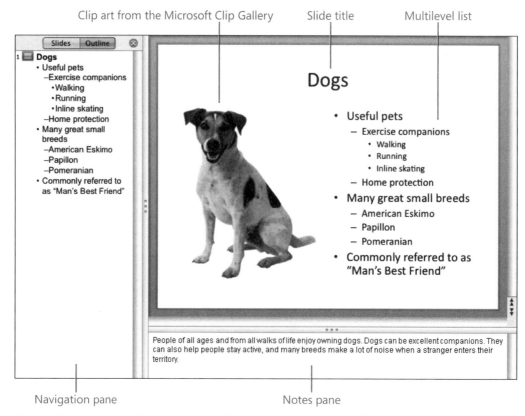

Navigation pane   Notes pane

The Outline page of the Navigation pane displays the text of all the slides.

> **Tip** If you enter more text in a text box than can comfortably fit at the default text font size, PowerPoint automatically changes the font size to fit the text into the box, and the AutoFit Options button appears. If you don't want PowerPoint to change the size of text that doesn't fit into a box (for example, if you intend to resize the text box to maintain the font size), click the AutoFit Options button and then, in the list, click Stop Fitting Text To This Placeholder.

See Also For information about adding tables to a slide, see "Work with Tables in PowerPoint 2008 for Mac" on the book's companion Web site at *www.microsoft.com/mspress/companion/ 9780735626171*. For information about images, charts, SmartArt graphics, and other graphic elements, see Chapter 12, "Create and Insert Graphics."

Modify Text

You can modify, add to, or remove the text you enter onto a slide. You can insert new text by clicking where you want to make the insertion and simply typing. Before you can change existing text, you have to *select* it by using one of the following techniques:

- Select an individual word by double-clicking it. The word and the space following it are selected. Punctuation following a word is not selected.
- Select adjacent words, lines, or paragraphs by dragging through them.
- Alternatively, position the insertion point at the beginning of the text you want to select, hold down the **Shift** key, and either press an arrow key to select characters one at a time or click at the end of the text you want to select.
- Select the title and all the text on a slide by clicking its slide icon on the **Outline** page of the Navigation pane.
- Select an entire list item by clicking its bullet or number on either the **Outline** page or the slide.
- Select all the text in a placeholder by first clicking inside the placeholder and then clicking **Select All** on the **Edit** menu or pressing **Command+A**.

Selected text appears highlighted in the location where you made the selection—that is, either on the slide or in the outline. To replace a selection, you type the new text. To delete the selection, you press the Delete key.

To move a selection to a new location, you can simply drag it. You can also move and copy text, and undo and redo changes, by using the same tools and techniques that you do in Word. You can work on the slide itself when moving or copying text within a slide, but it is more efficient to work on the Outline page of the Navigation pane when moving or copying text between slides.

Create a Presentation from the Project Gallery

Creating presentations from scratch is time-consuming and requires some skill and knowledge about PowerPoint. Even people with intermediate and advanced PowerPoint skills can save time by capitalizing on the work someone else has already done. When you don't need help with the content of a presentation but you do need help with its design, you can start a new presentation based on an *Office Theme template* or a *project template*, both available from the Project Gallery.

In Chapter 4, "Create Word Documents," and Chapter 5, "Create Excel Workbooks," we discussed the Project Gallery, from which you can create a variety of blank or purpose-specific Office documents from templates. By using the PowerPoint presentation templates that are available in the Project Gallery, you can create either a blank, themed presentation or a presentation containing content.

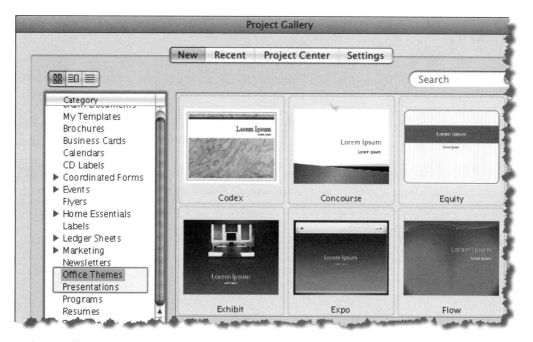

Only the Office Themes and Presentations categories include PowerPoint project templates.

Other than the blank presentation template available from the Blank Documents category, all the PowerPoint templates in the Project Gallery are in the Office Themes category and the Presentations category. (And, in the same vein, all the project templates in those categories are PowerPoint templates.)

Create a Presentation Based on an Office Theme Template

The Office Themes category includes 49 themes. Choosing a template in this category creates a presentation with an attractive, professional design template attached. (Opening the project template creates a presentation containing only a blank title slide. Slides you add to the presentation automatically pick up the fonts, colors, and backgrounds of the theme.)

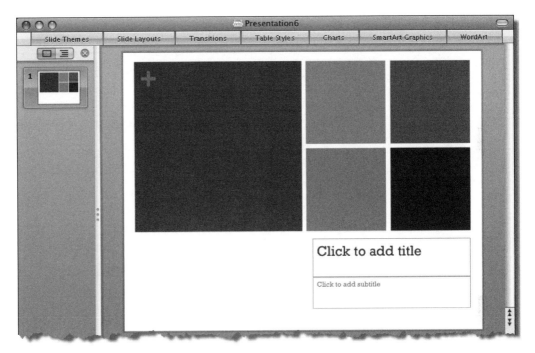

You can create presentations based on any of 49 Office Theme templates.

Create a Presentation Based on a Project Template

You can base a presentation on a project template from the Project Gallery, or you can design your own presentation and save it as a template.

See Also For information about saving your own templates, see "Create a Personalized Project Template" in Chapter 4, "Create Word Documents."

The Presentations category of the Project Gallery includes six templates that create pre-sentations containing instructional content that either teaches you about PowerPoint 2008 or teaches you how to modify the presentation with your information.

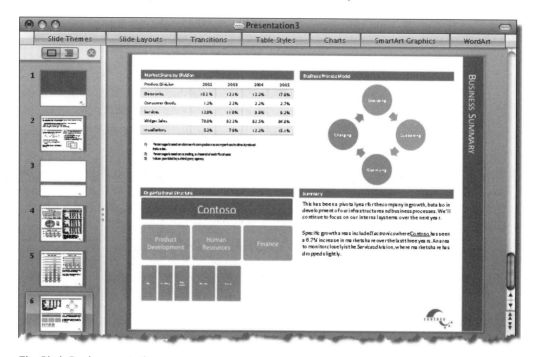

The Pitch Book presentation

The Presentations category includes templates to create the following stock presentations:

- **Classic Photo Album.** This presentation includes slide layouts for presenting from one to five images in a variety of arrangements, with corresponding captions. The default theme is intended for the presentation of black-and-white photos.

- **Contemporary Photo Album.** This presentation includes slide layouts similar to those in the Classic Photo Album. The default theme is intended for the presentation of color photos.

- **Introducing PowerPoint 2008.** This presentation is full of useful information about creating content in a PowerPoint 2008 presentation. It uses standard slide layouts and is intended more as a learning tool than as an actual template.

- **Pitch Book.** This is a structured presentation containing tightly packed text and graphics. Pitch books are usually intended for print, rather than on-screen, presen-tation. Pitch book slide layouts include an agenda slide that functions as a table of contents, and structured slides designed to present content in from one to five designated areas.

- **Quiz Show.** This presentation includes animated slide templates for presenting True/False, question/answer, multiple choice, and matching questions and answers to your audience.

- **Widescreen Presentation.** Slides in this presentation have an aspect ratio of 16:9 (10 inches wide by 5.63 inches high) to fit the widescreen flat panel monitors that are now available, rather than the default "on-screen show" aspect ratio of 4:3 (10 inches wide by 7.5 inches high).

See Also For information about slide aspect ratio, see "Change Standard Slide Settings" in Chapter 10, "Work with PowerPoint Slide Content."

Special Presentation Themes

The themes used by the project templates available from the Presentations category of the Project Gallery are not among the built-in themes available to other presentations. If you want to apply one of these specialized themes to another presentation, you can do so by following these steps:

1. Create a presentation from the project template that has the theme you want to apply to another presentation.

2. On the **File** menu, click **Save As**.

3. In the **Save As** dialog box, click **Office Theme (.thmx)** in the **Format** list.

   The location where the file will be saved changes to your *My Themes* folder.

4. In the **Save As** box, enter an appropriate name for the theme—for example, the same name as the original project template. Then click **Save**.

5. Open the presentation you want to apply the special theme to.

6. On the **Format** menu, point to **Theme**, and then click **From File**.

7. In the **Choose Themed Document or Slide Template** dialog box displaying the contents of your *My Themes* folder, click the theme you just saved, and then click **Apply**.

   PowerPoint applies the selected theme to the presentation and adds the theme's slide masters to the presentation's default set.

See Also For more information about themes, see "Work with Office Themes" in Chapter 7, "Work with Word Document Content."

Practice Creating Presentations

In this exercise, you'll create a themed presentation from the Project Gallery, and add slides to it. Then you'll populate the slides by entering text, both directly in slides and on the Outline page of the Navigation pane.

> **SET UP** From the Dock, or from the File menu of any Office program, open the Project Gallery.

1. In the **Category** list, click **Office Themes**.

2. Scroll the list of themes to view the available options. Then click the **Travelogue** thumbnail.

   The thumbnail depicts three white-framed photos on a gold background, with a title and subtitle below.

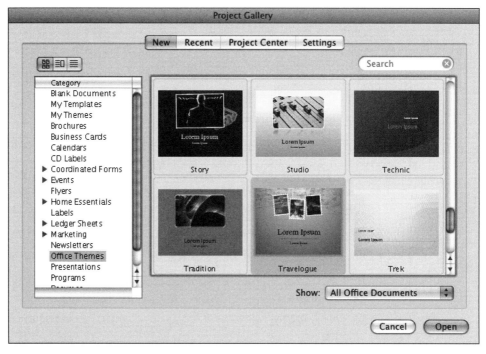

3. In the **Project Gallery**, click **Open**.

PowerPoint starts, if it wasn't already running, and a presentation based on the selected theme opens in Normal view. The Slides page of the Navigation pane shows that the presentation consists of only the title slide.

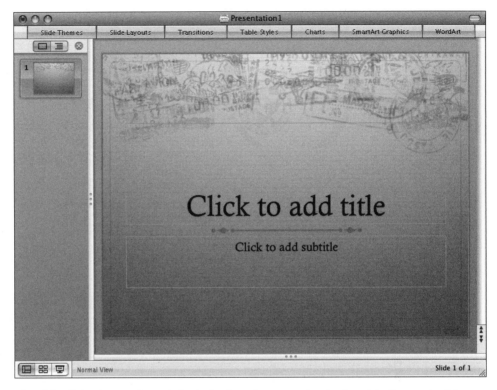

The title slide shown doesn't include the photographs depicted in the project template thumbnail. That title slide layout is not the default, but it is available from the Elements Gallery.

> **Note** We've hidden the toolbar area and the Notes pane to keep things tidy.

4. Click the **Slide Layouts** tab of the Elements Gallery to display thumbnail representations of the available slide layouts.

A red outline indicates the current slide layout. The name of the layout, *Title Slide*, is shown in the style name area at the top of the left pane of the gallery.

5. On the **Slide Layouts** tab, point to the third thumbnail, which depicts the title slide layout we saw earlier in the Project Gallery.

Title Slide with 3 Pictures appears in the style name area.

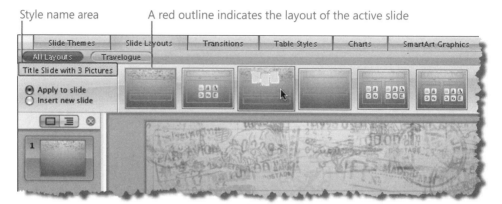

6. With the **Apply to slide** option selected below the layout title, click the **Title Slide with 3 Pictures** thumbnail.

PowerPoint changes the layout of the title slide displayed in the Slide pane. The red outline moves to the *Title Slide with 3 Pictures* thumbnail.

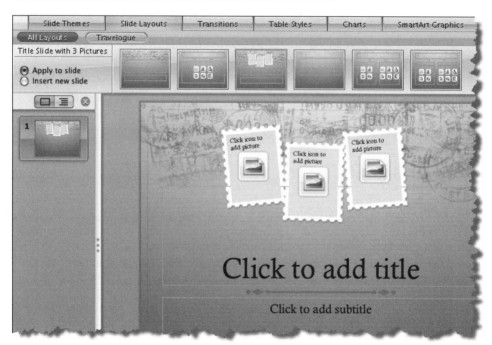

7. In the left pane of the gallery, below the style name area, click **Insert new slide**.

A white plus sign in a green circle appears in the upper-left corner of each slide layout thumbnail as a visual indicator that clicking the thumbnail will insert a slide.

8. In the gallery, click the second thumbnail, **Title and Content**.

A second slide, Slide 2, appears in the Navigation pane and in the Slide pane.

9. Scroll the gallery to display additional slide layouts. Click the **Picture with Caption** thumbnail, and then the **2 Pictures above Caption** thumbnail, to insert two additional slides.

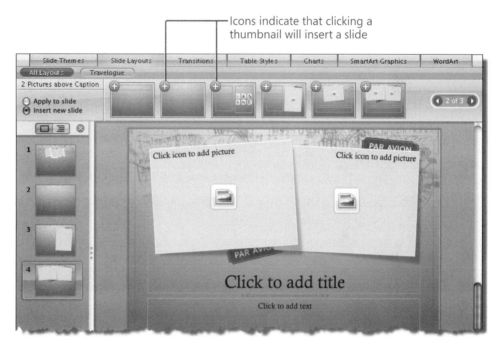

10. We're finished adding slides for now, so click the **Slide Layouts** tab once to close it.

11. In the Navigation pane, click **Slide 1**.

12. In the Slide pane, click the **Click to add title** placeholder.

A selection box surrounds the placeholder, and a blinking insertion point appears in the center of the box, indicating that the text you type will be centered in the placeholder.

13. Type My Vacation.

See Also For information about entering and editing text, see "Add Content to Slides" earlier in this chapter.

14. At the top of the Navigation pane, click the **Outline** button.

The text you typed also appears on the Outline page.

15. In the Slide pane, click the **Click to add subtitle** placeholder.

The subtitle placeholder becomes active.

16. Type Fun in the Sun!, and then press **Return** to move the insertion point to a new line in the same placeholder.

17. Type featuring Trinity Grace.

When you press the Spacebar after typing the first word, the AutoCorrect function changes it from *featuring* to *Featuring*, and a miniature version of the AutoCorrect Options button appears under the letter *F*. The button disappears by the time you type the rest of the text, but that's okay—we can get it back.

18. Click in front of the letter *F* to redisplay the miniature **AutoCorrect Options** button. Point to it and then, when it changes into the full-size **AutoCorrect Options** button, click it.

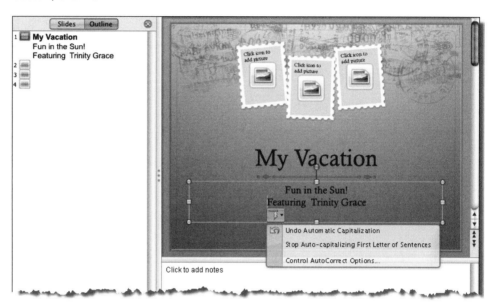

In the AutoCorrect Options list, you can choose to deal with this specific instance of automatic capitalization, with all instances of automatic capitalization, or with all AutoCorrect options.

19. In the **AutoCorrect Options** list, click **Undo Automatic Capitalization**.

The capital letter *F* reverts to lowercase.

 20. Below the vertical scroll bar, click the **Next Slide** button to display **Slide 2**.

21. In the slide title placeholder, type Where We Went. Then in the content placeholder, click the bulleted list item (not the bullet).

22. Type Olympia, and then press **Return**.

PowerPoint adds a new bullet at the same level.

23. Type Sequim, and then press **Return**.

24. Type Dallas, and then press **Return**.

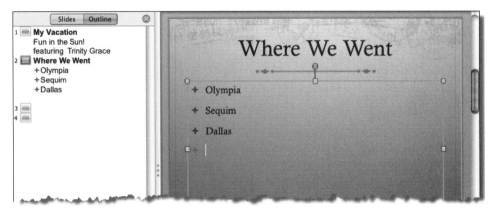

25. On the **Insert** menu, click **New Slide** (or press **Shift+Command+N**).

PowerPoint inserts a new slide following Slide 2, and displays it in the Slides pane. The new Slide 3 has the same slide layout as the slide you created it from.

26. In the Navigation pane, click to the right of the **Slide 3** icon. Then type What We Saw.

As you type in the outline, the text also appears on the slide. The insertion point is active only in the outline, not on the slide.

27. With the insertion point at the end of the new slide title, press **Return**.

PowerPoint inserts another new slide with the same layout.

28. Press the **Tab** key.

The new slide, Slide 4, changes into a bulleted list item on Slide 3. In the outline, the bullet is gray, to indicate that it is temporary, until you enter the list item text.

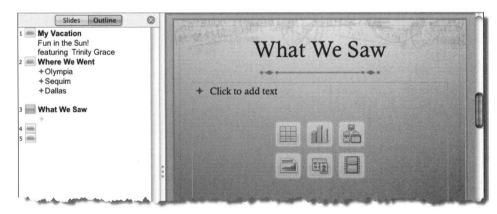

> **Tip** To convert a bulleted list item into a slide, press Shift+Tab.
>
> You can use the Increase Indent button on the Formatting toolbar to demote items (for example, to change slide titles to bulleted list items or first-level list items to second-level items), both on the slide and on the Outline page. You can also use the Decrease Indent button to promote items in both places. However, when you are entering text on the Outline page, it's usually faster to use key combinations—Tab and Shift+Tab—to perform these functions than it is to take your hands off the keyboard to use your mouse.

29. With the insertion point after the bullet in the outline, type Relatives, Friends, Dogs, and Horses, pressing **Return** after each word. Save the presentation in the *~/Documents/Microsoft Press/2008OfficeMacSBS/CreatePresentations/* folder, as My Vacation.pptx.

> **See Also** For information about saving presentations, see "Open, Save, and Close Office Files" in Chapter 2, "Practice Basic Office File Skills."

 CLEAN UP Close the *My Vacation* presentation.

Create a Presentation from a Word Document

If you find it simpler to organize your thoughts in a document than while creating slides, you can outline your presentation in a Word document, Word 98–2004 document, or Rich Text Format (.rtf) file, and then import the outline into PowerPoint to create a presentation based on the outline. PowerPoint uses the heading styles in the outline to create corresponding slide titles and bullet points.

To import an outline into PowerPoint, follow these steps:

1. In PowerPoint, on the Standard toolbar, click the **Open** button.

2. In the **Open** dialog box, browse to the folder containing the outline document you want to import.

3. Click the document, and then click **Open**.

   In a very short time, PowerPoint creates a presentation containing slides based on the outline document.

To export an outline from Word, follow these steps:

1. In the Word document, apply heading styles to the outline elements you want to use in the presentation. Use the Heading 1 style for slide titles, Heading 2 for first-level bulleted list items, and Heading 3 for second-level list items.

2. On the **File** menu, point to **Send To**, and then click **PowerPoint**.

   PowerPoint starts, if it wasn't already running, and creates a presentation from the outline.

If you want to use the text of a presentation in another program, or edit the presentation content, you can export the presentation outline as an .rtf file. You can open the .rtf file in Word or in a text editor such as TextEdit.

Part of an outline exported from a presentation

To export a presentation outline, follow these steps:

1. On the **File** menu, click **Save As** (or press **Shift+Command+S**).

   The Save As dialog box opens.

2. In the **Save As** box, specify the name of the file.

3. In the **Format** list, click **Outline / Rich Text Format (.rtf)**.

4. Navigate to the folder where you want to store the outline, and then click **Save**.

   PowerPoint saves an outline of the presentation in the designated folder. The original file remains intact.

Practice Exporting and Importing Presentation Outlines

In this exercise, you'll first export the outline of a presentation as an .rtf file, and then import the outline as a new presentation.

> **SET UP** Open the *Introducing* presentation located in the *~/Documents/Microsoft Press/ 2008OfficeMacSBS/CreatePresentations/* folder. This is an 18-slide presentation created from a project template.

1. Look through the presentation to become familiar with the slide content.

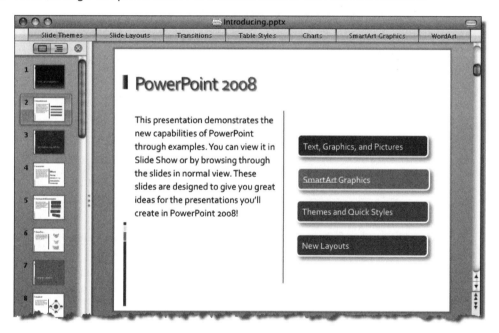

2. On the **File** menu, click **Save As** (or press **Shift+Command+S**).

   The Save As dialog box opens.

3. If the **CreatePresentations** folder is not already displayed in the **Where** box or in the *navigation area*, navigate to that folder.

4. In the **Format** list, click **Outline / Rich Text Format (.rtf)**.

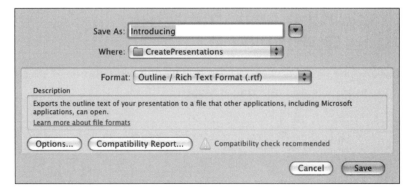

5. In the **Save As** dialog box, click **Save**.

The Save As dialog box closes, but there is no visible indication of whether the outline document has been created.

6. On the **File** menu, click **Open** (or press **Command+O**).

7. If the **Open** dialog box does not already display the contents of the *CreatePresentations* folder, navigate to that folder.

The *Introducing* .rtf file is visible in the *CreatePresentations* folder where you saved it in step 5.

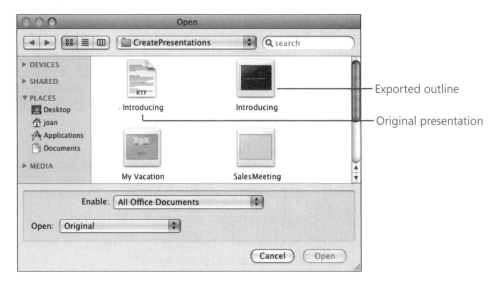

Exported outline

Original presentation

8. Click the *Introducing* .rtf file, and then click **Open**.

PowerPoint opens a new presentation based on the exported outline.

9. Compare the original presentation and the new presentation side by side to see the similarities and differences.

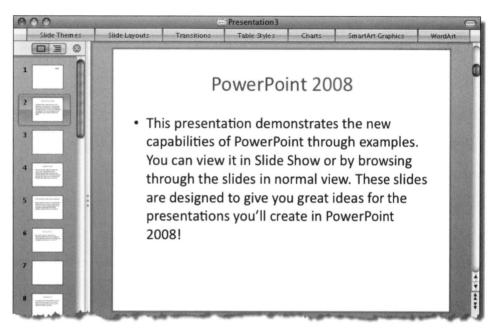

Like the original, the new presentation has 18 slides—but slides that originally contained only graphics are blank, and slides that contained text and graphics display only the text. The new presentation is built on blank slides, and the majority of the font formatting hasn't carried over from the original.

 CLEAN UP Close the open presentations. If you're not going to work on your own in PowerPoint, quit the program.

Key Points

- You can create presentations in many ways: from scratch, based on an existing presentation, based on an existing outline, or from a project template.

- A new presentation includes only the title slide. You add other slides that you want. An easy way to add a slide is by choosing a layout from the Elements Gallery.

- You can reuse a slide from another presentation by importing it. The imported slide automatically takes on the theme of the presentation you import it into.

- You can enter and edit text either on the Outline page of the Navigation pane or directly on a slide.

- Repurposing an existing presentation to fit the needs of a different audience is a useful technique that saves development time. Repurposing existing slides is another way to save time and ensure consistency.

Bonus Web Content

You can find the following articles about additional PowerPoint 2008 features on the book's companion Web site, at *www.microsoft.com/mspress/companion/9780735626171*:

- "Add Timings to Slides in PowerPoint 2008 for Mac"
- "Animate Slide Content in PowerPoint 2008 for Mac"
- "Animate Slide Transitions in PowerPoint 2008 for Mac"
- "Create a Self-Running Presentation in PowerPoint 2008 for Mac"
- "Practice Working with Slide Masters in PowerPoint 2008 for Mac"
- "Prepare Speaker Notes and Handouts for Presentations in PowerPoint 2008 for Mac"
- "Work with Tables in PowerPoint 2008 for Mac"

Part III

Work with Office File Content

7 Work with Word Document Content 213

8 Work with Excel Sheet Content. 259

9 Create Excel Formulas. 295

10 Work with PowerPoint Slide Content. 317

Chapter at a Glance

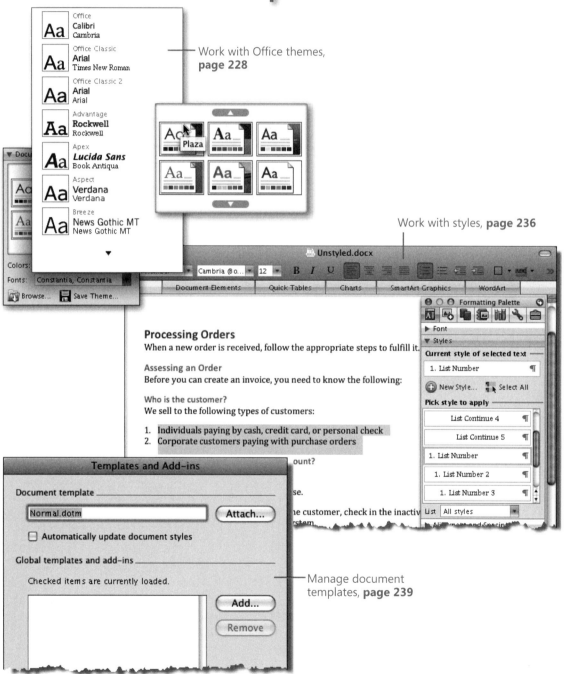

Work with Office themes, **page 228**

Work with styles, **page 236**

Manage document templates, **page 239**

7 Work with Word Document Content

In this chapter, you will learn how to

- ✔ Edit document text.
- ✔ Automatically display current information in a document.
- ✔ Work with Office themes.
- ✔ Work with styles.
- ✔ Manage document templates.
- ✔ Check spelling and grammar.

In previous chapters, you looked at documents, created documents, and created content in documents. The major advantage you have when creating a document in a word-processing program such as Microsoft Word 2008, rather than on a typewriter, is that you can cleanly and easily make changes to the document content after you enter it. Another advantage is that you can change the look of the document content and format it in ways that are likely to be more attractive than simple black letters on white paper.

In this chapter, we'll look at ways you can change the content that's already in a document. We'll take a twofold approach to this, first looking at the many ways you can insert, delete, select, cut, copy, and move text. You'll learn about the Clipboard, the Scrapbook, and the Spike, and which to use for the type of editing you want to do. Then we'll look at ways of formatting document content, by applying themes that govern colors and fonts, and by applying and modifying styles. Finally, we'll wrap up with a discussion of document templates and how you can use them to change the formatting of document content.

See Also You can find handy keyboard shortcuts, simple instructions for performing common tasks, and other useful information in the Quick Reference section at the beginning of this book.

 Practice Makes Perfect! The practice files you will use to complete the exercises in this chapter are in the *WorkDocuments* practice file folder. See "Using the Companion Content" at the beginning of this book for information about installing and locating the practice files.

Edit Document Text

You will rarely write a perfect document that doesn't require any editing. You will almost always want to insert a word or two, change a phrase, or move text from one place to another. You can edit a document as you create it, or you can write it first and then revise it. Or you might want to edit a document that you created for one purpose so that it will serve a different purpose. For example, you might change a cover letter for a job application to make it applicable to a different job opening.

Insert and Delete Text

Inserting text is easy; you click to position the insertion point, and begin typing. Any existing text to the right of the insertion point moves to make room for the new text.

Deleting text is equally easy. If you want to delete only one or a few characters, you can position the insertion point and then press the Delete key until the characters are all gone. Pressing Delete (the key at the right end of the row of number keys) deletes the character to the left of the insertion point; pressing Del (the key in the separate block of keys to the right of the Return key) deletes the character to the right of the insertion point.

> **Note** Different keyboards have different key layouts and labels. In this book, we'll do our best to identify keys by the names that will appear on a current Mac keyboard.

Select Text

To delete, format, move, or copy more than a few characters efficiently, you need to know how to *select* the text. Selected text appears highlighted on the screen. You can select specific items as follows:

- To select a word, double-click it. Word selects the word and the space following it. It does not select punctuation following a word.

- To select a sentence, click anywhere in the sentence while holding down the **Command** key. Word selects all the characters in the sentence, from the first character through the space following the ending punctuation mark.

- To select a paragraph, triple-click it.

You can select adjacent characters, words, lines, or paragraphs by positioning the insertion point at the beginning of the text you want to select, holding down the Shift key, and then pressing the Arrow keys or clicking at the end of the text that you want to select. To select words, lines, or paragraphs that are not adjacent, select the first block of text, and then hold down the Command key while selecting additional blocks.

As an alternative, you can use the selection area to quickly select various items. This is an invisible area in the document's left margin, where the pointer changes to a right-pointing arrow. You can use the selection area as follows:

- To select a line, click the selection area to the left of the line.
- To select a paragraph, double-click the selection area to the left of the paragraph.
- To select an entire document, triple-click anywhere in the selection area.

Selection area

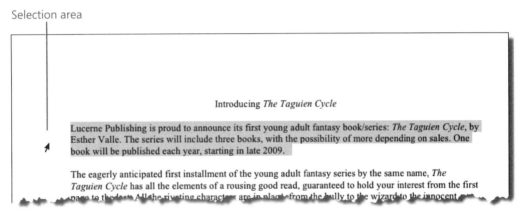

To select a paragraph, move the pointer to the selection area in the left margin of the document and then double-click.

Tip To release selected text, click in the document window anywhere other than in the selected text or selection area.

You can use the keyboard shortcuts described in the following table to select text and document content.

To select...	Press...
Multiple items that are not next to each other	Select the first item, press and hold the Command key, and then select the other items
One character to the right	Shift+Right Arrow
One character to the left	Shift+Left Arrow
One word to the right	Shift+Option+Right Arrow
One word to the left	Shift+Option+Left Arrow
To the end of a line	Shift+End or Command+Shift+Right Arrow
To the beginning of a line	Shift+Home or Command+Shift+Left Arrow
One line down	Shift+Down Arrow
One line up	Shift+Up Arrow
To the end of a paragraph	Command+Shift+Down Arrow
To the beginning of a paragraph	Command+Shift+Up Arrow
One screen down	Shift+Page Down
One screen up	Shift+Page Up
To the beginning of a document	Command+Shift+Home
To the end of a document	Command+Shift+End
To the end of a window	Command+Shift+Option+Page Down
The entire document	Command+A

Copy and Move Text

You can move or copy selected text to another area of the document, to another document, or to another Microsoft Office file, such as a Microsoft PowerPoint presentation.

To move or copy text only a short distance—for example, within a paragraph or line—use *drag-and-drop editing* (frequently referred to simply as *dragging*). Start by selecting the text. Then hold down the mouse button, drag the text to its new location, and release the mouse button. To copy the selection to the new location, hold down the Option key while you drag.

Use the *Clipboard*, *Scrapbook*, or *Spike* when you need to move or copy text between two locations that you cannot see at the same time—for example, between pages or between documents. Each of these temporary storage areas has a different purpose, which we explain in detail in this section. Here's an overview:

- To copy content from one location to another, you select the content you want to copy and then copy it to the Clipboard or Scrapbook. You then position the insertion point where you want to insert the clipping, and paste it from the Clipboard or Scrapbook.

- To move content from one location to another, you select the content you want to move and then cut it to the Clipboard. Then you position the insertion point in the location in which you want to insert the clipping, and paste it from the Clipboard.

- To move a series of noncontiguous content from multiple locations to another location, you cut each item you want to move to the Spike. When you have collected all the content you want to move, you position the insertion point where you want to insert the content collection, and then paste it from the Spike.

When you cut or copy information from a Word document, PowerPoint presentation, Microsoft Excel worksheet, or Microsoft Entourage item, it is temporarily placed as a clipping on the Clipboard. You can paste the most recent clipping from the Clipboard into any of these Office documents (even a document that's in a program other than the one from which you took the clipping). You can't view the Clipboard contents.

You can cut to or copy to and paste from the Clipboard by using the commands on the Edit menu, or you can use the keyboard shortcuts described in the following table.

To...	Press...
Copy a selection to the Clipboard	F3 or Command+C
Copy a selection to the Scrapbook	Command+Shift+C
Copy a selection to another location	Shift+F2, then click the target location and press Return
Cut a selection to the Clipboard	F2 or Command+X
Cut a selection to the Spike	Command+F3
Paste the current clipping from the Clipboard	F4 or Command+V
Paste the selected clipping from the Scrapbook	Command+Shift+V
Paste the Spike contents	Command+Shift+F3

If you want to store a clipping for later reuse, you can copy it to the Scrapbook, or insert the most recent clipping from the Clipboard into the Scrapbook. You can view saved clippings and files from the Scrapbook, which is part of the Toolbox.

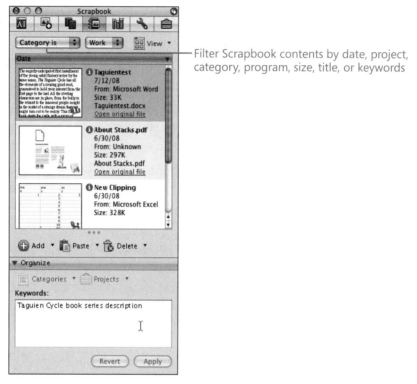

Filter Scrapbook contents by date, project, category, program, size, title, or keywords

Organize scraps by assigning categories and keywords.

You can assign each clipping stored in the Scrapbook to a *category* and associate *keywords* to help you organize and locate scraps (clippings and files stored in the Scrapbook). If you've created one or more projects in the Microsoft Project Center, you can also associate clippings with a project. These clippings appear on the Clippings tab of the Project Center, in Entourage.

You can copy to and paste from the Scrapbook by using the commands on the Edit menu or in the Scrapbook, or you can use these keyboard shortcuts:

- To copy a selection to the Scrapbook, press **Shift+Command+C**.
- To paste the most recent clipping from the Scrapbook into an Office document, press **Shift+Command+V**.

Note that the Scrapbook-related commands work only when the Scrapbook is open.

You can copy items and files to the Scrapbook by clicking the Add arrow in the Scrapbook and then, in the list, clicking Add Selection, Add File, or Add From Clipboard. (To automatically add all copied clippings to the Scrapbook, click Always Add Copy). You can paste a clipping from the Scrapbook into an Office document by selecting the clipping and then clicking the Paste button.

When you're working in Word, you can cut content from a document to the Spike (a dynamic *AutoText* entry that stores content until you empty it), and then later insert the Spike contents elsewhere. The Spike can store text, graphics, WordArt, and other elements, with the exception of structural elements, such as tables. You can't view the Spike contents.

You can cut to and paste from the Spike by using these keyboard shortcuts:

- To cut a selection to the Spike, press **Command+F3**.
- To paste all the collected content from the Spike into a document, press **Shift+Command+F3**.

Undo Changes

If you make a change to a document and then realize that you made a mistake, you can easily reverse the change. You can undo your last editing action by clicking the Undo button on the Standard toolbar. To undo multiple actions (up to 16), click the Undo arrow and then click the earliest action you want to undo. (Clicking an action will undo that action and all the actions that followed it; these will then move to the Redo list.)

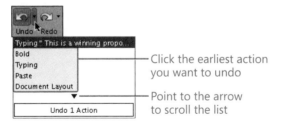

Click the earliest action you want to undo

Point to the arrow to scroll the list

Undo recent edits by selecting one or more changes from the Undo list.

> **Tip** You can return to the last three locations in which you entered or edited text by pressing Shift+F5.

If you undo one or more actions and then change your mind, you can click the Redo button on the Standard toolbar, or select from the Redo list the actions you want to revert.

Practice Manipulating Text

In this exercise, you'll select, replace, delete, cut, copy, paste, and move text within a document.

 SET UP Open the *SeriesDescription* document located in the *~/Documents/Microsoft Press/2008OfficeMacSBS/WorkDocuments/* folder.

 1. If non-printing characters are not already visible in the document, click the **Show** button on the toolbar.

2. On the third line of the first paragraph, click immediately to the left of the word *between*, hold down the **Shift** key, and then on the next line, click immediately to the right of the word *fifteen* (and to the left of the comma that follows it).

   Word selects the text between the two clicks.

   ¶

   • The Taguien Cycle¶

   •A Fantasy Series for Young Adults ¶
   The Taguien Cycle is the most exciting and promising new book project to have come before the committee in several years. It meets our two principal goals: Develop a book line that will appeal to young adult readers between the ages of twelve and fifteen, especially boys; and develop a book line that has the potential for media spin-offs that will contribute to future profits and on-going financial success. ¶

   Interest in the fantasy genre has increased steadily over the past ten years, a trend that shows no sign of reversal. Anecdotal industry sales statistics show an

3. Press the **Delete** key to delete the selection.

   Word also deletes the space before the word *between*, at the beginning of the selection.

   > **Tip** If Word doesn't delete the space, then your Edit Preferences setting has been altered from the default. See the sidebar on the facing page.

 4. To see an "instant replay" of your actions and watch Word delete the unselected space, click the **Undo** button on the toolbar, and then click the **Redo** button.

   Notice that when you undo the deletion, the text *between the ages of twelve and fifteen* is still selected, exactly as it was.

Let Word Take Care of the Details

Word inserts and deletes spaces when pasting and cutting text because this is one of the functions of the Use Smart Cut And Paste option. If you want to be able to control the spacing yourself, display the Preferences dialog box and, under Authoring And Proofing Tools, click Edit. Then on the Edit page, under Cut And Paste Options, click the Settings button next to Use Smart Cut And Paste.

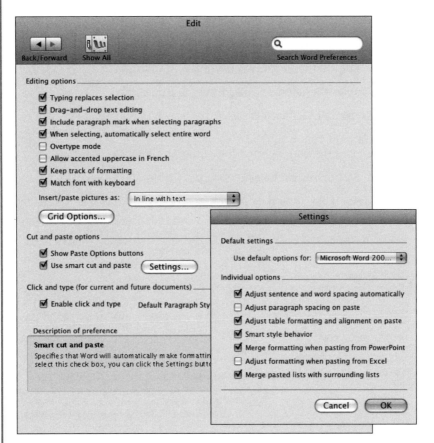

You can control a variety of automatic spacing and formatting functionality from the Smart Cut And Paste Settings dialog box.

Clear the check boxes of any functions you don't want Word to automatically handle for you, and then click OK in the Settings dialog box and on the Edit page of the Preferences dialog box.

5. In the first sentence of the first paragraph, double-click the word *book* to select it, and then press the **Delete** key.

6. In the second sentence of the same paragraph, double-click the word *principal*, and then replace it by typing primary.

   Notice that you don't have to type a space after *primary*. Word inserts the space for you.

7. Position the mouse pointer in the selection area to the left of the subheading *A Fantasy Series for Young Adults*. When the pointer changes from left-pointing to right-pointing, click once to select the entire line of text.

8. On the **Edit** menu, click **Copy** (or press **Command+C**).

   Word copies the selected line to the Clipboard.

9. At the bottom of the vertical scroll bar, click the **Next Page** button to move to the beginning of page 2, and then press the **Down Arrow** key twice to position the insertion point at the beginning of the paragraph (not the heading).

10. On the **Edit** menu, click **Paste** (or press **Command+V**).

    Word inserts the copied subheading, and the Paste Options button appears below and to the right of the insertion. You can click this button if you want to change the way Word pastes by default, but in this case, you can just ignore it.

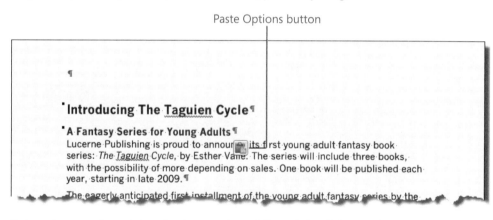

Paste Options button

11. Return to page 1, and then in the numbered list, triple-click anywhere in the *Bartimaeus Trilogy* entry to select the entire list item.

12. On the **Edit** menu, click **Cut** (or press **Command+X**).

    Word cuts the selection to the Clipboard and renumbers the list to reflect that it now has only four items.

13. Press the **Up Arrow** key once to move the insertion point to the beginning of the *Harry Potter series* paragraph. Then paste the *Bartimaeus Trilogy* item from the Clipboard.

You have switched the order of the first and second list items.

Bonus Web Content For more information about numbered lists, see "Organize Text in Lists in Word 2008 for Mac" on the book's companion Web site, at *www.microsoft.com/ mspress/companion/9780735626171*.

14. On the toolbar, click the **Undo** arrow and then, in the list, click the third action (**Paste**).

Word undoes the previous cut-and-paste operation and the pasting of the sub-heading at the top of the second page.

15. Verify that the subheading that was located at the top of page 2 no longer appears there. Then press **Command+Home** to move to the beginning of the document.

16. Move the pointer into the selection area adjacent to the second paragraph (the one beginning *Interest in the fantasy genre*), and double-click to select the paragraph.

17. Point to the selection, hold down the mouse button, and then drag the paragraph up, to the beginning of the paragraph above it.

As you drag, Word displays a transparent reference version of the dragged text. This can be more of a hindrance than a help if it obscures the target location.

Reference version of the text being dragged   Original text location

When you release the mouse, the text appears in its new location.

18. With the paragraph still selected, press the **End** key.

Word releases the selection and moves the insertion point to the end of the paragraph.

19. Press the **Spacebar**, and then press the **Del** key.

Word deletes the paragraph mark, and the two paragraphs become one.

20. Open the Toolbox and then, if the Scrapbook is not already displayed, click the **Scrapbook** button on the Toolbox menu bar.

21. Display page 2 of the *SeriesDescription* document. In the second paragraph of text, after the comma, point to the *e* in the word *The*. Click to the left of the *e* and then drag to select the second phrase of the sentence, beginning with *The Taguien Cycle* and ending with the period.

Although you started selecting text in the middle of the word *The*, Word automatically selected the entire word, as well as the space following the period.

22. On the **Edit** menu, click **Copy to Scrapbook** (or press **Shift+Command+C**).

A new clipping labeled *Series Description* appears in the Scrapbook. The clipping name is based on the name of the file the content was clipped from.

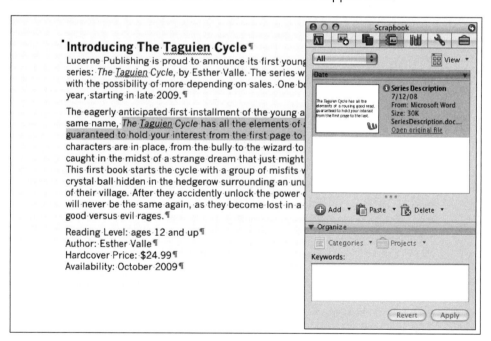

This clipping is now available for you to insert into any Office document.

 CLEAN UP Close the *SeriesDescription* document without saving your changes.

Automatically Display Current Information in a Document

If you are creating faxes, letters, or other dated documents from a project template, you can further reduce the amount of manual work you need to do each time you create the document, by inserting the date and/or time in the template as an automatically updating *field*. You can choose from a variety of formats with more or less detail.

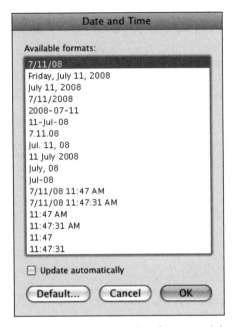

The available date and time formats might vary depending on the regional settings of your computer.

After you specify the format you want to use, Word retrieves the date or time from your computer's internal calendar or clock.

You can use the same process to insert the current date or time as static text in a document, if you don't want the information to change.

To insert the current date or time into a Word document:

1. On the **Insert** menu, click **Date and Time**.

2. In the **Date and Time** dialog box, under **Available formats**, click the date and/or time format you want.

3. To insert the date or time as a field rather than as static text, select the **Update automatically** check box.

4. Click **OK**.

If you selected Update Automatically, Word inserts the current information as a field. When you click information that is stored in a field, gray highlighting appears, to indicate the extent of the field.

To display the codes that control the information displayed in a field:

→ Right-click the field, and then click **Toggle Field Codes**.

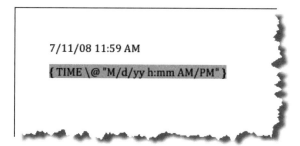

Codes such as those shown here control the display and formatting of the date and time in a field.

From the Field dialog box, which you display by clicking Field on the Insert menu, you can insert information other than the date and time as fields. For example, you can insert a field displaying a document property, such as the author, the file name, or the number of characters, words, or pages. You can also insert a limited number of mathematical formulas, and imbue text or graphics with functionality such as printing a document or moving between pages—for example, if you want to display a functioning Print or Go To Page button. For some fields, you can set options that Word will apply to the information displayed in the field.

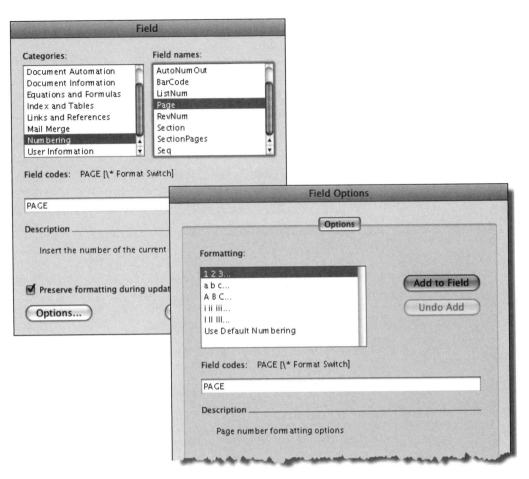

You can insert many types of fields and specify options for the display of information in the field.

Information that you insert from the Field dialog box is always set to update automatically, so you don't need to specify that option. The field updates automatically each time you open the document, or you can update it manually.

To manually update information in a field:

→ Right-click the field, and then click **Update Field**.

Work with Office Themes

When you create a document or presentation based on a template or a ready-made design, the file elements include a document theme—a combination of colors and fonts that give the file contents a cohesive look. Even a file developed from scratch has a theme, albeit one that consists of only a white background and a very basic set of font styles and sizes.

> **Note** In this topic, we discuss the process of applying and changing document themes in a Word document. You can use the same processes described here to work with document themes in a PowerPoint presentation. The same document themes are available in both programs.

An Office 2008 document theme has two primary elements: the color scheme and the font scheme.

The *color scheme* consists of 12 complementary colors designed to be used for the most common elements of a document or slide, as follows:

- Four Text/Background colors used for dark or light text on a dark or light background.
- Six Accent colors used for objects other than text.
- One Hyperlink color to draw attention to hyperlinks.
- One Followed Hyperlink color to indicate visited hyperlinks.

In the palette displayed in color galleries, such as the Font Color gallery in the Font panel of the Formatting Palette, the Theme Colors palette displays 10 of the 12 color scheme colors and gradients of each. (The two background colors are not represented in these palettes.) When you point to a color in the Theme Colors palette, a ScreenTip appears. The ScreenTip indicates the intended purpose of the color and the level of gradient.

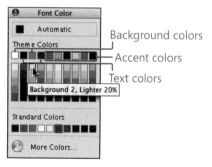

The current color scheme appears in the Theme Colors palette of the Font Color gallery.

Understanding color schemes can help you create professional-looking documents and presentations that use an appropriate balance of color. You are not limited to using the colors in a color scheme, but because they have been selected by professional designers based on good design principles, using them helps to ensure that your content will be pleasing to the eye.

> **Tip** Although working with the 12 colors of a harmonious color scheme enables you to create content with a pleasing design impact, you might want to use a wider palette. You can add colors that are not part of the color scheme by selecting the element whose color you want to change and then choosing a standard color from the Colors palette (available from any Color gallery, such as the Font Color gallery) or from the almost infinite spectrum of colors available in the Colors dialog box. After you add a color, it becomes available on all the palettes that appear when you click a button that applies color—for example, the Font Color button. The color remains on the palettes even if you change the theme applied to the presentation.

The *font scheme* consists of two font families: one that governs the appearance of headings and the other that defines the appearance of body text. You can apply other formatting to text within a document, but applying a paragraph style to selected text reverts it to the current font scheme.

See Also For information about paragraph styles, see "Work with Styles" later in this chapter.

In the Office 2008 programs, you work with the document theme and its color scheme and font scheme from the Formatting Palette of the Toolbox.

*From the Document Theme panel, you can select
a theme or a different set of colors or fonts.*

A thumbnail representing the current theme is shown in the gallery at the top of the Document Theme panel. You can view other themes by scrolling the panel.

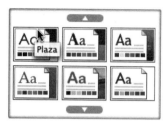

To display the name of a theme in a ScreenTip, point to its thumbnail.

Each theme thumbnail displays the following information, on a page formatted with the *Background 1* color (which is always white):

- An uppercase letter *A* formatted in the heading font.
- A lowercase letter *a* formatted in the body text font.
- Six blocks depicting the accent colors.

A second page, behind the first, depicts the Background 2 color and the title slide design of a presentation based on this Office theme.

The currently selected color scheme is shown in the Colors box. Clicking the Colors arrow displays a list of other color schemes. The correlation between the Office themes and the color schemes is one to one.

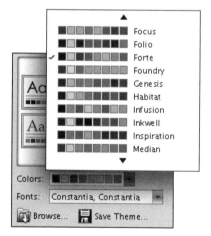

A check mark in the left margin indicates the current color scheme.

See Also For information about creating presentations based on Office themes, see "Create a Presentation Based on an Office Theme Template" in Chapter 6, "Create PowerPoint Presentations."

The currently selected font scheme is shown in the Fonts box. Clicking the Fonts arrow displays a gallery of available font schemes. Again, each Office theme has a font scheme.

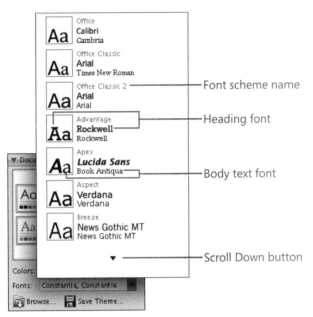

Each font scheme thumbnail displays samples of the heading and body text fonts.

Practice Applying Themes and Color Schemes

In this exercise, you'll change the theme applied to a document. Then you'll change the color scheme of the theme in the current document.

We'll work in a Word publication (the document type we discussed in "Work with Word Publications" in Chapter 4, "Create Word Documents," but you can use similar techniques when working in a Word document, a PowerPoint presentation, or an Excel workbook.

> **Note** In PowerPoint, theme thumbnails are also shown in the Elements Gallery.

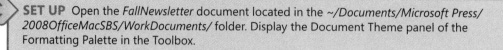

SET UP Open the *FallNewsletter* document located in the *~/Documents/Microsoft Press/ 2008OfficeMacSBS/WorkDocuments/* folder. Display the Document Theme panel of the Formatting Palette in the Toolbox.

Note The document opens in Publishing Layout view because it is a Word publication.

1. On the **View** menu, click **Navigation Pane**.

   The Navigation pane opens on the left side of the document window, displaying thumbnails of each page of this Word publication.

2. Scroll the Navigation pane to display the thumbnail of each of the four pages of the publication.

   Note the colors used throughout the publication—primarily red, orange, and yellow.

3. Click the thumbnail of page 4.

   Note the appearance of the text in the various text boxes.

4. In the **Document Theme** panel of the **Formatting Palette**, point to the thumbnail at the top of the theme gallery.

   The ScreenTip that appears says *Presentation22*. This is not one of the standard Office themes; this publication was created from the Microsoft Project Gallery and uses a theme associated specifically with the publication.

5. Point to the **Colors** box, and then to the **Fonts** box.

The ScreenTips for both elements are *Fall Newsletter*, which is the name of the template this publication was created from.

6. In the **Document Theme** gallery, click the **Advantage** theme thumbnail (the second thumbnail in the first row of Office themes).

   Word applies the Advantage theme to the publication. The colors of the heading text and background graphic on page 4 change, as do the colors shown on the page thumbnails in the Navigation pane.

   Text In Overflow icons indicate that the text boxes they're linked to contain more text than can be displayed. Because the fonts of the Advantage font scheme have wider characters, the placeholder text within some of the text boxes no longer fits.

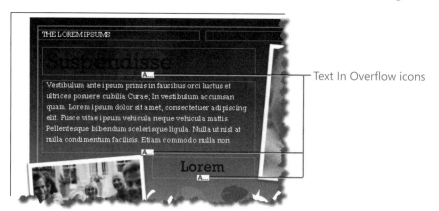

Text In Overflow icons

7. Click the **Fonts** arrow, scroll the list, and then click the **Infusion** font scheme.

   The publication fonts change, and the placeholder text now fits the text boxes.

8. Display page 1 of the publication.

   Near the upper-left corner of the page, the word *the* is shown in orange. This is one of the accent colors of the Advantage theme's color scheme.

9. Click the **Colors** arrow, scroll the list, and then click the **Opulent** color scheme.

   The colors of the text and graphics change to match the new color scheme. Near the upper-left corner, the word *the* no longer stands out against its background.

10. Double-click in the text box containing the word *the*.

    The insertion point appears in the text box, and the placeholder text disappears.

11. In the **Font** panel of the **Formatting Palette**, click the **Font Color** arrow.

    The Font Color gallery expands to display the Theme Colors palette and the Standard Colors palette. In the Theme Colors palette displaying colors associated with the current document theme, the second color from the right (Accent 5) is selected as the color for content in the active text box.

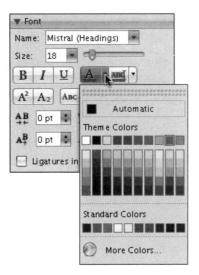

12. In the **Theme Colors** palette, click the last color square in the fifth column (**Accent 1, Darker 50%**).

13. Click the publication page to apply the color. Then in the text box, type The.

    The word appears in the newly selected color.

14. In the **Colors** list at the bottom of the **Document Theme** panel, select any other color scheme. Then with the word *The* selected, expand the **Font Color** gallery.

    Although the color of the word changed, it is still the color scheme equivalent of the color you chose earlier—Accent 1, Darker 50%.

 CLEAN UP Experiment more on your own. Then close the *FallNewsletter* document without saving your changes.

Work with Styles

Throughout this book, we've worked in documents that contain headings and other styles. Later, when we create tables of contents (TOCs), we'll talk about the importance of those styles, and the order they represent. Word 2008 for Mac has four categories of styles:

- **Paragraph styles.** You can use these styles to apply a consistent look to different types of paragraphs, such as headings, body text, captions, quotations, and list paragraphs.

- **Character styles.** You can use these styles to change the appearance of selected letters or words.

- **Table styles.** Word applies these styles when you create a formatted table. You can apply a different style to change the formatting.

- **List styles.** You can use these styles to govern the characteristics of lists, including the bullet characters, numbers, or alphanumeric characters that appear at the beginning of various list levels. You can also govern paragraph formatting such as tabs and spacing.

By default, a new document based on the Normal template has four styles available from the Styles pane: Heading 1, Heading 2, Heading 3, and Normal. However, the Normal template includes dozens of styles for elements, including various types of titles, headings, captions, and lists, as well as styles Word applies to content such as footnotes and endnotes, headers and footers, comments, index headings and entries, TOC entries, and more.

You apply and manage all four categories of styles from the Styles panel of the Formatting Palette. You can also apply styles from the Style list on the Formatting toolbar.

The Styles panel of the Formatting Palette

Tip You can display the entire list of styles available in a document by clicking All Styles in the List list at the bottom of the Styles panel.

The standard style for new text is Normal. The Normal style is the base on which most other styles are built. The font of the Normal style is determined by the current font scheme.

See Also For information about font schemes, see "Work with Office Themes" earlier in this chapter.

To apply a paragraph style, including list styles:

1. Position the insertion point in the paragraph you want to style, or select the paragraph.

2. In the **Styles** panel of the **Formatting Palette**, or in the **Style** list on the Formatting toolbar, click the style you want to apply.

To apply a character style:

→ Select the characters you want to format, and then click the style.

To create a new style:

1. In the **Styles** panel, click the **New Style** button.

2. Specify the name of the new style.

3. Specify the type of style you want to create.

4. If you choose to create a paragraph style, specify its base style (if any), and the style for paragraphs that follow it.

   If you choose to create a character, list, or table style, the dialog box changes to provide settings specific to that style type.

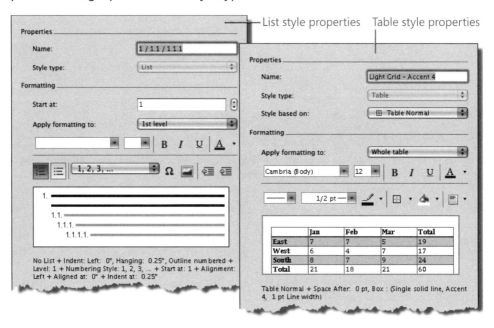

To modify an existing style:

1. In the **Styles** panel, point to the style you want to modify, click the arrow that appears, and then, in the list, click **Modify**.

2. Make simple changes to the formatting of the selected style from the **Modify Style** dialog box. To make more advanced changes, select the aspect you want to change from the **Format** list.

Manage Document Templates

Elsewhere in this book, we've touched on the concept of templates. Templates are Office files containing style definitions and/or content. Each program has template files, which can be identified by their file extensions, as shown in the following table.

Program	Extension	File types...
Word	.dotx	Word Template
	.dotm	Word Macro-Enabled Template
	.dot	Word 97–2004 Template
Excel	.xltx	Excel Template
	.xltm	Excel Macro-Enabled Template
	.xlt	Excel 97–2004 Template
PowerPoint	.potx	PowerPoint Template
	.potm	PowerPoint Macro-Enabled Template
	.pot	PowerPoint 97–2004 Template

Note Entourage also includes templates for creating messages and other Entourage items.

You can use a template in two ways:

- You can use a template as a starter file by opening the template. This creates a new file based on the template. The new file is not a template file; rather, when you save it, the program will prompt you to save it as a document, workbook, or presentation. (You can save it as a template, but that's not the default format.)

- You can apply the style definitions within a template to an existing file by attaching the template to the file.

In this book, we generally use the term *project templates* to refer to templates whose primary purpose is as starter files. These include the templates you open from the Project Gallery when you create a Word publication, an Excel ledger sheet, or a pre-populated PowerPoint presentation. We've worked with project templates in previous chapters. You can use templates in each of the primary Office programs, in the ways listed on the following page.

- When working in Excel, you'll primarily use templates as starter files for sheets.

- In PowerPoint, you'll use templates both as starter files and to apply different sets of themes and masters to a presentation.

- In Word, you can create documents and publications from starter templates. Another great use of document templates, however, is to change the look of document content, and to apply a consistent look to multiple documents, and that's the way we're addressing templates in this chapter.

A document template is a separate file in which paragraph, character, table, and list styles are defined. A document template can also include content, page formatting, headers and footers, and any other elements found in a document, but when you're attaching the template for the purpose of defining styles, that content is neither visible nor pertinent.

Every document you create is based on a document template. Unless you specify otherwise, all new documents are based on the Normal document template, which defines a few fairly plain styles, such as paragraph styles for regular text paragraphs, a title, and different levels of headings; and a few character styles that change the look of selected text. The styles from the Normal template appear in the Styles panel of the Formatting Palette when you create a new blank document. If you create a document based on a different template, the styles defined in that template appear in the Styles panel, and you can apply those styles to quickly format the text in the document.

You can change the look of document content by making changes to the style definitions within the attached template, or you can attach a different template that contains different definitions for the same styles to the document. You can create these additional templates or use templates provided to you by other people.

To create a document template, you simply save a file in the .dotx file format. You can distribute the file to other Word users to attach to their own documents, in the same way that you would distribute any electronic document—for example, by e-mail, through a shared drive, or on a portable disk or drive.

You can make a template available to Word by saving the template to any location and then loading it as a global template, or by saving the template to the standard template directory.

To attach a different template to a document:

1. On the **Tools** menu, click **Templates and Add-Ins**.

2. In the **Templates and Add-Ins** dialog box, click **Attach**.

3. In the **Choose a File** dialog box, locate and click the template you want to attach, and then click **Open**.

Practice Applying and Modifying Styles and Document Templates

In this exercise, you'll apply styles to document content, modify the content by modifying the styles, and then modify the content by attaching a different document template.

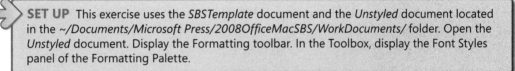

SET UP This exercise uses the *SBSTemplate* document and the *Unstyled* document located in the *~/Documents/Microsoft Press/2008OfficeMacSBS/WorkDocuments/* folder. Open the *Unstyled* document. Display the Formatting toolbar. In the Toolbox, display the Font Styles panel of the Formatting Palette.

1. Scroll through this simple one-page document to become familiar with its content.

   The document contains only simple text.

Style list   Current style indicators

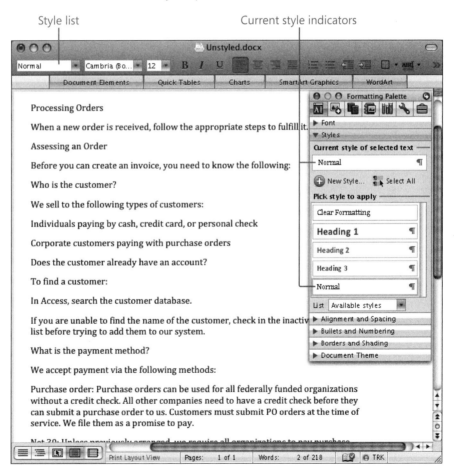

In the Style list on the Formatting toolbar, and in the Styles panel of the Formatting Palette, the style of the text at the current location of the insertion point is shown as Normal. (All text in the document is currently styled as Normal.) In the Pick Style To Apply list in the Styles panel, a light-blue outline surrounds the Normal style.

2. In the **Pick style to apply** list, point to **Heading 1**.

> **Note** From this point on, we'll refer to this more simply, as the Pick Style list.

A ScreenTip displays a description of the formatting associated with the style.

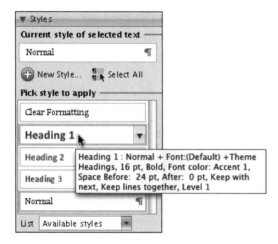

From the description we can ascertain that the style:

- Is based on the Normal style.
- Uses the default heading font associated with the current theme.
- Has a specific font size and weight.
- Has a color associated with the current color scheme.
- Has specific paragraph spacing characteristics.
- Indicates a first-level TOC entry.

3. With the insertion point in the first line of text, *Processing Orders*, click **Heading 1** in the **Pick style** list.

The text of the active paragraph changes to match the Heading 1 style depicted in the Pick Style list. In the Styles panel and on the Formatting toolbar, the current style is shown as *Heading 1*.

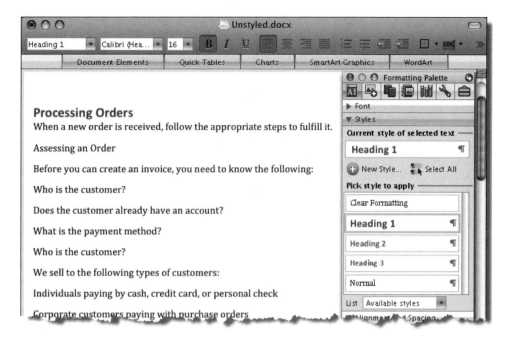

Because the Heading 1 style is a paragraph style, as indicated by the paragraph mark to the right of the style name, it isn't necessary to select specific text to apply the style to—it formats the current paragraph if the insertion point is active or, if part or all of multiple paragraphs are selected, all the paragraphs containing selected content.

4. Select the third line of text, *Assessing an Order*. On the Formatting toolbar, in the **Style** list, click **Heading 2**.

   The selected text changes to match the Heading 2 preview in the Styles panel.

5. Two lines below the selected heading, select the paragraph containing the question *Who is the customer?*. Press and hold the **Command** key, and then select the paragraphs containing the next two questions—*Does the customer already have an account?* and *What is the payment method?* Be sure to select the entire paragraph, not only the words.

   See Also For information about selecting paragraphs, see "Select Text" earlier in this chapter.

6. In the **Styles** panel, or in the **Style** list, click **Heading 3** to apply that style to the three questions.

   You've now used all the styles available in the Styles panel.

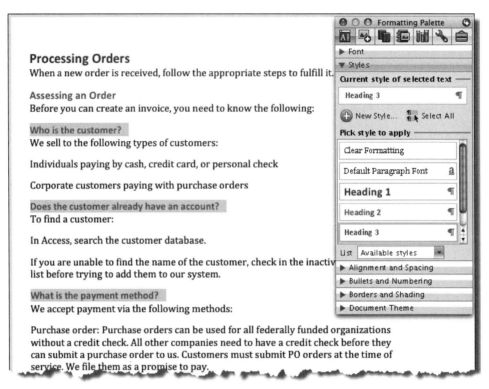

7. Below the first Heading 3–styled question, select the paragraphs beginning with *Individuals* and *Corporate*. Then, on the Formatting toolbar, click the **Bullets** button.

The selected paragraphs change to bulleted list items, and the List Paragraph style appears in the Pick Style list.

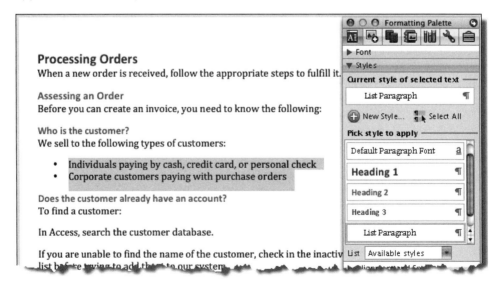

Bonus Web Content For information about bulleted and numbered lists, see "Organize Text in Lists in Word 2008 for Mac" on the book's companion Web site, at *www.microsoft.com/mspress/companion/9780735626171*.

8. At the bottom of the **Styles** panel, click the **List** arrow, and then click **All styles**.

   The content of the Pick Style list changes to include all the styles in the Normal template.

9. Scroll the **Pick style** list to view the myriad styles available. With the bulleted list items still selected, end by clicking the **List Number** style.

> **Note** The list icon to the right of the List Number style name indicates that it is a list style. The number *1* preceding the style name is part of the style preview. It indicates that the style will insert a dynamic number at the beginning of a paragraph and that consecutive List Number–styled paragraphs will be numbered consecutively, starting with the number *1*.

The selected bulleted list items change to numbered list items. On the Formatting toolbar, the Bullets button is no longer selected, but the Numbering button is.

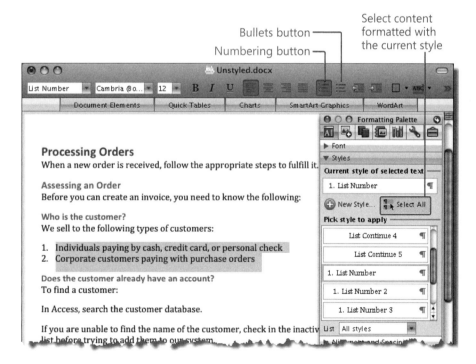

10. Place the insertion point in one of the Normal-styled paragraphs. In the **Styles** panel, under **Current style of selected text**, point to the **Normal** style preview. Then click the arrow that appears.

A list of tasks that you can perform with the current style appears.

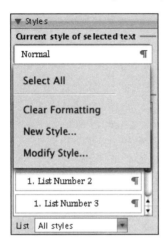

11. In the list, click **Modify Style**.

The Modify Style dialog box opens.

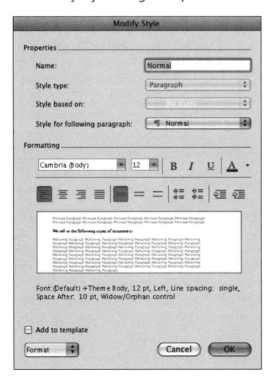

A description of the formatting associated with the style appears below the preview pane. Basic formatting options are available above the preview pane.

Take note of the information in the Properties section of the dialog box. We can see that this style is not based on any other, and that the paragraph created when you press Return to end this one will also be a Normal paragraph.

12. In the **Formatting** section of the dialog box, click the **Italic** button.

Our purpose here is to make a change that will be immediately obvious, which this one certainly is. All the text of the document changes to italic, but the other characteristics stay as they were.

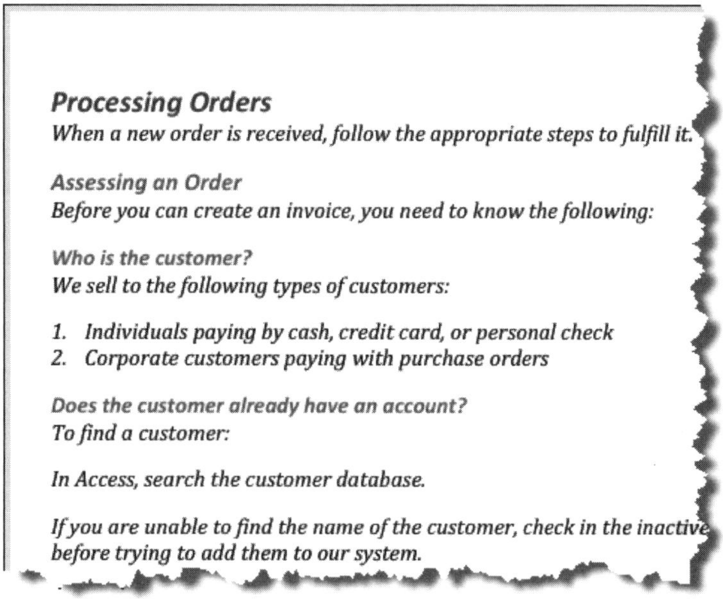

Processing Orders
When a new order is received, follow the appropriate steps to fulfill it.

Assessing an Order
Before you can create an invoice, you need to know the following:

Who is the customer?
We sell to the following types of customers:

1.   Individuals paying by cash, credit card, or personal check
2.   Corporate customers paying with purchase orders

Does the customer already have an account?
To find a customer:

In Access, search the customer database.

If you are unable to find the name of the customer, check in the inactive
before trying to add them to our system.

The reason that all the text changed is that the other styles in the document are based on the Normal style.

13. In the lower-left corner of the **Modify Style** dialog box, expand the **Format** list.

You can change any aspect of the paragraph format from the dialog boxes that
open when you click an item in the list.

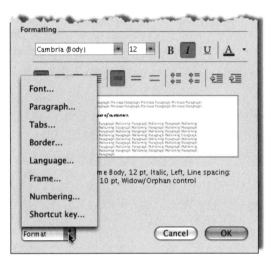

14. Click away from the list to close it, and then in the **Modify Style** dialog box, click **OK**.

    In the Styles panel of the Formatting Palette, many of the style previews are now
    italic.

15. Scroll the **Pick style** list.

    Notice that the styles now shown in italic are all based on the Normal style.

16. In the document, select any Normal-styled paragraph. Then, on the Formatting
    toolbar, click the **Bold** button.

    The text of the selected paragraph is now italic and bold. In the Style list on the For-
    matting toolbar, the style is indicated as *Normal*, but in the Styles panel, the current
    style is more precisely shown as *Normal + Bold*.

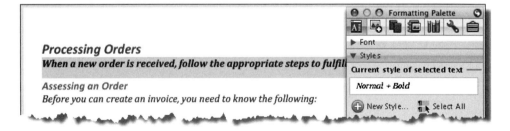

17. With the Normal + Bold paragraph still selected, in the **Styles** panel, just below the current style preview, click the **New Style** button.

The New Style dialog box opens. The Formatting section of the dialog box already reflects the formatting applied to the selected text.

18. In the **Name** box, replace *Style1* with My Style.

19. Scroll to the top of the **Style based on** list, and click **(no style)**.

> **Tip** If you don't want changes to other styles to affect a new style, select (no style) in the Style Based On list.

20. In the **Style for following paragraph** list, click **Style1**. Don't select the **Add to template** check box or the **Automatically update** check box.

> **Note** Because you haven't yet saved the renamed style, the program still knows this style as *Style1*. After you save the renamed style, this reference will update itself.

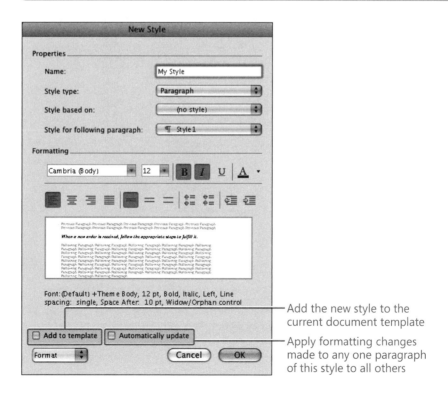

Add the new style to the current document template

Apply formatting changes made to any one paragraph of this style to all others

21. In the **New Style** dialog box, click **OK**.

    Normal + Bold still appears in the Current Style section of the Styles panel, because creating the new style didn't also apply it to the selection.

22. Click the **List** arrow at the bottom of the **Styles** panel and then, in the list, click **Available styles** to display a more manageable list of styles. Scroll the list to verify that it includes your new style.

    Because you did not select the Add To Template check box in the New Style dialog box, this style will appear only in this document.

23. Press the **End** key to position the insertion point at the end of the paragraph. In the **Pick style** list, click **My Style**. Then press **Return** to start a new paragraph, and type Let's see if this works.

    The new paragraph is also formatted with the style you created.

24. On the **Tools** menu, click **Templates and Add-ins**.

    The Templates And Add-ins dialog box opens.

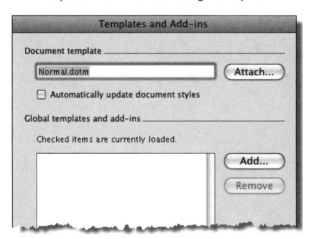

25. Click the **Attach** button.

    The Choose A File dialog box opens, displaying the contents of your default templates folder.

> **Tip** To make a document template readily available, store it in your User Templates folder, which is located in your *~/Library/Application Support/Microsoft/Office/* folder.

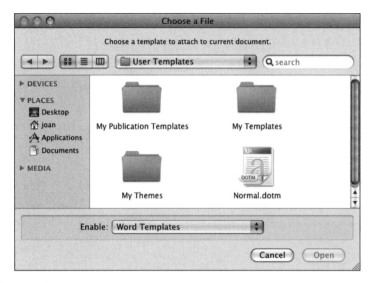

26. Click **User Templates** to display the folders on the path to this one and a list of recently accessed folders.

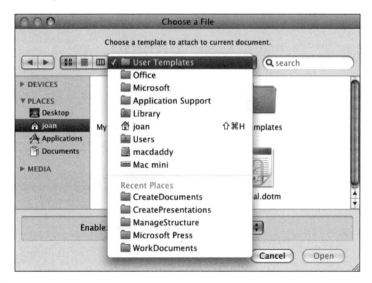

27. In the **Recent Places** section of the list, click **WorkDocuments**.

28. In the **Choose a File** dialog box displaying the contents of the *WorkDocuments* folder, click the *SBSTemplate* file, and then click **Open**.

29. In the **Templates and Add-ins** dialog box, select the **Automatically update document styles** check box so that the new template's styles will be applied to the document content. Then click **OK**.

The appearance of all the text in the document changes to reflect the style definitions contained in the template you just applied, and those styles appear in the Styles panel of the Formatting Palette.

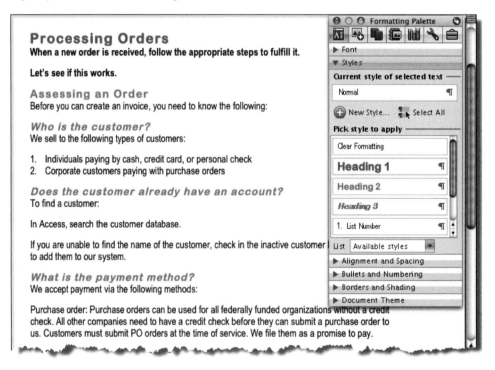

CLEAN UP Close the *Unstyled* document without saving your changes. If you're not going to continue working in Word on your own, quit the program.

Check Spelling and Grammar

In the days of handwritten and typewritten documents, people might have tolerated a typographical or grammatical error or two because correcting such errors without creating a mess was difficult. Word processors like Word have built-in spelling and grammar checkers, so now documents that contain these types of errors are likely to reflect badly on their creators.

> **Tip** Although Word can help you eliminate misspellings and grammatical errors, its tools are not infallible. You should always read through your documents to catch the problems that the Word tools can't detect.

Word provides two tools to help you with the chore of eliminating spelling and grammar errors: the AutoCorrect and Spelling And Grammar features.

Have you noticed that Word automatically corrects some misspellings as you type them? This is the work of the AutoCorrect feature. AutoCorrect corrects commonly misspelled words, such as *adn* to *and*, so that you don't have to correct them yourself. AutoCorrect comes with a long list of frequently misspelled words and their correct spellings. If you frequently misspell a word that AutoCorrect doesn't change, you can add it to the list in the AutoCorrect dialog box.

If you deliberately mistype a word and don't want to accept the AutoCorrect change, you can reverse it by clicking the Undo button on the Standard toolbar before you type anything else.

See Also For more information about the AutoCorrect feature, see "Word Tools and Preferences" in Chapter 1, "Explore and Manage the Office Interface."

Although AutoCorrect ensures that your documents are free of common misspellings, it doesn't detect random typographical and grammatical errors. For those types of errors, you can turn to the Spelling And Grammar feature for help. You might have noticed that as you type, Word underlines suspected spelling errors with red wavy underlines and possible grammatical errors with green wavy underlines. You can right-click an underlined word or phrase to display suggested corrections.

If you want to check the spelling or grammar of the entire document, it is easier to click Spelling And Grammar on the Tools menu than to deal with underlined words and phrases individually. Word then works its way through the document and displays the Spelling And Grammar dialog box if it encounters a potential error.

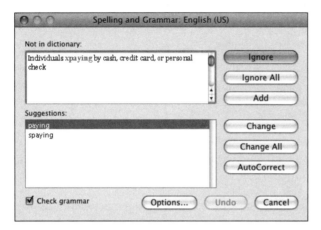

To change a flagged error, double-click a replacement in the Suggestions box, or type your own replacement into the Not In Dictionary box, and then click Change.

If the error is a misspelling, the Spelling And Grammar checker suggests corrections; if the error is a suspected breach of grammar, it tells you which rule you might have broken, and suggests corrections. The buttons available in the Spelling And Grammar dialog box are dynamic and change to those most appropriate for fixing the error. For example, for a grammatical error, you are given the opportunity to ignore the rule you have broken throughout the document.

You can change the Spelling And Grammar feature settings from the Spelling And Grammar page of the Preferences dialog box.

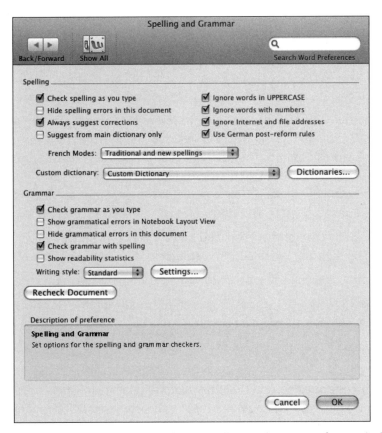

You can specify many settings for the Spelling And Grammar feature, including the writing style appropriate to the document.

To display the Spelling And Grammar page of the Preferences dialog box:

→ Click the **Options** button in the **Spelling and Grammar** dialog box.

→ Click **Preferences** on the **Word** menu, or press **Command+Comma**, and then under **Authoring and Proofing Tools**, click **Spelling and Grammar**.

See Also For more information about the Preferences dialog box in Word, see "Word Tools and Preferences" in Chapter 1, "Explore and Manage the Office Interface."

Key Points

- Made a mistake? No problem! You can undo a single action or the last several actions you performed by clicking the Undo button (or its arrow) on the toolbar. And if you change your mind, you can redo one or more of the actions you undid.

- You can cut or copy text and paste it elsewhere in the same document or in a different document. The Clipboard stores only the most recent clipping. The Scrapbook stores clippings from any Office program, as well as files, for later reuse. The Spike stores text, graphics, and other content cut from Word documents. Inserting the Spike contents into a document empties the Spike. Each of these storage mechanisms has its own set of keyboard shortcuts.

- You can quickly change the colors and fonts of a document by applying a theme or by changing the color scheme or font scheme of the current theme.

- You can provide a uniform look to document content by applying styles.

- You can quickly change the look of content by modifying the Normal style, which most other content styles are based on.

- You can entirely change the look of a document by attaching a different document template to it.

- You can use the Spelling And Grammar feature to locate misspelled words and phrases or sentences that might not meet standard grammatical guidelines.

Bonus Web Content

You can find the following articles about additional Word 2008 features on the book's companion Web site, at *www.microsoft.com/mspress/companion/9780735626171*:

- "Organize Text in Columns in Word 2008 for Mac"
- "Organize Text in Lists in Word 2008 for Mac"
- "Perform Calculations in a Table in Word 2008 for Mac"
- "Present Text in a Tabular List in Word 2008 for Mac"
- "Restructuring Content in Outline View in Word 2008 for Mac"
- "Work with Publication Elements in Word 2008 for Mac"
- "Work with Tables in Word 2008 for Mac"

Chapter at a Glance

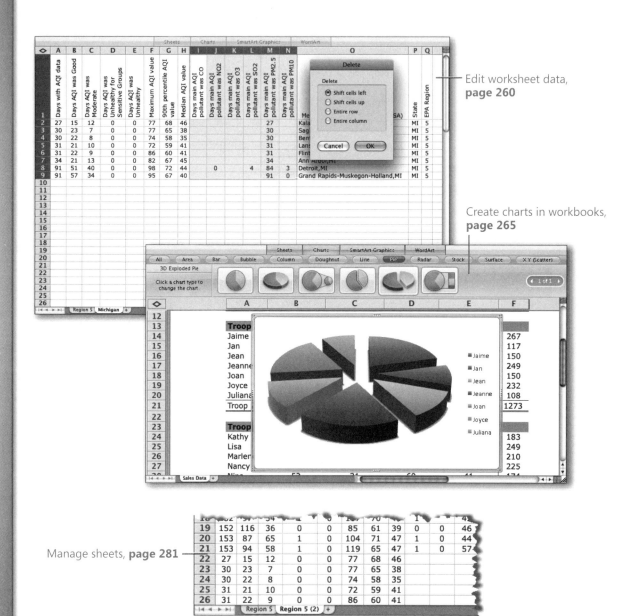

Edit worksheet data, **page 260**

Create charts in workbooks, **page 265**

Manage sheets, **page 281**

8 Work with Excel Sheet Content

In this chapter, you will learn how to

✔ Edit worksheet data.

✔ Restrict the content allowed in a cell.

✔ Automatically format cells based on content.

✔ Create charts in workbooks.

✔ Create charts in documents and presentations.

✔ Manage sheets.

You can use many of the file- and content-management skills you learned in Chapter 3, "Work in Office Programs," when working with Microsoft Excel workbooks and sheets. For the most part, the common functions will be self-evident when you are working in the Excel interface.

You can store many types of content in an Excel workbook, including alphanumeric text, images, and calculated formulas. From the stored data, you can easily generate informational charts.

In this chapter, you'll learn how to change the content of a worksheet by selecting, inserting, and deleting cells, columns, and rows. You'll learn how to use data validation and conditional formatting to restrict or format the contents of cells. You'll create and modify charts based on worksheet data and also learn how to create a chart directly in a document or on a slide, or link to an existing chart. Finally, you'll learn how to add, remove, hide, copy, move, organize, and rename individual sheets in a workbook.

See Also You can find handy keyboard shortcuts, simple instructions for performing common tasks, and other useful information in the Quick Reference section at the beginning of this book.

> **Practice Makes Perfect!** The practice files you will use to complete the exercises in this chapter are in the *WorkSheets* practice file folder. See "Using the Companion Content" at the beginning of this book for information about installing and locating the practice files.

Edit Worksheet Data

In Chapter 5, "Create Excel Workbooks," you entered data into a worksheet. Now we'll discuss ways in which you can change data that already exists in a worksheet cell.

Change Cell Content

In Chapter 5, you practiced inserting text into a blank cell by selecting that cell and then typing or pasting content. If you want to add to text that you already entered, change the text, or delete part of it, you must first activate the insertion point within the cell, either by double-clicking the cell (which places the insertion point at the cursor location) or by pressing Control+U (which places the insertion point at the end of the cell content). Then either click in the cell or use the keyboard navigation keys to position the insertion point where you want it.

After activating the insertion point in a cell, you can move around in the cell by clicking or by pressing the keyboard navigation keys (Home, End, Left Arrow, and Right Arrow). You can select text by dragging across it or by holding down the Shift key and pressing the navigation keys. You can cut, copy, or delete selected text by using the standard menu commands, keys, and keyboard shortcuts. To delete all the text in a cell, activate the cell by clicking it once, and then press Delete.

Minneapolis-St. Paul,MN-WI	WI	5
Cincinnati,OH-KY-IN	IN	5
Visalia-Tulare-Porterville,CA	CA	9
Davenport-Moline-Rock Island,IA-IL	IL	5
Fort Wayne,IN	IN	5
Flagstaff,AZ-UT	UT	8
Augusta-Aiken,GA	GA	4
Memphis,TN-AR-MS	MS	4
Atlanta,GA	GA	4

Selected text

You can select text by dragging or by holding down the Shift key and pressing the navigation keys.

Change Worksheet Structure

As you develop the data stored on a worksheet, you might find it necessary to add or remove columns, rows, or cells from the worksheet structure.

To insert a blank column, select the column that is in the location where you want to insert the new one. To insert multiple columns, select the columns located where you want the new ones. After selecting a column or columns, click Columns on the Insert menu. Excel then inserts the column or columns to the left of the selection.

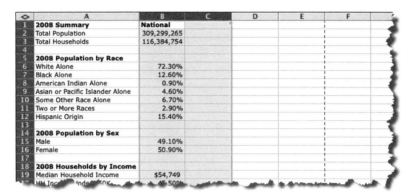

To insert multiple columns, first select the location in which you want to insert the new columns.

> **Tip** You can select the current column by pressing Control+Spacebar, and the current row by pressing Shift+Spacebar.

To insert one or more blank rows, select the row or rows above which you want to insert the new row(s), and then click Rows on the Insert menu.

To delete columns or rows, select the columns or rows (but not both at the same time) that you want to delete, and then on the Edit menu, click Delete. Excel deletes the column or row and all the data contained therein without asking you to confirm the deletion, so take care when making your selection.

> **Tip** As in other Microsoft Office 2008 programs, you can undo the last change you made by clicking the Undo button on the Standard toolbar (or by pressing Control+Z), and undo multiple changes by clicking the Undo arrow and selecting from the list the changes you want to undo.

To delete one or more cells, select the cell(s), click Delete on the Edit menu, and then in the Delete dialog box, specify the direction you want the remaining content to move to fill the gap left by the deleted cells.

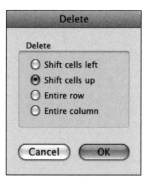

When you're removing cells from a worksheet, specify the direction you want to move the remaining content to fill the gap.

> **Tip** If you want to delete only the data within a column, row, or cell, without changing the worksheet structure, you can do so by selecting the column, row, or cell and then pressing the Delete key, instead of clicking Delete on the Edit menu.

To insert one or more blank cells within the current worksheet, select the range in which you want to insert the new, blank cells. Click Cells on the Insert menu, and then in the Insert dialog box, specify the direction in which you want to shift the selected cell(s) to make room for the new one(s).

Restrict the Content Allowed in a Cell

You can control the content entered in a list sheet column, and the formatting of each cell in the column, from the Column Settings dialog box, which you display by double-clicking the column name. In the Column Settings dialog box, you can specify formatting appropriate to the type of data you expect the column to contain. For example, you can specify the number of decimal places to display, the symbol that appears before currency values, the way dates or times are displayed, and formatting criteria. You can specify a value to appear by default in all the cells in the column by selecting the Default Value check box and entering the value in the text box. You can prevent the entry of duplicate values by selecting the Unique Values Only check box.

Restrict the type of data that can be entered

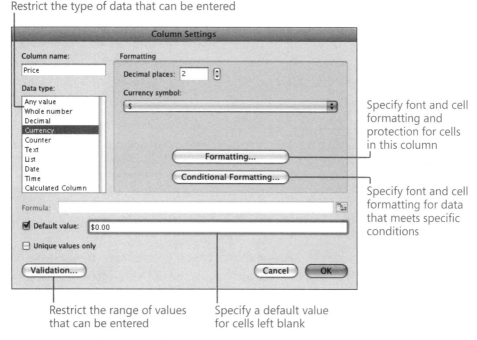

Specify font and cell formatting and protection for cells in this column

Specify font and cell formatting for data that meets specific conditions

Restrict the range of values that can be entered

Specify a default value for cells left blank

You can format the contents of each list sheet column to match a pattern, and specify a default value.

To further restrict the content that can be entered into a column cell, click the Validation button to display the Data Validation dialog box.

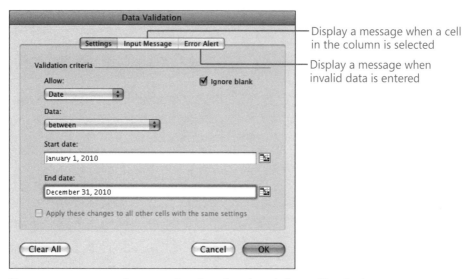

Display a message when a cell in the column is selected

Display a message when invalid data is entered

You can prevent users from entering data that doesn't fit specific criteria.

In the Data Validation dialog box, you can restrict the values that can be entered into a column cell. For example, you can specify that a date must fall within the current calendar year, that a number must be positive, that a text entry be no more than 30 characters, and other types of restrictions. If other people will be entering data in the list, you can inform them of the data entry restrictions by displaying an input message for each cell they select.

> **Tip** You can apply data validation to selected cells or to a column or row of cells in a worksheet by selecting the cells and then clicking Validation on the Data menu.

Automatically Format Cells Based on Content

You can differentiate cell values that meet specific conditions by using the Conditional Formatting feature. With this feature, you can instruct Excel to apply specific cell shading, cell borders, font styles, and font colors to cell content that matches the condition or conditions that you specify. For example, you can have Excel display the top 10 percent of all values entered in a column in red font; shade cells containing numbers within, higher than, or lower than a specific range of values in different colors; or format the text of all dates in a data range that fall within a specific date range in bold font. You can apply different conditions to different data ranges, and apply multiple conditions to one data range.

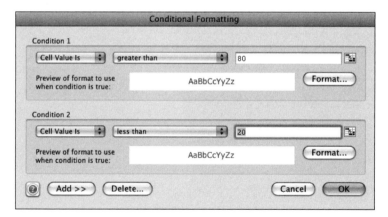

You can instruct Excel to apply special formatting to values that meet specific conditions.

> **Tip** You can apply conditional formatting to selected cells by clicking Conditional Formatting on the Format menu.

Create Charts in Workbooks

Excel is a wonderful program in which to store lots of data, but let's face it—data is only useful if you can do something with it. The point of having a lot of data is being able to analyze that data. Presenting data visually, in chart format, can greatly simplify the analysis process.

Choose a Chart Type

Excel 2008 provides 11 types of charts, each with multiple implementations, for a whopping total of 73 two- and three-dimensional chart formats that you can create instantly from data stored in a worksheet. The basic chart types are Area, Bar, Bubble, Column, Doughnut, Line, Pie, Radar, Stock, Surface, and Scatter. Although you can create any type of chart from a data selection, certain data is best represented by certain chart types. For example:

- Bar and column charts are good for showing the values of several items at a single point in time.

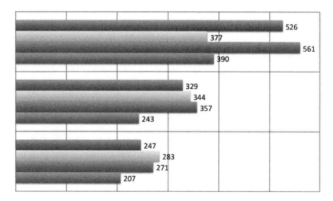

They're also good for showing how values change over time.

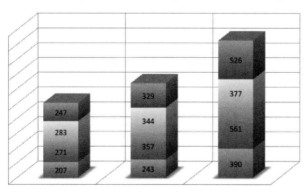

- Line graphs are good for showing erratic changes in values over time.

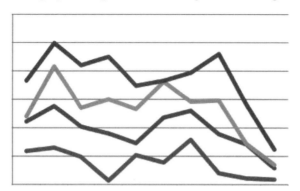

- Pie charts are good for showing how parts relate to the whole.

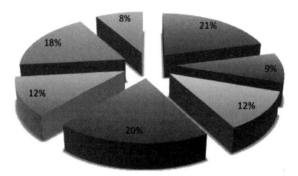

Creating a chart in a workbook is as simple as selecting the data you want to chart, and then clicking the chart type in the Elements Gallery. If, after you create a chart, you find that the chart type isn't appropriate to the data, you can change the chart type by activating the chart and then clicking another chart type on the Charts tab of the Elements Gallery.

Modify a Chart

After you create a chart, you can add data labels to help a person looking at the chart understand the data. You can also add a title, display axes and gridlines if appropriate to the chart type, and modify the chart or any of its elements, which include the following:

- *Chart area.* This is the entire area within the frame displayed when you click a chart.

- *Plot area.* This is the rectangular area bordered by the axes.

- *X-axis* **and** *y-axis*. The data is plotted against a horizontal x-axis—also called the *category axis*—and a vertical y-axis—also called the *value axis*. (Three-dimensional charts also have a *z-axis*—called the *series axis*—expressing the depth of the chart.)

- *Tick-mark labels.* These are labels along each axis that identify the data.
- *Data labels.* These are graphical representations of each data point in a data series.
- *Legend.* This key identifies the data series.

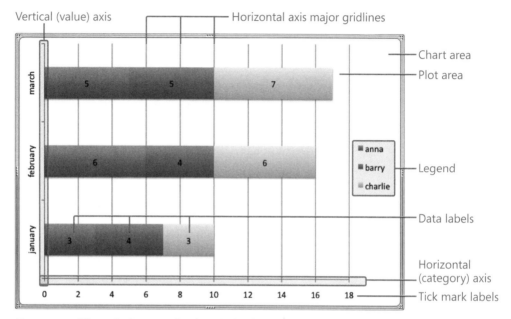

You can modify each element of a chart individually.

Practice Creating Charts from Worksheet Data

In this exercise, you'll create a pie chart from a data range and move the chart to its own sheet. You'll change the chart type and extend the data range on which the chart is based. Then you'll add labels to the chart to clearly present the data.

> **SET UP** Open the *CookieSalesByTroop* workbook from the *~/Documents/Microsoft Press/ 2008OfficeMacSBS/WorkSheets/* folder.

1. In the second table, select cells **A14:A20**. Press and hold the **Command** key, and then select cells **F14:F20**.

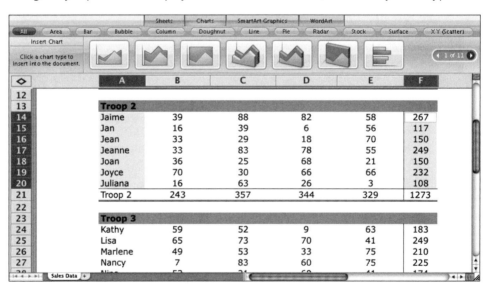

	A	B	C	D	E	F
13	**Troop 2**					
14	Jaime	39	88	82	58	267
15	Jan	16	39	6	56	117
16	Jean	33	29	18	70	150
17	Jeanne	33	83	78	55	249
18	Joan	36	25	68	21	150
19	Joyce	70	30	66	66	232
20	Juliana	16	63	26	3	108
21	Troop 2	243	357	344	329	1273
22						
23	**Troop 3**					
24	Kathy	59	52	9	63	183
25	Lisa	65	73	70	41	249
26	Marlene	49	53	33	75	210
27	Nancy	7	83	60	75	225
28	Nina	52	21	60	41	174
29	Patty	39	79	63	2	183
30	Rosemary	79	51	16	51	197
31	Sandra	20	69	59	82	230
32	Susie	11	60	1	69	141

2. Click the **Charts** tab of the Elements Gallery.

The gallery expands and displays all the available charts, ordered by chart type.

3. Click the **Area**, **Bar**, **Bubble**, **Column**, **Doughnut**, **Line**, **Pie**, **Radar**, **Stock**, **Surface**, and **Scatter** buttons to view the available chart types in each group. When you finish, display the **Pie** gallery.

4. Click the **3D Exploded Pie** chart type (the fifth thumbnail in the **Pie** group).

> **Tip** Point to any thumbnail to display the layout name and description in the style name area at the left end of the gallery.

Excel inserts a frame, containing a chart based on the selected data, into the worksheet. A legend appears to the right of the chart.

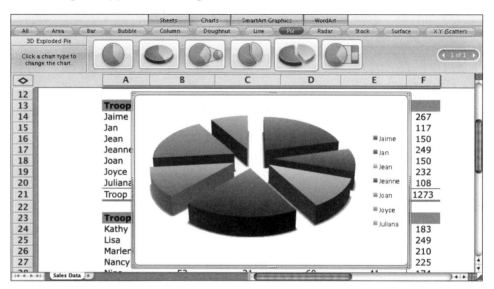

5. Right-click the chart frame, and then click **Move Chart**.

   The Move Chart dialog box opens.

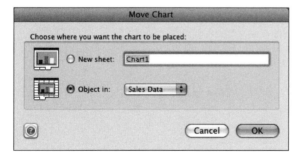

6. In the **New sheet** box, replace **Chart1** with Troop 2 by Girl. Then click **OK**.

> **Tip** Entering a chart name automatically selects the New Sheet option.

The chart, still in its frame, moves to its own chart sheet. The sheet tab reflects the name you entered in the Move Chart dialog box. The legend isn't legible in this format.

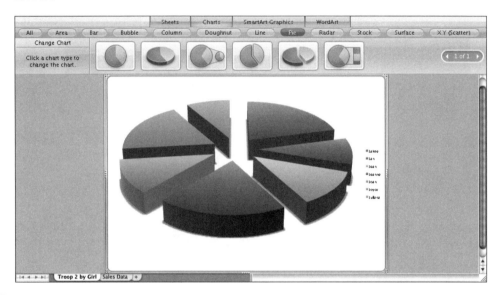

7. Right-click the legend, and then click **Format Text**.

The Format Text dialog box opens.

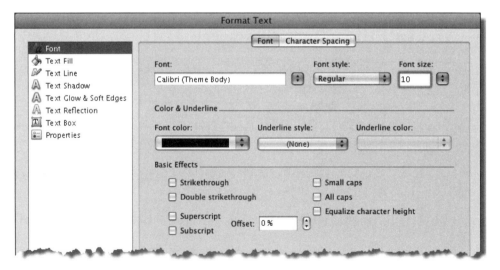

8. On the **Font** page, click **18** in the **Font size** list, and then click **OK**.

   The chart size changes to accommodate the larger legend.

9. Right-click the chart, and then click **Add Data Labels**.

   The total sales appear on each pie wedge but, again, the labels are too small to read.

10. Display the **Formatting Palette** in the Toolbox.

    While the pie wedges are selected, only the chart-related panels are visible.

11. Click any one of the data labels on the pie.

    The Font panel and the Alignment And Spacing panel appear in the Formatting Palette.

12. In the **Font** panel, change the **Size** to 20. Then click a blank area inside the chart frame.

    The legend and data labels are now easier to read.

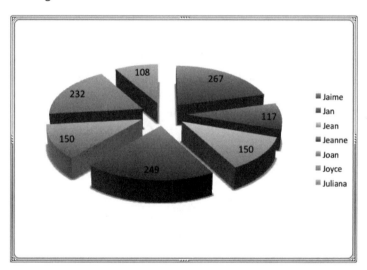

> **Note** You can also change the font size of the data labels from the Format Data Labels dialog box, which you display by right-clicking any data label and then clicking Format Data Labels. If you increase the font size beyond the size at which a label can fit on its pie wedge, the label moves away from the pie and a line connects the label to its wedge.

13. Display the **Chart Options** panel of the **Formatting Palette**. Under **Titles**, click the **Click here to add title** placeholder, and then type Troop 2 Sales by Girl.

The text that you enter in the Chart Options panel also appears at the top of the chart.

14. In the **Chart Options** panel, under **Other options**, click **Percent** in the **Labels** list, and then click **Top** in the **Legend** list.

The labels change to indicate the percent of total sales represented by each pie wedge, and the legend changes to a horizontal orientation across the top of the chart frame. Again, the chart size changes to fit the available space.

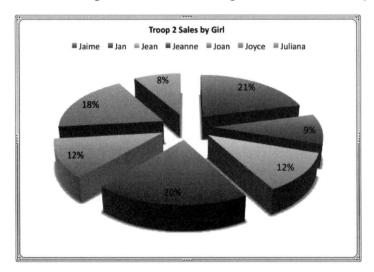

15. Click the **Sales Data** sheet tab. Select cells **A11:E11**, **A21:E21**, and **A34:E34**.

16. Display the **Charts** tab of the Elements Gallery. In the **Bar** group, click **3-D Clustered Bar**.

Excel creates a chart in the worksheet, depicting the number of each of the four cookie flavors sold by each troop.

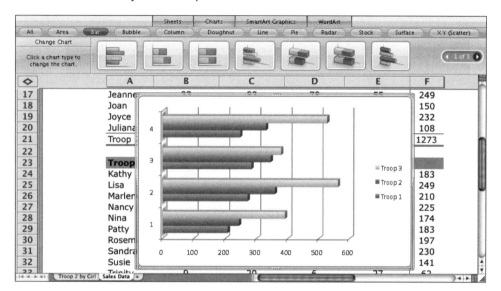

Because we didn't select the names of the cookies, they are identified on the y-axis of the chart only as *1*, *2*, *3*, and *4*.

17. Move the chart to its own sheet, named Cookies by Troop, and close the Elements Gallery.

18. Right-click the chart, and then click **Select Data**.

The Select Data Source dialog box opens, with the worksheet displayed behind it. The data range you selected in step 15 is still active in the worksheet, and is also displayed notationally in the Chart Data Range box.

Three data series are listed in the Series box. Clicking a series displays the corresponding worksheet cells containing the series name and Y values.

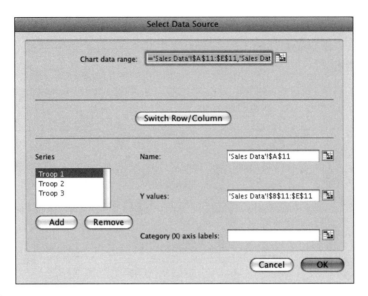

 19. In the **Series** list, click **Troop 1**. Then click the **Collapse Dialog** button to the right of the **Category (X) axis labels** box.

The Select Data Source dialog box minimizes to only a single input box, so that you can more easily access the data behind it.

20. Scroll the **Sales Data** worksheet until row **1** is visible. Then select cells **B1:E1** (the cookie names).

As you select the cells, they appear notationally in the Select Data Source input box.

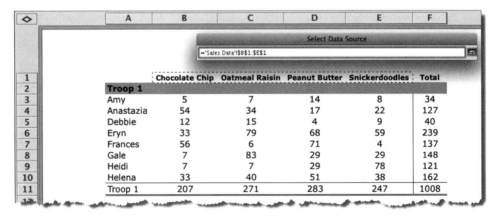

21. In the **Select Data Source** dialog box, click the **Expand Dialog** button.

    The dialog box expands to its normal format.

22. In the **Select Data Source** dialog box, click **OK**.

    The appropriate cookie names appear on the y-axis of the chart. The labels and legend are, again, not very legible.

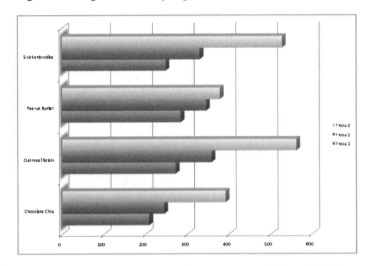

23. Right-click any one of the cookie names, and then click **Format Axis**.

    The Format Axis dialog box opens.

24. Display the **Text Box** page of the dialog box. In the **Text Layout** area, click **Rotate all text 270°** in the **Text direction** list.

    The change is visible on the chart behind the dialog box.

25. Display the **Font** page of the dialog box. In the **Font size** list, click **14**, and in the **Font style** list, click **Bold**. Then click **OK**.

    The cookie names appear vertical on the chart at a legible size.

26. Using the right-click method or the **Formatting Palette** panels, change the legend font size to **16**, and the legend placement to **Left**.

27. Point to the right end of any of the horizontal data bars.

A ScreenTip displaying the data series (troop), data point (cookie type), and value (total sales) represented by the data bar appears.

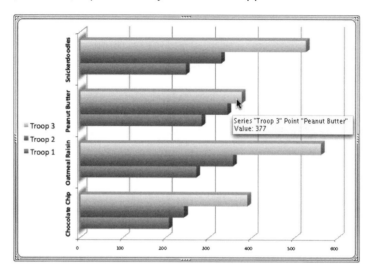

28. With the chart frame (rather than any chart element or group of elements) active, display the **Charts** tab of the Elements Gallery.

Rather than displaying the chart type, the style name area says *Change Chart*.

29. Apply the following chart types to the chart to see various ways in which you can present this data:

- In the **Area** group, apply the **3-D 100% Stacked Area** type.
- In the **Bubble** group, apply the **3-D Bubble** type.
- In the **Radar** group, apply the **Marked Radar** type.
- In the **XY (Scatter)** group, apply the **Smooth Marked Scatter** type.

Notice as you view the various chart types that some chart types automatically pick up the correct axis data, and others don't. If you change the chart type and Excel doesn't automatically pick up the data it needs, you can easily edit the chart to specify the data sources.

30. Experiment on your own with chart types and practice applying formatting by using the right-click method and the commands on the **Formatting Palette**.

31. Save the *CookieSalesByTroop* workbook as **My Charts**.

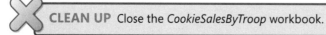

CLEAN UP Close the *CookieSalesByTroop* workbook.

Create Charts in Documents and Presentations

After you create a chart in Excel, you might want to display it in a document or presentation. You can present information in chart format in a Word document or on a PowerPoint slide in two ways:

- You can insert or link to an existing chart that you create in an Excel workbook.
- You can create a chart directly in the document or presentation. The data you create the chart from will be stored as part of the document or presentation, not as a separate file. You can edit the embedded chart data in Excel.

Insert or Link to an Existing Chart

A simple way to show an externally created chart on a document page or on a slide is to display both the chart and its destination, and then drag the chart by its frame from the worksheet or chart sheet to the page or slide. The inserted chart picks up the formatting of the document or presentation.

Alternatively, you can insert an existing chart from a workbook by following these steps:

1. In the workbook, ensure that the chart is saved on its own chart sheet.

2. In Word or PowerPoint, place the insertion point where you want the chart to be.

3. On the **Insert** menu, click **Object**.

   The Object dialog box opens.

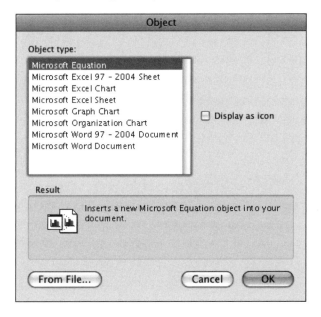

> **Tip** From the Object dialog box, you can insert a new object of one of the listed types by clicking the object type and then clicking OK.

4. In the **Object** dialog box, click **Microsoft Excel Chart**, and then in the lower-left corner, click **From File**.

The Insert As Object dialog box opens.

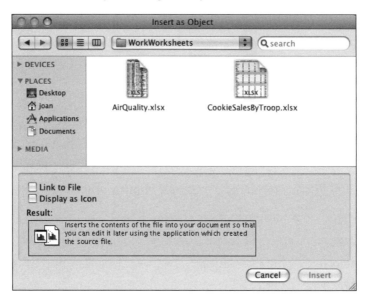

5. In the **Insert as Object** dialog box, navigate to and click the workbook containing the chart you want to insert.

6. If you want to maintain a link from the inserted chart to the source workbook, select the **Link to File** check box.

If you select this check box, changes to the chart in the source workbook will be reflected in the inserted chart. Otherwise, the data source for the inserted chart will be a separate copy of the original.

7. If you want to insert an icon linking to the source workbook, rather than inserting the chart itself, select the **Display as Icon** check box.

Selecting this check box inserts an icon representing the source workbook, and the source workbook name. Double-clicking the icon opens the source workbook if you also selected the Link To File check box, or a copy of the source workbook if you didn't.

8. In the **Insert as Object** dialog box, click **Insert**.

The first chart sheet in the selected workbook appears in the document or slide.

Double-clicking the embedded chart opens either the original workbook (if you linked to the file) or a copy of the original workbook (if you didn't). If the file contains other chart sheets, you can change the chart displayed in the Word document by activating that chart sheet and then closing the workbook window.

> **Note** In a Word document, charts aren't visible in Draft view or in Outline view; a blank space represents the area occupied by the chart.

Create a Chart on a Page or Slide

If you want to create a chart for use in only a specific document or presentation, you can create the chart directly from Word or PowerPoint (although you will still end up working in Excel). When you create a chart in a document or presentation, a sample chart is embedded in the document. The data used to plot the sample chart is stored in an Excel worksheet that is incorporated into the Word file. (You don't have to maintain a separate Excel file.) Then you modify the sample chart data to reflect the data you want to display, format the chart in the same way that you would in Excel, and you're done.

To create a chart directly in a document or presentation:

1. In a document, position the insertion point where you want the chart to appear.

Or

In a presentation, display the slide in which you want to insert the chart.

2. On the **Insert** menu, click **Chart**.

Or

Display the **Charts** tab of the Elements Gallery.

Or

On a slide that includes a content control, click the **Insert Chart** thumbnail.

3. Filter the **Charts** gallery to locate the type of chart you want to insert, and then click the chart thumbnail.

Excel starts, if it isn't already running, and displays a generic data table depicting four categories (x-axis values) and three series (y-axis values). The title bar indicates that the data you're viewing is linked to the chart in the Word document or PowerPoint presentation.

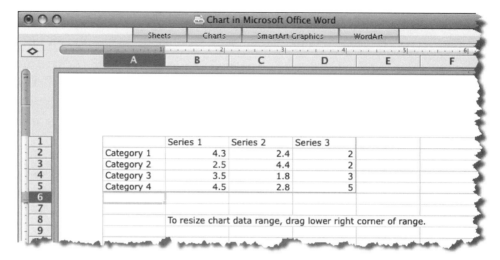

The corresponding chart appears in the document or slide, which is now behind the workbook.

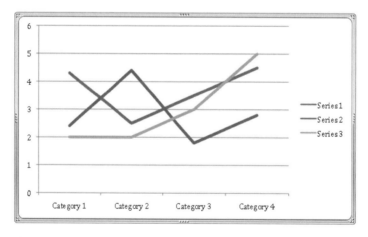

Changing the data in the data table dynamically updates the chart. You can resize and arrange the workbook and document or presentation windows to see the effect on the chart of changes you make to the data in the workbook.

Closing the *Chart in Microsoft Office Word* or *Chart in Microsoft Office PowerPoint* workbook returns you to the document or slide.

To make changes to an embedded chart:

● Right-click the chart, and then click **Edit Data** to open the workbook containing the chart data.

● Right-click any chart element (legend, axes, gridlines, and other element) to display formatting options for that element.

- Double-click a data series to display the **Format** dialog box for the data series, in which you can format the fill, line, shadow, scale, plot direction, data labels, or other settings appropriate to the chart type.

- On the **Charts** tab of the Elements Gallery, click a different chart type to change the chart without affecting the data.

In general, you can make changes to an embedded chart in the same way you would to a chart in a workbook.

Manage Sheets

Content in a workbook is stored on sheets. In addition to the basic blank sheet (which we'll refer to as a *worksheet* to differentiate it from the others), you can create chart sheets and list sheets. Each has a different appearance and purpose.

You can store and manage data in a worksheet, which has clearly defined cells and no built-in structure.

	A	B	C	D	E
1	**2008 Summary**	**National**	**ZIP 98008**	**ZIP 92127**	
2	Total Population	309,299,265	23,814	32,891	
3	Total Households	116,384,754	9,327	11,327	
4					
5	**2008 Population by Race**				
6	White Alone	72.30%	73.50%	71.10%	
7	Black Alone	12.60%	2.10%	2.70%	
8	American Indian Alone	0.90%	0.40%	0.40%	
9	Asian or Pacific Islander Alone	4.60%	16.70%	17.10%	
10	Some Other Race Alone	6.70%	3.60%	2.90%	
11	Two or More Races	2.90%	3.70%	5.70%	
12	Hispanic Origin	15.40%	7.80%	10.30%	
13					
14	**2008 Population by Sex**				
15	Male	49.10%	49.90%	48.50%	
16	Female	50.90%	50.10%	51.50%	
17					
18	**2008 Households by Income**				
19	Median Household Income	$54,749	$85,439	$99,273	
20	HH Income Under $50K	45.50%	20.60%	17.90%	
21	HH Income $50K-$100K	34.80%	39.50%	32.50%	
22	HH Income Over $100K	19.60%	39.90%	49.70%	
23					
24	**2008 Average Home Value**	**National**	**ZIP 98008**	**ZIP 92127**	
25		$260,559	$530,069	$633,176	

You can store and manage data, in any structure you want, in a worksheet.

> **Acknowledgment** The population statistics shown in the workbooks in this section are from the ESRI Community Data dataset. ESRI (originally named Environmental Systems Research Institute) is the original creator of geographic information systems (GIS) technology. GIS technology supports complex, geographically based data collection, management, and analysis. For more information, visit *www.esri.com*.

You can store and manage one set of data in a tidy list by using a list sheet, which has a built-in structure for entering columns of data. You can specify the name of each column and restrict the type of data that can be entered in the column. The column headings include built-in sort and filter functions. As you enter data into a list sheet, the cell structure of the specific data set becomes visible. You can create new columns (fields) and enter data in rows (records), but you can't enter data outside of the defined list structure.

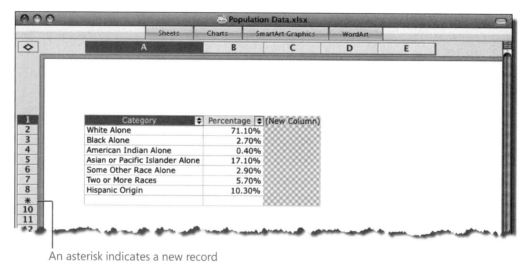

An asterisk indicates a new record

A list sheet provides a specific structure for entering data, as well as built-in sort and filter functions.

Add and Remove Sheets

A new workbook has only one sheet. This is sufficient for tracking simple data. If you want to track multiple data sets, divide a data set into logical groups, or display a different view of a data set (such as a chart), it's tidiest, and least confusing, to do this on multiple sheets within one workbook.

You can add a blank worksheet to an existing workbook by clicking the Insert Sheet button at the right end of the existing sheet tabs. You can add a blank chart sheet or list sheet by pointing to Sheet on the Insert menu and then clicking Chart Sheet or List Sheet. Other specialized sheets are available from the Project Gallery and from the Elements Gallery.

You can present a chart, independent of its data set, in a chart sheet. You can also embed a chart in its source worksheet (or another sheet). However, if you intend to present the chart to anyone, it will be more legible on a chart sheet.

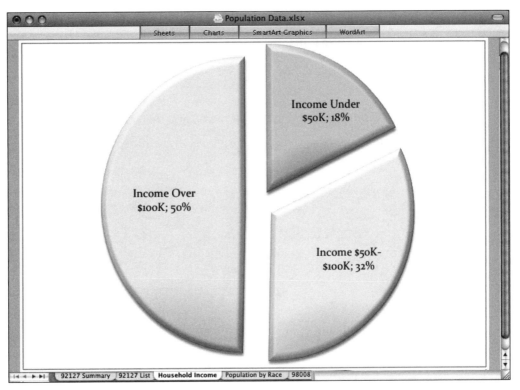

When you move a chart to its own sheet, it remains linked to its source data.

Hide Sheets

If you want to keep a sheet in a workbook but not display it, you can hide it. For example, you might want to display or distribute a workbook that contains data stored on worksheets, and charts generated from the worksheet data, on separate chart sheets. If you don't want to distract the audience with the raw data, you can hide the worksheets, leaving only the chart sheets visible.

To hide a worksheet, list sheet, or chart sheet:

1. Display the sheet you want to hide.

2. On the **Format** menu, point to **Sheet**, and then click **Hide**.

   The sheet disappears from view.

To redisplay a hidden sheet:

1. Point to **Sheet** on the format menu, and then click **Unhide**.

   The Unhide dialog box displays a list of the hidden sheets in this workbook.

2. Click the sheet you want to redisplay, and then click **OK**.

Hidden sheets retain their position within the workbook. You can redisplay only one sheet at a time.

Copy or Move Sheets

Another way of adding a sheet to a workbook is by moving or copying a sheet from one workbook to another. For example, you might want to compile related sheets from multiple workbooks into one, or use an existing dataset structure from one workbook in another. You can move a sheet between workbooks by displaying both workbooks and then dragging the sheet from one to the other. If you want to copy the sheet, hold down the secondary mouse button and drag the sheet. (We'll refer to this action as *right-click and drag.*) If it's not convenient to display both workbooks at the same time, open both workbooks, right-click the sheet you want to move, and then click Move Or Copy. In the Move Or Copy dialog box, you can specify the target location of the sheet.

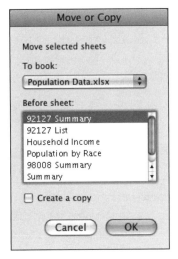

You can move or copy a sheet within a workbook or to another workbook.

Organize Sheets

You won't necessarily create sheets in a workbook in the order you want to present or access them. For example, Excel creates new sheets at the end of the existing sheets, but if the new sheet is the one you want to display most frequently, you might want to put it at the beginning.

You can change the order of sheets within a workbook by dragging their sheet tabs from one position to another. This method works well if the sheet you're moving is relatively close to its intended position. If it's difficult to find the target location this way, you can move a sheet by right-clicking its sheet tab and then clicking Move Or Copy.

Assign Sheet Names

At the bottom of each sheet, a sheet tab displays its name. New sheets have a name based on the type of sheet and the number of sheets of that type in the workbook. For example, the third chart sheet in the document is named Chart3.

The sheet name is not only a tab label. It might also be displayed and printed in the sheet *header* or *footer*, and is used in formulas referencing information on other sheets. For this reason, even if your workbook has only one sheet, it's a good idea to give each sheet a meaningful name. To select the sheet name for editing, double-click the sheet tab, or right-click the sheet tab and then click Rename. You can type a completely new name to replace the selected text, or click in the selected name to edit it. When you finish, press Return or click away from the sheet tab to save the new name.

A sheet name can be up to 31 characters, including spaces. The width of the sheet tab changes to match the sheet name. If you're managing multiple sheets within a workbook, you might want to keep the sheet names short so that you don't have to scroll the sheets to find the one you want.

Practice Working with Sheets and Data

In this exercise, you'll create a workbook from an existing worksheet, make a copy of the worksheet within the workbook, and rename the new worksheet. Then you'll delete rows of data and selected cells, shifting and reformatting the remaining data so that it's legible. Finally, you'll insert a new worksheet and populate it with selections of data from other sheets.

> **SET UP** Open the *AirQuality* workbook from the *~/Documents/Microsoft Press/2008OfficeMacSBS/WorkSheets/* folder. This workbook consists of eight worksheets: one containing data for all of the United States and the others for specific regions.

1. In the lower-left corner of the workbook window, at the left end of the sheet tabs, click the **Last Sheet** button.

   The sheet tabs shift within the tab area so that you can see the last sheet, *Regions 7-10*, and the Insert Sheet button.

2. Click the **Region 5** sheet tab.

This sheet displays air quality information from the United States Environmental Protection Agency for locations in one region of the United States. This region, referred to as *Region 5*, includes the states of Illinois (IL), Indiana (IN), Michigan (MI), Minnesota (MN), Ohio (OH), and Wisconsin (WI).

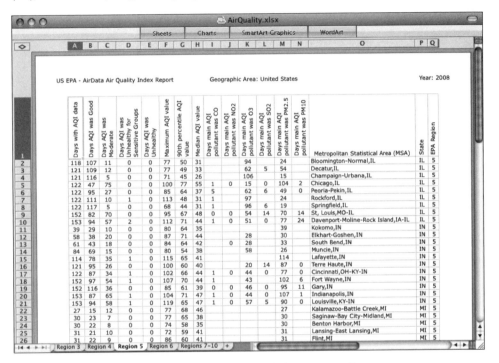

3. Right-click the **Region 5** sheet tab, and then click **Move or Copy**.

   The Move Or Copy dialog box opens. The To Book box displays the name of the current workbook. The Before Sheet box includes all the visible sheets in the active workbook.

   > **Note** If the workbook includes hidden sheets, they won't be shown in the Before Sheet box.

4. Click the **To book** list.

   The list expands. It includes all the currently open workbooks and a (new book) option.

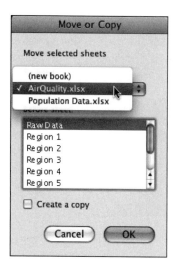

5. In the **To book** list, click **(new book)**.

   The Before Sheet box is now empty, because the new book doesn't yet have sheets.

6. Select the **Create a copy** check box, and then click **OK**.

   Excel creates a new workbook containing only the *Region 5* sheet. The workbook opens in the default Page Layout view.

7. On the **View** menu, click **Normal**.

   Later in this exercise, it will be simpler to work with the data in Normal view. By changing to Normal view now, all the copies you make of this worksheet will also be in Normal view.

8. Save the workbook in your *~/Documents/Microsoft Press/2008OfficeMacSBS/ WorkSheets/* folder as My Region 5.xlsx.

9. In the *My Region 5* workbook, right-click the **Region 5** sheet tab, and then click **Move or Copy**.

10. In the **Move or Copy** dialog box, click **(move to end)** in the **Before Sheet** box, select the **Create a copy** check box, and then click **OK**.

    Excel creates a copy of the worksheet, named *Region 5 (2)*.

19	152	116	36	0	0	85	61	39	0	0	46
20	153	87	65	1	0	104	71	47	1	0	44
21	153	94	58	1	0	119	65	47	1	0	57
22	27	15	12	0	0	77	68	46			
23	30	23	7	0	0	77	65	38			
24	30	22	8	0	0	74	58	35			
25	31	21	10	0	0	72	59	41			
26	31	22	9	0	0	86	60	41			

Region 5 Region 5 (2)

> **Note** The *Region 5* worksheet page orientation is landscape rather than portrait, because that is the orientation that was set for the *Region 5* worksheet in the original workbook. The default orientation of a new worksheet is portrait. By copying the worksheet rather than copying data to a new worksheet, you retain the page layout, column widths, and row heights of the original page.

11. Right-click the **Region 5 (2)** sheet tab, and then click **Rename**.

12. With the current worksheet name selected, type Michigan, and then press **Return**.

    Column P lists the state of each Metropolitan Statistical Area in Region 5. You will delete the data for Illinois (IL), Indiana (IN), Minnesota (MN), Ohio (OH), and Wisconsin (WI), leaving only the data for Michigan (MI).

13. On the **Michigan** worksheet, point to the row **2** heading. When the cursor changes to a solid right-pointing arrow, drag through the headings for rows **2** through **21** to select all the entries for the states of Illinois and Indiana.

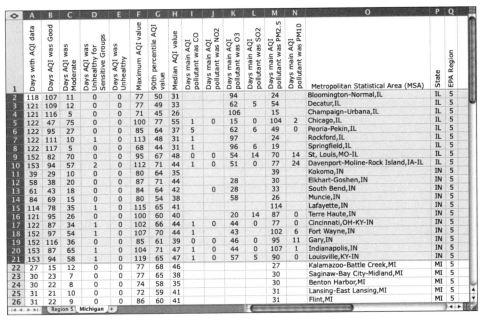

	A	B	C	D	E	F	G	H	I	J	K	L	M	N	O	P	Q
	Days with AQI data	Days AQI was Good	Days AQI was Moderate	Days AQI was Unhealthy for Sensitive Groups	Days AQI was Unhealthy	Maximum AQI value	90th percentile AQI value	Median AQI value	Days main AQI pollutant was CO	Days main AQI pollutant was NO2	Days main AQI pollutant was O3	Days main AQI pollutant was SO2	Days main AQI pollutant was PM2.5	Days main AQI pollutant was PM10	Metropolitan Statistical Area (MSA)	State	EPA Region
2	118	107	11	0	0	77	50	31			94		24		Bloomington-Normal,IL	IL	5
3	121	109	12	0	0	77	49	33			62	5	54		Decatur,IL	IL	5
4	121	116	5	0	0	71	45	26			106		15		Champaign-Urbana,IL	IL	5
5	122	47	75	0	0	100	77	55	1	0	15	0	104	2	Chicago,IL	IL	5
6	122	95	27	0	0	85	64	37	5		62	6	49	0	Peoria-Pekin,IL	IL	5
7	122	111	10	1	0	113	48	31	1		97		24		Rockford,IL	IL	5
8	122	117	5	0	0	68	44	31	1		96	6	19		Springfield,IL	IL	5
9	152	82	70	0	0	95	67	48	0	0	54	14	70	14	St, Louis,MO-IL	IL	5
10	153	94	57	2	0	112	71	44	1	0	51	0	77	24	Davenport-Moline-Rock Island,IA-IL	IL	5
11	39	29	10	0	0	80	64	35					39		Kokomo,IN	IN	5
12	58	38	20	0	0	87	71	44			28		30		Elkhart-Goshen,IN	IN	5
13	61	43	18	0	0	84	64	42		0	28		33		South Bend,IN	IN	5
14	84	69	15	0	0	80	54	38			58		26		Muncie,IN	IN	5
15	114	78	35	1	0	115	65	41					114		Lafayette,IN	IN	5
16	121	95	26	0	0	100	60	40			20	14	87	0	Terre Haute,IN	IN	5
17	122	87	34	1	0	102	66	44	1	0	44	0	77	0	Cincinnati,OH-KY-IN	IN	5
18	152	97	54	1	0	107	70	44	1		43		102	6	Fort Wayne,IN	IN	5
19	152	116	36	0	0	85	61	39	0	0	46	0	95	11	Gary,IN	IN	5
20	153	87	65	1	0	104	71	47	1	0	44	0	107	1	Indianapolis,IN	IN	5
21	153	94	58	1	0	119	65	47	1	0	57	5	90	0	Louisville,KY-IN	IN	5
22	27	15	12	0	0	77	68	46					27		Kalamazoo-Battle Creek,MI	MI	5
23	30	23	7	0	0	77	65	38					30		Saginaw-Bay City-Midland,MI	MI	5
24	30	22	8	0	0	74	58	35					30		Benton Harbor,MI	MI	5
25	31	21	10	0	0	72	59	41					31		Lansing-East Lansing,MI	MI	5
26	31	22	9	0	0	86	60	41					31		Flint,MI	MI	5

Region 5 | Michigan | +

14. Press the **Delete** key located on the keypad to the right of the **Return** key (not the **Delete** key in the upper-right corner of the alphanumeric keypad).

The data in rows 2 through 21 disappears, but the blank rows remain.

	Days with AQI data	Days AQI was Good	Days AQI was Moderate	Days AQI was Unhealthy for Sensitive Groups	Days AQI was Unhealthy	Maximum AQI value	90th percentile AQI value	Median AQI value	Days main AQI pollutant was CO	Days main AQI pollutant was NO2	Days main AQI pollutant was O3	Days main AQI pollutant was SO2	Days main AQI pollutant was PM2.5	Days main AQI pollutant was PM10	Metropolitan Statistical Area (MSA)	State	EPA Region
1																	
2																	
3																	
4																	
5																	
6																	
7																	
8																	
9																	
10																	
11																	
12																	
13																	
14																	
15																	
16																	
17																	
18																	
19																	
20																	
21																	
22	27	15	12	0	0	77	68	46			27				Kalamazoo-Battle Creek,MI	MI	5
23	30	23	7	0	0	77	65	38			30				Saginaw-Bay City-Midland,MI	MI	5
24	30	22	8	0	0	74	58	35			30				Benton Harbor,MI	MI	5
25	31	21	10	0	0	72	59	41			31				Lansing-East Lansing,MI	MI	5
26	31	22	9	0	0	86	60	41			31				Flint,MI	MI	5

Region 5 | Michigan

15. Press **Command+Z** to restore the deleted data. Then, with rows **2** through **21** still selected, click **Delete** on the **Edit** menu.

Excel deletes rows 2 through 21, moving the Michigan entries to the top of the data range.

16. Click the row **10** heading. Then scroll the window if necessary, press and hold the **Shift** key, and click the row **34** heading.

> **Tip** You can select adjacent rows, columns, or cells by selecting the first, holding down the Shift key, and then selecting the last. You can select non-adjacent rows, columns, or cells by selecting the first, holding down the Control key, and then selecting others.

17. Press the **Delete** key (again, the one on the keypad to the right of the **Return** key).

Excel deletes the Minnesota, Ohio, and Wisconsin entries, leaving only the eight Michigan entries. This method of deleting rows or columns of data works fine when no data follows the selected entries.

18. Drag to select cells **I1** through **N9**. Then on the **Edit** menu, click **Delete**.

The Delete dialog box opens.

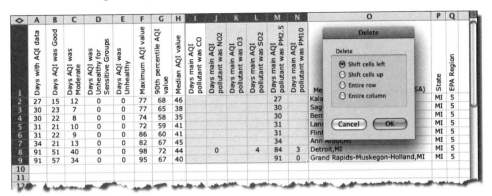

19. In the **Delete** dialog box, with **Shift cells left** selected, click **OK**.

Excel deletes the selected cells and shifts the remaining cells to the left to close the gap. Because we deleted cells rather than columns, the columns holding the shifted data aren't the same width as their original columns.

20. Double-click the column separator between columns **I** and **J** to resize column **I** to fit its contents.

21. Select row **1**, and then press **Command+C** to copy the column titles to the Clipboard.

22. At the right end of the sheet tabs, click the **Insert Sheet** button.

Excel creates a worksheet named *Sheet3*. The new worksheet is displayed in the default Page Layout view.

23. With cell **A1** of the new worksheet active, press **Command+V** to paste the column titles into row 1 of *Sheet3*.

The titles appear at the top of the sheet, with the Paste Options button visible below cell A1.

24. Click the **Paste Options** button and then, in the list, click **Keep Source Column Widths**.

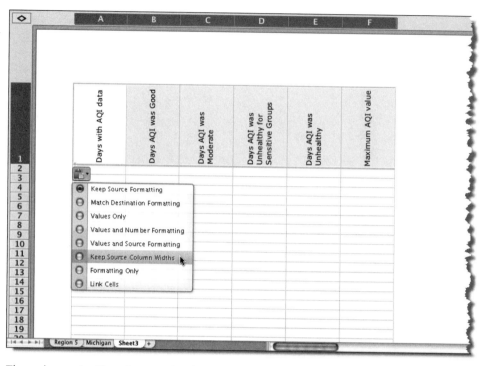

The columns in *Sheet3* are resized to match those in the *Michigan* sheet.

25. Change the name of *Sheet3* to Illinois.

26. Click the **Region 5** sheet tab. Drag to select cells **A2:H10** (A2 through H10). Then hold down the **Command** key and drag to select cells **O2:Q10**.

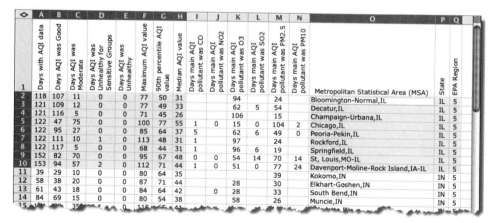

Tip The notational expression for a range of cells is the upper-left cell in the range, followed by a colon (no spaces), followed by the lower-right cell in the range.

27. Press **Command+C** to copy the selected data to the Clipboard.

> **Note** Shimmering dashed lines around the selected cells indicate that you've copied them to the Clipboard.

28. Click the **Illinois** sheet tab, click cell **A2**, and then press **Command+V** to paste the copied data into the *Illinois* sheet.

    Notice that Excel pastes the data into the *Illinois* sheet without including the gap for the cells you didn't select from the *Region 5* sheet. Pretty slick!

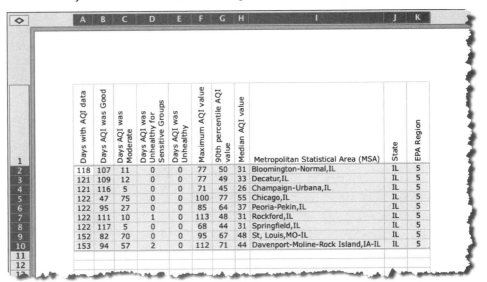

Days with AQI data	Days AQI was Good	Days AQI was Moderate	Days AQI was Unhealthy for Sensitive Groups	Days AQI was Unhealthy	Maximum AQI value	90th percentile AQI value	Median AQI value	Metropolitan Statistical Area (MSA)	State	EPA Region
118	107	11	0	0	77	50	31	Bloomington-Normal,IL	IL	5
121	109	12	0	0	77	49	33	Decatur,IL	IL	5
121	116	5	0	0	71	45	26	Champaign-Urbana,IL	IL	5
122	47	75	0	0	100	77	55	Chicago,IL	IL	5
122	95	27	0	0	85	64	37	Peoria-Pekin,IL	IL	5
122	111	10	1	0	113	48	31	Rockford,IL	IL	5
122	117	5	0	0	68	44	31	Springfield,IL	IL	5
152	82	70	0	0	95	67	48	St, Louis,MO-IL	IL	5
153	94	57	2	0	112	71	44	Davenport-Moline-Rock Island,IA-IL	IL	5

CLEAN UP Save the *My Region 5* workbook, and then close the *My Region 5* and *AirQuality* workbooks. If you're not going to practice on your own, you can quit Excel.

Key Points

- You can easily restructure data on a sheet, and move data within and between sheets and workbooks.
- By using the Data Validation feature, you can restrict the type of data entered in a list sheet by specifying conditions for each column.
- Using the Conditional Formatting feature, you can apply special font and cell formatting to cell values that meet conditions you specify.
- You can simplify the process of analyzing data by displaying the data in a chart.
- You can manage workbook content by adding or removing sheets, copying or moving sheets, or assigning names to sheets to make them easily identifiable.

Chapter at a Glance

Create simple formulas, **page 300**

B22			fx	=B21/SUM($B$21:$E$21)				

17	October	$	16,978	$	49,616	$	73,542	$	47,736
18	November	$	91,019	$	85,495	$	49,873	$	73,236
19	December	$	59,564	$	65,163	$	51,554	$	58,238
20	4th Quarter Total	$	167,561	$	200,274	$	174,969	$	179,210
21	Annual Total	$	669,419	$	684,734	$	715,313	$	738,745
22	Percentage of Sales		24%		24%		25%		26%
23	Change From Last Year								
24									

This Year | Last Year | +

Reference worksheets and workbooks, **page 304**

			fx	=B22-'Last Year'!B15				

◇	A		B		C		D		E
1			Region 1		Region 2		Region 3		Region 4
2	January	$	99,103	$	44,027	$	45,863	$	24,086
3	February	$	16,307	$	86,479	$	48,342	$	45,974
4	March	$	80,333	$	40,063	$	92,406	$	59,498
5	April	$	25,993	$	13,513	$	15,646	$	12,027
6	May	$	26,259	$	35,227	$	36,395	$	15,779
7	June	$	59,437	$	83,509	$	29,662	$	78,697
8	July	$	81,879	$	46,255	$	39,097	$	30,347
9	August	$	89,658	$	78,294	$	99,528	$	66,407
10	September	$	75,905	$	82,676	$	97,632	$	40,743
11	October	$	38,877	$	53,600	$	61,006	$	21,556
12	November	$	80,616	$	78,718	$	56,878	$	14,665
13	December	$	70,207	$	37,705	$	73,593	$	31,840
14	Annual Total	$	744,574.00	$	680,066.00	$	696,048.00	$	441,619.00
15	Percentage of Sales		29%		27%		27%		17%
16									

Use absolute and relative references, **page 305**

◇	A	B	C	D	E
1	Customer	Wingtip Toys			
2	Discount	0.2			
3					
4	Quantity	Price Each	Subtotal	Discount	Total
5	100	20	=A5*B5	=C5*$B$2	=C5-D5
6	200	20	=A6*B6	=C6*$B$2	=C6-D6
7				=C7*$B$2	=C7-D7
				=C8*$B$2	=C8-D8
				=C9*$B$2	=C9-D9

◇	A	B	C	D	E
1	Customer	Wingtip Toys			
2	Discount	20%			
3					
4	Quantity	Price Each	Subtotal	Discount	Total
5	100	20	2000	400	1600
6	200	20	4000	800	3200
7	300	20	6000	1200	4800
8	400	20	8000	1600	6400
9	500	20	10000	2000	8000
10					

9 Create Excel Formulas

In this chapter, you will learn how to

- ✔ Understand functions.
- ✔ Create simple formulas.
- ✔ Reference worksheets and workbooks.
- ✔ Use absolute and relative references.
- ✔ Reference named cells and ranges.

Formulas are equations that, in Microsoft Excel, calculate the content of a cell based on one or more criteria. Formulas in Excel can be made up of references to other cells or to ranges of cells, values that you specify or calculate, mathematical operators, and *functions*. Entire books have been written about Excel formulas, and this book isn't the place to get too deeply into that subject, but we can't let you go without at least a peek into this fascinating subject.

An Excel worksheet without a calculation is merely electronic accounting paper. Most worksheets contain at least simple calculations, such as one that adds the values of two cells together. Other Excel worksheets contain mathematic or date-driven formulas so daunting that it might seem as though only a computer scientist or mathematician could understand them. Although it is helpful to have some knowledge of the types of function-driven operations you are performing, Excel greatly simplifies the process of creating formulas by providing specific guidelines as you create any formula.

In this chapter, you'll learn about formulas and the functions you can use to work with alphanumeric data. You'll learn how to create simple formulas and how to include data from the same worksheet, another sheet in the workbook, or an external workbook, in a calculation.

See Also You can find handy keyboard shortcuts, simple instructions for performing common tasks, and other useful information in the Quick Reference section at the beginning of this book.

Practice Makes Perfect! The practice file you will use to complete the exercises in this chapter is in the *CreateFormulas* practice file folder. See "Using the Companion Content" at the beginning of this book for information about installing and locating the practice files.

Understand Functions

A function can be thought of as a service provided by Excel to do a specific task. That task might be to perform some math operation, it could be to make a decision based on information you give it, or it could be to perform an action on some text. A function is always indicated by the function name followed by a set of parentheses. For most functions, *arguments* inside the parentheses either tell the function what to do or indicate the values that the function is to work with. An argument can be a value that you type, a cell reference, a range reference, a name, or even another function. The number and type of arguments vary depending on which function you're using. It is important to understand the syntax of common functions and be able to correctly enter the function arguments. Fortunately, you don't have to memorize anything—Excel 2008 does an excellent job of walking you through the process of using a function within your formulas. You can type a function's syntax yourself if you want, but it's almost always easier to let Excel guide you through the process.

Excel 2008 includes over 200 functions that you can use to calculate, transform, retrieve, or otherwise manipulate alphanumeric data. Functions are available in the following categories:

- Database
- Date and time
- Engineering
- Financial
- Information
- Logical
- Lookup and reference
- Math and trigonometry
- Statistical
- Text

It looks as though Excel pretty much wipes out the need for high school math classes!

You can use formulas and functions to work with text, dates, and numbers. For example, at my company, we create project schedules in Excel that use formulas to help us determine when we need to do things, and calculate the date that a project will be completed. Within the same schedule, we use formulas to estimate the number of pages that each chapter of a book will be when it's in its final format, how many pages the entire book will be, how many pages the index should be to provide sufficient information to the reader, and whether the projected page count fits the page limitations required by the publisher.

In a typical book project schedule, we use these functions:

- DAY() to calculate the date that is a specific number of days beyond the date in the reference cell

- WORKDAY() to calculate the date that is a specific number of days, excluding weekends and holidays, beyond the date in the reference cell

- SUM() to add columns of numbers

- ODD(SUM()) to return an odd number closest to the result of the SUM calculation

- EVEN(SUM()) to return an even number closest to the result of the SUM calculation

- MAX() to return the largest number (or in this case, the latest date) in a referenced cell range

The types of functions and formulas you'll create depend largely on what you need to do.

We won't go into great detail about all the available functions here—you can find information about them in the Excel Help file. However, the following sections provide an overview of the available functions.

Numeric Functions

The functions in the following table can be used with any alphanumeric data. In the table:

- Any argument specified as a *number* can be a number that is entered directly, a text representation of a number (a number inside quotation marks), a cell reference, a cell range reference, or a *named reference*. Any cells that contain text that can't be translated to a number, that are empty, or that have an error are simply ignored by the function.

  See Also For information about named references, see "Reference Named Cells and Ranges" later in this chapter.

● Any argument specified as a *value* can be any type of value. In the case of COUNT, the function will simply ignore anything that it can't interpret as a number. In the case of COUNTA, the function will count everything that isn't empty.

● The *range* arguments are references to the set of cells that will be evaluated against the criteria. A *criteria* argument can be a number, an expression enclosed in quotation marks, or text enclosed in quotation marks. The *average_range* and *sum_range* arguments are references to the set of cells whose values will be averaged or summed. In the single criteria versions, if the *average_range* or *sum_range* argument is omitted, the function uses the values from the range. The *average_range* and *sum_range* arguments are not optional for the multi-criteria functions.

Function	Purpose	Arguments
AVERAGE()	Average a set of numbers	*number1,number2,...number255*
AVERAGEIF()	Average values that meet one condition	*range,criteria,average_range*
AVERAGEIFS()	Average values that meet multiple criteria	*average_range,criteria_range1,criteria1, criteria_range2,criteria2,...*
COUNT()	Count the number of cells that have numbers	*value1,value2,...value255*
COUNTA()	Count the number of cells that are not empty	*value1,value2,...value255*
COUNTIF()	Count cells that meet one condition	*range,criteria*
COUNTIFS()	Count cells that meet multiple criteria	*criteria_range1,criteria1,criteria_ range2,criteria2,...*
MAX()	Find the maximum value in a set of numbers	*number1,number2,...number255*
MIN()	Find the minimum value in a set of numbers	*number1,number2,...number255*
SUM()	Total a set of numbers	*number1,number2,...number255*
SUMIF()	Sum values that meet one condition	*range,criteria,sum_range*
SUMIFS()	Sum values that meet multiple criteria	*sum_range,criteria_range1,criteria1, criteria_range2,criteria2,...*

Text Functions

Excel provides several ways to work with text. The simplest text operation is concatenation—adding one text value to the end of another. This is useful when one part of the text value is the result of a calculation and another part is fixed or is the result of a different calculation. Some text functions help you to manage the capitalization of text. You can use the following functions on one cell at a time:

- LOWER() returns a text value in all lowercase letters.
- PROPER() returns a text value with an uppercase letter followed by lowercase letters.
- UPPER() returns a text value in all uppercase letters.

Resources Changing the case of text for more than one cell requires an array formula. These multi-dataset formulas are beyond the scope of this book, but you can find information about them in the Excel Help file.

Two functions are available to replace parts of a text value:

- REPLACE() replaces a specific number of characters in a text value.
- SUBSTITUTE() replaces one part of a text value with another (which could include an empty string, in order to delete part of a text value).

Generic Functions

The functions in the following table can be used with any alphanumeric data. In the table:

- The *lookup_value* argument is the value to be looked up. This argument can be a number, text, or a cell reference.
- The *table_array* argument is a reference to a range that has one or more rows, in the case of HLOOKUP, or one or more columns, in the case of VLOOKUP. Excel evaluates the first row or column of this range for the lookup value.
- The *row_index_num* and *column_index_num* arguments specify which row or column to return the value from. For example, in an HLOOKUP function, a *row_index_num* value of 1 would return the value from the first row, the same one being used for the lookup. A *row_index_num* value of 2 would return the value from the second row, and so on.

● The *range_lookup* argument is either TRUE or FALSE. If it is TRUE or omitted and an exact match is not found, the largest value that is less than the *lookup_value* argument is used as a match. If the *lookup_value* argument is smaller than any number in the first row (HLOOKUP) or column (VLOOKUP), a #N/A error occurs. If the *range_lookup* argument is FALSE, only an exact match is allowed. If an exact match isn't found, a #N/A error occurs.

Function	Purpose	Arguments
HLOOKUP()	Return a value from the column in which a value in the first row matches the criteria	*lookup_value,table_array,row_index_num,range_lookup*
VLOOKUP()	Return a value from the row in which a value in the first column matches the criteria	*lookup_value,table_array,column_index_num,range_lookup*
IF()	Return one value if a test is TRUE, and another if the test is FALSE	*logical_test,value_if_true,value_if_false*
AND()	Return TRUE if all arguments are true	*logical1,logical2,...*
OR()	Return TRUE if any arguments are true	*logical1,logical2,...*
NOT()	Reverse the logical value of the argument	*logical*
IFERROR()	Return a user-friendly message if a formula has an error due to user input	*value,value_if_error*

Create Simple Formulas

To apply a function, you create a formula that uses that function. If you know the formula you want to use, you can type it directly into a worksheet cell, or into the Formula Bar (which displays the cell content in a larger space). If you're uncertain about the specific function that will perform the calculation you want, or unsure about how to put together a formula using that function, you can call on the Formula Builder to help you put one together.

You can create a formula in any of these three ways:

→ Type the formula directly into the worksheet cell in which you want the results to appear.

→ Display the **Formula Bar**, and type the formula into the box.

As you enter the formula, prompts appear, to guide you through the formula-creation process.

> **Tip** To display the Formula Bar, click Formula Bar on the View menu. The Formula Bar opens at full-screen width. If you want, you can resize it by dragging its lower-right corner.

→ Display the **Formula Builder** in the Toolbox, and select the function you want to use.

After you select the function, the correct syntax appears in the Description box.

> **Tip** You can search for a function by typing basic information about what you want to accomplish into the Search For A Function box.

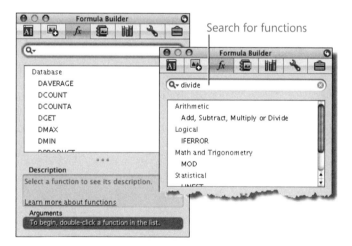

Search for functions

Double-clicking a function displays boxes at the bottom of the Formula Builder into which you can enter the required information. As you enter it, the Formula Builder builds the formula in the cell and (if it's displayed) in the Formula Bar.

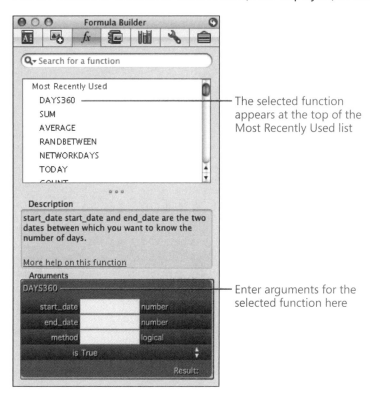

The selected function appears at the top of the Most Recently Used list

Enter arguments for the selected function here

Formulas in an Excel worksheet most often involve functions performed on the values contained in one or more other cells on the worksheet (or on another worksheet). In this chapter, when we refer to a cell in a formula, we'll call that cell the *reference cell*.

The basis of every formula is an equal sign (=). This symbol at the beginning of the cell content notifies Excel that the text following the equal sign is not what you want to display in the cell. The simplest formula takes the form of an equal sign followed by a cell reference. For example, this formula displays the contents of the reference cell A5:

=A5

> **Tip** You don't *have* to use a reference cell in a formula—you can perform functions on actual alphanumeric data. The beauty of performing functions on reference cells is that you can change the results of the function by changing the content of the reference cell, without having to edit the formula.

The next-simplest formula is one that performs a mathematical calculation based on the contents of one reference cell, but without using a function. For example:

=A5+1

returns a number, which could also be a date or time, that is one larger than the number in cell A5.

Formulas that use functions are built in this standard format:

=FUNCTION(argument1,argument2)

In this case, *argument* represents a reference cell, number, or other value that is required by the function. For example:

=MAX(A5,B5)

returns the value of cell A5 or of cell B5, whichever is larger.

Notice that the two arguments in the preceding example are separated by a comma. Excel evaluates whatever information is between the commas as one argument, so you can perform multiple calculations within a formula. For example:

=NETWORKDAYS(C2,TODAY())

returns the number of workdays (not counting weekends and holidays) between the date in cell C2 and today's date.

> **Tip** The TODAY function returns today's date. The function requires a set of parentheses following the name.

You can reference a range of cells in a formula by referencing the first and last cells in the range, divided by a colon. For example:

=AVERAGE(A1:B5)

returns the average of the values of the 10 cells included in the specified range (A1 through A5 and B1 through B5).

When you reference a cell or range of cells in a formula, you can enter the cell reference by typing it or—with the insertion point active in the formula where you want to insert the reference—by clicking a cell or dragging to select a range of cells.

Reference Worksheets and Workbooks

Within a formula, you aren't limited to referencing only cells on the same worksheet. You can reference cells on other worksheets by using syntax like this:

=SUM(A5,Sheet2!C5)

> **Tip** You reference a worksheet by whatever name appears on its sheet tab.

This formula adds the value in cell A5 of the current worksheet to the value in cell C5 of Sheet2.

As when referencing cells on the same worksheet, you can enter a reference to a cell on another worksheet by clicking the sheet tab and then clicking the cell.

> **Tip** In the absence of a mathematical operator, the SUM() function adds the numeric values that have been entered in the formula and separated by commas. You can use a plus sign (+) in place of the commas if you want to, but it isn't necessary. If you want to subtract numbers within a formula that uses the SUM function, insert minus signs (-) in place of the commas.
>
> You can use multiple mathematical operators within an operation, adding some numbers and subtracting others, as shown in the next example. It is not necessary to use the SUM function for these simple mathematical operations.

Similarly, you can reference cells in other workbooks by using syntax like this:

=A5+Sheet2!C5-'[Workbook2.xlsx]Sheet1'!D3

> **Tip** When referencing a workbook located in a folder other than the one your active workbook is in, enter the path to the file along with the file name. If the path includes a non-alphabetical character (such as the backslash in "C:\") in the file name, enclose the path in single quotation marks.

The simplest way to reference a cell in another workbook is to enter the formula elements leading up to the reference, and then activate the workbook and click the cell or range of cells you want to reference. Excel will enter the cell or range reference into the formula.

Use Absolute and Relative References

A reference that you make in a formula to the contents of a worksheet cell is either a *relative reference*, an *absolute reference*, or a *mixed reference*. It is important to understand the difference and know which to use when creating a formula.

A relative reference to a cell takes the form *A1*. When you copy or fill a formula from the original cell to other cells, a relative reference will change to indicate the cell having the same relationship to the formula cell that A1 did to the original formula cell. For example, if a formula in cell B1 references cell A1 and you copy the formula to cell B5, the formula in cell B5 references cell A5.

An absolute reference takes the form *$A$1;* the first dollar sign indicates an absolute reference to column A, and the second indicates an absolute reference to row 1. When you copy or fill a formula from the original cell to other cells, an absolute reference will not change—regardless of the relationship to the referenced cell, the reference will stay the same.

A mixed reference refers absolutely to either the column or row and relatively to the other. The mixed reference *A$1* will always refer to row 1, and *$A1* will always refer to column A.

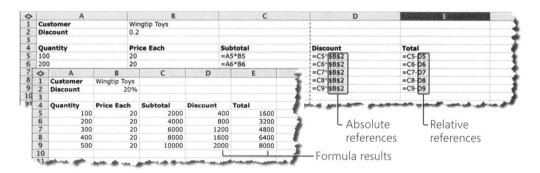

It's important to ensure that cell references are set up correctly, before you copy or fill a formula to other cells.

> **Tip** To display the formulas of a worksheet, as shown in the upper image, rather than their results, press Control+' (the accent grave character found under the tilde, in the upper-left corner of the keyboard).

Reference Named Cells and Ranges

A simple way to ensure that you're referencing the specific data you want to reference is by assigning a name to the cell, or more typically to a range of cells, that you want to reference. For example, the WORKDAY function allows an argument providing specific non-work days, such as holidays. This is very convenient because not everyone celebrates the same holidays.

To simplify the process of creating formulas that refer to a specific range of data, and to make your formulas easier to read and create, you can refer to a cell or range of cells by a name that you define. For example, you might use the name *Interest* for a cell containing an interest rate, or you might use the name *Holidays* for a range of cells containing non-work days. In a formula, you refer to a named range by name. Thus you might end up with a formula like this:

=WORKDAY(StartDate,DaysOfWork,Holidays)

A formula using named ranges is simpler to understand than its standard equivalent, which could look like this:

=WORKDAY(B2,B$3,Data!B2:B16)

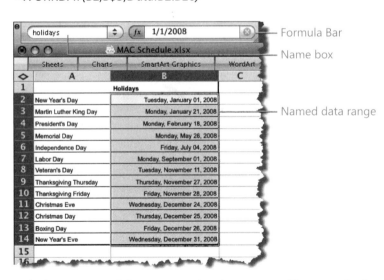

Referring to a named data range, rather than to a specific range of cells, is far simpler and also lessens the chance of error.

> **Tip** The range name is visible in the Name box at the left end of the Formula Bar, and in the various Names dialog boxes. If a cell is part of multiple named ranges, only the first name is shown in the Name box. The Name box displays the name of a multiple-cell named range only when all cells in the range are selected.

After defining a named range, you can change the range name or the cells included in the named range, or delete a range name definition, from the Define Name dialog box.

> **Note** Deleting a cell from a worksheet does not delete any associated range name.

To define a selected cell or range of cells as a named range:

→ In the **Name** box at the left end of the **Formula Bar**, type the range name, and then press **Return**.

Or

1. On the **Insert** menu, point to **Name**, and then click **Define**.

    The Define Name dialog box opens. The content of the upper-left selected cell is displayed in the Names In Workbook box as a suggested range name. The selected cells are displayed in the Refers To box.

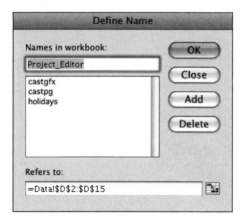

2. Verify or change the range name and cell range, and then click **Add**.

Practice Creating Formulas

In this exercise, you'll create a formula to calculate the difference between two cell values, duplicate the formula within a cell range, and then copy the formula to another table.

> **SET UP** Open the *AnnualSales* workbook from the *~/Documents/Microsoft Press/ 2008OfficeMacSBS/CreateFormulas/* folder. Display the Standard and Formatting toolbars.

1. If the **Formula Bar** isn't already open, click **Formula Bar** on the **View** menu.

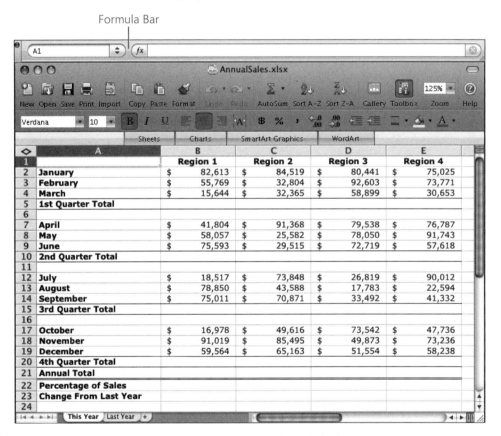

Formula Bar

2. Click cell **B5** to activate it. On the Standard toolbar, click the **AutoSum** arrow.

> **Note** Clicking the AutoSum button invokes the SUM() function, which we'll use, but at the moment we want to look at all the options.

The AutoSum list displays several simple functions. You can quickly create a formula that uses one of these functions by clicking the function and then verifying the data range Excel suggests that you base your calculation on.

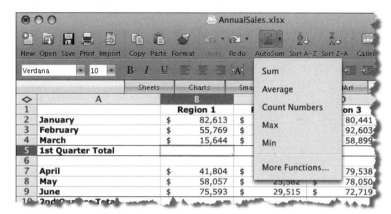

> **Note** Clicking More Functions in the AutoSum list opens the Formula Builder.

3. Press the **Escape** key to collapse the **AutoSum** list. Then click the **AutoSum** button.

Excel inserts a formula that uses the SUM() function to total the numbers immediately above the active cell. The cell references appear in the formula in blue text, and the corresponding cells are indicated in the worksheet by a shimmering blue outline.

	A	B	C	D
1		Region 1	Region 2	Region 3
2	January	$ 82,613	$ 84,519	$ 80,441
3	February	$ 55,769	$ 32,804	$ 92,603
4	March	$ 15,644	$ 32,365	$ 58,899
5	1st Quarter Total	=SUM(B2:B4)		
6				
7	April	$ 41,804	$ 91,368	$ 79,538
8	May	$ 58,057	$ 25,582	$ 78,050
9	June	$ 75,593	$ 29,515	$ 72,719
10	2nd Quarter Total			

The AutoSum functions default to the closest logical data range. You can change the cells referenced in the formula by dragging to select other cells, or by changing the cell references.

4. Press **Return** to accept the default formula.

The formula calculates the 1st Quarter Total of sales in Region 1. The result, $154,026, appears in cell B5, and cell B6 becomes the active cell.

5. Click cell **B5**, and then point to the fill handle in the lower-right corner of the active cell. When the pointer changes to a black plus sign, drag to the right through cell **E5**.

When you release the mouse button, the 1st Quarter Totals for Regions 2, 3, and 4 appear.

6. Click cell **E5**, and verify that the formula in the **Formula Bar** correctly calculates the 1st Quarter Total for Region 4 by adding cells E2 through E4.

	A	B	C	D	E
	E5		fx	=SUM(E2:E4)	
	A	Region 1	Region 2	Region 3	Region 4
1		Region 1	Region 2	Region 3	Region 4
2	January	$ 82,613	$ 84,519	$ 80,441	$ 75,025
3	February	$ 55,769	$ 32,804	$ 92,603	$ 73,771
4	March	$ 15,644	$ 32,365	$ 58,899	$ 30,653
5	1st Quarter Total	$ 154,026	$ 149,688	$ 231,943	$ 179,449

7. Drag to select cells **B5:E5**. Then on the Standard toolbar, click the **Copy** button.

   Excel copies the formulas in the selected cells to the Clipboard, and indicates the copied content with a shimmering blue outline.

8. Click cell **B10** (the 2nd Quarter Total for Region 1) and then, on the Standard toolbar, click the **Paste** button (or press **Command+V**).

   The 2nd Quarter Totals for the four regions appear in cells B10:E10.

9. Repeat step 8 two times, clicking cell **B15** the first time, and cell **B20** the second time. Then press the **Escape** key to release the selection.

   The four quarterly totals for the four regions are complete.

	A	B	C	D	E
1		Region 1	Region 2	Region 3	Region 4
2	January	$ 82,613	$ 84,519	$ 80,441	$ 75,025
3	February	$ 55,769	$ 32,804	$ 92,603	$ 73,771
4	March	$ 15,644	$ 32,365	$ 58,899	$ 30,653
5	1st Quarter Total	$ 154,026	$ 149,688	$ 231,943	$ 179,449
6					
7	April	$ 41,804	$ 91,368	$ 79,538	$ 76,787
8	May	$ 58,057	$ 25,582	$ 78,050	$ 91,743
9	June	$ 75,593	$ 29,515	$ 72,719	$ 57,618
10	2nd Quarter Total	$ 175,454	$ 146,465	$ 230,307	$ 226,148
11					
12	July	$ 18,517	$ 73,848	$ 26,819	$ 90,012
13	August	$ 78,850	$ 43,588	$ 17,783	$ 22,594
14	September	$ 75,011	$ 70,871	$ 33,492	$ 41,332
15	3rd Quarter Total	$ 172,378	$ 188,307	$ 78,094	$ 153,938
16					
17	October	$ 16,978	$ 49,616	$ 73,542	$ 47,736
18	November	$ 91,019	$ 85,495	$ 49,873	$ 73,236
19	December	$ 59,564	$ 65,163	$ 51,554	$ 58,238
20	4th Quarter Total	$ 167,561	$ 200,274	$ 174,969	$ 179,210
21	Annual Total				
22	Percentage of Sales				
23	Change From Last Year				
24					

This Year Last Year +

Next, we'll calculate the annual sales for each region by adding the quarterly totals.

10. Click cell **B21**, and then type = (an equal sign) to indicate the beginning of a formula.

11. Click cell **B5**.

A reference to the selected cell appears in the formula, in blue text, and a blue box outlines the cell.

12. Type + (a plus sign), click cell **B10**, type +, click cell **B15**, type +, and then click cell **B20**.

As you select each cell, a reference to the cell appears in the formula in a color different than the previous references, and a box of the same color outlines the cell.

◇	A	B	C	D	E
1		Region 1	Region 2	Region 3	Region 4
2	January	$ 82,613	$ 84,519	$ 80,441	$ 75,025
3	February	$ 55,769	$ 32,804	$ 92,603	$ 73,771
4	March	$ 15,644	$ 32,365	$ 58,899	$ 30,653
5	1st Quarter Total	$ 154,026	$ 149,688	$ 231,943	$ 179,449
6					
7	April	$ 41,804	$ 91,368	$ 79,538	$ 76,787
8	May	$ 58,057	$ 25,582	$ 78,050	$ 91,743
9	June	$ 75,593	$ 29,515	$ 72,719	$ 57,618
10	2nd Quarter Total	$ 175,454	$ 146,465	$ 230,307	$ 226,148
11					
12	July	$ 18,517	$ 73,848	$ 26,819	$ 90,012
13	August	$ 78,850	$ 43,588	$ 17,783	$ 22,594
14	September	$ 75,011	$ 70,871	$ 33,492	$ 41,332
15	3rd Quarter Total	$ 172,378	$ 188,307	$ 78,094	$ 153,938
16					
17	October	$ 16,978	$ 49,616	$ 73,542	$ 47,736
18	November	$ 91,019	$ 85,495	$ 49,873	$ 73,236
19	December	$ 59,564	$ 65,163	$ 51,554	$ 58,238
20	4th Quarter Total	$ 167,561	$ 200,274	$ 174,969	$ 179,210
21	Annual Total	=B5+B10+B15+B20			
22	Percentage of Sales				
23	Change From Last Year				
24					

This Year / Last Year +

By identifying each cell reference with a unique color, Excel makes it easier for you to locate cells referenced within a formula.

13. Press **Return** to complete the formula.

The Annual Total of sales for Region 1 appears in cell B21.

14. Fill the formula from cell **B21** to cells **C21:E21**.

The formula results are bold, because bold formatting was applied to row 21 in the original worksheet.

16					
17	October	$ 16,978	$ 49,616	$ 73,542	$ 47,736
18	November	$ 91,019	$ 85,495	$ 49,873	$ 73,236
19	December	$ 59,564	$ 65,163	$ 51,554	$ 58,238
20	4th Quarter Total	$ 167,561	$ 200,274	$ 174,969	$ 179,210
21	Annual Total	$ 669,419	$ 684,734	$ 715,313	$ 738,745
22	Percentage of Sales				
23	Change From Last Year				
24					

This Year / Last Year +

> **Tip** If you don't want to fill formatting from one cell to the next, click the Auto Fill Options button that appears in the lower-right corner of the fill zone, and then click Fill Without Formatting.

See Also For more information about the Auto Fill Options feature, see "Fill Cells with a Series of Data" in Chapter 5, "Create Excel Workbooks."

Next, we'll calculate the percentage of the total annual sales represented by each region, by dividing each region's annual sales by the total sales for all regions.

15. Click cell **B22**, and then click the **AutoSum** button.

Excel suggests a formula that sums only cell B21.

17	October	$	16,978	$	49,616
18	November	$	91,019	$	85,495
19	December	$	59,564	$	65,163
20	4th Quarter Total	$	167,561	$	200,274
21	Annual Total	$	669,419	$	684,734
22	Percentage of Sales	=SUM(B21)			
23	Change From Last Year				
24					

This Year / Last Year / +

16. Drag to select cells **B21:E21**.

The formula changes to reflect your selection.

17. In the **Formula Bar**, click to position the insertion point after the equal sign.

The cell range and surrounding parentheses, which were until this time black in the Formula Bar, become blue to indicate that you're actively working in the range. The insertion point is blinking in the Formula Bar. A non-blinking insertion point is visible in the formula in cell B22.

18. With the insertion point blinking after the equal sign, click cell **B21**, and then type / (a forward slash, used in formulas to indicate division).

In the Formula Bar and in the worksheet, the reference to cell B21 becomes blue and the reference to the cell range B21:E21 becomes green.

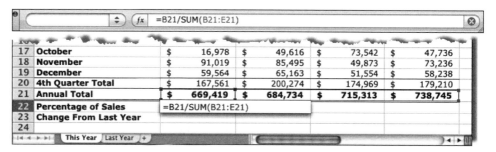

17	October	$	16,978	$	49,616	$	73,542	$	47,736
18	November	$	91,019	$	85,495	$	49,873	$	73,236
19	December	$	59,564	$	65,163	$	51,554	$	58,238
20	4th Quarter Total	$	167,561	$	200,274	$	174,969	$	179,210
21	Annual Total	$	669,419	$	684,734	$	715,313	$	738,745
22	Percentage of Sales	=B21/SUM(B21:E21)							
23	Change From Last Year								
24									

This Year   Last Year

19. Press **Return** to complete the formula.

The result is expressed in decimal notation.

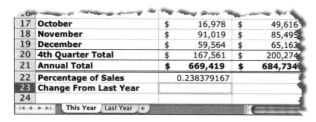

17	October	$	16,978	$	49,616
18	November	$	91,019	$	85,495
19	December	$	59,564	$	65,163
20	4th Quarter Total	$	167,561	$	200,274
21	Annual Total	$	669,419	$	684,734
22	Percentage of Sales	0.238379167		
23	Change From Last Year			
24				

This Year   Last Year

20. Click cell **B22**. Then on the Formatting toolbar, click the **Percent Style** button.

The number changes to a percentage, indicating that Region 1 sales were 24 percent of the total sales for the year.

Before filling the formula to the adjacent cells, we need to change the cell range reference from a relative reference to an absolute reference, so that the referenced cell range stays the same when we fill the formula.

21. In the **Formula Bar**, drag to select the cell range reference *B21:E21* (the green text). Then press **Command+T** to change the relative reference to an absolute reference, *$B$21:$E$21*.

22. Press **Return** to complete the formula. Then fill the formula from cell **B22** to cells **C22:E22**.

The results show that this year's sales were quite evenly spread between the four regions.

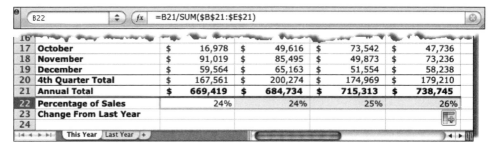

B22		fx	=B21/SUM($B$21:$E$21)						
16									
17	October	$	16,978	$	49,616	$	73,542	$	47,736
18	November	$	91,019	$	85,495	$	49,873	$	73,236
19	December	$	59,564	$	65,163	$	51,554	$	58,238
20	4th Quarter Total	$	167,561	$	200,274	$	174,969	$	179,210
21	Annual Total	$	669,419	$	684,734	$	715,313	$	738,745
22	Percentage of Sales		24%		24%		25%		26%
23	Change From Last Year								
24									

This Year / Last Year /

Next, we'll compare the division of sales this year to the division of sales last year. We'll subtract last year's sales percentages from this year's sales percentages, so that an increase in sales is expressed as a positive number and a decrease as a negative number.

23. Click cell **B23**, and then type = (an equal sign). Press the **Up Arrow** key to enter a reference to cell B22, and then type − (a minus sign).

24. At the bottom of the workbook window, click the **Last Year** sheet tab. On the *Last Year* worksheet, click cell **B15**, which displays the percentage of sales by Region 1 last year.

The cell in which you're building the formula isn't visible, but the formula is shown in the Formula Bar.

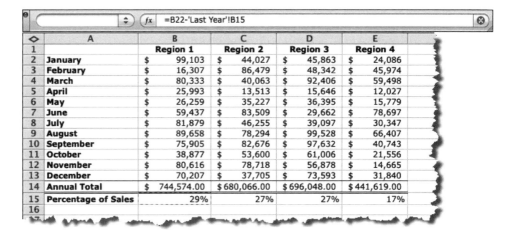

		fx	=B22-'Last Year'!B15					
	A		B		C		D	E
1			Region 1		Region 2		Region 3	Region 4
2	January	$	99,103	$	44,027	$	45,863	$ 24,086
3	February	$	16,307	$	86,479	$	48,342	$ 45,974
4	March	$	80,333	$	40,063	$	92,406	$ 59,498
5	April	$	25,993	$	13,513	$	15,646	$ 12,027
6	May	$	26,259	$	35,227	$	36,395	$ 15,779
7	June	$	59,437	$	83,509	$	29,662	$ 78,697
8	July	$	81,879	$	46,255	$	39,097	$ 30,347
9	August	$	89,658	$	78,294	$	99,528	$ 66,407
10	September	$	75,905	$	82,676	$	97,632	$ 40,743
11	October	$	38,877	$	53,600	$	61,006	$ 21,556
12	November	$	80,616	$	78,718	$	56,878	$ 14,665
13	December	$	70,207	$	37,705	$	73,593	$ 31,840
14	Annual Total	$	744,574.00	$ 680,066.00		$ 696,048.00		$ 441,619.00
15	Percentage of Sales		29%		27%		27%	17%
16								

25. Press **Return** to complete the formula.

Excel returns to the *This Year* worksheet and displays the formula result, which shows that Region 1 captured a lower percentage of sales this year than last year.

26. Copy the formula from cell **B23** to cells **C23:E23**.

The results of your calculations show that Region 4 made the biggest improvement this year.

	A	B	C	D	E
1		Region 1	Region 2	Region 3	Region 4
2	January	$ 82,613	$ 84,519	$ 80,441	$ 75,025
3	February	$ 55,769	$ 32,804	$ 92,603	$ 73,771
4	March	$ 15,644	$ 32,365	$ 58,899	$ 30,653
5	1st Quarter Total	$ 154,026	$ 149,688	$ 231,943	$ 179,449
6					
7	April	$ 41,804	$ 91,368	$ 79,538	$ 76,787
8	May	$ 58,057	$ 25,582	$ 78,050	$ 91,743
9	June	$ 75,593	$ 29,515	$ 72,719	$ 57,618
10	2nd Quarter Total	$ 175,454	$ 146,465	$ 230,307	$ 226,148
11					
12	July	$ 18,517	$ 73,848	$ 26,819	$ 90,012
13	August	$ 78,850	$ 43,588	$ 17,783	$ 22,594
14	September	$ 75,011	$ 70,871	$ 33,492	$ 41,332
15	3rd Quarter Total	$ 172,378	$ 188,307	$ 78,094	$ 153,938
16					
17	October	$ 16,978	$ 49,616	$ 73,542	$ 47,736
18	November	$ 91,019	$ 85,495	$ 49,873	$ 73,236
19	December	$ 59,564	$ 65,163	$ 51,554	$ 58,238
20	4th Quarter Total	$ 167,561	$ 200,274	$ 174,969	$ 179,210
21	Annual Total	$ 669,419	$ 684,734	$ 715,313	$ 738,745
22	Percentage of Sales	24%	24%	25%	26%
23	Change From Last Year	-5%	-2%	-2%	9%
24					

This Year / Last Year / +

CLEAN UP Close the *AnnualSales* worksheet without saving your changes. If you're not going to work further in Excel on your own, quit the program.

Key Points

- You can use formulas to calculate the content of a cell based on one or more criteria.

- Formulas can include references to other cells or to ranges of cells, values that you specify or calculate, mathematical operators, and functions.

- Excel 2008 includes over 200 functions that you can use to calculate, transform, retrieve, or otherwise manipulate alphanumeric data. Excel makes it easy to create formulas based on these functions, by modeling the required syntax for each function you work with.

Chapter at a Glance

Customize a slide background, **page 320**

Add a watermark to a slide, **page 321**

Change the layout of a slide, **page 337**

10 Work with PowerPoint Slide Content

In this chapter, you will learn how to

✔ Format slide text.

✔ Customize a slide background.

✔ Add a watermark to a slide.

✔ Change the layout of a slide.

✔ Change standard slide settings.

✔ Run a slide show.

In Chapter 6, "Create PowerPoint Presentations," we concentrated on the basic aspects of creating presentations and getting content into them. You can create very attractive and effective presentations by using the default presentation templates available in Microsoft PowerPoint 2008 for Mac. But you also have a lot of options for customizing the appearance of the slides in your presentation, and that's what we'll discuss now.

In this chapter, you'll learn to change the appearance of text on slides, and you'll customize slides with a variety of backgrounds. You'll learn several ways to change the appearance of individual slides, of groups of slides that share the same slide layout, and of all the slides in a presentation. Then you'll learn how to run a slide show of your presentation.

See Also You can find handy keyboard shortcuts, simple instructions for performing common tasks, and other useful information in the Quick Reference section at the beginning of this book.

> **Practice Makes Perfect!** The practice file you will use to complete the exercise in this chapter is in the *WorkSlides* practice file folder. See "Using the Companion Content" at the beginning of this book for information about installing and locating the practice files.

Format Slide Text

The standard PowerPoint slide text paragraph format is a bulleted list, but you're not limited to that format. You can change paragraph formatting in several ways, either before or after you enter text. Let's look at a few of them here, and then you can investigate more fully on your own.

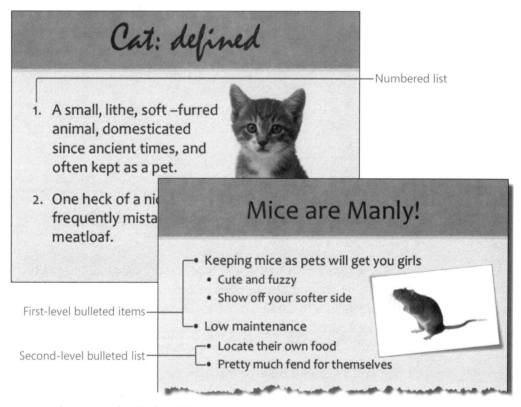

You can change standard bulleted list items to other paragraph formats.

To create a second-level bulleted list by indenting a list item:

→ Position the insertion point at the beginning of a list item, and then either press **Tab**, click the **Increase Indent** button on the Formatting toolbar, or click the **Increase List Level** button in the **Bullets and Numbering** panel of the **Formatting Palette**.

To outdent a list item:

→ Either press **Shift+Tab**, click the **Decrease Indent** button on the Formatting toolbar, or click the **Decrease List Level** button in the **Bullets and Numbering** panel.

To convert a bulleted (unordered) list to a numbered (ordered) list:

→ Select the list items you want to change, and then click the **Numbering** button on the Formatting toolbar or in the **Bullets and Numbering** panel.

You can change the style of the numbers or letters identifying ordered list items by making a selection in the Style list in the Bullets And Numbering panel, or on the Numbering page of the Format Text dialog box. From this page, you can also specify a color, size, and starting letter or number.

> **Tip** You can display the Format Text dialog box, either by clicking Bullets And Numbering on the Format menu, or by right-clicking the list and then clicking Bullets And Numbering.

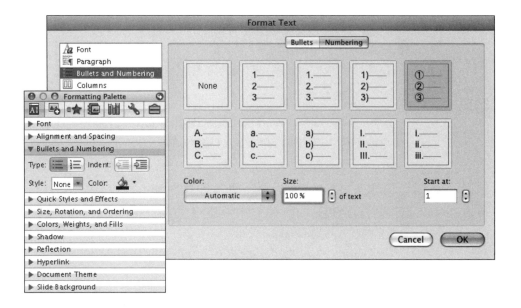

> **Troubleshooting** When you apply a number format to a multilevel list, PowerPoint uses the same format for all list levels. (This is different from the way Microsoft Word gracefully handles multilevel lists.) To differentiate the importance of the list levels, you can select and format the list items in each level separately.

See Also You can format the fonts and colors associated with a PowerPoint slide deck by applying or changing the theme. For more information, see "Work with Office Themes" in Chapter 7, "Work with Word Document Content."

To convert a bulleted list to normal text:

1. Click the active **Bullets** button in the **Bullets and Numbering** panel or on the Formatting toolbar to remove the bullet character or number.

2. If the text will be long enough to wrap to multiple lines, you'll need to remove the hanging indent from the paragraph. Start by displaying the **Paragraph** page of the **Format Text** dialog box in one of these ways:

   → On the **Format** menu, click **Paragraph**.

   → Right-click the selected text, and then click **Paragraph**.

3. On the **Paragraph** page of the **Format Text** dialog box, under **Indentation**, click **(None)** in the **Special** list, and change the **Before Text** measurement to **0"**.

Customize a Slide Background

In PowerPoint, you can customize the *background* of a slide by adding a solid color, a color gradient, a texture, or even a picture.

To format a slide background with a solid color:

→ In the **Slide Background** panel of the **Formatting Palette**, click the background color and, optionally, the style, you want.

Or

1. On the **Format** menu, click **Slide Background**.

2. On the **Solid** tab of the **Format Background** dialog box, expand the **Color** gallery and click the color you want.

3. Click **Apply** to apply the background to only the current slide, or **Apply to All** to apply the background to all slides in the presentation.

A color gradient is a visual effect in which two or more colors blend into each other. PowerPoint offers several gradient patterns—Linear, Path, Radial, Rectangular, and From Title, each with several variations. Standard gradients based on the presentation's color scheme are conveniently available from the Toolbox, or you can create your own gradient using from 2 to 10 colors.

If you want something fancier than a gradient, you can add a textured pattern or a picture to the slide background. PowerPoint comes with 24 preset textures that you can easily apply to the background of slides. You can add any picture to a slide's background, either as a single object stretched across the slide, or as a series of tiled images.

See Also For examples of color gradient, texture, and picture slide backgrounds, and step-by-step instructions for applying them, see "Practice Formatting Slide Backgrounds" later in this chapter.

Add a Watermark to a Slide

You can't create a simple textual watermark on a slide as you can in a document, but you can achieve a similar result by inserting WordArt and making it nearly transparent so that the slide content is visible through the WordArt text. Similarly, you can insert a shape, add text to it, and then adjust the transparency of the shape and the text to mimic a textual watermark. You can also format an image, such as a clip art image or a photo, as a watermark. The key difference between these methods and actual watermarks is that these methods place the nearly transparent watermark content in front of the slide content, rather than behind it, so the fake watermark could obscure the slide content.

See Also For information about textual watermarks, see the sidebar "Add a Watermark to a Document" in Chapter 14, "Add Finishing Document Elements." For information about inserting shapes, clip art, and photos, see Chapter 12, "Create and Insert Graphics."

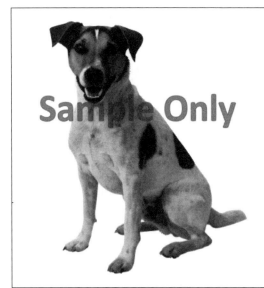

- **Useful pets**
  - Exercise companions
    - Walking
    - Running
    - Inline skating
  - Home protection
- **Many great small breeds**
  - American Eskimo
  - Papillon
  - Pomeranian
- **Commonly referred to as "Man's Best Friend"**

WordArt is the simplest tool for mimicking a watermark.

To insert a textual watermark on a slide by using WordArt:

1. Display the slide in Normal view.
2. From the **WordArt** tab of the Elements Gallery, select a WordArt style appropriate to your document.
3. Replace the *Your Text Here* placeholder with your watermark text.
4. Select the watermark text. In the **Colors, Weights, and Fills** panel of the **Formatting Palette**, set the **Fill Transparency** to a number between 65% and 90% (adjust the transparency to suit your preferences).

5. If the WordArt design includes an outline, set the **Line Transparency** to a number between 65% and 100%.

6. Size and position the WordArt where you want it to appear on the page. If you want the watermark to be diagonal, rotate the WordArt object by dragging the green rotation handle.

See Also For information about moving and rotating objects, see "Insert and Modify Shapes" in Chapter 12, "Create and Insert Graphics."

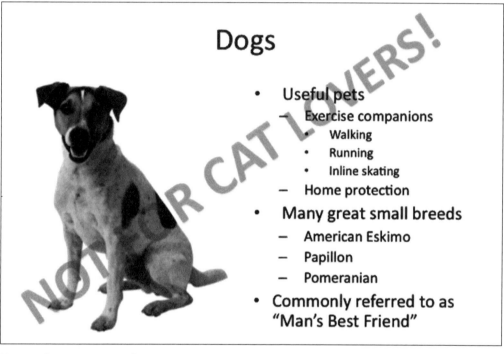

You can format text on a shape to act as a watermark.

To insert a textual watermark on a slide by using a shape:

1. Display the slide in Normal view.

2. From the **Object Palette** of the Toolbox, insert a rectangle shape. Then size and position the shape where you want it to appear on the page.

3. Add the watermark text to the shape.

Tip Some shapes allow you to type directly in them. You can activate others for text entry either by double-clicking in the center of the shape, or by right-clicking the shape and then clicking Add Text.

5. In the Toolbox, switch to the **Formatting Palette**.

6. Select the shape. In the **Colors, Weights, and Fills** panel, choose **No Fill** in the **Fill Color** list, and choose **No Line** in the **Line Color** list.

7. Select the watermark text. In the **Colors, Weights, and Fills** panel, choose the color you want the text to be. Then set the **Fill Transparency** of the text to a number between 65% and 90%.

8. If the inserted shape includes shadowing or any other formatting that is still visible, remove it by using the **Formatting Palette** tools.

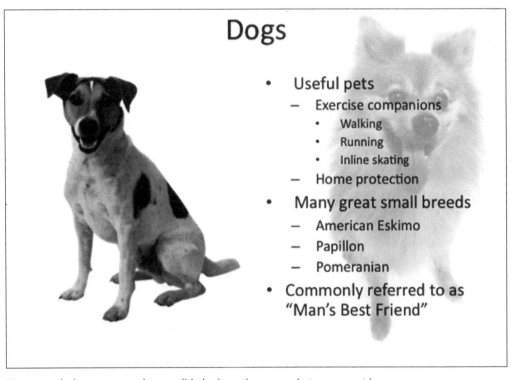

You can mimic a watermark on a slide by inserting a nearly transparent image.

To create a watermark on a slide by using an image or photo:

1. From the **Object Palette**, insert an image or photo.

2. Size and position the graphic object where you want it to appear on the page.

3. In the Toolbox, switch to the **Formatting Palette**.

4. With the image or photo selected, in the **Picture** panel, set the **Transparency** to a number between 65% and 90%.

Work with Presentation Color Schemes

The concept behind theme-specific color schemes is the same in PowerPoint as it is in Word. However, the way you work with the color scheme is a bit different.

See Also For information about working with theme color schemes in Word, see "Work with Office Themes" in Chapter 7, "Work with Word Document Content."

To display a presentation's color scheme:

→ On the **Format** menu, click **Theme Colors**.

The Create Theme Colors dialog box opens, displaying the four Text/Background colors, six Accent colors, and two Hyperlink colors. This is the same combination of colors that makes up a color scheme in Word.

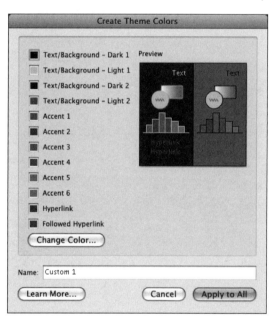

From this dialog box, you can change any of the theme colors and, if you create a color scheme that you want to reuse, save the custom color scheme.

To change a theme element to another color:

1. In the **Theme Colors** dialog box, dlick the colored square to the left of the theme element name, and then click the **Change Color** button.

2. In the **Colors** dialog box, select the color you want to use for the specified theme element from the **Color Wheel**, **Color Sliders**, **Color Palettes**, **Image Palettes**, or **Crayons** page, and then click **OK**.

   See Also For information about the pages of the Colors dialog box, see "Practice Formatting Characters" in Chapter 11, "Format Office File Content."

   In the Create Theme Colors dialog box, the icon of the selected color appears to the left of the theme element name, and is incorporated into the color scheme preview on the right side of the dialog box.

3. If the color of other theme elements doesn't work with the newly selected color—for example, if a background color and a hyperlink color are so similar that the hyperlink text wouldn't be visible against the background—change the colors of the other theme elements to create a balanced color scheme.

4. If you want to save the customized color scheme for reuse, enter a name for the color scheme in the **Name** box.

   You don't have to save the color scheme to apply it, at this time, to the presentation.

5. After you make all the changes you want to make, click the **Apply to All** button to apply your changes to the presentation content.

   If you changed the entry in the Name box before applying the theme colors, the custom color scheme is saved with that name.

To apply the custom color scheme to another presentation:

1. Save the custom color scheme as described above.

2. Open the presentation you want to apply the custom theme colors to.

3. In the **Document Theme** panel of the Toolbox, click the **Colors** arrow and then, in the list, click the custom color scheme.

Practice Formatting Slide Backgrounds

In this exercise, you'll format slide backgrounds with solid colors, custom gradients, textures, and pictures.

> **SET UP** Open the *MyVacation* presentation from the *~/Documents/Microsoft Press/ 2008OfficeMacSBS/WorkSlides/* folder, and display it in Normal view.

1. Display the Slides page of the Navigation pane, if it's not already open. Then adjust the width of the Navigation pane so that you can see several slides at once.

The background of each slide is a color gradient moving from a light color at the top of the slide to a darker color at the bottom of the slide. A graphic depicting several postmarks appears at the top of each slide. One or two graphics representing *Par Avion* (by airmail) stickers also appear on each slide other than the title slide. The postmark graphics on slides 1 and 4 are larger than the graphics on the others.

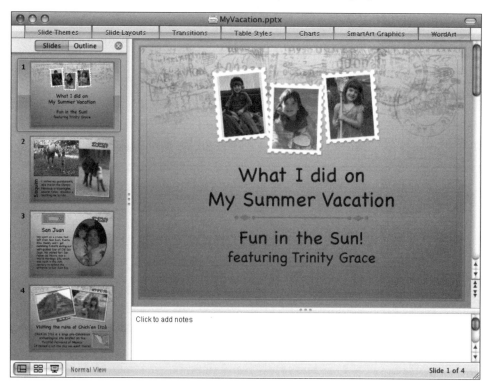

2. Display the **Formatting Palette** in the Toolbox, and expand the **Slide Background** panel.

The Slide Background panel of the Formatting Palette displays 12 slide backgrounds based on the Text/Background theme colors of this presentation (the PowerPoint equivalent of the theme-specific color scheme).

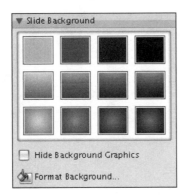

See Also For information about color schemes, see "Work with Office Themes" in Chapter 7, "Work with Word Document Content."

The top four backgrounds in the Slide Background panel (Style 1–Style 4) are solid versions of the Light 1, Light 2, Dark 1, and Dark 2 Text/Background colors. The middle four backgrounds (Style 5–Style 8) are three-color radial gradients, and the bottom four backgrounds (Style 9–Style 12) are two-color, centered, radial gradients.

3. With the presentation's title slide displayed, select the **Hide Background Graphics** check box in the **Slide Background** panel.

The postmark graphic disappears from the top of the title slide. In the Navigation pane, the postmark graphic is still visible on slides 2, 3, and 4.

> **Note** Although no Slide Background thumbnail is selected, the Style 5 background is the one currently applied to this slide.

4. In the **Slide Background** panel, click the **Style 3** thumbnail.

The backgrounds of this slide and the other slides in the presentation change to brown (the Text/Background - Dark 2 color), and the text changes to yellow (the Text/Background - Light 1 color).

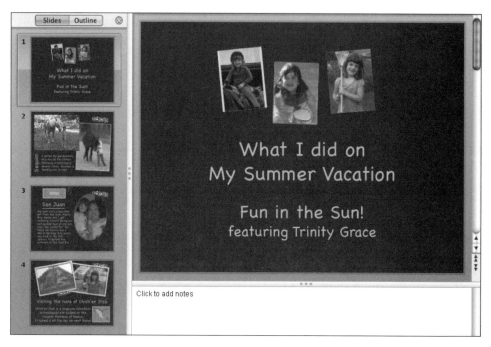

5. Display **Slide 3** of the presentation.

   The sticker graphic still appears on this slide. If you look closely at the top of the slide, you can see that the postmark graphic is still here, too. Its colors haven't changed, and they're difficult to see against this background.

6. In the **Slide Background** panel, click the **Style 10** thumbnail.

   The slide backgrounds change to a lighter brown color (the Text/Background – Light 2 color), with a sort of glow effect at the center. This effect is caused by the radial gradient that is part of this preset background.

The postmark graphic is more visible with this color scheme, as is the shadow effect that's been applied to the photo.

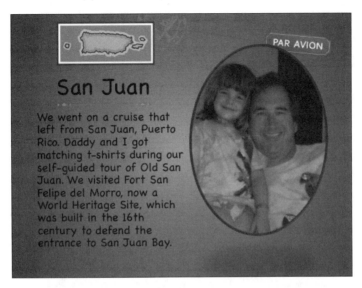

7. In the **Slide Background** panel, click the **Format Background** button.

The Format Background dialog box opens, displaying the Solid page. This dialog box always opens to the Solid page, regardless of the type of background applied to the active slide. The Color box at the top depicts an accurate representation of the current background formatting.

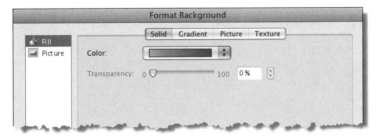

8. At the top of the dialog box, click the **Gradient** button.

The Gradient page displays the details of the current slide background. As mentioned earlier in this exercise, this is a two-color, centered, radial gradient.

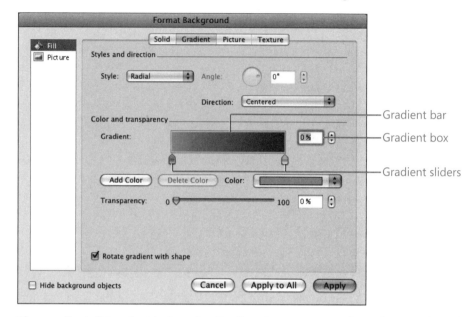

The gradient sliders just below the Gradient bar represent the colors used on the slide background and the way they blend into each other. (There are two sliders, so this is a two-color gradient.) The left slider is blue, indicating that it's active. The right slider is gray, indicating that it isn't active. The Color box displays the color of the active slider.

9. Click the right gradient slider to activate it.

The color shown in the Color box changes to the color represented by the right slider.

10. Click the **Color** box.

The Color palette expands. The 10 theme colors shown at the top are the same colors that appear in the Create Theme Colors dialog box discussed in the sidebar "Work with Presentation Color Schemes" earlier in this chapter.

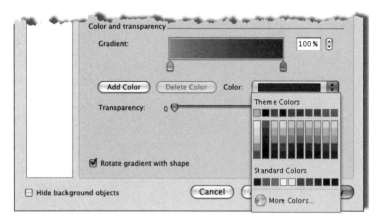

11. At the top of the **Theme Colors** palette, click the dark pink square (**Accent 2**).

    The Gradient bar changes to display a smooth gradient from a tan color to the dark pink color.

12. Drag the right gradient slider to the center of the **Gradient** bar, until the gradient box says **50%**.

    > **Tip** You can type a specific gradient percentage into the gradient box, or scroll the percentage by clicking the up and down arrows.

13. In the **Color and transparency** section of the **Gradient** page, click the **Add Color** button.

    A third slider appears, between the second slider and the right end of the Gradient bar. The color associated with the new slider is the same as the currently active slider—dark pink.

14. Click the **Color** box and then, in the larger **Theme Colors** palette, click the middle green square (**Accent 5, Lighter 40%**).

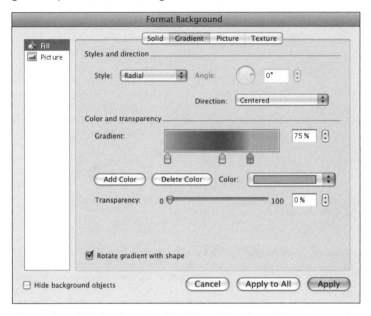

The active slide background and gradient box change to reflect your selection.

15. If necessary, drag the **Format Background** dialog box out of the way so that you can see the active slide or its thumbnail.

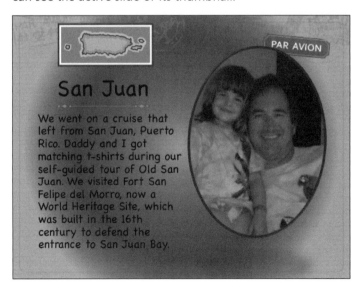

With this color combination, it's easier to see the effect of the centered radial gradient. It's basically a series of circles. The center of the slide is the tan color, surrounded by a larger red circle, surrounded by a larger green circle—but the green circle runs off the page, so we have to take that for granted.

16. In the **Styles and direction** section of the **Gradient** page, experiment with the other **Style** choices—**Linear**, **Rectangular**, **Path**, and **From Title**—looking at the effect of each. Experiment with different combinations of styles and directions, to see the varying results you can achieve.

> **Tip** Choosing None in the Style list resets the background to the most recent Slide Background panel selection.

The Direction list is active for only the Radial and Rectangular styles. The Angle setting is active for only the Linear style.

17. When you finish trying out the gradient slide backgrounds, find one that you like, and click the **Apply** button. Then in the presentation window, display **Slide 2**.

18. In the **Slide Background** panel of the **Formatting Palette**, click **Format Background**. Then in the **Format Background** dialog box, click the **Texture** button.

You can choose from 24 different "textures," or patterns, that generally represent patterns found in nature—marble, wood grain, and water—with a few fabric weaves and random patterns that look a bit like...linoleum patterns, perhaps. (It's hard to imagine what the criteria were for choosing these.)

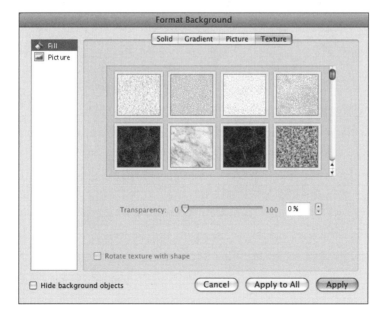

Pointing to a texture thumbnail does not display its name, but clicking a thumbnail displays the texture name, just below the thumbnail pane.

19. Scroll the texture thumbnail pane, and click any textures that interest you to see them previewed on the active slide. End by clicking the first thumbnail in the last row (**Cork**).

The selected texture appears on the active slide.

20. By moving the slider, typing in the box, or clicking the arrow buttons, set the **Transparency** to **15%**.

The cork lightens up a bit, providing a better contrast with the slide content.

21. In the **Format Background** dialog box, click **Apply**.

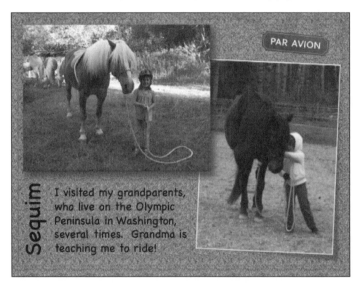

22. In the presentation window, display **Slide 4**.

23. In the **Slide Background** panel, click **Format Background**. In the **Format Background** dialog box, click **Fill** in the left pane, and then click the **Picture** button.

From the Picture page of the Format Background dialog box, you can add an image from the Clip Art Gallery storage location, or any image file, to the slide background. The image can stand alone on the slide or you can tile it to cover the entire slide.

24. On the **Picture** page, click the **Choose a Picture** button.

The Choose A Picture window opens, displaying the contents of the *Clipart* folder.

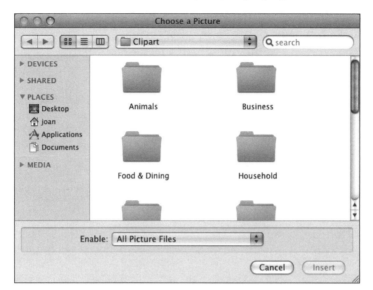

25. Scroll the window if necessary, and double-click the *Lines* folder to display its contents. Scroll the folder contents if necessary, click the **Stained Glass Line** icon, and then click **Insert**.

The Stained Glass Line image (a multicolored stripe) appears in the preview area of the Picture page, and also on the active slide—but on the slide, it appears as a series of colorful vertical stripes.

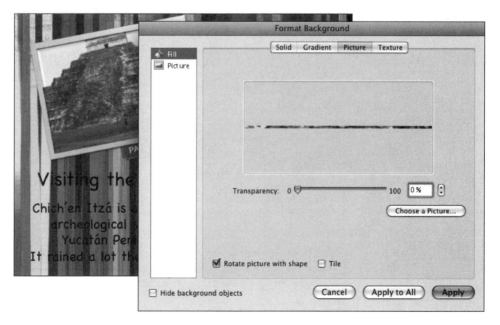

Many of the stripe colors are dark enough to make it difficult to read the writing on the slide. (And, let's face it, it looks a bit garish.)

26. On the **Picture** page of the **Format Background** dialog box, set the **Transparency** to **70%** to tone down the colors so the text is more visible.

The slide immediately reflects your change.

27. In the lower-left corner of the dialog box, select the **Hide background objects** check box to remove the somewhat distracting postmark and sticker images.

28. Finally, at the bottom of the **Picture** tab, select the **Tile** check box.

The stripes on the slide background change to a zigzag pattern.

29. In the **Format Background** dialog box, click **Apply**, and then survey the results of your efforts!

You've formatted the four slides in the presentation with four entirely different backgrounds.

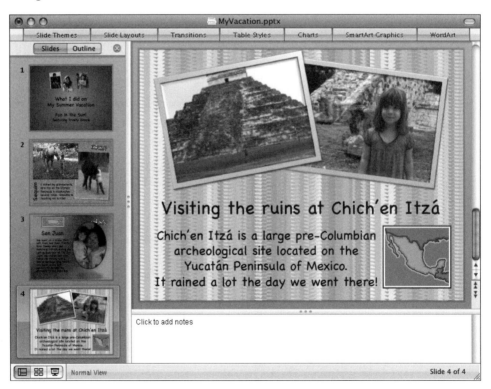

CLEAN UP Close the *MyVacation* presentation, saving your changes if you want to.

Move Slides in a Presentation

After you have created several slides, whether by adding them and entering text or by importing them from another presentation, you might want to rearrange the order of the slides so that they effectively communicate your message. You can rearrange a presentation in two ways:

- On the **Slides** tab, you can drag slides up and down to change their order.
- To see more of the presentation at the same time, you can switch to Slide Sorter view. You can then drag slide thumbnails into the order you want.

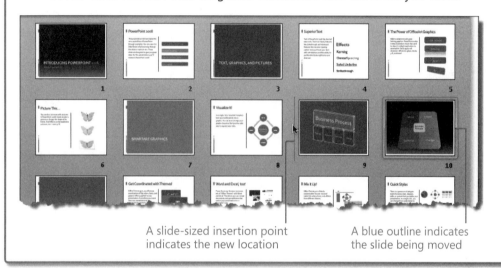

A slide-sized insertion point indicates the new location

A blue outline indicates the slide being moved

Change the Layout of a Slide

If you decide after you create a slide that you want it to have a different layout, you can easily change the layout by displaying the slide and then, on the Slide Layouts tab of the Elements Gallery, with Apply To Slide selected, clicking the layout you want.

You can make space on a slide for additional content by changing the slide layout to one that supports more content, or by adding a text box or graphic object. For example, if you want to add another layout placeholder to a Title And Content slide, you can do so by applying the Two Content slide layout, from the Slide Layouts tab of the Elements Gallery. You can add any graphic element to a slide, independent of a layout placeholder, by inserting it from the Insert menu. PowerPoint rearranges the existing content to fit the new layout.

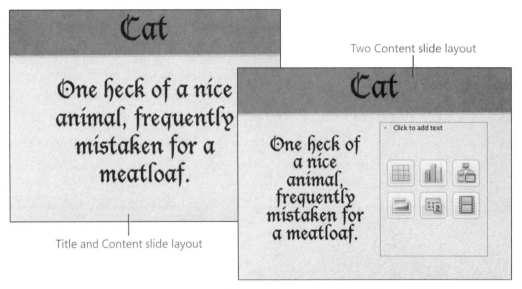

Two Content slide layout

Title and Content slide layout

PowerPoint rearranges the existing content for you when you apply a different slide layout.

You can move a layout placeholder on a slide by pointing to it and then, when the pointer changes to a four-headed arrow, dragging the placeholder to its new location. You can change the size of a layout placeholder by clicking its border to activate the resize and rotate handles, and then dragging the resize handles. If you don't like the change you made, you can reset the layout placeholders (while still preserving any content you've entered in them) by reapplying the original slide layout.

You can see both the original placeholder content and the changed content while dragging the resize handles.

Work with Slide Masters

Every slide layout corresponds to a slide master. Slide masters define the base content that appears on a slide, such as its background, its header and footer, and the default location and formatting of its text boxes and text.

You can work with slide masters in several ways:

- You can make changes to a slide master that are reflected on any slides based on the corresponding slide layout.
- You can create new slide masters for layouts that you can apply to new or existing slides.
- You can save a custom set of slide masters as a presentation template.
- You can add a slide master from one presentation to another by copying a slide based on the slide master into the destination presentation.

Bonus Web Content For more information about slide masters, see "Practice Working with Slide Masters in PowerPoint 2008 for Mac" on the book's companion Web site at *www.microsoft.com/mspress/companion/9780735626171*.

Change Standard Slide Settings

You can change the aspect ratio, size, and orientation of slides from the Page Setup dialog box. You can specifically size slides for:

- On-screen shows of different aspect ratios.
- Printing on standard U.S. paper formats (letter and ledger) and standard European paper formats (A3, A4, B4, and B5).
- Delivery on a 35mm slide projector or on an overhead projector.
- Printing as a banner, or at a custom size to fit any other purpose.

Troubleshooting When you resize slides, PowerPoint does its best to adjust existing slide content to fit the new space. If the new slide size is smaller than the original, some slide content might not comfortably fit on the slides. Be sure to check all of yours slides after you resize them to ensure that your content still appears the way you want it to.

Click Header/Footer in the Page Setup dialog box to set up standard header and footer content. You can apply changes you make in the Header And Footer dialog box to the current slide, to all slides in the presentation, or to all the printed handouts associated with the presentation.

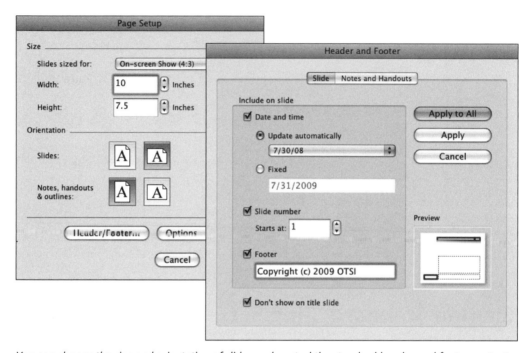

You can change the size and orientation of slides and control the standard header and footer content.

Run a Slide Show

After you put the effort into creating a fabulous PowerPoint slide show, you need to know how to present it to an audience.

To start a slide show from within PowerPoint, you can use any of the following methods:

→ Click **View Slide Show** on the **Slide Show** menu.

→ Click the **Slide Show** button on the Standard toolbar.

→ Click the **Slide Show** button on the **View** toolbar.

→ Press **Command+Return**.

The slide show starts with the slide that is currently displayed in PowerPoint. The on-screen show displays the slides at the largest size that can fit on your screen while maintaining the aspect ratio. Any leftover space is black.

Bonus Web Content   For information about practicing or presenting a slide show by using presenter tools, see the bonus Web article "Add Timings to Slides in PowerPoint 2008 for Mac" at *www.microsoft.com/mspress/companion/9780735626171*.

If you don't have an *Apple Remote Control,* the simplest way to move linearly between slides is to click the mouse button (anywhere on the screen) to move to the next slide, or press Control and click to move to the previous slide. You can also move between slides by using these keyboard commands:

- To move to the next slide, press the **Spacebar**, **Return**, **N**, **Page Down**, **Down Arrow**, or **Right Arrow** key.

- To move to the previous slide, press the **Delete**, **Page Up**, **Up Arrow**, or **Left Arrow** key.

- To move to the first slide in the presentation, press the **Home** key.

- To move to a specific slide, type the slide number, and then press **Return**. The number won't be visible on-screen.

- To move to the last slide in a presentation, press the **End** key.

You can end the presentation by pressing the Escape key.

 Another way to navigate through a slide show is by using the commands on the Slide Show menu, which you can display by clicking the inconspicuous button that appears in the lower-left corner of the slide each time you move the mouse. You can use commands on this toolbar in the following ways:

- Move between slides by clicking **Next**, **Previous**, or **Last Viewed**, or by clicking **Go To Slide** and then clicking the specific slide you want to display.

- To display the slides in a custom slide show, click **Custom Show**, and then click the show.

- To hide the slide show without closing it, click **Black Screen**. (To redisplay the slide show, click the screen, or press a key to redisplay the slide show and take the corresponding action.)

- To change an on-screen event, point to **Screen**, and then do one of the following:

  → Click **Pause** to pause a self-running presentation.

  → Click **Erase Pen** to remove annotations from the slide.

- To hide the pointer or change its form, point to **Pointer Options** and then do one of the following:

  → Click the pointer format you want.

→ Point to **Pen Color**, and then click the color you want. Choosing a pen color automatically changes the pointer to an annotation pen that you can use to write on slides during an on-screen slide show.

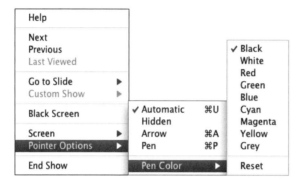

● To display a list of the many keyboard shortcuts available for carrying out slide show tasks, click **Help**.

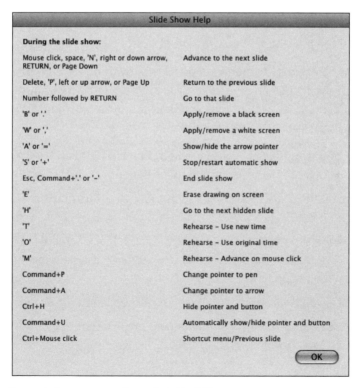

● To end the presentation, click **End Show**.

Key Points

- You can change slide text from the standard bulleted list to a numbered list, to a sublist, or to regular text that you can format in all the usual ways.

- You can choose from several types of slide backgrounds: solid colors and preset gradients linked to the presentation's color scheme; custom solid colors chosen from a variety of color palettes; custom gradients involving as many as 10 colors; clip art, photos, or other images; and a variety of textures. You can adjust the impact of each type of background by controlling its transparency.

- After you create a slide, you can easily modify its layout. You can do this by applying a different layout, by modifying existing placeholders, or by adding content directly to the slide.

- You can restore the default layout settings by reapplying the slide layout.

- You can change the order of slides by rearranging them in the Navigation pane or in Slide Sorter view.

Bonus Web Content

You can find the following articles about additional PowerPoint 2008 features on the book's companion Web site, at *www.microsoft.com/mspress/companion/ 9780735626171*:

- "Add Timings to Slides in PowerPoint 2008 for Mac"

- "Animate Slide Content in PowerPoint 2008 for Mac"

- "Animate Slide Transitions in PowerPoint 2008 for Mac"

- "Create a Self-Running Presentation in PowerPoint 2008 for Mac"

- "Practice Working with Slide Masters in PowerPoint 2008 for Mac"

- "Prepare Speaker Notes and Handouts for Presentations in PowerPoint 2008 for Mac"

- "Work with Tables in PowerPoint 2008 for Mac"

Part IV
Enhance Office File Content

11   Format Office File Content. .347

12   Create and Insert Graphics. .381

13   Review Word Documents. .413

14   Add Finishing Document Elements. 429

Chapter at a Glance

Format paragraphs, **page 353**

Add borders and shading, **page 356**

Format characters, **page 363**

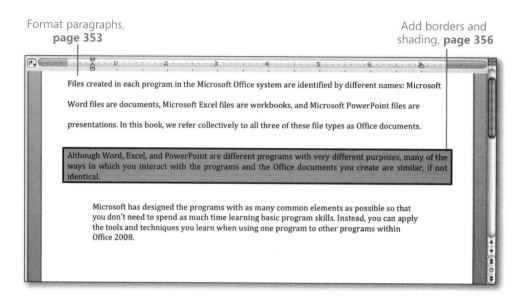

Files created in each program in the Microsoft Office system are identified by different names: Microsoft Word files are documents, Microsoft Excel files are workbooks, and Microsoft PowerPoint files are presentations. In this book, we refer collectively to all three of these file types as Office documents.

Although Word, Excel, and PowerPoint are different programs with very different purposes, many of the ways in which you interact with the programs and the Office documents you create are similar, if not identical.

Microsoft has designed the programs with as many common elements as possible so that you don't need to spend as much time learning basic program skills. Instead, you can apply the tools and techniques you learn when using one program to other programs within Office 2008.

TYPES OF BAMBOO

There are many different sizes and varieties of bamboo. It is both tropical and subtropical, growing in climates as diverse as jungles and mountainsides. Actually giant, woody grasses, it is very adaptable, with some species deciduous and others evergreen. Although there isn't yet a complete knowledge about this plant, there are believed to be between 1100 and 1500 different species of bamboo. The color range is from light green leaves and culms (stems) to dark, rich shades of green or some combination thereof.

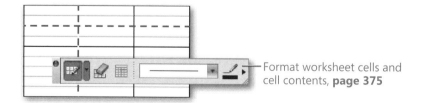

Format worksheet cells and cell contents, **page 375**

11 Format Office File Content

In this chapter, you will learn how to

- ✔ Control page setup.
- ✔ Insert page and section breaks.
- ✔ Format paragraphs.
- ✔ Add borders and shading.
- ✔ Format characters.
- ✔ Format worksheet cells and cell contents.

Earlier in this book, we discussed the basic processes for creating documents in Microsoft Word 2008 for Mac, workbooks and sheets in Microsoft Excel 2008 for Mac, and presentations and slides in Microsoft PowerPoint 2008 for Mac. In this chapter, we'll discuss ways of formatting and structuring documents and sheets to shape the appearance of on-screen and printed content.

In this chapter, you'll learn how to set up documents so that content appears correctly on-screen and when you print it. You'll change the size, shape, and appearance of paragraphs, and the font, font style, size, color, and character spacing of text. Then you'll learn specific techniques for formatting worksheet cells and the data they contain.

See Also You can find handy keyboard shortcuts, simple instructions for performing common tasks, and other useful information in the Quick Reference section at the beginning of this book.

 Practice Makes Perfect! The practice files you will use to complete the exercises in this chapter are in the *FormatContent* practice file folder. See "Using the Companion Content" at the beginning of this book for information about installing and locating the practice files.

Control Page Setup

When you work in a document in Print Layout view, the text and content of your document are shown on a page. Content is shown on the on-screen page exactly as it will appear on a printed page. The amount of content on a page, the location of line breaks within paragraphs, and the location of page breaks are determined by the page size, the page orientation, and the document margins.

Set the Page Size

By default, the pages of a document are set up to print on standard-sized paper, such as Letter (8.5 × 11 inches) in the United States, and A4 (210 × 297 millimeters) in countries that use the metric system of measurement—which would be pretty much every country other than the United States. You can create documents for other standard and custom formats by changing the Paper Size setting in the Page Setup dialog box. The page size setting is specific to each Office document, so you can change it in one document without affecting others.

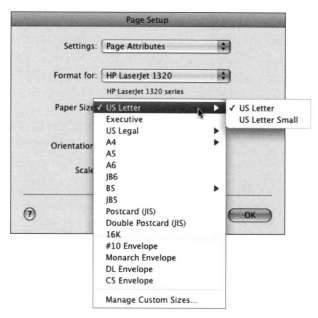

The Paper Size setting controls the size of the on-screen page and the printed page.

Set the Page Orientation

You can set up a document so that content is oriented vertically or horizontally on the page. A vertical orientation, in which the page is taller than it is wide, is called *Portrait* orientation. A horizontal orientation, with the page wider than it is tall, is called *Landscape* orientation.

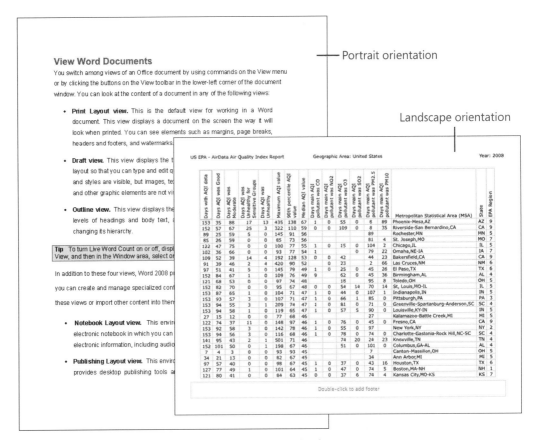

Choose the page size and orientation that best display the document contents.

Tip The pages of a document are all oriented the same way and all have the same margins unless you divide your document into sections. Then each section can have independent orientation and settings.

Set the Document Margins

You define the width and length of the print area (the portion of a page that printed content must fit into) by defining the size of the white space—the left, right, top, and bottom *margins*—around the text, rather than defining the area occupied by the text. By changing the margins of a document, you can control the amount of content that fits on a page.

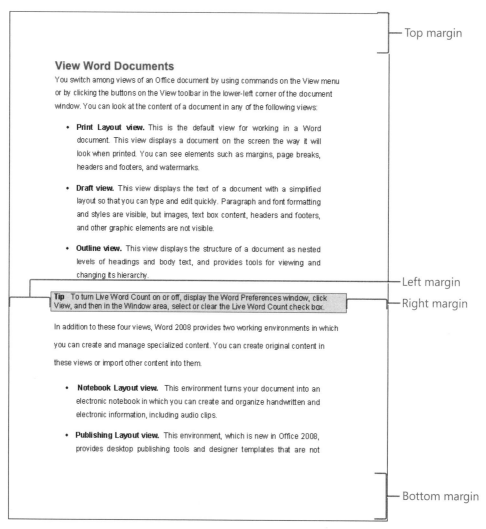

To define the content area of a document, you specify the amount of white space around its edges.

In Word, you can set the margins for an entire document from the Document Margins panel of the Formatting Palette. You can set the margins for a document or for only part of a document from the Margins page of the Document dialog box.

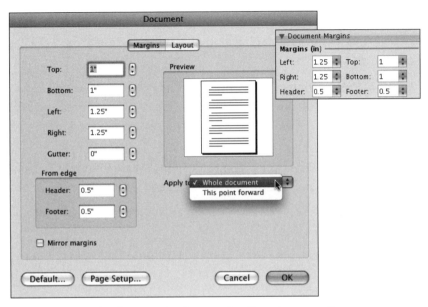

You can set margins for an entire document or for only one section.

Insert Page and Section Breaks

When you add more content than will fit within the document's top and bottom margins, Word creates a new page by inserting a soft page break. A *soft page break* produces separate pages in Print Layout view and is displayed as a horizontal line in Draft view.

If you want to control how pages break, you can insert a manual page break in either of these ways:

→ On the **Insert** menu, point to **Break**, and then click **Page Break**.

→ Press **Shift+Enter** (using the **Enter** key on the numeric keypad).

A *manual page break* produces separate pages in Print Layout view, and appears as a horizontal line, with the words *Page Break* at the midpoint of the line, in Draft view.

> **Tip** As you edit the text in a document, Word changes the location of the soft page breaks but not of any manual page breaks you might have inserted.

You can control whether page breaks leave widows and orphans—individual lines that appear on a different page from their paragraphs. A *widow* is the last line of a paragraph at the top of a page, and an *orphan* is the first line of a paragraph at the bottom of a page. These single lines of text can make a document hard to read, so by default Word specifies a two-line minimum. You can change the following options on the Line And Page Breaks page of the Paragraph dialog box displayed when you click Paragraph on the Format menu:

- **Widow/Orphan Control.** This option controls whether Word will break a page with the last line of a paragraph by itself at the top of a page or the first line of a paragraph by itself at the bottom of a page. This option is turned on by default for all new documents.

- **Keep With Next.** This option controls whether Word will break a page between the selected paragraph and the following paragraph.

- **Keep Lines Together.** This option controls whether Word will break a page within a paragraph.

- **Page Break Before.** This option controls whether Word will break a page before the selected paragraph.

> **Tip** You can apply the options in the Paragraph dialog box to individual paragraphs, or you can incorporate them into the styles you define for document elements such as headings. For more information about styles, see "Work with Styles" in Chapter 7, "Work with Word Document Content."

In addition to page breaks, you can insert section breaks in your documents. A *section break* identifies a part of the document to which you can apply page settings, such as orientation or margins, that are different from those of the rest of the document. For example, you might want to turn a large table sideways.

You can insert a section break by pointing to Break on the Insert menu and then clicking the type of section break you want to insert. The following types of section breaks are available:

- **Next Page.** This break starts the following section on the next page.
- **Continuous.** This break creates a new section without affecting page breaks.
- **Odd Page.** This break starts the following section on the next odd-numbered page.
- **Even Page.** This break starts the following section on the next even-numbered page.

A section break is not displayed in Print Layout view unless non-printing characters are turned on, in which case it appears as a double horizontal line from the preceding paragraph mark to the margin. In Draft view, a section break appears as a double horizontal line across the page. In both cases, the words *Section Break* and the type of section break appear in the middle of the line.

> **Tip** To remove a page or section break, click to the left of the break and then press the Del key, or click at the beginning of the content immediately following the break and press the Delete key.

Format Paragraphs

You create a *paragraph* by typing text and then pressing the Return key. The paragraph can be a single word, a single sentence, or multiple sentences. You can change the look of a paragraph by changing its alignment, its line spacing, and the space before and after it. You can also put borders around it and shade its background. Collectively, the settings you use to vary the look of a paragraph are called *paragraph formatting*.

Indent Paragraphs

Although the left and right margins are set for a whole document or section, you can vary the position of the text between the margins. The easiest way to do this is by changing the paragraph indent. You can indent paragraphs from the left and right margins, as well as specify where the first line of a paragraph begins and where the second and subsequent lines begin.

You can control the indentation of a paragraph from the Alignment And Spacing panel in the Formatting Palette, or by dragging the *indent markers* displayed on the horizontal ruler to indent text from the left or right margins as follows:

- **First Line Indent.** This indent setting begins a paragraph's first line of text at this marker.

- **Hanging Indent.** This indent setting begins a paragraph's second and subsequent lines of text at this marker. Paragraphs that are part of numbered and bulleted lists use a combination of a hanging indent and a tab stop to outdent the number or bullet character.

  Bonus Web Content For information about lists and tab stops, see "Organize Text in Lists in Word 2008 for Mac" on the book's companion Web site at *www.microsoft.com/ mspress/companion/9780735626171*.

- **Left Indent.** This indent setting indents the text to this marker.
- **Right Indent.** This indent setting wraps the text when it reaches this marker.

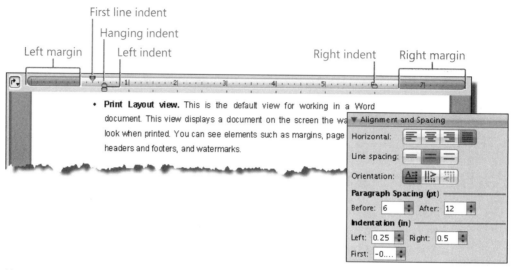

You can manage paragraph indents from the Ruler or from the Formatting Palette.

Align Text Horizontally

Most standard document text is left-aligned, but you can change the horizontal positioning of text between the left and right margins of a paragraph by changing the paragraph alignment.

From the Alignment And Spacing panel of the Formatting Palette, you can choose from these alignment options:

- **Align Text Left.** This setting aligns each line of the paragraph at the left margin, with a ragged right edge.
- **Align Text Right.** This setting aligns each line of the paragraph at the right margin, with a ragged left edge.
- **Center.** This setting aligns the center of each line in the paragraph between the left and right margins, with ragged left and right edges.
- **Justify.** This setting aligns each line between the margins, creating even left and right edges.

Tip When creating content in Print Layout view, if you know that you want to create a centered or right-aligned paragraph, you don't have to enter the text and then format it as centered or right-aligned. You can use the *Click and Type* feature to create text that already has the alignment you want. Move the pointer to the center or right side of a blank area of the page, and when the pointer's shape changes to an I-beam with appropriately aligned text attached, double-click to create a pre-aligned paragraph.

Align Text Vertically

To make text easier to read, or to fit more or less text onto a page, you can adjust the space between lines of text within a paragraph by changing the Line Spacing setting. To make it obvious where one paragraph ends and another begins, you can add space between paragraphs by changing the amount of space before or after a paragraph.

You can make changes to the alignment, indentation, and spacing of selected paragraphs all at the same time from the Paragraph dialog box, which you can display by clicking Paragraph on the Format menu.

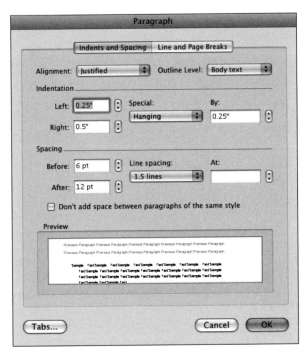

All the paragraph formatting settings are available from the Paragraph dialog box.

Tip To revert paragraph and character formatting to the document defaults, point to Clear on the Edit menu, and then click Clear Formatting.

Add Borders and Shading

In Word and Excel, you can add borders and shading to paragraphs and worksheet cells, to differentiate them from surrounding content or, in Excel, to indicate a mathematical operation.

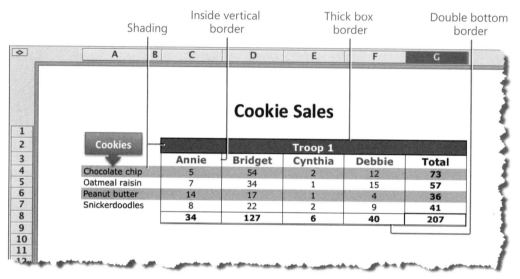

Borders and shading can help to define worksheet content.

To make a paragraph really stand out, you can put a border around it or shade its background. For real drama, you can do both. From the Borders And Shading dialog box or the Borders And Shading panel of the Formatting Palette, you can add borders of various sizes and patterns to any or all sides of a paragraph in a document, or of a cell in a worksheet. With or without a border, you can put a color or pattern behind the text of a paragraph or inside a worksheet cell.

> **Tip** A paragraph's formatting is stored with its paragraph mark. If you delete the paragraph mark, thereby making the paragraph part of the following paragraph, its text takes on the formatting of that paragraph. If you position the insertion point anywhere in the paragraph and press Return to create a new paragraph, the new paragraph takes on the existing paragraph's formatting.

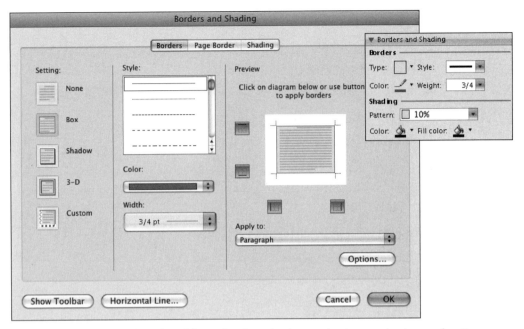

Make a paragraph stand out by adding a border, a background color, or a background pattern.

In a Word document, 12 standard border options are available from the Border Type gallery.

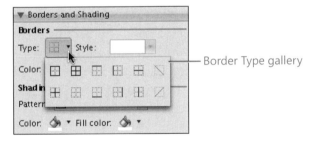

Border Type gallery

You can mix and match borders from the Border Type gallery.

Borders that you can apply to a paragraph of text are:

- Top Border
- Bottom Border
- Left Border
- Right Border
- Outside Border (applies Top, Bottom, Left, and Right borders)
- No Border (removes any border that's been applied)

Additional borders that you can apply to tables and to groups of worksheet cells are:

- Inside Horizontal Border
- Inside Vertical Border
- Inside Border (applies Inside Horizontal and Inside Vertical borders)
- All Borders (applies Outside and Inside borders)
- Diagonal Down Border
- Diagonal Up Border

In an Excel worksheet, six additional borders, most connoting mathematical operations, are available. They are:

- Top And Bottom Border
- Double Bottom Border
- Top And Double Bottom Border
- Thick Bottom Border
- Top And Thick Bottom Border
- Thick Box Border

You can build non-standard borders by clicking multiple buttons. For example, if you want to add borders to the top and bottom edges of a paragraph in a Word document, click the Top Border button and then redisplay the Border Type gallery and click the Bottom Border button. If you decide that you don't want a border that you added, you can't remove it by clicking the same button, as you can with some buttons. So if, in the previous example, you wanted to remove the top border and leave only the bottom border, you would need to click the No Border button to clear all the borders, and then click the Bottom Border button again.

Practice Changing the Size and Appearance of Paragraphs

In this exercise, you'll change the margins of a document. Then you'll change the indentation, alignment, line spacing, and paragraph spacing of text within the document. Finally, you'll add a border and shading to a paragraph.

Note Up to this point in the book, we've worked mostly with commands available from menus and toolbars. In this chapter, we'll primarily use the commands that are available from the *Toolbox*. Rather than listing all the places you can find a particular button or command, we'll reference only the Toolbox panel and button (unless the command isn't available from the Toolbox, in which case we'll reference the menu or toolbar instead). If you prefer to not use the Toolbox, feel free to locate and use the corresponding menu command, toolbar button, or keyboard shortcut.

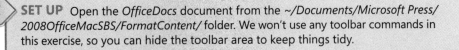 **SET UP** Open the *OfficeDocs* document from the *~/Documents/Microsoft Press/ 2008OfficeMacSBS/FormatContent/* folder. We won't use any toolbar commands in this exercise, so you can hide the toolbar area to keep things tidy.

1. If the Toolbox is not already open, or if it is open but not displaying the **Formatting Palette**, click **Formatting Palette** on the **View** menu.

2. In the **Formatting Palette**, expand the **Alignment and Spacing**, **Borders and Shading**, and **Document Margins** panels, and close the other panels. Arrange the document and Toolbox so that you can work with them.

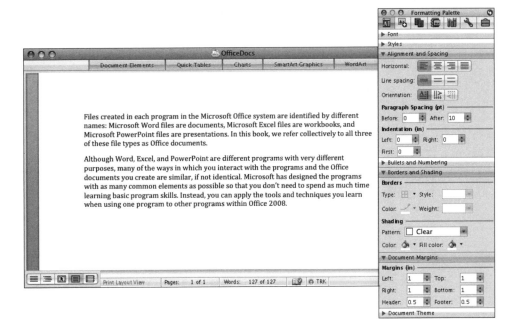

3. In the **Document Margins** panel, change the **Left** and **Right** settings to 0.5, and the **Top** and **Bottom** settings to 0.75.

> **Tip** To change the settings, you can type the new settings into the boxes or click the spin buttons.

The document text becomes wider and moves closer to the top of the page. Because this operation affects the document as a whole, it will have the same effect regardless of where the insertion point is or what is selected.

> **Note** The Ruler reflects changes you make to the document margins and to the paragraph indentations. If you have the Ruler hidden, as we do, you can temporarily display it by pointing to the top of the document window (to display the horizontal ruler) or the left side of the document window (to display the vertical ruler).

4. Click to position the insertion point anywhere in the first paragraph.

5. In the **Alignment and Spacing** panel, next to **Line Spacing**, click the **Double Space** button.

The spacing between the lines of text in the first paragraph increases, so that the space between the lines is as tall as the text of each line.

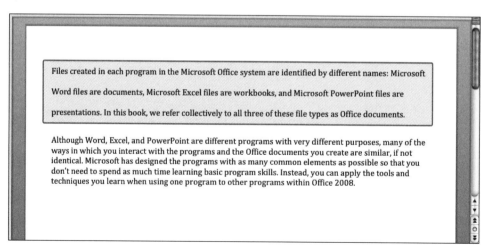

6. Click to position the insertion point anywhere in the second paragraph.

7. In the **Alignment and Spacing** panel, next to **Horizontal**, click the **Justified** button.

The space between the words expands so that each line of the paragraph exactly fills the space between the left and right margins. Whereas before, the space between each word was the same size on each line, now the spacing between words is evenly adjusted on a line-by-line basis.

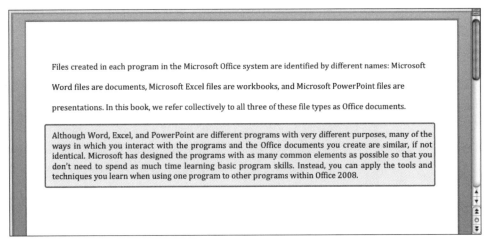

8. In the **Borders** area of the **Borders and Shading** panel, click the **Type** button and then, in the **Border Type** gallery, click the **Outside Border** button.

A one point–wide black box appears around the paragraph.

9. In the **Borders** area, in the **Weight** list, click **3 pt**.

The lines of the box become thicker.

10. In the **Shading** area of the **Borders and Shading** panel, click the **Fill color** button. Then in the **Fill Color** gallery, in the first row of the **Theme Colors** palette, click the green (**Accent 3**) square.

The selected color fills the box, behind the text of the paragraph.

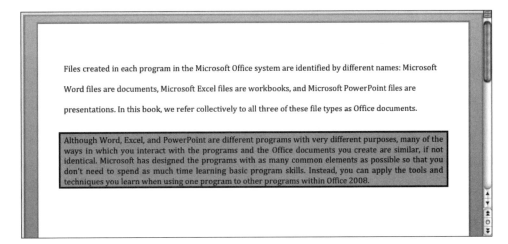

11. In the boxed paragraph, click to position the insertion point directly before the word *Microsoft*. Then press the **Return** key.

The boxed, shaded, justified paragraph becomes two shaded, justified paragraphs in one box. One box encompasses both paragraphs because the selected border type (Outside Border) doesn't include internal borders.

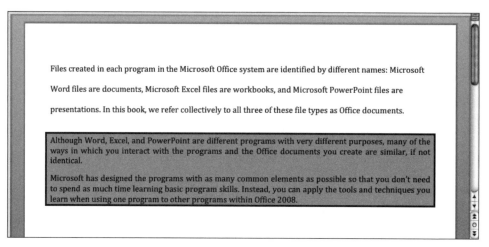

12. With the insertion point at the beginning of the new paragraph, point to **Clear** on the **Edit** menu, and then click **Clear Formatting**.

The new paragraph reverts to the default paragraph formatting for this document: single-spaced, left-aligned, with no border or shading.

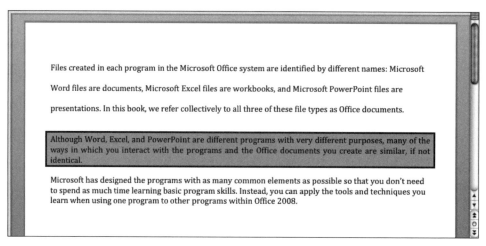

13. In the **Alignment and Spacing** panel, under **Indentation**, change the **Left** and **Right** settings to 0.5.

The left and right sides of the paragraph move in one-half inch.

14. Point to the top of the document window to display the horizontal ruler.

The indent markers on the ruler show the left and right indents you set in the Formatting Palette.

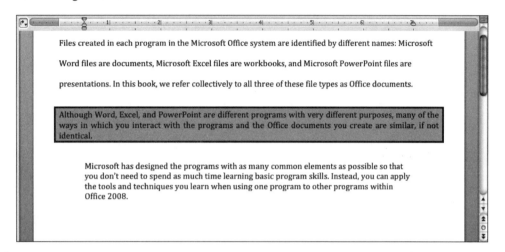

 CLEAN UP Close the *OfficeDocs* document without saving your changes.

Format Characters

The appearance of your documents helps to convey their message. By using Word, you can develop professional-looking documents whose appearance is appropriate to their contents. You can easily format your text so that key points stand out and your arguments are easy to grasp.

When you type text in a document, it is displayed in a particular font. Each *font* consists of alphabetic characters, numbers, and symbols that share a common design.

You can see samples of all the fonts installed on your Mac, in the Font Book.

> **Tip** You can open the Font Book from the */Applications/* folder.

The Font Book displays the alphabet in uppercase and lowercase, and the numbers 0–9, in whatever font you choose. When the Fit option is selected in the Size list, resizing the Font Book window (by dragging the resize handle) changes the size of the font shown in the right pane to the maximum size that fits in the pane. Dragging the Font Size slider changes the size of the font to whatever you specify. You can preview fonts at any size from 9 points to 288 points.

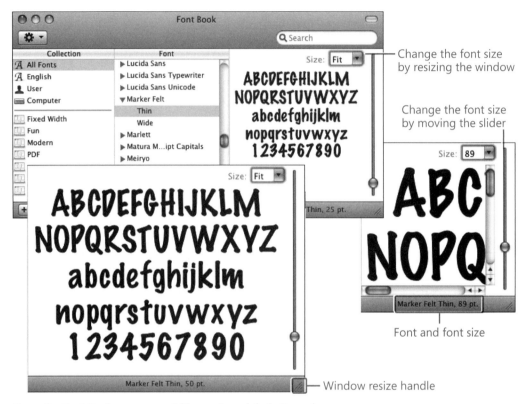

Change the font size by resizing the window

Change the font size by moving the slider

Font and font size

Window resize handle

From the Font Book, you can quickly preview alphabetic and numeric characters in all the fonts installed on your computer.

The default font for body text in a new Word 2008 document is Cambria, and the default font for heading text is Calibri. You can change the font of some or all of the text in a document at any time. Other common fonts include Arial, Verdana, and Times New Roman, but in the Office 2008 for Mac programs, you can choose from more than 100 fonts.

> **Tip** When you are viewing a document on-screen, the font will display correctly only if it is installed on the computer you're using. When creating a document that you intend to share electronically with people who might want to view it on a computer running the Windows operating system, choose fonts from the Windows Office Compatible collection. This collection contains about 60 fonts that are automatically installed with both Word 2008 for Mac and Word 2007 for Windows.

You can vary the look of a font by changing the following *attributes*:

- Almost every font comes in a range of *font sizes*, which are measured in *points* from the top of letters that have parts that stick up (ascenders), such as *h*, to the bottom of letters that have parts that drop down (descenders), such as *p*. A point is approximately 1/72 of an inch.

- Almost every font comes in a range of *font styles*. The most common are regular (or plain), italic, bold, and bold italic.

- Fonts can be enhanced by applying *font effects*, such as underlining, small capital letters (small caps), or shadows.

- A palette of harmonious *font colors* is available, and you can also specify custom colors.

- You can alter the *character spacing* by pushing characters apart or squeezing them together.

After you select an appropriate font for a document, you can use these attributes to achieve different effects. Although some attributes might cancel each other out, they are usually cumulative. For example, you might use a bold font in various sizes and various shades of green to make different heading levels stand out in a newsletter. Collectively, the font and its attributes are called *character formatting*.

In Word 2008, you can preview available font variations on the font-specific submenus of the Font menu.

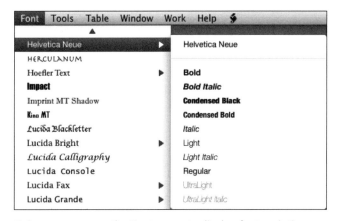

Point to arrows on the Font menu to display font variations.

Case and Character Formatting

The way you use case and character formatting in a document can influence its visual impact on your readers. Used judiciously, case and character formatting can make a plain document look attractive and professional, but excessive use can make it look amateurish and detract from the message. For example, using too many fonts in the same document is the mark of inexperience, so don't use more than two or three.

Bear in mind that lowercase letters tend to recede, so using all uppercase letters (capitals) can be useful for titles and headings or for certain kinds of emphasis. However, large blocks of uppercase letters are tiring to the eye.

Tip In Word and PowerPoint, you can change the case of selected text to uppercase, lowercase, and initial cap (where the first letter of each word is uppercase and the rest of the word is lowercase) by holding down the Shift key and pressing the F3 key. Pressing F3 repeatedly while holding down the Shift key cycles between the three case options. The programs in Office 2007 for Windows have a handy button that accomplishes the same thing; unfortunately this very convenient button didn't make it into Office 2008.

Where do the terms uppercase and lowercase come from? Until the advent of computers, individual characters were assembled to form the words that would appear on a printed page. The characters were stored alphabetically in cases, with the capital letters in the upper case and the small letters in the lower case.

Apply Existing Formatting to Other Content

The Format Painter is a handy feature you'll find in the Office 2008 programs.

As indicated by its name, you can use the Format Painter to apply formatting to content—actually, to copy the formatting of one paragraph, cell, shape, or other object and apply it to another. The Format Painter copies all the formatting of the source content, including the font, font size, font color, and (if the source content includes a paragraph mark) the paragraph alignment and spacing.

By using this tool, you can easily apply multiple format settings to content throughout a file. To copy formatting from selected content and apply it to only one other location:

1. On the Standard toolbar, click the **Format** button.
2. Click a single content item or drag across multiple contiguous items to apply the formatting.

To copy formatting from selected content and apply it to multiple locations:

1. On the Standard toolbar, double-click the **Format** button.
2. Click or drag across each item you want to apply formatting to.
3. When you finish, press the **Escape** key to release the Format Painter.

Practice Formatting Characters

In this exercise, you'll format the text in a document by changing its font, font style, size, color, and character spacing. We'll be working in a Word document, but you can use these same techniques when working with text on a worksheet or on a slide.

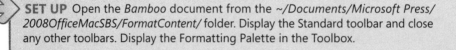

SET UP Open the *Bamboo* document from the *~/Documents/Microsoft Press/ 2008OfficeMacSBS/FormatContent/* folder. Display the Standard toolbar and close any other toolbars. Display the Formatting Palette in the Toolbox.

1. In the **Formatting Palette**, expand the **Font** panel, and close the other panels. Arrange the document and Toolbox so you can work with them.

   The Font panel displays information about the font at the current location of the insertion point. The font used in this document is 12-point Times New Roman.

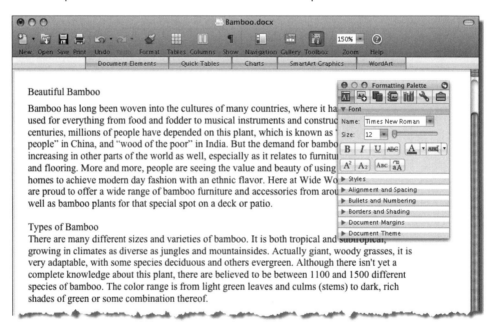

Note We've magnified the document text to make it easier to read.

2. In the *Beautiful Bamboo* heading, click anywhere in the word *Beautiful*.

3. In the **Font** panel of the **Formatting Palette**, click the **Underline** button.

   The word containing the insertion point is now underlined. Notice that you did not have to select the entire word to format it.

4. With the insertion point still in the word *Beautiful,* click the **Bold** button in the **Font** panel.

The word *Beautiful* is now bold and underlined.

5. On the toolbar, click the **Format** button to activate the Format Painter. Then move the pointer to the *selection area* to the left of the *Beautiful Bamboo* heading.

As you move the pointer across the text of the document, it changes to an I-beam with a plus sign to its left.

When the pointer is in the selection area, it changes to a right-pointing arrow.

6. Click in the selection area to the left of the *Beautiful Bamboo* heading.

Word "paints" the formatting of the word *Beautiful* onto the entire heading.

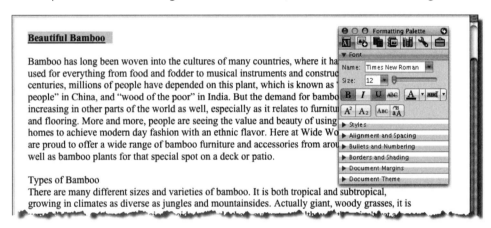

> **Note** The Format Painter carries both character formatting and paragraph formatting.

7. Click the **Format** button again, and then click in the selection area adjacent to the *Types of Bamboo* heading.

Word "paints" the formatting of *Beautiful Bamboo* onto *Types of Bamboo.* The font is bold and underlined, and the space after the paragraph increases to match that of the source paragraph. The active buttons on the toolbar and in the Toolbox indicate the attributes that you applied to the selection.

> **Tip** Information about the paragraph spacing is in the Alignment And Spacing panel of the Formatting Palette.

8. With *Types of Bamboo* selected, click the **Name** arrow in the **Font** panel.

The full Font list is available from the Toolbox.

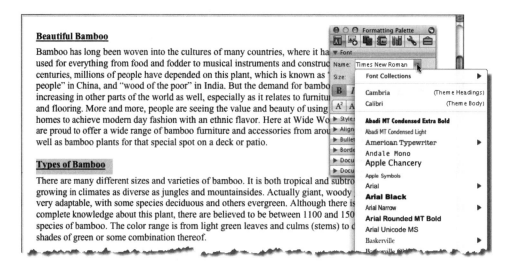

9. Point to the arrow at the bottom of the list to scroll down. Locate and click the **Stencil** font.

   The selected heading now appears in the new font.

10. Select the *Beautiful Bamboo* heading, and then click **Repeat Font Formatting** on the **Edit** menu (or press **Command+Y**)

    Word applies the Stencil font to the selected heading.

    > **Tip** The Repeat command changes to reflect the most recent action. (If the action can't be repeated, the Repeat command will be unavailable.) Commands that aren't available appear on a menu in gray letters instead of black letters.

11. In the **Font** panel, click the **Size** arrow and, in the list, click **26**.

    The size of the heading text increases to 26 points.

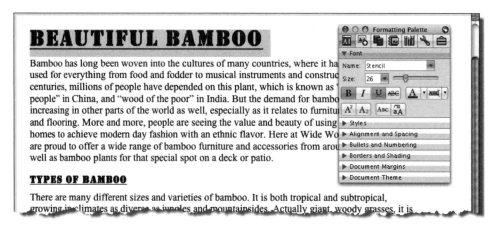

Tip In Word, you can increase or decrease the font size in set increments by sliding the Size control in the Font panel of the Word Formatting Palette.

Tip In PowerPoint, you can increase the font size by clicking the Grow Font button, and decrease the font size by clicking the Shrink Font button. Both buttons are found in the Font panel of the PowerPoint Formatting Palette.

12. On the **Format** menu, click **Font** (or press **Command+D**).

The Font dialog box opens. An example of the current font settings is shown in the Preview window at the bottom of the dialog box.

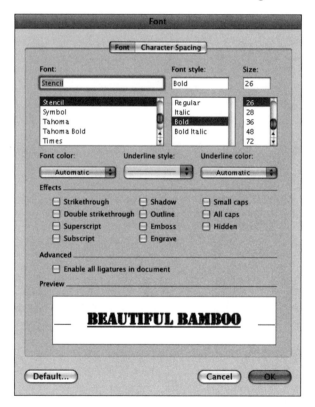

13. In the **Underline style** list, click **(none)**.

14. In the **Effects** area, select the **Outline** check box.

The Font sample in the Preview box changes as you make your selections.

15. At the top of the dialog box, click the **Character Spacing** button.

The Font dialog box changes to a page of character scale, spacing, and positioning options.

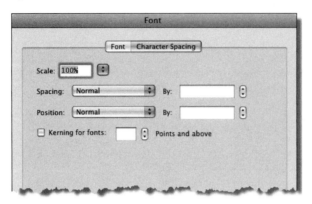

16. In the **Spacing** list, click **Expanded**. In the **By** box to the right of the list, enter 2 pt (or click the **Up** arrow to increase the number in increments of 0.1 point). Then click **OK**.

The selected text changes to reflect the font formatting you applied.

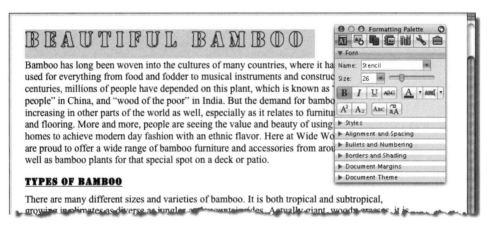

17. With *Beautiful Bamboo* selected, experiment with the other buttons in the Font panel. Then on the **Edit** menu, point to **Clear**, and click **Clear Formatting**.

The heading text returns to the default document font.

18. In the last sentence of the paragraph following the *Types of Bamboo* heading, select the words *light green*.

19. In the **Font** panel, click the **Font Color** arrow.

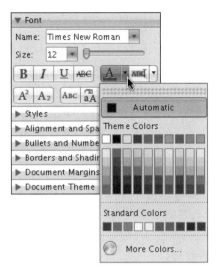

20. In the **Font Color** gallery, under **Standard Colors**, click the **Light Green** square (the fifth square from the left).

> **Tip** Pointing to a color in the Standard Colors palette displays the name of the color. Pointing to a color in the Theme Colors palette displays information about the purpose and intensity of that color.

The selected words are now light green. (To see the color, release the selection by clicking away from it.)

> **Tip** You can apply the color that currently appears on the Font Color button by clicking the button (rather than the arrow).

21. In the same sentence, select **dark, rich shades of green**. Click the **Font Color** arrow and then, at the bottom of the gallery, click **More Colors**.

The Colors dialog box opens. In this dialog box, you can choose colors from a color wheel, by moving color sliders, from a color palette, from an image palette, or from a box of crayons.

22. Click the buttons at the top of the dialog box to display the different color-selection interfaces. End by clicking the **Crayons** button.

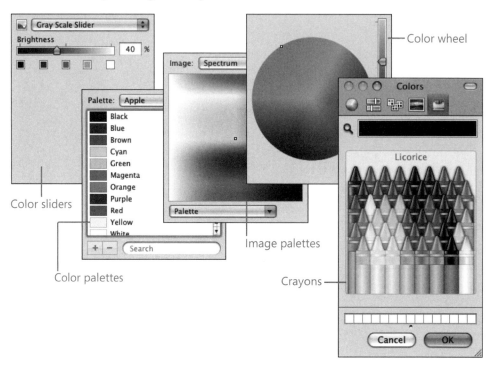

23. In the crayon box, click various crayons to display a sample of the color and its name. Finish by clicking the **Clover** crayon (the third crayon from the left end of the top row). Then click **OK**.

The color of the selected text changes to clover green.

24. In the same paragraph, select the phrase *there are believed to be between 1100 and 1500 different species of bamboo*. Then in the **Font** panel, click the **Highlight** arrow.

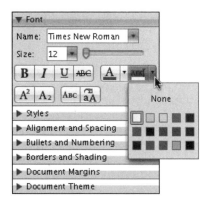

25. In the **Highlight** gallery, click the **Bright Green** square.

The highlighted phrase now stands out from the rest of the text.

> **Tip** If you click the Highlight button without first making a selection, the mouse pointer becomes a highlighter that you can drag across text to apply the currently selected highlight color, as indicated on the Highlight button. Click the Highlight button again, or press the Escape key, to turn off the highlighter.

TYPES OF BAMBOO

There are many different sizes and varieties of bamboo. It is both tropical and subtropical, growing in climates as diverse as jungles and mountainsides. Actually giant, woody grasses, it is very adaptable, with some species deciduous and others evergreen. Although there isn't yet a complete knowledge about this plant, there are believed to be between 1100 and 1500 different species of bamboo. The color range is from light green leaves and culms (stems) to dark, rich shades of green or some combination thereof.

CLEAN UP Close the *Bamboo* document without saving your changes.

Format Worksheet Cells and Cell Contents

Most of the document formatting techniques you use in Word work the same way in Excel. You can format fonts, align text horizontally and vertically, and indent text within a worksheet cell. Excel has a few additional formatting settings, which we'll discuss here.

Format Numeric Data

Excel is commonly used to store numeric data on which you can run a variety of calculations. Numeric data can take many formats, for example, whole numbers, numbers with one or more decimal places, currency values, percentages, and dates. You can more clearly express numeric data by applying a number format to it.

The simplest way to apply a numeric value is from the Number panel of the Formatting Palette.

Merge Cells

You can merge two or more cells to create one wide or tall cell. Merging cells joins the cell structure but not the cell content. When you merge multiple cells that contain content, Excel keeps only the content of the first cell; the rest is discarded.

Troop 1				
Annie	**Bridget**	**Cynthia**	**Debbie**	**Total**
5	54	2	12	**73**
7	34	1	15	**57**
14	17	1	4	**36**
8	22	2	9	**41**
34	**127**	**6**	**40**	**207**

— Merged cells

By merging cells, you can cleanly display content across multiple columns.

Draw Borders by Hand

You can apply borders to worksheet cells by using the same methods you use to apply borders to text paragraphs. You also have the option of "drawing" borders by hand. This is a convenient way to create non-standard borders.

— Border Drawing toolbar

You aren't limited to the standard borders—you can draw your own.

By using the tools on the Border Drawing toolbar, you can draw a single line by dragging along the cell separator where you want to draw the line, or you can create a set of lines by dragging diagonally across the range of cells in which you want to insert lines. You can control the line style, weight, and color of each line or set of lines that you insert.

To display the Border Drawing toolbar, click the Draw Border button in the Borders And Shading panel of the Formatting Palette.

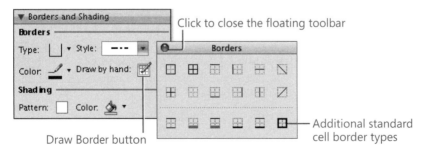

Click to close the floating toolbar

Draw Border button

Additional standard cell border types

In Excel, you can float the Borders menu independently of the Formatting Palette by clicking the move handle at the top of the Border Type gallery.

Set Up a Sheet for Printing

The Page Setup panel of the Excel Formatting Palette includes additional settings that control the appearance of worksheet or list sheet content on the printed page.

> **Note** The Page Setup panel isn't available in the Formatting Palette when a chart sheet is active.

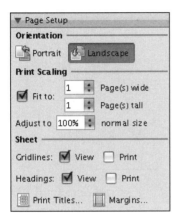

The Excel page setup options give you precise control over the printed page.

By using the commands available in this panel, you can:

- **Fit content to a printed page.** In both Word and Excel, you can adjust the way content fits onto a printed page by *scaling* the content, either to a specific percentage of the actual size or to fit onto a specific number of pages. Scaling content for print doesn't affect the size or appearance of the content when you're viewing the document or sheet on-screen.

- **Display and hide gridlines and headings.** For worksheets, you can specify whether gridlines and row and column headings appear on the printed page, independently of whether they appear on-screen.

- **Print titles.** When printing a multipage worksheet containing content that has row and column titles entered in the worksheet, you can instruct Excel to print the column titles at the top of every page and the row titles on the left side of every page. This greatly simplifies the process of reading content from a worksheet containing more than one page of printed content.

> **Tip** If you want to print only some of the content on a worksheet, you can define a specific selection of cells as the *print area*. When you print a worksheet that has a print area defined, only that range of cells is printed. To set the print area, first select the range of cells you want to print. Then point to Print Area on the File menu and click Set Print Area. You can modify or clear the print area from the same menu.

You control the appearance of chart sheet content on the printed page from the Page Setup dialog box, which you can open by clicking Page Setup on the File menu. The Excel version of the Page Setup dialog box has a specific Chart tab, but the only setting available on that tab is the option to print the chart in black and white.

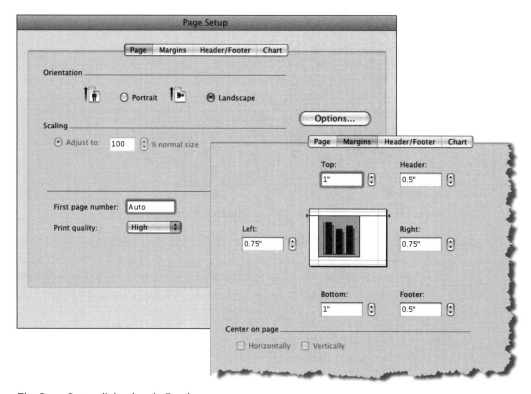

The Page Setup dialog box in Excel

From the Page tab of the Page Setup dialog box in Excel, you can control page orientation, scaling, and print quality, and set the page number for the first page of the sheet content. From the Margins tab, you can specify the amount of space to be reserved at the top and bottom of the page for the header and footer, and set the outer margins of the page, which define the print area. When printing worksheets and list sheets, you can instruct Excel to center the contents of each page horizontally, vertically, or (by selecting both check boxes) in the center of the page. From the Header And Footer tab, which is available only for worksheets and list sheets, you can specify the text, pictures, or file information that will appear in the page header and footer.

> **Tip** In Word and Excel, you can insert the date and time fields in a header or footer. The date and time shown on the screen update when you activate the header or footer containing the field, and when you print the file. The date and time shown on a printed page will always reflect the actual time at which the file was transmitted from Word or Excel to the printer.

Key Points

- The amount of content on a page, the location of line breaks within paragraphs, and the location of page breaks are determined by the page size, the page orientation, and the document margins.

- You can change the look of a paragraph by changing its alignment, its line spacing, and the space before and after it.

- In Word and Excel, you can add borders and shading to paragraphs and worksheet cells, to differentiate them from surrounding content.

- You can easily copy the font and paragraph formatting of one word, paragraph, or cell, and apply it to another, by using the Format Painter.

Chapter at a Glance

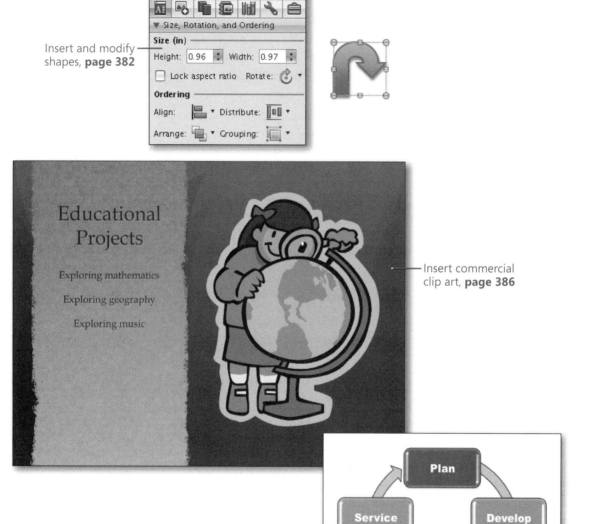

Insert and modify shapes, **page 382**

Educational Projects

Exploring mathematics

Exploring geography

Exploring music

Insert commercial clip art, **page 386**

Create professional diagrams, **page 401**

12 Create and Insert Graphics

In this chapter, you will learn how to

- ✔ Insert and modify shapes.
- ✔ Insert commercial clip art.
- ✔ Insert symbols as text or graphics.
- ✔ Insert your own photos.
- ✔ Create professional diagrams.

It's easy to think of the Microsoft Office programs—Microsoft Word, Microsoft Excel, and Microsoft PowerPoint—as programs for creating text-based content. But, in fact, each of these programs includes tools that make it easy to create or incorporate graphic elements into the documents, workbooks, and presentations you create. The 2008 versions of these programs include two new utilities—the Object Palette of the Toolbox and the extremely groovy SmartArt utility—with which you can quite easily add pizzazz to Word documents, Excel workbooks, and PowerPoint presentations.

You can insert shapes, symbols, pictures from your computer, and professional-quality art—including photographs, clip art, and animations—into a document, worksheet, or presentation from the Object Palette. You can create really amazing SmartArt diagrams depicting concepts such as processes, cycles, relationships, and hierarchies.

In this chapter, you'll explore the variety of pre-made graphics that you can insert into documents, worksheets, and presentations. Then you'll create a SmartArt graphic, insert content into it, and change the way it looks.

See Also You can find handy keyboard shortcuts, simple instructions for performing common tasks, and other useful information in the Quick Reference section at the beginning of this book.

> **Practice Makes Perfect!** The practice files you will use to complete the exercises in this chapter are in the *CreateGraphics* practice file folder. See "Using the Companion Content" at the beginning of this book for information about installing and locating the practice files.

Insert and Modify Shapes

Four types of graphic objects are available from the Object Palette: Shapes, Clip Art, Symbols, and Photos. The objects on each of these four pages are classified in categories. You can display all the objects of one type (such as Shapes) on a page, or filter the page to display only objects in a certain category (such as Equation Shapes).

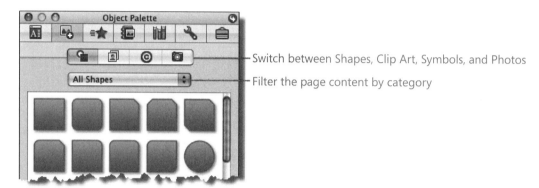

Switch between Shapes, Clip Art, Symbols, and Photos
Filter the page content by category

You can insert a variety of images from the Object Palette.

In Office 2008, shapes are very versatile graphic images. After you insert a shape in a document or worksheet, or on a slide, you can do things like change its size and color, rotate or flip it, and add text to it. You can stack or combine multiple shapes to create a graphic that exactly fits your needs.

You can combine shapes to make all sorts of pictures.

The Object Palette includes 130 general-purpose shapes in the following categories:

- Basic Shapes
- Block Arrows
- Callouts
- Flowchart Shapes
- Lines
- Stars And Banners

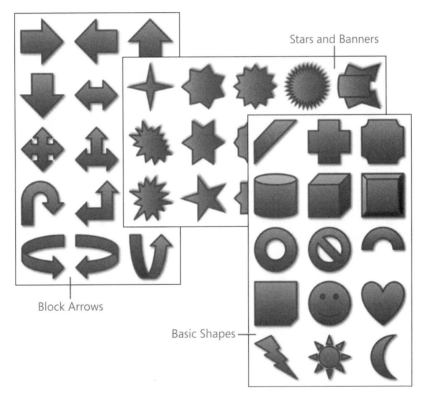

A wide variety of shapes are available.

Tip By holding down the Shift key while dragging a shape, you can restrict the shape to equal horizontal and vertical dimensions. For example, to draw a circle, click the Oval shape in the Object Palette, hold down the Shift key, and then drag to draw the circle.

In Excel and PowerPoint, the Object Palette includes additional Rectangles, Connectors, and Equation Shapes.

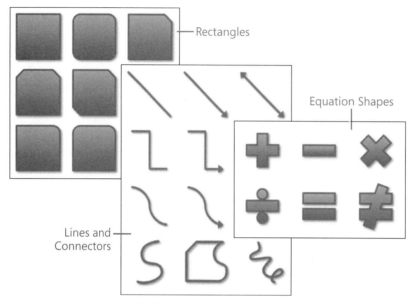

Additional shapes are available in Excel and PowerPoint.

You can insert a shape into an Office file by clicking the shape in the Object Palette and then, on the page, worksheet, or slide, clicking to insert the shape at its default size or dragging to draw a custom-sized shape.

By default, the shapes in the Object Palette are depicted in blue. When you insert a shape, it takes on the colors associated with the host document (or remains blue if there isn't an overriding color scheme). After you insert a shape, you can make any of the following modifications from the Formatting Palette (in Word, Excel, and PowerPoint), from the Format AutoShape dialog box (in Word), or from the Format Shape dialog box (in PowerPoint):

- Change the dimensions and angle of rotation.
- Change the fill color and outline color.
- Add shadows, glows, reflections, and three-dimensional effects.

> **Tip** You can use the Format Painter to copy colors and effects from one shape to other shapes. For information about the Format Painter, see the sidebar "Apply Existing Formatting to Other Content" in Chapter 11, "Format Office File Content."

To display the Formatting Palette:

→ In the Toolbox, click the **Formatting Palette** button.

→ On the **View** menu, under **Toolbox**, click **Formatting Palette**.

To display the Format AutoShape (or Format Shape) dialog box:

→ Right-click the shape and then click **Format AutoShape** (or **Format Shape**).

You can use the handles that appear around the outside of an active shape to modify it in the following ways:

- Drag a corner handle to resize a shape while maintaining its aspect ratio.
- Drag the top or bottom handle to change the height of the shape.
- Drag a side handle to change the width of the shape.
- Drag a green rotation handle to rotate the shape in a clockwise or counter-clockwise direction.

> **Tip** If a green rotation handle doesn't appear by default when you select a shape, display the Size, Rotation, And Ordering panel of the Formatting Palette, click the Rotate button, and then click Free Rotate. Multiple rotation handles will appear.

Some shapes also have yellow handles that you can drag to change the outer definition of the shape.

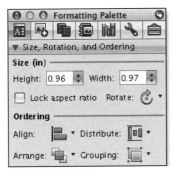

You can modify the size, shape, and location of any graphic object.

When working with overlapping shapes, you can change the order in which the shapes are stacked. You can also distribute shapes evenly within a space and align shapes vertically or horizontally with other shapes or with the page or slide the shape is on.

> **Note** When working with shapes in Excel, you don't have the option of automatically aligning a shape with the worksheet.

To add text to a shape:

1. Click the shape to select it.

2. Click in the text area of the shape to activate the insertion point.

3. Type the text that you want the shape to display.

> **Tip** If the text box on a shape doesn't become active when you click it, right-click the shape and then click Add Text.

You can change the attributes of the text in a shape from either the Formatting Palette or the Format Text dialog box. You have the same formatting options for shape text as you do for regular text.

To display the Format Text dialog box:

→ Right-click the shape and then click **Format Text**.

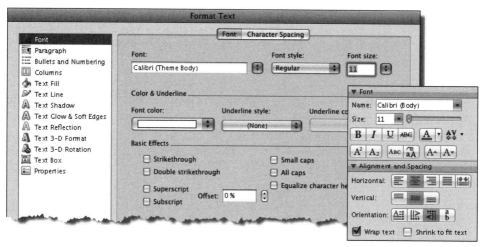

You can apply the same effects to the text on a shape as you can to the shape itself.

Insert Commercial Clip Art

From the Clip Art page of the Object Palette, you can view all the images stored in the Clip Gallery, which is installed with Office 2008. The Clip Gallery includes hundreds of illustrations, photographs, animations, and sounds. You can filter the Clip Art page to display a category of photographic images (Animals, Business, Food & Dining, Household, People, or Special Occasions), to display Animations or Clip Art (the Personal category contains extra clip art that you've added to the Clip Gallery), or to display photos in specific source folders.

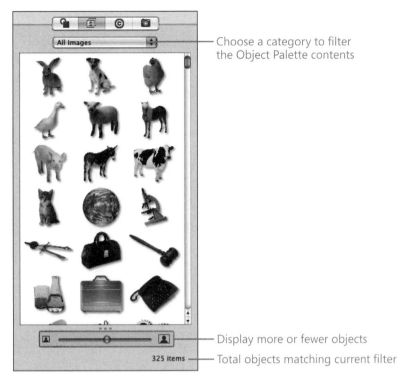

Choose a category to filter the Object Palette contents

Display more or fewer objects

Total objects matching current filter

The Object Palette makes it easy to view the available images. By moving the slider at the bottom of the palette, you can change the size of the images in the preview window.

Preview as many as 50 images in the Object Palette, or zoom in to see more detail.

Add Images to the Clip Gallery

The Object Palette draws its Clip Art content from the Clip Gallery. You can open the Clip Gallery independently of the Object Palette by clicking Clip Art on the Insert menu. You can add more clip art to the Clip Gallery from the Microsoft Office Online Web site, which you access by clicking the Online button in the Clip Gallery.

Download additional clip art
from Office Online

From Office Online, you can search for clip art and link to many different image providers. You can click any thumbnail to view a larger version of the clip, its associated keywords, and file information. When you locate a clip that you want to add to the Clip Gallery, select the Add To Selection Basket check box next to the clip either on the Office Online page or in the Preview window.

Add as many clips to the selection basket as you want. When you're ready to add your collected clips to the Clip Gallery, use the links in the Selection Basket pane on the left side of the screen to preview the selected clips and download them.

The downloaded files are available from the Downloads window on your Mac, or from the Downloads folder stored in your user profile.

To add clip art from the Downloads window or folder to the Clip Gallery:

→ Right-click the file and then click **Open**.

Extra clip art that you add by using this method is accessible from the Favorites category in the Clip Gallery, and from the Personal category on the Clip Art page of the Object Palette.

All the free clip art available through the Clip Gallery and from the Office Online site is available for you to use without restriction or license. Some third-party image providers that you link to from Office Online also offer licensed images (but these are not free).

Insert Symbols as Text or Graphics

The Symbols page of the Object Palette contains text and image symbols in the following categories:

- Currency
- Fractions
- Math
- Trade
- Special
- Keyboard

- Shapes
- Arrows
- Check Marks
- Music
- Greek
- Accents

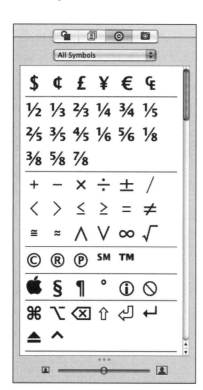

You can insert common symbols—as independent graphics or as text—in a document, in a worksheet cell, or on a slide.

When inserting a symbol into an Excel worksheet, you must first select a container to enter it in. Click a cell or shape and then, on the Symbols page of the Object Palette, click the symbol you want to insert. If you try (purposefully or otherwise) to enter a symbol into an element that doesn't accept symbols, Excel displays a *Reference is not valid* error. To clear the error, click OK to close the message box, and then press the Escape key. If you click around for too long trying to figure out what to do, your Mac might go into a tailspin, causing you to force Excel to quit and then restart the program, to regain control of your worksheet.

> **Tip** If a program isn't responding, first try to quit the program by clicking Quit on the program menu (or pressing Command+Q). If the Quit command doesn't work, you can bypass the issues that are preventing the program from closing by clicking Force Quit on the Apple menu (or pressing Command+Option+Escape). In the Force Quit Applications dialog box that opens, in the list of running programs, click the program, and click Force Quit. Then in the confirmation message box, click Force Quit one final time.

Insert Your Own Photos

The Photos page displays the contents of any image folder or iPhoto library you select for inclusion.

Search for metadata assigned to photos

You can quickly locate specific, tagged photos by searching for tag terms (metadata).

To add a folder or library to the Photos page:

1. In the category list at the top of the page, click **Other Library or Folder**.

   The Open Library Or Folder dialog box opens.

2. In the lower-left corner of the dialog box, select **Show iPhoto Libraries** or **Show Image Folders** to indicate the type of folder you want to navigate to.

   You can see folders of the type you don't select, but you can't choose them.

3. Navigate to the image folder or iPhoto library you want to add to the **Object Palette**.

As with other graphic objects, you can modify photos by using the commands in the Formatting Palette.

A photo, cropped to a pentagon shape, with outline, glow, and reflection effects

A lot of neat options are available, including the following:

- You can apply a variety of Quick Styles that resemble frames or make the photo into a three-dimensional object.
- You can crop the photo by using the rectangular cropping tool, or cut the photo into any of the shapes available from the Object Gallery.
- You can add shadows and reflections to the photo to give it depth.

- You can add an outline or glowing outline around the edge of the full, cropped, styled, or shaped photo.

- You can choose one color in the photo to become transparent, so you can see through the photo to whatever background it's sitting on.

Practice Inserting and Modifying Images

In this exercise, you'll insert and modify shapes, clip art images, symbols, and photos.

We'll work through this exercise in a PowerPoint presentation, but you can also apply the skills you practice here when working with Word documents or Excel worksheets.

> **SET UP** In this exercise, we'll use the *SummerActivities* presentation and the *Kids1* and *Panda1* images located in the *~/Documents/Microsoft Press/2008OfficeMacSBS/ CreateGraphics/* folder. Open the *SummerActivities* presentation, and display Slide 1.

1. Display the Toolbox, if it isn't already open, and on the button bar at the top, click the **Object Palette** button.

   The Object Palette opens, displaying the Shapes page. The unfiltered page contains 172 shapes.

2. Click the category list to display the shape categories.

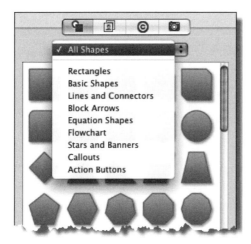

3. In the category list, click **Basic Shapes**.

   The filtered page displays 41 items.

4. Near the bottom of the page, click the sun shape.

5. In the Slide pane, point to the upper-right corner of **Slide 1**.

   The pointer changes to a plus sign to indicate that clicking the slide will add a graphic element.

6. Click in the space between the yellow stripe and the upper-right corner of the slide.

   A sun shape appears on the slide. The shape is selected for editing.

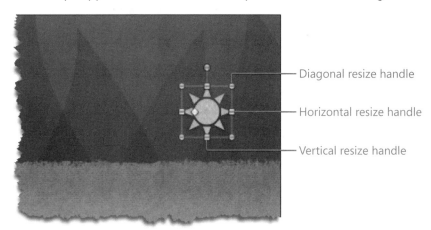

When inserted on the slide, the sun shape has a patterned yellow fill that it picked up from the *Habitat* theme attached to the presentation.

See Also For information about colors associated with themes, see "Work with Office Themes" in Chapter 7, "Work with Word Document Content."

7. Drag the round diagonal resize handles to enlarge the sun shape until it overlaps the yellow stripe.

8. Point to the round green rotation handle. When the pointer changes to a circular arrow, drag the handle to the left to rotate the shape by about 15 degrees.

> **Tip** To precisely rotate an object, right-click the shape and then click Format Shape. On the Size page of the Format Shape dialog box, you can set an exact degree of rotation.

9. Display **Slide 2**.

   This slide includes a multipurpose text and image box. You can insert text by clicking the placeholder at the top of the box. You can insert a table, chart, SmartArt graphic, picture, clip art image, or movie (through interfaces other than the Object Palette) by clicking the corresponding button in the center of the box.

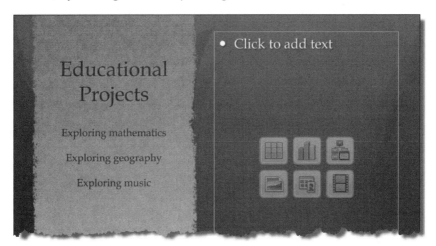

10. In the **Object Palette**, click the **Clip Art** button.

> **Note** The number in the lower-right corner of the Clip Art page in your Object Palette reflects the 319 basic clip art graphics that come with Office 2008 for Mac, plus any others that you've added.

11. In the category list, click **Clip Art**. Scroll about halfway through the pane, to the series depicting children's activities, and click the image of a girl looking at a globe.

12. Drag the selected clip art image from the **Object Palette** to the slide.

    As you drag the image, an Add icon (a green circle labeled with a white plus sign) appears on the pointer to indicate that releasing the mouse button will copy the image to that location. When the image is over a location where you can't drop it, such as a title bar, menu bar, toolbar, or scroll bar, the Add icon changes to a slashed circle to indicate that the operation is not allowed.

> **Tip** You can drag an image from the Object Palette to a slide, document, or worksheet to insert a copy of the image, or you can drag it to a storage location such as your desktop or a folder to insert a file containing the image.

13. Drop the image into the content box on the right side of the slide.

    A version of the image that is perfectly sized to fit the box appears, and the image buttons and placeholder text disappear.

 14. In the **Object Palette**, click the **Symbols** button. Then in the category list, click **Music**.

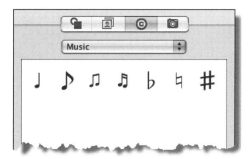

15. In the left pane of **Slide 2**, click to position the insertion point at the beginning of the phrase *Exploring music*.

16. Drag a musical note of your choice from the **Object Palette** to the active text box, and drop it at the insertion point.

PowerPoint inserts the symbol at the beginning of the line as a text character. It has the same formatting as the characters that follow it. As long as the insertion point is active in the text, dragging a symbol to the text box inserts it only within the existing text structure.

17. Click the text box frame (so that the insertion point stops blinking). Then drag a different musical note to the text box.

This time PowerPoint inserts the symbol as a movable, resizable image.

18. Display **Slide 3**.

The slide includes two picture placeholders.

19. In the upper photo frame, click the **Add Picture** icon.

The Choose A Picture dialog box opens.

20. Navigate to the *~/Documents/Microsoft Press/2008OfficeMacSBS/CreateGraphics/* folder. Click the *Kids1* photo, and then click **Insert**.

An appropriately sized photo, depicting two adorable children on a field trip, appears in the upper photo frame.

21. In the lower photo frame, click the **Add Picture** icon. In the **Choose a Picture** dialog box displaying the contents of the *CreateGraphics* folder, click the *Panda1* photo, and then click **Insert**.

An appropriately sized photo of a panda enjoying lunch appears in the lower photo frame.

22. Right-click the panda photo, point to **Arrange**, and then click **Bring to Front**.

The panda photo moves to the top of the photo stack.

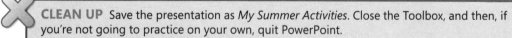

CLEAN UP Save the presentation as *My Summer Activities*. Close the Toolbox, and then, if you're not going to practice on your own, quit PowerPoint.

Check Whether Graphic Effects Are Compatible with Earlier Program Versions

Some of the fancy graphic effects that are new in Office 2008 won't look the same or have the same functionality in earlier versions of Office, due to an incompatibility between the technologies of the new and old program versions.

When you insert a shape that has effects that might not reproduce faithfully in earlier versions—such as transparency or shadows—Office 2008 immediately flags the fact in the Compatibility Report, which is available from the Toolbox. This causes the Compatibility Report button at the top of the Toolbox to flash red.

You can view a list of possible incompatibilities in the active document at any time by displaying the Compatibility Report. Clicking an item in the Results list activates the specific document element that generated the warning.

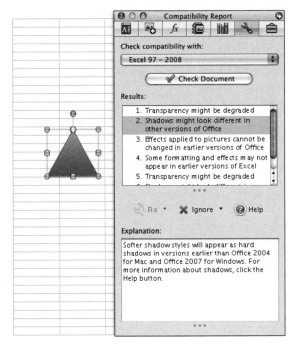

The Results list displays a separate warning for each instance of a specific incompatibility. You can remove warnings from the results list by clicking the Ignore arrow and then, in the Ignore list, clicking Ignore Once to remove the currently selected warning, Ignore All to remove all current instances of the warning, or Don't Show Again to stop generating the warning.

Create Professional Diagrams

When you need to clearly illustrate a concept such as a process, cycle, hierarchy, or relationship, you can create a dynamic, visually appealing diagram by using *SmartArt diagrams*. SmartArt is almost certainly the coolest new feature available in Word 2008 for Mac, Excel 2008 for Mac, and PowerPoint 2008 for Mac.

> **Note** To avoid confusion, in this book we refer to graphics created with the SmartArt engine as *diagrams*. In the program interface, you'll see references to SmartArt *graphics*. Both terms refer to the same thing.

From the extensive library of SmartArt layouts, you can create simple diagrams depicting simple concepts, or very complex graphics that earn their reputation as being "worth 1000 words."

A simple SmartArt graphic, using a Process layout

By using predefined sets of sophisticated formatting, you can almost effortlessly put together professional-looking diagrams that depict a variety of scenarios. Common types of diagrams include:

- **List diagrams.** These diagrams visually represent lists of related or independent information—for example, a list of items needed to complete a task, including pictures of the items.

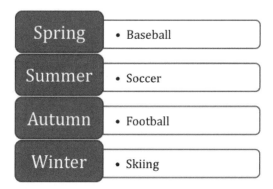

- **Process diagrams.** These diagrams visually describe the ordered set of steps required to complete a task—for example, the steps you take to process an order.

- **Cycle diagrams.** These diagrams represent a circular sequence of steps, tasks, or events; or the relationship of a set of steps, tasks, or events to a central, core element—for example, the importance of introducing the basic elements of a story in order to build up to an exciting ending.

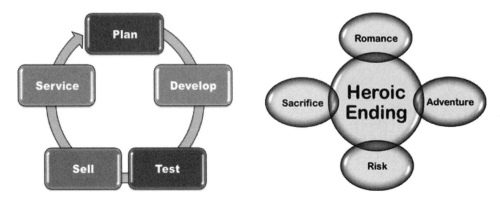

- **Hierarchy diagrams.** These diagrams illustrate the structure of an organization or entity—for example, the top-level management structure of a company.

Other diagram types include:

- **Relationship diagrams.** These diagrams show convergent, divergent, overlapping, merging, or containment elements—for example, how using similar methods to organize your e-mail, calendar, and contacts can improve your productivity.

- **Matrix diagrams.** These diagrams show the relationship of components to a whole—for example, the product teams in a department.

- **Pyramid diagrams.** These diagrams illustrate proportional or interconnected relationships—for example, the amount of time that should ideally be spent on different phases of a project.

Create a Diagram from Scratch

You create a SmartArt graphic directly in a document, worksheet, slide, or e-mail message by selecting the diagram layout you want from the SmartArt tab of the Elements Gallery. (You can leave the graphic in the document and it will remain editable.) You add text to the diagram either directly or from its Text pane.

The process of creating a SmartArt graphic is relatively quick, other than the time you'll spend choosing the layout you want and marveling over the many types of formatting you can apply to the graphic, the background, and the text.

SmartArt graphics are attractive simply as graphics, but because they are intended to convey specific information, they are specifically designed to incorporate text. Each SmartArt graphic has an associated Text pane. You can enter text into the Text pane or directly into the graphic; the text immediately appears in both locations.

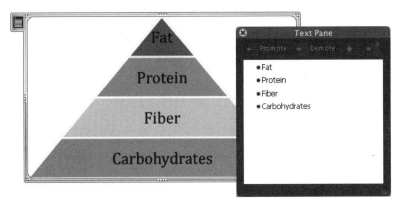

Text appears simultaneously in the diagram and in the Text pane.

Modify a Diagram

After you create a diagram, you can add and remove shapes, and edit the text that appears in the shapes, by making changes in the Text pane. If you scroll the file while the Text pane is open, the Text pane remains visible so that you can easily copy text between the file and the Text pane rather than retyping it.

You can also customize a diagram by using the options in the Formatting Palette of the Toolbox. You can make changes such as the following:

● Switch to a different layout of the same type or of a different type.

> **Tip** If the original diagram includes more text than will fit in the new layout, the text is not shown in the diagram, but it is retained in the Text pane so that you don't have to retype it if you switch to a layout that can accommodate it.

- Add shading and three-dimensional effects to all the shapes in a diagram.
- Change the color scheme.
- Change an individual shape—for example, you can change a square into a star to make it stand out.
- Apply a built-in shape style.
- Change the color, outline, or effect of a shape.

> **Tip** You can move a shape within a diagram by dragging it. You can remove a shape from a diagram by selecting it and then pressing the Del key.

Practice Creating and Modifying Diagrams

In this exercise, you'll create a SmartArt diagram in a document. Then you'll add text and format the diagram.

We'll work in a Word document in this exercise, but you can use the skills you practice in this exercise in Excel and PowerPoint.

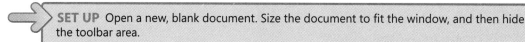

SET UP Open a new, blank document. Size the document to fit the window, and then hide the toolbar area.

1. In the **Elements Gallery**, click the **SmartArt Graphics** tab.

    The Elements Gallery displays all the available diagram layouts. You can filter the display by clicking the buttons at the top of the gallery.

2. Click the **List**, **Process**, **Cycle**, **Hierarchy**, **Relationship**, **Matrix**, and **Pyramid** buttons to view the available layouts in each group. When you finish, display the **Relationship** gallery.

3. Click the **Balance** layout (the first thumbnail in the **Relationship** gallery).

> **Tip** Point to any thumbnail to display the layout name and description in the style name area.

Word inserts a frame, containing the selected diagram, into the document. The diagram depicts a balance with shapes stacked on each side. Text placeholders appear in the shapes.

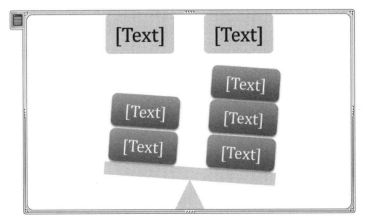

A floating Text pane opens next to the diagram frame. The Text pane contains the same placeholders, formatted as a bulleted list.

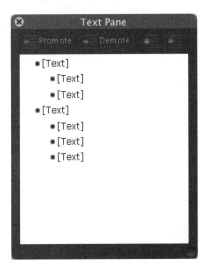

> **Troubleshooting** If the Text pane is not visible, click the Text Pane button located in the upper-left corner of the diagram frame.

4. In the Text pane, click the first **[Text]** placeholder, and then type Work.

When you click the placeholder, the upper-left diagram shape becomes active. As you type the letters, they appear simultaneously in the Text pane and in the active shape.

5. Press the **Down Arrow** key to move to the first second-level list item in the Text pane. The base shape on the left side of the balance becomes active.

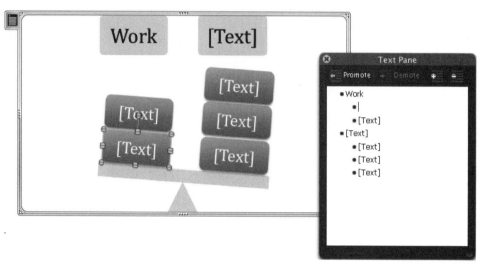

6. Type Time, press the **Down Arrow** key, type Toil, and then press **Return**.

   A third shape appears on the left side of the diagram, and the balance shifts to a state of equilibrium because each side now contains the same number of shapes.

7. Type Turbulence.

   When the word reaches a length where all the letters can't fit in the box, the font size used in that shape and all related shapes becomes smaller, until the widest word (*Turbulence*) fits its shape.

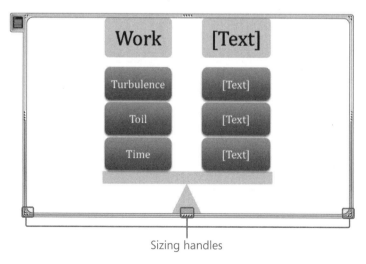

Sizing handles

> **Tip** You can manually resize a diagram by dragging the sizing handles of the frame. You can precisely resize it by right-clicking the diagram and clicking Format Shape, and then setting the height, width, or scale on the Size page of the Format Object dialog box.

8. Click the **[Text]** placeholder located in the upper-right shape of the diagram, and then type Play.

As you type, letters appear simultaneously in the shape and in the Text pane.

9. Click the shape at the top of the right stack, and type Fun. Click the next shape, and type Fitness.

10. Click the shape at the base of the right stack. In the Text pane, click the **Remove** button. Then click outside of the diagram frame to see the result.

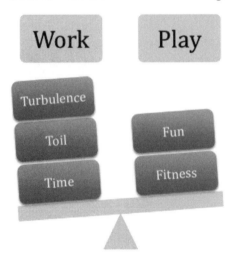

11. Click near (but not on) the diagram to activate the frame but not a specific shape. Then in the Text pane, click the **Close** button.

12. Display the **Formatting Palette** in the Toolbox. Expand the **SmartArt Graphic Styles** panel and the **Quick Styles and Effects** panel, and hide the others.

> **Note** You can apply the effects from many other Formatting Palette panels to the shapes in a SmartArt graphic. We'll focus on these two panels in this exercise, and you can experiment with others on your own.

The Styles tab of the SmartArt Graphic Styles panel displays a simple version of the current diagram layout with different styles applied to the diagram shapes.

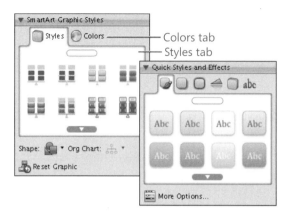

13. On the **Styles** tab, click the **Inset** thumbnail (the third thumbnail in the second row).

    The balance diagram changes to reflect the selected style. The shapes now take on a three-dimensional appearance.

14. Click the **Scroll Down** button at the bottom of the **Styles** tab to view more graphic styles. Apply other styles that look interesting. When you finish, click the **Polished** thumbnail (the second thumbnail in the second row).

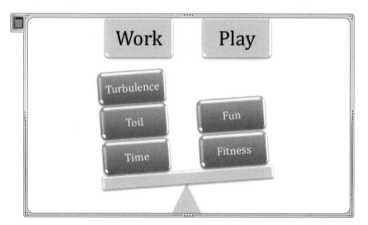

15. At the top of the **SmartArt Graphic Styles** panel, click **Colors**.

    The Colors tab displays the current diagram layout with 31 multi-color and single-color options reflecting the document theme colors applied to the diagram shapes.

16. Scroll down to view the color options.

    The first row of thumbnails depicts the multi-color options. The first *Colorful* option shows eight different theme-specific accent colors on the eight diagram shapes. The three *Colorful Range* options each show ranges of two accent colors across the eight shapes.

The six rows of single-color options each depict four patterns in one accent color.

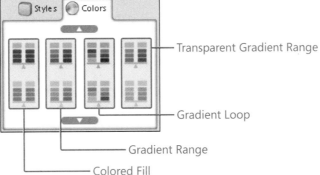

Transparent Gradient Range

Gradient Loop

Gradient Range

Colored Fill

The last row depicts three Dark options—two with only outlines, and one with filled shapes.

17. On the **Colors** tab, click the **Colorful** thumbnail. Then click away from the diagram to see the results.

The diagram changes from shades of blue to seven different colors.

> **Note** When the SmartArt diagram isn't active, the related panels disappear from the Formatting Palette.

18. In the diagram, click the triangle supporting the balance.

The triangle is selected for editing, and the options on the Quick Styles tab of the Quick Styles And Effects panel become active.

19. Press and hold the **Shift** key, and then click the rectangular shape balancing on top of the selected triangle, the **Work** shape, and the **Play** shape.

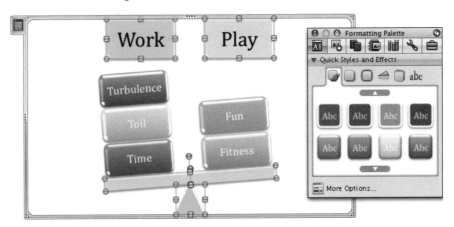

20. On the **Quick Styles** tab, click the **Colored Outline – Accent 4** thumbnail (the fourth thumbnail in the third row).

The four selected objects change to have only colored outlines.

> **Tip** The More Options button at the bottom of the Quick Styles And Effects panel opens the Format Shape dialog box (if one or more shapes are active) or the Format Object dialog box (if the frame is active). From these dialog boxes, you can apply Fill, Line, Shadow, Glow & Soft Edges, Reflection, 3-D Format And Rotation, Picture, and Text Box formatting to the active elements. From the Format Object dialog box, you can also control the size and layout settings of the diagram.

21. Click away from the diagram to see the results.

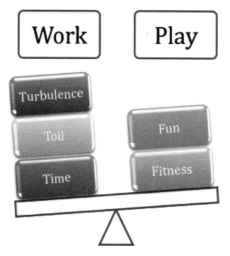

22. Experiment on your own with additional formatting options from the **Shadows**, **Glows**, **Reflections**, and **3-D Effects** tabs of the **Quick Styles And Effects** panel, and with options from the **Format Shape** dialog box. When you finish, right-click the diagram frame, and then click **Reset Graphic**.

The diagram returns to its original formatting.

CLEAN UP Save your diagram if you want to, and then close the document. If you're not continuing directly to the next chapter, or intending to practice on your own, quit Word.

Key Points

- When you insert a shape into a file, it takes on the color scheme of the file. Its color changes if you change the theme or color scheme, or you can select a specific color.

- You can change the size, orientation, and aspect ratio of a basic shape to the extent that it entirely changes its appearance. If the Object Palette doesn't contain the exact shape you want, look for a shape that resembles the shape you want to end up with, with the same number of corners and the same basic qualities.

- Hundreds of pieces of photographic, illustrated, and animated clip art come with Office 2008. You can download thousands more from the Office Online site.

- You can insert common symbols as freestanding graphics or as text.

- You can give an embedded photo a professional look by applying a frame or edge effects, or by changing it into another shape.

- SmartArt graphics are totally awesome! Using this cool new feature, you can create professional, dynamic diagrams that provide a strong visual message.

Chapter at a Glance

Revise a document, **page 414**

Once upon a time there was a prince who wanted to marry a princess; but she would have to be a real princess. He travelled all over the world to find one, but nowhere could he get what he wanted. There were princesses enough, but it was difficult to find out whether they were real ones. There was always something about them that was not as it should be. So he came home again and was sad, for he would have liked very much to have had a real princess.

Joan Preppernau 9/4/08 11:37 PM
Deleted: reel

One evening a terrible storm came on; there was thunder and lightning, and the rain poured down in torrents. Suddenly a knocking was heard at the city gate, and the old king went to

real princess could be as sensitive as that.

So the prince took her for his wife, for now he knew that he had a real princess; and the pea was put in the museum, where it may still be seen, if no one has stolen it.

There, that is a true story.

Joan Preppernau 9/5/08 12:38 AM
Formatted: Font:Italic

Main document changes and comments

Comment	Joan Preppernau	9/4/08 11:34 PM
Removing this would improve the readability of the sentence.		
Formatted	Joan Preppernau	9/5/08 12:38 AM
Font:Italic		

Give feedback on document content, **page 416**

It was a princess standing out there in front of the gate. But, good gracious! what a sight the rain and the wind had made her look. The water ran down from her hair and clothes; it ran down into the toes of her shoes and out again at the heels. And yet she said that she was a real princess.

Joan Preppernau 9/4/08 11:34 PM
Comment: Removing this would improve the readability of the sentence.

"Well, we'll soon find that out," thought the old queen. But she said nothing, went into the bedroom, took all the bedding off the bedstead, and laid a pea on the bottom; then she took twenty mattresses and laid them on the pea, and then put

13 Review Word Documents

In this chapter, you will learn how to

✔ Revise a document.

✔ Give feedback on document content.

When multiple people contribute to the creation of a document, or when you have cause to review a document written by another person, you can use the Track Changes and Comments features of Microsoft Word to simplify the process. The Track Changes feature marks insertions, deletions, and formatting changes made to a document so that other people can easily distinguish original content from changes and can choose to accept or reject the changes.

Using the Comments feature, you can insert remarks or additional information into a document for other reviewers to see, without affecting the actual document content.

In this chapter, you'll learn how to track the changes you make to a document and insert comments into a document. Then you'll review and process changes and comments by using various methods.

See Also You can find handy keyboard shortcuts, simple instructions for performing common tasks, and other useful information in the Quick Reference section at the beginning of this book.

 Practice Makes Perfect! The practice file you will use to complete the exercise in this chapter is in the *ReviewDocuments* practice file folder. See "Using the Companion Content" at the beginning of this book for information about installing and locating the practice files.

Revise a Document

When two or more people collaborate on a document, one person usually creates and "owns" the document and the others review it, adding or revising content to make it more accurate, logical, or readable. In Word, reviewers can turn on the Track Changes feature so that the revisions they make to the active document are recorded without the original text being lost. (Note that Track Changes affects only the active document, not any other documents that might also be open.) You then edit the text as usual, and your changes are recorded for later review.

To turn on the Track Changes feature:

→ On the status bar, click the **TRK** button.

Or

1. Point to **Track Changes** on the **Tools** menu, and then click **Highlight Changes**.
2. In the **Highlight Changes** dialog box, select the **Track changes** check box, and then click **OK**.

> **Tip** Regardless of the method you use to turn Track Changes on or off, the color of the dot on the TRK button indicates its status—a blue button indicates that the Track Changes feature is turned on, and a gray button indicates that it's turned off.

You manage the Track Changes feature from the Track Changes page of the Word Preferences dialog box.

By default, the Track Changes feature indicates revisions as follows:

- Inserted text is underlined.
- Deleted text is crossed out in Normal view or, in Print Layout view, displayed in *balloons* in the right margin.
- Formatting changes are displayed in balloons in the right margin.
- Any line of the document that contains a change is indicated with a vertical line in the left margin, so you can quickly scan a document for changes.

For each of these types of edits, you can choose other marking techniques—but unless these somehow conflict with an internal system, there's really no good reason to. These standard marks are used and recognized by Word users all around the world, and deviating from the standard could cause unnecessary confusion if the document is distributed to other people with the tracked changes shown.

By default, the color in which Word tracks insertions, deletions, and formatting changes is set to By Author. With this setting, Word assigns a specific color to each person who edits the document with change tracking turned on. Each reviewer will have a unique color assignment within the document, but that color assignment won't be the same among different documents.

> **Note** Word identifies reviewers by the user information stored on the User Information page of the Word Preferences dialog box. To view or edit the user information, open the Word Preferences dialog box and, under Personal Settings, click User Information.

If it's important to you that changes you make and comments you insert are always tracked in a specific color, you can specify that color by selecting it from a list. You can select different colors to indicate different types of changes.

You can display a ScreenTip identifying the name of the reviewer who made a specific change and when the change was made, by pointing to a revision or balloon.

You can work with revisions in the following ways by using the commands available from the Reviewing toolbar:

- If you want to track changes without showing them on the screen, you can hide the revisions by clicking **Final** in the **Display for Review** list. To redisplay the revisions, click **Final Showing Markup** in the **Display for Review** list. You can also display the original version, with or without revisions.

- When revisions are visible in the document, you can select the types of revisions that are displayed, from the **Show** list—for example, you can display only comments or only insertions and deletions. You can also display or hide the revisions of specific reviewers from this list.

- You can move forward or backward from one revision mark or comment to another by clicking the **Next** or **Previous** button.

- You can incorporate a change into the document by selecting the changed text and then clicking the **Accept** button.

- You can undo the selected change or restore the original text by clicking the **Reject** button.

- You can accept all the changes at once by clicking the **Accept** arrow and then clicking **Accept All Changes in Document**. To reject all the changes at once, click the **Reject** arrow and then click **Reject All Changes in Document**.

- You can accept or reject multiple changes by selecting a block of text containing changes you want to process and then clicking the **Accept** or **Reject** button.

- You can accept or reject only certain types of changes or changes from specific reviewers by displaying only the changes you want to accept or reject, clicking the **Accept** or **Reject** arrow, and then clicking **All Changes Shown** in the list.

Give Feedback on Document Content

In addition to tracking the changes made to a document, you can insert notes, or comments, to ask questions, make suggestions, or explain edits. To insert a comment, you select the text to which the comment refers, click the New Comment button on the Reviewing toolbar, and type what you want to say in the balloon that appears (in Print Layout view) or in the Reviewing pane (in Normal view). In Print Layout view, Word highlights the associated text in the document in the same color as the balloon and adds your initials and a sequential number to the balloon itself.

You can work with comments in the following ways:

- To display the reviewer's name and the date and time the comment was inserted, you point to either the commented text or the balloon.

- To review comments, you can scroll through the document, or in a long document, you can jump from balloon to balloon by clicking the **Next** or **Previous** button.

- To edit a comment, you simply click the balloon and use normal editing techniques.

- To delete a comment, you click the **Delete** button in the Comment balloon or click the **Reject Change/Delete Comment** button on the Reviewing toolbar.

- To respond to a comment, you can add text to an existing balloon. You can also click the existing balloon and then click the **New Comment** button to attach a new balloon to the same text in the document.

- If the complete text of a comment isn't visible in its balloon, you can view it in its entirety by clicking the **Reviewing Pane** button on the Reviewing toolbar. In addition to displaying comments, the Reviewing pane displays all the editing and formatting changes you have made to a document. Click the **Reviewing Pane** button again to hide the Reviewing pane.

- You can turn off the display of comment balloons by clicking **Comments** in the **Show** list.

If multiple people have reviewed a document and you want to see the comments of only a specific person, you can click the Show button, point to Reviewers, and then click the names of the reviewers whose comments you don't want to see.

> **Tip** To change the size of the Reviewing pane, drag its upper border by the Resize handle.

Practice Reviewing Documents

In this exercise, you'll track changes that you make to a document, and insert a comment. You'll review and resolve the revisions, and then hide the remaining comment.

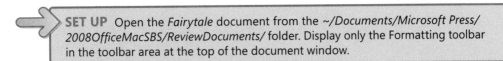

SET UP Open the *Fairytale* document from the *~/Documents/Microsoft Press/ 2008OfficeMacSBS/ReviewDocuments/* folder. Display only the Formatting toolbar in the toolbar area at the top of the document window.

1. On the **Tools** menu, point to **Track Changes**, and then click **Highlight Changes**.

    The Highlight Changes dialog box opens.

    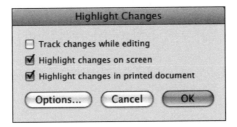

2. In the **Highlight Changes** dialog box, select the **Track changes while editing** check box. Then click the **Options** button.

    The Track Changes page of the Word Preferences dialog box opens. On this page, you can specify how you want Word to indicate changes made to the document. A preview of the marks selected for each type of edit (inserted text, deleted text, changed formatting, and changed lines) is shown at the right end of each section.

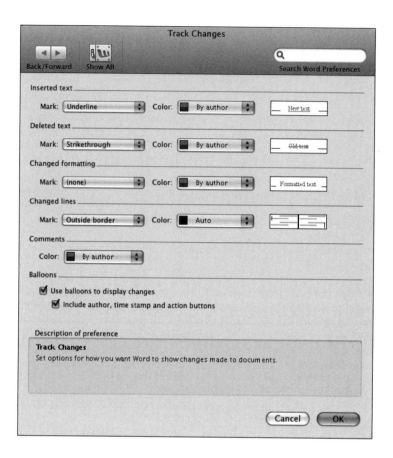

> **Tip** You can display the Track Changes page from Word by opening the Word Preferences dialog box (click Preferences on the Word menu, or press Command+Comma) and then, under Output And Sharing, clicking Track Changes.

In the Comments section, you can specify the color of the balloons that appear in the margin when you give feedback by using the Comment feature.

See Also For information about the Comment feature, see the previous topic, "Give Feedback on Document Content."

In the Balloons section, you can specify whether tracked changes should be shown in text balloons in the document margin, in addition to the inline underline and strikethrough formatting.

3. On the **Track Changes** page, click **Cancel** to close the page without making any changes. Then in the **Highlight Changes** dialog box, click **OK**.

The Reviewing toolbar opens in the toolbar area with the Track Changes button pressed, and the letters *TRK* appear near the right end of the status bar, with a blue dot next to the letters, indicating that change tracking is turned on. (A gray dot indicates that it's turned off.)

Reviewing toolbar

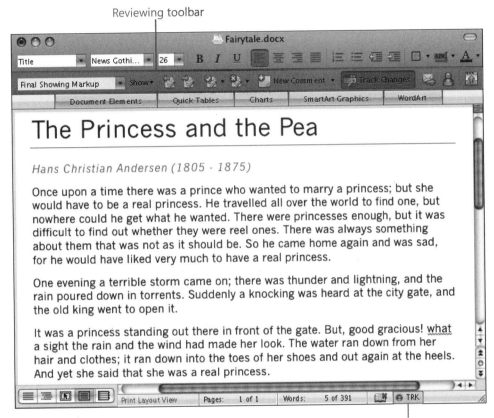

Track Changes status indicator

Note We've magnified the document to make the text more legible.

4. Point to each button on the Reviewing toolbar to display the button name in a ScreenTip.

Display or hide markup   Accept or reject changes

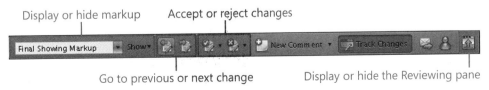

Go to previous or next change   Display or hide the Reviewing pane

5. Click the **Display for Review** arrow to expand the list of choices you have for displaying edited content.

> **Tip** When you're tracking your changes in a document, you might find it useful to display the Final version, rather than the default Final Showing Markup version. The Final version depicts the document as it will appear with all the tracked changes implemented. The Original version depicts the document as it would appear with none of the changes implemented. The two Showing Markup versions depict different views of the tracked changes.

6. Click the **Show** button to display the list of changes you can show or hide when displaying either of the Showing Markup versions.

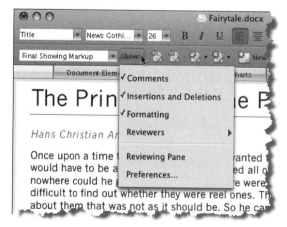

7. In the fourth line of the first paragraph of the story, select the word *reel*, and then type real.

The word *reel* changes to *real*. The word *real* is underlined (to mark it as inserted text), and is in the font color that Word has, just now, assigned to you for all changes you make, and comments you insert, in this document.

A balloon in the same color, on the right side of the page, indicates that the word *reel* was deleted by you, on the current date, and at the current time. The Deleted balloon is linked to the starting point of the deleted content. A vertical mark to the left of the line of text indicates that the line contains a change.

> **Tip** You can accept an edit from a balloon by clicking the check mark button, or reject it by clicking the X button.

8. In the last line of the same paragraph, position the insertion point at the beginning of the word *a*, which follows the word *have*. Type **had**, and then press the **Spacebar**.

Word inserts and underlines the word, but no balloon appears for this simple insertion.

> Once upon a time there was a prince who wanted to marry a princess; but she would have to be a real princess. He travelled all over the world to find one, but nowhere could he get what he wanted. There were princesses enough, but it was difficult to find out whether they were real ones. There was always something about them that was not as it should be. So he came home again and was sad, for he would have liked very much to have had a real princess.
>
> One evening a terrible storm came on; there was thunder and lightning, and the rain poured down in torrents. Suddenly a knocking was heard at the city gate, and the old king went to open it.
>
> Joan Preppernau 9/4/08 11:37 PM
> Deleted: reel

9. In the third paragraph, select the words *good gracious*, the comma and space preceding them, and the exclamation point that follows. Then, on the Reviewing toolbar, click the **New Comment** button.

> **Tip** You can insert a comment when the Reviewing toolbar is not visible, by clicking Comment on the Insert menu.

A balloon linked to the selected text opens on the right side of the page, ready to receive your input. The Comment balloon indicates that the comment was inserted by you, on the current date and at the current time. The blinking insertion point is visible in the Comment balloon.

10. Type **Removing this would improve the readability of the sentence.**

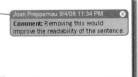

> It was a princess standing out there in front of the gate. But, good gracious! what a sight the rain and the wind had made her look. The water ran down from her hair and clothes; it ran down into the toes of her shoes and out again at the heels. And yet she said that she was a real princess.
>
> "Well, we'll soon find that out," thought the old queen. But she said nothing, went into the bedroom, took all the bedding off the bedstead, and laid a pea on the bottom; then she took twenty mattresses and laid them on the pea, and then put
>
> Joan Preppernau 9/4/08 11:34 PM
> Comment: Removing this would improve the readability of the sentence.

> **Tip** You can delete a comment by clicking the X button located in the upper-right corner of the Comment balloon.

11. In the third paragraph from the end of the story, position the insertion point at the end of *princes*, and then type the letter s.

Word inserts and underlines the letter.

12. Select the last paragraph of the story and then, on the Formatting toolbar, click the **Italic** button.

A Formatted balloon appears on the right side of the page, indicating that you applied italic font formatting to the text. The balloon points to the starting point of the formatting change.

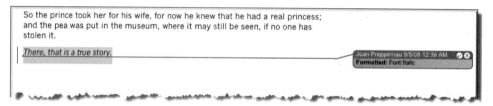

So the prince took her for his wife, for now he knew that he had a real princess; and the pea was put in the museum, where it may still be seen, if no one has stolen it.

There, that is a true story.

Joan Preppernau 9/5/08 12:38 AM
Formatted: Font:Italic

13. Press **Command+Home** to move to the beginning of the document. Then, on the Reviewing toolbar, click the **Next** button.

> **Tip** If a document contains both tracked changes and comments, clicking the Next or Previous button moves sequentially between both types of elements.

Word moves to the first tracked change, and selects the word *reel* in the Deleted balloon.

14. In the **Deleted** balloon, click the **Accept Change** button (the check mark).

The balloon disappears. The inserted text, *real*, is still indicated as a tracked change.

15. On the Reviewing toolbar, click the **Accept Change** button.

> **Tip** Clicking the Accept Change arrow displays a list of options. You can accept the current change, accept all the changes that are visible in the document (but none that are hidden), or accept all the changes in the document.

The underline disappears from the word *real*, and the font color changes to the default. The vertical marker on the left end of the line of text also disappears, indicating that there are no revisions or comments in this line.

16. On the Reviewing toolbar, click the **Next** button.

Word selects the word *had*. With a wavy green underline, Word's spelling and grammar checker has marked *have had* as grammatically incorrect.

17. On the Reviewing toolbar, click the **Reject Change/Delete Comment** button.

> **Tip** Clicking the Reject Change/Delete Comment arrow displays a list of options. You can reject the current change or delete the current comment, reject all the changes in the document or only those that are visible, or delete all the comments in the document or only those that are visible.

The word *had* disappears, as does the wavy green line.

18. On the Reviewing toolbar, click the **Next** button.

The focus moves to the comment. This comment will need to be addressed by someone else.

Now let's look at another way of reviewing revisions.

19. On the Reviewing toolbar, click the **Reviewing Pane** button.

The horizontal Reviewing pane opens across the bottom of the document window.

20. If the pane is quite short, drag the **Resize** handle in the center of the top border up, so you can see two items.

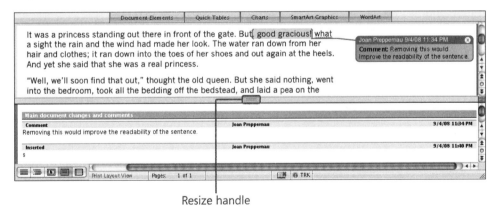

Resize handle

The first section of the Reviewing pane lists changes and comments in the main document. The first revision listed is the comment you just addressed. The colored heading above the revision text describes the type of revision (Comment), the person who made the revision (you), and the date and time of the revision.

21. In the **Reviewing** pane, click the next listed revision, the letter *s*.

The document shown in the window above the Reviewing pane moves so that the selected revision is visible. The insertion point is blinking in the Reviewing pane item.

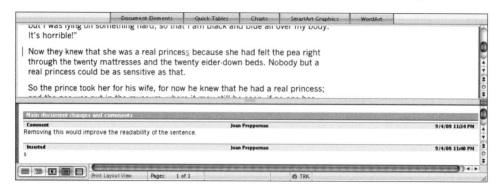

> **Tip** You can't resolve revisions from within the Reviewing pane. You have to use the buttons on the Reviewing toolbar, or the buttons in the balloons.

22. Click in the document body and position the insertion point immediately before the inserted letter *s*.

Now let's look at another, simpler way of moving between and resolving revisions.

23. On the **Tools** menu, point to **Track Changes**, and then click **Accept or Reject Changes**.

The Accept Or Reject Changes dialog box opens.

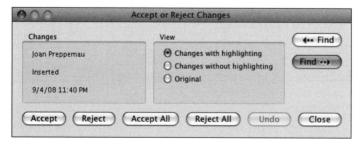

24. In the **Accept or Reject Changes** dialog box, click **Accept**.

Word accepts the change and moves immediately to the next change, the italic formatting. The accepted revision disappears from the Reviewing pane and the current revision is visible.

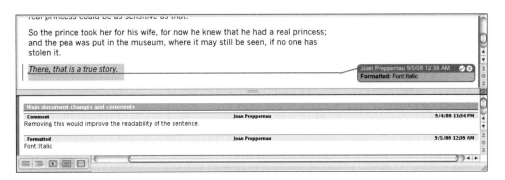

25. In the **Accept or Reject Changes** dialog box, click **Accept**.

A message box informs you that you resolved the last revision before the end of the document.

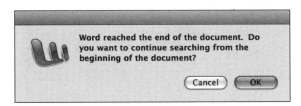

26. In the message box, click **OK**.

A message box informs you that you've resolved all the tracked changes in the document.

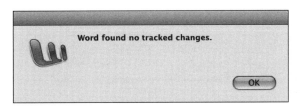

> **Note** The document still contains the comment we reviewed in step 18, but that isn't considered a "change."

27. In the message box, click **OK**. Then, in the **Accept or Reject Changes** dialog box, click **Close**.

28. In the **Reviewing** pane, click the comment that remains in the document, to move to that location.

29. In the **Display for Review** list, click **Final**.

The Comment balloon disappears, but the highlight remains, to signify to a reviewer that a comment is attached to that text.

30. In the **Show** list, point to **Reviewers**.

Your name appears in the list. You can hide all revisions and comments made by a reviewer by clearing the check mark from in front of his or her name on this list.

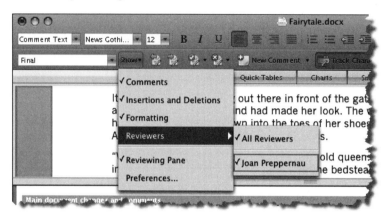

31. In the **Show** list, click **Comments**.

The highlight disappears from the comment, and it disappears from the Reviewing pane. It's not gone, though—it will be visible to any person displaying this document with comments shown.

 CLEAN UP Close the Reviewing pane, hide the Reviewing toolbar, and then close the *Fairytale* document. If you're not continuing directly to the next chapter, close Word.

Key Points

- You can track the changes that you make to a Word document, for later review and acceptance or rejection.

- Word automatically assigns a unique color to the revisions of each document reviewer. If you prefer, you can choose a specific color for the revisions that you make in any document.

- You can insert comments into a document. Word uses the same color system for comments that it does for tracked changes.

- You can view changes and comments in a Word document either in the balloons that appear in the margin in Print Layout view, or in the Reviewing pane.

- You can control the way your changes appear in documents by making selections in the Word Preferences dialog box. Your choices include the name attributed to your comments.

- You can move quickly between revisions, and accept or reject revisions, from the Accept Or Reject Changes dialog box.

Chapter at a Glance

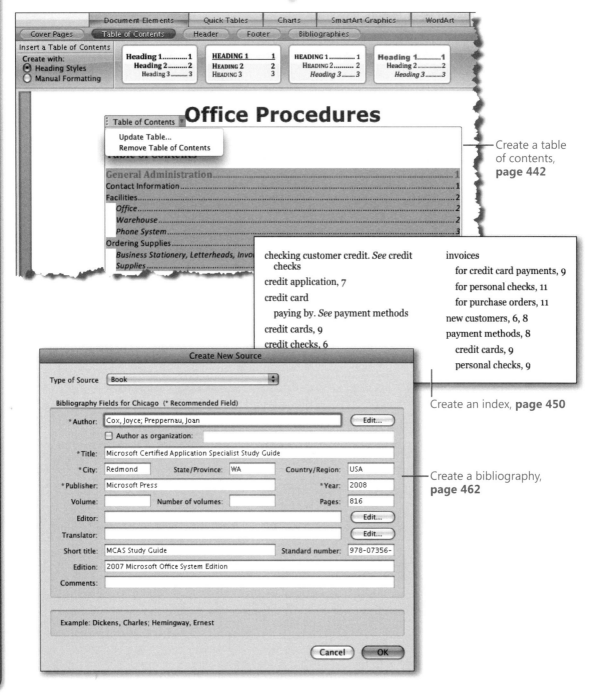

Create a table of contents, **page 442**

Create an index, **page 450**

Create a bibliography, **page 462**

14 Add Finishing Document Elements

In this chapter, you will learn how to

- ✔ Add professional cover pages.
- ✔ Add headers and footers.
- ✔ Create a table of contents.
- ✔ Create an index.
- ✔ Create a bibliography.

When you create a document that you plan to distribute to other people, you can make the document more attractive by adding a cover page, and more easily referenced by adding headers and footers that contain information such as page numbers, logos, and disclaimers.

After your document structure is final, you can create a table of contents to give readers an overview of the document content, and to help them easily locate topics of interest. To provide even more specific assistance in locating topics, you can create an index that directs readers to the specific pages on which they can find information about key subjects. If your document includes citations from external resources, you might also want or need to include a bibliography. Microsoft Word 2008 for Mac makes it easy to create precise reference elements such as these.

In this chapter, you'll add a cover page, headers, and footers to a document to give it a professional look. Then you'll create a table of contents, an index, and a bibliography.

See Also You can find handy keyboard shortcuts, simple instructions for performing common tasks, and other useful information in the Quick Reference section at the beginning of this book.

> **Practice Makes Perfect!** The practice files you will use to complete the exercises in this chapter are in the *FinishDocuments* practice file folder. See "Using the Companion Content" at the beginning of this book for information about installing and locating the practice files.

Add Professional Cover Pages

Word 2008 for Mac includes 17 professionally designed cover pages that you can add to a document to give it a professional appearance. The cover page designs are available from the Document Elements tab of the Elements Gallery. Each cover page features a partial or full-page graphic background, and placeholders for information such as the document title, document subtitle, author name, and organization. Word automatically inserts any of that information that is available from the document properties. You can change, add, remove, or modify the information and modify the graphics. The cover page graphics adopt the color scheme of the current document theme to provide a consistent visual experience.

A document can have only one cover page. Selecting a second style from the Cover Pages group of the Document Elements gallery will change the style of the existing page, but retain the information on it.

You can insert a cover page from anywhere in a document. Follow these steps:

1. Display the **Document Elements** tab of the Elements Gallery.

2. In the **Cover Pages** group, click the cover page design you want to insert.

Word inserts the selected cover page at the beginning of the document, checks the document properties, and inserts any information found there that is called for by the content placeholders.

 To delete a cover page from a document, point to any part of the page, click the button that appears near the upper-left corner of the page, and then click Remove Cover Page.

Practice Adding Cover Pages

In this exercise, you'll add a cover page to a document, enter information on the cover page, and then change the cover page design.

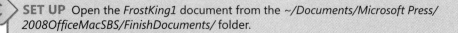

SET UP Open the *FrostKing1* document from the *~/Documents/Microsoft Press/ 2008OfficeMacSBS/FinishDocuments/* folder.

1. On the Standard toolbar, in the **Zoom** list, click **Two Pages**.
2. Click the **Document Elements** tab to expand the Elements Gallery.

   The Elements Gallery opens, displaying the Cover Pages gallery.

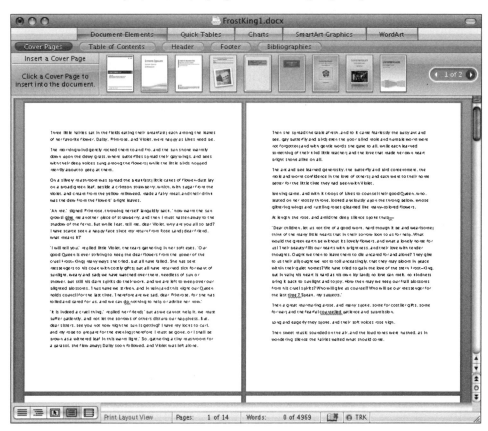

3. If necessary, click the right arrow to display additional cover pages, and then click the **Cover Page 13** thumbnail, which depicts a blue background with a pattern of pale blue dots.

The first page of the document moves to the right, and the selected cover page appears to its left. The cover page displays three text placeholders: [Document Title], [Document Subtitle], and [Author]. If your name is saved as part of your user information, your name appears in place of the [Author] placeholder.

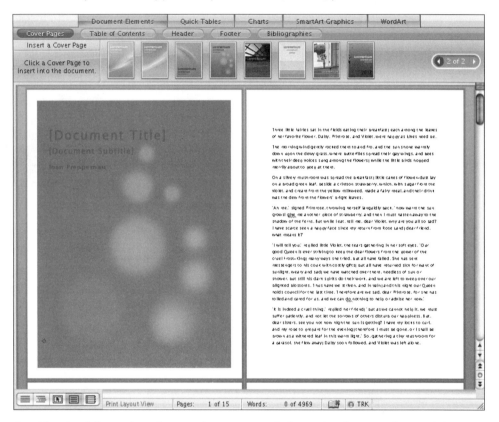

See Also For information about saving your user information for reuse in Word documents, see "Store Your Information for Reuse" in Chapter 1, "Explore and Manage the Office Interface."

4. Double-click the **[Document Title]** placeholder to select it, and then type The Frost King. Press **Tab** to move to the **[Document Subtitle]** placeholder, and then type A Flower Fable. Finally, press **Tab** to move to the **[Author]** placeholder (or your name) and type Louisa May Alcott.

5. In the **Cover Pages** gallery, click the **Cover Page 11** thumbnail. Then click the **Document Elements** tab to close the Elements Gallery.

Word applies the selected design to the cover page. Notice that the cover page has a different color scheme than the thumbnail—it has picked up the document theme's color scheme.

Notice also that Word retained the document title and the author's name, but reset the document subtitle to its original placeholder. This would appear to be a bug in the current version of Word 2008 for Mac, perhaps one that will have been addressed by the time you read this book.

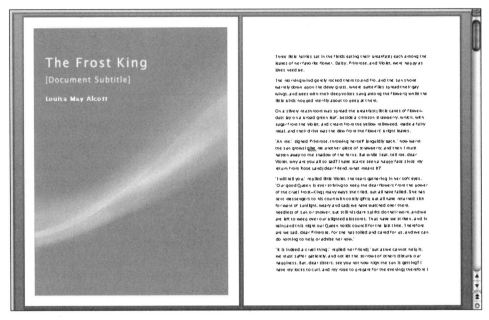

6. If Word reset the document subtitle or any other field, re-enter the appropriate information. Then save the document in the *FinishDocuments* folder as My Frost King.

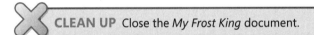

CLEAN UP Close the *My Frost King* document.

Add Headers and **Footers**

Headers and footers are areas at the top and bottom of a page in which you can insert additional information. For example, you might display a document's title, a company logo, or contact information in the header, and the page number in the footer. Other common footer content includes copyright and version information.

Every page of a document (other than the cover page) has an area at the top of the page that is designated for the header, and at the bottom of the page for the footer. In Print Layout view, you can edit the header or footer by double-clicking that area to activate it. In the active header or footer section, you can insert and format text and graphics.

When creating a header or footer, you can choose to have one that appears on all pages, one that is specific to the first page, one for odd-numbered pages and another for even-numbered pages, or some combination of these three options.

> **Tip** If your document contains section breaks, each successive section inherits the headers and footers of the preceding section unless you break the link between the two sections. If you do so, you can then create a different header and footer for the current section. For information about sections, see "Insert Page and Section Breaks" in Chapter 11, "Format Office File Content."

From the Document Elements tab of the Elements Gallery, you can insert any of three headers designed to display on all pages of a document, or any of 11 headers designed for display on every other page.

You can insert headers and footers from any location in a document. To insert a themed header or footer in a document, follow these steps:

1. Display the **Document Elements** tab of the Elements Gallery.

2. In the **Header** group or the **Footer** group, select from the **Insert as** list the pages you want the header or footer to appear on—**Even Pages**, **Odd Pages**, or **All Pages**.

   The available elements change to fit your selection.

> **Note** In general, Even Page content is aligned toward the left side of the page, and Odd Page content toward the right side of the page. This places information appropriately for double-sided documents.

3. In the **Header** gallery or **Footer** gallery, click the element you want to insert.

4. Scroll to a page displaying the header or footer, and replace any placeholders with the appropriate content.

> **Tip** While a header or footer is active for editing, the document text appears faded, to help draw your attention to the active document element. If you prefer to not see the document text at all while you're editing a header or footer, select the Hide Body Text check box in the Header And Footer panel of the Formatting Palette.

Insert and Format Page Numbers

If the only information you want to display in a header or footer is the page number, you can insert it by clicking Page Numbers on the Insert menu. In the Page Numbers dialog box, you can specify the position (Top or Bottom) and alignment (Left, Center, Right, Inside, or Outside) of the page numbers. You can select from various page number formats and set the starting page number.

If you want to use a numbering scheme other than arabic numerals, number pages by chapter, or control the starting number, you can do so by following these steps:

1. In the **Page Numbers** dialog box, click **Format**.

   The Page Number Format dialog box opens.

2. In the **Number format** list, click the number format you want.

3. If you want to precede page numbers with chapter numbers, select the **Include chapter number** check box and set the style and separator.

4. If you want to start at a page number other than 1, click **Start at** and enter the starting page number. Then click **OK**.

Practice Adding Headers and Footers

In this exercise, you'll add preformatted headers and footers to a document.

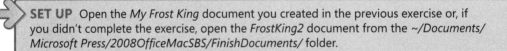

SET UP Open the *My Frost King* document you created in the previous exercise or, if you didn't complete the exercise, open the *FrostKing2* document from the *~/Documents/ Microsoft Press/2008OfficeMacSBS/FinishDocuments/* folder.

1. In Print Layout view, display page 2 of the document, and position the insertion point at the beginning of the first paragraph of the story.

   Page 1 is a cover page. The story starts on page 2.

2. Click the **Document Elements** tab of the Elements Gallery, and then click the **Header** category.

   The Header gallery opens, displaying thumbnails of some of the available preformatted headers. *Odd Pages* in the Insert As list indicates that these headers are specifically designed to appear on odd-numbered pages of a document. Notice that the page numbers—represented on the thumbnails by the number sign (#)— are all on the right side of these thumbnails.

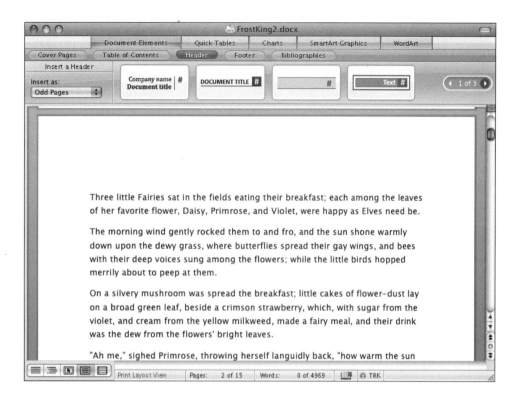

> **Tip** When printing a document double-sided, you can assign specific headers to odd and even pages to place information a reader might want to quickly see—such as page numbers—on the outside edge of every page. When flipping through a double-sided document (such as a book), a reader typically looks at the right page rather than the left page for reference information. For that reason, extra information is usually placed on odd-page headers rather than even-page headers.

3. In the **Insert As** list, click **Even Pages**.

The header thumbnails change to reflect the selected orientation. The content of the *Contrast* and *Edge* thumbnails, which on odd pages contain additional information, also changes.

4. Scroll through the gallery, noticing the variety of headers that are available, and then click the **Sideline (Even Page)** thumbnail.

> **Tip** As mentioned in earlier chapters, when you point to a thumbnail, the name of the associated gallery item appears in the style name area in the left pane of the gallery.

Word inserts the selected header at the top of page 2. The page number and the document title (which was saved with the document when it was entered on the cover page) appear automatically.

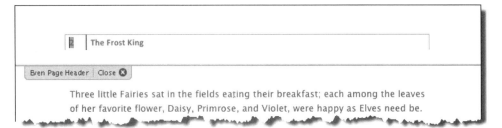

The text in the header is a different color from the text shown on the thumbnail in the Headers gallery, because headers and footers, like other document elements, adopt the color scheme associated with the current document theme.

See Also For more information about themes and color schemes, see "Work with Office Themes" in Chapter 7, "Work with Word Document Content."

5. In the **Insert as** list, click **Odd Pages**. Then, in the gallery, click the **Sideline (Odd Page)** thumbnail.

6. Display page 3, and verify that the matching odd-page header appears there.

7. In the **Document Elements** gallery, click the **Footer** category. Look at the footers available for odd pages (the current selection) and then, in the **Insert as** list, click **All Pages**.

The gallery displays the three footers available for all pages.

> **Note** The content in headers and footers designed for display on both odd pages and even pages is centered, rather than left- or right-aligned.

8. In the gallery, click the **Simple (All Pages)** thumbnail.

Word inserts the footer on all pages other than the cover page, and displays the first instance of it at the bottom of page 2.

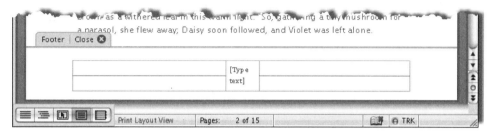

9. In the footer, click the **[Type text]** placeholder to select it. Then type Louisa May Alcott.

10. Display the **Formatting Palette** in the Toolbox. In the **Alignment and Spacing** panel, click the **Align Center** button.

Word centers the text you entered in the footer.

11. On the tab located at the upper-left corner of the footer, click **Close**. Click the **Document Elements** tab to close the Elements Gallery. Then scroll the document to view the finished headers and footers.

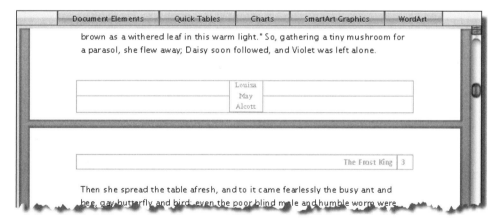

12. Save the document in the *FinishDocuments* folder as My Frost King. If you've been working in the *My Frost King* document from the previous exercise, replace it with this updated version.

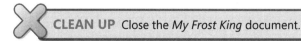

CLEAN UP Close the *My Frost King* document.

Add a Watermark to a Document

Sometimes, you might want words or a graphic to appear behind the text of a printed or online document. For example, you might want the word *CONFIDENTIAL* to appear faintly behind the text in a contract, or you might want a graphic to appear faintly behind the text in a press release. These faint background images are called *watermarks*. Watermarks are visible on-screen and in print, but because they are faint, they don't interfere with the readers' ability to view the document's main text.

To create a graphic watermark in a document:

1. On the **Insert** menu, click **Watermark**.

2. In the **Insert Watermark** dialog box, click **Picture**, and then click the **Select Picture** button.

3. In the **Choose a Picture** dialog box, navigate to and double-click the image file you want to display behind the document text.

   The preview pane displays a preview of the graphic as a watermark.

4. To display the graphic at its full color intensity, clear the **Washout** check box.

5. If you want the selected image to appear at a different scale than shown in the preview pane, change the percentage in the **Scale** box.

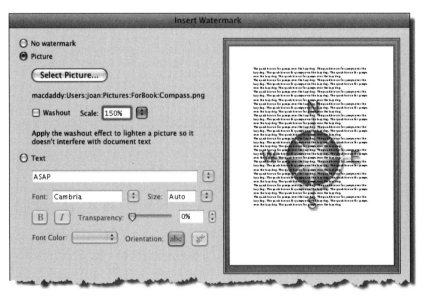

6. When you are satisfied with the preview, click **OK**.

To create an alphanumeric watermark in a document:

1. On the **Insert** menu, click **Watermark**.

2. In the **Insert Watermark** dialog box, click **Text**.

3. In the **Text** box, type the characters you want to display behind the document text.

   The preview pane displays a preview of the textual watermark.

4. Choose the font and font size. Apply bold and/or italic formatting if you want. Set the font color first, and then the transparency. Finally, choose horizontal or diagonal orientation.

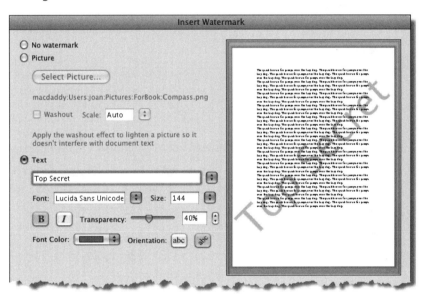

> **Note** You can choose to position the text horizontally or at a 45-degree angle, but not at any other orientation.

5. When you are satisfied with the preview, click **OK**.

See Also For information about using WordArt as a watermark, see "Add a Watermark to a Slide" in Chapter 10, "Work with PowerPoint Slide Content."

Create a Table of Contents

When working in a lengthy document, you can add a table of contents (TOC) to the beginning of the document to give your readers an overview of the document's contents and to help them navigate to specific sections.

In the TOC, you can indicate with a page number the starting page of each section. If the document is divided into sections by headings that are formatted with standard styles (Heading 1, Heading 2, and so on), the TOC can consist of an automatically generated list of the headings. If your document doesn't include headings, Word can generate a formatted table in which you can manually enter topics and page numbers.

To insert a table of contents, follow these steps:

1. Click to position the insertion point where you want to insert the TOC.

   > **Tip** If you want the TOC to appear on its own page, insert a page break *before* creating the table of contents, to ensure that the page numbers in the TOC are correct and remain that way.

2. Display the **Document Elements** tab of the Elements Gallery.

3. In the **Tables of Contents** group, with **Heading Styles** selected in the left pane, click the style of TOC that you want Word to generate from the document headings.

   Or

   With **Manual Formatting** selected in the left pane, click the style of TOC that you want to insert formatted placeholders for.

When you tell Word to create the table, Word identifies the TOC entries and inserts a frame containing the TOC. The frame is visible only when the TOC is active. You can move the TOC by dragging the frame's move handle (the three dots in the upper-left corner).

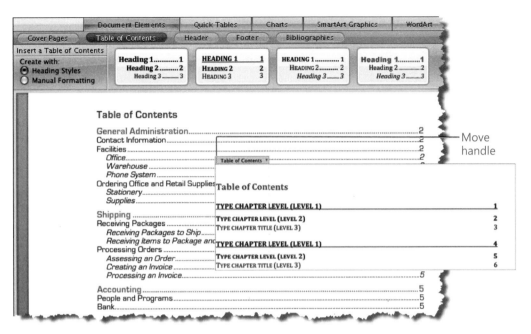

A TOC generated from headings, and the placeholders for a manually created TOC

The formatting of the entries in a TOC is controlled by nine levels of built-in TOC styles (TOC 1, TOC 2, and so on). By default, Word uses the styles that are assigned in the template attached to the document. If you want to use a different style, instead of clicking one of the standard options in the Table Of Contents gallery, you can click Index And Tables on the Insert menu. On the Table Of Contents tab of the Index And Tables dialog box, you can choose from several style variations, such as Classic, Modern, and Simple.

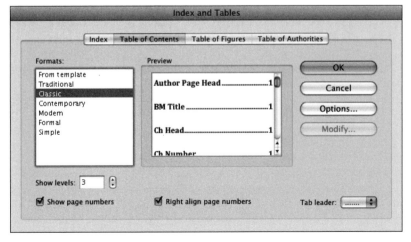

You can use the options in the Index And Tables dialog box to build a custom TOC.

To specify which styles the TOC contains, click the Options button. The Table Of Contents Options dialog box lists every paragraph style in the document. You simply place a number from 1 through 9 in the TOC Level box for any style you want to include in the TOC.

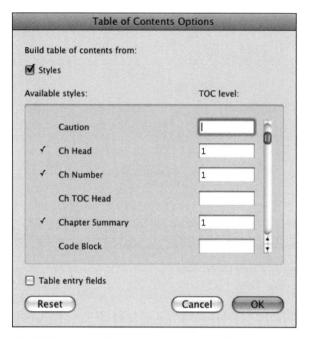

The TOC can include any style of paragraph in the document, organized in up to nine levels.

If you clear the Build Table Of Contents From check box and select the Table Entry Fields check box, Word builds the TOC based strictly on the nine standard heading levels.

> **Tip** If you create a TOC based on the document's template, you can customize the TOC styles during the creation process. On the Table Of Contents page of the Index And Tables dialog box, click Modify. The Style dialog box opens, displaying the nine TOC styles. You can modify the font, paragraph, tabs, border, and other formatting of these styles the same way you change any other style.

After you create a TOC, you can format it manually by selecting text and then apply-ing character or paragraph formatting or styles. You can edit the text of a TOC, but it is much easier to click the Update Table button and have Word do the work for you. You have the option of updating only the page numbers, or if you have changed, added, or deleted headings, you can update (re-create) the entire table.

Practice Creating Tables of Contents

In this exercise, you'll create a couple of different TOCs for a document, based on head-ing styles. Then you'll alter the document by inserting page breaks, and update the TOC to reflect your changes.

SET UP Open the *Contents* document from the *~/Documents/Microsoft Press/ 2008OfficeMacSBS/FinishDocuments/* folder. Display the document in Print Layout view.

1. Position the insertion point in front of the *General Administration* heading.

2. Click the **Document Elements** tab of the Elements Gallery, and then display the **Table of Contents** gallery.

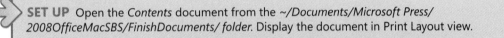

3. In the left pane of the **Table of Contents** gallery, click **Heading Styles** (if that option isn't already selected). Scroll the gallery if necessary, and then click the **Modern** thumbnail.

   After a short pause, Word inserts a TOC, with predefined styles, at the insertion point.

4. Scroll up to view the new TOC, and then point to any part of the table.

A pale pink background appears behind the TOC, indicating that this is a *field* rather than plain text.

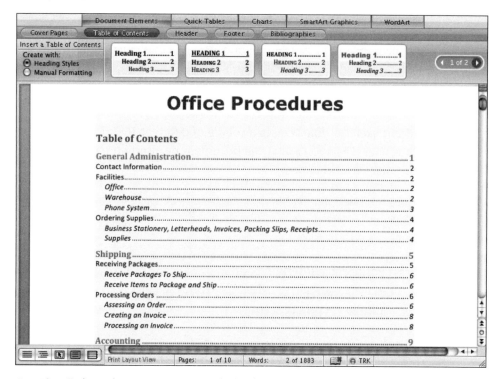

See Also To learn how to move to sections of the document from the TOC, see "Practice Creating Indexes" later in this chapter.

5. Click anywhere in the TOC.

   A border appears around the field contents. A tab containing a move handle and menu are in the upper-left corner of the field. The updatable field text is indicated by a gray background.

6. At the right end of the **Table of Contents** tab, click the arrow.

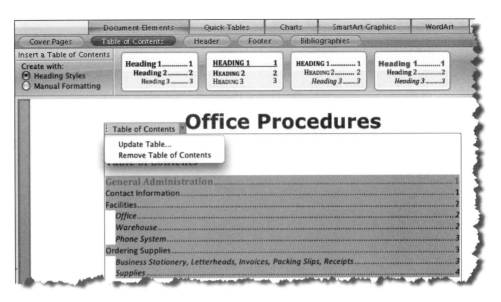

7. On the **Table of Contents** menu, click **Remove Table of Contents**.

   The TOC is deleted.

8. With the insertion point in front of the *General Administration* heading, point to **Break** on the **Insert** menu, and then click **Page Break**; or press **Shift+Enter** (the **Enter** key is on the numeric keypad).

   Word inserts a manual page break, and the General Administration heading moves to the next page.

   > **Note** When inserting a page break, Word also inserts two blank paragraphs, leaving a blank paragraph at the top of the new page.

   > **Tip** You can see manually inserted page breaks by displaying non-printing characters. To display non-printing and hidden characters, click the Show button on the Standard toolbar.

9. Press the **Up Arrow** key twice, to position the insertion point in front of the page break, immediately below the document title. Press **Return** to make space between the document title and the line on which you'll insert the new TOC.

10. On the **Insert** menu, click **Index and Tables**.

The Index And Tables dialog box opens.

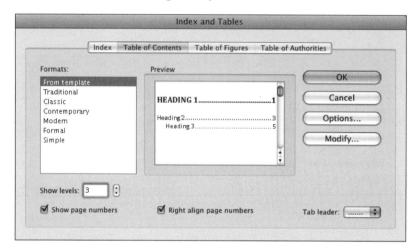

> **Note** If the Table Of Contents page of the dialog box is not displayed, click the Table Of Contents button at the top of the dialog box.

11. In the **Formats** pane, click **Classic**. In the **Show levels** list, click 2. In the **Tab leader** list, click **(none)**. Then click **OK**.

Word inserts a simple TOC displaying the page numbers of the first two levels of headings.

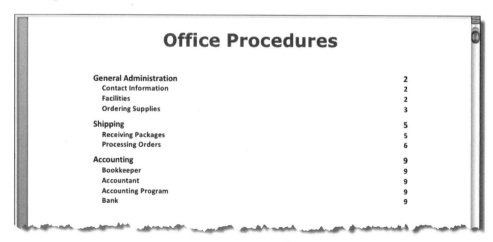

Notice that the TOC created from the Index And Tables dialog box doesn't include a title.

> **Tip** You can display *field codes*, rather than the calculated field contents, by pressing Option+F9.

12. Move to page 5, click at the beginning of the *Shipping* heading, and then press **Shift+Enter** to insert a page break.

The *Shipping* heading is now on page 6.

13. Move to page 9 and insert a page break before the *Accounting* heading to move it to the top of page 10.

14. Press **Command+Home** to return to the beginning of the document.

The page numbers in the TOC don't reflect the new page breaks.

15. Right-click anywhere in the TOC, and then click **Update Field**.

The Update Table Of Contents dialog box opens.

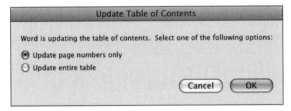

16. With the **Update page numbers only** option selected, click **OK**.

Word updates the TOC to reflect the new page numbers.

> **Tip** If you've added headings or other TOC elements to the document, choose the Update Entire Table option. Word regenerates the TOC rather than simply gathering current page numbers for the existing entries.

 CLEAN UP Close the *Contents* document without saving your changes.

Create an Index

To help readers find specific concepts and terms that might not be readily located by looking at a TOC, you can include an *index* at the end of a document. Word creates an index by compiling an alphabetical listing with page numbers based on *index entry fields* that you have marked in the document. As with a TOC, an index is inserted at the insertion point as a single field.

> **Tip** In documents that will be distributed electronically, readers can also use the Find feature to go directly to specific search terms.

In the index, an *index entry* might apply to a word or phrase that appears on a single page or is discussed for several pages. The entry might have related *subentries*. For example, the main index entry *shipping* might have below it the subentries *supplies*, *procedures*, and *packing*. An index might also include *cross-reference entries* that direct readers to related entries. For example, the main index entry *shipping* might have below it a cross-reference to *warehouse*.

checking customer credit. *See* credit
    checks
credit application, 7
credit card
    paying by. *See* payment methods
credit cards, 9
credit checks, 6
credit reference forms, 7

invoices
    for credit card payments, 9
    for personal checks, 11
    for purchase orders, 11
new customers, 6, 8
payment methods, 8
    credit cards, 9
    personal checks, 9

A simple index

To insert an index entry field in a document, you first display the Mark Index Entry dialog box. You can do this in one of two ways—by pressing Command+Option+Shift+X, or by following these steps:

1. On the **Insert** menu, click **Index and Tables**.

2. In the **Index and Tables** dialog box, click the **Index** tab.

3. Click **Mark Entry** to open the **Mark Index Entry** dialog box.

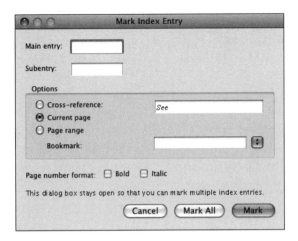

> **Tip** If, before you open the Mark Index Entry dialog box, you select text in the document that you want to mark as an index entry, that text will already appear in the Main Entry box.

From the Mark Index Entry dialog box, you can do any of the following:

- Add a main index entry or a subentry.

- Format the page number associated with that entry so that it appears in the index as bold, italic, or both.

- Designate an entry as a cross-reference, a single-page entry, or a page-range entry.

> **Tip** Cross-references appear in the index in the following format:
>
> *intercom. See phones*
>
> In this manner, you can direct readers to index terms that they might not think of when looking for specific information.

After you have set the options in the dialog box the way you want them, you can insert an index entry field adjacent to the selected text by clicking Mark, or adjacent to every occurrence of the selected text in the document by clicking Mark All. The Mark Index Entry dialog box remains open to simplify the process of inserting multiple index entry fields. You can move the dialog box off to the side so that it doesn't block the text you're working with.

> **Tip** When building an index, you should choose the text you mark carefully, bearing in mind what terms readers are likely to look up. For example, one reader might expect to find information about *cell phones* by looking under *cell*, whereas another might look under *mobile*, another under *phones*, and another under *telephones*. A good index will include all four entries.

Index entry fields are formatted as hidden; you can't see them unless you display hidden characters by clicking the Show button on the Standard toolbar. When an index entry field is visible, it appears in the document, enclosed in quotation marks within a set of braces, with the designator *XE* and a dotted underline.

Multiple index entries referencing the same location

Index entry

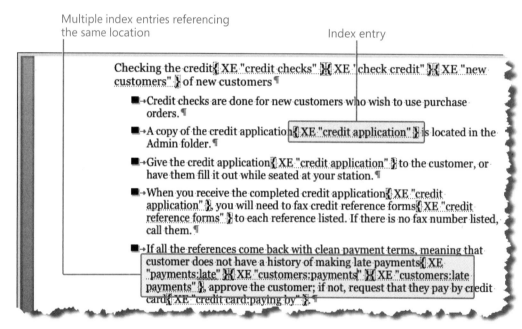

Insert multiple index entries to cover the many ways a reader might look for information.

> **Tip** You can hide any text in a document by selecting it, clicking Font on the Format menu, selecting the Hidden check box in the Font dialog box, and then clicking OK. When you print a document, Word doesn't print hidden text with the document unless you select the Hidden Text check box on the Print page of the Word Preferences dialog box. You can open this dialog box from within Word by clicking Preferences on the Word menu, or from the Print dialog box by clicking Word Options on the Microsoft Word page of the dialog box.

You can change the text of an index entry by editing the text within the quotation marks in the index entry field as you would any other. (You could also edit the text in the inserted index, but that change would not be permanent; regenerating the index or pulling index entry fields for another purpose would restore the original entry.) To delete an index entry, you select the entire hidden field and then press the Delete key. You can also move and copy index entries by using the techniques you would use for regular text.

> **Tip** Dragging through any part of an index entry field that includes one of the enclosing braces selects the entire field.

To create an index based on the index entries marked in a document, you position the insertion point where you want the index to appear, and then click Index And Tables on the Insert menu. From the Index page of the Index And Tables dialog box, you can specify the following:

- Whether the index formatting should use styles from the current template or be based on one of six predefined formats that you can preview in the Preview box.

- How many columns Word should create for the index. Because most index entries are very short, laying out an index in columns helps to evenly fill space on the page.

- Whether page numbers should be right-aligned, and if so whether they should have dotted, dashed, or solid *tab leaders*.

- Whether the index should be indented, with each subentry on a separate line below the main entries, or run-in, with subentries on the same line as the main entries.

- If your index terms include words beginning with accented letters, whether those should appear in a section specific to the accented letter rather than with the non-accented version.

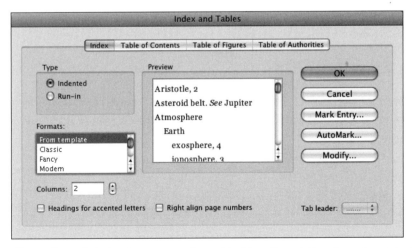

Choose from six index formats or a format built on the existing character styles in the document.

Clicking the Modify button opens a Style dialog box in which you can specify paragraph and character styling for each level of index entry. (Nine levels are available, but most indexes have only two or three.)

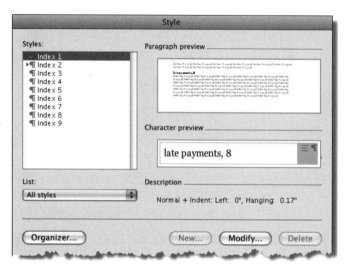

You can modify the appearance of each index entry level.

When you click OK in the Index And Tables dialog box, Word calculates the page numbers of all the entries and subentries, consolidates them, and inserts the index as a single field in the specified format at the specified location in the document. If the index is laid out in columns and the preceding (or following) content is not, the index will be set within its own section, with section breaks before and after it.

If you make changes to the document that affect its index entries or page numbering, you can update the index by right-clicking it and then clicking Update Field.

Practice Creating Indexes

In this exercise, you'll mark a few simple index entries and a cross-reference entry. Then you'll create and format an index, delete an index entry from the document, and update the index.

> **SET UP** Open the *Index* document from the *~/Documents/Microsoft Press/ 2008OfficeMacSBS/FinishDocuments/* folder.

1. In the TOC at the top of the document, point to the page number (2) following *Warehouse*.

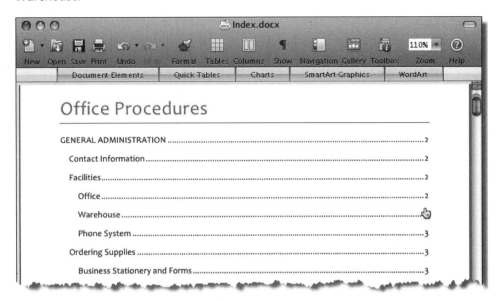

2. When the pointer changes to a pointing hand, click once to jump directly to the *Warehouse* heading at the top of page 3. Then on the Standard toolbar, click the **Show** button, to display hidden characters.

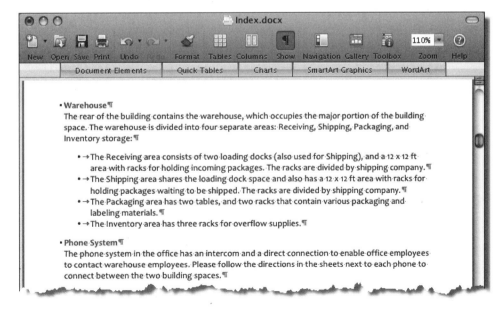

3. In the paragraph below the heading, select the word *Receiving*.

4. On the **Insert** menu, click **Index and Tables**. If the **Index** page isn't already displayed, click it.

The From Template format shown by default reflects the character formatting of the document.

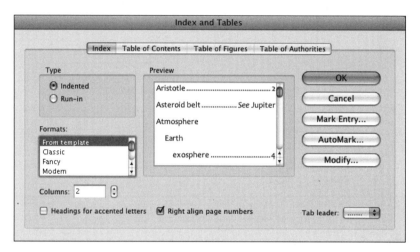

5. In the **Index and Tables** dialog box, click the **Mark Entry** button.

The Mark Index Entry dialog box opens. The selected text is already displayed in the Main Entry box.

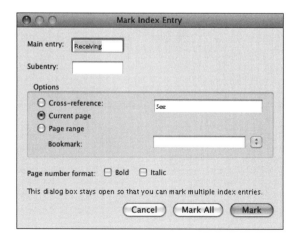

6. In the **Main entry** box, change *Receiving* to receiving (with a lowercase *r*). Then click **Mark All**.

> **Note** Index entries appear in the index exactly as they appear in the Mark Index Entry dialog box. For consistency, make all entries lowercase except those for proper nouns.

Word inserts hidden index entry fields adjacent to every occurrence of the word *Receiving* in the document.

> **Troubleshooting** The additional index entries might take some time to appear, or might appear only after you click around in the document. During the development of this exercise, additional entries consistently took a long time to appear; sometimes more than one minute. This seems to be a bug in the program.

> • Warehouse¶
> The rear of the building contains the warehouse, which occupies the major portion of the building space. The warehouse is divided into four separate areas: Receiving{XE "receiving"}, Shipping, Packaging, and Inventory storage:¶
>
> • →The Receiving{XE "receiving"} area consists of two loading docks (also used for Shipping), and a 12 x 12 ft area with racks for holding incoming packages. The racks are divided by shipping company.¶

> **Note** If this document contained instances of the word *receiving*, those would not be marked because their capitalization does not match the word you selected in step 6 (*Receiving*), even though you changed the index entry word to *receiving*.

7. Without closing the **Mark Index Entry** dialog box, select the word *Shipping* in the same paragraph.

8. Click anywhere in the **Mark Index Entry** dialog box to activate it.

Word automatically enters the selected text in the Main Entry box.

9. In the **Main entry** box, change the first letter of the word from uppercase to lowercase, and then click **Mark All**.

10. Repeat steps 7–9 for the words *Packaging* and *Inventory* in the same paragraph.

> **Troubleshooting** You might have to move the dialog box to see and select the words you want to mark.

11. In the paragraph under the next heading, *Phone System*, select the word *phone*. Change the entry in the **Mark Index Entry** dialog box to phones, and then click **Mark All**.

12. In the same paragraph, select the word *intercom*. In the **Mark Index Entry** dialog box, under **Options**, click **Cross-reference**.

The insertion point moves to the space after the word *See* in the adjacent box.

13. Without moving the insertion point, type phones.

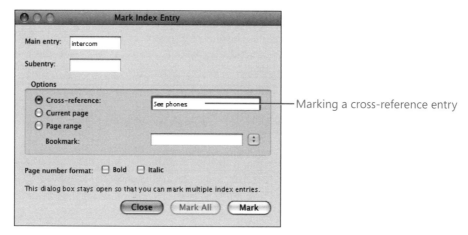
Marking a cross-reference entry

14. In the **Mark Index Entry** dialog box, click **Mark**.

A cross-reference to the *phones* index entry appears adjacent to the word *intercom*.

15. In the next heading, *Ordering Supplies*, select the word *Supplies*. In the **Mark Index Entry** dialog box, type ordering in the **Subentry** box, and then click **Mark**.

> **Troubleshooting** The index subentry functionality appears to have a bug. If you make a change to the word in the Main Entry box—for example, change the word or its case—and then move to the Subentry box, the main entry reverts to its original case. Steps 16–19 demonstrate a workaround to this, and will not be necessary if the bug is fixed in a service pack or other update released in the future.

Word creates an index entry/subentry pairing after the heading.

Subentry   Cross-reference entry

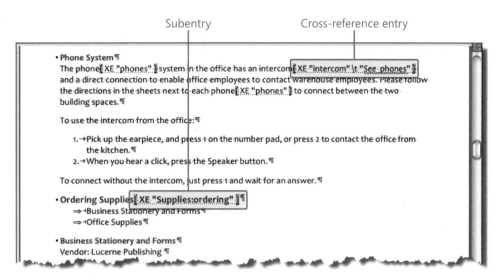

16. In the *Supplies:ordering* index entry you just created, replace the uppercase *S* with a lowercase s.

The capitalization of the main entry is now consistent with the *shipping* entry you created earlier.

17. Select the *{XE "supplies:ordering" }* entry, and then copy it to the Clipboard (by clicking **Copy** on the **Edit** menu or by pressing **Command+C**).

18. Move to the *Receiving Packages* heading near the top of page 6, (noting along the way the many index entries that you've created in the document). Position the insertion point after the word *Packages*, and then paste the copied index entry from the Clipboard.

19. In the second index entry, replace *ordering* with receiving.

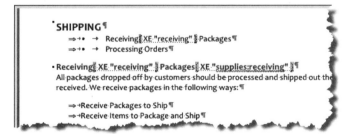

20. Close the **Mark Index Entry** dialog box.

21. Press **Command+End** to move to the end of the document, and then press **Shift+Enter** to insert a page break.

> **Tip** Use the Enter key on the numeric keypad, not the Return key. If your keyboard doesn't have an Enter key, point to Break on the Insert menu, and then click Page Break.

The insertion point moves to the top of the new page.

22. Type Index, and then press **Return** twice.

23. From the **Styles** panel of the Toolbox, apply the **Heading 1** style to the new heading. Then move to the second paragraph under the heading.

> **See Also** For information about applying heading styles, see "Work with Styles" in Chapter 7, "Work with Word Document Content."

24. On the Standard toolbar, click the **Show** button, to hide non-printing characters.

> **Tip** When hidden text is visible, the document might not be paginated correctly. Always turn off the display of non-printing characters before creating an index.

25. On the **Insert** menu, click **Index and Tables**.

The Index And Tables dialog box opens with the Index page active, because that was the most recent page displayed.

26. Make the following changes:

- In the **Columns** box, change the setting to **1**.
- In the **Formats** pane, click **Formal**.
- Clear the **Right align page numbers** check box.

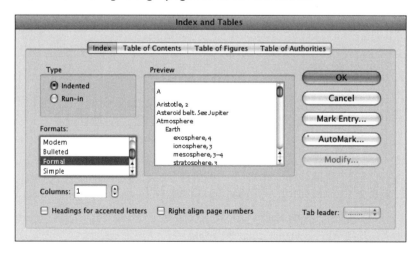

27. In the **Index and Tables** dialog box, click **OK**.

Word compiles a short index based on the few index entries you just marked. The index is formatted in one column with the page numbers adjacent to their index entries.

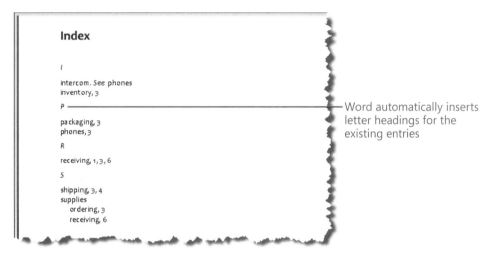

Index

I

intercom. *See* phones
inventory, 3

P ———————————————————— Word automatically inserts
letter headings for the
packaging, 3 existing entries
phones, 3

R

receiving, 1, 3, 6

S

shipping, 3, 4
supplies
ordering, 3
receiving, 6

28. Display non-printing characters, and then move to the *Phone System* heading on page 3.

29. Delete the entire *{XE "intercom" \t "See phones" }* cross-reference entry following *intercom*.

> **Tip** If you find it hard to select only the index entry, try pointing to the right of the closing brace (}) and dragging slightly to the left.

The cross-reference entry is deleted from the document.

30. Press **Command+End** to move to the end of the document.

31. Hide the non-printing characters. Then right-click the index, and click **Update Field**.

Word updates the index and removes the cross-reference.

CLEAN UP Save the *Index* document if you want to, and then close it. We won't be using Word again in this chapter, so if you aren't going to work in Word on your own, you can quit that program.

Create a Bibliography

A bibliography is a list of books, magazines, and other publications. You might use a bibliography to present a list of books and articles about a specific subject, a list of sources cited or quoted in a publication, or a list of sources consulted while preparing a document, book, or other text. Bibliographies are frequently required for school assignments, professional journal submissions, and scientific books.

Word 2008 automatically compiles a bibliography from the citations in a document. You insert citations from the Citations Manager palette of the Toolbox. First, you record information about the books or other sources you want to cite. Then you insert the citations into the document wherever necessary.

Bibliography citations follow one of a very few standard formats that are either required or appropriate for a given purpose. From Word 2008, you can create bibliographies that follow the American Psychological Association (APA), Chicago Manual of Style (Chicago), Modern Language Association of America (MLA), or Turabian style.

> **Note** Turabian style is based on the Chicago Manual of Style, and was developed by Kate Turabian for use in term papers, theses, and dissertations.

To record information about a citation source, follow these steps:

1. In the Toolbox, display the **Citations** palette.

2. If you want Word to show you the information required for a specific citation style, choose that style from the **Citation Style** list.

3. In the lower-left corner of the **Citations** palette, click the **Create New Source** button.

   In the Create New Source dialog box, information fields required for the currently selected citation style are indicated by asterisks. You won't be limited to citations of this style—the asterisks are only indicators of the information you would need if you were inserting a citation in this style.

4. Supply the necessary information (such as the author, title, and publisher of a book, or the title, director, and year of a film).

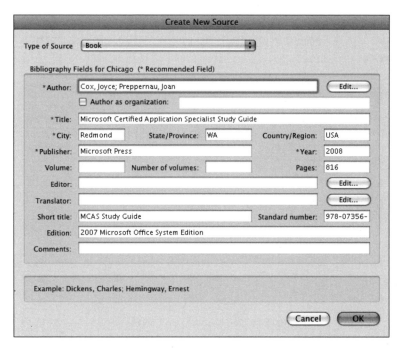

5. Click **OK** to display the citation in the **Citations Manager**.

To insert a citation reference into a document, follow these steps:

1. Position the insertion point in the citation location—usually immediately following the citation or in a footnote.

2. In the **Citations Manager**, select the citation style you want, and then double-click the source you want to cite.

   Word inserts the citation in the document. The inserted citation is not only text; it is an active field from which you can manage the citation and the source information.

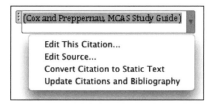

You can automatically generate a properly formatted bibliography that includes all the citations in a document from the Bibliographies group on the Document Elements tab of the Elements Gallery.

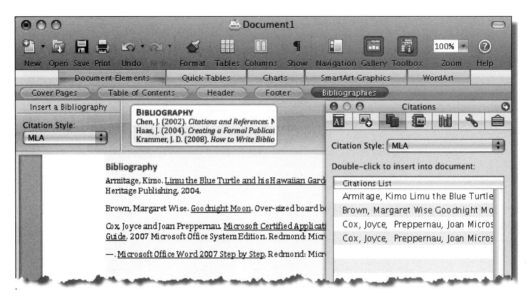

A typical bibliography generated from citations

To insert a bibliography into a document, follow these steps:

1. Position the insertion point at the end of the document or on a specific page you've chosen for the purpose.

2. Display the **Bibliography** group on the **Document Elements** tab of the Elements Gallery.

3. In the left pane, select from the list the citation style you want to use.

   The gallery thumbnails change to reflect the selected style.

4. In the gallery, click either the **Bibliography** thumbnail or the **Works Cited** thumbnail.

   Word inserts the citation references in the selected format.

Key Points

- Word 2008 for Mac includes 17 professionally designed cover pages that you can add to a document to give it a professional appearance.

- Every page of a document (other than the cover page) has an area at the top of the page that is designated for the header, and at the bottom of the page for the footer. You can insert text and graphics into the header and footer; either from the Elements Gallery or of your own design.

- If your document is long enough that it needs a table of contents to provide an overview and to identify specific sections, you can apply heading styles so that Word can create the TOC for you.

- By using the Bibliography feature of Word, you can track sources and compile a bibliography in the style you choose.

- Complex documents sometimes need an index to guide readers to discussions not easily located in a TOC. Word can use special hidden fields that you enter to create an index.

Part V
Stay In Touch and On Time

15 Communicate Online 469

16 Manage Contacts and Schedules 511

Chapter at a Glance

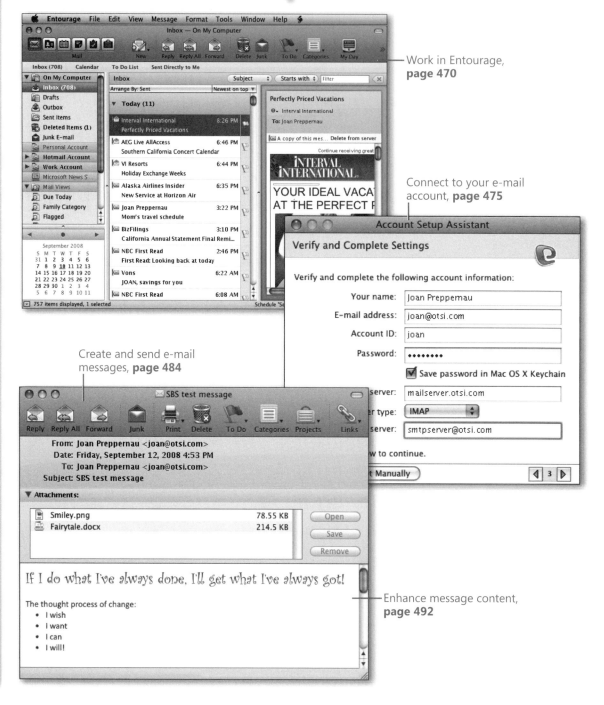

Work in Entourage, **page 470**

Connect to your e-mail account, **page 475**

Create and send e-mail messages, **page 484**

Enhance message content, **page 492**

15 Communicate Online

In this chapter, you will learn how to

- ✔ Work in Entourage.
- ✔ Personalize Entourage.
- ✔ Connect to your e-mail account.
- ✔ Create and send e-mail messages.
- ✔ Enhance message content.
- ✔ Reply to and forward messages.
- ✔ Delete messages.

Microsoft Entourage is an electronic communication and information management system designed specifically for the Mac. With Entourage 2008 for Mac, you can:

- Connect to multiple e-mail accounts.
- Send, receive, and manage e-mail messages.
- Store contact information for people and organizations.
- Keep track of appointments, meetings, and events.
- Store notes and general information.
- Keep track of tasks you need to do and your progress toward completing them.
- Centrally access messages and files related to a specific project.

Entourage 2008 for Mac represents a massive upgrade from the previous version, with lots of new features requested by users and, most importantly, a far more reliable and robust computing experience. The features we'll discuss in this chapter and the next are all part of the original release version of Entourage 2008. Historically, Microsoft has released a lot of program improvements through updates, so more upgrades might be on the way!

In this chapter, you'll learn about the Entourage program interface, and how to connect to your e-mail account. Then you'll learn about creating, sending, and managing e-mail messages.

See Also You can find handy keyboard shortcuts, simple instructions for performing common tasks, and other useful information in the Quick Reference section at the beginning of this book.

Practice Makes Perfect! The practice files you will use to complete the exercises in this chapter are in the *Communicate* practice file folder. See "Using the Companion Content" at the beginning of this book for information about installing and locating the practice files.

Work in Entourage

Entourage 2008 for Mac includes these six feature group modules:

- **Mail.** In this module, you display, organize, and manage received messages.
- **Address Book.** In this module, you manage contact information for people and groups.
- **Calendar.** In this module, you keep track of appointments, meetings, and all-day events.
- **Notes.** In this module, you store independent bits of information.
- **Tasks.** In this module, you keep track of things you need to do, when tasks need to be completed, and your progress toward completion.
- **Project Center.** In this module, you link Entourage items and files related to a specific project.

Only one of these modules is active within the Entourage program window at a time. You switch between modules by clicking the buttons that appear at the left end of the toolbar in every module.

Switch quickly between modules without losing your current view.

The Mail module is displayed by default each time you start the program.

The program window displays a different collection of tools for each module.

Certain program window features remain static regardless of the active module. These include:

- **Favorites Bar.** This bar provides quick links to specific views of your Entourage content. The default links are Inbox, Calendar, To Do List, and Sent Directly To Me. You can add a folder or view to the Favorites Bar by right-clicking it in the Folder list, and then clicking Add To Favorites Bar. You can remove a link by right-clicking the target folder or view, and then clicking Remove From Favorites Bar.

- **Content pane.** This view pane appears in the center of the window, and displays the content of the selected module—your e-mail messages, calendar, contacts, and other such content. You can sort and filter content within the pane.

- **Mini Calendar.** Located in the lower-left corner of the program window, this pane, which is available only when the Folder list is open, displays the calendar for the current month. You can move to other months by clicking the arrows on the left and right sides of the pane header, and return to the current month by clicking the dot in the center of the header. You can change the number of months displayed in the pane by dragging the horizontal divider at the top of the pane or the vertical divider on the right side of the pane.

> **Tip** Clicking the Expand/Collapse button at the left end of the status bar opens and closes the Mini Calendar.

- **Status bar.** Located at the bottom of the program window, the status bar displays statistics about the number of items displayed and selected in the current view, as well as notifications about upcoming program activities (such as the time until the next scheduled Send/Receive operation).

The following program window features are displayed by default in all modules, but change to reflect the module content:

- **Menu bar.** When working in the Entourage program window, you can access commands from the menus displayed here. The menu bar changes to display menus of commands relevant to the active module:

  - All modules include the Apple, Entourage, File, Edit, Format, Tools, Window, and Help menus.

  - The Mail, Notes, Tasks, and Project Center modules include View and Message menus.

  - The Address Book includes View and Contact menus.

  - The Calendar includes Calendar and Event menus.

  You can't hide the menu bar, but you can move it, docking it on any side of the program window or floating it anywhere on your screen.

● **Toolbar.** The Entourage program window has only one toolbar, but its contents change depending on the displayed module. The module buttons, Delete button, Categories list, and My Day button are displayed in all modules. You can hide or show the toolbar by clicking the Hide Toolbar Area button or by clicking Hide Toolbar or Show Toolbar on the View menu.

> **Tip** You can customize the toolbar in each module window by clicking Customize Toolbar on the View menu (or in the Calendar module, on the Calendar menu) and then, from the dialog box that appears, dragging commands to the toolbar. From this same dialog box, you can specify whether the toolbar should display the icon and text for each command (this is the default setting), the icon only, or the text only. When displaying the icon, you can choose the large version (the default) or the small version.

● **Quick Filter.** This area directly above the content pane provides a quick way to filter the module contents based on criteria such as subject, category, project, message sender or recipient, contact name, or task title or content.

● **Folder list.** This pane, which appears on the left side of the Entourage window, displays the module organizational structure and available filtered views. You can tailor the Folder list to suit your preferences:

   ● You can hide or show the pane by clicking **Hide Folder List** or **Show Folder List** on the **View** menu.

   ● You can change the width of the pane by dragging the vertical frame divider separating it from the content pane to its right.

   ● You can change the height of the pane by dragging the horizontal frame divider separating it from the Mini Calendar below.

● **Preview pane.** This pane displays the contents of a selected message or contact record. It is available in only the Mail module, in which you can display it to the right of or below the content pane, and the Address Book, in which you can display it below the content pane.

> **Tip** You might find that the default window arrangement is ideal for the way you work. But if you're viewing the program window on a low-resolution screen, don't need all the available tools, or would like more space for the main work area, you can display or hide workspace elements (other than the menu bar, which can't be changed) by using the commands on the View menu.

Personalize Entourage

As you can in other Office 2008 programs, you can change the way Entourage displays and handles information, from the Preferences dialog box.

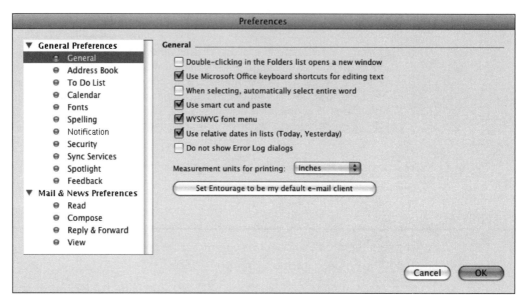

Oddball settings that don't fit in any other category are available from the General page of the Preferences dialog box.

You can specify your preferences for the following feature categories:

- **Address Book.** These settings pertain to the way Entourage formats addresses and phone numbers, whether to link contact records to messages sent to and received from contacts, and whether to color-categorize messages from contacts to match their contact records.

- **Calendar.** These settings govern the layout of the Calendar, how Entourage handles events, and the default reminder settings.

- **Fonts.** These settings control the font in which Entourage displays list items, HTML messages, and plain-text messages, and the font in which items are printed.

- **General.** These are the random settings that don't fit into any of the other categories. These settings govern the behavior of the Folder list, keyboard shortcuts, editing tools, font menu, dates, error logs, and units of measurement. In addition, from this page you can set Entourage as your default mail client, meaning that when you choose an option in another program to send something from that program, an Entourage message window will open.

- **Notification.** These settings govern whether a *desktop alert* appears when you receive a new mail item, and what information appears in the alert. You can also specify whether to sound audio alerts when you start Entourage, when new mail items arrive, when you send mail, when the mail system encounters an error, when Entourage checks for new mail items and there are none, and when reminders (for example, for appointments and tasks) appear.

- **Security.** These settings help to protect you from external threats. The default, most secure settings display warnings when an external application tries to send mail or access your Address Book, do not allow the display of complex HTML in messages, and do not download pictures in messages without your explicit approval, on a message-by-message basis.

- **Spelling.** These settings govern the behavior of the built-in spelling checker. You can turn the spelling checker on or off, check the spelling in all outgoing e-mail messages, display or restrict suggested corrections, and ignore certain types of text. You can also choose the dictionary language you want, from among 17 options.

- **Spotlight.** From this setting group, you can opt to include Entourage items (turned on by default) and attachments (turned off by default) in Spotlight search results. If Spotlight is having trouble locating Entourage items, you can rebuild the Entourage index that Spotlight references to quickly locate content.

- **Sync Services.** From this setting group, you can establish synchronization of your Entourage contacts, events, tasks, or notes with the .Mac system, the Mac Address Book, and the iCal tool, as appropriate.

- **To Do List.** These settings govern the default due date, reminder time, and reminder snooze time for new tasks.

In addition, you can specify preferences for the way Entourage displays mail messages and newsgroup items, and the way it performs when you are reading, composing, or responding to messages and newsgroup items.

To display the Entourage Preferences dialog box, click Preferences on the Entourage menu, or press Command+Comma.

Connect to Your E-Mail Account

You can connect to multiple accounts, and to multiple types of accounts, from Entourage 2008. If you're running the standard or Special Media Edition of Office 2008, you can connect to an *IMAP*, a *POP*, a Windows Live Hotmail, or a Microsoft Exchange Server account.

Work with Exchange Accounts

If you purchased Entourage as part of the Microsoft Office 2008 Home & Student Edition, you can't connect to an Exchange account by specifying it as such. However, if your Exchange mailbox is set up to allow IMAP and/or POP access, you can connect to the account by using that protocol. Connecting to an Exchange account through the IMAP protocol provides the structure and some of the functionality of the standard Exchange connection, but you won't be able to use any Exchange-related features, such as:

- Public folders
- Shared e-mail folders
- The Global Address List
- The Out of Office Assistant

Your Exchange administrator can provide you with alternative-protocol connection information.

If you previously connected to an Exchange account with another edition of Office for Mac, and you then install Office 2008 Home & Student Edition, you'll still be able to see the information that was in your Exchange account before you installed the Home & Student Edition, but you won't be able to work with it. If you later install the standard or Special Media Edition, the Exchange functionality will be restored to the already configured account.

You can configure Entourage to connect to an e-mail account by completing an interview process in the Account Setup Assistant or, if you're comfortable with the process of configuring an e-mail program, you can perform the configuration manually. The automatic setup functionality provided by the Account Setup Assistant is very convenient. In most cases, the only information you need is your e-mail address and password.

Before connecting from Entourage to an e-mail account, you will need to know the e-mail address, the account ID, and the account password. In addition:

- For IMAP and Exchange accounts, you'll need the incoming server name.
- For IMAP and POP accounts that use a separate *SMTP* server to process outgoing mail, you'll need to know the outgoing server name. If the outgoing server requires different *credentials*, you'll need the account ID and password for that server.

To configure a connection from Entourage to an e-mail account, by using the Account Setup Assistant:

1. On the **Tools** menu, click **Accounts**.

   The Accounts dialog box opens.

   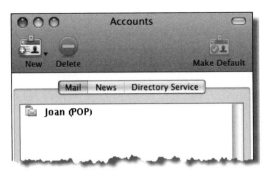

2. In the **Accounts** dialog box, click the **New** button, and then click **Mail** (or, to connect to an Exchange account, click **Exchange**).

   The Account Setup Assistant starts, and displays the Set Up A Mail Account page.

   > **Troubleshooting** If the New Account dialog box opens, click the Setup Assistant button.

3. In the **E-mail address** box, enter the e-mail account you want to connect to.

4. Click the **Next** button to submit the account for automatic configuration.

If Entourage successfully connects to the account without additional information, the Automatic Configuration Succeeded page appears.

If Entourage requires additional information to connect to the account, the Automatic Configuration Failed page appears.

5. If the automatic configuration was successful, click the **Next** button to display the **Verify and Complete Settings** page. Verify your name and e-mail address, and enter the password required to access the account.

Selecting the Save Password check box saves the password for automatic login.

6. If the automatic configuration was *not* successful, click the **Next** button to display a more complete version of the **Verify and Complete Settings** page. Enter the information required to access the account.

7. Click the **Next** button to display the **Optional: Verify Settings** page, and then click the **Verify My Settings** button.

    Entourage tests the connection to the account and reports the results.

8. If the verification fails, click the **Back** button to return to the **Verify and Complete Settings** page. The settings that failed verification are now indicated in red. Correct the information in these fields, and then click the **Next** button to return to the **Optional: Verify Settings** page.

9. After the verification succeeds, click the **Next** button to display the **Setup Complete** page. Enter the name by which you want to identify the account. If you want the account to appear in your Entourage contact record, and to be updated at regular intervals with other accounts, leave the check boxes selected; otherwise, clear the ones you don't want to apply. Then click **Finish**.

Entourage adds the newly configured account to the Accounts dialog box, creates a folder for the account in the Folder list, and creates the appropriate subfolders.

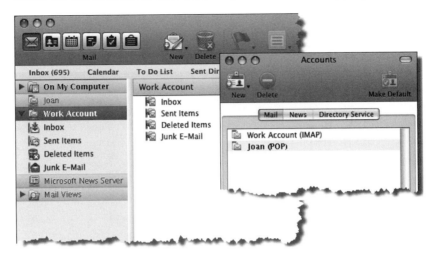

> **Tip** Each type of e-mail account other than POP has a specific base set of subfolders. (A POP account uses the folder structure under the On My Computer heading.) A Windows Live Hotmail account has Inbox, Sent Items, Deleted Items, and Junk E-Mail folders. An IMAP account has a Drafts folder in addition to the four basic folders. An Exchange account also has Calendar, Contacts, Journal, Notes, Outbox, RSS Feeds, Sync Issues, and Tasks folders.

To manually configure a connection from Entourage to an e-mail account:

1. On the **Tools** menu, click **Accounts**, and then click the **New** button (not its arrow).

   The New Account dialog box opens.

   > **Troubleshooting** If the Set Up A Mail Account dialog box opens, click the Configure Account Manually button.

2. In the **Account type** list, click the type of account you want to connect to (**POP,** **IMAP, Exchange,** or **Windows Live Hotmail**). Then click **OK.**

The Edit Account dialog box opens.

3. Enter the requested information in the dialog box.

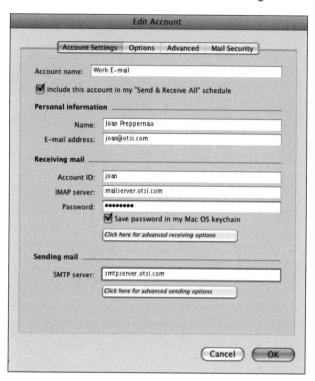

4. If your incoming server requires special information, click the **Click here for advanced receiving options** button in the **Receiving mail** section to display a box of options specific to the incoming server. Select the check boxes that are pertinent to your account, and then close the box.

Close button

☐ This IMAP service requires a secure connection (SSL)
☐ Override default IMAP port: 143
☐ Always use secure password

5. If your outgoing server requires special information, click the **Click here for advanced sending options** button in the **Sending mail** section to display a box of options specific to the outgoing server. Select the check boxes that are pertinent to your account, provide any additional information that is requested, and then close the box.

SMTP service requires secure connection (SSL)
Override default SMTP port: 25
SMTP server requires authentication
  ○ Use same settings as receiving mail server
  ● Log on using
  Account ID: [   ]
  Password: [   ]
    ☐ Save password in my Mac OS keychain
Domain for unqualified addresses:
[   ]

6. In the **Edit Account** dialog box, click **OK**.

After you connect to an account, a corresponding account group appears in the Folder list. If the account is an Exchange, IMAP, or Windows Live Hotmail account, the account folders appear under the account group.

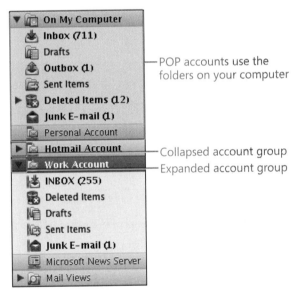

POP accounts use the folders on your computer

Collapsed account group

Expanded account group

Each account you connect to is available from the Folder list.

You can collapse or expand an account header by clicking the arrow to the left of the account name. Clicking the header itself displays the base content of the account in the content pane. For a POP account, the base content consists of messages. For other types of accounts, the base content is the folder structure—the same structure that appears when you expand the account group header.

Create and Send E-Mail Messages

Although Entourage is a full-service information management program, your primary use of it will probably be for e-mail. Regardless of the type of e-mail account you have (Exchange, IMAP, POP, or Windows Live Hotmail), as long as you have an Internet connection, you can send e-mail.

Address Messages

Addressing an e-mail message is as simple as typing the intended recipient's e-mail address into the To, Cc, or Bcc box. To determine the correct box, consider whether you want to send a message to more than one person, indicate a different level of involvement for certain recipients, or include certain people without other recipients knowing.

As you type a name or an e-mail address into the To, Cc, or Bcc box, Entourage searches the Address Book and your received mail for matching names or e-mail addresses, and displays them in a list below the box. If a name or address match is found, select it from the list, and then press Tab or Return to insert the entire name or address in the box.

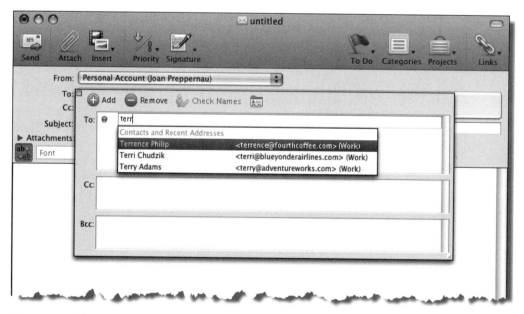

When you address a message, Entourage displays a list of possible address matches.

> **Tip** You can address a message sent from an Exchange account to another person on the same Exchange network by typing only his or her e-mail alias (the first section of the e-mail address)—the at symbol (@) and domain name aren't required.

To send a message to multiple recipients, separate their addresses with commas or press Return after each address to place the next recipient on a separate line of the address box.

To send a courtesy copy of a message to people, enter their addresses in the Cc box. This is commonly referred to as "CCing" a person. You might CC people to provide them with information but indicate that you don't require their involvement in the conversation.

To send a message to people without making it known to other recipients, enter their e-mail addresses in the Bcc box to send a "blind" courtesy copy (also known as "BCCing"). Addresses entered in the Bcc box can't be seen by other message recipients. They also aren't included in any replies to the original message. The Bcc field doesn't appear in the message header, but it's available from the pop-up box that appears when you click the To or Cc box.

> **Note** If you send a message with invalid or unresolved e-mail addresses among the recipients, Entourage delivers the message to the valid recipients, and eventually returns a failure notice listing the addresses the message couldn't be delivered to.

Attach Files

You can send files—Office files or other types of files—to people as message attachments. Most e-mail programs can receive message attachments. Some programs and *spam filters* will block attachments that could present a threat to the recipient's computer, such as executable files (.exe files) that might contain viruses or worms.

To attach a file to an outgoing message:

1. On the toolbar, click the **Attach** button.
2. In the **Choose Attachment** dialog box, select the file you want to attach, and then click **Open**.

Attached files are listed in the message header. You can expand the Attachments section to view more information about files and control settings related to the attachments.

Save Message Drafts

Until you save or send a message, it is only a temporary item. If you close the message before sending it, or close the program before sending the message, Entourage gives you the option of saving a copy of the message in your Drafts folder.

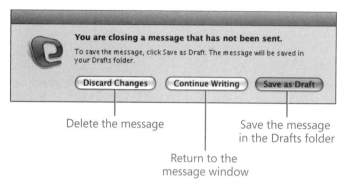

Delete the message — Discard Changes

Return to the message window — Continue Writing

Save the message in the Drafts folder — Save as Draft

Entourage prompts you to save drafts of unsent messages.

To restart work on a draft message, display the Mail module, click the Drafts folder in the Folder list, and double-click the message you want to open. Complete the message content, and then send the message as described in the following section.

Send Messages

If your profile includes multiple e-mail accounts, you can specify the account you want to use each time you send an e-mail message, by selecting the account in the From list, at the top of the message header. The From list is visible only when multiple accounts are configured within a profile.

 To send a message, click the Send button on the toolbar. And voila! You have communicated with the outside world!

Practice Creating and Sending E-Mail Messages

In this exercise, you'll compose an e-mail message, attach a file to it, and then send the message.

SET UP Start Entourage and configure your e-mail account. Display the Inbox that appears in the On My Computer group in the Folder list. We'll use the *Fairytale* document and the *Smiley* graphic in this exercise, from the *~/Documents/Microsoft Press/2008OfficeMacSBS/ Communicate/* folder.

Troubleshooting If you haven't configured an account that receives mail in the On My Computer group, you can perform this exercise in another account group without a problem. However, in the final exercise in this chapter, "Practice Deleting Messages," the process of setting up a schedule to automatically empty your Deleted Items folder will not work.

1. On the toolbar, click the **New Mail Message** button.

   A new message window opens, with the address box expanded.

   Tip Clicking the New arrow, rather than the button, displays a list of Entourage items. You can create any type of item, including messages, calendar events, tasks, notes, contact records, and groups, from the New list in any module.

2. In the **To** box, type your own e-mail address, and then press the **Return** key.

   The address box closes and the insertion point moves to the Subject box.

3. In the **Subject** box, type SBS test message. Then press **Return** to move to the content pane.

   Note The subject of this message begins with *SBS* so that you can easily differentiate it from other messages in your Inbox and Sent Items folders.

4. In the content pane, type If I do what I've always done, I'll get what I've always got! and press **Return** twice. Then type the following phrases, pressing **Return** once after each of the first four phrases (but not the last):

   The thought process of change:

   I wish

   I want

   I can

   I will!

5. Select the last four phrases (those beginning with the word *I*). Then, on the toolbar in the message header, click the **Bullets** button.

   Entourage converts the list of names to a simple bulleted list.

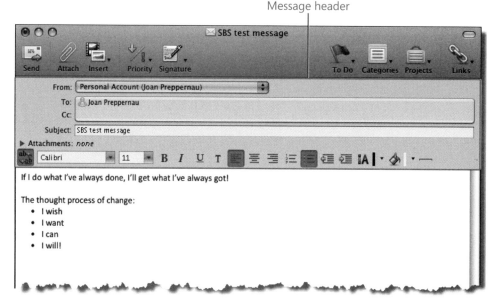

6. Press **Command+A** to select all the message content.

7. On the message header toolbar, click the **Font Color** arrow (not the button). Then in the **Font Color** list, click **Purple**.

   The color of the message text changes.

> **Note** Clicking Other at the bottom of the Font Color list displays the Colors dialog box. For information about the individual pages of the Colors dialog box, see "Practice Formatting Characters" in Chapter 11, "Format Office File Content."

8. Select only the first sentence. On the message header toolbar, in the **Font** list, click **Curlz MT**. In the **Font Size** list, click **18**. Then press the **Home** key to release the selection and display the results of your work.

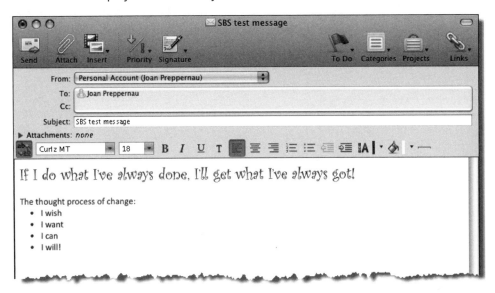

9. On the message window toolbar, click the **Attach** button.

The Choose Attachment dialog box opens.

10. Navigate to the *~/Documents/Microsoft Press/2008OfficeMacSBS/Communicate/* folder, click the *Smiley* image, and then click **Open**.

In the message header, the name of the attached file appears to the right of the Attachments label.

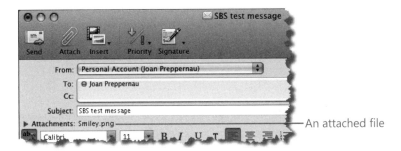

An attached file

11. Repeat step 10 to insert the *Fairytale* document. Then click the right-pointing triangle to the left of the **Attachments** label to expand the section.

The expanded list displays the file icon, name, and size of each attachment. You can add more attachments by clicking the Add button, or remove an attachment by clicking it and then clicking the Remove button.

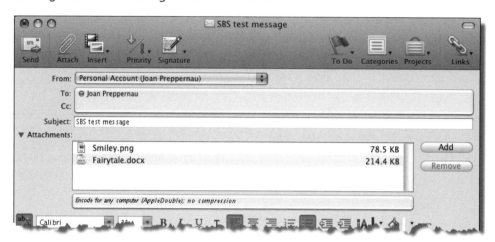

The box below the list displays the current encoding and compression settings for the attachments.

12. Just below the **Attachments** list, click the box to display the attachment options.

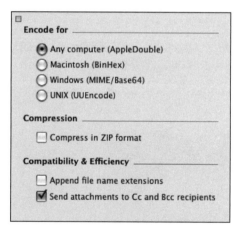

13. Review the **Encode for**, **Compression**, and **Compatibility & Efficiency** options you can set, and then close the box.

14. On the message toolbar, click the **Send** button.

Entourage closes the message window, encodes the attachments according to the specified settings, and moves the message to your Outbox. The next time Entourage sends and receives messages, this message appears in your Inbox.

See Also For information about the Entourage send/receive schedule, see the sidebar "Schedule Actions to Occur Automatically" later in this chapter.

When the message arrives in your Inbox, the icons in the message header give you information about the message and its contents, including the sender's name, the message subject, and the time you received the message. The paperclip indicates that the message has one or more attachments. The flag button at the right end of the message header is currently inactive (indicated by its gray color).

Message header   Preview pane

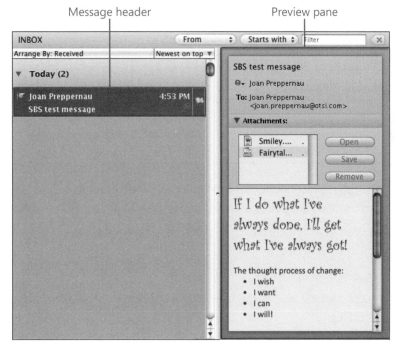

See Also For information about message flags, see "Flag Items for Follow Up" in Chapter 16, "Manage Contacts and Schedules."

The message contents are shown in the Preview pane. You can read the message and manage the attachments directly from the Preview pane, or you can double-click the message header to open the message in its own window.

> **Tip** If the Preview pane is not open, point to Preview Pane on the View menu, and then click On Right.

 CLEAN UP Keep the test message for use in the next exercise.

Enhance Message Content

You can personalize your outgoing messages in many ways, including the following:

- You can select the font, font style, and font color.

- You can format the text of your message to make it more readable by including headings and numbered or bulleted lists.

- You can format the background with a color or picture. (However, these won't always appear to e-mail recipients as you intend them to, and they can make your communications appear less professional.)

> **Tip** When you insert a background picture, Entourage tiles the picture to cover the entire message background. If your background picture isn't quite subtle, the tiled background will overwhelm the text of the message.
>
> After you insert a background picture, you can't remove it by clicking the Undo button. Instead, you have to click Remove Background Picture on the Message menu.

- You can represent information graphically by including charts you create in Microsoft Excel 2008 and tables you create in Microsoft PowerPoint 2008.

- You can insert clip art images, symbols, pictures, and other graphics from the Object Palette of the Toolbox.

- You can insert pictures, sounds, and movies directly into the message.

- You can attach files to the message and link the message to other Entourage items or to files.

- You can insert your contact information, or another message you want to deliver consistently, in the form of an *e-mail signature*.

While you're crafting a message, you can validate the words and phrases in the message by using the reference tools that are available in all the Office 2008 programs.

See Also For information about the Reference Tools palette, see "Research Words and Phrases" later in this topic.

Format Message Text

By default, the content of an Entourage message appears in black, 11-point Calibri (a very readable *sans serif* font), arranged in left-aligned paragraphs on a white background. You can change the appearance of a message by applying *local formatting* (text or paragraph attributes).

> **Note** You can't apply global formatting, such as themes and styles, to Entourage items.

The local formatting options available in Entourage 2008 are a subset of those available in other Office 2008 programs; if you've already worked through earlier chapters of this book, you're probably very familiar with them. Here's a quick review of the types of formatting changes you can make:

- **Font, size, and color.** More than 100 fonts in a range of sizes and in a virtually unlimited selection of colors.
- **Font style.** Regular, bold, italic, underlined, or fixed-width font.
- **Paragraph attributes.** Alignment and indentation.
- **List formats.** Numbered or bulleted lists.

Research Words and Phrases

The Entourage Toolbox includes only the Scrapbook palette, the Reference Tools palette, and the Object Palette. These function in Entourage the same way they do in other Office 2008 programs. We haven't yet discussed the reference tools, which are quite handy when you're composing an e-mail message or creating a Word document.

See Also For information about the Scrapbook, see "Edit Document Text" in Chapter 7, "Work with Word Document Content." For information about the Object Palette, see "Insert and Modify Shapes" in Chapter 12, "Create and Insert Graphics."

The Reference Tools palette provides easy access to the following reference tools:

- A thesaurus in which you can look up meanings and synonyms (alternative words) for a word or phrase.
- The Microsoft Encarta encyclopedia in which you can look up extensive information, in English or French, about a subject. The encyclopedia includes links to articles and resources on the Web.
- A dictionary providing definitions for English, French, German, Japanese, and Spanish words (not phrases).
- A multilingual dictionary providing definitions in Simplified Chinese, Traditional Chinese, English, French, German, Italian, Japanese, Korean, or Spanish for words (not phrases) in any of those languages.

> **Note** This is actually labeled in the Reference Tools palette as a *bilingual* dictionary, but it provides information in many more than two languages!

● A translation service (provided by an outside company named *WorldLingo*) that provides computer-generated translations into Simplified Chinese, Traditional Chinese, Dutch, English, French, German, Greek, Italian, Japanese, Korean, Portuguese (Brazilian), Russian, or Spanish for words or phrases in any of those languages. From the Translation panel, you can also link to information about a variety of translation services on WorldLingo's Web site.

You can display reference information for a word or phrase by entering it in the Search box at the top of the palette and then pressing Return. The available information appears in each panel of the palette.

To research alternatives for a word by using the thesaurus:

1. In the **Reference Tools** palette of the Toolbox, expand the **Thesaurus** panel.

2. In the Search box at the top of the palette, enter the word or phrase you want to look up, and then press **Return**.

   Available definitions of the word or phrase appear in the Meanings list. Alternative words for the selected meaning appear in the Synonyms list.

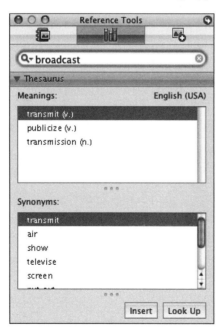

3. In the **Meanings** list, click the meaning that is most representative of the meaning you want to convey.

The Synonyms list changes to display alternatives for the selected meaning.

4. To further research a suggested synonym, click the word or phrase, and then click the **Look Up** button.

5. To insert a synonym from the list into the open message or document, click the word or phrase, and then click the **Insert** button.

> **Note** The selected synonym is inserted at the insertion point or, if text is selected, in place of the selected text.

To translate a word or phrase into another language:

→ Right-click the word, or select and right-click the phrase, and then click **Translate**.

Or

1. In the **Reference Tools** palette of the Toolbox, expand the **Translation** panel.

2. In the **Translation** panel, choose the original language in the **From** list, and the language you want to translate to in the **To** list.

3. In the Search box at the top of the palette, enter the word or phrase you want to translate, and then press **Return**.

Create E-Mail Signatures

When you create a paper-based message, you can add a signature at the end of the message by writing your name. When you create an e-mail message, you can add a *signature* at the end of the message by manually or automatically inserting a predefined block of information. An e-mail signature provides consistent information to message recipients. Your signature can include text, background pictures, inline pictures, graphics from the Object Palette, sounds, and even movies. You would commonly include your name and contact information but, depending on your needs and wants, you might also include information such as your company name, job title, a legal disclaimer, a corporate or personal slogan, or a photo.

You can create different signatures for use in different types of messages. For example, you might create a formal business signature for client correspondence, a casual business signature for interoffice correspondence, and a personal signature for messages sent from a secondary account. Or you might create a signature containing more information to send with original e-mail messages, and a signature containing less information to send with message replies. You can format the text of your e-mail signature in the same ways that you can format message text.

To create an e-mail signature:

1. On the **Tools** menu, click **Signatures**. Then in the **Signatures** dialog box, click the **New** button.

   An *Untitled* window opens.

2. In the **Name** box, enter a name by which you will identify this signature (such as Home, Work, Soccer Club, or whatever purpose the signature represents) and then press the **Tab** key to move to the content box.

   The window title changes to reflect the signature name.

3. In the content box, enter the text of your e-mail signature. Apply formatting by using the commands available on the toolbar above the content box.

4. If you want to insert a picture, background picture, sound, or movie into the signature, point to **Insert** on the **Message** menu, and then click the type of item you want to insert. In the **Choose a File** dialog box that opens, select the specific item, and then click **Choose**.

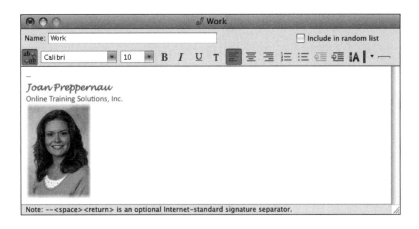

> **Note** You don't have much control over graphic elements after they're inserted into the signature content box. You can't resize or otherwise format the graphic, so be sure to take care of formatting issues before inserting it.

5. Close the signature window. If Entourage displays a dialog box prompting you to save the signature, click **Save**.

> **Note** If you previously dismissed the dialog box by selecting the Always Save Changes Without Asking check box, Entourage will automatically save your changes without prompting you to confirm them.

You can manually insert any signature you create in an e-mail message, but it's more common to instruct Entourage to automatically insert it for you. You do this individually for each e-mail account.

To specify a signature to be inserted on all new messages sent from a specific account:

1. Open the **Edit Account** dialog box by using one of these methods:

   → In the Folder list, right-click the account header, and then click **Edit Account**.

   → On the **Tools** menu, click **Accounts**. Then in the **Accounts** dialog box, double-click the account name.

2. In the **Edit Account** dialog box, display the **Options** page.

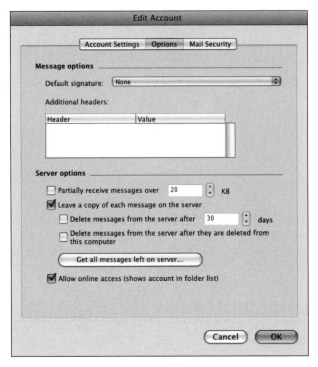

3. In the **Default signature** list, click the signature you want to appear at the bottom of each new message sent from this account. Or, if you're feeling a bit wild, click **Random** to have Entourage select one for you from a list of signatures you've designated for this purpose.

4. In the **Edit Account** dialog box, click **OK**.

   Entourage will now insert your signature into all e-mail messages, including replies and messages you forward, that you send from this account.

Tip You can remove the automatically inserted signature from a message by selecting and deleting it as you would any other text.

Reply To and Forward Messages

You can reply to or forward most e-mail messages that you receive by clicking the Reply, Reply To All, or Forward button either within the message window or on the Standard toolbar. When you reply to a message, Entourage fills in the To and Cc boxes for you, addressing the response either to only the original message sender or to the message sender and all other people to whom the message was addressed or copied (the recipients listed in the To and Cc boxes), depending on the reply option you choose. Entourage does not include recipients of blind courtesy copies (Bcc recipients) in message replies. You can add, change, and delete recipients from any reply before sending it.

To include all recipients of a message in your reply, click the Reply To All button. Entourage addresses your reply to the original message sender and any recipients listed in the To box of the original message, and sends a copy to any recipients listed in the Cc box of the original message.

Similarly, you can forward a received message to any e-mail address (regardless of whether the recipient uses Entourage) provided that the message was not sent with restricted permissions. When you forward a message, Entourage does not fill in the recipient boxes for you.

When responding to an e-mail message, take care to use good e-mail etiquette. For example, don't forward messages containing large attachments to people with low-bandwidth connections who don't need the attachment. If your response is not pertinent to all the original recipients of a message, don't reply to the entire recipient list, especially if the message was addressed to a distribution list that might include hundreds of members.

> **Tip** A simple way to prevent people from replying to multiple message recipients is to address the message to yourself and send blind courtesy copies to all other recipients. Then the recipient list will not be visible to anyone.

If the original message contains one or more attachments, be aware that replies do not include attachments, and forwarded messages do.

If you reply to or forward a received message from within the message window, the original message remains open after you send your response.

Practice Responding to Messages

In this exercise, you'll reply to and forward the message you sent to yourself in the previous exercise.

> **SET UP** In this exercise, you'll work with the *SBS test message* you created in the previous exercise. If you didn't do that exercise, you can work with any message in your Inbox, preferably one with an attachment. Display your Inbox, and we'll get started!

> **Troubleshooting** If you haven't configured an account that receives mail in the On My Computer group, you can perform this exercise in another account group without a problem. However, in the final exercise in this chapter, "Practice Deleting Messages," the process of setting up a schedule to automatically empty your Deleted Items folder will not work.

1. In your Inbox, double-click the *SBS test message* header.

    The message opens in its own window.

    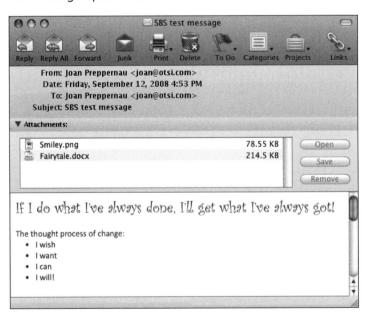

2. If a yellow bar displaying the message "This message has been partially downloaded" appears at the top of the message header, and the text of the file attachment information is gray rather than black, click the **Get entire message** link. If a yellow bar displaying the message "A copy of this message is on the server" appears at the top of the message header, you can ignore it.

3. Scroll the message window to the bottom, where you can see the image that you attached to the outgoing message.

> **Tip** You can collapse the Attachments pane by clicking the downward-pointing triangle to the left of the Attachments label.

4. On the toolbar, click the **Reply** button.

A new message window opens. Your name or e-mail address already appears in the To box. The text of the original message appears in the content pane, preceded by one line of information identifying the date, time, and sender of the original message. *Re:* appears at the beginning of the Subject line to indicate that this is a reply to an original message. The message has no attached files.

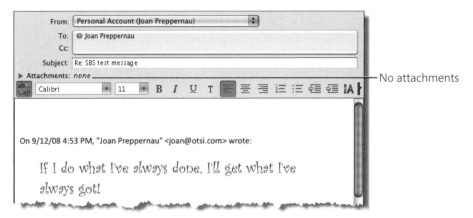
No attachments

5. Enter some reply text in the message if you want to, and then click the **Send** button.

Entourage sends the message and returns you to the original message window. A message appears at the top of the message header to let you know that you have replied to it.

6. On the message window toolbar, click the **Forward** button.

A new message window opens, with the address area active, and no recipients indicated.

7. Enter your e-mail address in the **To** box, and then press **Return** to close the address box.

The text of the original message appears in the content pane, preceded by the message header content of the original message. *FW:* appears at the beginning of the Subject line to indicate that this is a forwarded message. The *Smiley* and *Fairytale* files are attached to the message.

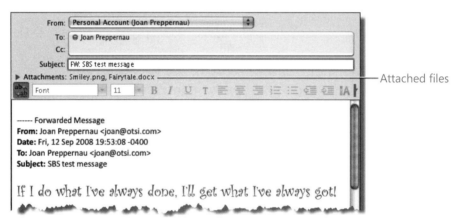

Attached files

8. Enter text in the message content pane if you want to, and then click the **Send** button.

Entourage encodes the attachments, sends the message, and again returns you to the original. The message at the top of the message header is replaced by one indicating that you forwarded the message.

9. Click the **History** link at the right end of the yellow bar to display a list of actions you've taken with this message.

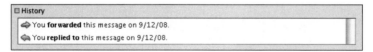

10. Close the original message, and return to your Inbox.

Colored arrows on the message header indicate that you've replied to and forwarded the message. (The arrows match those on the Reply and Forward toolbar buttons so that you can discern their meanings.) A paperclip icon on the header of the forwarded message indicates that it has attachments, whereas the lack of that icon on the reply message indicates that it doesn't.

This icon indicates that message content hasn't been downloaded

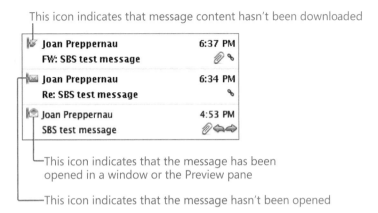

This icon indicates that the message has been opened in a window or the Preview pane

This icon indicates that the message hasn't been opened

 CLEAN UP Keep the three messages for use in the next exercise.

Delete Messages

When you delete a message, contact record, or any other item, Entourage temporarily moves it to the Deleted Items folder of your mailbox. Until you empty the Deleted Items folder, the items are still available to you. You can "undelete" an item by dragging it from the Deleted Items folder to the Inbox or to another folder.

You can empty the entire Deleted Items folder manually or automatically, or you can permanently delete individual items from it.

To permanently delete an individual item:

1. In the Folder list, click the **Deleted Items** folder to display its contents.

2. In the **Deleted Items** list, click the item (or select multiple items) that you want to delete.

3. On the toolbar, click the **Delete** button (or press the **Delete** key).

4. In the message box asking you to confirm that you want to delete the selected item(s), click **Delete**.

To manually empty the Deleted Items folder:

→ In the Folder list, right-click the **Deleted Items** folder, and then click **Empty Deleted Items**.

You can automatically empty the Deleted Items folder at regular intervals by setting up a schedule for this task. Schedules are mini-programs that tell your computer to take an action of your choosing at a specific time.

Schedule Actions to Occur Automatically

By using the Schedule feature, you can schedule any of the following events to take place automatically, on a consistent schedule.

You can set up any of the following as scheduled actions:

- **Receive Mail.** Check the mail server for new messages.
- **Receive News.** Check the news server for new messages.
- **Send All.** Transmit messages from all Outbox folders.
- **Delete Mail.** Purge the Deleted Items folder.
- **Delete Junk Mail.** Purge the Junk Mail folder.

> **Tip** Three additional actions are available from the scheduling tool, but are beyond the scope of this book. These are Excel Auto Web Publish, Launch Alias, and Run AppleScript.

You can schedule actions to occur at one or more of the following intervals:

- **At Startup.** Each time you start Entourage.
- **On Quit.** Each time you quit Entourage.
- **Timed Schedule.** At a specific time on a specific day, each week.
- **Repeating Schedule.** A specific number of minutes, hours, or days after the previous occurrence.
- **Recurring.** At a specific time on a specific day or date, each day, week, month, or year, for a specific number of occurrences or until a specific date.

By default, the Send All and Receive Mail actions are scheduled to occur when you start Entourage and every 10 minutes thereafter, while your computer is connected to the Internet.

Practice Deleting Messages

In this exercise, you'll use different methods to delete the three messages you created in the previous exercises, permanently delete a message from the Deleted Items folder, and set up Entourage to automatically empty your Deleted Items folder each time you quit the program.

> **SET UP** In this exercise, you'll work with the messages you created in the previous exercises. If you didn't do those exercises, you can work with any messages you are ready to delete from your Inbox.

> **Troubleshooting** If you haven't configured an account that receives mail in the On My Computer group, you can perform this exercise in another account group. However, the schedule you set up in steps 8–13 works only for the Deleted Items folder in the On My Computer group. It does not empty the contents of Deleted Items folders for other account groups.

1. In your Inbox, click the original *SBS test message* you sent to yourself.

2. On the toolbar, click the **Delete** button.

    Entourage moves the message from your Inbox to the Deleted Items folder.

3. Click the reply message (*Re: SBS test message*), and then press the **Delete** key.

4. Right-click the forwarded message (*FW: SBS test message*), and then click **Delete Message**.

    None of the SBS messages remain in your Inbox.

5. In the Folder list for the account you're using, click **Deleted Items**.

    The three messages are in the Deleted Items folder.

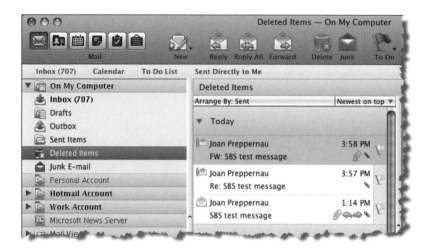

Other deleted items might also appear there. By default, the contents of the Deleted Items folder are sorted by the date and time you received them, not by the date and time you deleted them.

6. Click the *SBS test message*, and then press the **Delete** key.

Entourage prompts you to confirm that you want to permanently delete the message.

> **Note** If you've previously dismissed this message and selected the Don't Show This Message Again check box, Entourage will delete the message without additional confirmation.

7. In the message box, click **Delete**.

The selected message disappears from the Deleted Items folder. No one really knows where these go ... but after you delete an item it is no longer available to you from within the program.

> **Tip** You can employ any of the methods you used in steps 2–4 to permanently delete messages and other items from the Deleted Items folder.

Now we'll set up Entourage to automatically clean out your Deleted Items folder.

8. On the **Tools** menu, click **Schedules**.

The Schedules window opens. *Empty Deleted Items Folder* is one of the standard schedules. It's enabled (turned on), but doesn't show times in the Next Run or Last Run columns. This indicates that no specific schedule has been assigned to this action.

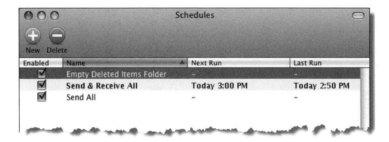

9. In the list, double-click **Empty Deleted Items Folder**.

The Edit Schedule dialog box opens. The schedule item instructs Entourage to delete mail from the Deleted Items folder—specifically, the Deleted Items folder in the On My Computer group in the Folder list. The schedule is currently turned on (as indicated by the selected Enabled check box), but is set to start manually rather than automatically.

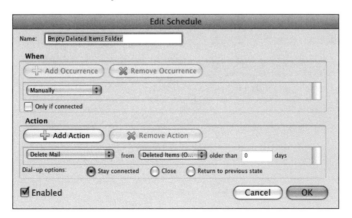

10. In the **When** area, click **Manually** to expand the list, and then click **On Quit**.

> **Tip** You can combine multiple requirements, such as *On Quit* and *Every Three Days*, or multiple actions, such as *Receive Mail* for multiple accounts.

11. In the **Action** section, in the **days** box to the right of the **Delete Mail** action, replace *0* with *3*.

This instructs Entourage to delete only the messages that are more than three days old, in case you realize after quitting the program that you still need access to a deleted file.

12. In the **Edit Schedule** dialog box, click **OK**.

On Quit now appears in the Next Run column of the Empty Deleted Items Folder action.

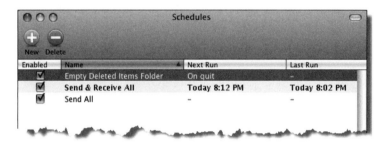

13. In the **Schedules** dialog box, click the **Close** button.

14. On the **Entourage** menu, click **Quit Entourage** (or press **Command+Q**).

The Entourage windows close, and a message box alerts you that the scheduled action will take place.

15. In the message box, click **Delete**.

A similar message box appears, for each account you're connected to, alerting you that Entourage will empty the Junk E-Mail folder.

16. Click **Delete** in each message box or, in the first of these message boxes, select the **Don't show this message again** check box and then click **Delete**.

When Entourage is completely shut down, the menu bar disappears from the top of your screen.

17. Start Entourage, open the **Deleted Items** folder, and confirm that it is empty.

 CLEAN UP If you're not continuing directly to the next chapter and you don't plan to work in Entourage on your own, quit the program.

Key Points

- Entourage includes six feature modules: Mail, Address Book, Calendar, Notes, Tasks, and Project Center.

- You can change the way Entourage displays and handles information, from the Preferences dialog box.

- You can configure Entourage to connect to multiple e-mail accounts, and to multiple types of e-mail accounts.

- You can personalize the content of outgoing messages in many ways, such as formatting message text or creating an e-mail signature.

- While you're crafting a message, you can validate the words and phrases in the message by using the reference tools that are available in all the Office 2008 programs. The Reference Tools palette of the Toolbox provides easy access to research tools, including a thesaurus that makes it easy to track down synonyms, bilingual dictionaries, and translation services.

- If you're interrupted before finishing a message, you can save a draft version of it for later.

- Replying to a message sends the text of the original message, but no attachments. Forwarding a message sends the message and all its attachments.

- Deleting a message moves it to the Deleted Items folder. Until you empty the folder or otherwise permanently delete items, they remain available to you.

Chapter at a Glance

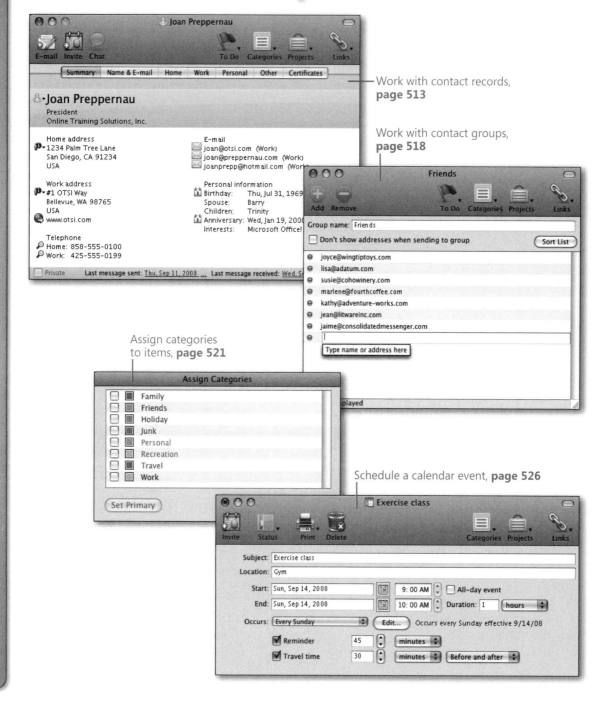

Work with contact records,
page 513

Work with contact groups,
page 518

Assign categories
to items, **page 521**

Schedule a calendar event, **page 526**

16 Manage Contacts and Schedules

In this chapter, you will learn how to

✔ Work in the Address Book.

✔ Work with contact records.

✔ Work with contact groups.

✔ Flag items for follow up.

✔ Assign categories to items.

✔ Work in the Calendar.

✔ Schedule a calendar event.

✔ Search for information.

In the previous chapter, we discussed sending and receiving messages, which is a primary motivator for using a program such as Microsoft Entourage. What differentiates Entourage from simple e-mail programs, though, are the additional information management modules: the Address Book, the Calendar, the Notes and Tasks modules, and the Project Center. In these feature modules, you can store or connect to pretty much all the information you need or want to have at your fingertips on a daily basis. But more importantly, you can easily locate information within what can be a monumental amount of data.

The two most commonly used features after messaging are storing information about people in *contact records* in the Entourage Address Book, and managing your schedule so that you can view and coordinate all your appointments, meetings, events, vacations, holidays, and special occasions in one place—the Entourage Calendar.

In this chapter, you'll learn about creating and viewing contact records in the Address Book, scheduling calendar events, and locating information in Entourage.

See Also You can find handy keyboard shortcuts, simple instructions for performing common tasks, and other useful information in the Quick Reference section at the beginning of this book.

Practice Makes Perfect! You won't need any practice files to complete the exercise in this chapter. See "Using the Companion Content" for information about practice files.

Work in the Address Book

The Address Book appears in the same program window that displays the Mail module we worked with in Chapter 15, "Communicate Online," but the toolbar and layout of the program window change to best display contact information.

Contact list   Column headings   Address Book pane

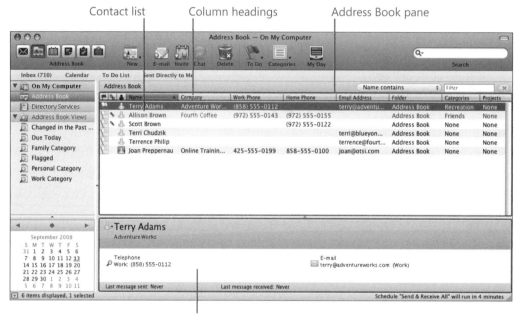

Preview pane displaying contact information and history

In the Address Book module, the program window reflects information and commands related to contact records.

View, Sort, and Filter Records in the Address Book

The Address Book displays contact records in a list format. By default, the following contact record fields are displayed in the Address Book:

- To Do Flag Status
- Links
- Contact Type
- Name
- Company
- Work Phone

- Home Phone
- Email Address
- Folder
- Categories
- Projects

You can display other fields by opening the contact record or by adding the field to the Address Book view. You can change the displayed fields by pointing to Columns on the View menu or by right-clicking any column heading and then clicking individual field names on the list that appears. The list of fields that you can display (and more importantly, that you can record information in) is quite impressive. Check marks indicate fields selected for display.

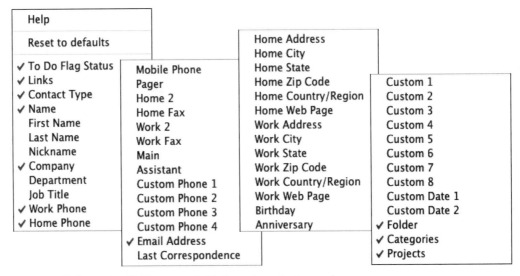

Dozens of information fields are available in each contact record.

> **Note** The fields that are selected are displayed regardless of whether any information is stored in them.

By default, Entourage displays contacts in order by last name (but displays the full name). You can change the order of the contact records by clicking the heading of the column you want to sort by, and the sort order of the column (high/low to low/high) by clicking the heading a second time.

Work with Contact Records

As shown in the previous topic, you can store dozens of pieces of information about a contact in the Address Book. The information you store about a person, company, or other entity is recorded in a contact record.

Work in the Contact Window

When you create or open a contact record, it opens in a *contact window*. The contact window has its own toolbar, displaying commands separate from those in the Entourage program window.

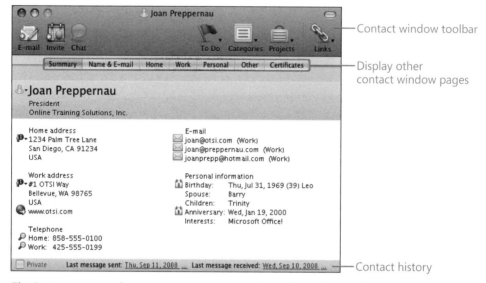

— Contact window toolbar

— Display other contact window pages

— Contact history

The Summary page of a contact record displays information collected from the other pages. You can't edit information from this page.

With the buttons and lists on the contact window toolbar, you can:

- Initiate e-mail or instant messaging communication with a contact.
- Invite a contact to a meeting.
- Flag a contact record to remind you to take action related to that person.
- Assign a category or project to a contact.
- Link a contact record to another contact or to a contact group, or link it to a message, calendar event, task, note, or file.

> **Tip** If you're using Entourage to connect to a Microsoft Exchange Server account, that organization's contact information is stored in the Global Address List (GAL). The GAL might include names, job titles, e-mail addresses, office locations, telephone numbers, and other contact information. It can also include organizational information (each person's manager and direct subordinates) and group membership information (the distribution lists and aliases each person belongs to). The GAL is administered as part of Exchange. Entourage users can view the GAL but not change its contents.

Create a Contact Record

For each person whose information you record in an address book, you can store the following types of general information:

- Name and e-mail information, including:
    - First and last names
    - Title (such as Mrs. or Dr.), suffix (such as Jr. or Sr.), and nickname
    - Work, home, and up to 11 other e-mail addresses
    - Thirteen instant messaging (IM) addresses
    - Two custom-labeled fields
- Home information, including:
    - Address details, from which you can display a map or driving directions
    - Web page
    - Two home phone numbers; mobile, pager, and fax numbers; and up to four custom-labeled numbers
    - Two custom-labeled fields
- Work information, including:
    - Company name, job title, and department
    - Address details, from which you can display a map or driving directions
    - Web page
    - Two work phone numbers plus numbers for the main switchboard and for an assistant; mobile, pager, and fax numbers; and up to four custom-labeled numbers
    - Two custom-labeled fields
- Personal information, including:
    - Birthday, age, and astrological sign
    - Anniversary date and spouse or partner's name
    - Interests
    - The names of up to 10 children
    - An image (most likely a photo of the person)

- Other information, including:

    - General notes (text only)

    - Two custom-labeled dates

    - Two custom-labeled fields

You can create a contact record containing only one piece of information (for example, a name or company name—but neither is required), or as much information as you want to include. You can quickly create contact records containing similar information—for example, for several people who work for the same company—by duplicating the contact record and then changing the details in the copy. And of course, you can add to or change the information stored in a contact record at any time.

To create a contact record:

1. On the Address Book toolbar, click the **New** button (or press **Command+N**).

> **Tip** You can create any type of item from any module by clicking the **New** arrow and then, in the list, clicking the item you want to create.

2. In the **Create Contact** window that opens, enter a basic name, e-mail addresses, phone numbers, and home or business addresses or, to store additional information in fields available from the full contact record window, click the **More** button (in the lower-right corner of the window).

3. After entering the information you want to store, click the **Close** button, and then in the message box prompting you to confirm that you want to save your changes, click **Save**.

To make changes to a contact record:

1. In the Address Book, double-click the contact record you want to edit.

2. In the contact record window, make any changes, additions, or deletions.

3. Click the **Close** button, and then click **Save** in the message box that appears.

> **Tip** When you send an e-mail message to a person whose contact information is stored in one of your address books, you can quickly address the message to that person by typing his or her name into the To, Cc, or Bcc box, or by clicking the adjacent button to open the Address Book window and then selecting the intended recipient's name.

Linking Entourage Items

You can associate contact records, or any type of Entourage item, with other Entourage items and with files. For example, you can link the contact records of two related people, link a contact record to the résumé of that person, or link a résumé to an interview appointment.

Links can be useful when you have a lot of information stored in Entourage and want immediate access to related items. You might find that it takes less time to open an item from the Links To window than it does to return to Entourage, change modules, and search for the item you want.

The Links list is located at the right end of the toolbar in each item window. You can create and display links from this list, and even simultaneously create and link items to the active item. You can open any linked item by double-clicking it in the Links To list.

To link a contact record to another item:

1. On the toolbar of the contact record window, click the **Links** button, and then click **Open Links**.

2. In the **Links To** window, click the **To New** button or the **To Existing** button and then, in the list, click the type of item you want to link to.

> **Tip** You can link to multiple items of one type by using Shift+Click (to select contiguous items) or Command+Click (to select non-contiguous items).

3. Select or create the item, and then close the open windows.

Linked records are indicated in the Address Book, Notes, and Tasks panes by a Link icon (a linked chain) in the Links column, and in the Mail pane by a Link icon in the message header. No indication of links is given in the Calendar pane or in any Preview pane. In the Address Book, Notes, and Tasks panes (which display information in list format), you can display and open existing links, and create additional links, by clicking the Links icon or in the Links column for the item you want to link.

Work with Contact Groups

If you frequently send messages to a specific group of people, such as members of a team you're on, or family members, you can simplify the process by adding them to a contact group. You can then address a message to the group (rather than to all the individual contacts) and it will go to all the group members.

To create a contact group:

1. On the Address Book toolbar, click the **New** arrow and then, in the list, click **Group**.

2. In the **Group** window that opens, enter the group name, and then click the **Add** button.

3. In the text box that appears, enter the name (if you have a contact record for the person) or e-mail address of each group member. Press **Tab** after each entry to start a new line, or **Return** to finish.

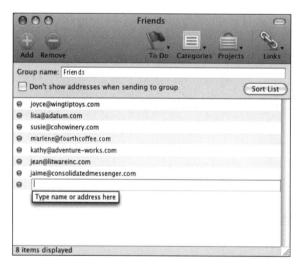

4. If you want the e-mail messages you send to this group to display only the group name, and not the addresses of the group members, select the **Don't show addresses when sending to group** check box.

> **Tip** The Don't Show Addresses When Sending To Group option is a good choice when you want to keep the group membership private or don't want recipients to reply to all of the group members—responses from 200 other group members can quite quickly flood your Inbox.

5. When you're done adding members to the group, close the window and, in the message box prompting you to save your changes, click **Save**.

Flag Items for Follow Up

You can add a To Do flag to any e-mail message or contact record, to indicate to yourself that you want to follow up on it. The flag can be a general reminder to take action at an unspecified time, or you can assign a specific due date or range of dates to it (Today, Tomorrow, This Week, or Next Week). The default due date is Today.

A flag icon appears at the right end of each message header in the Mail pane, and at the left end of each contact record in the Address Book pane. By default, the flag and surrounding background are gray, indicating that the message is not flagged. To flag a message for follow up, click the flag icon. The flag becomes red on a lighter red background to indicate that it's active. After you follow up on a flagged item, mark it as complete either by clicking its flag icon or by right-clicking the item, pointing to To Do, and clicking Mark As Complete. A green check mark on a lighter green background indicates a completed task or item.

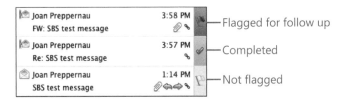

The flag icon indicates the follow-up status of a message or contact record.

After you flag a message or contact record, it appears on your To Do list, which is available from the Tasks module or from the Calendar.

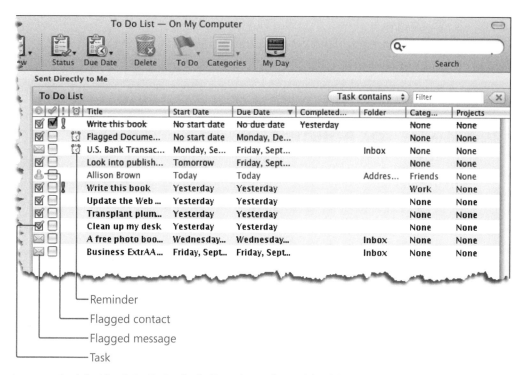

Icons on the left side of the To Do list indicate items flagged for follow up, as well as actual tasks.

If you'd like Entourage to remind you of a task, appointment, or flagged item, you can add a reminder. When the reminder time comes, a clock appears in the Dock and a desktop reminder appears. From the reminder window, you can dismiss the reminder completely, or click Snooze to have the reminder reappear later.

The clock that appears in the Dock indicates the number of reminders needing your attention.

To change a due date or set a reminder, right-click a flagged item, point to To Do, and then either click the due date you want or click Add Reminder to open the Dates And Reminder dialog box, in which you can set start and due dates for the flagged item and specify the date and time you want a reminder to appear.

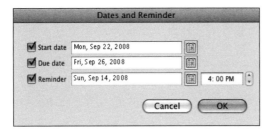

You can specify the date and time a reminder will appear.

Assign Categories to Items

Assigning categories to Entourage items can help you more easily locate information. Entourage 2008 for Mac uses color-coded categories, which combine named categories with color coding to provide an immediate visual cue when you are viewing your Inbox, Address Book, or other Entourage window.

Entourage 2008 has eight built-in categories: Family, Friends, Holiday, Junk, Personal, Recreation, Travel, and Work. You can change the names or colors of the existing categories to fit your needs, and you can create your own categories.

Assigning a category to an item displays the item header information in that category's color. You can assign a category to an item from the item window or from a module window.

To assign one category:

→ Right-click the item, point to **Categories**, and then click the category.

→ Select the item in the module window, click the **Categories** arrow on the program window toolbar, and then click the category you want to assign.

→ Open the item in its item window, click the **Categories** arrow on the item window toolbar, and then click the category you want to assign.

To assign multiple categories:

1. Click the **Categories** button on the program window or item window toolbar.

2. In the **Assign Categories** dialog box, select the check boxes of the categories you want to assign.

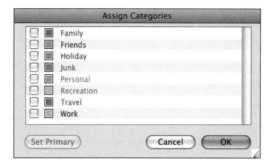

3. To assign a category and select its color as the one that will show on color-coded items, click the category name (before selecting its check box) and click the **Set Primary** button.

> **Note** If you don't set a primary color before assigning a category to an item, the item will appear in the color of the category you selected last.

4. In the **Assign Categories** dialog box, click **OK**.

You manage categories from the Categories window, which you can display by clicking Edit Categories in any of the Categories lists.

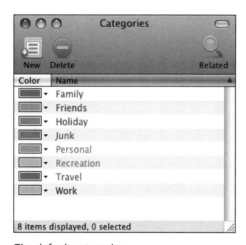

The default categories

In the Categories window, you can do any of the following:

● To create a new category, click the **New** button. Entourage inserts a new, untitled category with a color of its own choosing.

● To change the name of a category, double-click the name to select it for editing, change the name, and then press **Return**.

- To change the color associated with a category, click its color box, and then click the color you want.

- To delete a category and remove any assignments of that category, click the category name, click the **Delete** button, and then in the message box prompting you to confirm the deletion, click **Delete**.

A compelling reason to use categories is that you can very quickly filter the information stored in a module to display only items with a specific category assigned to them, by clicking the category name in the Views section of the Folder list. Only the categories that are currently assigned to items appear in the Views list.

Work in the Calendar

The Calendar appears in the same program window that displays the Address Book, but the toolbar and layout of the program window change to best display calendar event information.

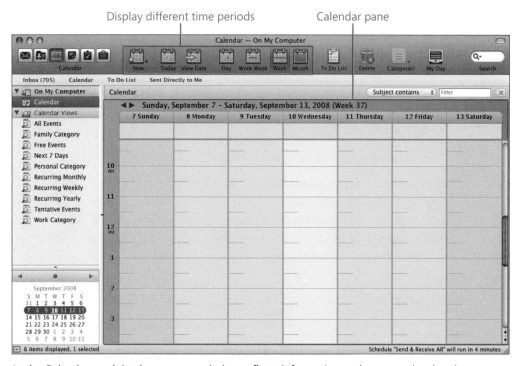

In the Calendar module, the program window reflects information and commands related to calendar events.

Display Different Views of a Calendar

To help you stay on top of your schedule, you can view your calendar in a variety of ways:

- **Day view.** This view displays only one day at a time.

- **Work Week view.** This view displays only the days that are part of your work week, which by default is defined as Monday through Friday from 9:00 A.M. to 5:00 P.M. You can define your work week to include whatever days and hours you want, from the Calendar page of the Preferences dialog box.

> **Note** In the Calendar, time slots that fall within your work week are shaded in a different color from non-work timeslots.

- **Week view.** This view displays one week (Sunday through Saturday) at a time, divided into days.

> **Note** In Day view, Work Week view, and Week view, each day is represented by an individual column that is divided into half-hour timeslots.

- **Month view.** This view displays five weeks at a time.

> **Note** In any of the above views, you can move to the current day by clicking the Today button on the toolbar.

- **List view.** This view displays a simple list of your current and future calendar items.

The currently displayed time period is shown at the top of the calendar content pane, below the Quick Filter. You can move to the previous or next time period by clicking the left and right arrows that appear to the left of the time period. You can display a specific date or range of dates by clicking or dragging to select them in the Mini Calendar in the lower-left corner of the Calendar window.

You can change the Calendar view by clicking the toolbar buttons or by clicking, on the Calendar menu, the name of the view you want to display. You can also change the time period displayed in the large calendar by selecting time periods in the Mini Calendar. Here's how:

- To display the month that appears in the Mini Calendar, click the name of the month.

- To display a week that appears in the Mini Calendar, click the margin to the left of that week.

> **Tip** Week numbers are used in some countries to reference events, vacations, and other specific dates. Week 1 is the calendar week (Sunday through Saturday) in which January 1st falls, Week 2 is the following week, and so on through to the end of the year. Because of the way the weeks are numbered, a year can be made up of Weeks 1 through 53. In Entourage 2008 for Mac, the week number is displayed, to the right of the specific dates, in Week view.

● To display a day, click that day.

In module views that include the Mini Calendar, increasing the width of the Folder list also increases the number of months shown in the Mini Calendar. You can allocate up to 50 percent of the program window to the Folder list.

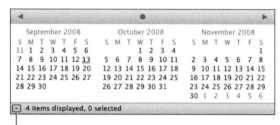

Expand/Collapse button

The Mini Calendar is available in any module window. Click the Expand/Collapse button to show or hide it.

Display Your To Do List

Entourage keeps a To Do list for you of all the items you've flagged for follow up. You can display your To Do list in the Calendar window, by clicking the To Do List button on the toolbar.

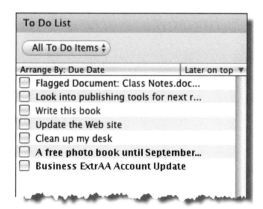

The To Do List pane opens on the right side of the Calendar window.

Here are some of the ways you can work in the To Do list:

● You can add a task to the To Do list (and simultaneously to the Tasks list) by enter-ing it in the **Create a task** box at the bottom of the **To Do List** pane. To assign a due date to the task as you create it, enter the task description in the box, click the **Options** button, and then click the due date you want to assign.

● You can open any To Do list item in its original item window by double-clicking it.

● You can assign color-coded categories to list items. The color is visible in the To Do list and in the item's original module. To assign a category to an item, right-click the item, point to **Category**, and then click the appropriate category.

Schedule a Calendar Event

In Entourage, entries you record in the Calendar are collectively referred to as *calen-dar events*, regardless of their length or whether other people are invited. A calendar event might be a day-long block of time, such as a holiday, or an appointment with specific start and finish times. You can make it a meeting by inviting other people to the appointment. (You can also invite people to day-long events.)

By default, Entourage displays a desktop reminder 15 minutes prior to the start of the event.

See Also For more information about reminders, see "Flag Items for Follow Up" earlier in this chapter.

You can create an event when viewing your calendar in Day view, Week view, or Month view. To create a calendar event:

1. In the **Calendar** window, click the **New** button on the toolbar (or press **Command+N**).

   A New Event window opens.

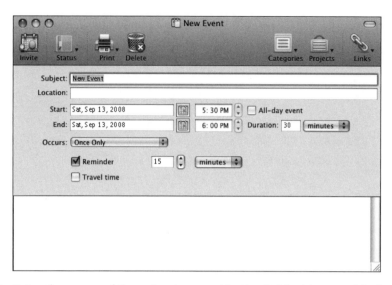

2. Enter the name of the calendar event in the **Subject** box, and its location in the **Location** box.

3. In the **Start** box, select the date of the event or, if it's a multi-day event, the first day.

4. If the event is not tied to a specific time span, select the **All-day event** check box. If it starts and finishes at specific times, enter that information in the **Start** and **End** boxes.

5. If the event will recur on a regular schedule, such as a monthly meeting or a weekly exercise class, click the **Occurs** list, and then click the frequency of the recurrence.

6. If you want to change the reminder time, select the units and number of units in the lists to the right of the **Reminder** check box. Or, if you prefer that Entourage not display a desktop reminder, clear the **Reminder** check box.

> **Note** The maximum reminder time is 999 days in advance of the calendar event, which probably wouldn't be a very helpful reminder!

7. If you want to block out time on your schedule before and after the event for traveling to and from the event location, select the **Travel time** check box. Then from the lists that appear, select the amount of travel time required and whether the time is required before, after, or before and after the event.

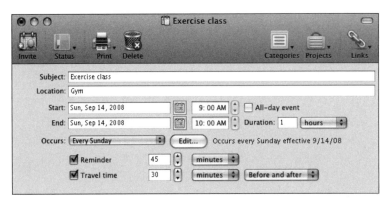

8. After you complete the information in the event header, click the **Status** button and then, in the list, click **Busy**, **Free**, **Tentative**, or **Out Of Office** to indicate whether you're available for other appointments or meetings during the event.

9. Add any notes or other information you want to save with the event in the text area at the bottom of the event window. Then click the **Close** button, and click **Save** in the message box that prompts you to confirm that you want to save the changes.

10. Display the event date in the Calendar and confirm its details.

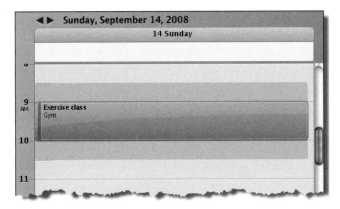

Practice Working with Your Calendar

In this exercise, you'll schedule an event and convert it to a recurring event. There are no practice files for this exercise.

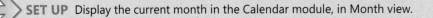

SET UP Display the current month in the Calendar module, in Month view.

1. In the calendar, double-click the first Wednesday of the next month.

   An untitled calendar event window opens. The Start and End boxes display the selected date, and a time period of 9:00 A.M. to 10:00 A.M. The event is scheduled to occur only once, and a reminder is set to appear 15 minutes before the event starts.

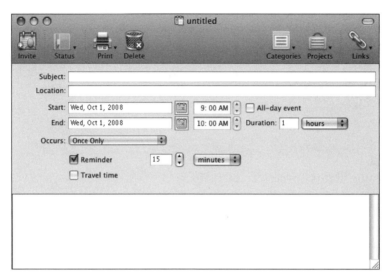

2. In the **Subject** box, enter SBS study session.

   As you type, the window title changes to reflect your entry.

3. Press the **Tab** key to move to the **Location** box, and then enter Coffee shop.

4. Click the **Occurs** list to display the recurrence options.

   Entourage has incorporated the specific weekday and date into the list.

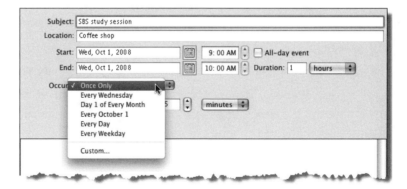

5. In the **Occurs** list, click **Every Wednesday**.

   The selected frequency appears in the event window header, to the right of the Occurs list.

6. On the event window toolbar, click the **Status** button to display a list of options for indicating your availability during the scheduled event.

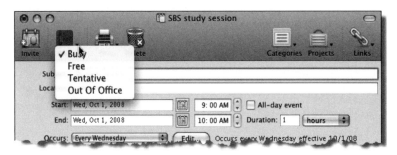

7. In the **Status** list, click **Out Of Office**.

> **Note** No visible sign of the status appears in the event window.

8. In the **SBS study session** window, click the **Close** button.

   A message box appears, asking you to confirm that you want to save the calendar event.

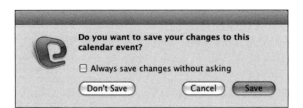

9. In the message box, click **Save**.

   The appointment appears on your calendar, at 9:00 A.M. every Wednesday.

10. Scroll the calendar back one month and forward one month, to confirm that the first instance of the appointment is the first Wednesday of the current month, and that the appointments continue out into the future.

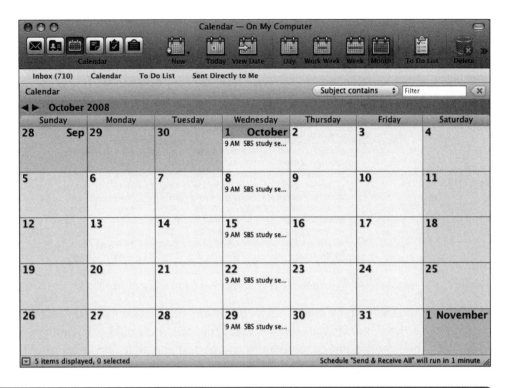

 CLEAN UP If you're finished working with Entourage, you can quit the program.

Search for Information

And now, saving the best for last, we'd like to share one final bit of information with you before we go.

From the Search box that appears in the upper-right corner of the Entourage program window, you can instantly locate any Entourage item containing a specific search term. Enter the search term into the box. As you type, Entourage filters the content pane to display only items containing that term. From the Quick Filter just above the content pane, you can refine the scope of the search results—your Inbox, all messages, or all types of items.

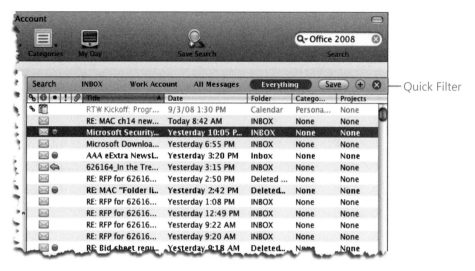

Quick Filter

You can instantly locate any Entourage item matching a search term.

You can sort the search results list by any of the column headings, and you can work with any item in the search results list just as you would in its module. You do this either by selecting one or more items and performing an action, or by double-clicking an item to open it in its original item window.

You can save the search and return to it later. When you return, the results update automatically to reflect the current content.

Key Points

- You can store a tremendous variety of information about a person in a contact record. You manage contact records from the Address Book.

- You can simplify the process of sending messages to multiple people by creating a contact group, and then addressing the message to the group rather than to the individual members.

- You can assign a color-coded category to any Entourage item to make it easier to locate visually. You can filter modules to display only a certain category of items.

- You can keep track of all your appointments, meetings, and events in the Calendar module. You can indicate your availability, including travel time, for any type of event.

- You can instantly display a list of Entourage items containing specific search terms, by entering the term in the Search box. You can filter the results list to display results from one module or from all modules, and work with items in the results list just as you would in their original modules.

Glossary

Apple Remote Control An infrared-based transmitter that you can use to control features such as iTunes and DVD Player.

attribute Structural information about data that describes its context and meaning.

AutoCorrect A feature that automatically detects and corrects misspelled words, grammatical errors, and incorrect capitalization. You can also add custom AutoCorrect entries.

AutoText A storage location for text or graphics you want to use again, such as a standard contract clause or a long distribution list. Each selection of text or graphics is recorded as an AutoText entry and is assigned a unique name.

background The screen background image used on a graphical user interface (GUI). Any pattern or picture that can be stored as a bitmap (.bmp) file can be set as a screen background.

balloon A box containing a comment, deletion, or formatting change that appears to the right of a document when Track Changes is turned on.

body text Text that is not formatted with a built-in heading style (Heading 1 through Heading 9) or an outline-level paragraph format (Level 1 through Level 9). In outline view, Word displays a symbol to the left of body text.

category A group to which you can assign Entourage items for the purpose of sorting or filtering related items.

cell A box formed by the intersection of a row and column in a worksheet or a table, in which you enter information.

character formatting Formatting you can apply to selected text characters.

character spacing The distance between characters in a word or line of text. Scaling, spacing, and kerning can be changed to adjust the space between characters.

chart area The entire area occupied by a chart, including the legend and any titles.

Click and Type A feature that allows you to double-click a blank area of a document to position the insertion point in that location, with the appropriate paragraph alignment already in place.

Clipboard A temporary storage area. Information clips (such as text, files, graphics, sound, or video) can be copied to the Clipboard from one program or location and pasted elsewhere. The Clipboard can hold only one piece of information at a time. Each clip cut or copied to the Clipboard replaces the previous clip.

color scheme A set of balanced colors that you can apply to enhance the appearance of documents, worksheets, presentations, and messages.

column heading In Excel, the gray box at the top of a sheet column, displaying the column letter. See also *row heading*.

command An instruction that tells a program to perform an action.

comment A note or annotation that an author or reviewer adds to a document. Word displays the comment in a balloon in the margin of the document or in the Reviewing pane.

contact record In the Entourage Address Book, a collection of information about a person that might include business and personal contact information and other information you want to store.

contact window In Entourage, the program window displaying the form in which you enter information about a contact to create a contact record.

credentials An electronic set of information that includes identification and proof of identification, used to gain access to online resources. Examples of credentials are user names and passwords, smart cards, and digital certificates.

cross-reference entry In an index, an entry that refers readers to a related entry.

data label A number that appears in a chart next to the bar or marker that it represents.

data point A point that represents the value of a single item.

data series Related data points that are plotted in a chart. A chart can plot one or more data series.

desktop alert A window that appears on screen in response to an event, such as a task due date, an appointment, or an incoming e-mail message.

document template A predefined set of text, formatting, and graphics, stored in a special type of document that can be used as the basis for other documents. A basic Word 2008 document template has the extension *.dotx*.

drag-and-drop editing A way of moving or copying selected text by dragging it with the mouse pointer.

dragging A way of moving objects by pointing to them, holding down the mouse button, moving the mouse pointer to the desired location, and releasing the button.

drop zone An area of a document or slide designated for the placement of an image or other element.

e-mail signature A block of text, sometimes accompanied by a graphic, that is appended to the end of a message you send.

field A set of codes that instruct a program to automatically insert text, graphics, page numbers, and other information into a document. For example, the DATE field inserts the current date, the TOC field inserts a table of contents, and the INDEX field inserts an index of tagged terms.

field code A code that controls the display and formatting of the information in a field.

filling In Excel, the action of copying the contents of one cell into adjacent cells by dragging the originating cell's fill handle.

Finder On a Mac, the program you use to locate and manage files, disks, network volumes, and other programs.

Folder list The left pane of the Entourage program window in which groups, folders, and views are listed.

font A set of characters of the same typeface (such as Garamond), style (such as italic), and weight (such as bold). A font consists of all the characters available in a particular style and weight for a particular design.

font color One of a range of colors that can be applied to text.

font effect An attribute, such as superscript, small capital letters, or shadow, that can be applied to a font.

font scheme Two font families: one that controls the appearance of headings and another that controls the appearance of other text elements.

font size The height (in points) of text characters, where one point is equal to approximately 1/72 of an inch.

font style An attribute that changes the look of text. The most common font styles are regular (or plain), italic, bold, and bold italic.

footer A set of static text, images, lines, rectangles, borders, background color, and background images that repeats on the bottom of each page of a document, worksheet, or slide.

Format Painter A tool you can use to transfer the character and paragraph format settings of a selection to another block of text.

function A prewritten formula that takes a value or values, performs an operation, and returns a value or values. Use functions to simplify and shorten formulas on a worksheet, especially those that involve lengthy or complex calculations.

gallery A grouping of thumbnails that display options visually.

greeked text Placeholder text used to hold the position of text that will be inserted by a user.

group An organizational element of the tabs of the Elements Gallery. Each group contains thumbnails representing the document element you can insert or apply by clicking the icon.

header A set of static text, images, lines, rectangles, borders, background color, and background images that repeats on the top of each page of a document, worksheet, or slide.

IMAP Internet Message Access Protocol. A standard mail server for the Internet.

import The process of having a program pull information from an existing file into the document, worksheet, or presentation you are working on.

indent marker A marker on the horizontal ruler that controls the indentation of text from the left or right side of a document.

index An alphabetical list of concepts and terms and the page numbers where they are found.

index entry A field code that marks specific text for inclusion in an index. Index entries are formatted as hidden text.

index entry field The field that defines an index entry. It includes the XE code and the entry enclosed in braces ({}).

interface The point of communication between two entities—in this case, Office 2008 and the user. The interface consists of all the elements designed to make using the Office programs easy and intuitive.

interface element Any of the screen elements of Office 2008 that facilitate communication between the Office programs and the user.

key combination A combination of two or more keys that perform an action when pressed together.

keyword A word or phrase that helps you organize and locate clippings or files such as clip art.

layout placeholder A text box on a slide with dimensions and formatting that are predefined by the presentation's slide master. See also *placeholder*.

legend A table, usually displayed to the right or at the bottom of a chart, that identifies information in the chart.

local formatting Formatting applied at the text or paragraph level.

macro-enabled A file in a format that allows it to contain macros—small programs that run from within the file. Only files with extensions ending in *m* (*.docm*, *.xlsm*, and *.pptm*) are macro-enabled.

manual page break A page break inserted to force subsequent information to appear on the next page.

margin The part of a page—top, bottom, and sides—outside the main body of text.

named reference A cell or group of related cells defined by a name you can use to reference the cell(s) in a formula.

navigation area The area of a dialog box, such as the Save As or Open dialog box, in which you locate the file you want in a Finder-like structure.

Office file The term used to refer collectively to Word documents, Excel workbooks, and PowerPoint presentations.

Office Theme template A template in the Office Themes category of presentations in the Project Gallery. A presentation based on one of these templates has an attractive, professional design template attached.

orphan The first line of a paragraph printed by itself at the bottom of a page.

palette A set of colors from which you can choose the one you want , or a tool (such as the Formatting Palette, the Object Palette, or the Reference Tools palette) displayed in the Toolbox.

panel A component of the Toolbox. Each program's Toolbox includes multiple palettes, and each palette can include multiple panels of commands. You can choose which panels appear on each palette by opening and closing them.

paragraph In word processing, a block of text of any length that ends when you press the Return key.

paragraph formatting Formatting that controls the appearance of a paragraph. Examples include indentation, alignment, line spacing, and pagination.

paragraph selector In a Word notebook, the round dot that appears in the left margin adjacent to the first line of the current paragraph. You can select a paragraph by clicking its paragraph selector.

placeholder Text that you replace with your own information. See also *Layout placeholder*.

plot area In a 2-D chart, the area bounded by the axes, including all data series. In a 3-D chart, the area bounded by the axes, including the data series, category names, tick-mark labels, and axis titles.

point The unit of measure for expressing the size of characters in a font, where 72 points equals 1 inch.

POP A maildrop service that allows a client to retrieve mail that the server is holding for it.

presentation The product created in PowerPoint. Also called a *slide show*. Presentations consist of a series of slides containing text, graphics, and other content designed to convey information to an audience.

primary mouse button The mouse button you use for clicking and double-clicking screen elements. The primary mouse button is the left button on most mice and trackball devices, and the lower button on some trackball devices, but you can switch the function of the buttons from within the operating system.

print area In Excel, an optional definition of specific sheet cells that will display when the sheet is printed. Content outside a defined print area is not printed.

Project Gallery A program installed with Office 2008 from which you can create files based on simple or professionally designed project templates, and custom templates located in the default User Templates folder. You can also access Office files you've recently worked in.

project template A file that stores text, character and paragraph styles, page formatting, and elements such as graphics for use as a pattern in creating other documents.

property A file detail, such as an author name or project code, that helps identify the file.

read-only A setting that allows a file to be read or copied, but not changed or saved. If you make changes to a read-only file, you can save your changes only if you give the document a new name.

row heading In Excel, the gray box at the left end of a sheet row, displaying the row number. See also *column heading*.

ruler An on-screen scale marked off in inches or other units of measure and used to show line widths, tab settings, paragraph indents, and so on.

sans serif A style of typeface with no ornamentation on the upper or lower ends of the characters.

scaling The process of adjusting the way content fits onto a printed page. Scaling content for printing doesn't affect its size or appearance when you're viewing it on-screen.

Scrapbook A central storage location for content snippets and files that you want to reuse elsewhere. The Scrapbook is shared by Word, Excel, and PowerPoint, so you can retrieve stored content from a program other than the one you saved it in.

secondary mouse button The mouse button you use for right-clicking screen elements, primarily to display shortcut menus of commands specific to a selected item. The secondary mouse button is the right button on most mice and trackball devices, and the upper button on other trackball devices, but you can switch the function of the buttons from within the operating system.

section A part of a document. You create sections so that you can apply page settings, such as orientation or margins, that are different from those of the rest of the document.

section break A marker that indicates the beginning or end of a section. A section break stores the section formatting elements, such as the margins, page orientation, headers and footers, and sequence of page numbers.

select To highlight an item in preparation for making some change to it.

selection area An area in a document's left margin in which you can click and drag to select blocks of text.

slide master The slide that stores the base content of each slide layout—the default position of layout placeholders, the default fonts and colors of text within text placeholders, and any background graphics that appear on all slides of a certain type.

smart button A button that is displayed when refining options are available for an action you have just performed. For example, clicking the Auto Fill Options button displays a menu of options tailored specifically for the type of data series you're filling.

SmartArt diagram A professional business graphic easily created within a document, worksheet, presentation, or message by using SmartArt technology. Diagrams can depict relationships, hierarchies, processes, and other business functions.

SMTP A TCP/IP protocol for sending messages from one computer to another on a network. This protocol is used on the Internet to route e-mail.

soft page break A page break that Word inserts when text reaches the bottom margin of a page.

spam filter A utility that identifies junk e-mail messages and blocks attachments that might contain viruses or worms.

Spike In Word, a tool you can use to move a collection of content from multiple locations to another location. You cut each item you want to move to the Spike, position the insertion point, and then paste the content collection from the Spike.

splash screen A transitional screen image that appears as a program is in the process of launching.

Spotlight On a Mac, the desktop search engine that quickly locates files, programs, and features by searching a virtual index of all items and files on the system.

subentry An index entry that falls under a more general entry. For example, the index entry *planets* could have the subentries *Mars* and *Venus*.

tab In a document, a character with which you can specify the amount of space preceding or following a section of text, and its alignment.

tab leader A repeating character (usually a dot or dash) that separates text before the tab from text or a number after it.

table Information presented in a grid that consists of a series of cells laid out in columns and rows.

template A file that stores text, character and paragraph styles, page formatting, and elements such as graphics for use as a pattern in creating other documents, worksheets, and presentations.

thumbnail A miniature version of an image or page that is often used for quickly browsing through multiple images or pages.

tick-mark label A label on an axis of a chart that identifies the axis value or category.

title bar The top frame of a program, file, item, dialog box, or other window. You can move a window by dragging the title bar.

Toolbox A convenient collection of tool palettes specific to each Office 2008 program. The Toolbox displays in its own window that you can position independently of the program window, so the tools you use most often are always available. The Toolbox palettes include Formatting, Object, Scrapbook, Reference Tools, and several others. Commands on a palette are arranged on panels. See also *panel*.

watermark A picture or phrase that appears behind the text in a document or on a slide.

workbook An Excel file containing one sheet, or a collection of related sheets, that you create for the storage and analysis of data on which you can perform calculations.

widow The last line of a paragraph printed by itself at the top of a page.

workspace An area of the program window in which you perform most tasks with documents, worksheets, and presentations.

x-axis The horizontal plane in a chart; also called the *category axis*.

y-axis The vertical plane in a chart; also called the *value axis*.

z-axis The plane that represents depth in a chart; also called the *series axis*.

Index

Symbols and Numbers

* (asterisk), as Word Find and Replace wildcard, 61
= (equal sign), to start formula, 302, 338
? (question mark), as Word Find and Replace wildcard, 61
#N/A error, 300
35mm slide projector, slide settings for, 339
3D Exploded Pie chart, 268

A

absolute cell references, 305
   changing relative to, 313
accent colors, in Word theme, 228
Accept Or Reject Changes dialog box, Q-37, 424
accepting changes, Q-36
Account Setup Assistant
   Automatic Configuration Succeeded page, 478
   completing interview process, 476
   saving password in, 479
   Set Up A Mail Account page, 477
   Verify And Complete Settings page, 478
Accounts dialog box, 477
Accounts worksheet templates, 173
active cell, 163
active document, name of, 6
adding data to charts, Q-46
Address Book (Entourage), 470, 512–523
   contact records, 511
   displayed fields, changing, Q-74
   to select e-mail recipient, 516
   settings, 474
   toolbar, New button, 516
   viewing, sorting, and filtering records, 512
addressing e-mail messages, Q-77, 484–485
Advanced settings, in PowerPoint, 26
alignment of text
   changing, Q-13
   horizontal, 354
   vertical, 355
alphanumeric watermark, creating, 441
American Psychological Association (APA),
      bibliographic style, 462
AND( ) function, 300

annotation pen in PowerPoint, 342
Apple icon, on menu bar, 10
Apple menu, Force Quit, 391
Apple Remote Control, G-533
applications, 4
appointment reminders, Q-80
arguments, for functions, 296
Arial font, 364
Arrange dialog box, 58
Arrange Windows dialog box (Excel), 101
arranging document windows, Q-53, 58
arrows, toolbar buttons with, 14
ascenders, 365
aspect ratio, for slides in PowerPoint, 339
Assign Categories dialog box, 521
assigning categories for Entourage items,
      Q-75, 521
asterisk (*), as Word Find and Replace wildcard, 61
attaching files to e-mail, Q-78, 485, 489, 499
attaching template to document, Q-29, 240
attributes, G-533
attributes of fonts, 365
   in shapes, 386
audio notes, in Notebook, 141
Audio toolbar, 141
Auto Fill feature, in Excel, 161
Auto Fill Options menu (Excel), 162, 167
   Fill Without Formatting option, 312
auto fitting in PowerPoint, Q-60
AutoComplete settings, in Excel, 25
AutoCorrect, Q-10, G-533
   in PowerPoint, Q-60, 200
   word list, 129
AutoCorrect group on Word and PowerPoint
      Preferences page, 22
   customizing, 28
AutoFormat As You Type settings, in Word and
      PowerPoint, 22
automatic page breaks, 89
Automator, 11
AutoRecover, 28
   save frequency, Q-16
AutoText, 125G-533
   Spike for, 219
   in Word, 23
AVERAGE( ) function, 298, 303
AVERAGEIF( ) function, 298
AVERAGEIFS( ) function, 298

B

background, G-533
background, document
  color, 228, 361
  saving in Office Theme, 93
background, e-mail, 492
background, Notebook workspace, 139
background, paragraph (shading), 356
background, slides
  color gradient, Q-61, 326
  image for, Q-61, 334
  in slide master, 339
  textures, Q-61, 333
  transparency for, Q-61, 334, 336
backward data series in Excel, Q-48
balloons for Track Changes feature, 414, 421, G-533
  color of, 418
  Formatted, 422
  turning off display, 416
bar charts, 265
Bcc box, 485
  and message replies, 499
beginning of document, moving to in Word, 78, 80
Beige Plastique display, for Notebook Layout
    view, 138
bent arrow, in Word display, 124
bibliography
  creating, Q-26, 462–464
  inserting, 464
binary file format, saving workbook as, 156
Bitmap file format, exporting presentation
    slide as, 115
Black Screen, in PowerPoint, 341
black slide, ending slide shows with, Q-64, 116
blank documents, in Word, 126
blank slides
  adding to presentation, 183
  layout, 183
"blind" courtesy copies, 485
  and message replies, 499
.bmp file format, exporting presentation
    slide as, 115
body text, G-533
  default font, 364
  font for, 229
bold font, 365, 369
Border Drawing toolbar, 376
Border Type gallery, 357, 361
borders
  in Excel, Q-49, 358, 376
  for paragraphs, Q-26, 356
Bright Academic display, for Notebook Layout
    view, 138
brochure template, 144

Budget worksheet templates, 173
bulleted text
  converting to normal text, Q-62, 320
  converting to numbered list, Q-62, 319
  converting to slide, 203
  creating second-level PowerPoint, 318
  entering on slide, 189

C

calculations, Excel settings for, 25
    See also formulas in Excel; functions
  data limitations, 157
Calendar (Entourage), 470, 511, 523–531
  displaying different views, 524
  practice exercise, 528–531
  scheduling events, Q-74, Q-80, 526
  settings, 474
Calibri font, 364, 492
Cambria font, 364
capitalization, Q-31
  automatic, 201
cascading windows, 58, 102
case of characters, Q-31
  recommended use, 366
categories, G-533
categories for Entourage items
  assigning, Q-75, 521
  creating, 522
  in To Do list, 526
categories for Scrapbook clippings, 218
category axis of chart, 266
Category list, for Project Gallery, 134
Cc box, 485
  and message replies, 499
cell, G-533
cell references, Q-51
  absolute or relative, 305, 313
  color for, 311
  display in Formula Bar Name box, 99
  for named cells and ranges, Q-50, 306
  range of cells, 303
  workbooks from different folder, 304
  worksheets and workbooks as part of, 304
cells in Excel worksheet, 159
  activating insertion point within, 260
  borders, 358, 376
  changing content, 260
  deleting, 261
  filling with data series, 161
  formatting automatically, based on content, 264
  indicator for active, 163
  inserting, 262
  merging, Q-48, 375
  moving to last occupied, 99

names, 160, 306
referencing. *See* cell references
selecting, Q-52, 290
centering text, Q-31, 354
in footer, 439
change tracking. *See* Track Changes feature
character styles, Q-29, 236
applying, 237
for index entries, 454
characters. *See also* non-printing characters
formatting, 363–365, 366, G-533
formatting (practice exercise), 368
maximum visible in Excel cell, 157
spacing for, Q-29, 365, G-533
chart area, 266, G-533
Chart settings, in Excel, 24
chart sheets in Excel, 283
appearance on printed page, 378
hiding, 284
charts in documents and presentations, creating,
Q-26, 277–282
charts in workbooks, 265
choosing type of, Q-46, 265, 276
creating, Q-46, 267–276
data limitations, 157
font size, 271
formatting, Q-46
including in e-mail, 492
inserting or linking to, Q-26
modifying, 266
sheets for, 156
Chicago Manual of Style, for bibliography, 462
Chinese dictionary, 493
Choose A File dialog box (PowerPoint), 185
Choose A Picture dialog box, 398
for watermark, 440
Choose Attachment dialog box, 485, 489
circle, drawing, 383
circular references, resolution setting in Excel, 25
citations
inserting, Q-26, 462
recording information about source, 462
Citations palette (Word), 18
Classic Photo Album presentation template, 194
click action for mouse, 5
Click And Type feature, 355, G-533
clip art, Q-10
inserting, 386
Clip Art Gallery
image for slide background, 334
opening, 388
Clipboard, Q-11, G-533
copying line of text to, 222
to move or copy text, 217
clock, in Dock, 520

closing
document windows, Q-6, 6
Elements Gallery, Q-7
files, Q-6, 47
workbooks in Excel, 55
codes for information fields, displaying, Q-33
collaboration. *See* Track Changes feature
color
adding when not part of scheme, 229
of alphanumeric watermark, 441
of annotation pen in PowerPoint, 342
of balloons, 418
for cell references, 311
changing, of theme element (PowerPoint), 325
changing scheme for, Q-18
in diagrams, 408
of e-mail message, 488
of Entourage category, 522, 523
Excel settings for, 24
of fonts, 365, 373
for Office programs, 31
of paragraph background, 228, 361
of pen for notebook Scribbles, 140
PowerPoint slides, Q-61
saving scheme in Office Theme, 93
of shapes, 384
when tracking changes, 414
color gradients in PowerPoint, 320, 326
color schemes, 228, G-533
applying, 231–235
for cover page, 433
currently selected, 230
for headers and footers, 438
for PowerPoint, Q-62, 324
Colors dialog box, 373
Colors palette, 373
column charts, 265
column headings in Excel, 159, G-533
hiding, 96
Column Settings dialog box, 262
column view in Save As pane, switching
between other views and, 47
column_index_num argument, in functions, 299
columns in Excel
deleting, 261
hiding, 161
inserting, 260
maximum width, 157
resizing, Q-46, 160, 166, 291
selecting, Q-52, 159, 166, 290
comma separated values (.csv) file format, 105
Command key, 9
commands, 9, G-533
accessing to control Mac, Q-18
with ellipsis (...), 130
gray, 370

comments, Q-28, 413, G-533
  deleting, 416
  inserting, Q-27, 416
  reviewing, 416
commercial clip art, inserting, 386
compatibility issues, Q-10
Compatibility Report, Q-11
  settings related to, 29
Compatibility Report palette, 17
compiling bibliographies, Q-26, 462–464
concatenation of text, 299
Conditional Formatting, in Excel, 264
configuring e-mail accounts, Q-76
contact groups, Q-76, 518
contact records in Entourage, 29, 511, 513, G-533
  creating, Q-74, Q-76, 515
  display order, Q-74
  editing, Q-76, 516
  linking, 517
  Summary page, 514
  To Do flag for, 519
contact window, 514, G-534
Contemporary Photo Album presentation
    template, 194
Content pane (Entourage), 471
contiguous slides, selecting, 184
Continuous section break, 352
converting file format, for sharing files, 46
Copy Cells option, for Auto Fill, 162
copy of file, creating and opening, 44
copying
  cells in Excel worksheet, Q-48
  with Clipboard, Q-11, 217
  files, Q-8, 44
  formatting, Q-13, 367
  index entries, 452. 459
  line of text to Clipboard, 222
  into Scrapbook, Q-28
  sheets in Excel workbook, Q-52
  text in Word, 216
  worksheets in Excel, 285
COUNT( ) function, 298
COUNTA( ) function, 298
COUNTIF( ) function, 298
COUNTIFS( ) function, 298
courtesy copies
  and message replies, 499
  sending e-mail as, 485
cover pages, Q-28, 430–434
  color scheme for, 433
  deleting, 430
  in Elements Gallery, 38
Create Contact window, 516
Create New Source dialog box, 462
Create Theme Colors dialog box, 324, 325

credentials, G-534
criteria argument, for functions, 298
cropping photos, 392
cross-reference entries in index, 450, 451,
    458, G-534
.csv file format, 105
current day, moving to, in Calendar, 524
current information, automatic display in Word
    document, Q-33, 225
Custom Animation palette (PowerPoint), 18
custom fill series, 161
Custom Lists, Excel settings for, 25
custom tab stops, 86
customized color scheme, saving in
    PowerPoint, 325
customized project templates in Word,
    creating, 147
  practice exercise, 148–291
cutting and pasting, with Clipboard, Q-47, 217, 222
cycle diagrams, 402

D

data, in Excel
  charting. *See* charts in workbooks
  workbook storage maximums, 157
  working with, 286
data definitions, 159
data entry in worksheet, 158–159
  filling with data series, 161
  setting restrictions, 262
Data Interchange Format, 105
data labels in charts, 267, G-534
  formatting, 271
Data menu (Excel), 24
data points in Excel worksheet, 159, G-534
data series in Excel, Q-48, 159, G-534
  filling cells with, 161
  Format dialog box for, 281
data sets, creating custom, in Excel, 25
Data Validation dialog box, 262
date, inserting, Q-33, Q-49, 225
date fields, in header or footer, 379
Dates And Reminder dialog box, 520
datum, 158
DAY( ) function, 297
Day view for Calendar, 524
days of week, Auto Fill in Excel, 161
decimal places in cells, specifying, Q-50
default document template, in Word, 122
default font, for body text, 364
default location
  for Excel worksheets, Q-52
  for PowerPoint files, Q-66, 26
  for saving files, Q-16

default orientation, of worksheets, 289
default settings, for paragraph and character formatting, reverting to, 355, 362
default tab stops, 86
default view, in Excel, Q-53, 92
Define Name dialog box (Excel), 307
Delete dialog box (Excel), 291
Deleted Items folder, 505
  emptying, 503
  schedule for emptying, 507
deleting
  background picture from e-mail, 492
  cells in Excel worksheet, Q-47, 261
  columns or rows in Excel, Q-47, 261
  comments, 416, 422
  cover pages, Q-28, 430
  custom formatting in Word, 362
  data from worksheet, 290
  e-mail messages, Q-78, 503
  e-mail messages (practice exercise), 505–509
  e-mail signature, Q-79
  Entourage category, 523
  folders from Favorites Bar, Q-79
  index entries, Q-32, 452
  page breaks, Q-34
  paragraph marks, 224
  rejecting changes, Q-36
  section breaks, Q-35
  selected text, 220
  slides in PowerPoint, Q-62
  table of contents, Q-36, 447
  text in cell, 260
  text in Word, Q-11, 214
  text on slide, 191
descenders, 365
desktop, starting programs from, Q-8
desktop alerts, 475, G-534
Details pane, for template information, 143
Details view, of Project Gallery, 134
diagonal watermark, 322
diagrams, 401
  creating from scratch, 402
  inserting, Q-17
  modifying, Q-17, 403
  practice exercise, 404
  sizing, 407
  types, 401
dialog boxes, moving, Q-6
.dic file format, 93
dictionaries, 493
  Reference Tools palette to access, 17
.dif file format, 105
displaying. See hiding or displaying
distribution, changing, Q-13

Dock
  clock in, 520
  Microsoft Project Gallery icon in, 132, 142
  program icons, 4, 32
docking toolbars, 12
  in PowerPoint, 26
  in Word, 21
.docm file format, 46, 92
document compatibility, checking, Q-10
Document dialog box (Word), 128
document elements, inserting, from Elements Gallery, 15
Document Elements tab, 38, 431
  Bibliographies group, 464
  cover page designs, 430
  Cover Pages group, 38
  headers, 435, 436
  Table of Contents, 38, 442, 445
Document Map, Q-37, 87
document page setup, Word
  margins, 350
  numbering, 436
  orientation, 349
  size, 348
document templates, 122, 239–240, G-534
  applying, 241–252
  creating, 240
Document Theme panel, 230, 325
  Advantage theme thumbnail, 234
  Colors list, 235, 325
document windows, 6
  changing size, 7, 34
  closing, Q-6, 6
  hiding, Q-6
  opening more than one, Q-19
  resizing, Q-6
  splitting and arranging, 58
  title bar, 6, 33
  typical configuration, 8
documents (files)
  checking compatibility of, Q-10
  closing, Q-6, 47
  copying, Q-8
  double-clicking in Finder to start program, 4
  inserting in Excel worksheets, Q-49
  inserting in Word document, Q-33, 125
  opening, Q-7, Q-9
  printing contents of, Q-15
  saving, Q-7
  saving multiple versions, 47
  viewing multiple, Q-19
documents (files) in Word, 43
  attaching template, Q-29, 240
  automatic display of current information, 225

documents (files) in Word (*continued*)
cover pages, 430–434
creating, Q-33, 121, 122, 126–132
creating chart in, 277–282
creating from project template, 132–135, 142–146
editing text, 214
headers and footers, 434, 436
hierarchical view of headings, 87
inserting or linking to external content, 125
moving around in, Q-37, 77–86, 90–91
moving to specific page, Q-37, 144
opening, 44, 49
page and section breaks, 351–353
PowerPoint presentation created from, 203
properties, Q-28, 121
red wavy line for errors in, 129
reviewing, 414–426
saving, 45, 93
selecting entire, 215, 216
table of contents, 442–447
text entry, 124
undo changes, 219
unsaved, 127
versions, 420
viewing, 76
watermark for, Q-38, 440
.docx file format, 46, 92
.dot file format, 92, 239
.dotm file format, 92, 239
.dotx file format, 92, 239, 240
double-sided printing, 145
downloading clip art from Microsoft Online
site, 389
Draft view (Word), 76
and charts, 279
horizontal line, 351
drafts of e-mail messages, Q-78, 486
drag action for mouse, 5
drag-and-drop editing, 216, G-534
dragging, G-534
to add image, 396
paragraphs, Q-12, 223
drop zone, G-534
due date, for To Do item, 520

E

Edit Account dialog box, 482, 497
Edit commands, customizing, 28
Edit menu, 10
Clear, Clear Formatting, 362, 372
Copy To Scrapbook, 224
Delete Slide, 184
Find, 60, 64
Replace, 62

Edit Schedule dialog box, 507
editing text in Word, 214
practice exercise, 220
program behavior for, Q-12
Elements Gallery, 14–16
Charts tab, 266, 268, 276, 279
closing, 97
color scheme changes, 31
Document Elements tab. *See* Document
Elements tab
managing behavior and appearance, Q-7
opening and closing, Q-7
Publication Templates tab, 136
setting for opening automatically, 31
Sheets tab, 174, 178
Slide Layouts tab, 183, 197, 337
SmartArt tab, 402, 404
tabs in, 15
WordArt tab, 321
ellipsis (...), commands with, 130
e-mail accounts
configuring, Q-76
connecting to, 475
e-mail messages
Address Book for selecting recipient, 516
addressing, Q-77, 484–485
color of, 488
deleting, 503, 505–509
etiquette, 499
formatting, 492
history of actions, 502
Inbox for, 491
personalizing content, 492–495
Schedule for checking server for, 504
starting new, Q-77
To Do flag for, 519
e-mail messages, creating and sending, Q-74,
484–491
addressing, Q-77, 484–485
attaching files, Q-78, 485, 489
practice exercise, 487
saving drafts, Q-78, 486
sending messages, 486
e-mail signature, 492, G-534
automatic insertion, Q-79, 497
creating, Q-79, 496
embedded charts, making changes to, Q-27, 280
emptying Deleted Items folder, 503
schedule for, 507
Encarta encyclopedia, 493
Reference Tools palette to access, 17
End key, 90
Entourage
assigning categories, 521
capabilities, 469

contact groups, 518
contact record creation, 29
deleting messages, 503
editing user information in, Q-19
e-mail messages, creating and sending, 484–491
flagging items for follow up, 519
linking items, 517
modules, Q-76, 470
personalizing, 474
program window features, 472
replying to and forwarding messages, 499–502
replying to and forwarding messages
   (practice exercise), 500
search for information, 531–532
Toolbox, 493
verifying connection settings, 479
equal sign (=), to start formula, 302, 338
equations. *See* formulas in Excel; functions
Error Checking, Excel settings for, Q-48, 25
errors, specific
   #NA, 300
   "Reference is not valid," 390
errors in Word documents, red wavy line for, 129
ESRI Community Data dataset, 282
EVEN( ) function, 297
Even Page section break, 352
even pages, header or footer for, 435, 436–437
events. *See* Calendar (Entourage)
Events category, of templates, 143
Excel
   borders in, Q-49, 358, 376
   data entry restriction, 262
   date and time fields in header or footer, 379
   file formats, 104
   Find and Replace in, 64
   formatting, 375
   Formula Builder palette, 18. *See also* Toolbox
   importing data, 159
   inserting document elements from Gallery, 15
   inserting symbols, 390
   magnification range, 57
   maximizing screen working space, 96–97
   menu bar, 9
   menu bar and program windows, 9
   Object Palette shapes, 384
   opening workbook in, 51
   Preferences dialog box, 28
   quitting, 55
   ScreenTips in, for formula syntax, 99
   Search box for program settings, 27
   selecting text, 260
   shapes in, 385
   templates, 104, 240
   toolbars, 11
   tools, 24–25
   user information stored by, Q-19, 29
Excel Add-In file format, 104
Excel Preferences dialog box, Q-53, 24, 92, 100
   Custom Lists page, 161
   General page, default font changes, 165
   View page, 96
Exchange accounts, 476
   folder structure, 481
exporting
   outline from Word into PowerPoint, Q-65, 204
   presentation outline, in .rtf file format, 204, 205
   presentation slide, as image, 115
external content in Word document, inserting or
   linking, 125

F

Favorites Bar (Entourage), Q-79, 471
feedback, on document content, 416
Feedback commands, settings related to, 29
field codes, G-534
Field dialog box, 226
fields, G-534
   automatic updating in Word, 225
   for citations, 463
   for contact records, 512
   displaying codes, 449
   manually updating information, 227
   for table of contents, 446
file formats, 46
   in Excel, 104
   in PowerPoint, 114
   in Word, 92
File menu, 10
   Close, 47
   Open, 44
   Open Recent, 101
   Print, 69
   Project Gallery, 142, 182
   Properties, 127
   Quit, 47
   Save, 44
   Save As, 47, 49
   Send To, PowerPoint, 204
files. *See* documents
Fill Color gallery, 361
Fill Formatting Only option, for Auto Fill, 162
fill handle in Excel, 167
Fill Without Formatting option, for Auto Fill,
   162, 312
filling cells, Q-48, G-534
filtering Address Book records, 512
Final Showing Markup version of document, 420

Final version of document, 420
Finance Tools worksheet templates, 172
Find and Replace, Q-12, 60–68
  in Excel, 64
  in PowerPoint, 65
  practice exercise, 66
  in Word, 60–64, 144
Finder, G-534
  starting programs from, Q-8, 4, 32
First Line Indent, for paragraph, 353
flagging Entourage items for follow up, Q-80, 519
floating toolbars, Q-9, 12
  in Excel, 24
floating Toolbox, 18
  in Word, 21
Folder list (Entourage), Q-80, 473, G-534
folders
  adding to Clip Gallery photos page, 392
  Favorites Bar (Entourage), Q-79
  Photos page, Q-14
  for saving files, Q-8, 45
Font Book, 363
  opening, Q-13
font color, G-534
Font Color gallery, 235, 373
Font dialog box, 371
font effect, G-534
Font menu (Word), 20, 365
font scheme, 228, 229, G-534
  currently selected, 230
font size, G-534
font styles, 365, G-534
fonts, 363, G-534
  for alphanumeric watermark, 441
  attributes of, 365
  changing for selected text, Q-14
  changing scheme for, Q-18
  changing size to fit text in slide placeholder, 190
  for charts, 275
  color, 365, 373
  default for Excel worksheet, Q-48, 165
  displaying list, 369
  effects, 365
  in Entourage, 474
  in Normal style, 237
  in PowerPoint slides, Q-64
  saving in Office Theme, 93
  size in charts, 271
  in slide master, 339
footers, G-534
  date and time fields in, 379
  in Excel, 157, 286
  page numbers in, Q-34
  in slide master, Q-64, 339
  themes for, Q-31
  in Word, Q-28, 434, 438

Force Quit Applications dialog box, 391
forcing programs to quit, Q-6
Format AutoShape dialog box (Word), Q-17, 384, 385
Format Axis dialog box, 275
Format Background dialog box (PowerPoint), 329
  Color And Transparency section, 331
  Gradient page, 330
  Picture button, 334
  Styles And Direction section, 333
  Texture button, 333
Format Data Labels dialog box, 271
Format dialog box, for data series, 281
Format menu, 10, 37
  Document, 128
  Hide/Unhide Sheet, 284
  Paragraph, 320, 355
  Theme Colors, 324
  Unhide, 284
Format Object dialog box, 410
  Size page, 407
Format Painter, 367, 369, G-535
  for shapes, 384
Format Shape dialog box, Q-17, 384, 410
Format Text dialog box, 270, 319
  Paragraph page, 320
  for text in shapes, 386
Formatted balloon, 422
formatting
  applying existing to other content, 367
  cells in Excel worksheet, Q-47
  characters, 363–365
  characters (practice exercise), 368
  charts, Q-46
  copying, Q-13
  e-mail messages, 492
  legend in charts, 270
  numeric data in Excel, Q-48, 375
  pictures, Q-15
  removing from paragraphs, Q-26
  replacing, Q-13
  searching for, Q-29
  shapes, Q-17
  slides inserted from other presentations, 187
  text in PowerPoint slides, 318
  tracking changes to, 414
formatting, Excel, 262, 375
  automatically based cell on content, 264
formatting, Word
  in Find and Replace, 62
  page numbers, 436
  page numbers in index, 451
  paragraph marks and, 124, 356
  paragraphs, 353
  replacing, 62

Formatting Palette, Q-14, 16, 17, 37, 385
  Alignment And Spacing panel, 271, 353, 360, 362, 439
  Borders And Shading panel, 361
  Bullets And Numbering panel, 318
  for changing shapes, 384
  Chart Options panel, 272
  for customizing diagram, 403
  Document Margins panel, 351, 360
  Document Theme panel, 233
  Font panel, 235, 271, 368, 371
  Grow Font button, 371
  for modifying photos, 392
  in Notebook Layout view, 140
  Number panel, 375
  Page Setup panel, 96
  Quick Styles And Effects panel, 407, 410
  Scribble panel, 141
  Shadow panel, 141
  for shapes, 323
  Shrink Font button, 371
  Slide Background panel, 327, 329
  SmartArt Graphic Styles panel, 407
  Styles panel, 237, 242
Formatting toolbar, 11, 12
  Bullets button, 244
  Percent Style button, 313
  Style list, 242
  in Word, 36, 128
Formula Bar in Excel, Q-49, 99, 301, 312
  hiding, 96
Formula Builder, 18, 300
  displaying, 301
formulas in Excel, 295. *See also* cell references
  creating, Q-49, 300–303
  creating (practice exercise), 308–315
  displaying, Q-49, 100–103, 305
  functions in, 303. *See also* functions
  reference cell for, 302
  referencing range of cells, 303
  referencing worksheets and workbooks, 304
  ScreenTips for syntax, 99
forwarding e-mail messages, Q-78, 499
frames, for table of contents, 442
French dictionary, 493
functions, 296–300, G-535
  categories, 296
  in formulas, 303
  generic, 299
  numeric, 297
  searching for, 301
  text, 299
  value as argument, 298
Fundraising worksheet templates, 172

G

GAL (Global Address List), 514
galleries, 13, G-535
  color scheme, 31
  customizing commands, 28
  displaying or hiding, Q-6
General dialog box, Measurements Units, 86
generic functions, 299
German dictionary, 493
.gif file format, exporting presentation slide as, 115
Global Address List (GAL), 514
global template, 240
goal seeking, iterations setting in Excel, 25
Go To, 79,95
gradient sliders, for slide background, Q-61, 330
grammar checker, Q-35, 423
Graph Paper worksheet templates, 172
graphics. *See also* images; shapes; SmartArt utility
  compatibility with earlier Office versions, 400
  for e-mail background, 492
  in e-mail signature, 496
  including in e-mail, 492
  resizing, Q-13
  rotating, Q-13
  for watermarks, Q-38, 440
Graphics Interchange Format (.gif), exporting presentation slide as, 115
gray commands, 370
Greek, 494
greeked text, in Word template, 135, G-535
gridlines, displaying and hiding, 377
group, G-535
groups, in Elements Gallery, 15

H

handwritten notes, in notebook, 140
hanging indent, removing from presentation text, 320
Hanging Index marker, for paragraph, 353
headers, G-535
  date and time fields in, 379
  in Excel, 157, 286
  page numbers in, Q-34
  in slide master, Q-64, 339
  themes for, Q-31
  in Word, Q-28, 434, 436, 438
headings in document
  displaying and hiding (Excel), 377
  font for, 229, 364
  hierarchical view, 87
  jumping to, Q-37
  styles for outline, 204
Help menu, 10

hidden characters, displaying, 452, 455
    and document pagination, 460
Hide Toolbars button, 6, 12
hiding or displaying
    columns and rows in Excel, Q-47, 161
    document windows, Q-6
    formulas in Excel, Q-49, 100–103, 305
    galleries, Q-6
    headings in worksheet, 377
    index entry fields, 452
    mouse pointer in PowerPoint, 341
    non-printing characters, Q-38, 88, 220, 452, 460
    program elements, Q-15
    rulers, Q-34
    selected text, Q-32
    sheets in Excel workbook, Q-52, 284
    slide background, Q-61, 334, 336
    slide show in PowerPoint, 341
    status bar in Excel, 93, 97, 100
    text in Word, 452
    toolbars, Q-9, 12, 35, 39, 47
    Toolbox, 18
    worksheet gridlines, 377
hierarchy diagrams, 402
Highlight Changes dialog box, 414, 417
highlighting text, Q-30
history of actions, for e-mail message, 502
HLOOKUP( ) function, 299, 300
Home Essentials category, of Excel templates,
    170, 172
Home key, in Word, 78, 90
horizontal scroll bar, 6
    hiding in Excel, 97
horizontal window arrangement, 58
.htm file format
    in Excel, 105
    in PowerPoint, 115
    in Word, 93
hyperlinks, color in Word theme, 228

I

icon view in Save As pane, switching between
    other views and, 47
icons
    as links to charts, 278
    for Word document types, 126
IF( ) function, 300
IFERROR( ) function, 300
images
    adding to Clip Gallery, Q-10
    adding to PowerPoint slides, Q-65
    creating watermark with, Q-68, 323
    formatting, Q-15

inserting and modifying, Q-14, 393, 396
    for slide background, Q-61, 320, 334
IMAP, G-535
    for Exchange mailbox access, 476
    folder structure, 481
importing data, G-535
    into Excel, 159
    outline into PowerPoint, Q-65, 203
Inbox, message in, 491
indent markers, on ruler, 85, G-535
indented index, 453
indenting paragraphs in Word, Q-31, 353, 362
Index And Tables dialog box, 448, 450, 453, 460
    Table Of Contents page, 444
index entries, 450, G-535
    case of, 457
    copying, 459
    editing, 452
    selecting, 461
    styles for, 454
index entry fields, 450, G-535
    hiding and displaying, 452
    inserting, Q-32, 450
indexes, 450–461, G-535
    creating, Q-32, 453
    creating (practice exercise), 454–461
    cross-reference entries, 450, 451, 458
    formatting page numbers, 451
    indented or run-in, 453
    non-printing character display and document
        pagination, 460
    subentries, 450, 458
    term selection, 452
information fields, Q-33
Infusion font scheme, 234
Insert As Object dialog box, 278
Insert File dialog box, 130
Insert menu, 10
    Break and Page Break, 351, 352, 447
    Chart, 279
    Clip Gallery, 388
    Columns, 260
    Comment, 421
    Date And Time, 226
    Field, 226
    Index And Tables, 448, 450, 453, 456
    New Slide, 183
    Object, 277
    Slides From, Other Presentation, 185
    Watermark, 440, 441
Insert Watermark dialog box, 440, 441
inserting
    bibliography, 464
    cells in Excel worksheet, 262

charts in documents and presentations, Q-26, 277
citations, Q-26
clip art, Q-10
columns in Excel, 260
comments, Q-27, 416
commercial clip art, 386
content in PowerPoint placeholder, 189, 395
cover pages, Q-28
document elements, from Elements Gallery, 15
e-mail signatures, Q-79, 497
external content in Word document, 125
files into Excel, Q-49
files into Word, Q-33
images, 393
index entry fields, Q-32, 450
manual line break, 124
page breaks, Q-34
page numbers in Word, Q-34, 436
rows in Excel, 261
section breaks, Q-35
shapes, Q-17, 382
sheets in Excel workbook, Q-52
slides in other presentations, 184
symbols, as text or graphics, 390
table of contents, 442
text in Word, Q-11, 214
textual watermark on slide, 321
themed header or footer, 435
insertion point
    activating within cell, 260
    blinking in Word, 124
    displaying location on status bar, 78
    moving in Word, 78
instant messages, sending, Q-74
instructions, in Monthly Home Budget
    worksheet, 176
interface, G-535
Introducing PowerPoint 2008 presentation
    template, 194
inviting contacts to meetings, Q-74
Invoices worksheet templates, 174
Italian dictionary, 493
italic font, 365

J

Japanese dictionary, 493
JPEG images, exporting presentation slides as, 115
jumping to specific page, Q-37
justified text, 354, 360

K

Keep Lines Together option, for page breaks, 352
Keep With Next option, for page breaks, 352
key combination, G-535
keyboard commands, for moving between slides
    when running slide show, 341
keyboard shortcuts, 9
    for copy, cut, and paste, 217, 218, 219
    to move around, 78, 94, 107
    for PowerPoint Slide view, 106
    for selecting in Word, 216
    for slide show tasks, 342
keywords, G-535
keywords, for Scrapbook clippings, 218
Korean dictionary, 493

L

Landscape orientation, 349
last slide, setting as black, 116
layout for PowerPoint slides, Q-60, Q-67
layout placeholders. *See* placeholders
Ledger Sheets category, of Excel templates,
    170, 173
Left Indent marker, for paragraph, 354
left-aligned text, in Word, 354
legends in charts, 267, G-535
    formatting, 270
levels of items on slides, Q-62
libraries, adding to Photos page, Q-14
licensing, for clip art from Microsoft Online
    site, 389
line break, manual, inserting, 124
line graphs, 266
lines of text
    copying to Clipboard, 222
    selecting in Word, 215, 222
    spacing, Q-31, 360
Link icon, 517
linking
    to charts, inserting icon for, 278
    charts in documents and presentations, Q-26, 277
    to contact records, Q-76
    Entourage items, 517
    external content in Word document, 125
    to files, Q-33
    text boxes, 136
Links To window, for address, 517
list diagrams, 401
list sheets in Excel, 156, 282
    hiding, 284
    printing, 379

list styles, Q-29, 236
List view
   for Calendar, 524
   for Project Gallery, 134
   in Save As pane, switching between other
      views and, 47
Lists worksheet templates, 174
Live Word Count feature, 78
local formatting, of e-mail message, 492, G-535
lookup_value argument, in functions, 299
LOWER( ) function, 299
lowercase characters, 366
Lucent Glass display, for Notebook Layout
     view, 138

M

macro-enabled template, 122, G-535
Mactopia Downloads page, 22
magnification level, Q-19, 57
   in Excel, 96
   in Word, 80
Mail (Entourage), 470
mail server, Schedule for checking, 504
manual line break, inserting, 124
manual page breaks, 89, G-535
   inserting, 351
margins, G-535
   of chart sheet, 379
   of document, Q-28, 350, 360
   on ruler, 85
Mark Index Entry dialog box, Q-32, 450, 456
master pages in Word publications, 137
   viewing, 146
Match Case option, in Word Find and Replace, 61
mathematical calculations. See formulas in Excel
matrix diagrams, 402
MAX( ) function, 297, 298, 303
maximum data storage in Excel, 157
measurement units
   changing, Q-35, 86
   on rulers, 86
meetings, inviting contacts to, Q-74
menu bar, 9
   Apple icon on, 10
   in Entourage, 472
menus, 9
merging cells in Excel, Q-48, 375
Message menu, Remove Background Picture, 492
.mht file format
   in Excel, 105
   in Word, 93
mice, 5
microphone, for audio notes, 141

Microsoft Customer Experience Improvement
     Program, 29
Microsoft Encarta encyclopedia, 493
   Reference Tools palette to access, 17
Microsoft Entourage 2008 for Mac. See Entourage
Microsoft Excel. See Excel
Microsoft Messenger for Mac, 3
Microsoft Office 2008 programs
   personalizing functionality, 27–31
   starting, 4
   updating and enhancing, 22
Microsoft Office Compatibility Pack for Word,
     Excel, and PowerPoint 2007 File Formats, 46
Microsoft Office document, 4
Microsoft Office files, 43
   opening, 44
   printing, 69
   viewing, 56
Microsoft Office Fluent user interface Ribbon, 14
Microsoft Office OneNote for Windows, 138
Microsoft Office Online Web site, adding clip art
     from, 388
Microsoft PowerPoint. See PowerPoint
Microsoft Visual Basic for Applications (VBA)
   macros, 92
Microsoft Word. See Word
MIN( ) function, 298
Mini Calendar (Entourage), Q-80, 472, 524
Minimize button, of document window, 6, 34
minimizing Toolbox, 18
misspellings, adding to AutoCorrect list, Q-10
mixed reference, 305
Modern Language Association of America (MLA),
     bibliographic style, 462
Modify Style dialog box, 246
modules, Microsoft Entourage 2008 for Mac,
     Q-76, 470
month, displaying in Calendar, Q-80, 524
Month view for Calendar, 524
Monthly Home Budget worksheet,
     instructions, 176
months of year, Auto Fill in Excel, 161
mouse, 5
mouse buttons, primary/secondary, 5
mouse pointer
   as pen in Scribble mode, 140
   in PowerPoint, hiding or changing, 341
.mov file format, 115
Move Chart dialog box, 269
move handle, for table of contents frame, 442
Move Or Copy dialog box (Excel), 285, 287
moving
   charts, Q-46
   via Clipboard, Q-12
   dialog boxes, Q-6

by dragging, Q-12, 223
events in Calendar, Q-80
floating toolbars, Q-9
index entries, 452
between objects, 79
between pages, Q-37, 79
placeholders on slide, 338
selected text on slide, 191
sheets in Excel workbook, Q-52
between slides, Q-67
slides in PowerPoint, Q-65, 337
table of contents, Q-36
text in Word, 216
through slides in running slide show, Q-63, 341
worksheets in Excel, 285
moving around open Excel worksheets, 95
moving around open Word documents, Q-37,
    77–86, 90–91
  to specific page, 144
multilevel list, PowerPoint formatting for, 319
multilingual dictionary, 493
My Publication Templates folder, 148
My Templates folder, 147
My Themes folder, 148

N

#N/A error, 300
named cells and ranges, 306–307
named references, Q-51, G-535
names
  of active document, 6
  of Excel cell, 160
  of sheets in Excel workbook, Q-52, 286
Names dialog box, 307
navigating. *See* moving around open Word
    documents
navigation area, G-535
Navigation pane, PowerPoint, 106, 111
  Delete Slide, 184
  Outline page, 112, 190
  Slides page, 197
Navigation pane, Word, 87
  Document Map, 87
  thumbnail of publication pages, 233
NETWORKDAYS( ) function, 303
New Account dialog box, 481
new blank document, creating in Word, Q-33, 122
New Blank Document icon, 126
New Blank Notebook Layout Document icon, 126
New Blank Publishing Layout Document icon, 126
New Folder dialog box, 55
New page, in Project Gallery, 133
New Style dialog box, 249
Next Page button, 91

noncontiguous slides, selecting, 184
noncontiguous text, cutting and moving, 217
non-printing characters
  bent arrow, 124
  displaying, Q-38, 88, 220, 452, 460
  paragraph marks, 124
Normal document template, 240
  listing all styles in, 245
  styles in, 236
Normal style, 237
Normal view (Excel), 92, 96
Normal view (PowerPoint), 106, 108
  layout placeholders, 188
Normal.dotm template, 122, 128
NOT( ) function, 300
Notebook Layout view (Word), 76, 138, 148
notebooks in Word, 138–172
  handwritten notes in, 140
  printing, 149
Notes (Entourage), 470
notes, inserting, 416
Notes pane, in PowerPoint, 106
Notification settings, in Entourage, 475
number format, for page numbers, 436
numbered list, converting bulleted list to,
    Q-62, 319
numbering
  pages in Word, 436
  weeks, 525
numeric data, formatting in Excel, Q-48, Q-50, 375
numeric functions, 297

O

Object dialog box, 277
Object Gallery, shapes with integrated text
    boxes, 136
Object Palette, 17, 381
  Clip Art page, 386, 396
  graphic objects available, 382
  opening, 393
  Photos page, 391
  shapes, 383, 393
  Symbols page, 390
objects, moving between, 79
ODD( ) function, 297
Odd Page section break, 352
odd pages, header or footer for, 435, 436–437
Office files, G-536. *See also* documents (files);
    PowerPoint presentations; workbooks, in Excel
  closing, Q-6
Office Open XML File Format Converter
    for Mac, 46
Office Open XML Formats, 46, 104

Office theme
    for PowerPoint presentation, 115, 182
    saving, 93
Office Theme template, G-536
    for presentation, 192, 193
    saving presentation as, 195
OneNote for Windows, 138
"open apple" key, 9
Open dialog box, 44, 48
Open Library Or Folder dialog box, 392
opening
    contact records, Q-74
    document in Word, 49
    Elements Gallery, Q-7
    files, Q-7, Q-9
    Font Book, Q-13
    Office files, 44
    presentations in PowerPoint, 53
    Project Gallery, Q-9
    workbooks in Excel, 51
Opulent color scheme, 235
OR( ) function, 300
order of sheets in workbook, changing, 285
ordered lists. See numbered list, converting
    bulleted list to
orientation
    of page, 349
    of worksheets, default, 289
orphans, from page breaks, 352, G-536
outdenting slide list item, 318
outline, adding to photos, 393
outline in Word
    heading styles for, 204
    importing to PowerPoint, Q-65, 203
Outline page, in PowerPoint Navigation pane,
    Q-67, 109, 112, 190
Outline view (Word), 76
    and charts, 279
overhead projector, slide settings for, 339

P

Page Break Before option, for page breaks, 352
page breaks
    in Excel, Q-50
    in Word, Q-34, 351–353
    automatic or manual, 89
    deleting, 353
Page Layout view (Excel), 92, 163
Page Number Format dialog box, 436
page numbering in Word, Q-34, 436
    formatting in index, 451
page picker, 84
page setup, control, 348

Page Setup dialog box (Excel), 378
Page Setup dialog box (PowerPoint), 339
    Header/Footer, 340
Page Setup dialog box (Word), 123, 348
Page Width magnification level, 85
pages
    moving between, Q-37, 79
    moving insertion point to next, 84
    scaling content to fit, 377
    viewing simultaneously, Q-38
pagination of document, non-printing character
    display and, 460
palettes, in Toolbox, 17, G-536. See also Toolbox
panels of commands, 17, G-536
paper format, for printing slides, 339
Paragraph dialog box (Word), 355
    Line And Page Breaks page, 352
paragraph formatting, G-536
paragraph marks
    deleting, 224
    displaying, 88
    and formatting, 356
    in Word display, 124
    in Word Find and Replace, 62
paragraph selector on notebook page, 149, G-536
paragraph styles in Word, Q-29, 236
    applying, 237
    Heading styles as, 243
    for index entries, 454
paragraphs in PowerPoint, formatting, 318
paragraphs in Word, G-536
    background color, 361
    borders and shading, Q-26, 356
    combining, Q-11
    creating, Q-11
    dragging, 223
    indenting, Q-31, 353, 362
    removing formatting from, Q-26
    selecting, 214, 215
    starting new, 124, 129
    white space between, 355
paragraphs in Word, formatting, 353
    horizontal text alignment, 354
    indenting, 353
    practice exercise, 358
    vertical alignment, 355
parentheses, for functions, 296
password protection for Excel worksheets, Q-50
pasteboard, in Word Notebook Layout view, 139
pasting
    with Clipboard, Q-11, 217
    column titles in worksheet, 291
    keyboard shortcuts for, 217, 218, 219
    into Scrapbook, Q-28
pause, when running slide show, 341

.pdf file format
  in Excel, 105
  in PowerPoint, 115
  in Word, 93
pen, for notebook Scribbles, 140
Pen Color, for pointer as annotation pen in
    PowerPoint, 342
personalized project templates in Word,
    creating, 147
  practice exercise, 148–151
photos
  in Clip Gallery, 386, 391
  creating watermark with, 322
  presentation templates for, 194
Photos page, folders in, Q-14
phrases, reference information for, Q-16
picture. *See* images
Picture panel, 323
pie charts, 266
  creating, 267–276
pink background, for table of contents, 445
Pitch Book presentation template, 194
PivotTable toolbar (Excel), 24
placeholders, G-535, G-536
  on cover page, 430, 432
  moving on slide, Q-65, 338
  in PowerPoint Normal view, 188, 189, 395
  in Word template, 135
plain text file format, 93
Planners worksheet templates, 173
plot area, 266, G-536
plotting data. *See* charts in workbooks
.png file format, exporting presentation
    slide as, 115
point action for mouse, 5
points, 365, G-536
POP account, G-536
  for Exchange mailbox, 476
  folder structure, 481
population statistics, 282
Portable Document Format (PDF)
  in Excel, 105
  in PowerPoint, 115
  in Word, 93
Portable Network Graphics file format, exporting
    presentation slide as, 115
Portfolios worksheet templates, 174
Portrait orientation, 349
Portuguese (Brazilian), 494
.pot file format, 114, 239
.potm file format, 114, 115, 239
.potx file format, 46, 114, 239
PowerPoint
  AutoCorrect function in, 200
  changing character case in, 366

color schemes for, Q-62, 324
creating chart in, 277–282
Custom Animation palette, 18
exporting outline as .rtf file, 204, 205
file formats, 114
Find and Replace, 65
Find and Replace (practice exercise), 66
inserting chart, 277
inserting document elements from Gallery, 15
magnification range, 57
menu bar and document windows, 9, 182
Object Palette shapes, 384
Preferences dialog box, 28
quitting, 55
saving customized color scheme, 325
switching between views, 107
templates in, 240
toolbars, 11
tools, 26
user information stored by, Q-19, 29
viewing and moving around, 106–107
views, 56
PowerPoint package, 115
PowerPoint Preferences dialog box, 26
  AutoCorrect group, 22
PowerPoint presentations, 43, G-536
  adding slides, 183
  advancing, 116
  creating, Q-64, 181, 182, 196
  creating from Project Gallery, 192
  creating from Word document, 203
  custom set of slide masters as template, 339
  ending with black slide, 116
  exporting as outline, Q-65
  hiding, 341
  moving around in, 108
  opening, 44, 53
  pausing, 341
  removing slides, 184
  running, 340–342
  saving, 55
  special themes, 195
  stopping, 116, 342
PowerPoint slides
  adding content, Q-60, 188
  adding to presentation, Q-60, 183
  background customization, Q-61, 320
  bulleted text on, 189
  changing standard settings, 339
  converting bulleted list to, 203
  exporting as images, 115
  formatting backgrounds, 326–336
  formatting text, Q-64, 318
  inserting in other presentations, 184
  layout changes, Q-60, 337

PowerPoint slides (*continued*)
  layout of inserted, 202
  moving, 337
  moving between, 107
  moving placeholders, 338
  paper format for printing, 339
  removing from presentation, 184
  reusing in another presentation, 184
  selecting, 184
  selecting text, 191
  slide masters, 339
  text entry, editing, 191
  titles of, 189
  watermark for, 321–323
.pps file format, 115
.ppsm file format, 114, 115
.ppsx file format, 46, 115
.ppt file format, 114
.pptm file format, 114, 115
.pptx file format, 46, 114
Preferences dialog box, Q-7, 27. *See also* Word
    Preferences dialog box
Preferences dialog box (Entourage), 474, 475
preferences pages, displaying, Q-7
presentations. *See* PowerPoint presentations
Preview pane (Entourage), 473
  for e-mail, 491
preview, print, Q-15, 72
primary mouse button, 5, G-536
primary Office programs, 3
print area, of worksheet, Q-50, 378, G-536
Print dialog box, 69
  Copies & Pages page, 71
Print Layout view (Word), 76, 80, 348
  adding header, 436
  editing header or footer in, 434
printing, Q-14
  chart sheets in Excel, 378
  double-sided, 145
  file contents, Q-15
  hidden text, Q-32
  notebooks in Word, 149
  Office files, 69
  slides in PowerPoint, paper format, 339
  titles in worksheet, 377
  workbooks in Excel, settings for, Q-50
  worksheets in Excel, setup, 377
.prn file format, 105
process diagrams, 401
program menu, 10
programs, 4
  quitting, Q-6, 391
  starting, Q-7, Q-8

Project Center (Entourage), 470
Project Center page, in Project Gallery, 133
Project Gallery, 132, G-536
  behavior and appearance, Q-16
  creating presentation from, 192
  default page displayed, 143
  Excel templates, 170, 175
  opening, Q-9
  Presentations category, 194
  views, 134
project management notebook, creating generic,
    149–150
Project palette, 17
project templates, 239, G-536. *See also* templates,
    in Word
  creating workbook or sheet from, 170–174
  for PowerPoint presentation, 192, 193
PROPER( ) function, 299
properties, G-536
  of styles, 247
  of Word documents, Q-28, 121
Properties dialog box (Word), 123, 127
protecting worksheets, Q-50
publications in Word, 136–137
Publishing Layout view (Word), 76, 136, 137
pyramid diagrams, 402

Q

question mark (?), as Word Find and Replace
    wildcard, 61
Quick Filter (Entourage), 473
Quick Preview pane, 72
QuickTime player, file from PowerPoint for, 115
quitting
  Excel, 55
  forcing programs to quit, Q-6
  PowerPoint, 55
  programs, Q-6, 391
Quiz Show presentation template, 195

R

range of cells
  as function argument, 298
  notational expression for, 292
  referencing in formula, Q-50, 303, 306
  selecting for printing, 378
range_lookup argument, in functions, 300
read-only files, 44, G-536
Recent page, in Project Gallery, 133
red wavy line, in Word documents, for errors, 129
redo changes, Q-12

reference information, Q-16
"Reference is not valid" error, 390
Reference Tools palette, 17, 493
   Thesaurus panel, 494
   Translation panel, 495
referencing cells for formulas, Q-51, 302. *See also*
   cell references
reflections, adding to photos, 392
rejecting changes, Q-36
relationship diagrams, 402
relative cell references, 305
   changing to absolute, 313
reminder
   changing time for Calendar event, 527
   from Entourage, Q-80, 520
renaming. *See* names
Repeat command, 370
REPLACE( ) function, 299
Replace dialog box, 60, 62
Replace Font dialog box (PowerPoint), 68
replacing. *See* Find and Replace
replying to and forwarding messages
   (practice exercise), Q-78
Reports worksheet templates, 174
resize handle, 7, 34
resizing
   columns in Excel, Q-46, 160, 166
   document windows, Q-6
   graphics, Q-13
   layout placeholders, Q-65
Restore button, of document window, 6, 34
Results list
   removing warning from, Q-11
   warning of incompatibility instances, 400
Return key
   in Excel, 165
   for new paragraph in Word, 124, 129, 353
reviewers
   displaying name, 416
   identifying, 415
   viewing comments of specific, 417
reviewing document. *See also* comments
   Track Changes feature for, 413, 414
Reviewing pane, displaying, Q-28
Reviewing toolbar, 415, 419
   New Comment button, 416, 421
   Reviewing Pane button, 416, 423
Ribbon (Office 2007 for Windows), 14
Rich Text Format, 93
Right Indent marker, for paragraph, 354
right-aligned text, in Word, Q-31, 354
right-click action for mouse, 5
right-click and drag action for mouse, 5, 285
rotating graphics, Q-13

rotation handle
   for shapes, 385, 395
   for WordArt object, 322
row headings in Excel, G-536
   hiding, 96
   selecting, 159
row_index_num argument, in functions, 299
rows in Excel
   deleting, 261
   hiding, 161
   inserting, 261
   resizing, Q-46, 160
   selecting, Q-52, 159, 290
.rtf file format, 92
   exporting presentation outline in, 204, 205
rulers, 33, 360, G-536
   displaying or hiding, Q-34, 84
   for Excel worksheet, 164
   indent markers, 353
   margins on, 85
   measurement units, 86
run-in index, 453
running slide show in PowerPoint, 340–342
   pause, 341
Russian, 494

S

sans serif, G-537
Save As dialog box
   in Excel, 168, 176
   in PowerPoint, 195
   in Word, 131, 146
   for templates, 147
Save As pane, 44, 49
   expanding, 54
   switching views in, 47
Save commands, customizing, 28
saving
   customized color scheme, 325
   default location for, Q-16
   e-mail message drafts, Q-78, 486
   files, Q-7, 44, 104
   personalized project templates in Word, 147
   presentations in PowerPoint, 55
   as templates, Q-29
   user information, 29
   Word document, 45, 93, 127
   workbooks in Excel, Q-54
scaling, 377, G-537
Schedule
   for emptying Deleted Items folder, 503
   for event in Calendar, Q-80, 526
scheduling calendar events, Q-74, Q-80, 526

schemes for PowerPoint colors, Q-62, 324
Scrapbook, Q-28, 17, 218, G-537
  to move or copy text, 217
screen working space in Excel, maximizing, 96–97
ScreenTips
  for buttons, 13
  in Excel, for formula syntax, 99
  for identifying reviewer making change, 415
  for Office themes, 233
  in PowerPoint, 109
  for style formatting description, 242
Scribbles, in notebook, 140
scroll arrows, 6
scroll bars, 6, 59
  controlling, Q-15
  hiding in Excel, 97
  in Word, 77
scrolling, Q-19
Search box for program settings, 27
search of Entourage, for information, Q-81, 531–532
searching for a term, Q-12
searching for formatting, Q-29
secondary mouse button, 5, G-537
section breaks in Word, Q-35, 351–353, G-537
  deleting, 353
  and headers and footers, 435
  inserting, 352
sections, G-537
  of Word notebook, 138
security, Excel settings for, 25
Security settings, in Entourage, 475
Select Browse Object button, 79, 91
Select Data Source dialog box, 273
selected text
  deleting, 220
  hiding, Q-32
  moving on slide, 191
selecting, G-537
  in Excel, Q-52, 159, 166, 260
  in Excel, for printing, Q-50, 378
  highlighting text, Q-30
  index entry, 461
  line of text, 222
  rows, columns or cells in Excel, 290
  slides in PowerPoint, Q-66
  text, in general, Q-8
  text in Word, 214, 216
  text on slide, 191
selection area, G-537
  moving pointer to, 369
  in Word, 215
sending e-mail messages, Q-78, 486
sentence, selecting in Word, 214
series axis of chart, 266

series data in Excel, Q-48, 159, G-534
  filling cells with, 161
  Format dialog box for, 281
settings, basic, Q-15
Settings page, in Project Gallery, 133
settings pages, displaying, Q-7
shaded background, in Word, 356
shaded pages, in Excel Page Layout view, 163
shadows
  adding to photos, 392
  for fonts, 365
shadows for paragraphs, Q-26
shapes, Q-17
  adding text to, Q-17, 386
  changing order of stacked, 385
  color of, 384
  in diagrams, 404
  handles for, 385
  inserting and modifying, 382
  for inserting textual watermark on slide, 322
  with integrated text boxes, 136
  rotating, 395
  sizing, 385, 394
sharing files, converting file format for, 46
sheets in Excel workbook, 155. *See also* chart
    sheets in Excel; list sheets in Excel; worksheets
    in Excel
  adding and removing, Q-52, 282
  creating, from project template, 175
  hiding, 284
  managing, 281
  moving or copying, Q-52, 285
  names, 286
  organizing, 285
  working with, 286
signature. *See* e-mail signature
Signatures dialog box, 496
Simple Contemporary display, for Notebook
    Layout view, 138
size. *See also* resizing
  of diagrams, 407
  of font, 364, 370
  of font (in charts), 271
  of shapes, changing, 385, 394
Slide Background panel, Format Background
    button, 329
slide masters, Q-67, 188, G-537
Slide pane, in PowerPoint, 106
slide show in PowerPoint, Q-63. *See also*
    PowerPoint presentations
Slide Show menu (PowerPoint), 26, 341
  View Slide Show, 340
Slide Show view (PowerPoint), 106
Slide Sorter view (PowerPoint), 106, 337
Slide view (PowerPoint), 106, 113

slides. *See* PowerPoint slides
.slk file format, 105
small capitals, 365
smart button, 162, G-537
Smart Cut And Paste Settings dialog box, 221
SmartArt utility, 381, 401, G-537
   creating diagrams from scratch, 402
   diagram types, 401
   modifying diagram, 403
SMTP, G-537
SMTP server, name of, 476
Snow Gloss display, for Notebook Layout view, 138
soft page break, 351, G-537
Software Update, Q-18, 22
sorting Address Book records, 512
Sounds Like option, in Word Find and Replace, 61
source information, recording, Q-26
Space Delimited Text file format, 105
spaces
   between characters, Q-30, 365
   displaying, 88
   between lines of text, Q-31, 360
   Word insertion and deletion, 221
spam filters, G-537
   and blocked attachments, 485
Spanish dictionary, 493
speaker notes, in PowerPoint, 106
special characters
   finding, Q-12
   in Word Find nd Replace, 62
Speller Custom Dictionary file format, 93
Speller Exclude Dictionary file format, 93
spelling, Q-35
   settings in Entourage, 475
   settings to correct common mistakes, 28
Spelling And Grammar feature, Q-35
Spelling settings, in PowerPoint, 26
Spike, G-537
   cutting content from document to, Q-28, 219
   to move or copy text, 217
splash screen, 8, G-537
splitter bars, in PowerPoint, 106
splitting, document windows, 58
Spotlight, 27, 40, G-537
   settings, 475
stacked shapes, changing order, 385
stacking order, changing, Q-13
Standard toolbar, 12, 35
   Format Painter button, 367
   Gallery button, 38
   Help button, 10
   Print button, 69
   Redo button, 219, 220
   Show button, 447, 455
   Slide Show button, 340

   Undo button, 219, 220, 261
   Zoom list, 57
Standard toolbar (Excel)
   AutoSum, 308
   Copy, 310
   Import button, 159
   Paste, 310
starting number in lists, setting, Q-62
starting Office 2008 programs, Q-7, Q-8
static text, current date or time as, 225
status bar, 6
   controlling display of information, Q-18
   hiding and displaying in Excel, 93, 97, 100
   insertion point location displayed on, 78
   TRK button, 414
status bar (Entourage), 472
status bar (Word), Customize Workspace, 139
stopping slide show in PowerPoint, 116, 342
Style dialog box (Word), 123
styles, Q-29, 236–238
   applying, 241–252
   categories, 236
   creating, 238
   displaying list of available, 237
   modifying, 238
   for page numbers, 436
   for table of contents, 444
   from template, applying to document, 252
Styles panel
   List, All styles, 245
   Pick Style To Apply, 242
subentries in index, 450, G-537
SUBSTITUTE( ) function, 299
SUM( ) function, 297, 298, 304, 309
SUMIF( ) function, 298
SUMIFS( ) function, 298
Summary page, of contact record, 514
Symbolic Link format, 105
symbols
   changing character combinations to, 28
   inserting, Q-18
Sync Services settings, in Entourage, 475
synonyms, 495
System Preferences window
   Appearance page, 6
   Software Update, 22

T

tab characters, G-537
   in Word Find and Replace, 62
tab leader, G-538
tab stops, 86
table, G-538
table delimiters, displaying, 88

Table menu (Word), 20
table of contents, Q-35, 442–447
  practice exercise, 445
Table of Contents group, in Elements Gallery, 38
Table of Contents menu, Remove Table of
    Contents, 447
table styles, Q-29, 236
table_array argument, in functions, 299
tabs
  displaying, 88
  in Elements Gallery, 15
Tasks (Entourage), 470. *See also* To Do List
    (Entourage)
  reminders for, Q-80
templates, G-538
  custom set of slide masters as, 339
  in Excel, Q-54
  in PowerPoint, Q-65
templates, in Word
  applying styles to document, 252
  attaching to document, Q-29, 240
  Category list display, 135
  changing sort order, 144
  creating document from, Q-29, 132, 142–146
  creating personalized, 147, 149–150
  file formats for, 92
Templates and Add-ins dialog box, 250
text
  adding to shapes, Q-17, 386
  changing font and appearance, Q-14
  deleting, Q-11
  inserting, Q-11
  in PowerPoint, formatting, Q-60, 318
  on PowerPoint slide, editing, 191
  selecting, Q-8
  in SmartArt graphics, 403, 405
  in Word, 228, 452
text boxes, Q-60
  linking, 136
  location and formatting, in slide masters, 339
text entry, in Word documents, 124
text functions, 299
Text Import Wizard, 159
Text In Overflow icons, 234
textual watermarks, Q-38, 322
textures, for slide background, Q-61, 320, 333
Theme Colors palette, 235, 373
themes, Q-18, 228–231
  applying, 231–235
  colors, 324
  for headers and footers, Q-31
  special for presentations, Q-63, Q-66, 195
  thumbnails of, 230

thesaurus, Q-16, 493, 494
  Reference Tools palette to access, 17
.thmx file format, 93, 115
  saving presentation as, 195
three-dimensional charts, 266
thumbnails, G-538
  in Elements Gallery, 15
  in Navigation pane, 87
  of themes, 230
  of Word documents, 35
Thumbnails view of Project Gallery, 134, 135
  sort order, 144
tick-mark labels in charts, 267, G-538
tiled windows, 58
  in Excel, 102
time, inserting, Q-33, Q-49, 225
time fields, in header or footer, 379
Times New Roman font, 364
title bar, G-538
  of document window, 6, 33
  in Excel, Maximize button, 96
  of floating toolbar, 13
title slide
  for presentation, 199
  for presentation template thumbnail, 197
titles
  of slides, 189
  of worksheet columns, copying to Clipboard, 291
  of worksheet columns, printing, 377
To Do flag, for e-mail message or contact
    record, 519
To Do List (Entourage)
  adding tasks, Q-81, 526
  displaying, Q-81, 525
  settings, 475
TOC. *See* table of contents
TODAY( ) function, 303
toggling codes for information fields, Q-33
toolbar (Excel), New button, 163
toolbars, 11–14
  appearance and content, Q-9
  button descriptions, 13
  buttons with arrows, 14
  for contact window, 514
  docking vs. floating, 12
  in Entourage, Q-81, 473
  in Excel, hiding, 97
  hiding and displaying, Q-9, 12, 35, 39, 47
  Navigation button, 87
  Open button, 44
  Show button, 88, 220
  in Word, 21, 126, 138
  Zoom arrow, 80

Toolbox, 16–18, 37, 359
    appearance and content, Q-9
    Citations Manager palette, 462, 463
    Citations palette, 18, 462
    Compatibility Report, 400, G-538
    Custom Animation palette, 18
    Document Theme panel, 325
    Entourage, 493
    Formatting Palette. *See* Formatting Palette
    Formula Builder palette, 18, 300, 301
    hiding and displaying, 18
    minimizing, 18
    Object Palette, 322, 381
    Objects Gallery, 136
    Project Palette, 17
    Reference Tools palette, 17, 493
    Scrapbook button, 224
    Scrapbook palette. *See* Scrapbook
    Theme Colors palette, 253, 313
Toolbox Settings pane, 18
Tools menu, 10
    Accounts, 481
    Schedules, 507
    Templates And Add-ins, 250
    Track Changes, 414, 417, 424
Tools menu (Entourage)
    Accounts, 477, 497
    Signatures, 496
Track Changes feature, Q-36, 413, 414
translation between languages, Q-16, 495
translation tool, Reference Tools palette
        to access, 17
transparency
    of image watermark, 323
    of photo color, 393
    of shape watermark, 323
    of slide background, Q-61, 334
    of slide image background, 336
    of text materials, 321
Travel Tools worksheet templates, 173
TRK button, on status bar, 414
Turabian bibliographic style, 462
Two Pages magnification level, in Word, 82
.txt file format, 93, 105
typing errors, settings to correct common
        mistakes, 28

U

underlining, 365, 368
    for Track Changes feature, 414
undo changes in Word, Q-12, 219
    changes in document review, 415
unhiding columns and rows in Excel, 161

units of measurement, changing, Q-35, 86
unordered lists. *See* bulleted text
unresponsive programs, forcing to quit, Q-6
Update Table Of Contents dialog box, 449
updating indexes, Q-33
updating information fields, Q-33
updating Office 2008 programs, Q-18, 22
updating table of contents, Q-36
UPPER( ) function, 299
uppercase characters, 366
Use Smart Cut And Paste option, 221
User Information dialog box (Word), 30
user information, storing for reuse, Q-19, 29
user interface, G-535
user interface elements, 3, 9, G-535
UTF-16 Unicode Text, 105

V

value, as argument for function, 298
value axis of chart, 266
VBA macros
    and Excel 2008, 104
    and PowerPoint 2008, 114
    and Word 2008, 92
Verdana font, 364
vertical alignment of text, in Word, 355
vertical scroll bar, 6
    hiding in Excel, 97
vertical window arrangement, 58
View dialog box (Excel), 100
View menu, 10, 77, 107
    Customize Toolbar, 473
    Formatting Palette, 359
    Formula Bar, 99, 308
    Navigation pane, 232
    Normal, 288
    Ruler, 84
    Slide Show button, 113, 340
    Toolbars, 12, 35, 128
    Web Layout, 90
View settings, customizing, 28
View toolbar, 7, 77, 93
    Draft View button, 89
    Normal View button, 100, 106
    Slide Sorter View button, 112
viewing Address Book records, 512
views, Q-19, 79
    in Calendar, 524
    changing, 56
    in Word, 76
VLOOKUP( ) function, 299, 300

W

watermark, G-538

watermarks for slides in PowerPoint, Q-68, 321–323

  creating textual on slide, Q-68, 322

  creating with image or photo, 323

  transparency for, 323

watermarks for Word documents, Q-38, 440

  alphanumeric, 441

  graphics, 440

Web Layout view (Word), 76, 90

Web Page file format

  in Excel, 105

  in PowerPoint, 115

  in Word, 93

week, displaying in Calendar, 524

Week view for Calendar, 524

white space

  margins, 350

  between paragraphs, 355

Whole Page magnification level, in Word, 82

whole word searches, in Word Find and Replace, 61

Widescreen Presentation template, 195

widows, from page breaks, 352, G-538

wildcards, in Word Find and Replace, 61

Window menu, 10

  Arrange, 101

  Bring All To Front, 59

  New Window, 101

windows for documents. *See* document windows

windows in Entourage, rearranging, 473

Windows Live Hotmail account, folder structure, 481

Windows Logo key, 9

Windows Office Compatible collection of fonts, 364

Word, Q-65

  changing character case in, 366

  Citations palette, 18. *See also* Toolbox

  copying and moving text, 216

  creating charts in, 279

  date and time fields in header or footer, 379

  document properties, Q-28, 121

  document windows, 9

  editing text in, 214

  editing text in (practice exercise), 220

  exporting outline from, Q-65, 204

  file formats, 92

  inserting chart, 277

  inserting document elements from Gallery, 15

  magnification range, 57

  moving around open document, 77–86

  Preferences dialog box, 28

  print settings, 69

  saving document, 45

  Search box for program settings, 27

  selection area in, 215

  templates in, 240. *See also* document templates

  toolbars, 11, 21

  user information stored by, Q-19, 29

word forms, finding all in Word Find and Replace, 61

Word Macro-Enabled Document file format, 92

Word Macro-Enabled Template file format, 92

Word menu, Preferences, 86

Word menu bar, 9, 20

  Font menu, 20

  Table menu, 20

  Work menu, 21

Word Preferences dialog box, 21, 39

  Authoring And Proofing Tools, 86, 221

  AutoCorrect group, 22

  Personal Settings, 30

  Print page, 452

  Track Changes tab, 414, 418

  User Information tab, 415

  View tab, 78

WordArt, for slide watermark, Q-68, 321

words

  reference information for, Q-16

  selecting in Word, 214

Work menu (Word), 21

Work Week view for Calendar, 524

workbook windows, splitting and arranging, 58

workbooks in Excel, 43, 155, G-538

  adding worksheet, 283

  changing order of sheets, 285

  closing, 55

  creating, Q-50, 156

  creating (practice exercise), 163

  creating from project template, Q-54, 170–174

  creating with copied worksheet, 288

  limits for data storage, 157

  opening, 44, 51

  printing setup, 377

  protecting, Q-50

  referencing from different folder, 304

  referencing in formula, 304

  rulers, 164

  viewing and moving around, 92

  viewing and moving around (practice exercise), 98

WORKDAY( ) function, 297, 306

worksheets in Excel, 156, 281

  adding to workbook, 283

  changing structure, 260

  creating, 291

  default font, 165

  default orientation, 289

  editing, 260

editing cell content, 260
gridlines, displaying and hiding, 377
hiding, 284
hiding tabs, 97
maximum size, 157
merging cells, 375
moving around in, 95
moving or copying, 285
print area of, 378
printing, 379
referencing in formula, 304
selecting all, 159
workspace, G-538
  in Word Notebook Layout view, 139
WorldLingo, 494

X

x-axis (charts), 266, G-538
.xla file format, 105
.xlam file format, 104, 105
.xls file format, 104, 176
.xlsb file format, in Excel, 105
.xlsm file format, 104
  in Excel, 105
.xlsx file format, 104, 156, 176
.xlt file format, 104, 105, 239
.xltm file format, 104, 239
.xltx file format, 104, 239
.xml file format, in Excel, 105
XML Open Format, Office, 92

Y

y-axis (charts), 266, G-538
  names on, 275

Z

z-axis (charts), 266, G-538
Zoom dialog box, 57, 83
Zoom list (Standard toolbar), 57
Zoom setting in Word, 80

What do you think of this book?

We want to hear from you!

Do you have a few minutes to participate in a brief online survey?

Microsoft is interested in hearing your feedback so we can continually improve our books and learning resources for you.

To participate in our survey, please visit:

www.microsoft.com/learning/booksurvey/

...and enter this book's ISBN-10 or ISBN-13 number (located above barcode on back cover*). As a thank-you to survey participants in the United States and Canada, each month we'll randomly select five respondents to win one of five $100 gift certificates from a leading online merchant. At the conclusion of the survey, you can enter the drawing by providing your e-mail address, which will be used for prize notification only.

Thanks in advance for your input. Your opinion counts!

* Where to find the ISBN on back cover

ISBN-13: 000-0-0000-0000-0
ISBN-10: 0-0000-0000-0

Example only. Each book has unique ISBN.

Microsoft®
Press